HENRY DAVID THOREAU

HENRY DAVID

THOREAU

A Life

LAURA DASSOW
WALLS

THE UNIVERSITY OF CHICAGO PRESS

CHICAGO AND LONDON

The University of Chicago Press, Chicago 60637
The University of Chicago Press, Ltd., London
© 2017 by The University of Chicago. All rights reserved.
For more information, contact the University of Chicago Press,
1427 East 60th Street, Chicago, IL 60637.
Published 2017
Printed in the United States of America

26 25 24 23 22 21 20 19 18 17   1 2 3 4 5

ISBN-13: 978-0-226-34469-0 (cloth)
ISBN-13: 978-0-226-34472-0 (e-book)
DOI: 10.7208/chicago/9780226344720.001.0001

Library of Congress Cataloging-in-Publication Data
Names: Walls, Laura Dassow, author.
Title: Henry David Thoreau : a life / Laura Dassow Walls.
Description: Chicago : The University of Chicago Press, 2017. | Includes bibliographical
    references and index.
Identifiers: LCCN 2016053416 | ISBN 9780226344690 (cloth : alk. paper) |
    ISBN 9780226344720 (e-book)
Subjects: LCSH: Thoreau, Henry David, 1817–1862. | Authors, American—19th century—
    Biography. | Naturalists—United States—Biography.
Classification: LCC PS3053 .W28 2017 | DDC 818/.309 [B]—dc23 LC record available at https://
    lccn.loc.gov/2016053416

♾ This paper meets the requirements of ANSI/NISO Z39.48–1992 (Permanence of Paper).

To Richard von Dassow (1939–1967)
Artist and poet
who went before

"Be thou my Muse, my brother—"

Contents

PART II
THE MAKING OF WALDEN

IMAGE GALLERY FOLLOWS PAGE 332

Preface

What youthful philosophers and experimentalists we are!
There is not one of my readers who has yet lived a whole human life.
HENRY DAVID THOREAU, *WALDEN*

Everyone who comes to Thoreau has a story. Mine begins in a neighborhood bookstore where I pulled a book off the shelf simply because it was small and green—like the little green book I'd been carrying around (filched from my father's library) by a writer named Ralph Waldo Emerson. "There is one mind common to all individual men," it opened. "Of the works of this mind history is the record." To a restless, idealistic teenager, this was catnip. And here was a second green book! This one had a double title, *Walden and Civil Disobedience*: "I have lived some thirty years on this planet," I read, "and I have yet to hear the first syllable of valuable or even earnest advice from my seniors." That made sense. Don't trust anybody over thirty, we were all saying, for the adult world was clearly mad. Every afternoon I brought the newspaper in off the front porch and read the headlines: how many soldiers had died in Vietnam, where the latest riots were burning, which of my heroes had just been assassinated. "Here is life," continued the new green voice, "an experiment to a great extent untried by me; but it does not avail me that they have tried it."[1] More catnip! I bought the book and brought it to school. Next time I was marched to the mandatory football rally, I split off at the door, sat on a grassy rise nearby, and opened my copy of *Walden*, holding it high so my teachers could see the title. They left me alone, and I've been stepping to the music of that different drummer ever since.

I began this biography to return to the figure who opened up that space for independent thinking, to learn how he had opened up that space for himself. "A man is a bundle of relations, a knot of roots, whose flower and fruitage is the world," wrote Emerson.[2] Thoreau's roots were in Concord, Massachusetts, where he was born in 1817— far from the Seattle of 1970. Yet had Thoreau lived a normal life span, my grandmother could have shaken his hand; our world is that close, in many ways the flower and fruitage of his. Two hundred years ago, American democracy still felt raw, experimental, and uncertain, especially in Concord, where America was a family affair, earned by one generation and about to pass to the next. Thoreau felt the weight of that responsibility more than most, and when he returned home from college, he set about reexamining the roots of democracy for himself. For it was clear to him that the American Revolution was incomplete: inequality was rife, materialism was rampant, and the American economy was wholly dependent on slavery. Yet in a terrible irony, his elders seemed content to let this state of things, from which they all benefited, continue. No, they were not to be trusted; he must try the experiment for himself.

By the time Thoreau built his house on Walden Pond at the edge of town, he had come of age among a circle of radical intellectuals called "Transcendentalists," for their belief in higher ideas that "transcended" daily life. Emerson was their leader; he had moved to Concord while Thoreau was at Harvard, class of '37. Back home, Thoreau found his new neighbor declaring America's intellectual independence, even as his own household had become a hotbed of antislavery activism. Thoreau joined the new revolution, but by 1844 he was less certain that Emerson, now his mentor, had all the answers. The dilemma that pressed upon him was how to live the American Revolution not as dead history but as a living experience that could overturn, and keep overturning, hidebound convention and comfortable habits. Moving to Walden Pond thus had a double purpose: it offered a writer's retreat, where Thoreau could follow his calling as spiritual seeker, philosopher, and poet; and it offered a public stage on which he could dramatize his one-person revolution in consciousness, making his protest a form of performance art.

In writing *Walden*, Thoreau encouraged his readers to try the experiment of life for themselves, rather than inheriting its terms from others—including himself. When he returned from Walden and became, once again, a working member of a large family in town, he tried to bring into the heart of workaday America his belief in life as a quest toward higher truth. Thoreau is often said to have turned to "Nature," but what he actually turned to was, more exactly, the "commons"—spaces that, back then, were still open to everyone: woods, fields and hilltops, ponds and blueberry thickets, rivers, meadows, trails up nearby mountains, the long open beaches on the Atlantic shore. Nearly all his writings use landforms and watersheds to explore the commons, expanding our shared natural and intellectual heritage until it touches the Cosmos itself. When Thoreau sailed on the Concord and Merrimack Rivers, he traveled the deep stream of time; when he walked the shore of Cape Cod, he dabbled his toes in a wild ocean stretching around the globe; when he stood on the shoulder of Mount Katahdin, he breathed the thin chill air of a planet in stellar space.

This viewpoint—deep time, planetary space—structured Thoreau's thinking from his Harvard years onward. He read at least six languages; to him, literature was *world* literature, beginning with the written word itself—Homer, Virgil, the Bible, the ancient scriptures of India and China, Old English poetry—on through the latest in German philosophy and science, French histories of the New World, England's most advanced Romantic poetry, and Scotland's most vigorous prose. Thoreau filled dozens of notebooks with extracts from hundreds of volumes, creating his own working library: poetry, history, science, anthropology, travel, and exploration. His ferocious curiosity meant the least detail in his own backyard could speak to him of faraway times and places: farmers working their fields evoked Virgil's *Georgics*; Arctic explorers helped him analyze winter in New England; Irish laborers showed him the Bhagavad Gita in the waters of Walden. Through the 1840s and '50s, Thoreau's commitment to social activism deepened as he linked the actions of his Northern neighbors to the perpetuation of slavery in the South, a connection that led to his famous acts of protest: his night in jail for nonpayment of taxes, his essay "Civil Disobedience," his furious denunciation of "Slavery in Massachusetts," his passionate support for John Brown's attempted insurrection. When death stilled his voice just after the onset of the Civil War, Thoreau's friends mourned not only him, but also the loss of all the work he had begun and never lived to complete.

→>—<←

When I began writing this book, the term *Anthropocene* was a novelty: human beings, scientists were suggesting, had become a geological force changing the planet itself. As I worked, I realized that Thoreau's life span, though short, had been long enough to witness and record the arrival of the Anthropocene epoch in America. He was born on a colonial-era farm into a subsistence economy based on agriculture, on land that had sustained a stable Anglo-American community for two centuries and, before that, Native American communities for eleven thousand years. People had been shaping Thoreau's landscape since the melting of the glaciers. By the time he died, in 1862, the Industrial Revolution had reshaped his world: the railroad transformed Concord from a local economy of small farms and artisanal industries to a suburban node on a global network of industrial farms and factories. His beloved woods had been cleared away, and the rural rivers he sailed in his youth powered cotton mills. In 1843, the railroad cut right across a corner of Walden Pond, but in 1845 Thoreau built his house there anyway, to confront the railroad as part of his reality. By the time he left Walden, at least twenty passenger and freight trains screeched past his house daily. His response was to call on his neighbors to "simplify, simplify." Instead of joining the rush to earn more money for the latest gadgets and goods from China, Europe, or the West Indies—feeding an economy that grew mindlessly, he wrote, like rank and noxious weeds—he called for mindful cultivation of one's inner being and one's greater community, a spiritual rather than material growth through education, art, music, and philosophy. When he wrote that "a man is rich in proportion to the number of things which he can afford to let alone," he meant not an ascetic's renunciation, but a redefinition of true wealth as inner rather than outer, aspiring to turn life itself, even the simplest acts of life, into a form of art. "There is Thoreau," said one of his closest friends. "Give him sunshine, and a handful of nuts, and he has enough."[3]

Thoreau's own family rose from penury to middle-class respectability after his father founded a small pencil factory. Thoreau was fond of machinery, and his inventions and improvements to the manufacturing process brought prosperity to his family. To pay his own expenses—including the bills for living in the family's boardinghouse—he worked as a day laborer and eventually built up his own business as a land surveyor. When he wasn't laying out property bounds, he was crossing those bounds in his own private enterprise as a walker and writer, earning just enough from publishing and lecturing to cover travel expenses. The more closely Thoreau lived and worked in nature, the more he was drawn to science, for the workings of things always fascinated his engineer's mind; his quest to understand nature's "bundle of relations" made him a pioneer of ecological science well before the field existed. Yet the more deeply he understood natural science, the more intensely he longed for something beyond understanding—what he called "the wild." In "Walking," one of his most famous essays, Thoreau declared his credo: "In Wildness is the preservation of the world." In later years, he kept a detailed journal to record his observations of nature (including human nature), noting the date each flower bloomed, the date the ice melted on Walden Pond, when leaves turned color, and the dates and depths of snowfalls. He bragged that from looking at the flowers, he could tell the day of the month within two days. Scientists are now using his meticulous records to track with precision the ever-earlier onset of spring and the lingering of fall, as year by year climate change shrinks winters and alters the composition of Walden's plant communities.[4]

But today, as those scientists have shown, Thoreau's flower

calendar is deranged, for the synchronies he documented are falling out of rhythm. His records thus help us measure the arrival of the Anthropocene epoch that threatens to overturn everything he believed. Thoreau could look to "Nature" as an eternal fountain of renewal and regeneration, a sacred force capable of healing even the deepest acts of human destruction, including slavery, war, and environmental devastation. He ended *Walden* with an ecstatic vision into the regenerative forces of the Cosmos, and late in life, when he took up Darwin's *Origin of Species,* he saw in a flash that the theory of evolution meant nature was a "constant *new* creation," a creative principle unceasingly at work, all around, every day. That the actions of human beings and the ancient fossil fuels they dug out of the ground to feed the engines of industry could fundamentally alter those natural processes—changing the chemistry of the atmosphere and of the encircling oceans, melting the poles, killing winter, killing life itself—was beyond Thoreau's reckoning. Can his faith live on after nature, at least nature as he knew it, has ended?

I think it can and will. Thoreau could speculate that even a slight shift in natural processes—a little colder winter, a little higher flood—might put an end to humanity, so dependent are we on a wild nature that gives us no guarantees. Hence he emphasized living "deliberately"; that is, living so as to perceive and weigh the moral consequence of our choices. "Civil Disobedience" insists that the choices we make create our environment, both political and natural—*all* the choices, even the least and most seemingly trivial. The sum of those choices is weighed on the scales of the planet itself, a planet that is, like Walden Pond, sensitive and alive, quick to measure the least change and register it in sound and form. To Thoreau this was cause for tremendous optimism: as the village expanded and the old trees fell, he planted new ones and reveled in the young forest. If the English settlers had wiped out many of New England's animals—beaver, wolf, bear and cougar, moose and deer, wild turkey—still there was much remaining, enough to assure him the wild was everywhere, ready to reseed and reclaim what it had lost. His last, unfinished works, *Wild Fruits* and *The Dispersion of*

Seeds, emphasize how the smallest of seeds, let loose on the winds or carried by the least of beings, could transform the world. All humans need to do is learn to work with instead of against the vital currents of life. The books Thoreau didn't live to finish are about building a community of life, and he died in the faith that his words, like seeds, would take root and grow. Exactly insofar as we, today, share his belief in the future of life and act on it, will he continue to speak to us.

➤➣◄

Henry Seidel Canby, in his 1939 biography of Thoreau, listed half a dozen biographies he might have written instead: Thoreau as creative artist, mystical Pan of Concord, rustic local boy who made good, Transcendentalist in conflict with modern science, individualist in conflict with society.[5] As Canby recognized, Thoreau has never been captured between covers; he was too quixotic, mischievous, many-sided, paradoxical. Even the friends who knew him best despaired of getting any truthful portrait on paper. Yet each generation has attempted to bring Thoreau alive in their own way. In line with this tradition, I attempt to bring Thoreau alive for our time, basing my story primarily on the journals, letters, and writings of Thoreau and his associates. There are many gaps in the record; I groaned when I read Sophia Thoreau's account of burning the Thoreau family letters as the "sad duty" of the last surviving family member![6] But much remains. Indeed, as this biography threatened to swell into two volumes, I realized that making it accessible to a wide readership required making tough choices. I couldn't include the full interior story told by Thoreau's massive Journal, which would have required a second volume. Nor could I include, here, extended critical readings of Thoreau's many books and essays, which would have added hundreds of pages. Thankfully, many rich and various interpretations of his works are already available.[7]

What I offer instead is a reading of Thoreau's life *as a writer*—for, remarkably, he made of his life itself an extended form of composition, a kind of open, living book. I hope my readers are inspired to turn to Thoreau's own words, to see for themselves how he wrote his life. Interested readers will also find many additional incidents and shades of meaning in earlier biographies. As another of his biographers once remarked, different biographies do not "cancel out or fully supplant each other" but provide particular emphases, information, and insights that continue the ongoing conversation about the "elusive, complex, and gifted man and writer who was Henry Thoreau." I fully agree, and I hope my own effort will further that ongoing dialogue.[8]

The biographies closest to mine are Walter Harding's *The Days of Henry Thoreau,* an exhaustive chronicle of the known events and documents; Robert D. Richardson's *Henry David Thoreau: A Life of the Mind,* an indispensable intellectual biography of Thoreau that traces in detail the movement of his mind as he lived, read, and wrote; and David Robinson's *Natural Life: Thoreau's Worldly Transcendentalism,* a deep and wise spiritual biography of Thoreau's life in nature. All are exemplary, and I have learned immensely from them. My many additional debts and recommendations are registered in the notes. These, too, could have been much longer, for given that Thoreau's writings are all autobiographical, virtually every study of his work takes up some aspect of his thought in the context of his life. The true student of Thoreau and his time will want to explore them widely.[9]

Still, the Thoreau I sought was not in any book, and so I wrote this one. Today, two hundred years after his birth, we have invented two Thoreaus, both of them hermits, yet radically at odds with each other. One speaks for nature; the other for social justice. Yet the historical Thoreau was no hermit, and as Thoreau's own record shows, his social activism and his defense of nature sprang from the same roots: he found society in nature, and nature he found everywhere, including the town center and the human heart. Thus where others see schism, I see Emerson's "bundle of relations" and "knot of roots"—roots of which Thoreau's life and writings are the flower and fruit. The sweep of his life takes in the deep, even geological, time of the land he walked and studied and the social history of his family, town, and nation, which were already part of a global network.

Thoreau himself embodied this intertwined narrative so deeply that at his death, his friends said his truest memorial was Concord itself. It's true that he often lived in tension with his townsfolk, but he was always near them, and often among them—a gadfly not above stinging his neighbors to wake them up. This relationship shaped his every word, for as his ideas outran his time, Thoreau often found his voice silenced and censored—so often that I sometimes marveled he found courage to keep speaking at all.

In short, Thoreau struggled all his life to find a voice that could be heard despite the din of cynicism and the babble of convention. That he was a loving son, a devoted friend, a lively and charismatic presence who filled the room, laughed and danced, sang and teased and wept, should not have to be said. But astonishingly, it does, for some deformation of sensibility has brought Thoreau down to us in ice, chilled into a misanthrope, prickly with spines, isolated as a hermit and nag. He could of course be icy, prickly, occasionally her-mitous, and even a nag—features that I hope this biography makes clear, perhaps understandable. My real question is how he could be all that and also be a writer of world-class achievement; a natural scientist who gave us the deep poetry of nature writing; a political activist who, in the name of the common good, gave the weak their most powerful tool against the strong; and a spiritual seeker who encouraged every one of us to enter into the great experiment of life. Thoreau earned the devotion of friends who saw in him no saint, but something perhaps more rare: a humane being living a whole human life.

NOTES ON USAGE

The word *Indian*, a blanket term used by the invading Europeans for all the Native nations and peoples of North and South America, is today controversial, and no single, satisfactory replacement has emerged. I have, whenever they are known, referred to specific tribal affiliations; this, the preferred usage today, respects the continuing struggle for Native cultural persistence and political sovereignty. When I am speaking in my own narrative voice, I have used the words *indigenous* or *Native*; but when I am using the voice of Thoreau and his contemporaries, I use, as did they, the term *Indian*. To do otherwise would not only be anachronistic, it would ignore the limitations that existed in Thoreau's day—limitations that constrained what he could think, even as he wrestled to think beyond "the" Indian to see Indians, in the plural, as individualized, intellectually sovereign, and vital to any vision of America.

Regarding the difference between *Nature* and *nature*: This term was often used as a transcendentalized or universalized expression of a divine or sacred ideal, in contrast with "garden-variety" nature. This is a distinction Emerson holds to, and Thoreau, of course, often follows Emerson here. I capitalize *Nature* when it names a divine or holy essence, but stay with lowercase *nature* when the word is used in our modern, secular way.

HENRY DAVID THOREAU

Land of the Grass-Ground River

The Germans say—Es ist alles wahr wodurch du besser wirst.
(Everything is true through which you become better.)
HENRY DAVID THOREAU, OCTOBER 22, 1837

TAHATAWAN'S ARROWHEAD

One Sunday evening, late in September 1837, something happened that young Henry Thoreau couldn't get out of his head. For a month it teased him, until finally he wrote it down in his new Journal. Was it worth recording? Maybe. He tried it out: after spending the day looking for Indian relics, he and his brother John strolled to the river-bank to watch the sunset. Henry, seized by inspiration and gesturing wildly, broke into "an extravagant eulogy on those savage times": "'There on Nawshawtuct,' said I, 'was their lodge, the rendezvous of the tribe, and yonder, on Clamshell hill their feasting ground.'" How often the Indians must have stood on that very spot, at that very hour—just like John and Henry!—watching the sunset over the Musketaquid River, communing with the spirits of their fathers gone before them. "'Here,' I exclaimed, 'stood Tahatawan; and there, (to complete the period), is Tahatawan's arrowhead.'" Down they sat, and Henry, "to carry out the joke," threw out his hand to seize a random stone—and lo! It "proved a most perfect arrowhead, as sharp as if just from the hands of the Indian fabricator!!!!"[1]

It's a lighthearted story, just two brothers playing Indian. But when Henry's hand grasped something real, his youthful fantasy caught hold of an adult truth. The arrowhead, hard and sharp, didn't feel like a relic from the past, but like a live thing handed to him by an elder—as if Tahatawan himself had materialized at his elbow and offered him a choice: you may laugh this off as superstition, or you may take it up as truth. In the act of committing this story to his Journal, Henry made a choice: he would *make* it true. This choice will set him off from family, friends, and neighbors—unlike them, Henry David Thoreau would be a *writer*. This meant taking up the writer's double consciousness, splitting the self who lives from the self who writes, opening up a double vision: present and past, white and Indian, civil and wild, man and nature. Jumping that gap had been the point of the joke to begin with, the kind of playacting that usually ends when childhood is over. But Thoreau, fingering in the nick of time the stone blade's edge, felt that gap snap shut. Time folded together, and for an instant, he straddled both sides, beholding two realities in one.

He wasn't quite there yet on that Sunday watching the sunset from the riverbank. He came closer a month later when he opened his Journal to answer Emerson's call: "'What are you doing now?' he asked, 'Do you keep a journal?'—So I make my first entry today." There, he's begun. But what does it mean to be a writer? At first Thoreau was tentative; he had many years ahead of him. In this little experiment, he turned his story of the arrowhead into a story about *himself telling* a story, feeling a little silly about it, but also feeling genuine awe. The next step was the crucial one: he knew he was "making" the arrowhead story—just as the arrowhead itself was made, or "fabricated," by the hand of the Indian. But precisely because he knew he was making it, it became real to him, invested, a commitment. Could it be true? Yes, Emerson had told him. So at the end of his first entry, Thoreau wrote down what Emerson said: "*Es ist alles wahr wodurch du besser wirst.*" Everything is true through which you become better.[2]

Thoreau was learning how to make things speak, learning his path as an artist. But where were the living Indians? Nashoba, the town Tahatawan helped build, had been swept off the map in King Philip's War: in 1675, as terror spread among the English, the colonial government ordered all Praying Indians confined. Nashoba's fifty-eight residents were evacuated to John Hoar's house in Concord (now the Alcott's Orchard House), where Hoar and the Nashoba people built a stockade together to protect their new homes and workshops. Hoar insisted to the rest of Concord that the Nashoba were peaceful and industrious, posing no threat—even though several Concord soldiers had been killed in a nearby massacre. One Sunday, an army captain came to church to whip up hatred against the Indians, and the people of Concord listened and kept silent. Hearing no objection, the captain and his troops led a mob of "a hundred or two" to John Hoar's house, broke down the door, seized the fifty-eight Indians inside—mostly women and children—plundered their clothing, shoes, dishes, and food stores, and marched them to the Deer Island prison camp in Boston Harbor. After a long miserable season subsisting on clams and seaweed, they were sold into slavery.[3] Thus vanished Tahatawan and his people.

Or so the story ran. Actually, many of Concord's Native people survived, working their way into Concord's ordinary life. In 1676, for instance, one of them, Tom Doublet, helped redeem Mary Rowlandson from her famous captivity. But in 1734, Sarah Doublet, the last inheritor, old and blind, sold the last of her family's land to pay for her care. Family by family, acre by acre, the land base of Concord's Native people was nibbled away on the marketplace. Yet they lived on, quietly maintaining their customs and kinship networks. Some became farmers who hunted and fished as of old. Many put to sea as whalers, as readers of Melville's *Moby-Dick* will recall. Others worked as laborers or in manufactures. Some wove baskets, brooms, and mats, selling them door to door, often on established routes to repeat customers.[4] Tellingly, *Walden* opens with "a well-known lawyer" turning away such an Indian selling his baskets. The lesson, says Thoreau, is not to stop weaving baskets but "to avoid the necessity of selling them"—to subvert the modern marketplace. But the irony goes deeper: the lawyer was Samuel Hoar, a descendent of John Hoar and the patriarch of Concord's leading family. In 1813, Hoar found himself defending three men charged with murdering an Indian, who escaped execution thanks to the pressure of popular prejudice against Indians as wild creatures to be hunted and destroyed.[5] If Indians could be seen only as wild beasts, no wonder Thoreau's neighbors could not recognize, amid the farmers and laborers living quiet lives among them, Tahatawan's people. But they were there, as Thoreau knew, and many live there still.

ENCLOSURES AND COMMONS

The wild beasts, on the other hand, really had disappeared forever. In 1855, Thoreau perused with wonder and dismay a colonial account of the landscape that had greeted Concord's English founders: the meadow grasses were taller, the berries bigger and thicker, the forests more open with great trees whose trunks reached thirty feet or more before branching. There were "lions" or cougars, bears, moose, deer, porcupines, wolves, beavers, martens and raccoons, lynx and maybe wolverines; heath cocks and turkeys, snow geese and swans—"Think of that!" marvels Thoreau.[6] By 1855, they were all gone, yet the land did not seem impoverished to Thoreau, who could barely keep up with what creatures remained—the woodchucks and muskrats, turtles and frogs, owls and hawks and smaller birds—or with the farmers' cycles of planting and harvest. Still, when he traveled to Maine, he felt as though he had traveled back in time, and the contrast startled him into some of his most intense and creative thinking. Domestic and wild: he loved them both, he longed for both, though they seemed like polar opposites. For there was no escaping the fact that the English had made the Musketaquid Valley into a wholly different world.

It had started badly; the English almost gave up the Musketaquid's rank and swampy bottomlands in disgust. Many moved a few miles north to found Chelmsford on higher ground. Those who stayed reengineered what they could change and adapted to what they could not: dredging the river to improve the drainage, clustering their houses by the millpond, plowing the Indians' planting grounds, keeping the uplands open as a commons for grazing cattle and cutting timber and firewood. To survive New England's shockingly long and bitter winters, they built barns to shelter their live-stock, which they fed all winter with the rank wild meadow grasses, cut and cured into hay. In spring they carted manure to the fields, and wherever the land looked lean, they fattened it with cartloads of muck hauled from the swamps and meadows. Each family needed at least twenty cords of firewood a year, which required at least twenty acres of woodland, which meant leaving about a third of Concord's land in forest. For two centuries, large swaths of woodland stayed that way. The largest were the great woods around Walden Pond, where the dry and gravelly glacial tills grew excellent pine and oak, but little else. These woods reminded the English of "the Weald," or "forest," of their homelands, the name they gave to the deep blue lake at their center: "Walden." Thoreau was delighted to discover a branch of his family traced to the English town of Saffron Walden; Walden Pond was a family relation.[7]

Given the diversity of this crazy-quilt landscape, no single prop-erty could include all the resources a colonial family needed to sur-vive. So there amid an American forest, the immigrants set down a sixteenth-century English common village in all its intricate com-plexity: each family owned bits and pieces scattered miles apart—a field here, a little forest there, a bog or two—while everyone worked together to manage the all-important meadows and grazing lands as a community commons. The wealthiest proprietors underwrote the town's expenses and were paid in land accordingly. One was Thomas Flint, a London merchant who received 750 acres next to Walden Pond before returning to London, where he died and bequeathed his land to his sons and "his perfect Yankee surname" to his pond. "*Flint's Pond!*" taunted Henry Thoreau; what did Flint know of the pond? "Such is the poverty of our nomenclature."[8]

The result was a complex system of enclosures and commons that required farmers to work closely together, regulating and maintain-ing both rights and boundaries. Instead of "farms" in today's sense—large contiguous plots of land devoted to commercial agriculture—Concord featured a system of mixed husbandry: livestock, crops, and woodlands were interwoven in tight balance, and conflicts over water rights and flowage often led neighbors to court. This was less a story of Europeans conquering and settling the American wilderness than of a tight-knit group of English immigrants importing a premodern English agricultural system and replacing the Musketaquid's landscape with their own. Where Tahatawan's people had lived on and with the land, nudging it in directions they preferred and moving fluidly across its various seasons and resources, the English settled and possessed, planting bounds and issuing titles, building houses and outbuildings of stout oak timber that would endure for centuries. And endure it all did—long enough for Thoreau to live in it, study it, and write about it, even as it all melted away.

For Thoreau witnessed the final collapse of this two-hundred-year-old system.[9] When he went to Walden Pond in 1845, change was visible everywhere: the new railroad cut right across Walden's prettiest cove; the traditional subsistence farms nearby were failing, eroded away by the global marketplace. Few of his neighbors still cooked and heated with open wood fires, built with local oak timber, ate homegrown "rye 'n' Injun" bread, or wore homespun "linsey-woolsey." Now they cooked on stoves, heated with coal, built with Maine white pine, cut their woodlots to fuel the railroads, planting them in English hay to feed the new breeds of cattle they slaughtered for the Boston market and packed for the West Indies. They filled their pantries with China tea, slave-grown sugar, prairie wheat flour, tropical oranges and pineapples; they wore Georgia cotton, China silks, Canada furs, British woolens.

The railroad whistle across Walden Pond sounded the death knell of an old world and the birth of something new. What it would be, no one yet knew; today geologists call this epoch, when fossil fuels put global economies into hyperdrive, the Anthropocene. Thoreau thus saw the end of one geological epoch and the beginning of the next, and the unease he felt is rampant today, infecting the headlines and blocking our own imagination of the future he believed he was helping to realize. Thoreau could see the ground was shifting, and, in the sheer audacity of his genius, he decided it was up to him to witness the changes and alert the world. From his watchtower by the railroad, deep in Walden Woods, he would sound the alarm and point to a better way.

THE GENESIS OF MUSKETAQUID

No American writer is more place centered than Thoreau. Take him away from Nawshawtuct Hill rising behind Egg Rock, where Concord's three rivers meet; or from the gentle Musketaquid, or "Grass-Ground" River, which the English renamed Concord; or from the "here!" of grasping Tahatawan's arrowhead, and Thoreau is a different person. He learned this himself when he moved to New York City and tried to be like other writers, mobile and market driven. It was a disaster. But back home the smallest things—like the way the sandy soil breaks through the grass, "the naked flesh of New England her garment being blown aside"—moved him to rhapsody: "And this is my home—my native soil, and I am a New Englander. Of thee o earth are my bone & sinew made—to thee o sun am I brother.... To this dust my body will gladly return as to its origin." Nor could he ever forget who came before.[10] What the Indian had by birth, Thoreau claimed through art, a spiritual rebirth for himself and his own immigrant people. His longing for a deep connection with the land would make *Walden* into the great American fable of alienation, regrounding, and rebirth.

Thoreau used the specifics of place to embody deeper and more universal truths. Take Walden Pond: thank goodness, he wrote, it was made deep and pure for a symbol. Had he built instead over the hill on Sandy, or "Flint's," Pond, that broad, shallow lake with its old Yankee surname, *Walden* would have been a different book. With no sandy soil, there would have been no beanfield; with no New England winter to freeze the pond, there would have been no spring thaw to melt the soul; with no railroad to carve the Deep Cut, his fable of creation must find a different shape. To grasp Thoreau means grasping where he was and how it became that way.

Walden Pond is deep—at 102 feet (by Thoreau's measure) the

deepest natural lake in Massachusetts—and steep sided, "a clear and deep green well," he called it, "a perennial spring in the midst of pine and oak woods." It has a self-contained feel, a "walled-in" look like a mountain tarn, which in a way it is. Walden is a kettle pond, formed when a huge block of ice fractured off the face of a retreating glacier and melted slowly away while ice-cold meltwaters pooled and flowed around it, layering a thick mantle of gravelly sediment studded with rounded cobblestones. At its birth Walden was not a pond at all, but a pile of dirt-covered ice—a genesis perhaps recorded in the oral memories of the first peoples to live there, for the oldest say that "anciently the Indians were holding a pow-wow upon a hill here, which rose as high into the heavens as the pond now sinks deep into the earth."[11] This, geologists have remarked, is a pretty accurate description.

To imagine Walden then, go to the snout of a glacier today and look around. Until roughly 13,000 years ago, Concord was under a mile of ice that had been scouring the land for nearly 10,000 years before melting slowly northward, ending the most recent of four cycles of glaciation and warming that shaped North America for 600,000 years. Meltwaters poured off the ice face and gullied through ice canyons carrying sand, silt, and stones, outwashing to form shallow Sandy Pond and broad Fairhaven Bay. Other stranded ice blocks melted to form White Pond, Goose Pond, and countless kettle bogs. For about a thousand years, the retreating glacier blocked the land's northward drainage, so the silty meltwaters pooled in great glacial lakes where the fine gray silt settled into broad flats. English newcomers were drawn to the edge of one of those ancient lakes, digging caves for shelter into the high moraine ridge pushed up by the ice face. The glacier ground down but could not smooth away rocky promontories like Fairhaven Hill and Emerson's Cliff, where Thoreau loved to sit and gaze upon the hills and valleys rippling away westward. As it melted, the glacier left behind a hard-packed stony till carved into long hills—Nawshawtuct, Punkatasset—and smaller "drumlins," like the low hummock that gives Goose Pond the shape of a butterfly.[12]

Thus Thoreau's world was shaped by ice, rock, and water: ice that ground and scoured and shoved, rock that resisted the ice, meltwaters that smoothed and spread. The result is scenery "on a humble scale," as he admitted—not grand, not much to look at. But it's a land riddled with surprises: rocky cliffs break out over sandy plains, and wide valleys sparkle with broad open river bays. Steep slopes plunge into hidden lakes or slide into deep gullies seeping with moisture and running with spring-fed brooks, giving way to chains of pocket bogs percolating with tea-colored juices. Slow, meandering rivers interlace the whole, widening into meadow wetlands recharged by the dark muck rich with nutrients that the spring floods leave behind.

As the ice retreated north, plants pushed up from the south, creating a tundra landscape of sedges, grasses and shrubs whose remnants Thoreau would explore in the kettle bogs: cranberry, cotton grass, Labrador tea. Trees took hold slowly. By 11,000 years ago, Concord had become an open woodland of spruce, fir, and willows—good browse for the caribou and mastodon hunted by Concord's first people, who fished and foraged and built trade networks stretching from Tennessee to Maine; it was they who saw Walden melt from hill to lake. As the climate warmed, hardwoods replaced most of the evergreens (though some, like the mysterious dark hemlocks Thoreau loved, never left): oaks with nutritious acorns; hickories with rich, oily nuts; hazelnuts, butternuts, and groundnuts; birches and beeches; pine in sunny uplands and hemlock in shady copses. By then the mastodon were long gone, but deer and turkey were plentiful, and in spring migrating fishes filled the willow fishweirs. The people adapted, using fire to create good browse for the deer, keep back the juniper and hemlock, and encourage their favorite hardwoods for nuts and acorns. They made pots to store grains, grew hard-shell gourds to carry liquids, and feasted on freshwater shellfish, leaving clamshells behind in great middens. About two thousand years ago, squirrels—and perhaps people, too—brought in chestnuts from the Mississippi Valley over the Allegheny Mountains, and soon the people were planting chestnut trees.

A dramatic change came a thousand years ago: the still-warming climate allowed new crops needing long hot summers to come in from the west and south. With farming, the population grew tenfold. The earliest Europeans found an indigenous civilization growing corn, beans, and squash, planted together in untidy hillocks where they strengthened one another, replenished the soil, and, when eaten together, produced a complete protein. These farms did not stay put behind fixed fences but migrated among favored sites, allowing the Massachusetts Indians to take advantage of New England's sharp seasonal changes. In summers they lived in light, movable shelters, growing crops and picking berries in the warm uplands. Fall meant gathering mast from the forests while moving into snug wigwams on the milder coasts, sheltering from bitter winters and eating shellfish from the tideflats. Spring meant following fish migrations upriver to weirs that trapped alewives and salmon. The land abounded with food: cattails and water lilies, cranberries, wild onions, wild rice; a dozen kinds of nuts and acorns; turtles, freshwater clams, muskrat and beaver, deer and turkey—all part of the feasts Thoreau imagined on Clamshell Hill, a huge midden heap built over the millennia. For 11,000 years, indigenous people adapted to this evolving landscape, modified it to meet their needs, cultivated and shaped it into a physical expression of their culture and artistry. Story and song, elaborated into distinctive cultures, tied them to their history and bound them to one another and their homelands via "a rich spiritual and ceremonial calendar that defined their place in the created world."[13] In Thoreau's world, the people were as old as the forests.[14]

THE COMING OF THE ENGLISH

Thoreau knew little of all this. Indeed, we know hardly more, for by the time the English arrived, the Native world was in such chaos that no clear understanding of how they once lived survives. Around 1616, just before the Pilgrims landed at Plymouth Harbor, an epidemic burned through the coastal communities inland to the Musketaquid Valley and beyond, reducing the Native population by roughly 90 percent. This much Thoreau knew from reading Lemuel Shattuck's *History of Concord* (written for the town's 1835 bicentennial), where he learned that the first Pilgrims attributed this "great mortality" to Divine Providence, who thereby made room for civilization.[15]

Tahatawan was one of the few survivors. He was a leader, though not a "prince" or "king"; his people lived in loose kinship groups that gathered or split as occasion called, governed by family leaders and guided by sachems whose authority was granted by the people. Their base was a lodge on Nawshawtuct Hill, "hill between the rivers," and they called the main river *Musketaquid*, grass-ground or marsh-grass river, from the same root that gives us the word *mosquito*. The name pleased Thoreau for its descriptive precision; he liked to say the Meander River "musketaquidded," for it runs so lazily that, as Hawthorne joked, one couldn't tell which way it flowed. Nawshawtuct Hill divides the north fork, or Assabet—"drinking-water stream," since it runs brisk, strong, and clear—from the lazy south fork, or Sudbury, which pools behind Concord's Main Street, making a convenient boat launch. The Musketaquid Indians grew corn in the light sandy soils above the riverbanks or on the old lake-bottom flats the English dubbed the Great Field, still some of Massachusetts's most productive agricultural land. They built a fishweir in the Mill Brook to trap migrating alewives in spring and salmon in summer. Once or twice a year they burned off the underbrush, keeping the forests open and the blueberries growing thick on the upland hills.

->-<-

Tahatawan knew quite a bit about the English newcomers. In 1620, when the Pilgrims arrived in Massachusetts Bay, they were greeted in English by Native Americans who had been trading with Europeans for a century or more and could bargain in several European languages. Not until 1634 did the English venture inland: Simon Willard, hoping to make money in the fur trade, followed an Indian trading road to Musketaquid Valley, which the epidemic had left vacant and overgrown—the perfect site for a new town. Willard teamed up with the wealthy Peter Bulkeley, and in 1635 the first band of English moved to Musketaquid, which they optimistically renamed "Concord." Bulkeley took possession of the fishweir, which he dammed up to power a grist mill for grinding corn, giving birth to the millpond that would delight young Henry Thoreau. Willard moved in next door to Tahatawan on Nawshawtuct Hill, where he set up a fur trading post with perfect access, via the three river highways, to the interior, whence came Indians with canoes full of deer hides and beaver and marten pelts.

Land that proved bountiful to the Indians seemed barren to the English. The latter survived that first winter by burrowing earthen shelters into the south-facing hillside along Mill Brook—the remains of the ancient glacial lake—whose broad green meadows turned out, disappointingly, to be too marshy for corn. They bartered with the Indians for venison and raccoon, which they thought not so good as lamb; they complained of the strange Indian diet of corn, pumpkin, and squash; they watched in horror as their sheep and cattle died and wolves devoured their pigs. The next year they built board houses (some of them still standing), and in later years they would proudly call themselves America's first western pioneers, who began the march leading all the way to the Pacific. Concord launched America's Manifest Destiny; it was, quite literally, America's first West.[16]

Not until 1637 did the English formalize their relationship with the Musketaquid Indians. That May, a group led by Tahatawan, Squaw Sachem, her husband Wibbacowett, and Natanquatick met Concord's English leaders at the town square under Jethro's Tree, still thriving in Thoreau's day. In an official ceremony, the Musketaquid accepted useful objects—hatchets, hoes, knives, cotton cloth, shirts—plus a parcel of wampum, the shell beading manufactured on the New England coast that the Native Americans used to keep records and the English repurposed into currency: literally, the first American money. Thus the English taught the Indians that in this new world, things had not merely value, but a *price*. Accordingly, the English believed they were purchasing, fair and square, a six-mile-square plot of land. But the Indians' entire economic system was *ecological*, so intricately tied to the land base as to be inseparable from it; they believed they were receiving payment for usage rights, including cultivation, fishing, hunting, and gathering seasonal produce. Since land could not be owned, it could not be sold. This fact is still recorded in their place names, which were not markers of ownership (as in "Flint's Pond") but signposts to ecological relationships. To know Native names was to know the shape of the land and the patterns of seasonal change.[17] Thoreau would seek out and use Indian names to help keep alive the indigenous knowledge of place.

The tragedy for Tahatawan and his people started under Jethro's Tree. Since they hadn't "sold" their land, they didn't leave it; they lived their lives alongside the English as before. But Willard's trading post was tutoring all the Indians within three rivers' reach about money. Trade turned beaver and deer into commodities, giving Indians a powerful incentive to kill animals and purchase a place in the English economy. The beaver population crashed, creating far-reaching changes in the land as beaver dams rotted and wetlands became fields; wild turkey, that Thanksgiving staple, vanished, and deer became scarce. Thoreau never saw a deer in Concord, and was amazed when George Minott told him his mother had once seen a deer in her childhood. While Native food sources collapsed, the English ate well—better than ever, for as deer disappeared, so did their predators: the cougar, lynx, and wolves that also preyed on cattle and pigs. When one wild commodity crashed, the English turned to another or simply lengthened their trading networks to reach communities where ecological diversity still reigned. As the ecological communities Native Americans had shaped and nurtured for thousands of years melted away, their way of life disintegrated. Without deerskins, for example, they needed English cloth and blankets, which took money to buy—as did axes, knives, hoes, and kettles, not to mention guns, which they needed more and more for self-defense as well as hunting. Even arrowheads became commodities for purchase.

In the face of all this, Tahatawan's people proved remarkably resilient. In 1644, only seven years after their bargain with the English, they petitioned to become Christian subjects of the English crown—a good sign, thought the English, especially in the wake of the terrible Pequot War of 1636–37. Local governments were ordered to care for local Indians by civilizing them in English ways and teaching them Christian theology. In 1646, the Reverend John Eliot, who argued for books over guns as civilizing agents, took advantage of the Indians' initiative by preaching a series of sermons. Tahatawan and his family were among those who converted to Christianity, and they petitioned for a town of their own. The English Puritans would not agree unless the Indians gave up their religious rites, or powwows, and their games—as well as howling as an expression of grief, lying, theft, polygamy, and all conflict. They must wear their hair "comely as the English do," improve their time, pay their debts, pray in their wigwams, say grace before and after meals, and always knock before entering an Englishman's house. The Musketaquid people agreed to these conditions, asking in return for a little land: eastward in Lincoln perhaps, or between Flint's Pond and Walden.

The English balked—but Walden was a commons open to all, and Indians were already living there, wearing the paths Thoreau saw encircling Walden Pond and leaving the arrowheads he plowed up in his beanfield. Years went by until finally, in 1654, the Musketaquid were granted a township a few miles northwest of Concord for a "Praying Town," Nashoba. Tahatawan and his family moved there, and in 1660 his son John Tahatawan became Nashoba's leader; Tahatawan himself had become a missionary, often traveling with John Eliot.[18] Not all the neighboring Indians approved. Many distrusted the English and tried to hold on to their old ways—but that meant keeping the English at bay, and only guns could do that. Tahatawan chose instead the path of books: his people would become readers and writers, not warriors, and use mastery of the word to make a place within the English economy. In Nashoba they planted corn and apple orchards, and raised cows and pigs. They wore English clothing, cut their hair short, prayed and sang hymns, and made buttons and brooches to sell. Caught between two worlds, accepted by neither, the Musketaquid carved out a middle space to call their own—a space destroyed two decades later. This was the story told by Tahatawan's arrowhead.

LIVING THE REVOLUTION

For Thoreau, looking around meant looking back, seeing the future through eyes educated by the past—including that past to which others seemed blind. But all his neighbors had their eyes on America's Revolutionary past, for it was the key to Concord's unique identity, its great role on the world stage. Thoreau's generation was the last to know the American Revolution as a living memory. The Reverend Ezra Ripley had been Concord's spiritual guide since the Revolutionary War, and he still walked the town in stockings and knee breeches. As a boy, Thoreau soaked up the thrilling stories told by his grandmother, a proud Tory who had married and buried two Patriots in succession. All true Concordians knew exactly what their parents had done to win American independence. The sons and daughters inheriting that legacy also inherited that beautiful, terrible question: What have *you* done to deserve it? For Concord reeked with self-importance, to the annoyance of neighboring Lexington, where the British had first fired and American blood had first been shed—a sore subject in 1825, when young Henry watched Concord celebrate the Revolution's fiftieth anniversary.

Concordians were proud they had stood virtually united, vowing to defend their liberty with their lives: "Our fathers left a fair inheritance to us, purchased by a waste of blood and treasure. This we are resolved to transmit equally fair to our children after us. No danger shall affright, no difficulties intimidate us"—not even death.[19] By 1775 the town was a military post, storing food, weapons, gunpowder, and ammunition for a war the colonials knew would be long and desperate. On April 19, 1775, when the British finally moved to put down the rebellion, they marched to Concord to seize those stores; likewise, Paul Revere and William Dawes rode toward Concord to sound the alarm. As eight hundred British redcoats came down upon them, weapons glittering in the April sunshine, Concord's minister, the Reverend William Emerson, roared out to the Concord Minutemen, "Let us stand our ground! If we die, let us die here!" And by the Concord River, farmers, artisans, and shopkeepers from all the region gathered to face the British and return fire, changing in that moment from colonists to Americans.

Everywhere Thoreau looked, he saw the Revolution. The fiery Reverend Emerson's grandson, Ralph Waldo Emerson, gave the grand oration for the town's two hundredth birthday; two years later, on July 4, 1837, Thoreau stood with the chorus singing Emerson's "Concord Hymn," declaring that *here*, nowhere else, Americans fired "the shot heard round the world"—right by the Old Manse where Reverend Emerson had lived, where Reverend Ripley still lived, and where Ralph Waldo Emerson had begun his great book *Nature*—the *intellectual* shot heard round the world. On top of the Old Hill Burying Ground, above the town square, one could stand in the footsteps of the attacking English and look out at it all. Or one could look down and read the gravestone of John Jack, "a native of Africa" enslaved in Concord, put there by Daniel Bliss, Concord's lone Tory, in a fit of anger at his town's hypocrisy:

> Tho' born in a land of slavery,
> He was born free.
> Tho' he lived in a land of liberty,
> He lived a slave.

Thoreau never got over his surprise that he had been born "into the most estimable place in all the world, and in the very nick of time, too."[20] Was there a better place to ask how liberty coexists with slavery, how the past challenges the present, how one's actions now shape the future? As Thoreau watched the sunset on Nawshawtuct and fingered Tahatawan's arrowhead, this simple question commanded his future: Which way did Tahatawan's arrow point? Toward the past, or toward the future? Answering that would take him on a lifetime of journeys—all leading home, to the land of the grass-ground river.

PART ONE

THE
MAKING OF
THOREAU

CHAPTER ONE

Concord Sons and Daughters

Minott, Lee, Willard, Hosmer, Meriam, Flint
Possessed the land which rendered to their toil
Hay, corn, roots, hemp, flax, apples, wool, and wood.
Each of these landlords walked amidst his farm,
Saying, "'Tis mine, my children's, and my name's:
How sweet the west wind sounds in my own trees!"
RALPH WALDO EMERSON, "HAMATREYA"

COMING TO CONCORD

Emerson found poetry in Concord's ancient names. Among them—"Minott, Lee, Willard, Hosmer, Meriam, Flint"—one will not find Thoreau, though of all Concord's authors he alone was born there. His family were newcomers among neighbors with houses weathered by a hundred New England winters. The very name Thoreau was novel—foreign, French, part of a Revolutionary wave of restlessness that carried European immigrants into New England's market towns and industrial centers. Henry's upright Aunt Maria insisted that her father, Jean Thoreau, was a merchant who emigrated from Jersey to Boston, but Franklin Sanborn, who knew the family well, said Jean was a sailor, shipwrecked from a Jersey privateer off the coast of New England, who was rescued and brought to Boston, with no intention of staying.[1] The year, both agree, was 1773. Jean was only nineteen. Whatever his intentions, he plunged into life on the Boston docks, and soon was fighting with the Patriots.

Perhaps returning to Jersey was not an option for an adventurous younger son. The Thoreaus—or "Tiereaus," or perhaps Toraux or Thaureaux—were Huguenots forced to flee Catholic France in 1685.

When French dragoons began to terrorize their home in Poitou, Henry's great-great-grandfather[2] swept up his young son Pierre and escaped to the nearby island of Jersey, a protectorate of England and a haven for Huguenot refugees. Here the Thoreaus maintained their Protestant faith and their French language and traditions, part of a global network of Huguenot enclaves preserving their identity until they could at last return home. Some of Pierre's many children carried the Thoreau name to London, New Zealand, and eventually even to Denver; but Philippe, his fourth son, remained on Jersey, a prosperous wine merchant in the port of St. Helier. It was his second son, Jean, who took to sea and landed, by chance or design, in Boston.

Jean must have written home, but it was wartime. Only three letters remain, sent by his younger brother Pierre Thoreau from Jersey starting in 1801. Aunt Maria treasured these letters and passed them on to Henry, who copied them into his Journal—precious relics from his French great-uncle, slender threads to his own past.[3] Thoreau was proud to be "of French extract"; it set him apart from his Yankee neighbors. Later in life he spent years investigating the French foundation of the New World, until he could prove that "the Englishman's history of *New* England commences, only when it ceases to be, *New* France." His friends remarked that he pronounced "the letter *r* with a decided French accent" such that "his speech always had an emphasis, a *burr* in it."[4]

Henry's grandfather Jean Thoreau was short but stout, strong enough to set a hogshead of molasses upright single-handedly. He worked first on a sail loft, then apprenticed with a Boston cooper. When the British blocked Boston harbor, he could give his men no more work, so Jean went to war, helping fortify Boston harbor.[5] As an experienced sailor at the epicenter of the Revolution, however, he soon became a privateer. For a time Jean was based at Castle Island (soon renamed Fort Independence) under the command of fellow Huguenot Paul Revere ("Rivoire"); when Revere captured the *Minerva*, Jean shared in the bounty.[6] Without privateers—pirate ships licensed to prey on enemy vessels—the Revolutionary War would have gone quite differently. By April 1776 privateers had captured enough British ships off Boston to break the British occupation. Two years later, the alliance with France opened French ports to America, and Jean worked this dangerous cross-Atlantic passage, too. In November 1779, when John Adams sailed to France on the frigate *La Sensible* to negotiate peace with Britain, the ship hailed an American privateer off the Grand Banks. When the privateer couldn't make out their name, a lone sailor ran out onto the frigate's bowsprit before the situation escalated, shouting, "*La Sensible!*" Henry noted proudly in his Journal, "That sailors name was Thoreau."[7]

Most wartime fortunes were squandered in luxury goods or lost to runaway inflation, but Jean saved enough to set up a store on Boston's Long Wharf, the heart of America's busiest port. His grandson was pleased to encounter a Captain Snow, who "remembered hearing fishermen say that they 'fitted out at Thoreau's'—remembered him."[8] As Jean's fortune grew, so did his family. In 1781 he married Jane "Jennie" Burns, whose Boston Quaker mother, Sarah Orrok, had refused to accept the hand in marriage of Jennie's father-to-be, a Scottish immigrant, until he divested himself of the ruffles that covered it.[9] Jennie bore ten children in their house on Prince Street. Eight survived to adulthood.[10] In 1787, following Huguenot custom, they named their first son John, after his father. John followed the custom in turn, and gave his second son a name with a French cognate, "Henri." Four of John's sisters grew up to fill Henry's life with maiden aunts: Elizabeth (Betsy) and Sarah Thoreau ran a boardinghouse on Concord's town square; Jane and Maria Thoreau lived in Boston, paying long, frequent visits to Concord. A fifth sister, Nancy, married Caleb Billings and settled with him in Bangor, giving the Concord Thoreaus a virtual second home in Maine.

Family stories preserve only glimpses of these early years. Boston was still so rural that, as John remembered, the family "had milk of a neighbor, who used to drive his cows to and from the Common every day." Boiled green corn was sold piping hot out of "large baskets on the bare heads of negro women, and gentlemen would stop, buy an ear, and eat it in the street." Jean Thoreau would rise before dawn and share his breakfast with John before opening the store, the father eating the undercrusts of biscuits and his son the upper.[11] There were also memories of a darker cast. One of the Thoreaus' future neighbors, recalling her Boston childhood, said her mother always respected Jean Thoreau because he was a religious man; he used to ride to their house "when they made cheeses, to drink the whey, being in consumption." Once, he asked where blue vervain grew, "which he wanted, to make a syrup for his cough," and she ran and gathered some.[12] That cough was an ominous sign. Like so many New England men and women, Jean Thoreau was cursed with tuberculosis, the insidious disease named "consumption" for the way it consumed its victims from within. The first of several tragedies came when Jennie's father died while in Scotland trying to claim an inheritance; Jennie herself died only six weeks after giving birth to her tenth child, David, in 1796.[13] Jean found himself alone with eight children to care for and his Long Wharf store to run.

A year later, Jean Thoreau married Rebecca Hurd Kettell of Concord, thus solving both their problems: his orphaned children had a new mother, and she escaped a widow's poverty. They met perhaps through church—she was religious, too—or perhaps through commerce, for Rebecca's sister was married to Deacon John White, who owned Concord's most prosperous store at the town square's busy crossroads. In 1799, Jean bought the house next door—today, it forms the north end of the Colonial Inn—and in 1800 the Thoreaus moved in. Soon young John was studying at the Lexington Academy, and his parents, having joined the First Parish Church, were hosting the Reverend Ezra Ripley for tea.[14] The Thoreaus arrived as one of Concord's best families. Everything promised happiness and prosperity.

It was over in months. According to family tradition, Jean Thoreau was out patrolling the Boston streets in a severe rainstorm and caught a cold that inflamed his tuberculosis; he died weeks later, on March 7, 1801, just forty-seven years old.[15] His eight orphaned children found themselves in the care of their stepmother Rebecca, widowed once again. It should have worked out better than it did: Jean left a huge estate, $25,000 all told, including houses in Concord and Boston and cash and securities worth $12,000. But by the time the pious Rebecca died in 1814, the houses were mortgaged and the money was gone. Her brother Joseph Hurd, a Charlestown merchant who administered the estate, had used it up paying himself legal fees and expenses, leaving Jean Thoreau's children to grow up in deepening penury. Fourteen-year-old John, who upon his father's death became the man of the family, had to leave school to juggle relentless creditors while hoping to duplicate his father's success as a merchant.

For a while John clerked in Deacon White's store, but in 1807 he went to Salem, one of the world's leading ports for Chinese ceramics, silks and cottons, furniture, and spices, to learn the dry-goods trade. This was shooting for the top: imported goods required a large investment. In 1808, he came of age at twenty-one; he borrowed $1,000 on his anticipated inheritance to open his own store, partnering with Isaac Hurd Jr., who'd been to Canton and knew the China trade. His family must have had high hopes when John opened the "yellow store" on the square, but somehow the partnership soured. When John sought to dissolve it, Hurd took him to court, and though Hurd lost the case, in the legal mess John lost his store.[16] In the meantime, John's sister Nancy had married Caleb Billings and gone north to Bangor, where Billings opened his own store. John, his hopes ruined, followed them for a spell, "selling to the Indians (among others)." Meanwhile, his neighbor Moses Prichard bought John's old inventory for their own "green store" across the square, and when the United States declared war on Great Britain in 1812, the value of that inventory skyrocketed. Then Prichard's store was named the local post office too. For twenty years, the "green store" was the hub of Concord, with two hundred customers on the books and so much trade they didn't bother to advertise.[17] It must have hurt.

Caleb and Nancy Billings hung on and made a go of it; their daughter Rebecca would later marry George Thatcher, whose invitations to explore the Maine Woods changed Henry Thoreau's life. But John Thoreau didn't stay in Bangor. There were still four unmarried sisters to look out for, and he'd bought a bit of farmland out on Virginia Road, too, next door to Captain Jonas Minott's farm. When exactly did he meet Minott's stepdaughter Cynthia? Perhaps while chatting over the back fence, or at church. For something drew him back to Concord—likely the tall, accomplished, "handsome, high-spirited woman . . . with a voice of remarkable power and sweetness in singing," who helped run Captain Minott's Virginia Road farm and raised her voice every Sunday in Ezra Ripley's First Parish Church.[18]

✦━◆━✦

Cynthia Dunbar came to Concord about the same time as John, but by a very different road. While John's Patriot father was sailing the high seas, Cynthia's mother, Mary Jones Dunbar, was caught in a civil war between her Tory father, the immensely wealthy Colonel Elisha Jones, and her Patriot husband, the witty and genial Reverend Asa Dunbar. Mary's father, a fierce Royalist, had set himself against the insurgents; as the violence escalated, he even raised a private army to defend his Weston estate until, defeated, he fled to occupied Boston. Trapped in Boston, Elisha Jones watched as the Americans destroyed everything he'd built. He collapsed and died in March 1776, just as George Washington was about to drive the British out of Boston. Colonel Jones thus "escaped banishment by death," but most of his fourteen sons escaped death by banishment, either joining the British army or fleeing to Canada. The Jones family lost everything. Their immense fortune—including farms, estates, and acreages scattered across Massachusetts—was confiscated.[19]

And Mary? After her splendid wedding in 1772, she and the Reverend Asa Dunbar had settled in Salem, where her husband became pastor of the First Congregational Church. When all hell broke loose, they rushed back to her family estate in Weston so Mary could care for her bereft mother and help her Tory brothers. On that fateful day of April 19, 1775, it was her brother Stephen who showed British soldiers the short way to Lexington so they could reinforce the retreating British troops. Later, her brother Josiah was captured and jailed for bringing food to the British in Boston. Seventy-seven years later, Henry Thoreau recalled what happened after his grandmother carried ripe cherries to her jailed brother: "They secreted knives furnished them with their food sawed the grates off & escaped to Weston. Hid in the cider mill. Mary heard they were in the mill put on her riding hood—was frightend." She captured "Old Baldwin's the sheriff's horse," harnessed him up to the family chaise, and drove to her brother, who with his two fellow escapees whipped up the horse all the way to Portland and "pawned him for 2 bushels of potatoes—wrote back to Baldwin where he'd find his horse by paying charges." No word on whether Baldwin ever got his horse back.[20]

Thoreau's grandfather stayed loyal to his treasonous wife even though his own sympathies were with the Patriots. Asa Dunbar must have had a golden tongue, for when suspicion turned on him, he protested his innocence and was believed.[21] When deteriorating health forced him to resign the Salem ministry, he reinvented himself as a lawyer. In 1782 he resettled his family in the frontier town of Keene, New Hampshire, where his nephew was the Episcopal minister. For a few years the family throve: Asa became a charter member (and the first Master) of a Masonic Lodge and was elected first town clerk and then selectman. It was a bustling, full household when Mary gave birth to her sixth child, Cynthia, on May 28, 1787.[22] But not a month later, Asa took ill, and in two days he was dead. The town, shocked, buried him with full Masonic honors.

Mary Jones Dunbar was now a widow with a houseful of children, little money, and no family. Resourceful as ever, she turned her house into a licensed tavern; her children served the customers. Keene, the county seat, was a favorite stop on the road to Boston, and Mary's tavern stood on the highway in the heart of town. Captain Jonas Minott regularly traveled that highway. A Concord farmer with property in New Hampshire, Captain Minott had earned his title before the American Revolution—indeed, it was he who warned the British that American militia were expected "to meet *at one minutes warning* equipt with arms and ammunition." When the alarm came and his own militia arrived late, Minott was suspected of lingering Tory sympathies—a failure that led, ironically, to the town's signature: the Concord Minutemen.[23] Minott, a widower since 1792, married the plucky Mary Jones Dunbar in 1798. Mary moved her family into his farmhouse on Virginia Road, where Cynthia Dunbar, then eleven years old, finished growing up.

Cynthia long remembered the quiet on the eastern edge of Concord's Great Field. All she heard on summer nights was "the lowing of cows, or cackling of geese," or perhaps Joe Merriam whistling to his team; "she used to get up at midnight and go and sit on the door-step when all in the house were asleep, and she could hear nothing in the world but the ticking of the clock in the house behind her." Virginia Road was named, according to tradition, for "Old Virginia," a freed slave who built his cabin on the outskirts of Concord and wore the footpath walking to town. Today its curves have been smoothed to speed cars on their way to corporate parks and shopping malls, but in those days it was "an old-fashioned, winding, at-length-deserted pathway" with mossy banks and tumbling stone walls. In 1798, the farm was already 150 years old, and the fine high-style farmhouse, built decades before, had already seen one generation grow up and leave. Now the old house was filled again, with a new generation carrying on what was, and remains today, one of America's oldest farms.[24]

Cynthia also remembered Cold Friday: January 19, 1810, when "the people in the kitchen . . . drew up close to the fire, but the dishes which the Hardy girl was washing froze as fast as she washed them, close to the fire. They managed to keep warm in the parlor by their great fires."[25] Jack Garrison, one of the laborers keeping warm that night in Cynthia's kitchen, was new in town, an escaped slave from New Jersey. Soon he would marry and establish his own farm nearby; he and Henry Thoreau would often work together. John Thoreau was not by Cynthia's fire that night, for his store was still disintegrating and he still had ahead of him his adventure selling to the Indians in Bangor. But by 1811, John was back in Concord, and the romance quickened through the harvest and into the winter months. By February 1812, Cynthia was pregnant with Helen. Three months later, on May 11, Rev. Ezra Ripley married Cynthia Dunbar and John Thoreau at the First Parish Church. By the time Helen Louisa Thoreau was born on October 22, her parents were living in the Virginia Road farmhouse and carrying on the farm, while John clerked at Josiah Davis's store in town. The years ahead were crowded with uncertainties, but from then on, John and Cynthia Thoreau faced them together.

THE EARLY YEARS OF
JOHN AND CYNTHIA THOREAU

John Thoreau would be remembered as a quiet man, unambitious and too decent to press the hard bargains needed for success in the cash-poor early republic. But time and again, he met defeat by taking a forward leap, such as opening his own store, and when it failed, trying again in Maine. Now, back in Concord, he was again looking to the future. For her part, Cynthia had grown into a shrewd observer of humanity. Horace Hosmer, who knew them both, always insisted Cynthia was "a most exacting woman, who never would accept a second rate article of any kind if a better was obtainable, but that John Thoreau satisfied her." There was a certain quality to John: Hosmer said he was "French from the shrug of his shoulders to his snuff box. . . . healthy, fine boned, fine trained, well bred, a gentleman by instinct, so clean hearted and clean tongued that his wife recognized his superiority." And she, being Cynthia, "was not afraid to speak her mind."[26] For if few noticed John, everyone noticed the indomitable Cynthia, who stood a head taller than her husband and was one of the most famous talkers of the day, full of wit and anecdote spiced with sarcasm, and blessed with that brisk efficiency New Englanders called "faculty."

If the refined John and fearless Cynthia had looked forward to some quiet years on the farm, events proved otherwise. Five weeks after their wedding, on June 18, 1812, the United States declared war on Great Britain in retaliation for the British depredations on American trade strangling American commerce. The war dragged on for two and a half years, choking off imports and creating chaos along the coastline; British ships raided American ports at will, climaxing with the burning of the White House and the attack on Baltimore memorialized in "The Star-Spangled Banner." Up north, the Thoreau relatives lived through days of terror as the British reclaimed Maine, invading Bangor in the fall of 1814 and setting all the ships in the harbor ablaze—in one stroke reducing Bangor's transportation system and economic base to ashes. Aunt Nancy, pregnant with their first son, survived the attack only to die with infant Caleb in childbirth. The British also harassed ships in Massachusetts Bay, but thanks to the guns of Fort Independence, Boston stayed secure. Just as Jean had done before him, John Thoreau took a turn as commissar at the fort, supplying groceries to the soldiers.[27]

Back on the Virginia Road farm, Helen was only five months old when the bottom fell out from under them: on March 20, 1813, Captain Jonas Minott died in the night, and Cynthia's mother Mary awoke to find herself widowed a second time. As before, this spelled calamity for mother and children. By English common law and American legal practice, women could not inherit personal property, so instead of passing to his widow, all of Captain Minott's effects were auctioned off less than a month after his death, stripping the house virtually bare. Mary managed to buy back a bedspread and some green-edged china. As for real estate—the farm, woodlot, house and outbuildings—the custom of "widow's thirds" gave sixty-five-year-old Mary the right to use one-third of her deceased husband's property until she died or remarried. Surviving legal documents spell out in excruciating detail exactly what that meant: Mary and her family were allowed to use the east end of the house, including the front room and chamber and the garret above; they could go in and out of one-half the grand front entry and all the back door; they could use the oven, the well, the backyard, half the wood, and the upstairs bedroom facing the sunrise, the room where her grandson Henry would be born.[28]

Mary walked away from it all. She mortgaged her right to the property for $129 to Joe Merriam of the musical whistle and moved, with her bachelor son Charles and her unmarried daughter Louisa, into the "Red House" on Lexington Road, rented from the store-keeper Josiah Davis, her son-in-law's employer. Years later, Emerson's apple orchard would stand across the street. Eventually Mary repaid the mortgage, allowing Cynthia and John to return to her third of the farmhouse. Where had they gone in the meantime? Henry had the impression they decamped to Boston, from where John wrote a letter to his Bangor relatives sometime in 1815, with baby John (born July 5, 1814) "on his knee." Meanwhile, Mary had to plead for charity to the Reverend Ripley. In a letter on her behalf, the minister pointed out that she had been "peculiarly unfortunate" in the settlement of her late husband's estate and in her straitened circumstances, "feeling the weight of cares, of years and of widowhood to be very heavy, after having seen better days, she is induced by the advice of friends, as well as her own exigencies, to apply for aid to the benevolence and charity of the Masonic Fraternity."[29] The Masons passed the hat, and with their help Mary lived on just long enough to impress her grandson Henry, who collected her stories in his Journal. When she died in 1830, Aunt Louisa and Uncle Charles would move in with John and Cynthia.

But not to their home on the farm. Commerce had brightened once the war was over, but still, life on Virginia Road required John to split his time between working the farm and tending store in town—and with two young children, the widows' third was growing cramped. Had the crops been good, perhaps they might have made a go of it. But everything they planted in the spring of 1816 was doomed. By May the farmers complained of a "backward" spring, with daily temperatures below freezing; early in June, an Arctic cold front froze the ground solid from Ohio, across New England, and as far south as New Jersey, with snow across the northern tier. The apple crop was destroyed, and the corn, potato, and vegetable crops were devastated. As one historian has written, "No one was ready. People donned winter clothes and watched the blackened fields and gardens or gathered in dismay around fires."[30] Whatever survived or was replanted was hit again by hard frosts in July and August; on September 28, a hard killing frost destroyed what was left. After that, the weather turned mild, mocking the blackened and ruined fields. With nothing left to feed the livestock, hogs and cattle were slaughtered, glutting the markets and driving down prices that rebounded to record levels as winter approached. New England was still a relatively local economy, and crop failures meant starvation.

The strange weather was worldwide: 1816 was the notorious "Year without a Summer," a global climate collapse unaccountable then, but explained today by the 1815 eruption of Indonesia's Mount Tambora, the largest volcanic event in over 1,300 years. The following spring, a strange high fog dimmed the sunlight, reddening sunsets and making sunspots visible to the naked eye—a weird spectacle that Concord's newspaper said was "the burthen of almost every conversation." Average global temperatures dropped by nearly 1.5 degrees Fahrenheit, a seemingly trivial amount, but enough to make the difference between prosperous harvests and famine from Europe to North America to China. An estimated 200,000 New Englanders had to sell or abandon their farms and move west.[31]

By the autumn of that terrible year, Cynthia was pregnant for the third time. Under these unprecedented conditions, keeping her family fed and herself healthy through the winter must have taxed even her famous thrift. She once told Henry that she bought "no new clothes for John until he went away into a store, but made them of his father's old clothes," causing Henry to remark that in a pinch, country boys could always rob scarecrows. Thanks to such economies they made it through, and on July 12, 1817, Cynthia gave birth to a healthy baby boy. They called him Henry, but then, only six weeks later, John's little brother David died, just after coming of age at twenty-one. So on October 12, when it came time to bring their infant son to the First Parish Church for baptism, they followed family custom and kept the name alive: the Reverend Ezra Ripley baptized their second son David Henry Thoreau. Remarkably—at least, the family remarked on it—little Henry "did not cry."[32]

Henry Thoreau's first biographer thought it "lovely he should draw his first breath in a pure country air, out of crowded towns, amid the pleasant russet fields." Lovely indeed, but he would not grow up amid the farm's pleasant fields.[33] John and Cynthia survived one more crop cycle, but the world climate in 1817 was hardly better. In March 1818, as spring planting approached, they gave up the farm for good. For a time the young family rented the other half of the Red House, where Grandmother Jones was living out her final years in genteel poverty. Henry recalled that Aunt Sarah taught him how to walk here, at fourteen months of age. While the family recuperated, John tidied up his precarious finances and planned their next move. He'd finally paid off the vexed loan on his inheritance the previous August, giving up his share of the Prince Street house in Boston, and in September 1818 he sold their share of the Virginia Road house to pay off funds due to Jonas Minott's estate. Perhaps that was when John sold even his gold wedding ring.[34]

It was time for a fresh start. John decided to return to the business he knew best: keeping store. In October 1818 they moved ten miles north to the quiet rural village of Chelmsford, renting a house and shop next door to the village church, where the town stored their gunpowder in the garret. In those days no store could attract trade without selling rum; as Horace Hosmer remarked, "Church buildings were cold, and sermons were long," and everyone, even the ministers, drank it. The reliable Reverend Ripley helped out by certifying John had "sustained a good character" and was "a man of integrity, accustomed to store-keeping, and of correct morals."[35] That got John his liquor license, and on November 15 he opened for business, selling groceries and spirits and painting signs while Cynthia waited on customers.

John and Cynthia lived in Chelmsford for two and a half years. They never quite forgave the town for not removing the gunpowder next door, but other than that, stories show the young family coming to life. Here Sophia was born, on June 24, 1819, making four children in all, born regularly two years apart. All four grew to adult-hood, though Henry, a toddler now, gave the family plenty of scares. Once, he swung from the stairs, fell, and knocked himself out, "and it took two pails of water to bring me to." Another time, while playing with an axe, he cut off part of a toe. He got himself tossed by a cow, "knocked over by a hen with chickens, etc., etc." Best was the story about the cow they took on trial. When Cynthia tried to milk her, the cow kicked over the pail. The neighbor laughed at Cynthia as a city girl, but when he tried, the cow "kicked him over, and he finished by beating her with a cowhide shoe." By the time John got home, the cow "needed much to be milked," so he thought he'd "'brustle right up to her'"—but she kicked him "'fair and square right in the muns,'" knocked him flat, and broke his nose "which shows it yet." John drove her home to the seller, the blood still running down his face, as passersby scrambled over walls to save themselves from her horns. It was a barefoot, knockabout childhood—rough, unfussy, and close to the soil, with animals everywhere. Livestock roamed freely in those days, and Henry always remembered when the cow wandered into the house after the pumpkins.[36]

Had they stayed, Henry Thoreau would have gotten his first lessons from Ralph Waldo Emerson. In 1825, Emerson spent autumn and winter living on a Chelmsford farm, recovering from the eye-strain that had temporarily blinded him and teaching thirty or forty boys at the Chelmsford school. Years later he looked back fondly on the village's "plain homely land, sandy fields which the Merrimack washes," where apples covered the ground and "the chestnut forest spread its brown harvest on a frosty morning." Those Chelmsford farmers were the "original authors of liberty," but, added Emerson, they were also "all orthodox Calvinists, mighty in the Scriptures" who "read in no romances, but with the pulpit, on one hand, & poverty & labor on another, they had a third training in the town meeting."[37] Whether it was the poverty, the Calvinism, or the intransigence at town meetings isn't clear, but something brought the Thoreaus' rural idyll to an end. In March 1821, they once again pulled up stakes, moving this time into "Pope's House," a ten-footer in the south end of Boston. Here John tried schoolteaching, and Henry started school; in September, with winter coming on, they moved to "Whitwell's House" at 4 Pinckney Street, staying until March 1823.[38] In contrast to the Chelmsford years, the two years in urban Boston left barely a trace in Henry Thoreau's memory.

What Henry did remember was a vision of still, clear water among the pines. During a visit to Grandmother Jones, the Thoreau family took an outing to Walden Pond. Looking back, Henry dated his life from this moment: "Twenty three years since when I was 5 years old, I was brought from Boston to this pond, away in the country. . . . That woodland vision for a long time made the drapery of my dreams." Even as a child, his spirit longed for "that sweet solitude," for "that speaking silence that my ears might distinguish the significant sounds." Not in Boston, "that tumultuous and varied city," but here on the outskirts of Concord, where "sunshine & shadow were the only inhabitants that varied the scene," would this wild child find the nursery for his spirit.[39]

MAKING CONCORD HOME

Uncle Charles made it all possible. Cynthia's elder brother had grown into an eccentric bachelor with a habit of disappearing for weeks or months at a time, "cutting hay on a farm in northern Vermont . . . or wandering through a village on the coast of Maine," reappearing without warning to play card tricks in the tavern, twirl his hat up to the ceiling and catch it on his head every time, or "burst" the tough local farmers in wrestling matches.[40] In October 1822, on one of his rambles, Charles came across a plumbago deposit in Bristol, New Hampshire, in the foothills south of the White Mountains. The term *plumbago*, for lead, is now obsolete; what Charles had found was a greasy, slate-gray form of carbon that we today call graphite. Mixed with clay, it makes crucibles for molten metals. In an age of heavy industry, graphite lubricant stands up to high heat and keeps ball bearings rolling smoothly; in an age of iron, graphite paint prevents rust and polishes wood stoves. Above all, as suggested by the word's derivation from *graphein* (Greek for "to write"), graphite is the key ingredient in pencils.

Charles had stumbled upon black gold. He staked a mining claim and sent off some samples for testing. A Dr. Mitchell in New York certified the Bristol graphite's high quality and value, congratulating Charles on "the discovery of such a treasure in our country." James Freeman Dana, Dartmouth College's first professor of chemistry and mineralogy, declared Charles's graphite to be far superior to any other found in the United States, as fine as England's peerless Borrowdale ore.[41] Back in Concord, Charles formed a partnership with Cyrus and Nathan Stow, manufacturers of soap and candles, and they started to work the mine. Unfortunately Charles had acquired mining rights for only seven years. He needed help, someone with marketing experience and ingenuity, able to drop everything and jump onto a new enterprise fast. He called upon John Thoreau. In March 1823, the Thoreaus moved into the "Brick House" on the corner of Walden and Main, next to Concord's Mill Dam. Charles passed the business over to his brother-in-law, who named the fledgling firm "John Thoreau and Co." and set up shop on the corner of Walden and Everett Streets overlooking the millpond. John knew exactly what to do with this rare, pure graphite of such extraordinary quality: pencils. On this flash of insight he built the Thoreau family fortune.

The Industrial Revolution was about communication as much as machinery. Everyone needed a reliable, cheap, and portable writing instrument, something better than quill and ink. Since the sixteenth century, the Borrowdale mine in England had supplied the British, then all of Europe, with graphite, starting with simple sticks of it encased in wood. Horace Hosmer, a pencil-maker who worked for John Thoreau, thought the American pencil started with a Concord woman who pushed the pith out of elder twigs with a knitting needle, to fill them with pencil leads made from Borrowdale graphite scraps pounded fine and mixed with glue. Given the exorbitant cost of imported British pencils, it was better than nothing. William

Munroe, a Concord furniture maker, took the next step: after sales slumped during the British embargo leading to the War of 1812, he started casting around for alternative products. Munroe ground the graphite with a hammer, mixed it into a paste in the head of a spoon, and encased the leads in cedar. When he had thirty pencils, he brought them to Boston. They sold immediately.

Munroe returned home with an order for five gross more; over the next year and a half he cleared over $4,000 on 1,200 gross of pencils—a stunning profit. Terrified of competition, he kept his process secret from everyone but his wife. But once the war ended, the British flooded the market with the stockpiles jamming their warehouses, including pencils far better than Munroe could make. He went back to crafting cabinets and clock cases, but on the side he kept fiddling with pencils, haunted by that giddy profit margin. By 1819 Munroe had something workable, and he opened up a pencil factory on Concord's Mill Dam. Soon he was marketing pencils as far away as Kentucky. By 1825 he'd relocated his factory to Barrett's Mill and was turning out more pencils in four days than he'd made in a month before. Thus was born the first industrial pencil factory in the United States.[42]

The mystery is how John Thoreau caught up so fast. Like Munroe, he kept his trade secrets to himself. But where Munroe had spent years developing his process, only seven months later, in October 1823, Thoreau pencils won a premium at the Massachusetts Agricultural Fair. John sold six gross of them to Moses Prichard, whose store became his major local retail outlet. By October 1824 John was displaying his pencils at the Massachusetts Agricultural Society, earning words of praise from the *New England Farmer*: "The Lead Pencils exhibited by J. Thorough & Co. were superiour to any specimens exhibited in past years." Such stunning progress indicates either a brilliant engineering mind, cheap imitation (as Munroe complained), or collusion with someone who broke Munroe's trade secret. Two years later Munroe countered by unveiling his new, improved, and elegantly packaged pencils, winning a silver medal and a stack of endorsements. Soon he was marketing three grades of pencils—"best quality," "premium," and "common"—and John Thoreau was pressed to upgrade his own product. Competition pushed them both to success, and by the 1830s, "the two firms together were manufacturing 3,000 to 6,000 gross of pencils annually." Although Munroe fretted about overproduction, the market kept expanding and both firms prospered, making Concord, for a time, the center of American pencil-making.[43]

By today's standards, early American pencils were crude affairs. The graphite was ground and mixed with bayberry wax, whale spermaceti, and glue, heated and pressed into grooves cut in a slab of fine-grained cedar wood, dried, covered with a second slab, cut, and shaped. Edward Emerson remembered them as "greasy, gritty, brittle, inefficient."[44] But John's graphite pencils sold well enough (along with red and blue pencils, stove polish, battery plates, sandpaper made of white Walden sand, and fine, marbled paper for bookbinding, plus a side in clock repair) to lift the Thoreau family into the respectable middle class. Of John's two sons, it was Henry who got involved in the business; like his father, he was intrigued with machinery and loved to work with his hands. Thanks to Henry's improvements, for a time Thoreau pencils were the best in America, sought by artists, engineers, surveyors, architects, carpenters, and writers—everyone who depended on a good pencil. Thoreau's own working method coevolved with the family pencils. Selling them helped fund his writing, but more important, the pencil allowed him to take notes out in nature, in wind or heat or bitter cold—notes he inked into his notebooks back home. Quite literally, Thoreau's writing career rested on the humble pencil, so much a part of him that, when he drew up a list of travel essentials, he forgot to mention a pencil, the same way he forgot to mention air to breathe or water to drink.

→>-<-

John may have been too gentle to drive hard bargains in a general store, but he "loved to sit in the shops or at the post-office and read the papers," and he spent the rest of his life happily ensconced in the heart of town, offering fellowship to everyone. His business allowed him to socialize, drawing on his knowledge of markets and men, while devoting himself to making things both useful and beautiful. Henry said his father studied "how to make a *good* article," refusing to make "a poor one" for money, "as if he labored for a finer end."[45] John loved music and played the flute—his elegant flute books from around 1800, filled with music transcribed by a journeyman, still survive—and his name, in exquisite copperplate handwriting, is inscribed in some of the finest books in Henry's library. Horace Hosmer said, "He was an Artist . . . even if he never touched a brush or chisel." John avoided town politics and never joined Concord's elite Social Circle, yet whenever the Circle launched a new project, John pitched in, donating books to the library, joining the Society of Middlesex Husbandmen and Manufactures, becoming secretary of the Concord Fire Society (the volunteer fire department), and giving time and money to the Ornamental Tree Society, which lined Concord's streets with elms, sycamores, and maples to make "the barren spot and way-side smile and blossom" for future generations.[46]

If John avoided controversies, Cynthia, the vocal defender of liberal causes, courted them. Her sharp eye and caustic wit delighted her friends but provoked her more conventional neighbors. Despite the "edge" of what Ralph Waldo Emerson called her "malicious wit," his son Edward never forgot her great kindness, "especially to young people, often shown with great delicacy." One neighbor averred Cynthia's readiness to condemn a fault "was done in all honesty to bring about a reform." Those reforms started at home: though her table was attractive and the food abundant, they did without such luxuries as tea, coffee, and sugar to afford a piano for the girls and a Harvard education for their talented younger son. To bring in extra money, Cynthia ran the family home as a boardinghouse, yet neighbors who could afford no return were always welcome at her table. Like John, she sought out community service, joining the Concord Female Charitable Society and regularly hosting their meetings, at which ladies sewed clothing and linens for families in need while they talked over who could use a gift of shoes or schooling, payment of a doctor's bill, extra food, or a little tobacco to make the day go easier. From this busy group (the "*chattable* society," some of the men unkindly called it) evolved the Concord Female Anti-Slavery Society, one of the earliest and most active in the nation.[47] Before abolitionism reached the media and the lecture hall, it lived in family homes where mothers and wives, sisters and daughters met to stitch together the fabric of their community.

Helen, the eldest, grew into a bookish young woman—elegant, graceful, earnest, and quiet, the family's moral lodestar. She was the first teacher in the family, setting the career path followed by her siblings, and she took the outrages of social injustice most deeply to heart, dedicating herself to ending slavery in America. She became a friend of Frederick Douglass, and at her tragically early death, William Lloyd Garrison eulogized her in the *Liberator*. Sophia, the youngest, had her mother's wit, tempered with her father's sweetness. In her gravity, speech, and appearance, many thought she resembled Henry, with whom she shared many interests. In later years, whenever Henry found something interesting, he called Sophia to come look. She loved plants and filled the house with sunshine and flowers; her conservatory by the dining room became a neighborhood showpiece. She knew the wild plants, too, and more than once beat her brother to a rare wildflower. Sophia was also an artist of limited training but real talent, whose drawing of Henry's house at Walden became the famous frontispiece of her brother's book.

But all that lay in the future. For now the star of the family was John Jr. He was gregarious, bold, charismatic; Horace Hosmer declared that John Jr. was "his father over again with the sunny side turned to the world where all men might see it." He was strong and quick, a natural athlete who would "throw somersaults, wrestle with the boys, jump high, walk on his hands, laugh, shout, and roll over on the grass in mock fights at recess," or regale them by the hour with stories so funny their sides ached with laughter, "as chock full of fun as an egg is of meat."[48] But while John dove into boyhood games with zest and uninhibited glee, his little brother held back, observing with a sober gravity that Horace's brother Joseph called "perfectly unaccountable and disgusting." Young Henry puzzled everyone. He was gentle and obliging to the boys, even as they mocked him as "the Judge," "the old maid," or "the fine scholar with a big nose," and they shied snowballs at him as he stood by the brick schoolhouse watching their pranks. Yet though they could scoop him every time at high-spy, standing on their heads, or "in a good square yell," Henry scooped them all in class: "He had a better understanding of the subject matter of the books at twelve than most of the class at sixteen."[49]

What was this quiet, watchful boy thinking? In adulthood he remembered being quite capable of defending himself when he thought it mattered, as when he found a potato that had sprouted and, on his mother's advice, planted it in his own little plot in their kitchen garden. Soon afterward, John came in holding his sprouted potato, then Sophia, then even Helen—until Henry came in crying that someone had taken *his* potato, whereupon "it was restored to me as the youngest and original discoverer," and it grew "in *my* garden, and finally its crop was dug by myself and yielded a dinner for the family." He also recalled the dreamy child who would stare out the window, gazing upon the clouds "and, allowing my imagination to wander, search for flaws in their rich drapery that I might get a peep at that world beyond." His mother told a friend how, when Henry and John still slept together in a trundle bed, "John would go to sleep at once, but Henry often lay long awake. His mother found the little boy lying so one night, long after he had gone upstairs, and said, 'Why, Henry dear, why don't you go to sleep?' 'Mother' said he, 'I have been looking through the stars to see if I couldn't see God behind them.'"[50]

Henry's journeys were not always taken alone. He reminisced in college that "in the freshness of the dawn my brother and I were ever ready to enjoy a stroll" to Fairhaven Hill, climbing the highest rocky peak together to "catch the first ray of the morning sun." From childhood on, nature structured and furnished Thoreau's inner mindscape. His friend Ellery Channing said that in their walks together, Henry never remarked on the childhood houses they passed, but he did recall a particular field as the one to which he drove the family cow to pasture, returning, like the other barefoot village boys, to drive her home again for milking. And he often "let fall some memory of the 'Milldam' when he was a boy and of the pond behind it, now a meadow."[51] Though the millpond was long since drained, Henry's friends recalled that in wintertime it made "a skating ground for the older boys and a sliding place for us young-sters," where the boldest boys would play "kittlybenders," crowning with victory the last one to safely skate across the thinning ice.[52] Thoreau never wrote an autobiography (Channing said he didn't like to dwell on the past), but around 1837 he sketched some notes for a memoir: "Gardening—Chickens—First ramble a graping—First fishing expedition—skaiting—berrying—hunting—Bare Garden hill &c—fireflies—Indian wigwam—old mill—music—Squantum feasts in the fields with one companion only—Bread and butter on the garden fence—Books and Reading—Sleepy Hollow—Character of my companions—Visit to Walden—Drive to lecture—birch swinging and potatoe roasting—."[53] What pages he could have written of his earliest years.

Nature, to Thoreau, began as a family, communal event. Dr. Josiah Bartlett, the village physician, often led neighborhood chil-dren on swimming and fishing expeditions; and on summer after-noons, young men and women got up "walking parties" to climb Fairhaven Hill or stroll around Walden Pond.[54] Cynthia and John, renowned for taking long walks together, fit right in: rumor had it one of their children was nearly born on Nawshawtuct Hill. A neighbor recalled how Cynthia set off on grand picnics, cooking supper on an open fire and boiling water in a little tin teapot, and leading them all home by twilight. Cynthia, "with her keen delight in nature ... trained her children's eyes and ears." She would take them outside and make them listen to the birds, "framing little verses of exclamation cheerful or plaintive to fit the accent of the outbursts from the various little feathered throats." Soon the boys were out on their own: "when John and Henry came running into the house slamming the doors," Cynthia reminisced, "I knew that Ben Hosmer or Joseph had come, and that the boys would take their luncheon and not be home till night, being off for Walden, Fairhaven Cliffs, Egg Rock or down the river." Decades later, when Horace Hosmer saw Henry and Sophia ramble out together, he with his notebook, she with her sketchpad, he thought "they were father and mother over again, Nature and Art lovers, son like the mother, daughter like the father."[55]

But life couldn't be all skating contests and picnic suppers. One day Cynthia led John, Henry, and little Sophia to Miss Phoebe Wheeler's "infant school," startling Miss Wheeler's other pupils with the entrance of her "big barefoot boys." Mothers routinely sent their young children to such neighborhood "school dames," spinsters or widows who supported themselves by running what amounted to daycare centers, teaching their charges the ABCs while baking bread or working at the spinning wheel. Young Henry spent many days in the bare rooms of Phoebe Wheeler's "old unpainted weather beaten house" shaded by big buttonwood trees, furnished with unpainted seats and stools, a bed in the corner for tired children to nap on, and a row of half-eaten apples "turning rusty in the sunshine," waiting to be returned at recess. The children learned their lessons pinned to Miss Wheeler's knee by their aprons. Henry Thoreau remembered asking Miss Wheeler the prescient question, "Who owns all the land?", as well as winning a medal for geography, only to ask his mother afterward, "Is Boston in Concord?" He was quite sure that had he remained with Miss Wheeler a little longer, he would have received "the chief prize book 'Henry Lord Mayor.'"[56]

To a small boy, Concord must have seemed huge. Living by the Mill Dam put the Thoreaus next door to a thriving industrial park, where the clang of the blacksmith's trip hammer rang out over ramshackle shops built on pilings and squeezed between factories and foundries. Here Henry could watch the gristmill's great stone wheels grind flour for "rye 'n' Injun," peer behind the stacks of raw cowhides into the stinking tannery vats, and feel the scorching heat of the foundry fire, where men cast molten brass into bells for horse-drawn sleighs and fittings for the clockmakers across the street. Out on the street were mounds of leather scraps, horse stables, teams of oxen in front of busy stores, raucous taverns, and the old Thoreau home, which Henry's aunts, "the Misses Thoreau," ran as a popular boardinghouse, with many a party catered by Shattuck's store next door. On the corner next to the grand Middlesex Hotel, with stagecoaches at the door and the jail behind, were the irresistible windows of Montefiori's candy store. Four times a year on court days, the town bells summoned a parade of sheriffs, judges, and lawyers from the Middlesex Hotel across the commons to the courthouse. Concord center was a microcosm of the world: young Henry, roaming free, would have absorbed more in a day on the Mill Dam than in a month in the schoolroom.[57]

Sometimes the world came to Concord, too—like the time the Marquis de Lafayette, the hero of the Revolution, passed through town during his farewell tour. This was rather more interesting than it sounds. On August 31, 1824, a cavalcade of Concord's worthies ushered the aging Lafayette to Concord's town square, announcing his arrival with a twenty-four-gun salute and the pealing of bells. Dignitaries were shepherded to a posh reception under a tent by the First Parish Church, where they munched delicacies and listened to a succession of fine speeches. The space around the tent was supposed to remain open, but the townspeople, anxious to see the great man, pressed past the barriers. As armed militia pushed them back, the crowd raised a chorus of angry voices: Didn't they have a right to be there, too? Perhaps their clothes were not so fine or their manners so polished, but hadn't their fathers fought in the Revolution? What, after all, had they been fighting for? A riot was barely averted, and though Lafayette's party deep inside the tent never noticed, the anger and bitterness festered for years, kept alive by what some thought were "crafty demagogues" using social alienation to further their own selfish purposes.[58] Such mounting resentment against the rising elite led by the wealthy Samuel Hoar and the powerful John Keyes—whose sons were among Henry Thoreau's playmates—meant the boundaries being drawn were unavoidably personal.

Young Henry witnessed Concord's jubilee as well, the fiftieth anniversary of the Concord Battle, held on April 19, 1825, around the corner from his home. The logical site by the Old North Bridge, where the battle had been fought, was mired in debates with Ezra Ripley, who lived in the Old Manse, even as commercial interests in the village pushed for a monument in the town center. So instead, after a thirteen-gun salute and the pealing of the town's bells, Concord's Masonic leaders laid, with due ceremony, the foundation stones for a mighty monument in the town square. Speeches followed in the First Parish Church (including a toast by Ralph Waldo Emerson honoring his grandfather William, who had rallied the minutemen fifty years before). Late one night soon afterward, town dissenters heaped on the cornerstone a twenty-foot mock-monument of tar barrels. The next night, town rowdies set it ablaze. The huge bonfire delighted the children, alarmed their parents, and cracked the foundation stones, ruining the monument. The ignominious heap stood for years, a favorite climb for schoolboys and, for their parents, a troubling reminder of the cracks in their community.[59]

While the mild-mannered John Thoreau steered clear of such conflicts, Cynthia soon found herself and her family square in the bull's-eye, torn between two factions.[60] Since its foundation, the church—still an official branch of town governance—had held Concord together. Every Concord household was taxed to pay Reverend Ripley's salary and maintain his meetinghouse; no other church was permitted or even contemplated. But the old-time Puritanism had liberalized over the years. Church membership had once required a full confession of one's sins; now it asked only a public profession of one's faith. Cynthia had done this in 1811, and at various times so had Henry's aunts Betsy, Jane, and Maria. But beyond Concord, protests were mounting against such liberalizing moves, and the evangelist Reverend Lyman Beecher (father of Harriet Beecher Stowe) rose to leadership in Boston by mustering the saints against the sinners, even as Boston's liberal icon, the Reverend William Ellery Channing, pleaded for tolerance and unity. The Reverend Ripley finally lost control of his flock in May 1826, when nine unhappy members

of his congregation banded together to found a new, more conservative church of their own, a "Trinitarian" church standing for the full
divinity of Christ within the mystery of a triune God. The liberals,
in response, rallied under the banner of "Unitarianism," insisting
that God could only be One, single, infinite Being.

Henry's aunts Betsy, Jane, and Maria were three of the nine original dissenters. Cynthia was deeply torn, but soon she, too, sought
to join the Trinitarians. When the new Trinitarian minister, Rev.
Daniel Southmayd, and his wife Joanna arrived in Concord in spring
1827, Cynthia welcomed them into her home. By then the Thoreaus
had moved yet again, across Main Street into the large, gracious
Shattuck House. To help meet their increased expenses, Cynthia
took in boarders. The Southmayds were among the first, and all that
spring, abstruse theological debates unfolded at the dinner table and
spilled into the parlor. Cynthia began to waver. Searching conversations with Joanna Southmayd convinced her that she must not yield
in her conviction that God was One, not Three, and Christ was
not divine, but God's embodiment in human form. The Trinitarians could not accept someone admitting such doubts, and Ripley
proudly welcomed Cynthia back to his fold. The new Trinitarian
meetinghouse continued to rise, directly across the millpond from
the First Parish Church, the twin steeples marking the moment New
England religion pluralized. Massachusetts dissenters pushed the
legislature for formal disestablishment of the church, and in November 1833, when it was put to a vote, Massachusetts citizens agreed.
From then on, the state's churches were private and voluntary. Their
ancient role in uniting a community was over.

The grave and observant young Henry took all this in. He grew
up in a profoundly religious household, where Sabbath for a small
boy meant endless dreary days indoors, banned even from the dis-
traction of books, staring out the window longing for sunset and
searching the sky for a hawk or two who might bear his thoughts
away "from earthly things." Fast days meant games of baseball out
at Sleepy Hollow, wondering how many services there would be
for his family, and whether there would be "an ordinary dinner,

an extraordinary dinner, or no dinner at all." The historian Robert Gross suggests the young Thoreau derived some important lessons from watching his household struggle over religion: first, that no one should sacrifice the claims of his or her own conscience to another—not to authority, and not to family, either. And second, that in its search for purity, religion had devolved into "a battlefield of squabbling parsons and warring churches."[61]

Henry's response was deep, even visceral: reject it all. The meetinghouse must be unbuilt, for the true church lived in no building and could be confined to no institution. Thoreau became an exacting student of the Bible, and he went beyond it to read the scriptures of other major religions, including Hinduism, Islam, and Buddhism, seeking for the true fountainhead of spiritual truth. When angry readers shook the New Testament in his face, Thoreau shot back that New England hadn't heard a single word of it: "Let but one of these sentences be rightly read from any pulpit in the land, and there would not be left one stone of that meeting-house upon another." Religion, to be true, must be founded anew, not on some cracked cornerstone but on "a hard bottom and rocks in place, which we can call *reality*, and say, This is, and no mistake."[62] That quest would lead Thoreau not to the meetinghouse and not to the courthouse, but to his house of one, out on the shore among the pines that made the drapery of his dreams.

CHAPTER TWO

Higher Learning
from Concord to Harvard

(1826–1837)

It is only when we forget all our learning that we begin to know.
HENRY DAVID THOREAU, OCTOBER 4, 1859

A CONCORD EDUCATION

Concord liked to boast of its schools. Ever since 1647, Concord's citizens had taxed themselves to make free public education available to all its children. Once Henry outgrew Phoebe Wheeler's lessons, he was at the grammar school on the town square at 9:00 a.m. sharp, having bowed to the master and taken his seat in one of the eighty wooden desks. Attendance was voluntary, and spotty; had all the eligible children shown up at once, Henry would have had to fight for a seat. Girls and boys of all ages and abilities crowded together into the one-room schoolhouse to pick up what they could from the perpetual curriculum: spelling and grammar, enough arithmetic for bookkeeping and enough trigonometry for elementary surveying, perhaps a taste of Latin and Greek for those few who aspired to college.

Most of the town's schoolteachers saw teaching as merely a convenient way station between college and a career. They weren't much older than their students, and they taught as they had been taught, by oral recitation: each student read a stanza or a paragraph aloud, passing the book along, waiting as the lesson crawled up and down the rows of desks. On Saturdays, children stood up to "speak pieces"—memorized bits of lyric or oratory. The schoolroom was heated by a single wood stove, whose fumes and stench were sealed in by windows shut against the cold, and the day's two brief recesses were needed as much to ventilate the room as to reinvigorate the children. Worst of all was the classroom's real goal: not education, but discipline. Teachers suspected that boys fresh off the farm would submit to authority only after testing its limits. So every teacher placed, right on top of their desk where everyone could see it, a "ferule," a thin, flat stick of wood about two feet long, ready to strike disobedient children on the palm of the hand, inflicting what one teacher admitted was "very great suffering." Inside the desk would be hidden "a cowhide for gross cases," and the rowdier boys could expect to be tied up and flogged for insolence or disruptive behavior.[1]

This was hardly the way to educate leaders for the new republic, and Concord's town fathers knew it. One of Thoreau's teachers, Edward Jarvis, joined the school committee and led a reform movement, hoping to replace authoritarian fear with mutual respect and courtesy. It helped, for a few years. Meanwhile, a group of concerned citizens had another idea: open a private-pay school whose cost (five dollars per term) would screen out "the lower-class rowdies" and give Concord's most promising young men and women a high-quality secondary school education.[2] Thus was born, in 1822, the Concord Academy, dedicated to fitting young men for college admission and both women and men for careers as schoolteachers. The academy had a full curriculum: Latin and Greek, plus French and Italian, English rhetoric and composition, mathematics, some chemistry and natural philosophy, a little history and geography. A parade of teachers came and went until September 1827, when the academy's directors hired Phineas Allen, Harvard class of '25. Allen saw teaching as his life's work, literally—he stayed in the classroom until he dropped dead of pneumonia at eighty-three, whereupon his obituaries honored him as the oldest teacher in the state's history. During his years at the Concord Academy, Phineas Allen shaped the intellectual horizons of a generation of Concord's youth, the generation that included Henry Thoreau.[3]

Although Allen taught an imposing roster of great men, including judges, senators, and at least one famous writer, his students did not think of him as a great teacher. "The poorest teacher and the worst school," one of them snorted. After a boy seized the ferule and broke it over Allen's head, smashing his gold glasses, discipline was over and the school "degenerated into a merely useless machine." Thoreau himself joked that "I was fitted, or rather made unfit, for College, at Concord Academy & elsewhere, mainly by myself, with the countenance of Phineas Allen, Preceptor."[4] Yet Allen was hardworking and anxious to be a model teacher. In a letter to the local newspaper, he admonished his successors to be mild and gentle, neat in person and dress, "conscientious in the smallest matters," and to encourage virtue rather than punish vice. Despite these worthy ideals, Allen's obituaries praised him for two things: being a "veritable encyclopedia" of information, and missing—in all his fifty-eight years of teaching—only five days on account of illness.[5]

As Thoreau hinted, his real education happened elsewhere, among the remarkable cohort of young women and men who grew up together and bonded during their academy years. "How I enjoyed it all!" sighed one classmate. "How we studied in school, and how we strolled to the cliffs and love lane in afternoons & recesses or skated on the shallow ponds. . . . We thought ourselves an uncommon lot." Thoreau, too, listed a cornucopia of pleasures: "Amusements at school—Swimming—boating—Virgil and Salust—Gardening—Squantums—nutting—Books and reading—coasting and skating music—and Society—."[6] Thoreau and his friends shared a common sensibility: they worried that commerce was overtaking American ideals; they longed for authenticity; they disdained the commands of convention and the dictates of fashion; they resolved to forge their own independent paths. This was the restless and hopeful new generation who listened so intently to Emerson, whose dreams and ideals were forged at the very moment when an explosion of newspapers, magazines, and books reinforced hopes for reform—a moment when lyceums and debating societies, libraries, musical groups, and antislavery societies opened up a new world of ideas competing in a burgeoning global marketplace.[7]

The Concord Academy itself was part of Concord's transition into this new era. Even as the old consensus was splintering and the new church was welcoming religious dissenters, Phineas Allen was offering the most promising youths of Concord a new, secular intellectual center. At that very moment, the same town fathers who founded the academy set about the remaking of Concord itself. In 1825, a group of Concord's wealthiest men constituted themselves as an unofficial chamber of commerce to clean up the Mill Dam's ramshackle shops and noisy, stinking factories. They tore down the gristmill and opened up the dam, "redeeming" (in the word of the day) the swampy, mosquito-breeding wetlands upstream that Thoreau loved, but everyone else deemed pestilential. The noxious tannery and factories were replaced with fine, high-columned, white-painted Federal-style buildings where artisans and craftsmen shared space with banks and insurance brokers who provided capital for the newly prosperous center of commerce. They widened the narrow old Mill Dam road (a notorious bottleneck) into an inviting thoroughfare, and all along the streets, the Ornamental Tree Society planted elms, sycamores, maples, and ashes—whip-lean saplings that in a quarter century would grow into the graceful arching colonnades Thoreau celebrated in "Autumnal Tints."

The result was the classic, picturesque New England village: lofty steeples and white-pillared buildings clustered around a convenient town center amid a leafy canopy of trees, surrounded by gracious neighborhoods and a few outlying farms. When Jean Thoreau had settled in Concord Center, it was a messy, improvised colonial hub of commerce, industry, and government. A few years later, his son John watched Concord remade as an attractive planned village, in the country but not of it. In 1843, when developers diverted the new railroad through town, Concord completed its evolution into a quiet, green residential town a world away from the urban noise and jostle of Boston, where few remembered the days when cows grazed on the commons. Concord was once again a trendsetter, and the vision realized by its city planners—order and stability, all the advantages of commerce in a quiet country retreat—would draw the rest of the famous Concord authors: Emerson, Hawthorne, the Alcotts, Channing, Sanborn.

Concord's town planners believed education was a civic necessity for everyone, not just the wealthy. Phineas Allen took an important step in October 1828, when he founded the Concord Academic Debating Society to give his male academy students practice in forensics: the thrust and parry of political argument, the foundation of civic democracy. Academy debaters crossed swords over such questions as whether gunpowder was a benefit to humankind or whether America would always be free. A month after its founding, John Thoreau Jr. was debating the question, "Are good novels preferable to good histories?" A year later his younger brother was taking the affirmative against Ebenezer Rockwood Hoar on the question, "Does it require more talents to make a good writer than a good extemporaneous speaker?" Allen scored it against Thoreau, who thus lost his first debate, at age twelve, to a future Massachusetts chief justice. Henry's performance was little better a month later when he came poorly prepared and won only because his opponent hadn't prepared at all. The secretary, the jailer's son George Moore, recorded his disgust: "Such a debate, if it may be called so, as we have had, this evening, I hope never again will be witnessed in this house, or recorded in this book." Henry then teamed up with George (who no doubt gave him some pointers) to win the negative in a debate over the usefulness of lotteries. The academy lads must have wanted out from under Allen's governance, however, for in January 1830 they started a new debating club of their own: the Young Men's Society for Mutual Improvement.[8]

But far more exciting was the new Concord Lyceum, which became one of the organizing centers of Thoreau's life. The lyceum movement had been founded by Josiah Holbrook. Electrified by a lecture on chemistry and geology, the Massachusetts schoolmaster envisioned an America where all workingmen—nay, all citizens!—

could be inspired by knowledge of science—nay, knowledge of all things!—the arts and letters and history as well, all that was *useful*, that could be linked to everyday life. After Holbrook published his manifesto in October 1826, he led his movement with the fervor of a crusader: lyceums would be local associations for mutual, hands-on instruction, where citizens would speak to one another of what they knew, sharing local knowledge and community resources, and linking to nearby communities for support and exchange of speakers across growing networks—all toward "raising the moral and intellectual taste of our countrymen."[9] After founding the first lyceum in the industrial town of Millbury (near Worcester) in November 1826, Holbrook traveled from town to town, organizing new ones wherever he touched down until his lyceum movement reached right across the nation.

Only a week after this "Johnny Appleseed of the Lyceum" came to Concord in October 1828, the Concord Debating Club—the adult model for Allen's student version—took up the question of founding a lyceum in Concord, and decided in the affirmative. On December 3, a large crowd of Concord citizens voted unanimously to make the Concord Lyceum a reality. A month later the newspaper was proclaiming its pride that Concord, "whose ancestry were among the foremost and boldest assertors of civil and political liberty," would stand among the first to emancipate its citizens "from vice and ignorance." For two dollars a year—half that for those who had to travel from farther away—every town citizen could bring "2 ladies and if married his children in addition" to weekly meetings that alternated lectures with debates. The fees covered expenses for out-of-town speakers, plus a cabinet of minerals, scientific apparatus, and a library, all made available (by way of the lyceum secretary Phineas Allen) to the students of the Concord Academy, and to the town's public school students, too—providing their teachers paid the dues.[10] Since Allen's students were all eligible to attend lyceum events, Thoreau's lifetime membership may be said to have begun at the age of eleven.

Soon the town was assembling at the Concord Academy to hear

weekly debates on such politically charged questions as whether the State should build a railroad from Boston to Albany (yes), whether corporal punishment in the schools should be abolished (no), and whether it was right to remove Indian tribes from their ancestral lands to regions beyond the Mississippi (no decision). Lyceum lectures consistently drew a full house, eager to learn about geography and history, politics, theology, and the sciences; in 1829, a course of lectures on chemistry attracted an audience of a hundred. For decades the Concord Lyceum was one of the largest and most active in the nation. Thoreau attended regularly and took several turns as curator and secretary, which allowed him to direct the town's attention to topics he thought were important, such as the abolition of slavery. He lectured there himself nearly twenty times in as many years, testing out his ideas before a live audience who, having seen him grow up from boyhood, were unawed by his growing fame and freely expressed their amusement, skepticism, and often their appreciation. "Civil Disobedience" was born at the Concord Lyceum; so were *Walden, The Maine Woods, Cape Cod*, and the late natural history essays. The importance of the lyceum to Thoreau is incalculable. It bound him to the town, and bound the town to him; whenever Thoreau wrote for the wider public, the faces he saw in his mind's eye were those of his friends and neighbors.

To all this the Thoreau household was integral. John's pencil business was important to Concord's commercial success, and Phineas Allen, who taught three of the Thoreau children, joined the household for a time. But the family's involvement went beyond this. The Thoreaus often hosted, and always attended, the lively parties held for academy students and their families. They were regulars at the lyceum, often escorting the speakers and putting them up for the night. And their household was growing: after Grandmother Jones died in 1830, the colorful Uncle Charles and the round and loving Aunt Louisa moved in, to stay for the rest of their lives. Cynthia always had final say over who could board at her home, and she made sure her boarders were people of quality who could educate her children in the newest ideas sweeping the nation, and who added to the intellectual life of the community as well.[11] Henry Thoreau hardly needed to leave Concord to see the world; staying home in Concord meant the world came to him.

A HARVARD PORTRAIT

There was one thing Henry Thoreau could not get in Concord, however: a college degree. It was not immediately obvious that he needed one; the family considered apprenticing him to a cabinet-maker—a logical choice, given he liked to work with his hands.[12] But his aptitude for Phineas Allen's bookish curriculum opened up a new possibility. Cynthia was proud and ambitious for her boys and determined to send at least one of them to Harvard, where her father, Asa Dunbar, had launched his career. In the end Phineas Allen would, in the quaint phrase of the time, offer for admission to Harvard not her lively and charismatic elder son John, but the quiet and studious Henry.

George Frisbie Hoar thought getting into Harvard was easy. Why, in a couple of years, any reasonably bright boy of fourteen could master the entrance requirements. But George Moore the jailer's son steeled himself to get up at 4:00 a.m. every morning to read his lessons, and all summer of 1830 he flogged himself without mercy through Latin reviews, Jacobs' *Greek Reader*, and the New Testament gospels before sitting for Harvard's August entrance exams: Latin and Greek, algebra and arithmetic, geography, the Greek New Testament. In the end, he passed with only a single "condition," in Sallust.[13] By contrast, Thoreau spent a good part of *his* pre-exam summer building his first boat, the *Rover*, and taking excursions up the river. On August 24, 1833, he rode into Cambridge for a long grueling day of testing by tutor after tutor in all the branches of learning. Years later he still stung under the embarrassment: "One branch more," President Quincy told him, "and you had been turned by entirely. You have barely got in." Thoreau had been conditioned in Greek, Latin, and mathematics—Harvard's three principal subjects! But get in he did, and graduate he did, even if, as he admitted, "Those hours that should have been devoted to study, have been spent in scouring the woods, and exploring the lakes and streams of my native village."[14]

Why Harvard? For a Concord son, it was the inevitable choice, the highest aspiration for the town's best and brightest boys. Founded in 1636, only a year after Concord itself, Harvard had grown into a center for education in theology, medicine, law, and the liberal arts. Its ties to Concord were deep: when the American army laid siege to British-occupied Boston, it was to Concord that Harvard's faculty and students decamped, and one of those students, Rev. Ezra Ripley, returned to Concord, where he became a proud advocate of the rationalist, liberal wing of New England's ancestral Congregational Church, of which Harvard was the national leader. This made Harvard a lightning rod as well: when the 1805 appointment of the liberal icon Henry Ware (with whom Thoreau himself would study) as professor of divinity turned orthodox Calvinists into open enemies of Harvard, they fled to competing colleges—Andover, Dartmouth, Princeton, Yale. This split reinforced Harvard's position as the great bastion of Unitarianism, as well as the mother ship for Concord's own First Parish Church.

That Harvard was state supported hardly meant it was open to everyone. Even the most gifted women were categorically excluded. Frisbie Hoar was prepared for Harvard by Sarah Alden Ripley, whom he called "one of the most wonderful scholars of her time, or indeed of any time." Even Harvard's President Edward Everett said that Ripley "could fill any professor's chair at Harvard." Except, of course, she couldn't—she couldn't even attend classes. Instead, she tutored Harvard students, boys trying to gain entrance or who'd been "rusticated" for some offense, in mathematics, Greek and Latin, German and Italian, and natural philosophy (in which Ripley particularly excelled). She gave them, thought Hoar, better instruction than they got in Cambridge.[15] The same was true of the formidable Margaret Fuller, who also tutored Harvard students and who also, like Ripley, became become one of Thoreau's most respected colleagues—

but only after he was released from Harvard Yard to a world where women of intellect could make their mark.

Cost was another barrier. At roughly $200 a year for tuition, room and board, plus other expenses, at a time when a typical wage for a laborer was less than a dollar a day, a Harvard education was out of reach for most. Even the Thoreaus—with a solid family business plus the boardinghouse—found it a financial stretch. To make ends meet during Henry's final two years at Harvard, his family had to give up the fine but expensive Shattuck House and squeeze back in with the Misses Thoreau on the town square, where they lived from spring of 1835 to the spring of 1837. Henry Thoreau was, in short, a scholarship boy. For each of his four years he received small but essential funds from the legacy of James Penn, designated for disadvantaged students who worked hard, kept up their grades, and stayed out of trouble. For three of those four years, his hard work earned him some of the coveted prize money awarded at commencement in lieu of honors.[16] The instant the college passed a regulation allowing students to take a thirteen-week leave to earn extra money by teaching school, Thoreau applied and was accepted, even though this absence put him behind in his coursework. Thoreau could never forget that not only had he barely gotten in, he barely *stayed* in: for him there was no room for carelessness or slacking off, no cushion for risky high-jinks.

→-◄-

On August 30, 1833, a week after his entrance exams, Henry Thoreau rose early in the morning to take the stage to Cambridge. The carriage rattled over the Lexington hills, past the cattle market at Porter Square, and down "a solitary country road, till the college buildings came in sight, grey with age, but the yard gay with students and the life of the opening term." Once he arrived at the back entrance, Thoreau carried his few possessions to red-brick Hollis Hall, where he roomed with his academy classmate Charles Stearns Wheeler, the ruddy-cheeked son of a Lincoln farmer. It was a good match: under Wheeler's quiet and studious good cheer was an intellect burning with high ambition.[17] Their uncarpeted room lacked all the comforts of home: the only furnishings were a pine bedstead; a washstand, washbowl, and pail; a table and two plain chairs; a lamp and perhaps a desk. Students' rooms were heated by an open wood fire and an old cannonball, which on cold days was cooked red hot and set on a skillet or stand, and on warm nights was occasionally encouraged to roll down the stairs, carefully timed so as to "bisect a proctor's night-sleep." Students made their own fires, drew their own water, and polished their own boots, unless they could afford the extra dollars to hire a bootblack.[18] Thoreau's stripped-down life at Walden was hardly less luxurious.

The day's schedule was rigidly prescribed. Students attended prayers at six in the summers, half past in winters, in the unheated college chapel, where faculty overseers noted every absence and infraction. Students who failed to show up in the mandatory black coat were docked points—except, curiously, Thoreau, whose green coat went unpunished; likely President Quincy understood that the scholarship boy could afford no other.[19] The day's first recitations followed; then breakfast at the college commons, where students fueled up on hot rolls, butter, and coffee, supplemented perhaps by a slice of yesterday's meat pinned by a fork to the underside of the table. Another class came after, followed by a coarse but hearty dinner at half-past noon, then afternoon recitations, except on Saturdays. After evening chapel at six the students regrouped for a third time to the commons for cold rolls and tea. Then the dormitories rang with laughter and song until the study bell rang curfew at eight. Sundays were workdays, with mandatory attendance at morning and evening chapel. Only Saturday afternoons offered a window of freedom to venture off campus—though any who missed evening curfew were threatened with a penalty. After five weeks of this, Thoreau and Wheeler were homesick enough to risk it. They walked home for a visit—a long walk; Thoreau's shoes blistered his feet so badly that he took them off, wincing the last two miles to Concord in bare feet.[20] Hardly had he said hello than he had to turn back to Cambridge.

Harvard's curriculum was equally rigid. The College was at a low point in its history; critics fretted it was "falling behind the age," too aristocratic, expensive, and hidebound to attract the really interesting students from the lower and middle classes, and too resistant to reform.[21] It was also very small, just over a dozen professors for two hundred students. Numbers fluctuated, but Thoreau's class of '37 never had more than about fifty students. Fortunately this small set included some lively minds: Richard Henry Dana returned from his "two years before the mast" to join the class of '37, and Horatio Hale left it early to sail with the Wilkes Exploring Expedition. Charles Dall would marry Caroline Healey, contributing to a second generation of Transcendentalism. Others, such as the poets Jones Very ('36) and James Russell Lowell ('38), overlapped on campus, but class years were strictly segregated; the same few students cycled together for term after term through the same standard courses offered by the same dozen professors, seldom hearing other points of view. Harvard's professors did not socialize with the students, who regarded them as "their natural enemies." Should a student seek out a professor for help or advice, it was by night and in secret, for it was a high crime to enter a classroom early or stay late to ask a question; anyone caught doing that was ostracized as "a fish." Thoreau found himself in a barely larger version of the Concord Academy: youths thrown together learned from one another and bonded into a tight cohort, a little world to itself laced with rivalries and friendships that were remembered, though they might not last, for a lifetime.[22]

There were advantages to this. As President Everett remarked, in a mere four hours "a young man of any capacity at all" could easily accomplish the day's tasks, leaving him lots of time to pursue his own bent "unimpeded."[23] For Thoreau this meant walking off into the countryside to observe birds or hunt for nests and eggs. In a letter from Walden to a young naturalist, he fondly recalled paying his daily respects to a weasel living in a hollow apple tree, and with his friends annually raiding the nest of a long-suffering flicker who "steadily supplied the loss like a hen, until my chum demolished the whole with a hatchet." It also meant daily trips to Harvard's tremendous library, the best in the nation. On his deathbed, Thoreau would advise Edward Emerson that Harvard's library was perhaps "the best gift Harvard had to offer." There in the stacks Thoreau began his lifelong habit of keeping a permanent record of his reading by copying extracts into commonplace books. He developed a passion for English poetry from Chaucer to Shakespeare—a mine he worked, as his classmate John Weiss sneered, "with a quiet enthusiasm, diverting to it hours that should have sparkled with emulation."[24]

Emulation, indeed: in this environment, the social pressure to compete was intense. Another classmate remembered Thoreau as "bright and cheerful," but Weiss thought him oddly dressed, "cold and unimpressible," his hand "moist and indifferent," his "prominent, gray-blue eyes" roving down the path just ahead of his feet in "his grave Indian stride"—already living at some interior Walden Pond, hiding his genius, for none of *them* could see it.[25] While Weiss was busy sneering, others enfolded Thoreau into a lively circle of loyal friends, starting with his academy classmates Stearns Wheeler and Henry Vose (who became a Superior Court judge), and Sam Hildreth, the class poet, so poor he lived on the charity of friends, so eloquent he was hired upon graduation as Harvard's new professor of elocution. Hildreth's best friend was William Allen, to whom Thoreau inscribed his precious first copy of Emerson's *Nature*. James Richardson, Thoreau's sophomore roommate, was a good-hearted daydreamer who wrote poetry for the *Harvardiana* and died nursing soldiers in the Civil War. There was Augustus Peabody, a lover of nature who became a doctor in Maine, and Charles Russell, who became a law professor at Boston University, and Charles Rice the blacksmith's son, who became a lawyer in Georgia. This talented circle borrowed books from one another, debated one another formally in the Institute of 1770 and informally in bull sessions, and traded letters that were by turns cheerful, anxious, and just plain silly.

John Shepard Keyes tumbled into Thoreau's circle when the nervous and overawed Concord Academy student arrived for his entrance exams. Thoreau greeted him at the gate and led him to his room, whereupon Thoreau's classmates burst through the door and set about teasing the two Concordians "in all sorts of amusing ways, and took down some of our local pride, and Concord self-conceit for which I soon found out that my host was as distinguished in college as afterwards." Amid these "roaring seniors," Keyes forgot all about the impending terrors of the exam, and there, piled together in his dorm room, Thoreau and his rollicking friends gave him the lowdown on student life at Harvard—including, most important of all, the insiders' story of the notorious Dunkin Rebellion, which, as Keyes drily observed, "varied essentially from the home notion."[26]

Harvard still remembers the Dunkin Rebellion of spring 1834 as one of the worst student riots in its history. Thoreau and his classmates were just freshmen, but that didn't protect them from the riots or from the punishments that followed. Student rebellions were a Harvard tradition: the recent Great Rebellion of 1823 had inspired President Kirkland to institute reforms, including a new grading system intended to be fair and transparent. But in 1828, after Kirkland was forced to resign, the overseers brought in Josiah Quincy to tighten the ship. Tighten he did—too tight; his methods made things worse. By the time Thoreau arrived, students were protesting Quincy's eight-point "Scale of Merit" used to rate every single class, recitation, and assignment, with points deducted for the least infraction. Quincy himself kept score, deputizing the faculty as his police force: every hour, day and night, Harvard's professors and tutors watched, judged, and scored, penalizing such offences as "grouping" in the college yard—two students constituted a group, which explains why Keyes was entertained behind closed doors—and wearing clothing of the wrong cut or color, meaning anything but black. While Thoreau was mocked for his green homespun, James Russell Lowell was docked for reporting to chapel in a brown coat. The least offense could be terminal: Thoreau watched as a student two years behind him was suspended for cracking walnuts in chapel.[27]

Marshall Tufts, who participated in the Great Rebellion, wrote, "Should not liberty of conscience be consulted in education as well as religion?"[28] Thoreau agreed, and Tufts's words became a rallying cry. In March 1834, Thoreau, along with most of his classmates, signed a petition calling for the abolition of Quincy's point system, arguing it fostered not real learning but "the petty emulation of the schoolboy." Thoreau had walked right into a tinderbox. The match was lit when a sophomore quarreled with the Greek tutor Christopher Dunkin. After several students were punished for insubordination, the campus erupted: students threw rocks through Dunkin's windows, smashed his furniture, broke into the bell tower, and rang the campus bell in the middle of the night. Quincy called on county authorities to investigate, but no one would identify the guilty parties, leaving no one liable for the $300 in damages. So Quincy dismissed virtually the entire sophomore class.[29] The result was all-out student riot. Every shutter in reach was ripped off to feed bonfires of classroom furniture; the chapel was bombed, and Quincy was hanged in effigy from the Rebellion Tree while a black flag fluttered over the campus. The day after, students stepped gingerly around mounds of broken glass, heaps of smashed furniture, and the smoldering ashes of bonfires. Many left for good, and new enrollments plummeted.

Where, in all this mess, was Henry Thoreau? Nowhere, accused John Weiss, who'd grown into a hotheaded radical preacher. But this isn't quite correct. A month into the cleanup, Dr. Henry Ware informed President Quincy that members of Thoreau's class had made "offensive noises" at prayers. The faculty voted to smoke out the miscreants by examining each freshman individually. Their inquisition indicted one Joseph Huger of South Carolina, and one Giles Henry Whitney. But Whitney protested his innocence and pleaded that Thoreau and Wheeler both be reexamined on his behalf. The faculty refused. Whitney was dismissed from Harvard, whereupon his dismayed father petitioned for a new hearing, submitting in his son's defense letters from Thoreau and Wheeler—which, alas, have not survived. The two letters failed to move the faculty, who voted 8 to 2 to let Whitney's dismissal stand.[30]

In short, Thoreau put himself on the line to defend his classmate's innocence in person, and when he was refused, he wrote a letter of testimony, which the faculty read, discounted, and apparently destroyed. He may not have smashed windows and trashed classrooms, but he did stand up for a friend who, in his view, had been unjustly accused and punished, at a time when students had been dismissed for far less.

Thereafter, for three more years, Thoreau was one of only nineteen students in his class who were never once called in for disciplinary action. Whatever his thoughts, he was very careful not to risk his class standing. This was not mere schoolboy obedience. Even Weiss, who blamed Thoreau for disappearing while "our young absurdity held its orgies," grudgingly admitted that "there is nothing so conventional as the mischief of a boy who is grown large enough to light bonfires," but not large enough to pay the bills for his "anarchy."[31] The Dunkin Rebellion gave the sixteen-year-old Thoreau occasion to think about who pays the costs for riotous anger and what courage even a modest act of civil disobedience requires. He started a slow burn: though he was consistently among the college's better students, by his senior year, his professors, suspicious of his attitude, docked his final prize money as punishment. One can only imagine what they would have done had Thoreau exposed them to the fullness of his scorn.

→>-<←

So what exactly was this "Harvard education" for which Thoreau worked so hard and his family sacrificed so much? The hot-button controversy over "emulation" gives a clue: Harvard's ranking system rewarded gentlemanly behaviors and discouraged eccentricities. The classroom forensics, endless recitations, and declamations all encouraged each student to measure his performances constantly against his classmates'; those who could never measure up simply stopped trying. In lectures, where much of the actual instruction occurred, students took copious notes, which they copied into their records to memorize.[32] While Quincy's rankings seemed arbitrary and punitive to the rebels, they were designed to tell each student at the end of the term precisely where he stood, who was ahead of him, and who was behind him. All Harvard's rewards were based on these assessments.

The core of a Harvard education was total immersion in the long-dead languages of ancient Greece and Rome. Today this seems incomprehensible; even then it was controversial. As one graduate complained, ancient literature may well have been the ark that saved civilization from the deluge of barbarism, "but we do not read, that Noah thought himself obliged to live in the ark after the deluge had subsided."[33] Thoreau, though, was indeed obliged to live in that ark. Having been conditioned in Latin and Greek, he worked hard to catch up, plunging into Livy, Horace, Seneca, and Cicero, Rome's great orator and moral philosopher; he read the great orations of Demosthenes calming the threat of mob rule, and the austere tragedies of Sophocles illustrating the sublime poetics of Aristotle, and Homer's *Iliad*, called the bible of the Greeks, showing the universality of manly virtue—all, of course, in the original Greek. This education shaped Thoreau profoundly, teaching him to measure the moderns by the standards of the ancients, and it enabled him to lean hard into every word he wrote, hearing echoes of meaning layered across a multitude of languages and ringing down through the ages.

Thoreau went on to make languages his special project. George Ticknor had turned modern languages into Harvard's "live literary center," and Thoreau took everything available: Italian from the banished political dissident Pietro Bachi, who read his beloved poets with such beauty that "it was like hearing a sweet and soft music";[34] four terms of French, until he passed the required exam; German from the political exile Hermann Bokum; the smattering of Spanish and Portuguese offered by the immaculately dressed and powdered Frenchman Francis Sales. Having missed the great Ticknor, Thoreau nearly missed his replacement, Longfellow, as well: in his final term he sat in on the poet's inaugural lectures on German and Northern Literature, but caught under a crushing course load, he soon dropped out. By the time he graduated, Thoreau could read at least five foreign languages—Latin, Greek, Italian, French, and German—plus a little Spanish and Portuguese. On his own he studied Wampanoag, the Native American language of eastern Massachusetts; he may have been inspired by his classmate Horatio Hale, who while still a student published a monograph on Penobscot languages based on interviews he conducted with a group of Penobscot encamped on Harvard's grounds.[35] It's possible that Thoreau, so fascinated with both languages and with Native Americans, went along.

Mathematics was another Harvard signature, and here Thoreau was lucky: his newly hired professor, Benjamin Peirce, was the foremost mathematician of his day and the leading theorist and practitioner of surveying and practical navigation; soon he would also be superintendent of the US Coast Survey. Or perhaps Thoreau was unlucky—as Frisbie Hoar laughed, not one person in the room understood Peirce's lectures. "He would take the chalk in his hand and begin in his shrill voice, 'if we take,' then he would write an equation in algebraic characters, 'then we have,' following it by another equation or formula," covering the board in a transport of delight, smearing his clothes with chalk, and leaving his bewildered students far behind. Yet Thoreau's flair for mathematics might have put him in the advanced study group who met at Peirce's home in the evenings. In *Walden* he professed astonishment at being informed, upon graduation, "that I had studied navigation!—why, if I had taken one turn down the harbor I should have known more about it."[36] Nevertheless, his successful career as Concord's town surveyor began under Peirce, in whose classroom he acquired a rich trove of navigational metaphors.

Thoreau would have flourished in science courses, too, had there been any. Instead he was taught physics and astronomy by a tutor who marched them through recitations in outdated French treatises without a single laboratory demonstration and without once looking at the stars. More amusing were the chemistry lectures of Professor John Webster, whose fondness for blowing things up earned him the name "Sky-rocket Jack." During one of his demonstrations, a copper vessel exploded with such force that a chunk flew into the back row, where it would have killed the student sitting there had he not chanced to be absent that day. Webster was only mildly repentant: "The President sent for me and told me I must be more careful. He said I should feel very badly indeed if I had killed one of the students. And I should."[37] Webster's nonchalance perhaps foreshadowed his shocking crime: one day in November 1849, Professor George Parkman unaccountably disappeared; a week later, a suspicious janitor unearthed human body parts in a brick vault underneath Webster's chemistry lab. Thoreau's former professor was tried for murder, confessed, and hanged.

The man who truly introduced Thoreau to science was not a professor at all, but the college's shy and modest librarian, beloved by generations of students: Thaddeus William Harris. When Harvard had an open position in natural history but no funds to hire anyone, Harris agreed to cover the required course in natural history, dutifully drilling his students in Harvard's outdated textbooks. But Harris's passion for natural history was real, and he was building one of the best insect collections in America. In May 1837, he joined forces with Thoreau and friends to found Harvard's Natural History Society, leading them on field excursions around Cambridge in pursuit of plants, birds, and insects. Students long recalled Harris's "beauty loving soul," his enthusiasm at their discoveries "as if he had never seen the like before," and his willingness to lend books and help "with a kindness and patience beyond praise." One student recalled how every spring Harris's eyes would kindle over a "plain little orchid" that grew "in a certain field near the Observatory"; he led their annual quest for it with an enthusiasm that cast the Holy Grail itself into insignificance.[38] Thoreau's rambles to flickers' nests and weasel dens were thus not lonely escapes from society, but expressions of shared passion and mutual instruction amid a circle of friends. Harris himself would remain Thoreau's friend and mentor until his death, in 1856.

Harvard taught history and philosophy as extensions of Greece and Rome, conceived not as dead civilizations but as living expressions of art, culture, and history—the springboard into the democratic politics necessary to govern the new American republic. Tho-

reau arrived at Harvard just as Charles Beck and Cornelius Conway
Felton were leading this national New Humanist revolution; Beck,
who taught Latin, was a German émigré who brought the latest
German scholarship straight from Tübingen; Felton became the
Eliot Professor of Greek Literature in 1834, making Thoreau among
the first to study Greek under America's most influential scholar of
classics. The New Humanists hadn't yet been able to toss out Harvard's antiquated Latin textbooks, which Felton joked had defeated
generations of students more thoroughly than the Roman Legions
had ever defeated the Carthaginians. But they did open a new vista
by insisting that one not merely learn *about* Greece and Rome, but
to speak and write in Greek and Latin, inhabit the language itself, to
become Greek or Roman. Felton famously led his students away from
the stern civic virtue of republican Rome to an emotive, Romantic
Hellenism meant to cleanse the self of the toxins of modernity and
remake the soul, laying the foundation for a lifetime of self-culture.
Athens, not Rome, was the true mirror of America, offering American democracy a deeper and more authentic past. While Rome had
risen only to fall, America would learn from the past to build a literature, a culture, and a nation that would last, surpassing all that
had come before.[39]

   With all this, Thoreau was completely at home: when Concord's
town fathers had swept away the creaky shops and odious factories to erect those fine, white-columned neoclassical monuments,
they were deliberately embodying neoclassic republican virtue in
wood and paint, just as the architects of Washington, DC, did in
marble and granite. The Concord Academy itself, where sons and
daughters learned leadership by imbibing Latin and Greek, was part
of this national movement toward a new, secular civic culture, an
America modeled on the measured and timeless self-sacrifices of
the ancients. This is the sweeping vista behind the small moment
in *Walden* when, on a Sunday morning, Thoreau's "Homeric" man,
the French Canadian immigrant Alek Therien, takes the *Iliad*, the
bible of Greece, in his hands while Thoreau translates for him Achil-
les's reproof to the grieving Patroclus. "He says, 'That's good.'"[40] In

that simple passage, the promise of a democratic American future is borne forward out of the deepest historical past.

To set up this scene on Walden's shores took all the resources of Harvard: even as Thoreau was mastering the classics in depth, he was being marched through world history up to the American Constitution, offered as the capstone to world progress. He was immersed in John Locke, the foundation of American political philosophy, then steeped in William Paley's *Moral Philosophy* and Scottish Common Sense philosophy, and enjoined by the aging and saintly Henry Ware Sr. to admire Paley's *Evidences of Christianity*. All this was rounded off in the senior year by Ware's lectures on the Greek New Testament.[41] By the time he graduated, Thoreau was saturated with Harvard rationalism at its finest, even as outside the classroom he was finding his way to the very writers and intellectuals who were about to topple it all.

✦

Every teacher has been baffled by the mysterious alchemy of education. Given a dozen or a hundred or a thousand students, there will be the one who trots in harness with the rest only to blossom—often quite suddenly—into a genius wholly unexpected. Of Harvard's professors, it would seem one above all held the key to this genius: the man who taught (or tried to teach) Thoreau how to write. Every term for three long years, Edward Tyrrel Channing, the Boylston Professor of Rhetoric and Oratory, issued Thoreau a long series of assignments, every one of which he collected, corrected, and returned, scored on Quincy's merciless eight-point scale. If Thoreau kept a journal through these years, it is lost; if he wrote letters home, they are gone; when he ventured into poetry, his verses mostly vanished.[42] What survives are his essays for Channing. They disappoint. Plodding, creditable, wooden and conventional, they pleased Channing well enough, but to us, they say little. In Henry Seidel Canby's succinct phrase, Harvard "nearly ruined him as a writer."[43]

Nearly—but not quite. Channing assigned topics that forced students out of their comfort zones and taxed their ingenuity to think of something—anything!—to say. This was Channing's intention; he wanted his students to discover themselves by exploring the broader universe of their reading. As Emerson (also a Channing student) insisted, "One must be an inventor to read well." The problem wasn't Channing's method or his topics but his withering sarcasm, which destroyed any youthful flicker of originality. Week by week he called each author to the front of the room and made him sit, humiliated, while Channing read his worst passages aloud to the class. It was a terrible ordeal, and students wrote as little as possible so as to give the least occasion for offense. Typical was the time he called one student to the dreaded chair and read aloud, in his shrill voice, "'The sable sons of Afric's burning coast.' You mean negroes, I suppose." Yes, admitted the student, whereupon Channing crossed out the offending phrase and wrote "negroes" above it, to the student's everlasting mortification.[44] It took a tough mind to survive his methods, and, perhaps as a result, Channing had a profound effect not just on his students but on American literature. Three full years of Channing's minute criticisms bled out all emotional excess, all frivolous ornament, all exaggeration, in the name of a balanced and sober style that could draw on the world's classic literature to forge citizens capable of thoughtful deliberation and sound, well-informed political decisions. One editor remarked that he could always tell a Channing student: no one exposed to the fire of his ridicule ever forgot it.[45] The young and earnest Henry Thoreau learned so well how to write for his teacher that it took ten years and a move to Walden Pond to shake himself free.

Not until June 1837, the eve of graduation, did Thoreau dare reveal the crackle of his wit. Channing's topic was to define the standard by which a nation "is judged to be barbarous or civilized." One more dull assignment—but Thoreau's response is not dull: "A nation may be ever so civilized and yet lack wisdom," he snaps to his teacher. "Wisdom is the result of education, and education being the bringing out, or development, of that which is in a man, by contact with the Not Me, is safer in the hands of Nature than of Art. The savage may be, and often is, a sage. Our Indian is more of a man than the inhabitant of a city. He lives as a man—he thinks as a man—he dies as a man."[46] Was Channing pleased with his pupil? The economy of phrasing, the taut parallelism of that final sentence, the worldly assurance of one who finds civilization wanting only after weighing it first, all owe to Channing. But the sass is all Thoreau's. And the philosophy? Straight out of Emerson. The tight little eggshell of Harvard was cracking open.

LEARNING TO LEAVE HARVARD

Thoreau the freshman got off to a good start. In his first term he missed only a handful of classes and made up all his work; the only chapels he missed were the morning and evening of the Saturday he walked home with Wheeler. By the end of his second term, he had earned enough of Quincy's precious points to put him sixteenth out of fifty students, and by the end of the year he'd racked up enough to walk away with twenty-five dollars, a major share of the freshman class's prize money. Only two students earned more: Hildreth, the class poet, and the remarkable Horatio Hale were each awarded thirty dollars. Thus during the notorious year of the Dunkin Rebellion, Thoreau distinguished himself as one of his class's top students, earning him election to the Institute of 1770. He was one of only seven freshmen to be elected on the first round. Ten more were admitted a week later, and soon all his best friends were members.

Election to the Institute of 1770 radically opened up Thoreau's world. It had been founded on the eve of the Revolution by students who wanted extra practice in public speaking. They held biweekly meetings and set up a schedule of formal debates, with plenty of time for discussion. Members gave lectures to each other, composed poetry and read it aloud, and shared book reviews. Thoreau paid his annual two dollars regularly, seldom missed a meeting, and jumped right into debates, starting in September 1834 when he joined his old academy buddies Wheeler and Vose to debate the freedom of the press. Members could check out two books at a time from the institute's growing library—more if they donated the complete works of some author, which Thoreau, who often carried away three or four books, must have done. The institute's library may have been dwarfed by Harvard's, which was the nation's largest with 41,000 volumes by 1840, but the institute filled major gaps, offering the latest scientific works, the major literary journals—and the daring, the foreign, the forbidden, and the avant-garde. By spring 1837, Thoreau was hauling away armfuls of Goethe, Coleridge, Victor Cousin, and, of course, Emerson's *Nature*, the great manifesto of Transcendentalism, which he borrowed from the Institute in April and again in June, after giving his own copy away.[47]

Thoreau kept up his honors record right through his sophomore year, ironically benefiting from an error Quincy made in his favor, which briefly raised him to sixth in his class.[48] Emerson himself helped examine Thoreau in February 1835, and while neither impressed the other, Thoreau did well enough to be awarded a "detur," a specially bound book.[49] By school year's end he'd dropped a bit, to eleventh—still strong enough to earn another twenty-five dollars in prize money and a speaking role in the college's Exhibition Day: Thoreau translated into Greek and helped perform a dialogue in which he played Cato delivering a defiant message to Caesar.[50] Altogether he was holding his own, momentum he kept up right through fall of his junior year, when he loaded up on no fewer than eight different classes. Quincy docked him for a variety of petty offenses (chiefly tardiness and absences) and under the load he slipped to fourteenth—still respectable.

→—◄—

The trouble started in November 1835, when the overseers passed a rule allowing students to take a term off to earn extra money by teaching. Henry's family had just given up their home of eight years to move in with the Aunts Thoreau, suggesting real financial strain, and Henry lost no time in applying for a teaching position. On December 2, he traveled to Canton, Massachusetts, for an interview with the Unitarian minister Orestes Brownson. Something clicked:

the slight and wiry Harvard junior with the downcast gray eyes and the tall, lean, firebrand radical with the booming voice stayed up talking straight through to midnight, spurred by Brownson's famous bottomless cups of coffee. Brownson informed the Harvard Overseers that Henry Thoreau had been examined, and would do, and would live with him for the term.[51] Sometime after—the dates are lost to history—Thoreau joined the household: Orestes, his wife Sally, and their four children. In the daytime he kept the Canton grammar school, leading some seventy young people through their paces, and after hours, when he wasn't tutoring the Brownson boys, he and Orestes studied German together and continued their ferocious conversations. This was Thoreau's first encounter with a free-range intellectual for whom ideas snapped and crackled, who moved easily in the circles of the great and the near great. His term with Brownson broke the spell of Harvard.

Brownson was a Vermonter who had grown up in poverty, the orphaned son of a farmhand. He became a preacher, writer, and editor in upstate New York, a vocal supporter of the radical left, and a relentless religious seeker. By the time Thoreau met him, he had passed from Calvinist Presbyterianism all the way through the fires of atheism to Unitarianism; in 1844, he would complete his religious journey by converting to Catholicism. In 1834 he had named his third son William Ellery Channing, after the preacher who, in his great sermon "Likeness to God," had said it was God within each of us who opens our eyes to see God in the world around us. Brownson went straight to Boston to tell Channing in person that his sermon had saved him from atheism. Though Channing kept his distance from the intense young outsider, his follower George Ripley embraced Brownson as a fast friend. Soon the two were trading the latest books from Europe and pounding out their plans to save the world. In 1841 Ripley went all in, founding the utopian community Brook Farm. Emerson and Thoreau both declined to join it, but Brownson sent his son Orestes Jr., as well as the idealistic religious seeker Isaac Hecker.

The Brownson who took Henry Thoreau under his wing was still simmering from the controversy of July 1834, when he had declared at an Independence Day address that in America, equality existed only on paper: "A free government is powerless without a free people." Government must not lead, but follow; it must let the people alone; it must leave the people free to lead it. Years later, Thoreau opened "Civil Disobedience" with a tip of the hat to Brownson: "For government is an expedient by which men would fain succeed in letting one another alone; and, as has been said, when it is most expedient, the governed are most let alone by it." As Brownson stormed on: "We have equality in scarcely any sense worth naming. Will you say that we are equal while all our seminaries of learning are virtually closed to all except the rich?" To Thoreau, the scholarship boy struggling to pay his tuition bills, Brownson's words hit home. To Brownson, education was the key to creating true equality, which meant the key to remedying all the evils of society. He didn't mean reading, writing, and ciphering; he meant real education, "the *formation of character*, the moral, religious, intellectual, and physical training, disciplining, of our whole community."[52]

Thoreau was living with Brownson at the very moment he was writing his breakthrough book, *New Views of Society, Christianity, and the Church*, which soon joined Emerson's *Nature* as a founding text of Transcendentalism. When Thoreau arrived back at Harvard, he began working through Brownson's reading list: the latest European literature and philosophy—Goethe and Coleridge, Heine, Cousin, Constant. He bought Brownson's *New Views* and Emerson's *Nature* for his personal library, even though he didn't have a dollar to spare. When Channing assigned an essay on government-supported education, Thoreau let fly: "I maintain that the Government ought to provide for the education of all children who would otherwise be brought up, or rather grow up, in ignorance. In the first place the welfare of the individual, and in the second that of the community, demand it. . . . The duty in this instance amounts to a moral obligation."[53]

Nearly two years later, when he was defining his own path as an educator, Thoreau wrote Brownson a remarkable letter. The six weeks they lived together were, Thoreau told him, "an era in my life—the morning of a new *Lebenstag*"—meaning one's moral and intellectual birth, the day one's life as a philosopher begins. Brownson, at a chance meeting with Henry's brother John, passed along his "great regard" for Henry. "Young men!" he had urged, "Ye who are full of the future . . .'tis yours to hasten that day. Your fathers have done nobly. They have begun a magnificent work, but it is yours to finish it."[54] Thoreau took Brownson's call to heart. The Henry who returned to Harvard was a new man: the sleepy student had woken up.

The road back was a bumpy one. Thoreau's absence from the winter term meant he'd earned no points, and by Quincy's harsh reckoning, his rank plummeted. By March 20, 1836, he was back in the classroom for the spring term, loading up on classes (another eight in all) to make up for the lost time. But in April he was struck down by a lingering illness, probably his first bout with tuberculosis. By May twenty-first he was forced to withdraw from school, and for a few summer weeks it was unclear whether he had the strength—or his family the funds—to return. They debated whether Henry should drop out. It could not have helped that Quincy's ranking system penalized Thoreau for his absences due to illness, too, and the few points he'd managed to earn before his health collapsed were, by some oversight, not counted. By the end of his junior year, the honors student had sunk to the bottom half of his class. When his talented friends gathered once again to collect their Exhibition Day prize money, Thoreau's name was nowhere to be found.

While his family fretted about his future, Henry recreated himself by building a new and better boat, which he dubbed *Red Jacket* after the Seneca chief whose landmark "Speech to the U.S. Senate" had insisted on Indians' right to practice their own religion without interference. His Harvard chums tried to cheer him up with long newsy letters: "Everything goes on here as regular as clock work" and "as dull as one of Dr. Ware's sermons," one reassured him, a claim belied by his hilarious account of doings at the student's chemistry club, where a fireworks display had brought Tutor Bowen storming out of his room to quell the riot and send the instigators up to Quincy for punishment. Then the noxious fumes of Professor Webster's volcano demonstration had emptied the classroom. After class, two students cooked up some "laughing gas," nitrous oxide. One dose and the sobersides Stearns Wheeler cut loose in a dance; two doses and Sam Hildreth raved on in conversation with Shakespeare. High times indeed! It was too much to miss. On July 5, 1836, a lonely Thoreau wrote a playful dialogue to Henry Vose vowing to be back for classes and asking his "chum" to have Wheeler secure a dorm room for him. A month later, another worried friend, also sick at home, wrote to commiserate, asking what interesting Indian artifacts Henry had dug up lately; why not come for a visit, so they could explore Indian sites together? Henry answered with an "extract from the log-book of the Red Jacket, Captain Thoreau," which in its maiden voyage had lost her mast in a terrible squall and been cast ashore on Nawshawtuct beach, where the astonished natives appeared "a harmless inoffensive race, principally devoted to agricultural pursuits." Henry closed with good news: his health was better and he hoped to return; meanwhile, do come for a visit.[55]

These happy, warm, playful letters show that it was more than academics that drew Henry back to Harvard. As he remarked in *Walden*, while college demands money for tuition, it makes no charge for "the far more valuable education" of associating with one's classmates. Nevertheless, there was still the business of money. To cover tuition, Henry traveled to New York City with his father to help open up a new market for Thoreau pencils.[56] By September 12, 1836, he was finally back in Cambridge, just in time to join two hundred other undergraduates, thirteen hundred alumni and eighty invited guests to celebrate Harvard's bicentennial. The festivities started with students and alumni parading to the Unitarian Church, where they sat through Quincy's two-hour speech before emptying out into Harvard Yard for "toasts, libations, and a meal" that lasted until curfew, when students adjourned to dorm rooms whose windows were lit with lamps arranged in patterns and mottos.[57]

At some point during the day, four of those alumni slipped away to a nearby hotel for a private meeting. They had been called together by Frederic Henry Hedge, visiting from his ministry in Maine, and Ralph Waldo Emerson, who had been corresponding with Hedge all summer long about starting a discussion group. New ideas were bubbling up everywhere: Brownson's *New Views*, Emerson's *Nature*, and Thomas Carlyle's *Sartor Resartus* were just out, and Elizabeth Peabody and Bronson Alcott were turning heads with their radical new approach to education in *Record of a School*. Hedge and Emerson invited George Ripley and George Putnam, a Unitarian minister from Boston, to join them. Even as the self-congratulations went on at Harvard, four of its own graduates were secretly discussing how to unsettle it all and lead America forward to a radically new intellectual life. The meeting went well; they called a second for a week later at George and Sophia Ripley's home in Boston, inviting, among others, Orestes Brownson, Amos Bronson Alcott, Theodore Parker, and Emerson's new protégé—Charles Stearns Wheeler. These meetings went on for four years, bringing together the loose group of intellectuals and reformers dubbed "the Transcendentalists." Thoreau was not yet invited, although Brownson had already ignited him and Wheeler filled him in on the discussions. Thoreau was testing out Transcendentalism on his own well before it existed as a movement.

All through his senior year, Thoreau worked furiously to make up the time, points, and classes lost the year before. This was Harvard's capstone year, and the load was heavy: recitations in philosophy (natural, moral, and intellectual), Channing's assignments plus lectures in rhetoric, Ware's sleepy theology lectures, Harris's classes in natural history and botany, plus anatomy and mineralogy, German and Italian, a little Spanish and Portuguese, and required exercises in oratory—intended to teach the leaders of the future how to fill large rooms with their voices and read written addresses with the fresh energy of original creation. All year Thoreau beavered on, earning an astonishing 2,285 points in his final term—twice the normal accumulation—for a grand total of 14,397 by Quincy's erratic reckoning. It was not enough to recapture his earlier high ground, to be sure, but it was enough to put him nineteenth of forty-one, securing him a speaking part at commencement and a twenty-five-dollar prize—but only after Emerson wrote to Quincy on his behalf. Quincy replied that he'd done all he could for Thoreau, who was "indifferent, even to a degree that was faulty" to the rules. Yet Quincy had long felt a certain respect for Thoreau, so he managed to get him a sum only "*ten*, or at most *fifteen* dollars" less than he would have received had no objections been made.[58] In short, Thoreau worked hard but had a bad attitude—unlike Wheeler, who earned the grand prize, sixty dollars. Harvard was not ready to forgive Henry Thoreau for becoming his own man.

For his part in the ceremony, Thoreau was assigned a role in a "conference" of three addresses on the topic "The Commercial Spirit of Modern Times, considered in its Influence on the Political, Moral, and Literary Character of a Nation." This meant homework to complete during the traditional six-week senior holiday. As soon as classes were over, Henry returned to Concord, where John and Cynthia had just moved again, this time out of the old cramped townhouse on the square to the gracious Parkman house near Main Street. Henry arrived just in time to help dedicate the new Revolutionary Monument on the Fourth of July; after a dozen years of debate, everyone had agreed to Reverend Ripley's proposal that a granite obelisk be erected behind his Old Manse. On that hot afternoon, Henry Thoreau joined the long procession up Monument Street to the site of the Old North Bridge, where three hundred men, women, and children gathered on the grass in the sun—the trees that would turn the bleak road into a shady lane had yet to be planted—to hear prayers and a speech by Samuel Hoar and to sing in chorus Emerson's "Concord Hymn." In old age, John S. Keyes still remembered the last stanza's invocation of the heroes who dared "to die or leave their children free."[59]

That last word, "free," must have stayed in Henry's mind as well, for he opened his address by invoking it as the keynote of the modern epoch: "perfect freedom—freedom of thought and action." This was indeed his summer of perfect freedom: after the Fourth of July, he and Wheeler moved into a cabin Wheeler had built the summer before, perhaps with Thoreau's help, on his family's property on Flint's (or Sandy) Pond. For six weeks the two friends loafed by the shore, reading, writing, and dreaming aloud while the leaves rustled overhead and the summer sun sparkled off the broad lake waters all around, walking to the family farmhouse for their meals. Wheeler brought their other college friends to this cabin, too. The following summer one would vow there, in this "beautiful and secluded spot . . . in communion with Nature and her God," to "forsake all lower ambitions, and to devote himself to His service."[60] One could say that Henry Thoreau made a similar vow. His experiment at Walden Pond had its origin here, in these weeks spent living and writing with Charles Stearns Wheeler.

The topic Thoreau meditated on this blissful summer, "the commercial spirit," was on everyone's mind. It was especially on the minds of that year's unfortunate college graduates, who found themselves turned loose to hunt for jobs during the Panic of 1837, the worst financial crash America had yet seen. Westward expansion had fueled massive speculation, and the storm broke in May when all of New York's banks were closed, followed by bank closures across the nation. As the bubble in real estate burst, property values collapsed overnight; factories closed, and starving workers rioted in the streets. Prospects for the class of '37 were bleak beyond all anticipation, and as their three classmates stood to speak about the economic crisis, the graduates must have leaned in to listen. Charles Rice the blacksmith's son had drawn the "political" side of the question, and he came out swinging as a good Democrat, blaming the calamity on rampant speculation and the corruption of hard work and hard-earned gains by sheer greed. His fear was the Jacksonian one, that legislators would use the Panic to widen government power when the proper remedy was to leave the people alone so they could cultivate true self-reliance. Henry Vose, who drew the literary side, wrote a Whiggish hymn to commerce, which unites all the regions of America and all the peoples of the earth, feeding the growing energies of the American people and spreading wealth and enterprise among all. Without commerce, Vose closed, there is no freedom, and no true America.[61]

Standing before this audience of hundreds—which included Massachusetts Governor Edward Everett, an assemblage of congressmen and senators, the Harvard Overseers, and President Quincy, as well as the young rebel's professors, graduating classmates and their families, plus the merely curious—"David-Henricus Thoreau" (in the Latinate formality of the commencement program) tackled the moral question head-on. Commerce, he told them, destroys moral freedom. But freedom must come first, for freedom generates commerce, not the other way around. From "an observatory in the stars," would America's "beehive" of commercial activity really look like freedom? Hardly. "There would be hammering and chipping, baking and brewing, in one quarter; buying and selling, money-changing and speech making, in another." By tying us to material goods, commerce does not free us but enslaves us, turns us into brutes. To be human is to cast off these material desires and walk forth, freely, into paradise.

Right there, Thoreau laid the foundations for *Walden*: "The order of things should be somewhat reversed,—the seventh should be man's day of toil . . . and the other six his Sabbath of the affections and the soul." Caught between Jacksonian democracy and Whig cheerleading, Thoreau struck out a third, radically different path. Some in the audience scorned his path as a flight from reality. But Thoreau himself was about to wrestle hard with that same reality and to watch his classmates—whom he loved, he wrote in his Class Book Autobiography, with a love too sacred for words—struggle, too.[62] "The mass of men lead lives of quiet desperation," he would eventually tell them, "but it is characteristic of wisdom not to do desperate things." In front of the whole wide world, for everyone in authority to hear, Thoreau was staking out his most sacred commitments. How could any man, in the teeth of this world, hope to keep such vows?

CHAPTER THREE

Transcendental Apprentice
(1837–1841)

"What are you doing now?" he asked, "Do you keep a journal?"
—So I make my first entry today.
HENRY DAVID THOREAU, OCTOBER 22, 1837

SIC VITA

On August 31, 1837, a bold new voice rang out over Harvard Yard from the First Parish Church: "In self-trust, all the virtues are comprehended. Free should the scholar be,—free and brave." Crowds packed the church, spilled out the door and gathered under the open windows to hear the address Oliver Wendell Holmes called "America's Intellectual Declaration of Independence." The speaker was Ralph Waldo Emerson, and the speech, "The American Scholar," would make him a star.[1] There, standing next to President Quincy and facing an audience of Harvard dignitaries, Phi Beta Kappans, faculty, students, and the curious, Emerson leveled his first powerful blow at the foundation of the education Thoreau had just completed.

Thoreau was not in the audience. The day before, he had stood on that same stage and championed "perfect freedom—freedom of thought and action." As soon as he finished, Thoreau had put his principles into action and vanished. "I hardly saw you again at all," complained his old roommate; "I liked much" your speech, but "neither at Mr Quincy's levee, neither at any of our Classmates' evening entertainments, did I find you" to say goodbye. The Phi Beta Kappa address, held the day after commencement, was a tradition honored with much pomp and ceremony. Thoreau and his classmates were all expected to attend; his absence could only have been deliberate. Emerson had recently interceded on Thoreau's behalf over the prize money, and for months Thoreau had been under the spell of *Nature*. Why didn't he linger for a few more hours to see him and hear his philosophy in person? Thoreau must have asked himself the same question, for he answered it a few months later: "One goes . . . to a commencement thinking that there at least he may find the men of the country," only to find those men completely merged in the occasion, "so that he is fain to take himself out of sight and hearing of the orator, lest he lose his own identity in the non-entities around him."[2] To see Emerson like this—one of them faceless in the crowd, the other merged in the ceremony—was not part of Thoreau's plan.

He had an awkward homecoming. His striving self-consciousness comes out in "Sic Vita," with its odd story: one morning that May, one of the Thoreaus' boarders, Lucy Jackson Brown, found a poem, wrapped around a bunch of violets and sorrel and tied with a straw, tossed through her open window:

> I am a parcel of vain strivings tied
>> By a chance bond together,
>
> .   .   .   .
>
>
> A bunch of violets without their roots,
>> And sorrel intermixed,
>> Encircled by a wisp of straw
>> Once coiled about their shoots,
>>> The law
>>> By which I'm fixed.[3]

Thoreau was flirting, but hardly serious; Lucy was twice his age and married with children, although her husband had recently abandoned her. Henry would become something of a son to her, helping her around the house and writing her letters in the same wistful, teasing tone. But for now, his whimsy combining the language of flowers—violets for modesty, sorrel for ill-timed wit—with an intricate and learned verse form was more a bid for attention from Lucy's brother-in-law, Ralph Waldo Emerson. Feeling rootless and cut off from the person he had been, Thoreau was confessing anxiety over his new identity as a Harvard graduate and a young man of promise. It was around this time that he changed his name, reversing the baptismal "David Henry" to his preferred "Henry David." Not everyone in Concord accepted this act of self-definition. One local farmer cracked up visitors by insisting, "His name's *Da*-a-vid Henry and it ain't never been nothing but *Da*-a-vid Henry. And he knows that!" But from now on he was, as the locals said, "Henery."[4]

Henry's immediate concern was earning a living. His commencement speech may have prophesied the one-day workweek, but the new graduate still had to work six days a week, like everyone else. But unlike his friends, forced by the Panic of 1837 to scramble for jobs, he walked into one of the best: teacher of Concord's Center Grammar School, with ninety students and an annual salary of $500—making him one of the hardest-working and best-paid schoolteachers in town. On Wednesday, September 6, a week after skipping Emerson's address to American educators, Henry Thoreau entered the classroom.[5] He almost certainly planned to stay for some years, for he saw education as democracy's highest civic calling, a calling reflected in the building itself: an ornate two-story brick schoolhouse in the town center.[6] Through its elaborate portico Thoreau entered an amphitheater-shaped classroom, sat at his desk, and watched the children of storekeepers, bank directors, lawyers, farmers, millers, carriage-makers, and cobblers file through the back door and take their seats, boys on one side, girls on the other. He was to teach them how to read and speak well, write correctly, calculate sums, grasp a little geography, history, natural philosophy—even how to carve barnyard goose quills into writing instruments that served for a page or two before needing repair. His classroom was well equipped: blackboards, spelling cards, celestial and terrestrial globes, world maps, and wall posters outlining rules of grammar.

Pupils worked at their desks, grouped by age and studies, while small groups came forward to review their lessons.

In the decade since Thoreau had attended this same school, educational reforms led in part by Edward Jarvis, his former teacher, called for teaching through example and appeals to moral elevation rather than corporal punishment. Thoreau made clear when he was hired that he would not flog his students for disobedience, but "talk morals as a punishment instead." But unfortunately the reformers had moved on, and by 1837 the Concord school committee had shrunk to three of its most conservative members. One of them, Barzillai Frost, had tutored Thoreau at Harvard and likely approved of his teaching methods, but Deacon Nehemiah Ball did not. The committee's senior member and a formidable presence in town governance, Ball stopped by late in Thoreau's second week to judge the new schoolmaster's conduct. As the story goes, Deacon Ball "sat through one session with increasing disapproval, waiting for corporal chastisement, the corner-stone of a sound education."[7] When Thoreau failed to comply, the Deacon took him to task: the teacher must flog, or the school would spoil.

What Thoreau did changed his life forever. He couldn't actually flog anyone—he didn't even own a cowhide—but he did possess a ferule, and that afternoon he used it. Accounts vary: some said he struck one or two students; some said as many as thirteen. Only two are recorded: Eliza Jane Durant, the Thoreau family's maidservant, who left their employ soon after, and Daniel F. Potter, who vividly recalled the thrashing and declared as an old man, "It smarts still!" He was ten, and he'd just come from a district school where he'd been taught to put his book away, fold his arms, and sit quietly when finished with his lesson. To his astonishment, Thoreau called him up and feruled him for putting away his book and doing nothing. "I was so mad that I said to myself, 'When I'm grown up, I'll whip you for this, old feller.' But," chuckled Potter, "I never saw the day I wanted to do it.—Why, Henry Thoreau was the kindest hearted of men." So perhaps it was only the two, Jane and Daniel, one girl and one boy, but that was enough. That evening, having completed his act of "uncivil obedience," Thoreau went before Deacon Ball and resigned. Next day he returned to tell his students that punishing with force went against his conscience: "He wouldn't keep school any longer, if that was the way he had to do it."[8]

Thus ten days after it began, Thoreau's career as a public school-teacher was over. The annoyed school committee hired his friend William Allen in his place, and the term resumed almost immediately. Thoreau, out of a job, wrote Henry Vose, "fellow soldier of the campaign of —37," to ask after any openings near Butternuts, New York, where Vose had found a teaching job. "Pens to mend, and hands to guide. / O, who would a schoolmaster be?" quipped Henry. Sorry, answered Vose, no openings near Butternuts. To his family, Henry talked largely about getting "an academy or private school where he can have his own way."[9] But an academy couldn't be whistled up for the asking. For now, with the school year already under way, it was just talk. Town gossip burned through the scandal. Was young Thoreau a quitter, or too cavalier with a good job? Or was Deacon Ball too meddlesome, and in a bad cause, too? While the gossip moved on, Henry Thoreau did not. Rootless still, a sudden martyr to conscience, he needed help.

Now, at last, he was ready for Emerson.

TRANSCENDENTAL SELF-CULTURE

It's unclear exactly when Emerson and Thoreau met. Emerson thought it was around Thoreau's graduation in 1837, perhaps in May when Lucy showed him "Sic Vita," or as early as April, after she showed him the bit of Henry's journal that sounded so much like himself. It could have been as late as that summer, when Wheeler and Thoreau were living on Sandy Pond. "The nonchalance of boys who are sure of a dinner & would disdain as much as a lord to do or say aught to conciliate one, is the healthy attitude of human nature," Emerson jotted approvingly.[10] For his part, Thoreau carefully commemorated Sunday, October 22, 1837, as nothing less than his second

Lebenstag, the day that gave him birth as a writer. Across the top of the first page of a new blank book, he wrote: "'What are you doing now?' he asked, 'Do you keep a journal?'—So I make my first entry today."[11] Few doubt that "he" was Emerson. His query sounds casual, a kindly expression of interest in the youthful and newly unemployed Harvard graduate. This quiet conversation announces a momentous change in Thoreau's life: from this day on, he had an interlocutor. His lifelong dialogue with Emerson, by turns loving, inspired, hostile, angry, and reconciled, would turn Thoreau into a great and wholly original writer. Thoreau's creativity was realized not alone but in partnership, as Emerson fanned his creativity into genius.

Thoreau's next wish was for solitude: "I seek a garret. The spiders must not be disturbed, nor the floor swept, nor the lumber arranged." This also was Emerson's advice, straight from the lectures he was writing then on "Human Culture": first, "sit alone. In your arrangements for your residence see that you have a chamber to yourself, though you sell your coat and wear a blanket." Second, "keep a journal. Pay so much honor to the visits of Truth to your mind as to record those thoughts." Emerson's point was that solitude and journal-keeping work together: solitude is not for empty reverie but for the productive habit of exploring, pen in hand, "what facts of moment lie in the memory," facts that would illumine the gross and heedless world into meaning and life. Likely Thoreau had already been keeping some sort of journal. Spiritual self-examination was an honored New England tradition; journals were often shared with friends and family, and Professor Channing had encouraged his Harvard students to record their daily progress. But the professor's moral accounting did not catch and hold Thoreau's imagination— not like Emerson's call to see how the inexhaustible waters of life roll through the catch of every moment.[12] Thoreau's response to that call inaugurated a monumental life's work, an epic journey of over two million words, sustained as long as he could hold a pen.

With garret secured and pen in hand, Thoreau transformed himself from Harvard graduate to Transcendental apprentice. The key was "Self-Culture." To culture, or cultivate, is to make something grow, whether plant, animal, or mind; while they all grow, only humans can turn that principle of culture upon themselves. To be human is to search for one's unique inner powers and then consciously unfold, guide, and nourish them. In most people those powers lie dormant; to awaken, to become fully human, is to see that of all creation, humans alone carry God's nature within. As William Ellery Channing wrote, "We see God around us, because he dwells within us. It is by a kindred wisdom, that we discern his wisdom in his works."[13] Over the years, the Transcendentalists would argue with one another and follow many paths, but all held firm to the belief that a divine principle dwells within every person. This insight proved absolutely transformative: it meant that slavery was an abomination to be stopped at any cost; that the political and social inequality of women must end; that children must never be punished as sinners nor trained as workers, but educated to unfold and foster that divine spirit within; and that spiritual seekers could read divine wisdom directly in nature and so enjoy, as Emerson proclaimed in *Nature*, "an original relation to the universe." The new view reshaping everything—philosophy, theology, science, law, the trades and professions—had, in Emerson's words, "as yet attained no clearer name than *Culture*."[14]

The gracious village of Concord, with its leafy streets, neoclassical pillars, and welcoming pathways to ponds and hilltops, seemed to Emerson the perfect place to pursue this new project of Culture. In 1835 he bought a large white house on the busy Cambridge Turnpike, to which he brought his bride Lidian. Emerson's home quickly became the center of American intellectual culture: the very evening of his triumphant "American Scholar" address, the Emersons returned to Concord with a virtual university in their train, who all stayed the night for a huge party the next day—the gala day when the small Transcendentalist circle opened at last to friends and sympathizers, including women. Margaret Fuller and Elizabeth Peabody were there, as were Thoreau's neighbors Elizabeth Hoar and Sarah Alden Ripley. Lidian made sure it was a true festival, for, as she wryly noted, even Transcendentalists liked to eat well: "beef . . . a noble great piece for the Spiritualists," mutton with caper sauce, ham and tongue, corn, "beans tomatoes macaroni cucumbers lettuce and *applesauce*," plus puddings, with custards and pears, raisins and nuts for desert.[15] But Henry Thoreau was not there. In a coincidence that must have felt like destiny, he found himself neighbored by a virtual force of nature. But he would gain entrance not as a local boy, son of a pencil-maker whose mother kept a boardinghouse, but only as Emerson's intellectual equal—and that must be by Emerson's invitation.

That invitation was not long in coming. Emerson opened his "Human Culture" lecture series in Boston on December 6, 1837, and gave his young neighbor tickets. Thoreau walked the nineteen miles to Boston's impressive Masonic Temple, where he heard Emerson sorrow, in words that echoed Thoreau's own commencement speech, "to see men blind to a beauty that is beaming on every side of them." The student who loved mathematics and read through stacks of old English poetry heard Emerson ask, "Cannot a man know the mathematics, and love Shakespear also?" And the boy who dreamed of Walden Pond heard Emerson declare that "Culture in the high sense" turned to *nature* to awaken humankind— not to "the trimming and turfing of gardens," but *wild* nature, "the true harmony of the unshorn landscape, with horrid thickets, wide morasses, bald mountains, and the balance of the land and sea." Thoreau was hooked. And now, at last, so was Emerson. Someone told him that his young neighbor had walked all the way to Boston to hear him speak. Emerson's response was to invite Thoreau to his home, where he was giving private readings of these same lectures to family and close friends.[16]

By February 1838, Thoreau and Emerson were companions. "I delight much in my young friend, who seems to have as free & erect a mind as any I have ever met," wrote Emerson. Thoreau made the solitary afternoon "sunny with his simplicity & clear perception.... Every thing that boy says makes merry with society though nothing can be graver than his meaning," for he is "spiced throughout with rebellion."[17] By April they were taking walks together, and by

ı's transformation was complete—at least according to
.ssell Lowell, whom Harvard had suspended and sent to
.ord to "rusticate" for a spell. "I saw Thoreau last night," he
giggled to a friend, "and it is exquisitely amusing to see how he imi-
tates Emerson's tone and manner. With my eyes shut I shouldn't
know them apart." Thoreau's resemblance to Emerson dogged him
for the rest of his life, however unfairly: one visitor declared he was
"even getting up a caricature nose like Emerson's"![18] A decade later,
Lowell publicly mocked Thoreau as a pickpocket pilfering Emerson's best fruit: "Fie, for shame, brother bard; with good fruit of
your own, / Can't you let Neighbor Emerson's orchards alone?" Yet
William Ellery Channing insisted that imitation was necessary to
self-culture: "We need connexions with great thinkers to make us
thinkers too."[19] Once his apprenticeship was over, Thoreau would
fight hard to grow beyond Emerson's influence, but the paradox
was built into the heart of Emerson's philosophy. How could the
disciples of the great Apostle of Originality declare their own originality without parroting their teacher?

CONCORD SOCIAL CULTURE

While Thoreau was sharpening the cross-grained banter that won
him a place with the Emerson family, he was also working out a new
role in his own family, who had sacrificed so largely to send him to
Harvard and who expected more than a smart tongue in return. The
Thoreau family compound in the Parkman house now included his
parents, his three siblings (when they weren't away teaching), Aunt
Louisa and Uncle Charles Dunbar, Aunts Maria and Jane Thoreau
(when they were visiting, which was often), and now Aunt Maria's
elderly friend Prudence Bird Ward and her daughter Prudence as
well—plus such long-term residents as Lucy Jackson Brown, various temporary boarders, and one or two live-in maidservants. In
addition, the pencil factory out back occupied a growing series of
sheds. It was a large and active household composed almost entirely

of women, bustling with meetings and missions, meals to be cooked, tables to be set and cleared, gardens to be tended (this job fell to Henry) and the factory to be managed (he helped out here as well). No wonder the budding writer hungered for solitude. Henry took a room in the attic—what he called his "upper empire," from whose "perspective window" he could look out on the sunrise and see "all things . . . in their true relations."[20]

There in that upper empire he wrote up his first lecture for the Concord Lyceum, on April 11, 1838, on "Society." It was a grumpy lecture: men "have not associated, they have only assembled," he would tell the assembly; as for himself, he was only acting a part in "the great farce" of life."[21] His Journal records glimpses of that "farce," as in a sketch titled "A Sunday Scene" delineating family representatives of "the gender feminine": Mrs. Ward, "born in days that tried men's souls," never let him forget her husband was a colonel in the Revolutionary War ("For time was when I conversed with greater men than you," she'd say); and Aunt Maria, perfectly willing to rest her elbow on the Bible, spurned Henry's scandalous foreign book "'Germany by De Stael', as though a viper had stung her." But in his letters he clowns around: one day a big, mysterious box arrived in the mail from John. The honor of opening it fell to Henry: "What could it be? Some declare it must be Taunton herrings." He crawled around the carpet, sniffing the box from corner to corner—no herring. Milking the family guessing game, s-l-o-w-l-y he pulled out one nail, then another, until someone howled "rip it off"!—and at last the contents, Indian relics, were revealed, examined, and distributed to their delighted recipients.[22]

Even when he was away, John was the "bright spot everywhere; the life of every gathering." He graced the family parlor with a fancy album to record bird sightings, listed carefully by month starting at on one end, and by scientific families at the other, leaving plenty of blank space for new entries. Henry added a few, and Sophia, busy learning botany from Prudence Ward, added some pressed plants. As was the custom, John did his bird-watching with a gun; ironically, when a neighbor winged a male scarlet tanager, the family tried to keep the poor thing alive by feeding him worms, which he ate "voraciously" until he died three days later.[23]

Playing Indian with John fostered a deep bond between them. In December 1836, the brothers carved and erected a memorial to Tahatawan on Fairhaven Hill—"Tahatawan's cliff": here, "A Son of Nature, TAHATTAWAN, Sachimaupan, The Last of the Indians, has hunted, in this stream he has fished," Henry inscribed, in his best college Latin. "This crag shall be his cenotaph," declared the brothers; "Oh Indian! Where have your people gone?" In answer Henry added the words of Psalm 2.8, in Wampanoag: "Ask of me, and I shall give thee the heathen for thine inheritance, and the uttermost parts of the earth for thy possession."[24] In November 1837, when John was teaching in Hopewell, Henry wrote him an elaborate letter dated "Musketaquid two hundred and two Summers—two moons—eleven suns since the coming of the Pale Faces. Tahatawan—Sachimaupan—to his brother sachem—Hopeful—of Hopewell—hoping that he is well." Henry's counterfeit Indian mimicked the speeches of Red Jacket: "Brother, it is many suns that I have not seen the print of thy moccasins by our council fire. . . . Brother. I have been thinking how the Pale-Faces have taken away our lands." His elaborate satire of Concord politics mounted a protest in the name of the alienated and excluded, who found no representative in the town meeting: "There is no seat for Tahatawan in the council-house."[25] The mask of the Indian allowed Henry to play a visible dissenter, returning from the past to hold the present to account.

In the midst of writing this letter, Henry learned that one of the last survivors of the American Revolution, Anna Jones, was on her deathbed, and he walked to the poorhouse to interview the elderly and destitute woman. Faithfully he recorded her disconnected memories: the president of Harvard living at her farm house; Reverend Emerson's wartime sermons; the song her sweetheart used to sing; how the miller, Mr. Buttrick, was captured by the British, who told him they would send him to hell, and who replied, Do as you please, I haven't long to live at any rate. This deathbed oral history resulted in Thoreau's first publication, an obituary of Anna

Jones in the *Freeman's Gazette*, though the published version suppressed most of the information he took down, as well as his closing assertion: "And who shall say that her religion was not a reality? that under much that was hollow and conventional there burned not a living and inextinguishable flame?"—a singular remark and a red flag to the self-righteous, signaling Thoreau's dawning Transcendentalism.[26]

While Henry was groping for a role and a voice, the women in his family were finding theirs. When the Wards joined the Thoreau household late in 1833, they brought along their radical abolitionism and their subscription to William Lloyd Garrison's antislavery newspaper, the *Liberator*. Women, proclaimed Garrison, held the destiny of slaves in their hands. Once Prudence discovered Concord was too stuffy and timid to hear such "hard things," she and her friends set about waking people up. In 1834, three of Concord's most prominent citizens formed the Middlesex County Anti-Slavery Society, and by 1835—the year a mob attacked Garrison, trashing his newspaper office and nearly killing him—Helen and Sophia Thoreau were involved in abolitionism. So were Elizabeth Hoar and Mary Moody Emerson, who drew in Lidian and Waldo (as Emerson was known to his friends). In short, Henry Thoreau returned from college to find his home a hotbed of radical abolitionism. The week he began teaching public school, the antislavery activists Angelina and Sarah Grimké spoke at Concord's Trinitarian Church, where Prudence thought they won over even some of the men. A few weeks later, a group of Concord women—including Cynthia, Helen, and Sophia Thoreau, both the Wards, and Lidian Emerson—formally founded the Concord Female Anti-Slavery Society.[27] Henry Thoreau was too preoccupied with his "upper empire" to sign on, but simply walking through his front door put him in the midst of America's great and growing crisis over slavery.

Henry was also preoccupied with making a living. As a boarder he was bound by honor and duty to contribute to the family income. If he couldn't teach, at least he could work at the pencil factory, which he did, turning the task into an intriguing intellectual problem: Why were American pencils so terrible? They functioned, more or less, but were coarse, brittle, greasy and scratchy. Leads were still made from a warm paste of ground graphite, bayberry wax, glue, and whale oil, pressed into grooves cut in slats of cedar wood, topped by a second slat, cut, and finished. But imported French Conté pencils were far superior, and unlike the English pencils of pure-cut natural graphite, the French pencils were graded, from hard to soft. Thoreau went to work to figure out how the French did it. It has been said he found the clue in an encyclopedia article on German pencil-making, but no such article has been located, and the Germans hadn't yet cracked the secret, either.

Somehow Henry made the leap. Perhaps his father suggested the idea, or perhaps he read how crucibles were manufactured by mixing graphite with clay, which was heat-resistant. In any case, over the next few months he figured it out: first, use just the right kind of clay (Warren Miles, who later worked in their factory, said the Thoreaus used the fine Bavarian clay imported by glassblowers). Second, vary the proportions: the more clay, the harder the pencil lead. Third, grind the graphite finer than anyone had managed to before. To do that, Henry invented a new graphite mill, a tall churn that used airflow to sift out the finest particles, leaving the rest in the chamber for further grinding. Fourth, mold the graphite-clay mix and fire it in a kiln.[28] The result was a completely new kind of pencil lead: a kiln-fired ceramic that could be cut and set into grooves to make pencils graduated in hardness from 1 to 4. Artists, surveyors, and engineers paid a premium for them. The Thoreaus added a rich blue pencil to their product line, plus other styles and sizes, such as flat carpenters' pencils that wouldn't roll away. As their business grew, so did the series of manufacturing sheds behind the Parkman house. To keep their trade secrets, father and son wrote nothing down and kept their mouths shut. For some years, no one in America made better pencils.[29]

Yet Thoreau felt his calling was not pencil-making, but teaching. He detailed his teaching philosophy in a long letter to Orestes Brownson: education should be a pleasure both for teacher and student, and discipline should be the same in the classroom as in the street; that is, not the cowhide whip but life itself. "I have ever been disposed to regard the cowhide as a nonconductor. . . . Not a single spark of truth is ever transmitted through its agency." To transmit that spark, the teacher should be a student, too, learning with and from his pupils. But such teaching "supposes a degree of freedom which rarely exists"—the freedom to liberate the self. Brownson was too preoccupied with his new journal, the *Boston Quarterly Review*, to respond, so Thoreau kept working his contacts, following up rumors of a job here or there.[30] Nothing.

By mid-March he was ready to explode. "We should start in company for the West and there establish a school jointly," he wrote John—or at least find positions together. Why, their former teacher, now in Kentucky, had listed "nearly a dozen schools which I could have." It was high time to get started. "Go *I* must at all events." Henry started calling in all his forces, and soon he had letters of support from George Ripley, Ralph Waldo Emerson, and Harvard's President Quincy—an impressive portfolio. Even as Cynthia flurried around packing to send her sons West, Quincy alerted Thoreau to a plum opening in Virginia.[31] But the Virginia lead fizzled, and John accepted a position in West Roxbury, near Boston, so Henry turned to Maine. In May 1838, with a hundred dollars borrowed from Emerson, he headed to Bangor to work his family connections.

This two-week venture was Thoreau's first trip beyond the Boston area. Midnight of May 3 found him on a ship to Portland, "head over the boat's side," gamely declaring that being seasick heightened the effect of the moon's brightness. Elbowing his way into strange towns and begging for work from strangers did not come naturally to Thoreau, but on the mail coach to Brunswick, he forgot his awkwardness and grew absorbed in the succession of villages rolling past, each a world to itself, each deserving a separate study. Of his Bangor relatives he left no record, but he detailed his conversation in Oldtown with an old Indian who sat on a scow, "striking his deerskin moccasins against the planks." He was "the most communicative man I had met. —— Talked of hunting and fishing—old

times and new times. Pointing up the Penobscot he observed—
'Two or three miles up the river one beautiful country!'"—words
Thoreau would never forget.[32]

THE THOREAU SCHOOL

By May 17, 1838, Thoreau was back home, still jobless; he'd been
either a month too late or three months too early. After spinning
plans all spring to leave Concord, perhaps for far away and perhaps
for good, in the end he stayed home. Ellery Channing told a family story of a youthful Henry asking his mother which profession
to choose, whereupon Cynthia replied, "You can buckle on your
knapsack, and roam abroad to seek your fortune." As Henry's eyes
watered and tears rolled down his cheeks, Helen put her arm around
him, kissed him and said, "No, Henry, you shall not go: you shall stay
at home and live with us."[33] Which was, for the time being, exactly
what he did. In mid-June, 1838, Henry Thoreau opened a school of
his own, right in the Parkman House.

The solution to Henry's travail seemed to unfold like magic.
Soon he had four students, with another engaged, and was keeping
school hours: classes from eight to twelve, a break for lunch, then
two to four in the afternoon, followed by some reading in Greek or
English or, for variety, a stroll in the fields. When the schoolmaster
of Concord Academy resigned, the trustees hired Thoreau as the
new academy instructor. By September 15, he was announcing openings in Concord's two newspapers for "a limited number of pupils,
of both sexes" for instruction in "the usual English branches" and
preparation for college, six dollars per quarter. When enrollments
got off to a slow start, his family grew worried: early in October,
at Helen's and John's urging, Henry inquired into an opening in
Taunton, admitting his present school was "not sufficiently lucrative." But his pupils' fathers —Samuel Hoar, John Keyes, the lawyer
Nathan Brooks—were prominent men in Concord, and word was
spreading. Enrollment grew. By the end of winter quarter, the acad-

emy required a second teacher, and on February 9, John joined his younger brother. As senior teacher, John took the title preceptor, with Henry assisting him "in the classical department." Under the Thoreau brothers, Concord Academy soon reached capacity, with twenty-five students.[34]

Henry was now free to put his liberating educational principles into practice, and the "Thoreau School" became one of the most important of the nation's early educational experiments, combining intellectual rigor and a demanding curriculum with the revolutionary Transcendentalist notion of "Culture." While Transcendentalism has been called a religious movement, the first and most electrifying application of its principles was education: the lifelong process of "educing," or unfolding, each individual's inward, God-given spiritual nature.[35] As Emerson had announced in "The American Scholar," the movement's great manifesto, in the right state the scholar is "Man Thinking." Every human being is forever a student, and all things exist to draw out each person's latent abilities. "The main enterprise of the world for splendor, for extent, is the upbuilding of a man," declared Emerson; "in yourself slumbers the whole of Reason."[36] What did this mean for an aspiring teacher? First, teaching was a vocation to which one could dedicate one's life. Second, joining this revolution meant one's own education would never end: one should find discussion groups and forge networks to explore and share new thought, such as the twice-monthly teachers' meetings Thoreau attended at Emerson's home. Third, it took real courage to break with generations of convention and ignite students' love of learning. As Emerson warned, the true teacher could not instruct, but only provoke. The actual learning was in the hands of the students themselves.

There were few guidebooks to this revolution in education, but Thoreau owned the best: *Record of a School*, Elizabeth Peabody's account of Bronson Alcott's innovative Temple School in Boston, which Peabody helped Alcott found in 1834. She, too, became a great educational reformer, introducing American readers to the progressive European educators Pestalozzi and de Gérando, popularizing

the radical European idea of the "Kindergarten," and opening a
Boston bookstore to help spread Transcendentalism to the world
and introduce radical books and journals to America. But educational reform didn't come easily. By the time Thoreau met Alcott
in 1839, his Temple School was dying a protracted death. Scandal
had erupted in 1837 when Alcott's *Conversations with Children on the
Gospels* showed him drawing out his pupils on such off-limits topics
as human sexuality and Christ's humanity. Enrollment plunged, and
Alcott relocated his school. Enrollment collapsed altogether when
he admitted a free black child and white parents withdrew their children en masse. It's all the more remarkable, then, that the Thoreau
school succeeded, enrolled to capacity and fully supported by Concord's mainstream community. Unlike Alcott, the Thoreau brothers
taught both older and younger children, with the Harvard-trained
Henry taking the most advanced classes. This meant combining a
rigorous college prep curriculum—mathematics, natural philosophy, Greek, Latin, and French—with "the usual English branches"
taught by John. Yet the Thoreaus dispensed with conventional methods of rote memorization, recitation, and endless drills under threat
of physical punishment. How did they do it?

The process began with an admission interview. "You say you
would like to enter our school," John would begin; "why do you
wish that?" To learn Latin, Greek, and mathematics, the child would
reply. "If you really wish to study those things," John would say, "we
can teach you, if you will obey our rules and promise to give your
mind to your studies; but if you come to idle and play, or to see
other boys study, we shall not want you for a pupil. Do you promise,
then, to do what we require?" The student who disobeyed would
be reminded of the promise, in a process of moral suasion the students found seamless. "It was a peculiar school," recalled Horace
Hosmer. "There was never a boy flogged or threatened, yet I never
saw so absolutely military discipline. How it was done I scarcely
know. Even the incorrigible were brought into line." Where Henry
was "strict," John could "govern and get the good-will of the most
unruly boys of Concord," even those expelled from other schools. At

most, John might call a misbehaving student to his desk to reprove him in a voice so low only the culprit could hear it. Once, Hosmer was called up, and instead of punishment he came away with two new books. As for Henry, one student remembered him barreling through the door and commencing work "at once in his peculiar odd way," with no mercy to the child who had not got his lesson. Frisbie Hoar recalled how they used to call him "Trainer Thoreau, because the boys called the soldiers the 'trainers,'" and Henry had a soldier's erect carriage and long, measured stride.[37]

On Saturday afternoons, Henry's long stride would lead the students on weekly field trips, to the *Yeoman's Gazette* to see how newspapers were made; to the gunsmith's to try making their own gunflints; on long walks to Walden, Fairhaven, or Sleepy Hollow for field lessons in botany, geology, and natural history; or boating on the rivers in the *Musketaquid*, the new boat Henry and John built their first spring at the academy, which the students helped to keep clean and watertight. Sometimes the lessons were practical, like the trip to Fairhaven so Henry could show the students how surveyors worked and have them try out the instruments. One student recalled the day when, sailing through the Great Meadows, Henry landed them all on shore. "Do you see," he asked the children, "anything here that might attract Indians to this spot?" One boy pointed to the river for fishing, another to the woodland for hunting. "Anything else?" prompted Henry, pointing to a rivulet flowing from a nearby spring, then to a hillside offering shelter. Then, taking a spade, he struck it into the soil, sampling places, until everyone began to despair. Suddenly his spade struck a stone, then it struck another. Soon Henry had uncovered the fire-scorched stones of an Indian campfire, proving the students' conjectures. Before they left, he carefully replaced the turf to cover up their find, "not wishing to have the domestic altar of the aborigines profaned by mere curiosity."[38]

The school itself was divided into two rooms, with John in charge of the "lower" school on the main floor while Henry taught the advanced classes upstairs. One of the brothers would open with a morning prayer, not a reading of scripture but an extemporaneous address "to put their minds in proper trim for the work of the day." Thomas Hosmer remembered Henry speaking of the beauties of the seasons, engaging the students so intensely that "you could have heard a pin drop in the School room." Another morning, Henry asked them to imagine walking into a shop to see the "wheels, pinions, springs and frame pieces" of a watch spread out on a bench, then returning to find them all "exactly put together and working in unison" to show the passage of time—would they believe this happened by chance? Or that "somebody with plan and thought and power" had been there? One of Henry's addresses was on profanity: "Boys, if you want to talk to a man and he insisted on thrusting a word having no connection with the subject into all parts of every sentence—*Boot-jack* for instance—wouldn't you think" he was trifling with your time? Henry went on to illustrate by inserting "Boot-jack" violently and frequently into a sentence—and young Thomas never forgot the lesson.[39]

Writing was central to the curriculum. Everyone had to complete a composition each week, taking half the day with no other lesson. Henry would read some of them aloud to general laughter. While Channing had assigned arcane topics that puzzled his students, Henry did the opposite: write on something you know, something before you. "What their hands find to putter about, or their Minds to think about,—that let them write about," he suggested to his sister Helen, his fellow schoolteacher: note what passes in the street, or gaze into a fire, or study a corner "where there is a spider's web, and philosophize—moralize—theorize, or what not." Students were encouraged to keep journals of their thoughts and activities, too. The journal of twelve-year-old Edmund Sewall still survives: "I study in the morning. I did Geometry, Geography and grammar and in the afternoon read, spell or say definitions from the reading lesson, say Latin & Algebra. I write every other morning. Saturday is given to writing compositions." Horace Hosmer recalled another writing exercise "called defining, but defiling would describe it better. Poetical gems were mangled and then rolled in the mud" as students translated them into their own words. One student translated

Cowper's poem "Needless Alarm" into four words—"Look before you leap," at which "John sprang from his chair and shouted Good, *very good* indeed."[40]

At noontime the day students would run home for dinner, but Horace, who lived nearly two miles away, remembered how sometimes John would take him by the hand "and say, I must eat dinner with him, and you may be sure I was willing to obey. I shall never forget those dinners while reason lasts." Cynthia and John Sr. presided over a table loaded with "an abundance of fruit and vegetables, puddings and pies," and best of all, delicious fresh bread and butter. "There was an absence of heat, noise, fat greasy meat, of everything unpleasant, and I learned to love Mr. and Mrs. T. quite as well as their food." The Thoreau brothers were famous for their melon patch, and once Horace returned from dinner to find "a piece of green melon in my desk." He almost threw it out in disgust until the smell enticed him to eat it: "I was astonished and delighted." When watermelons were ripe, the brothers brought a bushel to school, and at recess— which they often extended far past the prescribed ten minutes—all shared in the treat.[41]

Many students openly preferred John, who played with them at recess as if he were still a boy, or gathered them around and told stories. By contrast, Henry seldom mixed with the children; he seemed "rather on his dignity," thought one. Another remembered how they made fun of him, cutting a picture of a booby out of an almanac and passing it around because, they giggled, it looked just like their teacher.[42] Yet Henry's quieter style touched some students deeply. One of the Hosmer boys said that though Henry avoided children in groups, he took an interest in individuals: "I have seen children catch him by the hand as he went away to walk with him & hear more." He had "something beyond the dollar," "an interest in teaching, His heart in the undertaking."[43] When he visited Thoreau at Walden Pond years later, his former teacher asked what use he'd found his school studies in life. Frisbie Hoar, too, counted him a lifelong friend, who never ceased to teach even after he'd left the classroom.

Thoreau had written to Brownson that the classroom should never be separate from the street, and the greatest success of the Thoreau school was the brothers' ability to integrate the school with their community. Why, wondered Thoreau, should we "leave off our education when we begin to be men and women"? "It is time that villages were universities," *un*common schools where citizens could pursue liberal studies for the rest of their lives, banding together to fund the arts and learning, and make not a village with a few noblemen, but "noble villages of men"—a classroom so open that everyone would be welcome.[44] It was a goal he would never surrender.

"THERE IS NO REMEDY FOR LOVE BUT TO LOVE MORE"

In 1839, Henry Thoreau's life blossomed. He rose to a position of standing and honor in his community; he went on the adventure of a lifetime; he began polishing poems and essays for the Transcendentalists' new literary journal; and to top it all off, he fell in love—twice. Teaching at the Concord Academy did more than give Thoreau a respectable job: it put him at the center of Concord's cultural life, as Phineas Allen had been a decade before. At the first meeting of the Concord Lyceum's new season, Thoreau was elected secretary, and thereafter he proudly recorded lyceum proceedings in his finest handwriting. When one of the lyceum curators resigned, Thoreau was elected to fill his place, too. This meant helping to arrange twenty-five lectures over the six-month season: choosing speakers, writing letters persuading them to come, handling schedule and travel arrangements, securing payments, and returning forgotten articles, all on a tight budget. This was genuine service, the kind that earned Thoreau the right to suggest, in *Walden*, that villages could indeed become "universities." Lyceum members showed their appreciation by reelecting him to double duty for a second year. They tried to reelect him for a third year as curator, but, overwhelmed, Thoreau begged off—only to be reelected again two years later, in November 1842, over his protests.

Altogether, Thoreau's social world was exploding. He dropped by the Emersons' every few days to greet their constant stream of visitors, including, about this time, Margaret Fuller and Bronson Alcott. When Emerson tried to lure Fuller to Concord, in February 1839, he sent Thoreau to find her a suitable house. To their disappointment she chose Jamaica Plain instead. With Alcott they had better luck: he arrived on April 29, 1839, just in time to witness Emerson's marriage of Sam Staples, the bartender and future jailer, to Lucinda Wesson, the innkeeper's daughter. Alcott liked the simple ceremony, and he liked how Emerson spoke from the soul—a good start to days of walking and talking. When Emerson lectured at the lyceum, Thoreau, as curator, no doubt joined them at the Emersons' afterward; two days later Alcott held one of his formal "Conversations" at "Mrs. Thorows," where he launched into "Knowledge, Memory, Hope, Pre-existence, Faith, Elements of the Soul, Incarnation, Miracles," stunning the normally voluble Thoreaus into silence. Alcott, disappointed, recorded Emerson's criticism that "the people were stupid, and that I did not meet them wisely." Nevertheless, a year later he moved his family to Concord, going to work as a woodcutter and enrolling his eldest daughter, Anna, in the Thoreau school. Thus did Alcott and Thoreau begin their lifelong conversation. To Thoreau's delight, he could now, in a few steps, go from the agricultural "Scythia" of his farmer friend George Minott to the philosophical "Athens" of Mr. Alcott and his family.[45]

To top it off, Henry was again writing poetry. In "Sic Vita" he had been cut off, rootless and uncertain; now he imagined himself as one voice in a duet of two—like a woman singing her songs from the shore over the waves until she hears the voice of "a kindred soul out of the distance" answering, or floating on the waves, all strife dissolved away: "Drifting in a sultry day on the sluggish waters of the pond I almost cease to live—and begin to be. . . . I am dissolved in the haze."[46] Three times that year Henry would float unmoored and dissolved by joy: first with Edmund Sewall; then with Edmund's sister Ellen; and finally with his brother John.

On June 17, 1839, Caroline Ward Sewall brought her eleven-year-old son Edmund from Scituate for a weeklong visit with her sister,

Prudence Ward, and her mother, Mrs. Ward. Henry was immediately drawn to the boy: "I have within the last few days come into contact with a pure uncompromising spirit" who, all unconscious, carried "the air and conviction of virtue. . . . Such it is impossible not to love." They went sailing together on the river and walking to the Cliffs and Walden Pond, just as the brothers often did with students and other visitors. This time, though, Henry ventured a poem: "Lately alas I knew a gentle boy, / Whose features all were cast in Virtue's mould." The poem, "Sympathy," elegized a friendship that could never be: drawn together like two planets by unconscious sympathy, the emotion proved too strong. The speaker's love, springing to consciousness, forced the two apart, "beyond each other's reach," leaving Henry alone to love not the boy himself, but "that virtue which he is." Alas, he added, "I might have loved him, had I loved him less."[47] Seldom has the pain of Platonic passion burned more brightly.

The Sewalls were delighted with the poem, and Edmund was so proud of it that his five-year-old brother George suffered in jealousy until Henry, with his unerring sympathy for the quieter, younger ones, inscribed to the boy a copy of his other great poem about love and loss, "The Bluebirds." Emerson loved "Sympathy," too, calling it "the purest strain & the loftiest, I think, that has yet pealed from this yet unpoetic American forest." He sent a copy to Samuel Gray Ward, suggesting he pass it along to Margaret Fuller, and alerted both Thomas Carlyle and Mary Moody Emerson that Concord at last had a genuine poet "who writes the truest verses," "that rarest product of New England wit."[48] But by the time Edmund returned in March 1840 as a boarding student, Henry's passion for him was spent. Edmund's earnest diary records a lively array of excursions, but mostly with John, who attended to the serious boy like an affectionate older brother.

Ellen Devereux Sewall arrived for her own family visit on July 20, three weeks after her brother's departure. Since she, too, was part of the extended family circle, Henry and John had often seen her before; Edmund found her initials carved in the "red bridge" between the initials of John and Henry Thoreau, dated 1830 and 1835, with Henry's initials "cut very neatly and deep."⁴⁹ But by 1839, things were different. Ellen was now seventeen, the cultivated daughter of Scituate's Unitarian minister Edmund Quincy Sewall, and an exceptionally handsome young woman. A daguerreotype taken of her about this time shows her poised and alert, with a strong, angular nose and deep-set, level eyes, barely resisting an ironic smile. Henry the dreamer, Emerson's grave jester, erupted into poetry: "Come let's roam the breezy pastures," he invites in his first poem to Ellen. "One green leaf shall be our screen, / Till the sun doth go to bed, / I the king and you the queen / Of that peaceful little green." Four days later, the flirtation turned romantic: "Our rays united make one Sun, / With fairest summer weather." And on July 25, he recorded but a single line that entirely reversed the tortured distance of his poem to her brother: "There is no remedy for love but to love more."⁵⁰

Henry and Ellen did all the things vacationing young people did then (chaperoned, of course, by Cynthia or Prudence). On Monday Henry took her to see a giraffe on display in Concord; on Tuesday he took her rowing up the Assabet River—"Forward press we to the dawning, / For Aurora leads the way"—and on Wednesday, a school holiday, John, Henry, and Ellen all walked together to the Cliffs and beyond to Fairhaven Bay. Cynthia, John, Ellen, and Henry all took tea at the Reverend Barzillai Frost's. They went a-berrying, and walked to Walden Pond. Henry took Ellen for a drive, and they went sailing on the Concord River. Her visit nearly over, Ellen wrote to her father, with perhaps intentional double-meaning, "I can not tell you half I have enjoyed here." That same evening her lover was showing his new poems to Emerson, who was telling him that under the inspiration of love Thoreau had become, at last, America's true poet.

For two weeks Henry went everywhere with Ellen—or nearly everywhere. He did refuse to accompany her to church, an ominous sign for a minister's daughter. Nor was he there when, the morning after he showed Emerson his new poems, Aunt Prudence escorted Ellen through Captain Abel Moore's fine gardens. John S. Keyes, on vacation from Harvard, happened to be there as well, and he was instantly infatuated: he walked Ellen home, then returned after dinner, hoping to see her again. Missing her then, he found her that night at a party and, in his words, "pounced upon" her, escorting her to supper and again walking her home. The next afternoon he found her again at tea, pried her away from the Thoreaus, and walked her home for a third time. The attention was overwhelming; the next morning, on the stagecoach home, Ellen cried all the way to Lexington. When she reached Scituate, she wrote Aunt Prudence that her two weeks at the Thoreaus had been some of the happiest of her life.[51]

In the aftermath of Ellen's visit, Henry's Journal lapses. He could dismiss the cocksure Keyes, but he had to weigh the rivalry with his own brother: John the sunny extrovert, gregarious, witty, and athletic; John the elder, who took over as senior teacher even though Henry had the Harvard education and had started the school.[52] The tension simmered even as they embarked on their great adventure. They'd built the *Musketaquid* that spring, roomy and strong, to take a trip together down the Concord River and up the Merrimack to the White Mountains, climb Mount Washington, then float home. To celebrate, the brothers held a melon party for the entire neighborhood. Keyes got the grand tour of "all the minutiae of packing" and affirmed Henry had "all things arranged prime and will have a glorious time if he is fortunate enough to have good weather." After admiring the table spread "in the very handsomest style with all kinds and qualities of melons," Keyes and the fellows "attacked them furiously" until "what with wine & all" he had quite as much as he could carry home. Late-summer melon parties became a Thoreau tradition: after another one years later, Elizabeth Hoar reported that Henry had adorned the table "with sunflowers, cornstalks, beet leaves & squash blossoms. There were forty-six melons, fifteen different kinds; & apples, all the production of his own garden." To her amusement, Cynthia, having spread it around town that Henry detested parties, felt she had to apologize when he threw one himself.[53]

→>⊰⊦

Saturday morning, August 31, dawned gloomy and drizzly, but as the skies cleared into a mild summer afternoon, the brothers unchained their boat from the wild apple tree and shoved off into the open waters of the Concord River. The *Musketaquid* was well loaded with potatoes, melons and other supplies; two masts, one doubling as a tent pole; a cotton tent that doubled as a sail; and a buffalo hide to sleep on. The gaily painted boat, green below with a border of blue above, made a picturesque sight for the family and friends gathered on shore to see them off, and as the brothers raised their guns and fired a farewell volley, the hills rang with echoes. As they floated past the Old North Bridge battleground, they meditated on the din of war, and at the Great Meadows, when they spotted a rare and spectacular hibiscus in bloom, they hailed a farmer and gave him a blossom with instructions to carry it to church on the morrow for their botanist friend Prudence Ward. They made seven miles that day, pitching their tent on a patch of high ground near Billerica, picking huckleberries for their supper of bread and sugar, then sipping hot cocoa made with river water while they watched their shadows lengthen and the sun set.

Sunday morning their campfire smoke mingled with the thick morning fog, which had burned off by the time they reached the Middlesex Canal. They walked the towpath, drawing their boat behind, under the censorious gaze of Sunday churchgoers. After being locked to the swift Merrimack, they turned upriver, nooning in the shade near Chelmsford, where they gathered wild plums, then passing Wicasuck Island, the lost home of the Penacook Indians, where they refused a ride to two lost men anxious to get to Nashua. At Tyngsboro they made camp by twilight under an oak by the stream, and all night they drowsed while the river eddied and Irish railroad workers kept them awake with "boisterous sport."[54] That night, Henry reported, one sailor was beset in his dreams "by the Evil Destinies" while the other "passed a serene and even ambrosial or immortal night," awakening the next morning to soothe and reassure with his good cheer. Need we guess which was which?

Monday, September 2, they navigated the busy ferry passage

as their countrymen stirred about their workweek. One brother brought the boat around the river's lazy oxbow curves while the other cut across, collecting well water and reports of the countryside. They hailed a canal boat, tied up alongside, and floated in company, chatting with the boatmen. Later they stopped to explore an ancient Indian homesite exposed when fishermen had broken the bank pulling out the brush; the sand had blown ashore, creating a pocket desert. As they passed Nashua's falls and factories, they cast longing eyes at the blue heights of Wachusett and Monadnock beyond, but stayed river-bound, camping near Nashville, New Hampshire under a pine wood by a deep ravine, where they fell asleep listening to a distant drummer practice for a muster of country militia.

By 3:00 a.m. they were under way again, and by dawn they had been rowing for hours past woods, pastures, and fields of corn, potatoes, rye, oats, and English hay. At the locks around Cromwell's Falls—"the Nesenkeag of the Indians"—they picked up arrowheads on the bank while waiting their turn, listening to the locktender's stories of buried treasure, and witnessing the end of an era; soon the railroad, not the canals, would carry the region's freight.[55] That noon they watched a flock of passenger pigeons and shot exactly one. They plucked and broiled it with some squirrels, but the poor, skinned bodies were so disgusting they threw them away and ate rice instead. At Bedford they camped in a sheltered spot above the waterfalls; next morning, they found they were blocking the workmen's path to the locks, the only time their campsite was observed by human eyes.

Above Bedford the river was rocky and broken by falls—a refreshing change—but they hastened past Manchester, a village even then hammering away on the new foundations of an industrial city. In the canal beyond, they agreed to let a canal boat take them in tow until they learned this meant taking the *Musketaquid*, too heavy to lift, on board. So the canal men challenged the brothers to a race, taunting them until the brothers mounted their sail, doubled up on their oars, and shot gleefully past, taunting the canal men in return. That night the brothers reached the limit of their river journey, pitching their tent just below Hooksett Pinnacle, exactly where a party of

Penobscot Indians had camped a few summers before. John went off to find a farmhouse for provisions and returned with young Nathan Mitchel the farmer's boy, who longed to join them. Come along! they said, but Father said no, then compensated with a tour of his farm and permission to store their gear in his barn. That night Henry dreamed of "a difference with a Friend" that was, in dream space, resolved, leaving him "unspeakably soothed and rejoiced."[56]

Next morning, September fifth, dawned to the "ominous" sound of raindrops on their cotton rooftop. They walked ten miles through the rain to Concord, New Hampshire—"*new* Concord," they joked with the friends who put them up for the night—where they caught the morning stage to Plymouth, on the verge of the White Mountains. From there it was fifteen miles up Pemigewasset Valley to James Tilton's Inn in Thornton.[57] The next day, the seventh, they walked through Peeling (now Woodstock) and Lincoln to Franconia to see the Notch and the famous Old Man of the Mountain (a craggy formation now lost in a rockfall). On the eighth they walked to Crawford House, from where they set off next morning to explore the mountains, reaching the summit of Mount Washington the next day. Back at the bottom they caught the stage to Conway and for two days retraced their steps to their campsite in Hookset, which they reached on September 12—a week to the day after they stored their gear in Mitchel's barn. They didn't linger: after packing up their boat and purchasing young Nathan's prize watermelon, the largest on the farm, for ballast, they set off homeward. Thanks to the strong current and friendly winds, they made it all the way downstream to an island north of Merrimack, New Hampshire, where they pitched their tent for the last time.[58]

Long before daybreak on their last day together, Friday, September 13, the brothers lay awake listening to a fresh autumn wind rustle the leaves overhead. The season had turned in the night: "We had gone to bed in summer," wrote Henry years later, "and we awoke in autumn."[59] It was fifty miles to Concord, but with the north wind at their backs, they made the distance in a day, flying down the Merrimack past the sites of their upward journey, watching them fade one after another into memory. At noon, their old friend the locktender let them back into the Middlesex Canal, and they rowed up the gentle Concord River, a long pull in a dreamy mood through sunset into darkness until, "far in the evening, our boat was grating against the bulrushes of its native port, and its keel recognized the Concord mud."[60] The Thoreau brothers leaped out and fastened the *Musketaquid* to the wild apple tree. They were home.

→>-<←

Henry had penciled a few notes, but he didn't copy them into his Journal until the following summer.[61] The trip was a summer lark, not a literary vehicle, although when Emerson heard about it, he thought it a fine commentary on the "death-cold convention" on education he had suffered through the day before, shivering with boredom at the very moment when Henry and John were skimming with delight down the Merrimack, the wind filling their sails. "We are shut up in schools & college recitation rooms for ten or fifteen years & come out at last with a bellyfull of words & do not know a thing," muttered Emerson. We don't know an edible root in the woods, we can't tell our course by the stars or the time by the sun. "Now here are my wise young neighbors who instead of getting like the wordmen into a railroad-car where they have not even the activity of holding the reins, have got into a boat which they have built with their own hands with sails which they have contrived to serve as a tent by night, & gone up the river Merrimack to live by their wits on the fish of the stream & the berries of the wood."[62] This would make a fine story. Meanwhile, it was time to spread the word: young writers like Henry Thoreau needed a place to publish their new poems and their radical ideas without prejudice or censorship.

Emerson and his friends had been toying with the idea of a new journal since 1832. When the topic came up yet again in May 1839, the lack of a literary journal in Boston—the supposed literary center of America—had become an embarrassment.[63] Now the time felt right. On September 18, 1839, the Transcendentalists held a meeting to discuss founding a journal of their own. Emerson wasn't there, but Alcott was, and he came up with a name: the *Dial*, for the gnomon on the sundial that always shows the true, celestial time. Nothing happened until October 19, when Orestes Brownson forced the issue by suggesting to Alcott that the two branches of Transcendentalism, his and Emerson's, should join forces, and *The Dial* should merge with Brownson's *Boston Quarterly Review*. Consternation followed; Brownson's militant self-righteousness had already split the Transcendentalist coterie, and Emerson's friends agreed that his new proposal had to be squelched. The next morning Alcott swept up Margaret Fuller and the two dashed off to Emerson's house to press the point: there must be a journal, the *Dial*, and it must be kept out of Brownson's hands. By day's end the *Dial* was born. Fuller would edit it, George Ripley would be the business manager, and Emerson would assist as needed. By mid-November, before Fuller had even begun to think of contacting potential contributors, Emerson had in hand their very first submission: "Sympathy," Thoreau's elegy to his love for Edmund Sewall.

The perilous fortunes of the *Dial* are a story unto itself. Suffice it to say that after months of jostling, the project had devolved into the hands of Fuller, Emerson, and their closest friends, which included, of course, Bronson Alcott and Henry Thoreau, both busy writing up their contributions. Alcott was at work on "Orphic Sayings," and Thoreau was finishing up "Aulus Persius Flaccus," an essay on an obscure Roman satirist. When the *Dial's* first issue was published, on July 1, 1840, it included both his poem and his essay. Reviewers greeted the new journal with ridicule and hostility, but Thoreau, at least, could pride himself on success: "Sympathy" was picked up and reprinted in the *Boston Morning Post* for July 5, 1840. His summer of poetry had, just a year later, borne its first fruit. Encouraged, he began drafting passages on the river journey, testing out the excursion's literary potential.

→>–<←

John, meanwhile, had been making his own plans, and was now actively pursuing Ellen. On September 30, he took the stage to Scituate and knocked on her door, unconscious of the awkwardness he created: her parents were away on a two-week trip to Niagara Falls, leaving Ellen to care for Edmund and George; otherwise only the occasional maid was present. It was a scandal—there was John, quite immovable, with no chaperone in sight. Ellen did not send him away, nor did she tell her parents of his visit. To Aunt Prudence, who knew all about it, Ellen insisted the maid was there, even though she had sent her away (it being much more pleasant without "a stranger" in the house for John's visit!).

It must have taken some time to clear the air after the Sewalls learned from the neighbors that their daughter had been entertaining a young gentleman in their absence. John tried to smooth things over with a second, courtesy visit during Thanksgiving, so that Ellen's parents could look him over themselves. For Christmas, Prudence brought both brothers to Scituate. Both came bearing gifts: John brought South American opals for Ellen's mineral collection, and Henry brought a volume of Jones Very's poems. His gift exemplified Transcendentalism at its most formally elegant and most doctrinally dangerous: Very had been dismissed from Harvard after proclaiming himself Christ resurrected. Perhaps Henry thought he had little to lose, for at this point John was fully in the lead. That fall Henry gloomed in an essay on "Friendship" that to be "actually separated from that parcel of heaven—we call our friend—with the suspicion that we shall no more meet in nature—is source enough for all the elegies that were ever written. . . . My friend will be as much better than my-self as my aspiration is beyond my attainment."[64]

There matters rested until June, when Ellen visited Concord again. Henry had her to himself for an afternoon: "The other day I rowed in my boat a free—even lovely young lady—and as I plied the oars she sat in the stern—and there was nothing but she between me and the sky." The moment didn't last long. July 20 was the first anniversary of Ellen's arrival in their universe, and John decided to act. He went with the Wards to Scituate, and while walking on the beach, led Ellen out of Prudence's hearing long enough to propose marriage. Ellen said yes. What happened next is conjecture—Ellen scissored these pages out of her diary—but remorse set in immediately. She said she loved not John, but Henry. When her mother, horrified, insisted she break the engagement out of respect for her father, she did. By the time John returned to Concord two days later, it was all over. In his Journal Henry wrote, "These two days that I have not written in my Journal have really been an aeon in which a Syrian empire might rise and fall—How many Persias have been lost and won in the interim—Night is spangled with fresh stars."[65]

Now it was John's turn to gloom, and he did. "Tonight I feel doleful, somewhat lachrymose, and desponding 'Bluey,'" he wrote in his own journal, "not absolutely suicidal. . . . Can say with truth I think this the vilest world I have ever been in." It couldn't be, he joked mordantly, that he was "crossed in love"—no, it must be that "indigestible compound" concocted by "the Kitchen Cabinet" wasn't sitting right; "wouldn't be uncharitable, but certainly things in my chemical laboratory don't assimilate kindly; rather more Chyme than than [sic] Chyle I fear, or something of that sort: hence my gloomy feelings."[66]

John's famous gift for gab jollied him out of disappointment, but Henry's gift for words may have been his own undoing. Henry should have gone to Scituate to press his case with Ellen in person, as John had done; instead he tried to woo her long-distance with poetry. In November, he wrote Ellen proposing marriage. The letter does not survive, but his Journal preserves a few words of the draft. They suggest he opened by alluding to his love poem "The Assabet," Ellen's favorite, in which he imagines the two of them voyaging together into the dawn: "I thought that the sun of our love should have risen as noiselessly as the sun out of the sea, and we sailors have found ourselves steering between the tropics as if the broad day had lasted forever. You know how the sun comes up from the sea when you stand on the cliff, and doesn't startle you, but every thing, and you too are helping it."[67] Ellen had kept the poem and treasured it. But she could hardly turn down one brother and then accept the other—and her father, an old-school Unitarian minister, refused to allow his daughter to marry a Transcendentalist. The notoriety after Emerson's scandalous "Divinity School Address" made that

impossible, and besides, Thoreau's work as a teacher hardly produced a solid income. Ellen's letter refusing Henry's proposal has
not survived, although her letter to Prudence suggests she followed
her father's order to make it "*short, explicit* and *cold*":

> I wrote to H.T. that evening. I never felt so badly at sending a letter
> in my life. I could not bear to think that both those friends whom I
> have enjoyed so much with would now no longer be able to have the
> free pleasant intercourse with us as formerly. My letter was very short
> indeed. But I hope it was the thing. . . . It is all over now. We will say
> nothing of it till we meet. . . . Burn my last.[68]

Henry's reaction does not survive, though this was far from the end
of their story.

Although she grieved at being "deprived of one whose society I
loved and would have cherished," Ellen was soon being courted by
the much more eligible Joseph Osgood, a Unitarian minister. They
were married in her father's church on March 20, 1844, and Ellen told
their children she would have married their father no matter what
her father said. In later years Henry Thoreau became a close family
friend, visiting the Osgoods several times.[69] His portrait hung in the
entry of their parsonage home, his books were family favorites, and
the poems he had given to Edmund, George, and Ellen became family heirlooms. As for Henry, having tried the experiment of romantic
love once, he seemed quite satisfied not to repeat it. In his later years,
though he cherished many close friendships with women—Lucy
Jackson Brown, Lidian Emerson, Mary Russell—he never again
proposed marriage. Sophia Thoreau claimed that on his deathbed,
when Ellen's name came up, her brother said, "I have always loved
her." But on this question Thoreau himself never broke his silence.[70]

COMPENSATIONS

The great public event of July 4, 1840, was Concord's huge rally for
William Henry Harrison, the Whig party's "Log Cabin" presidential

candidate whose catchy slogan "Tippecanoe and Tyler too" cleverly positioned the elderly Harrison as a bold Indian fighter (in 1811, Harrison had defeated Tecumseh's warriors at Indiana's Tippecanoe River). Concord's streets overflowed with "Tippecanoe clubs" from the neighboring towns, with banners, flags, and marching bands starting from the Old North Bridge battleground all the way to the speaker's stand in Sleepy Hollow. Horace Hosmer, the lone Democrat in the Thoreau school, felt left out when John Thoreau, an ardent Whig, made sure all the boys had "canes with hard cider barrels for heads, there were Log Cabin medals, and breast pins, Log Cabin Hats made of Rattan . . . and hard cider flowed everywhere." The campaign rally for "Old Tip" featured a twelve-foot red-white-and-blue ball drawn by ropes so that, as it rolled majestically along, everyone could read the songs and slogans written on it: "O'er every ridge we'll roll this ball, / From Concord Bridge to Faneuil Hall," read one; "Farewell poor Van, / You're not the man / To guide our Ship. / We'll try Old Tip," opined another. It seemed a shame, Henry thought, that men did not move with such "dignity and grandeur" as the ball did.[71]

The great intellectual event that week was the debut of the *Dial*, with Thoreau's "Sympathy" and "Aulus Persius Flaccus," his first major essay. Emerson thought Thoreau's first published poem was "good enough to save a whole bad number"; as for the essay, he had asked Fuller to include it as "a piece of character," and she had agreed.[72] Getting the *Dial* off the ground proved hard work, in part because not everyone in the Transcendental Club was willing to commit to print. Hedge feared the *Dial* was too radical, while Brownson scoffed it was hardly radical enough. So they reached out to new and younger voices: Fuller, Thoreau, Alcott, and Ellery Channing, an unknown poet writing from Cincinnati. By now Thoreau was ready to come on board as a full-fledged Transcendentalist, and on May 13, 1840, he attended his first meeting of the Transcendental Club, at Emerson's house. The topic was tailor-made for him: "the inspiration of the Prophet and Bard, the nature of Poetry, and the causes of the sterility of Poetic Inspiration in our age and country."[73] Alcott, Emerson, Hedge, and some of the older members were there, along with Jones Very and Margaret Fuller—the first time Thoreau and Fuller definitely met face-to-face.

The reviews of the *Dial* were bad to the point of malice—so vicious and damaging that America's first great literary magazine, though it would struggle on valiantly for another four years, never really recovered. The *Boston Times* hooted that "duck tracks in the mud convey a more intelligible meaning." Alcott's "Orphic Sayings" in particular was the butt of more ridicule than it could shake off. Henry's elegant poem was reprinted, but few noticed his earnest essay or its attempt to practice what Fuller called "comprehensive" literary criticism, based not on personal taste but on universal aesthetic principles. When the *Dial*'s editorial board met in August, Theodore Parker called the essay "foolish" and told Thoreau to keep himself out of mischief by writing for newspapers instead. When Emerson protested that "Persius" was full of life, Parker retorted that indeed it was, but the life was all Emerson's. And when Fuller turned her skeptical eye to Thoreau's next submission, "Stanzas," she saw much she didn't like. Her red pencil provoked a tiff: Thoreau "boggled" at the way she smoothed his opening line, and Emerson had to intercede, begging Fuller, "Our tough Yankee must have his tough verse."[74] He got it, but not until Fuller was good and ready: the second issue of the *Dial* included nothing from Thoreau, and the third, published in January 1841, had only this one poem, its "tough" opening line intact. Thoreau's great career as a poet was off to a rocky start.

It got worse. Just when he found his way into the Transcendental Club, it fell apart. That September, defiant in the face of growing national hostility, they held two more meetings to discuss organizing a new and more liberal church of their own. The split in their ranks opened wider: Would such a church be Christian? Or would it articulate new, post-Christian, universal principles? The deepening fractures destroyed what was left of their common ground, and the Transcendentalists never met again. What remained was the *Dial* and the coterie Fuller and Emerson had pulled together of young avant-garde writers eager to share their thoughts and poetry with like-minded friends.[75] It was a narrow public, but it was still a public, and Thoreau wanted in. He worked up a long, ambitious essay, "The Service," plus a new poem, "Wachusett," in an experimental and still more rugged style, and sent both to Fuller.

Fuller was having none of it. She wrote Thoreau two letters of rejection, each devastating in its own way. "The Service," she admitted, was rich in thought, but those thoughts were "so out of their natural order, that I cannot read it through without *pain*. I never once feel myself in a stream of thought, but seem to hear the grating of tools on the mosaic." Of "Wachusett" she granted "a noble recognition of nature," two or three "manly thoughts," and a moment of "plaintive music," but it, too, lacked flow: thoughts were "too detached," verses were "startling, as much as stern," unconnected with life; "there is a want of fluent music." The author seemed, she told Thoreau, "healthful, sane, of open eye, ready hand, of noble scope," but "as yet a somewhat bare hill which the warm gales of spring have not visited."[76] After Fuller spiked "The Service," Thoreau shelved it for good; it was never published in his lifetime. He salvaged the rugged "Wachusett" only by inserting it, years later, into his essay "A Walk to Wachusett" and then into his self-published first book. Fuller accepted only two more of Thoreau's poems: his early, metaphysical verses "Sic Vita" and "Friendship."[77] The poet Emerson had hailed as America's purest and loftiest had published, at the end of two years, exactly four poems.

A lesser writer would have been discouraged. But Fuller's real point, that his talent was far greater than his execution, was not lost on Thoreau. He was a genius, no doubt, but he had yet to learn his craft. This was precisely the lesson Thoreau needed to hear, and it was Fuller who gave it to him. As she admonished him, while "it is true as Mr. E says," that essays much poorer than "The Service" had found their way into the *Dial*, "those are more unassuming in their tone, and have an air of quiet good-breeding which induces us to permit their presence. Yours is so rugged that it ought to be commanding."[78] The challenge she offered was tremendous: no models existed for what Thoreau was attempting. He was on his own, bearing the potential for greatness but also the knowledge that getting to that greatness meant a leap to originality—a leap he didn't know how to make.

Fuller's harsh criticism of "The Service" came into Henry's hands barely two weeks after Ellen's curt letter of refusal. The following months were tense. Henry was in a withdrawing mood: early in November he withdrew his name from reelection as the lyceum curator, and early in January 1841, he formally withdrew from the First Parish Church, freeing him from paying the tax the town levied for its support. As he put it in *Walden*, he told them that "I, Henry Thoreau, do not wish to be regarded as a member of any incorporated society which I have not joined."[79] Worst of all, John was ill and not recovering: consumption, the dreaded New England curse, had him in its jaws. As he weakened, it fell to Henry to take over the "lower" school. Horace Hosmer, who always remembered John as the light of his life, was miserable in Henry's classroom: "He never mixed with the schoolboys; he was hated. The bell tolled instead of rang, when he taught alone during John's illness."[80] As John weakened further, it became painfully clear that at the end of winter term, they must close their school. They would both be out of work.

Thoreau had to find a lifeboat. Early in March 1841 he rejected one possible solution, joining Brook Farm, the utopian community getting under way in West Roxbury. "As for these communities—I think I had rather keep batchelor's [*sic*] hall in hell than go to board in heaven," he grumbled. A few days later he applied for a teaching job at the world-famous Perkins School for the Blind,[81] but knowing the odds, he cast around for alternatives. In February he started to think about buying some farmland, though as spring advanced, he fretted about losing his freedom by becoming a farmer and a landowner. "What have I to do with plows—" he wrote truculently; "I cut another furrow than you see." Despite his doubts, on April 16 he actually did buy an old farm on the Sudbury River, but the deal, and his hopes, fell through when the farmer backed out of the sale.[82] Chaffering with the local farmers was sobering: "I must confess I am startled to find everywhere the old system of things so grim and assured. Wherever I go the farms are run out, and there they lie, and the youth must buy old land and bring it to." Whether Thoreau was up to the physical demands of farming must have been another worry, for he, too, was sick with "bronchitis," probably a flare-up of his own incipient tuberculosis, through much of February.[83]

The Thoreau school was formally closed on April first. In his Journal, Henry tried to buck himself up: "Again foul weather shall not change my mind. / But in the shade I will believe what in the sun I loved." By April 20, he was trying to keep a stiff upper lip while shoveling manure: "To day I earned seventy five cents heaving manure out of a pen, and made a good bargain of it. If the ditcher muses the while how he may live uprightly, the ditching spade and turf knife, may be engraved on the coat of arms of his posterity."[84] Coincidentally, at that very moment his future friend Nathaniel Hawthorne, who had joined Brook Farm, was doing the very same thing and thinking similarly optimistic thoughts. As he wrote his fiancée, Elizabeth Peabody's sister Sophia: "After breakfast, Mr. Ripley put a four-pronged instrument into my hands, which he gave me to understand was called a pitch-fork; and he and Mr. Farley being armed with similar weapons, we all three commenced a gallant attack upon a heap of manure. . . . Dearest," he concluded, "I shall make an excellent husbandman. I feel the original Adam reviving within me."[85]

→>–<←

While Hawthorne shoveled away at Brook Farm, Emerson devised a solution for Thoreau: Come live with me. Emerson, too, had rejected Ripley's invitation to join Brook Farm, stating that he had "builded and planted" his *own* utopian community—namely, his household and town. At home he was already reforming "labor and self-help" by trying "some domestic & social experiments," including "a common table" where the servants would sit and eat with the Emersons as equals. He'd invited the Alcotts to move in, too, so they could all forge their own united utopian "Association." Emerson's plans didn't go quite as he'd hoped. The maid agreed to eat at the common table, but the cook refused; caught in the middle, the maid decided to dine with the cook. As for the Alcotts moving in, Bronson was all for it, but Abigail was dead set against it. But the idea was planted. In two years they would go off to their own utopian community, Fruitlands.[86]

Meanwhile, Emerson had a convert in Henry Thoreau, who joined his household on April 26, "to live with me & work with me in the garden & teach me to graft apples."[87] The arrangement would last over two years: Thoreau became Emerson's live-in gardener and handyman, and tutor and caretaker to the Emerson children. Ellen, their eldest daughter, was still an infant, but Thoreau played daily with their young son Waldo Jr., whose winsome curiosity captured all hearts. In exchange, Thoreau had free run of Emerson's library, free rein to entertain Emerson's endless stream of visitors, and free time to study, write, and roam as he pleased. Thoreau's mood lifted immediately.

On move-in day he sketched in his Journal a vision of his new role: "At R.W.E.'s. The charm of the Indian to me is that he stands free and unconstrained in nature—is her inhabitant—and not her guest—and wears her easily and gracefully." As he added, sensing new possibilities, "It is a great art to saunter."[88] In his inscribed copy of Emerson's new *Essays*, he could read, in "Self-Reliance," Emerson's first public portrait of the person he saw in Henry: "A sturdy lad . . . who in turn tries all the professions, who *teams it, farms it, peddles*, keeps a school, preaches, edits a newspaper, goes to Congress, buys a township, and so forth, in successive years, and always, like a cat, falls on his feet, is worth a hundred of these city dolls. He walks abreast with his days, and feels no shame in not 'studying a profession,' for he does not postpone his life, but lives already." Here "my brave Henry" (as the passage read in the original) could be a resident "Indian" in Emerson's world, learning to wear that world with ease and grace.[89] It was a fortunate move that allowed Thoreau to grow, as Fuller had hinted, from mere apprentice into his own command.

The benefit was mutual. On May 30, Emerson wrote to Carlyle that in his house now dwelled "a poet whom you may one day be proud of:—a noble, manly youth, full of melodies and inventions. We work together by day in my garden, and I grow well and strong." A week later Thoreau took Emerson rowing at sunset, and the man who by day had been annoyed by life on the dusty turnpike was enchanted by night as "the good river-god" in "the form of my valiant Henry Thoreau" introduced him "to the riches of his shadowy starlit, moonlit stream, a lovely new world lying as close & yet unknown to this vulgar trite one of streets & shops as death to life or poetry to prose."[90] Thoreau was in a river-god mood: a few days before, he'd been drifting in his boat on Walden Pond, playing his flute, watching the charmed perch hover around him and "the moon travelling over the ribbed bottom." He felt then "that nothing but the wildest imagination can conceive of the manner of life we are living." By August he was sailing on the Assabet at night, again with his flute, "and my music was a tinkling stream which meandered with the river—and fell from note to note as a brook from rock to rock." When Margaret Fuller came for a visit, he took her out on the pond one night. She wrote to her favorite brother, Richard, that Henry rowed her before "a sweet breeze full of apple blossom fragrance which made the pond swell almost into waves. I had great pleasure."[91]

Thoreau's flute became a general favorite. On June 7, Emerson sent him a note inviting him up to the Cliff, "where our ladies will be greatly gratified to see you & the more they say if you will bring your flute for the echo's sake." The "ladies" included Lidian, Lucy, Margaret Fuller, and Mary Russell, a friend of Lidian's who was spending summer at the Emersons', running a small school. After she returned home, Henry sent her a poem, "To the Maiden in the East": "Whatever path I take, / It shall be for thy sake."[92] It was almost Ellen all over again, except this time no proposal came between them. Mary eventually married Thoreau's friend from Harvard, the Transcendentalist sympathizer Benjamin Marston Watson, and Thoreau became a lifelong friend of the family, making many visits to the Watsons' famous garden and orchard in Plymouth.

That fall Margaret Fuller, who was impressed with Thoreau himself if not his poetry, brought yet another friend into his life: her brother Richard, who had just quit the dry-goods business hoping to enter Harvard. Margaret asked Henry to tutor Richard in Greek while he boarded nearby and fortified himself with Lidian's famous meat pies. The treatment worked: Richard entered Harvard, inoculated with just enough Transcendentalism to become something of a writer but not so much as to prevent him settling into a stable and prosperous life as a lawyer, Christian, and family man.[93] It was while tutoring Richard, in October 1841, that Henry received Margaret's critique of "Wachusett," with its sisterly advice to open himself to the "harmonizing influences of other natures," and learn not to say so constantly of nature, "She is mine." For, as Fuller continued (showing how acute was her sympathy for Thoreau), "She is not yours until you have been more hers. Seek the lotus, and take a draught of rapture. . . . I apprehended you in spirit, and you did not seem to mistake me as widely as most of your kind do." Henry must have confided deeply in her. "Let me know whether you go to the lonely hut," she closed, "and write to me about Shakespeare, if you read him there."[94] Clearly Thoreau had confided to Fuller what he had barely confessed to himself: he longed to go away and live by the pond and be the writer he dreamed of becoming.

Under Emerson's roof, Thoreau consolidated his sense of himself as above all a writer—not a dilettante who published occasionally, but a true and focused professional patterned after Emerson's own model, which Thoreau now witnessed daily. He was, he wrote, in "the mid-sea of verses," which rustled about him like autumn leaves and rose around him "verse on verse, far and near, like the mountains from Agiocochook." Among those leaves was the rugged "Wachusett," plus a major new poem cycle that would push his ambition to the limit.[95] As he pushed with ferocious energy toward a breakthrough he could not see, he took the massive bulk of his Journal—over a thousand pages—and tore it to shreds, transcribing a few "gleanings" into fresh volumes and destroying the rest. Meanwhile, Emerson was promoting him to the publisher of a major anthology of new American poetry, to whom Thoreau sent "Sic Vita," "Sympathy," and "Friendship"—his three best poems, but all old ones. The publisher ignored him. So Emerson had another idea: Thoreau would go to Harvard, ransack the library, and select the best of British poetry for an anthology—the "old" to America's "new"—learning his craft by total immersion in the discipline of poetry. Late in November Thoreau moved to Cambridge, rooming with his old friend Wheeler. There he checked out great stacks of Old and Middle English poetry, carrying books to Concord two weeks later, illegally.[96]

If Emerson expected an epiphany, he was disappointed. Certainly Thoreau was. "When looking over the dry and dusty volumes of the English poets," he wrote in his new Journal volume, "I cannot believe that those fresh and fair creations I had imagined are contained in them." One look out the window made the whole of English poetry, from Gower on down, seem "very mean." Oppressed by sadness, Thoreau ransacked his books for any "living word." From time to time he found something—in Chaucer, say, or in the old Scottish poet Gawin Douglas—but it made him wonder what he was doing. They all seemed so tame and civil, as if not a one of them had seen so much as "the west side of any mountain"—why, even "Wordsworth is too tame for the Chippeway." Thoreau felt more "kith and kin" with the lichen on the bare winter branches than with anything in these books. His yearning for wildness struck him as peculiar, his one redeeming quality, even as it isolated him from all of literary history.[97]

On Christmas Eve 1841, surrounded by mountains of dusty books and the rustling dead leaves of his old poems, Henry Thoreau looked out the window and brooded. In his Journal he wrote, "I want to go soon and live away by the pond. . . . But my friends ask what I will do when I get there? Will it not be employment enough to watch the progress of the seasons?" On New Year's Eve, brooding still, he vowed, "To the soul that contemplates some trait of natural beauty no harm nor disappointment can come."[98] It was a noble affirmation of his emerging faith—a faith about to meet its hardest test.

"Not till We Are Lost"

(1842–1844)

Not till we are lost, in other words, not till we have lost the world, do we begin to
find ourselves, and realize where we are and the infinite extent of our relations.
HENRY DAVID THOREAU, *WALDEN*

THE DEATH OF JOHN THOREAU

In April 1841, Ellen Sewall recorded sad news about her friend John Thoreau: "Poor fellow, his health is poor & he cannot keep school." After the brothers closed their school, John traveled to New Hampshire for a spell, and not until he returned did Henry move in with the Emersons. Through the summer of 1841 into the fall, John helped out around the house, working at the pencil shop and taking on garden chores, his future still uncertain. Thus things stood on New Year's Day 1842. Out at the Emersons', Henry was giving himself a pep talk—"Let him remember the sick in their extremities," he wrote in his Journal, "but not look thither as to his goal"—while back home, John was going about an ordinary Saturday afternoon.[1] While stropping a razor, he chanced to slice off a bit of skin on his left ring finger, just deep enough to draw blood. Without thinking twice he replaced the loose skin, bound the wound with a rag, and went on with his day.

It was an insignificant cut, and no one suspected anything wrong. But it was deep enough to let tetanus spores enter John's body; only decades later would doctors realize that tetanus bacteria can lurk in animal droppings and soils treated with manure, the very setting of John's daily chores. Two or three days later his finger began to hurt. The following Saturday he found the skin he'd replaced had "mortified," and, alarmed, he walked over to see Dr. Bartlett, who reassured him, dressed the wound, and sent him home. But the neurotoxins released by the incubating bacteria were already at work. Walking home, John felt strange pains throughout his body and barely made it to the door. Even as he collapsed inside, Henry, a few blocks away, was writing: "Am I so like thee my brother that the cadence of two notes affects us alike?" Something, or someone, called him home, for the next morning he told Lidian Emerson he'd been helping out his family, since John's cut finger disabled him from his usual labors.[2] Everyone was taking everything in stride. But that very evening—Sunday, January 9—the Thoreaus' neighbor Nathan Brooks pounded on the Emersons' door: Henry, you must come home immediately. John has the symptoms of lockjaw.

The end was swift and terrible. Tetanus neurotoxins disable muscle contractions, causing spasms that start in the jaw muscles—hence the name "lockjaw"—and spread rapidly throughout the body, which goes into violent and agonizing convulsions. The instant Henry arrived home, he became John's constant nurse. On Monday, someone was sent to Boston to fetch another doctor. When he arrived, he could do nothing but tell John that his death was upon him. A friend recalled John's response: "'Is there no hope?' he said. 'None,' replied the doctor. Then, although his friends were almost distracted around him, he was calm, saying, 'The cup that my Father gives me, shall I not drink it?' He bade his friends all goodbye."[3] The convulsions continued through the evening, all that night, and all the next morning. Finally, at 2:00 p.m. on Tuesday, January 11, John Thoreau, twenty-six years old, died in Henry's arms.

One can hope the end was peaceful. Likely a contraction kept John from drawing breath, or his heart stopped from lack of oxygen. Lidian reported that he retained his power of speech to the last, though exactly what he and Henry may have said to each other, Henry never revealed. "He was perfectly calm, ever pleasant while reason lasted," Henry told a friend, "and gleams of the same serenity and playfulness shone through his delirium to the last." That evening Henry went to the Emersons' to see Ralph Waldo alone, and would talk to no one else. He came by again the next morning to collect his clothes and tell Lidian he did not know when he would return. Even then Lidian had been writing a letter to her sister Lucy, telling "the strange sad news" of John's death, which at first seemed "terrible" but then, thanks to his calm resignation, "not terrible but beautiful. . . . I feel as if a pure spirit has been translated." After Henry left, she added, "I love him for the feeling he showed and the effort he made to be cheerful. He did not give way in the least but his whole demeanor was that of one struggling with sickness of heart."[4]

The funeral service was held Sunday, January 16. Rev. Barzillai Frost's sermon made John sound eerily like Henry's double: "He had a love of nature, even from childhood amounting to enthusiasm. . . . There is not a hill, nor a tree, nor a bird, nor a flower of marked beauty in all this neighborhood that he was not familiar with, and any new bird or flower he discovered gave him the most unfeigned delight." John was also deeply involved with the human community: "He had a heart to feel and a voice to speak for all classes of suffering humanity; and the cause of the poor inebriate, the slave, the ignorant and depraved, was very dear to him." He loved music, and "the sound of his favorite flute mingling with and softening the voices of his friends, was but an emblem of his spirit," preparing him for heaven; as to that, Reverend Frost admitted some qualms over his dalliance with "revolutionary opinion" and "transcendental views"—which under other circumstances would have made his brother smile—but, he concluded soberly, John's "principles and religious feelings were always unshaken." In Concord's liberal First Parish Church, the state of one's heart mattered most, and John's heart was just and good.[5]

Henry's struggle to feign good cheer and not give way to unmanly grief resulted, at first, in a strange calm that incubated for a week. Then, to his family's horror, he, too, collapsed with the terrible symptoms of lockjaw, his body seized by violent and uncontrollable convulsions. Emerson, away in Boston, returned home to the shocking news that the Thoreaus feared they were losing their second son as well: "It is strange—unaccountable—" he wrote his brother William, "yet the symptoms seemed precise and on the increase. You may judge we were all alarmed & I not the least who have the highest hopes of this youth." Days later Henry's affliction was easing and the emergency was past. Yet it was another month before he could get out of bed, and all that spring he was too weak even to garden. Deep in depression, he lapsed into passivity, sitting in the house, able to do nothing. His sisters tried to walk him outside into nature, hoping to revive something of the old Henry, but it didn't help. Friends, Henry had written exactly a year before, "are not two united, but rather one divided."[6] When John died, it seemed half of Henry died with him.

＋＞＜＋

Once Henry began to reawaken, he learned the Emersons had suffered their own cruel blow. On January 24, their son Waldo Jr. was showing signs of scarlet fever; three days later, young Waldo died, just five years old. His father's grief was raw and bottomless. A dozen times or more he had to write out the same words, in letter after letter: "Our darling is dead." "Our little Waldo died this evening." "Shall I ever dare to love any thing again." Emerson had endured tragedy before, but this was different—the pain was keener, the loss baffling, incomprehensible. A dark reckoning with all his philosophy followed, culminating in his great, brooding essay "Experience."[7] The double blow numbed them both and brought them closer together: Waldo Jr. had been Thoreau's special charge; he loved the boy as his own. Emerson, tormented by sweet memories, recalled how Thoreau had played with Waldo every day, charming him "by the variety of toys whistles boats popguns & all kinds of instruments which he would make & mend; & possessed his love & respect by the gentle firmness with which he always treated him." Thoreau loved the boy's way of asking unanswerable questions, "the same which you would ask of yourself." Emerson lingered on the moment Waldo said, "My music makes the thunder dance," for it chanced to thunder once when Waldo was blowing his willow whistle—one of the little toys Thoreau had fashioned for him.[8]

For almost six weeks Thoreau could not bear to open his Journal. "When two approach to meet they incur no petty dangers but they run terrible risks," he finally wrote on February 20. "I feel as if years had been crowded into the last month," he added the next day. Time seemed deranged; he couldn't find his way back into the present, or even into his own body: nothing else in nature, he confessed, seemed so strange to him as his body. Walks into nature only intensified his estrangement. "She always retreats as I advance," he lamented; he felt like a feather floating, ungrounded, with "depth unfathomable" on every side, soul and body tottering along together "tripping and hindering oneanother [sic] like unpracticed Siamese twins—They two should walk as one."[9] But how? His answer is extraordinary, and central to his rebirth: "walking as one" would not mean walking "into" nature, penetrating it on his quest for unity only to drive nature ever farther away, but something far riskier: stopping. Still the mind, open the body, clear the senses. Thoreau called this *listening*, beyond sound itself: "I was always conscious of sounds in nature which my ears could never hear—that I caught but the prelude to a strain." To listen truly meant cultivating a new sense, a deeper hearing: "Will not this faith and expectation make to itself ears at length." Here is his pathway forward. "The death of friends should inspire us as much as their lives," he reminds himself. "How can any good depart. It does not go and come but we. Shall we wait for it? is it slower than we?"[10]

No, we are the slow ones; we lag behind while the good waits for us ahead. John had always gone before and was before him still. To John, Henry wrote his most achingly personal poem:

> Brother where dost thou dwell?
>   What sun shines for thee now?
> Dost thou indeed farewell?
>   As we wished here below. . . .

His questions mount: Where can he feel John's presence? "Along the neighboring brook / May I thy voice still hear? . . . What bird wilt thou employ / To bring me word of thee?" The birds John loved become messengers to his brother—but they are silent still. "They have remained to mourn / Or else forgot."

Yet in a second ending, Henry ventures to hope:

> When on the pond I whirl
>   In sport, if sport may be,
> Now thou art gone
>   May I still follow thee?
>
> For then, as now, I trust,
>   I always lagg'd behind,
> While thou were ever first,
>   Cutting the wind.[11]

To "lag behind" is now to "follow." From now on, following John into the woods and along the rivers was no longer to pursue a Nature forever retreating "away behind and behind," but to *advance* into Nature, following the tracks of the beloved who has gone before, drawing nearer to him, listening for the messages he sends. Henry, still struggling at twenty-five to find his voice as a poet, heard John calling to him from the places they loved and shared together. In life, John overshadowed his shy brother. In death, John became his brother's muse. The Henry who felt he was half of one could never have grown out of John's shadow. Now he had to grow to fill John's absence; he had to make ears to hear him and voice to speak. John's death became Henry Thoreau's birth—the birth of the writer who would voice Nature to the world.

It was another week before Henry could write to his friends. He turned first to the kind-hearted Lucy: "What right have I to grieve, who have not ceased to wonder?" This sense of wonder allowed Thoreau to accept what Emerson refused: nature's inhuman onwardness, as the winter ice melts despite all and the morning birds sing.

"I do not wish to see John ever again—I mean him who is dead," he confided to her, but only that "other" John, the one whom he must now strive to become. His second letter, to the grieving Emerson, was harder. To his friend's bitterness Henry offers the glacial comforts of Transcendentalism: "Nature . . . finds her own again under new forms without loss." But then Henry takes a green turn: "Every blade in the field—every leaf in the forest—lays down its life in its season as beautifully as it was taken up." It startles to hear this abrupt outcropping, in young Henry, of the older Thoreau, who in "Autumnal Tints" anticipates his own death. Here it seems premature, a faith he has yet to earn. But to Emerson, the intellectual father who had feared for his life, Henry needed to avow his new faith, with a sincere promise to live up to it: "After I have imagined thus much will not the Gods feel under obligation to make me realize something as good?"[12]

To others, Thoreau confessed he had been harrowed. He was no longer the same person, and he would never fully heal. For the rest of his life Henry fought nightmares on the anniversary of John's death. Whenever John's name was mentioned, he grew pale and excused himself from the room. Yet in these early months the gravity of the experience was thrilling and challenging; he recovered by reshaping himself in the most fundamental way. The comparison with Emerson is revealing: for all his private agony, Emerson declared publicly in "Experience" that Waldo's death changed nothing: "I seem to have lost a beautiful estate,—no more. . . . It was caducous," falling away as easily as a leaf in autumn. "I grieve that grief can teach me nothing, nor carry me one step into real nature." By contrast, Thoreau avowed that he "could not have done without this experience," that it made him who he was.[13] It taught him that his deep empathy for others made him terrifyingly vulnerable. Thoreau could feel another's pain as his own, could suffer that pain beyond endurance. To buffer himself against such shocks, he erected a protective shield that could make him seem crusty and distant. Emerson noted Elizabeth Hoar saying around this time, "I love Henry, but do not like him; and as for taking his arm, I should as soon take the arm of an elm tree."[14]

But his deep empathy also opened Thoreau up radically to the world. Injustice to another made him storm with the passionate and sleepless rage that powered his great writings of political protest, and the natural world spoke to him of the spiritual ideals he and John had shared. "I live in the perpetual verdure of the globe—I die in the annual decay of nature," he wrote that March. On this scale, every being and phenomenon in nature rang with meaning like a struck bell. Only if he could articulate these meanings could Henry, the aspiring poet, find a common world and a common language by which he might speak to all. A week later, he leaned into his hopes: "I have no private good—unless it be my peculiar ability to serve the public—this is the only individual property."[15] He'd offered himself up to death, and lived. Why? What was his mission? What good had the gods commissioned him to realize?

"SURELY JOY IS THE CONDITION OF LIFE!": NEW FRIENDS, NEW VENTURES

Emerson would open the path. In mid-March, Margaret Fuller sent him an alarming letter: exhausted, about to collapse from overwork, she was resigning as editor of the *Dial*. The Transcendentalists' literary journal had steadily improved under her care, but its publisher had gone bankrupt. The new publisher, Elizabeth Peabody, had opened the account books to find it had only three hundred subscribers and could not possibly make a profit. Fuller, after working without pay for two years, told Emerson that unless he took over immediately, the *Dial* was dead. Emerson reluctantly accepted, unwilling to kill the one hope for publication left to his young flock of experimental writers. Pressed for copy to fill the July issue, he happened across a series of natural history reports published by the State of Massachusetts. He assigned them to Thoreau; setting the moping Henry on a review that would draw on his "woodcraft boatcraft & fishcraft" might cheer him up. The assignment was just a potboiler, but Thoreau plunged in. In a month he had fifty pages or so, and he summoned Emerson to a reading. "I do not like his piece very well," he grumbled, but he needed to fill the issue, so in it went.[16]

"The Natural History of Massachusetts" was no ordinary book review. Thoreau dismissed the books themselves as little more than an inventory of the state's "natural riches," useful in their way but "not interesting to the general reader"—but their very failure set him on fire. He pushed aside his stacks of old English poetry and combed his Journal for the best moments, the wild outdoor moments he longed to live again. "Surely joy is the condition of life!" he exclaimed: "the butterfly carrying accident and change painted in a thousand hues upon its wings," the loon whose "wild laughter" makes the woods ring, foxes whose curving tracks seem "coincident with the fluctuations of some mind," fish that call to his sympathy, snakes that send a mute appeal. The spring catkins become his "little vegetable redeemers"; summer's green leaves and winter's ghost-leaves of ice seem "creatures of but one law."

Yes, the books were dry, but Thoreau knew the spirit behind them was not: Thaddeus Harris himself had written the volume on insects. Thoreau paid tribute to the "quiet bravery" of science, and to his Harvard teacher's real lesson: "Nature will bear the closest inspection; she invites us to lay our eye level with the smallest leaf, and take an insect view of its plain. She has no interstices; every part is full of life." The key was to stay alert to that life in even the driest of facts: "Let us not underrate the value of a fact; it will one day flower in a truth." This was Thoreau's new motto, and his new method, too: "Let *us*." "She invites *us*." He'd been taught to lecture from on high. Now he was guide and companion, extending a hand, inviting us to come along and share his joy.[17] Here, whipped out in a month's inspiration, was a proto-*Walden*, rough and imperfect but leaping with life. It was like nothing Thoreau had written before; in places, it was like nothing *anyone* had written before. What he read aloud to Emerson that evening was nothing less than his first original writing.

This makes it all the more revealing that Emerson didn't much like it. Bronson Alcott loved it, declaring it "worthy of Isaac [*sic*]

Walton himself." After reading it, Nathaniel Hawthorne decided that Thoreau "is a good writer . . . with real poetry in him."[18] What Emerson did like was the strange, dark story he solicited from his new friend, Charles King Newcomb: "The Two Dolons," a mystical Gothic fantasy in which a thinly disguised Waldo is stalked in the woods by a cave-dwelling Druidical hermit with an eerie resemblance to Henry, who sacrifices the boy on an altar by driving a knife into his breast. Today Newcomb's overwrought tale is almost unreadable, but Emerson loved it so much that he pestered Newcomb endlessly for part two, the "second" of "The Two Dolons," without success: Newcomb's genius was spent. The creepy allegory of his son's bloody sacrifice by an uncanny woods-god must have allowed Emerson to exorcise certain demons. By July, with the issue in print, Emerson's own uncanny river-god had moved back to the alcove at the top of the stairs, once again serving as handyman and now the *Dial*'s editorial assistant as well.

This put Thoreau back at the heart of Emerson's growing circle of friends and associates. Indeed, so many visitors took to dropping by that the Emersons' cook threatened to post a sign on the front gate: "This House is not a Hotel." Their daughter Ellen remembered how in those "Transcendental Times," "All sorts of visitors with new ideas began to come to the house, the men who thought money was the root of all evil, the vegetarians, the sons of nature who did not believe in razors nor in tailors, the philosophers and all sorts of come-outers."[19] Hawthorne chuckled to see how Emerson conjured up such "hobgoblins of flesh and blood" who were drawn to his "intellectual fire, as a beacon burning on a hill-top"—"bats and owls, and the whole host of night-birds, which flapped their dusky wings against the gazer's eyes, and sometimes were mistaken for fowls of angelic feather." "Never," he concluded hilariously, "was a poor, little country village infested with such a variety of queer, strangely dressed, oddly behaved mortals."[20]

One of them, arguably, was Hawthorne himself. After heaving manure for eight months at Brook Farm, he'd concluded to resume a more ordinary relation to society. Just as he was looking for a place to bring his bride-to-be, Sophia Peabody, the Reverend Ezra Ripley passed on to his heavenly reward, leaving the Old Manse open. Hawthorne signed the lease, and by June 1842, Cynthia Thoreau and Elizabeth Hoar had made the old gray parsonage "all new & bright again as a toy" for the newlyweds. By then Henry was strong enough to help Jack Garrison's son John work up some land alongside the avenue to the Manse, planting it with beans, peas, cabbages, and squash, both summer and winter, as his wedding gift to Nathaniel and Sophia. They moved into the Old Manse on July 9, 1842—the afternoon of their wedding day.

Soon afterward Emerson and Thoreau paid their formal call. It was awkward—three great writers sitting bolt upright, each struggling to break the silence with something profound—but when Thoreau returned alone, he and Hawthorne found their friendship growing. At first Hawthorne thought "Mr. Thorow" (spelling the name as Concord pronounced it) "a singular character . . . ugly as sin, long-nosed, queer-mouthed, and with uncouth and somewhat rustic, although courteous manners." But his ugliness, Hawthorne judged, was "honest and agreeable," suiting him better than beauty. His new friend lived "a sort of Indian life" as part of Emerson's family, and showed himself "a keen and delicate observer of nature—a genuine observer, which, I suspect, is almost as rare a character as even an original poet."[21]

Thoreau sold his boat, the beloved *Musketaquid*, to Hawthorne— "being in want of money," thought Hawthorne, although Thoreau was grateful to shed this reminder of his grief. After a test paddle, Hawthorne paid the seven dollars, and the next morning Thoreau gave the author a rowing lesson. Hawthorne marveled how the boat, "as docile as a trained steed" under "Mr. Thorow's" management, at first went in every direction but the one he intended. He renamed it the *Pond Lily*, and soon his journal filled with idyllic river excursions. Eventually he passed the old fisherman's dory along to Ellery Channing, under whose care it rotted away into honorable oblivion. In the winter, boating gave way to skating, and Sophia Hawthorne recorded the three friends setting off down the ice, Thoreau "figuring dithyrambic dances and Bacchic leaps," Hawthorne, wrapped in his cloak, moving "like a self-impelled Greek statue, stately and grave," and Emerson "evidently too weary to hold himself erect, pitching headforemost, half lying on the air." Twice the Hawthornes would move away from Concord, and both times on their return Nathaniel and Henry would renew their friendship. When they laughed together, said Channing, "the operation was sufficient to split a pitcher."[22]

→>-<+

Another young idealist drawn to Emerson, that "prime minister" of the spirit, was Margaret Fuller's younger brother Richard.[23] Fuller's tutorials in Concord gained him midterm admission to Harvard, and in July 1843, eager for a summer break, he walked from Cambridge to Emerson's house. After being roundly examined "to see if I yet surrendered to Imagination," the next morning he and Thoreau shouldered knapsacks and set off for Mount Wachusett, thirty miles away on the western horizon. They planned it as a literary excursion: Richard kept a running record of his thoughts, and Henry's notes grew into his next original essay, "A Walk to Wachusett." From childhood on, Thoreau's eyes had rested on the dim blue outline of Wachusett. He even addressed a poem to the mountain—the one Margaret Fuller had so firmly rejected. Now this walk with her brother would be itself a form of composition, using the approach she had recommended: nature will not be yours, she had said, until you have been more hers. "Seek the lotus, and take a draught of rapture."[24]

After setting out in the cool dawn twilight, they paused to cut stout walking sticks, then again to chat with mowers in the meadows. As they walked on westward, Thoreau's excitement grew at the locals' "truer and wilder pronunciation": "not Way-tatic, Way-chusett, but Wor-tatic, Wor-chusett." What a letdown that evening when at that wild western inn, the innkeeper handed them a copy of the Concord newspaper! Next morning they left in the gray twilight to hike the remaining four miles to the mountain's base; as they ascended, the trees got smaller, then vanished altogether on the summit, where on the ruins of an old observation tower they read Virgil and Wordsworth and ate wild blueberries washed down with fresh milk from a farm below. From on high they watched the sun set and night creep over the land, until "the sun's rays fell on us two alone, of all New England men." As the moon rose, they kindled their campfire, visible for thirty miles around, and at dawn the whole of Massachusetts lay "spread out before us, in its length and breadth, like a map." At noon they descended eastward into the dusty abodes of men, stopping at Harvard village to reflect on the sunset and spend the night. Next morning they parted, Henry for Concord and Richard to join his family.[25]

Back at the Emersons', Henry opened the "Nature Notes" album in which John had recorded his trophies: birds seen, specimens collected. Earlier that spring, the grieving Henry had taken out the long-untouched album and, alongside John's elegant script, inserted a few scraggly jottings of his own. Then, early that June, something astonishing happened. While out walking, Henry came upon a brood of partridge chicks squatting in the leaves. He cradled them in his hand, where they lay unflinching, then set them gently back among the leaves, touched when one accidently fell over and stayed that way. Recording the sighting in John's elegant album, Henry struggled to capture why he was so moved: "The innocent yet adult expression of their eyes I shall not soon forget. There was the clarified wisdom and cunning of the sphinx and sybil in their clear eyes. When the mind is born then is not the eye born . . . coeval with the sky it reflects."[26] The effect is uncanny: Henry's raw and angular handwriting spills down the page, ripping open a vortex in John's tidy checklist, inscribing a moment of rapture that would become one of *Walden*'s most beautiful passages—indeed, a touchstone for *Walden* itself, as Thoreau took the vulnerable young bird into his hand, saw the birth of cosmic intelligence in its limpid eye, laid it back among the leaves, and, with that same hand, ignited a routine entry into radiance.

A few blank pages remained in John's parlor album, and Henry overwrote them with a draft of "A Walk to Wachusett," elevating his pedestrian excursion into an epic mountaintop revelation. From now on, he vowed, heaven would indeed be under his feet: whenever he gazed on Wachusett on the horizon, his eyes could rest "on the very rocks where we boiled our hasty pudding amid the clouds," reminding him that "there is elevation in every hour, as no part of the earth is so low that the heavens may not be seen from it." Hawthorne had just published a sketch in the stylish new *Boston Miscellany*, and it was surely Hawthorne who tipped Thoreau off that his picturesque travel narrative was just the thing for that high-class popular magazine. If he sent it there instead of the *Dial*, he would gain a national audience—and get paid! In January 1843, the editors published "A Walk to Wachusett," Thoreau's first piece to reach the wider world.[27] It seemed he was pointed toward commercial success. But publishing was a chancy world; the promising startup folded with the next issue. Thoreau was never paid, despite repeated attempts and both Emerson's and Peabody's intercessions. Still, he'd found his voice, and he'd found an audience too. A career as a professional author seemed well within his grasp.

--><--

In summer 1842, Emerson drew into his orbit yet another young idealist: Ellery Channing. In the fall of 1839, Emerson had received a portfolio of poems in which he recognized a new and important unknown poet. Their author was the nephew of the "Pope" of Transcendentalism himself, William Ellery Channing, and also the family's black sheep. In 1834, Ellery Channing dropped out of Harvard after a single term and fled Boston altogether to homestead on the Illinois prairie, which was where Emerson's ecstatic greeting reached him: "I have seen no verses written in America that have such inward music, or that seem to be such authentic inspiration." Ellery agreed to let the *Dial* publish his poems, and Emerson introduced the unknown poet with a flourish: the Muse, he proclaimed, had finally found a voice in America.[28] Thereafter nearly every issue of the *Dial* would feature poems by Ellery Channing, and Emerson would help collect them into a book—even as Henry Thoreau worked away, dreaming he himself would someday blossom into Emerson's Great Poet.

Ellery Channing did not present himself to Emerson in person until summer 1842. By then he was part of the Transcendental family—literally. After giving up the Illinois farm, he married Margaret Fuller's younger sister Ellen, much to her family's dismay. The happy if penniless couple considered joining Brook Farm, but instead stayed in Cincinnati until Ellery decided he must meet Emerson in person. Margaret arrived for her July visit to find her brother-in-law already there, fast friends with Henry. Where would they live? Margaret suggested the Old Manse. Absolutely not, said the Hawthornes. Emerson thought Ellery, Henry, and Richard Fuller should all buy a farm together, grow produce, and peddle it from a wheelbarrow on the street, like Marston Watson in Plymouth. Instead the Channings moved in with Margaret in Cambridge, until Ellery concluded he must live next to Emerson, nowhere else. Thoreau located a little red cottage just down the street, in poor repair and overpriced, but Channing took a fancy to it. In April 1843, Channing the poet sent Thoreau the handyman a long list of repairs: painting, stoning the cellar, building new stairs, clearing and resetting the well, moving the privy, fencing the property—enough to keep a crew busy for weeks. "O beloved Thoreau!" he exclaimed in May as the family was moving in. "So many have been your benevolences that my wish is too shallow to know how to bring you into my debt."[29]

Ellery Channing was not the easiest of friends. He could be sweet, funny, and sardonic, or rude, moody, and cranky—"a great genius with a little wretched boy trotting beside him," said Margaret Fuller, who saw "a touch of the goblin in his beauty."[30] Hawthorne thought he was a perfect example of the "queer and clever young men" Emerson was "continually picking up by way of a genius"—yet he, too, found Channing irresistible. With him, their talk "up-gushed" like "the babble of a fountain. The evanescent spray was Ellery's," and so, too, were the deep gold nuggets of thought "that lay glimmering in the fountain's bed."[31] More than once Channing lured the reclusive Hawthorne out of the Old Manse for a fishing excursion in the *Pond Lily*, though for really long walks he counted on Thoreau. From the very beginning, the two became each other's closest friend, inseparable companions—"a pair of knights in homespun"—who lived in nature with a religious intensity.[32]

→‒‹‐

Bronson Alcott was on his epic trip to England this busy and sociable summer, hoping to spread the "Newness" and persuade some of England's most radical "living minds" to come to America.[33] America might not have allowed Alcott to keep a school, but England honored him as a prophet. His followers modeled their school, Alcott House, directly on his Temple School, and they welcomed him with such enthusiasm that Alcott began to dream of founding a whole New American Eden. In October 1842, he returned to Concord with two of his English disciples: Henry Wright, the director of Alcott House, and Charles Lane, a journalist and reformer. Emerson introduced them around town, where everyone took to calling them "the Englishmen," for "they always go in platoon." Thoreau listened to them spin plans for a new utopian community, just as soon as they could purchase a farm. His own family were won over—or at least, entertained: "We find the Englishmen very agreeable," wrote Prudence Ward, and the Thoreau women all agreed they liked to hear Mr. Lane talk—Alcott all over, with a British accent—for "it makes a pleasant variety . . . to have these different thinkers near us."[34]

Six weeks later the town suddenly had a lot more to talk about. In 1838, Bronson Alcott had become a founding member of the New England Non-Resistance Society, founded in reaction to a proslavery mob's murder of the abolitionist Elijah Lovejoy. The society's leader, William Lloyd Garrison, announced their principles in the *Liberator*: one must not oppose force with force. This meant rejecting all institutions based on fear or coercion: no wars, no voting, no holding of government offices, no imprisonment, and, of course, no payment of taxes. Alcott brought the nonresistance movement to Concord; in January 1841, the lyceum held a debate on whether it was ever proper to offer forcible resistance. Alcott argued no—against John and Henry Thoreau.[35] As a conscientious nonresister, Alcott had refused to pay his taxes ever since arriving in Concord in 1840. The authorities let the matter slide until January 17, 1843, when the new tax collector, Sam Staples (whose wedding Alcott had witnessed in 1839) showed up to collect. When Alcott refused, Staples led him to the Middlesex County Jail, but the jailer was nowhere to be found. While they waited, Staples fed him supper while Alcott made his case. Sam wasn't convinced, but he told Helen Thoreau, "I vum—I believe it was nothing but principle—for I never heard a man talk honester." After a couple of hours, a messenger announced the tax had been paid, by Samuel Hoar, so Staples let Alcott go. "Thus we were spared the affliction of his absence and he the triumph of suffering for his principles," wrote Abigail.[36] Next time, her family, anxious to keep the peace, prepaid her husband's taxes.

That night, at least, the peace was not entirely kept. While Alcott, Lane, and Thoreau ate supper and awaited the receipt for payment, they conspired: with Alcott in jail, Lane and Thoreau would "agitate the state." But later that evening, Thoreau arrived at the lyceum to find Alcott in the audience, a free man after all; "my fire all went out—and the state was safe as far as I was concerned." But Lane's fire still burned hot. The speaker happened to be Charles M. Spear from the American Peace Society, a onetime Universalist preacher. The instant he finished, Lane leaped to his feet to proclaim his outrage at Alcott's arrest. Then Alcott stood, too, and delivered "a 'My Prisons' which made us forget Silvio Pellico himself." An annoyed Mr. Spear protested that the Concord radicals were wrong; as he muttered in his journal, "The Saviour's example seems to be in favor of taxes."[37] But Lane wasn't done. The next day he mailed his righteous defense of Alcott to the *Liberator*: the issue was not whether tax money went to iniquitous purposes. After all, some went to support education, and no one supported that more fervently than Alcott himself. No, opposition to payment of taxes "is founded on the moral instinct which forbids every moral being to be a party, either actively or permissively, to the destructive principles of power and might over peace and love." The State was diabolical when it used brute force, even—no, *especially*—when that force was sanctioned by majority opinion.[38]

Lane's argument may not have carried Mr. Spear, but it did carry Henry Thoreau, who by then had also stopped paying his taxes. Lane himself would be arrested that December, when he happened to be taking the stagecoach through town; Staples spotted him, demanded he pay up, and, when Lane refused, clapped him behind bars. Then it was Samuel Hoar's son Ebenezer Rockwood Hoar who paid the debt, and the liberated Lane, "sad & indisposed," drooped over to Emerson's house to retail his troubles. Emerson, who paid his own taxes regularly, was unconvinced.[39] By the time Henry Thoreau's turn came three years later, he had plenty of time to plot how his own "My Prisons" would agitate against the State.

→►◄←

All year long, Thoreau's energies were on the upswing. In August 1842, right after returning from climbing Wachusett, he joined Emerson and other prominent neighbors to found the Concord Athenaeum, a subscription reading room conveniently located in the vestry of the First Parish Church.[40] And that November, when the Concord Lyceum again reelected Thoreau as a curator, he accepted, helping to invite Orestes Brownson as well as regional luminaries— Horace Greeley, Charles T. Jackson, Theodore Parker, Wendell Phillips—and such locals as Charles Lane, Ephraim Bull (who was about to earn fame for commercializing the Concord grape), the Reverend Barzillai Frost, and, of course, Emerson. It was a solid season, and Thoreau was proud that of the $109.20 allocated for the year, they spent exactly $100 for fees, rent, lighting, and heat, returning the remaining $9.20 for next year. "How much might be done for a town with $100," he crowed. "I myself have provided a select course of twenty-five lectures for a winter, together with room, fuel, and lights, for that sum,—which was no inconsiderable benefit to every inhabitant."[41]

Thoreau was on the program, too, for a February 8 lecture on "Sir Walter Raleigh." It was his first time speaking in public as a full-fledged town citizen, and Emerson, away on a lecture tour, sent his blessing: may "the brightest star of the winter shed its clear beams on that night!" Lidian returned word that Henry's lecture "pleased me much." Others liked it, too, and the Concord newspaper noticed it as "a production very creditable to its author." "Henry," Lidian urged her husband, "ought to be known as a man who can give a Lecture. You must advertise him to the extent of your power. A few lyceum fees would satisfy his moderate wants" and give "improvement and happiness" to him and to his audiences. Thoreau himself wrote Emerson cheerfully, "It was as bright a night as you could wish."[42] Raleigh, in his treatment, became nothing less than a tragic Emersonian "American Scholar" executed by the State: an explorer of New World nature, a writer whose prose lay across the page vivid as "a green bough," but whose real poems were written in action, with ships and fleets—altogether, a heroic ideal for the writer's life. Thus it is puzzling that, when Thoreau submitted it to the *Dial*, Emerson never published it.

Being a lyceum curator gave Thoreau power to help set the agenda for town discussions, and he used it. Concord's antislavery activists were led by women, including all the women in Thoreau's family; but women were prohibited from speaking in public. If abolitionism were to take hold, the men would have to step up— and Thoreau did, by helping invite Wendell Phillips to the lyceum. This meant taking a stand with the radical wing, who had just split from the conservatives over the question of women's rights. The split cut across Thoreau's family, for Aunts Maria and Jane followed the conservatives in opposing voting rights for women, while Cynthia, Helen, and Sophia remained staunch Garrisonians, proud that women now had the right to vote at their meetings. To silence the radical wing, both the Trinitarian and the First Parish churches banned the radicals from speaking. Helen Thoreau was so incensed that she never went to church again. In defiance, the radicals brought to town the nation's most radical speaker of all to keynote their

October 1842 meeting: Frederick Douglass, the escaped
was riveting audiences with his thunderous denunciation
With Douglass came William Lloyd Garrison and Wend
the two activists about to introduce Douglass's *Narrati..*
of Frederick Douglass to the world, as well as Abigail Alcott's brother
Samuel May. Garrison and May stayed with the Alcotts, while Douglass stayed with the Thoreaus; from this visit forward, Douglass and
Helen Thoreau were friends and correspondents.[43]

Out of this October 1842 meeting, someone—Thoreau's mother
or sisters, or Lidian Emerson, or perhaps Henry Thoreau himself—
suggested that Phillips be invited back to speak at the Concord
Lyceum. This was a canny choice, for Phillips knew precisely how
to use well-modulated logic to unsettle a conservative audience. But
when it was announced to the lyceum membership that Phillips
would speak on slavery, the Honorable John Keyes rose to protest:
the lyceum was no place for "the vexed and disorganizing question of Abolition or Slavery." Keyes moved to cancel the lecture. He
was outvoted, and on December 21, 1842, Wendell Phillips spoke as
scheduled. Almost certainly Phillips stayed with the Thoreaus, and
as a curator, Henry Thoreau may have ushered him to the lecture
hall and introduced him. Though the speech was not recorded, the
town's reaction suggests the tenor of his words: the indomitable
Mary Brooks, the leader of the Concord radicals, beseeched Phillips
to return and refute Keyes's "gross barefaced malignant misrepre-
sentation" and his charge that Phillips was a traitor to his country.[44]
Phillips would return, but not for another year. The stage was set
for round two.

Thoreau was gaining confidence as a literary professional, which
is one reason he was ready to step into town affairs. When Fuller
resigned from the *Dial*, Emerson realized he needed to find "some
friendly Hercules who will lend a shoulder to uphold the little
world." He found Thoreau, who helped Emerson with his second
issue. The results were uneven. When the last batch of printer's copy
arrived late in September during a stretch of "mild sweet perfect
days," Emerson handed off the pages to his friendly Hercules and

left on a two-day walk with Hawthorne. Weeks later, when Fuller received her October *Dial*, she was furious: her essay on Tennyson had been spoiled by an outrageous misprint. Tennyson's lines were supposed to read "O'er the deep mind of dauntless *infancy*," but instead it read "dauntless *infamy*." Was this a *joke*? she demanded—all the more vexed because she'd counted on sharing her review with Tennyson himself. For that and certain other embarrassing errors, replied Emerson, the fault belonged to "Henry T." He considered bumping Henry T. for someone else, but Henry was still jobless, so Emerson kept him on.[45]

Henry's limitations as an editor were one thing; his shortcomings as a poet were another. Fuller had rejected almost all his poetry, and now Emerson rushed to put it before the world: the October 1842 *Dial* printed no fewer than eight Thoreau poems, and only one by the usual favorite, Ellery Channing. This, too, pained Fuller, who complained that Thoreau's tin ear had ruined his best poem, whereas Channing's "Dirge" was "more and more beautiful" the more she read it—as everyone at Brook Farm agreed. This, the peak of Thoreau's career as a poet, was the beginning of the end. An embarrassed Emerson sat him down and critiqued his poems, pulling no punches. For all their "honest truth" and "rude strength," they lacked beauty. "Their fault is, that the gold does not yet flow pure, but is drossy & crude. The thyme and marjoram are not yet made into honey; the assimilation is imperfect."[46] After five years dedicated to poetry, Thoreau was devastated. Emerson never printed another Thoreau poem. Thoreau himself slipped in three more when he edited the April 1843 issue, including two of his greatest, "Smoke" and "Haze." But from then on, Emerson's designated poet would be Ellery Channing.

→>-<←

For Thoreau, Emerson had something else in mind: selecting, editing, and translating hard-to-find literature from such old and foreign books as Anacreon's graceful lyrics and Aeschylus's tragedy *Prometheus Bound*. Thoreau's translation of the latter was used as a trot by generations of Harvard students; he worked hard to embody in English the genius of the ancients, hoping to inspire a modern poetry deeper and truer than Tennyson's sugared rhymes.[47] Emerson also asked Thoreau to collect "Ethnical Scriptures," a new feature offering selections from world ethical and religious writings. Emerson led off with extracts from the *Panchatantra*, a collection of animal fables by the ancient Indian scholar Vishnu Sharma. "What is religion?" one of them asked. "Compassion for all things which have life. . . . What is philosophy? An entire separation from the world." Ever since the 1830s Emerson had steeped in the religious writings of Asia—ancient Hindu scriptures, the sayings of Confucius, Zoroastrian works, the *Arabian Nights*—reading them not for exotic ornamentation, but as guides to the rebirth in America of ancient and honorable spiritual traditions: the origins of perennial philosophy, universal ethical truths that could guide individual moral belief and action.[48]

When Thoreau found these books in Emerson's library, he was entranced. For the *Dial* he went back to his early favorite, "one of the oldest compositions extant": *The Laws of Menu* (or *Manu*, from the same root as *mind* and *man*), scripture literally from the dawn of civilization. Thoreau filled nine pages with its wisdom: "The resignation of all pleasures is far better than the attainment of them." "The hand of an artist employed in his art is always pure." "Whatever is hard to be traversed, whatever is hard to be acquired, whatever is hard to be visited, whatever is hard to be performed, all this may be accomplished by true devotion; for the difficulty of devotion is the greatest of all." These, he wrote in his Journal, were "the laws of you and me—a fragrance wafted down from those old-times, and no more to be refuted than the wind." Thoreau found his India in New England, for these laws were true wherever there was solitude and silence: "In my brain is the sanscrit."[49]

He also collected the "Sayings of Confucius" ("Having knowledge, to apply it; not having knowledge, to confess your ignorance; this is real knowledge") and the "Chinese Four Books," which introduced the fundamentals of Confucianism to America: "Sincerity is the Taou or way of heaven. To aim at it is the way of man." Next was the Nepalese text "The White Lotus of the Good Law," detailing the path to Buddha—enlightenment or awakening. For Thoreau these scriptures were absolutely foundational, and he dreamed of reviving ancient "Oriental" wisdom in the modern world. He also vowed to follow his own devotional path: "The Bráhmen is the ideal man."[50] It struck him as singular that even as the tide of religion was withdrawing and religious scholars were "picking to pieces its old testaments, here are some coming slowly after on the sea-shore picking up the durable relics of perhaps older books and putting them together again." To truly renew this ancient spiritual wisdom, he must first find a way to live it—he must attempt to be a Brahman, to be awakened, Buddha. He must attempt a devotion so complete that he would be a teacher not merely in his writings, but in his life. As he would tell his first disciple, "To some extent, and at rare intervals, even I am a yogin."[51]

All through 1842 Thoreau's vision was deepening and clarifying, but his moods were often ungovernable. January 1843, the first anniversary of John's death, found him ill with "bronchitis." He dumped a glum self-assessment in his Journal: "What am I at present? A diseased bundle of nerves standing between time and eternity like a withered leaf that still hangs shivering on its stem." Yet he could look back on a year of real growth: a stack of publications, including two original essays; a growing role in Concord's civic affairs; increasing responsibility as coeditor of a respected journal; important, lifelong friendships begun and nurtured. The very same day he dumped his misery into his Journal, he wrote Richard Fuller a warm, loving letter, trimming an osprey feather he'd been saving for "some state occasion" to thank him for his New Year's gift, a music box. It "seems to be playing just for us two pilgrims marching over hill and dale of a summer afternoon," he wrote, recalling their happy days together. Lidian was charmed with Henry's "child-like joy" in his new possession. After dancing across the carpet with Edith, not quite two years old, he dashed off to play it for his mother and sisters.[52]

→►◄←

That winter Emerson was away lecturing, and he placed his family and possessions into Thoreau's care, an overwhelming degree of trust. After three weeks as surrogate father to the Emerson children, Thoreau wrote Emerson a letter of thanks: "I have been your pensioner for nearly two years and still left free as under the summer sky . . . as free a gift as the sun or the summer." He wasn't the easiest person to have around—early on Emerson had said he admired Henry's "perennial threatening attitude," but how long could that have lasted?—and Thoreau admitted he'd "sometimes molested you with my mean acceptance." But with Emerson away, Thoreau visibly relaxed. Lidian reported that "after breakfast the little girls all petitioned to have some pop-corn parched," and Henry played master of ceremonies, holding the warming pan over the fire and enjoying the frolic as much as any child. Henry, too, reported on the children's progress: "Edith takes rapid strides in the arts and sciences . . . as well as over the carpet," and had taken to calling him "papa." The older Ellen "declares every morning that 'Papa *may* come home to-night.'" As for Lidian, she "almost persuades me to be a Christian"—indeed, confided an astonished Lidian, after they talked over his "heresies," Henry had actually gone to church.[53]

Lidian continued to host Transcendental gatherings. Once, she looked on, amused, as Alcott and Lane proclaimed "the Love of Nature" to be "the most subtle and dangerous of sins," an idolatry so refined it deluded its sinners into unconscious degradation. "Henry frankly affirmed to both the wise men that they were wholly deficient in the faculty in question, and therefore could not judge of it." Alcott rejoined that they were filled with *spiritual* love, "as Mr. T. was not." "It was ineffably comic," smiled Lidian. "Henry was brave and noble; well as I have always liked him, he still grows upon me." As for Henry, he was, as he wrote Lucy Brown, very happy, even though it was "a strangely mixed life" there among the "brooms and scouring and taxes and house keeping." But, he added with a smile, "even Valhalla must have its kitchen."[54]

Emerson had confided the *Dial*, too, to Henry's care. Buoyed by the vote of confidence, Thoreau soon had the issue in hand: Lane's essay on Alcott; a report from Charles Stearns Wheeler beavering away in Heidelberg; pieces by Fuller, Lydia Maria Child, and Fuller's friend James Freeman Clarke; more from Alcott and the inevitable

Ellery Channing; plus his own essay on the "Dark Ages." "As for poetry," he snapped back to Emerson, "I have not remembered to write any for some time—it has quite slipped my mind—but sometimes I think I hear the muttering of the thunder," though in fact, he did slip in those three poems.[55] Emerson returned in March to finish off a solid and notably cosmopolitan issue, completing his first year as editor. Lately the *Dial* had drawn some good reviews, and in England, said Alcott, it was regarded as "quite an Oracle." But Peabody had more bad news. They were down to 220 paying subscribers, which couldn't pay even the cost of paper and printing. For weeks Emerson fretted while his friends argued: Keep it going, begged Lane and Alcott. Let it go, said Elizabeth Hoar, so its best writers could publish elsewhere. One more year, pleaded Fuller, to please "wellwishers" in the distance "or even in the Future."[56]

Thoreau was ready to bail. It wasn't just the unpaid service as editorial assistant; the whole arrangement as Emerson's "pensioner" was wearing thin. On March 1, 1843, he wrote Emerson, who was then visiting his brother William on Staten Island, to say he was feeling better than he had been, "and am meditating some other method of paying debts than by lectures and writing. . . . If anything of that 'other' sort should come to your ears in N.Y. will you remember it for me?" Emerson hated New York, but he had a notion that the land of Wall Street was ready to hear a little Transcendentalism. He talked it over with William, and together they came up with a plan: Henry would tutor William's son Willie. He'd be a good influence on the boy, and he could take him to the woods and into the city. In exchange, Henry would get room, board, and $100 a year for expenses. Henry liked the idea, but asked if there wasn't some way to earn a little money beyond expenses. Perhaps he could do some clerical work in William's law office on Wall Street, or in some other office—at least until he got a little literary work going? He could leave right away, as soon as April 1, only two weeks away.[57]

A move from Waldo Emerson's Concord pensioner to William Emerson's Wall Street scrivener might not sound very promising. Had he been able to reach into the future and read Melville's portrait in "Bartleby, the Scrivener: A Story of Wall Street," Thoreau might have been more wary. But his career had reached a dead end. Life on Staten Island would put him at last beyond Emerson's orbit and well within reach of the New York literary market. Thoreau was willing to take the gamble. He packed up his life in Concord and planned a new beginning in New York City, the heart of American commerce, not suspecting it would be his second near-death experience.

THOREAU ON STATEN ISLAND

Hawthorne was still looking out for his friend. "The man has stuff in him to make a reputation of," he'd told the editor of the *New Monthly Magazine* in October 1842. That magazine folded and the editor never replied, but in January 1843 Hawthorne tried again, when his friend John O'Sullivan, the New York publisher of the *Democratic Review*, visited him at the Old Manse. Hawthorne invited Thoreau to meet them at the athenaeum, where O'Sullivan's journal was on prominent display, and they took tea together at the Old Manse before Thoreau escorted O'Sullivan to the lyceum. Thoreau wasn't especially impressed with O'Sullivan himself, but he was very impressed when "he made a point of asking me to write for his Review, which I shall be glad to do."[58] The *Democratic Review* published some of the nation's best-known writers: Hawthorne, of course, and also Bryant, Whittier, Longfellow, Lowell, and Catherine Sedgwick. It was, in fact, the publishing arm of the reformist, liberal-minded "Young America" group, sympathetic to Transcendentalism: "The Best Government Is That Which Governs Least," trumpeted the cover. With a circulation of 3,500, anything Thoreau placed there would multiply his *Dial* audience fifteen-fold. Thoreau bookmarked the offer to bring with him to New York, along with a special Journal volume he'd begun in the summer of 1842, dubbed the "Long Book" for its large pages, into which he'd been copying and arranging entries relating to his 1839 river voyage with John. Thoreau was making long plans.

Soon he was telling Richard Fuller, "I expect to leave Concord, which is my Rome—and its people, who are my Romans, in May." Early in April he dropped in on Hawthorne to leave Fuller's music box in his care. Thoreau's move would be a good one, thought Hawthorne, though he'd miss Thoreau's combination of "wild freedom" with "classic cultivation"; Thoreau "is physically out of health, and, morally and intellectually, seems not to have found exactly the guiding clue." After Emerson's visit, Hawthorne wryly added that Emerson "appears to have suffered some inconveniency from his experience of Mr. Thoreau as an inmate." Perhaps Thoreau was better met "occasionally in the open air" than as "a permanent guest at table and fireside."[59]

The goodbyes mounted as the day approached: Hawthorne and Thoreau took the *Pond Lily* on one last row upriver, where they boarded an ice floe and rode it all the way home, towing the dory behind them. Prudence Ward gave Henry a small microscope for his natural history studies, and Elizabeth Hoar gave him a pen and inkstand, and her hope that the pen "may be made sometimes the interpreter of friendly thoughts to those whom you leave beyond the reach of your voice." Emerson advanced him twenty dollars for supplies and new clothes, and another seven dollars for traveling expenses. He wrote William with a trace of anxiety, "And now goes our brave youth into the new house, the new connexion, the new City. I am sure no truer & no purer person lives in Wide New York"—though he might pester one with "some accidental crotchets and perhaps a village exaggeration of the value of facts." Little Willie, he hoped, would value Thoreau "for his real power to serve & instruct him."[60]

On Saturday, May 6, Henry Thoreau and William Emerson's wife, Susan Haven Emerson, journeyed together from Concord to Staten Island, stopping in Boston to collect the sum owed him by the bankrupt *Boston Miscellany*. It wasn't just the principle of the thing; Thoreau really needed the money, though he still didn't receive it. Their ship ran aground at low tide in New London, Connecticut, but otherwise the long ride was without incident. At ten o'clock Sunday morning, Thoreau and Mrs. Emerson stepped onto the wharf at the Battery in New York City, where they were instantly besieged by "an army of starving cab-men," "a confused jumble of heads, and soiled coats dangling from flesh-colored faces, all swaying to and fro, as if by a sort of undertow," each sighting along their buggy whips to the harried couple, all growing more insistent by the minute: "Want a cab sir?" "You want a cab sir." Thoreau held them off with a stare and escorted Mrs. Emerson and their baggage to the Staten Island Ferry landing.[61]

They were soon home at the long, low, brown-shingled house Waldo Emerson had dubbed "The Snuggery," tucked behind a grape arbor and surrounded by gardens and a tree-shaded lawn.[62] It was green and rural, overlooking woods stretching south to the sea. From the hilltop above Thoreau could see all of New York, Brooklyn, Long Island, the Narrows from Sandy Hook to the New Jersey Highlands, and over the Atlantic to ships on the horizon nearly a day's sail away. Staten Island was William's rural retreat from his Manhattan law offices. He was a man of stature, the Richmond County judge of the Court of Common Pleas, and Fuller thought he was "as unlike his brother as possible": very much the gentleman, clearheaded, amiable, but "a mere business man" with no love for Transcendentalism.[63] Thoreau was tasked with tutoring seven-year-old Willie and perhaps with helping the toddlers Charles and Haven as well. Days were rigid: breakfast at six thirty, lunch at noon, dinner at five, schoolmastering from nine to two. He found Mr. and Mrs. Emerson "irreproachable and kind" but "not indeed my kith or kin in any sense." Waldo had insisted Thoreau have a room of his own, "be it never so small . . . wherein to dream, write, and declaim alone. Henry has always had it and always must." But it wasn't heated, so whenever Henry needed a room with a fire, he had to juggle with Judge Emerson for the library or the basement parlor.[64]

→►◄←

Off-duty, he explored the neighborhood, alternating between the "two things I hear. . . . The roar of the sea—and the hum of the city." The Island's natural history drew him first: sweetgum and tulip trees, wild garlic that grew everywhere and flavored the cows' milk, seventeen-year locusts that filled the air with their din—"Phar-r-r-aoh—Pha-r-r-aoh"—and fattened the local dogs, cats, and chickens.[65] He walked all over Staten Island from Telegraph Hill to the sailor's Snug Harbor to the old elm tree on the shore where the island's first settlers, the Huguenots, landed in 1661. The sea drew him most. "I like it much," he wrote Emerson. "Everything there is on a grand and generous scale—sea-weed, water, and sand; and even the dead fishes, horses and hogs have a rank luxuriant odor. Great shad nets spread to dry, crabs and horse-shoes crawling over the sand."[66] He watched men draw their boats up onto the sand with teams of oxen, "stepping about amid the surf, as if it were possible they might draw up Sandy Hook," and he made friends with old Captain Smith the fisherman, who drew up nets full of "moss-bonkers," or menhaden, which he sold by the thousand to fertilize the Island's lean soil. From shore Thoreau could watch immigrant ships stop at the nearby quarantine quay, where children ran races and swam while their parents stretched their limbs and took the air, waiting for the ships to be purified. "They are detained but a day or two, and then go up to the city, for the most part without having *landed* here."[67]

For the most part, neither had he. To go "up to the city" was a half-day's trip. The boat ran five or six times daily, and catching it meant a half-hour walk up Richmond Road or nearly a mile along the beach. From the south tip of Manhattan, it was another two- or three-mile walk on hard pavement to anywhere, and only were it to "rain shillings" could Thoreau afford the omnibus. "You see," he wrote his parents, "it is quite a day's training to make a few calls in different parts of the city."[68] His first Saturday, he called on Prudence Ward's brother George, who told him about setting up a daguerreotype studio; then he met with Emerson's young friends Giles Waldo and William Tappan, clerks in the national credit bureau that Tappan's father, the abolitionist Lewis Tappan, ran. "A kind of intelligence office for the whole country," Thoreau explained to his father, a business about to employ thousands. Saturday being a workday, the two took Henry to a neighborhood alehouse for a quick visit. He finished with some sightseeing: the *Great Western*, the first transatlantic passenger steamship, which cut the crossing to Europe from several dangerous weeks to a few safe days; the Croton Waterworks, to see how water was piped in from forty miles away, making such urban density possible; the National Academy of Design, where he saw landscapes by Asher Durand and Emanuel Leutze's career-making *Return of Columbus in Chains* (his *Washington Crossing the Delaware* would soon follow).[69] It was a heady introduction to technologies on the vanguard of modernity: photography, a global economy, urban expansion, his first glimpse of modern art.

The Thoreau who loved machinery was fascinated, but the Thoreau homesick for Concord was appalled. Like Poe and Hawthorne, the crowd struck him as "something new and to be attended to," but the more he saw of the city, the worse he liked it. "I am ashamed of my eyes that behold it. It is a thousand times meaner than I could have imagined. It will be something to hate that's the advantage it will be to me," he pronounced. "When will the world learn that a million men are of no importance compared with one man." Impressions overwhelmed him. "Persons and things flit so rapidly through my brain now a days that I can hardly remember them."[70] It didn't help that as soon as he returned from the city, a cold he caught while traveling worsened to "bronchitis," keeping him inside for a week. He rallied after that, but in June he worried to Emerson that he was failing the family: "I do not feel myself especially serviceable to the good people with [whom] I live, except as inflictions are sanctified to the righteous." Nor did he and Willie hit it off: "I am not attracted toward him but as to youth generally." But he tried as best he could. In July he reported, "My pupil and I get on apace," and in August William Emerson assured his brother that "Thoreau makes us all like & respect him, & he is doing William much good."[71]

As for cultivating a literary career, here, too, Thoreau started off with a good will. Emerson was eager for him to meet Henry James, "an independent right-minded man" and "the best apple on the tree," assuring James that once he got past Thoreau's "village pedantry & tediousness of facts," he would find "a profound mind and a person of true magnanimity." James reached out immediately with a warm invitation, and as soon as he was well enough, Thoreau visited his home on Washington Square, where he perhaps looked in on the newborn Henry James Jr., the future novelist, and his infant brother William, the future philosopher. For the first time in New York, Thoreau was genuinely happy: "I have been to see Henry James and like him very much. . . . he is a refreshing forward looking, and forward moving man, and has naturalized and humanized New York for me." After three hours' talk, James told Thoreau to make "free use of his house," and Thoreau returned at least once—until suddenly James and his family boarded the *Great Western* to be spirited away to Europe. "I am the more sorry because you liked him so well," Emerson commiserated, adding in a letter to James that losing him was a "great disappointment." He had hoped James would move his family to Concord.[72]

Losing Henry James so soon was yet another in a series of unlucky breaks. But one lucky break occurred when Thoreau entered the Mercantile Association Library and found his old Harvard tutor Henry McKean working therein, who immediately granted him full access to the library's reading room. In a second lucky break, right on the library's steps he ran into the era's leading utopian reformers: Henry Wright, the other half of "the Englishmen" Alcott had brought to Concord, now living in New York; Albert Brisbane, the era's leading Fourierist; and William Henry Channing, a cousin of Ellery Channing, busy preaching in the city and editing the Fourierist reform journal the *Present*. Thoreau was dubious about their "Associationist" schemes to reorganize society according to the new principles of social science, but he respected W. H. Channing enough to visit him at home for "a few pleasant hours, discussing the all absorbing questions—what to do for the race." From then on, Thoreau would address their arguments with the confidence of a man who had looked his opposition in the face—which, he remarked of Channing's face, would "break with a conchoidal fracture," so much had Channing made up his mind to find humanity disappointing.[73]

The luckiest break of all came when Thoreau called on Horace Greeley, editor of the *New-York Tribune*, whose weekly edition was fast becoming the nation's largest and most influential newspaper. Also an Associationist, Greeley had helped fund Brook Farm, and he put his weight and enthusiasm behind nearly every reform movement of the day, including Transcendentalism. Greeley adored Emerson and promoted the *Dial*, so when Thoreau dropped into his busy office, naturally he jumped right up and made him welcome: "Now be neighborly," he greeted the lonely Thoreau, who in return thought him "a hearty New Hampshire boy as one would wish to meet."[74] When Thoreau completed his first major work—an essay on Carlyle—he sent it to Greeley, who placed it and made sure Thoreau got good money for it. From then on, he would be Thoreau's friend and tireless literary agent, championing his work to the world and, in private, cajoling an often discouraged writer to be of good cheer and write on. Forging this one friendship made the Staten Island venture, for all its disappointments, worthwhile.

--><--

The first real setback came when John O'Sullivan rejected Thoreau's essay. Thoreau had written a feisty review of J. A. Etzler's *The Paradise Within the Reach of All Men, without Labor, by Powers of Nature and Machinery*. Emerson had wanted the review for the *Dial*, but buoyed by their promising tea at the Old Manse, Thoreau sent "Paradise (To Be) Regained" to O'Sullivan's *Democratic Review* instead. It was a savvy move, but risky: O'Sullivan supported the communitarian social reforms Etzler promoted—reforms that Thoreau skewered without mercy. There in New York, he'd seen a new world a-building where every social problem had a technological solution. Why bother to make *ourselves* better, when we can simply remake the world instead? In Etzler's giddy vision of a geo-engineered planet, man would harness the winds, tides, and sun itself to power machines that will grind down the hills, grade the earth flat, pave it smooth, lay canals and roads, light up the night sky, and thrill the air with nonstop music. Why stop there?—jeers Thoreau. Why not "run the earth off its track into a new orbit, some summer, and so change the tedious vicissitude of the seasons?" Or why bother with the earth at all? Why not "migrate from the earth, to settle some vacant and more western planet"? Etzler, explains the man who understands both labor and machines, forgot to calculate three little things: "time, men, and money." But technology requires all three: no magic wand would turn Etzler's fantasy world into reality. What's more, the future is not an engineering problem but a *human* problem: "Nothing can be effected but by one man. . . . In this matter of reforming the world, we have little faith in corporations; not thus was it first formed."[75]

A hard look at the corporate world being born in New York's streets and offices confirmed Thoreau's Transcendentalist convictions: nature permitted no shortcuts; reform must start with the inner self, not the outer circumstances. O'Sullivan could hardly agree, but he could see Thoreau had written a lively and pointed essay. Perhaps, he mildly suggested, Thoreau might make "some additions and modifications"? Or send him something less controversial— perhaps some of his private little interviews with nature? After all, the journal's "collective 'we'" required "a certain pervading homogeneity." Thoreau responded humbly but did not back down. In the end, remarkably, O'Sullivan relented and ran the Etzler review in his November issue. He also ran, in the October issue, Thoreau's character sketch "The Landlord," honoring the country innkeeper who feeds and shelters all comers out of his love for human nature, a portrait of hospitality based on the inn near Wachusett where he and Fuller stayed. This "public" interview with nature made for an interesting experiment, but no one much liked it. When Thoreau's family asked for a copy, he replied that he had none to send, since he couldn't afford the fifty cents it cost.[76]

This was the summit of Thoreau's success in the New York literary market. Early in June he'd written hopefully, "I have not set my traps, yet, but I am getting the bait ready." Four months later he had to admit that "my bait will not tempt the rats; they are too well fed."[77] To his family he spilled out the grim details: he was pounding New York's streets without effect, pushing into the offices of every bookseller and publisher, only to be told they had no money to pay contributors, or if they did—like the Harper brothers, on their way to founding a publishing empire—they were unwilling to chance an unknown writer. To Emerson he was blunt: "Literature comes to a poor market here, and even the little that I write is more than will sell." The popular journals "are overwhelmed with contributions, which cost nothing, and are worth no more." The best journal, the *Knickerbocker*, excluded Transcendentalism on principle, but they'd gotten Thoreau out their door by pleading poverty instead. "Only the Ladies Companion pays"—"but I could not write anything companionable," he joked mordantly with his mother.[78]

There was other trouble as well. Thoreau had recovered from "bronchitis" only to find himself attacked by something more insidious: narcolepsy, the "demon" said to haunt his mother's side of the family. When Uncle Charles nodded off midsentence, it was a family joke, but for Henry it was growing desperate. "This skirmishing interferes sadly with my literary projects," he confessed to his anxious mother, "and I am apt to think it a good day's work if I maintain a soldier's eye till night-fall." A month later he was no better: "I find it impossible to write or read except at rare intervals." By then he had to admit to Emerson that being unable to keep his eyes open rendered him an invalid.[79]

His narcolepsy may have been congenital, or another symptom of latent tuberculosis, but it also registered real psychic conflict and pain. Thoreau was deeply unhappy at Judge Emerson's and thoroughly frustrated with the obstacles palisading around him on the streets of Manhattan. Worse, Emerson's expectations for him put him in an impossible bind. On the one hand, he was supposed to carry Transcendentalism into the heart of America's commercial center and make a national name for himself; on the other hand, Emerson wanted him to bolster up the *Dial*. The Etzler review—a sharp satire on a hot-button issue, targeting the Associationist

reformers on their home ground and in their house journal, too—
was calculated to kick Transcendentalism up a notch into a national
controversy. For all his complaining, Thoreau now had O'Sullivan's
ear, and Greeley's, too. He'd even begun a new essay, "A Winter's
Walk," a dreamy, evocative, intimate love letter to the tough New
England winter and the metaphysical fire that burned underneath
it, deep in nature's Puritan heart. O'Sullivan and Greeley would have
snapped it up in a New York minute, earning him national attention,
but Emerson wrote him that "Our Dial is already printing, and you
must, if you can, send me something good by the 10th June certainly,
if not before." And so "A Winter's Walk" disappeared instead into
the back pages of the *Dial*.[80]

Even worse, Emerson hated it. "H.D.T. sends me a paper with
the old fault of unlimited contradiction," he sniped. "The trick of his
rhetoric is soon learned. It consists in substituting for the obvious
word & thought its diametrical antagonist. . . . It makes me nervous
& wretched to read it, with all its merits."[81] So he edited out his
worst objections, smoothing Thoreau's phrasing and softening his
meaning—editorial interference that would, in time, drive Thoreau
wild with fury, but not now, and not from Emerson. "I see that I was
very blind to send you my manuscript in such a state," he replied
abjectly. "There are some sad mistakes in the printing."[82] And when
Emerson saddled him with a new assignment—translations of Pindar (as suggested by Newcomb)—Thoreau could not refuse. "I . . .
wish he were better worth translating," he replied wearily. Would
Emerson take instead the Aeschylus tragedy *Seven Against Thebes*?
Send *something*, pleaded Emerson. In October his tone is still more
demanding: "Where are my translations of Pindar for the *Dial*?
Fail not to send me something good & strong." Thoreau complied,
and Pindar appeared in the *Dial*'s last two issues. His Aeschylus
translation, dramatizing resistance to civil government, was never
published.[83]

Had Emerson wished to undermine Thoreau's confidence and
sabotage his nascent career, he might have chosen just such means.
He might also have furthered his designs by singing the praises of

the young men who had replaced Thoreau in his affections—which he did. Charles Newcomb was, as ever, irresistible; Ellery Channing was happily settled into the house next door—the one Thoreau had fixed up for him—and "works very steadily thus far & our intercourse is very agreeable to me."[84] For a time Emerson's new "genius" was Benjamin West Ball, "a prodigious reader & a youth of great promise" who might, "with a little more repose of thought . . . be a great companion."[85] More lasting was his infatuation with the two young men who had ushered Thoreau to the alehouse on his first day in the city, William Tappan and Giles Waldo. Emerson had entreated Thoreau to meet Tappan, "a lonely beautiful brooding youth," and the "young Washington phoenix, Giles Waldo," and share in their "beautiful friendship."[86] Thoreau found them congenial, but no more. Giles Waldo withered under his inquisition: "My interview with Thoreau has shown me how desperately ignorant I have been content to remain of books," he wrote Emerson dejectedly. Tappan's "more reserved and solitary thought" earned more of Thoreau's respect, but just as yet, he wrote Emerson acidly, "the heavens are not shivered into diamonds over their heads." Perhaps, Emerson replied testily, Thoreau was being unfair.[87]

-+><-+-

Word was troubling on other fronts as well. On May 25, Bronson Alcott and Charles Lane bought a ninety-acre farm near Harvard village. Early in June they set off in good spirits to found their utopian community, Fruitlands. As Louisa May Alcott recalled, they made up in idealism what they lacked in practical knowledge, which was nearly everything. Lane tried to recruit Thoreau, writing him that their beautiful green landscape wanted only "a Thoreau's mind to elevate it to classic beauty." They could use his practical experience, too—and, as Lane perceptively added, "I have some imagination that you are not so happy and so well housed in your present position as you would be here amongst us."[88] But Thoreau stayed put. Then came a bitter blow from abroad. In Leipzig, Germany, while pursuing the studies that should have made his name, Charles Stearns

Wheeler, Thoreau's Harvard roommate and most trusted friend, died suddenly of gastric fever. On July 21, in a letter to Helen, Thoreau wrote a eulogy of his brave friend: Wheeler's "patient industry and energy—his reverent love of letters—and his proverbial accuracy" would have done such good for the world, giving it "a sort of connecting link between men and scholars of different walks and tastes." "So much remains," Thoreau sighed, "for us to do who survive."[89]

As autumn approached, Thoreau pushed himself hard. "I'm a good deal more wakeful than I was," he reassured Cynthia, "and growing stout in other respects, so that I may yet accomplish something in the literary way." Desperate to earn money, he tried peddling subscriptions to the *American Agriculturalist*. On his first go, he got caught in a historic rainstorm and sheltered for the night with Giles Waldo. His absence alarmed William Emerson, and in reporting to his brother, Thoreau had to downplay the incident. "I could heartily wish that this country wh. seems all opportunity, did actually offer more distinct & just rewards," Waldo Emerson wrote back, but it looked "more like crowded England & indigent Germany, than like rich & roomy nature. . . . But," he added unhelpfully, "the few cases are deceptive." After all, Thoreau's friends in Concord were doing fine. Emerson's reassurance only drove the knife deeper.[90] Thoreau's letters home, once resolute, became wistful, then acutely homesick. At first he'd missed the Emersons, but more and more he wrote long, newsy, nostalgic letters to his own family. In one, he envisioned the parlor on a Sunday evening: Cynthia poring over "some select book, almost transcendental perchance"; "Father has just taken one more look at the garden" before absorbing himself in the newspaper; "Helen has slipped in for the fourth time to learn the very latest item"; Sophia is away visiting the Thoreau cousins in Maine, "but Aunt Louisa without doubt is just flitting away to some good meeting." On October first, he dropped a hint: "I don't know when I shall venture home."[91]

The answer was not long in coming, for he was clearly miserable. The few surviving pages from his Journal evoke his despair: "I walked through New York yesterday—and met no real and living person." "I hate museums. . . . They are catacombs of Nature." Most telling of all is a bleak portrait, dated October 21, of what must have been William and Susan Emerson's house: "O I have seen such a hollow glazed life as on a painted floor which some couples lead—with their basement parlor with folding doors—a few visitors cards and the latest annual." The very children seemed to cry "with less inwardness and depth than in the cottage," here where people did not live, only resided. "There is no hearth in the center of the house."[92] Desperate for a hearth, Thoreau decided to come home for Thanksgiving. Bring a lecture for the lyceum! responded Emerson. Soon Thoreau was back in Concord, taking tea with Emerson and Orestes Brownson, escorting Brownson to the lyceum, introducing his old mentor to the curators and enjoying his lecture on "Demagogues." On Thanksgiving Eve, it was the turn of "H. D. Thoreau, of New York city," who spoke on "Ancient Poets." But H. D. Thoreau was no longer "of" New York. On December 2, Emerson paid him ten dollars for his contributions to the *Dial*. Thoreau used the money to return to Staten Island, pack up, and come home.

Still, he did investigate one other possibility: on his way back to New York, he spent several nights at Brook Farm.[93] It was a moment of decision. Not only was he suddenly at loose ends, but while in New York he'd been immersed in the excitement over Charles Fourier's proposals to reorganize society according to the new principles of social science. Now, after two years, Brook Farm was staggering under mounting debt, and voices from New York—W. H. Channing's new journal the *Present*, Albert Brisbane's journal the *Phalanx*—were converging to produce an existential crisis: Should Brook Farm reorganize as a Fourierist Phalanx? This would mean financial support to keep Brook Farm alive. It would also mean abandoning their original, founding Transcendentalist principles. It's unclear exactly why Thoreau veered to Brook Farm: Was he merely curious, or was he trying to influence the decision? After all, he'd just published an essay skewering the very kind of utopian social engineering they were debating. Perhaps he was considering a move to Brook Farm?

If so, he changed his mind. George Bradford posted a worried letter to Emerson: friend Thoreau had gone off in the very midst of a snowstorm, and to Bradford's shame, not one person had offered to drive him to the railroad station. The insult was bad enough—"we accused ourselves of great thoughtlessness or want of hospitality" (had there been an argument?)—but what really tortured Bradford was the fear that Thoreau, in "delicate" health, had "suffered in his throat in consequence." Thoreau's health was fine, but he never went back. A month later Brook Farm formally voted to go Fourierist. The decision split the Brook Farmers, and many left, including Bradford himself, who clearly was on Thoreau's side: "We are quite indebted to Henry for his brave defense of his thought which gained him much favor in the eyes of some of the friends here who are of the like faith."[94]

Meanwhile, Fruitlands, the other Transcendentalist utopia, was in the final grim stages of collapse. "They look well in July, we shall see them in December," the skeptical Emerson had commented. Lane didn't last even that long: late in November, feeling betrayed by the Alcotts, he retreated to Boston, where early in December he wrote Thoreau a warm note of commiseration: "That from all perils of a false position you may shortly be relieved and landed in the position where you feel 'at home' is the sincere wish of yours most friendly Charles Lane."[95] Thus there was now exactly one place left to try, one place where Thoreau might feel "at home"—home. He went back to the Parkman house, to John and Cynthia and his sisters, where he had not lived for nearly four years. On December 17, Waldo Emerson wrote his brother William that Thoreau, who thanked him for the payment, had brought away all the possessions he valued and that anything left in his chamber could be disposed of. The Pindar he'd borrowed would be returned through Waldo. That was that. The Thoreau who'd left in May so full of hope returned in December in defeat.

So it appeared. A failure this complete slammed the door on a literary career—or at least, on the kind of literary career Thoreau had been pursuing since 1837, when *he* had been Emerson's bright new genius. Now he was back in Concord, worn down and tarnished, but *home*. His months in New York drained the city of both its romance and its power to intimidate. From its mean crowded streets, shabby offices, and hollow parlors, Thoreau had finally seen what he'd said before but not quite believed: Concord truly was his Rome, its citizens his Romans. "Defeat is heaven's success," he told himself once. Abroad he'd met only defeat. Now it was time to see if success resided at home.

THE ROAD TO WALDEN

Thoreau plunged into life in Concord with renewed energy and vigor. In the heat of the New York summer, he'd longed for "those walks in the woods in ancient days—too sacred to be idly remembered," and now he was back on sacred ground. "Yesterday I skated after a fox over the ice," who cantered before him at top speed until he sat on his haunches as if spellbound "and barked at me like a young wolf." The spell bound Thoreau as well—it cheered him to see any wild nature, a "free forest life" far in advance of the courts and the pulpits.[96]

Yet the home he had known was gone forever. In January 1842, town leaders lobbied hard to divert the Boston-Fitchburg railroad through Concord. By late April 1843, even as Thoreau was packing to leave, the great "Locomotive Demon" filled the Concord woods with engineers and Irish railroad workers. In June Emerson warned Thoreau, "The town is full of Irish & the woods of engineers with theodolite & red flag singing out their feet & inches to each other from station to station." By August, silent meadows unvisited since Concord's founding were swarming with laborers straining with work, and by September Emerson was fretting that "the humanity of the town suffers with the poor Irish who receives but 60 or even 50 cents for working from dark till dark."[97] A village of Irish shanties crowded Walden's shore, and everywhere on the forest paths one encountered laborers, "explosions all day, & now & then a painful accident," excused with vague promises of what the railroad would "do & undo for the town hereafter." By September the deep cut from Walden to the new depot was eighteen feet high and going forward at two rods a day. "So that you see our fate is sealed," reported Emerson. For his part, he hadn't yet advertised his house for sale, but he feared the railroad would soon drive him away. Thoreau teased his sister Sophia: "I hope *you* will not be washed away by the Irish sea."[98]

Thoreau had observed the immigrants on the streets of New York with sympathy and interest: Norwegian farmers carrying their tools, English factory workers seeking a little sun and wind, sunburned families cooking dinner on the pavement. His friends and family fretted on about the invading Irish until Thoreau finally silenced them: "The sturdy Irish arms that do the work are of more worth than oak or maple. Methinks I could look with equanimity upon a long street of Irish cabins and pigs and children reveling in the genial Concord dirt, and I should still find my Walden wood and Fair Haven in their tanned and happy faces."[99] Hawthorne, at least, found his Walden there: on an October stroll he was charmed to find "a little hamlet of huts or shanties" built on Walden's prettiest cove, Irish houses of rough boards with earth heaped to the roof, forming "small natural hillocks" tucked among the trees as naturally as anthills or squirrels' nests. But reared up against the picturesque hamlet was the "torment" of "the great, high, ugly embankment of the rail-road," thrusting right into the pure Walden water. Margaret Fuller, too, who visited Thoreau in September, alerted him that "the cottages of the Irish laborers look pretty just now but their railroad looks foreign to Concord." What indeed would the new railroad "do & undo"? Everyone worried and hoped.[100]

Yet the mechanic who'd invented a better pencil was hardly anti-technology. That spring Thoreau was working again in the family pencil factory: their pencils had been selling well enough, but they were still gritty, and the grading from hard to soft needed refinement. The square lead annoyed him, too—to sharpen evenly, a pencil lead should be cylindrical. To tackle the first problem, Thoreau further refined their milling process that used an air current to lift out only the finest graphite powder, a secret process that placed the Thoreaus at the head of American graphite manufacture.[101] The second problem was harder: the old way was to cut a square groove into the pencil casing, fill it with lead paste, and glue on the cap. After long days experimenting with machinery, Thoreau dreamed all night of wheels and gears.[102] Finally he figured out how to turn out a round wooden case, drill a hole in it halfway (to leave a handle and avoid wasting graphite), extrude the graphite lead as a perfectly sized cylinder, and insert the hardened lead into the drilled hole. It's unclear if his new machine was practical for scaled-up production—the few surviving Thoreau pencils all have square leads—but they may have produced a few. For the Thoreaus now made pencils of every variety—fancy drawing pencils and common pencils "of every quality and price," "Mammoth" round and "Rulers, or flat," in a bewildering array of packaging and labels—a pencil for every need.

By the middle of May 1844, Henry Thoreau had a new and improved pencil ready for testing. Emerson sent some to an artist friend: Did she agree they were as good as the English drawing pencils? Yes, she replied: "excellent,—worthy of Concord art & artists and indeed one of the best productions I ever saw from there." She would certainly recommend them to all her friends, and hoped "to destroy great numbers of them myself—Is there one softer than S—a SS. well as H.H.?"[103] By June the Thoreaus had testimonials from the scientist Charles T. Jackson (Lidian's brother), who recommended the harder pencils to engineers for their fine, even points, and from a Boston artist and engraver who pronounced them the best made in America and the equal of any made in London. The Thoreaus printed up these shining endorsements into a showy advertising flyer and started entering contests: in 1847, the Massachusetts Charitable Mechanic Association awarded a diploma to "John Thoreau and Son" for their lead pencils, and in 1849 the Salem Charitable Mechanic Association awarded them a silver medal.[104] At her Boston bookstore, Elizabeth Peabody sold fine Thoreau pencils for 75 cents a dozen. For a time, one could have purchased there both writings by Henry Thoreau and a "John Thoreau and Son" pencil with which to mark them.

→>-<←

"Henry will never be a writer," Ellery Channing scoffed to Emerson; "he is as active as a shoemaker."[105] Yet even as he was dreaming of wheels and gears, Thoreau was staking out his principles for poetry. His newest essay at first sounded exactly like Emerson—"A man bears a poem as naturally as the oak bears an acorn, and the vine a gourd"—but soon he added a Thoreauvian twist: the true poet "weaves into his verse the planet and the stubble." Works of *true* genius (like his own?) will not be varnished and gilded but "rough-hewn from the first" with an "ingrained polish, which still appears when fragments are broken off, an essential quality of its substance. Its beauty is at the same time its strength, and it breaks with a luster." Poetry, it turns out, is not at all like an acorn or a gourd, but exactly like an arrowhead knapped from stone, which, like the ideal poem, "anticipates the lapse of time"—a fossil with a blade sharp as steel.[106]

Edged tools, edged words: Wendell Phillips was on his way back to Concord. Once again, John Keyes rose to protest, asserting that Phillips's previous address was "vile, pernicious, and abominable" and that he should be allowed back only if he spoke on a nonpolitical topic. The lyceum curators held firm, and on January 18, 1844, Phillips's treasonous words again held his Concord audience rapt. Furious, Keyes and Samuel Hoar called a meeting of the town at the First Parish Church, where they offered a resolution condemning Phillips, that arrogant "stripling" who had captivated the "silly" and ignorant women of Concord. Someone tipped off Phillips, who waited quietly in the back pew until the town fathers had finished. He then stood and addressed the assembly: "Stripling as I am, I but echo the voice of ages, of our venerated fathers, of statesman, poet, philosopher. The last gentleman has painted the danger to life, liberty, and happiness that would be the consequence of doing right. That state of things is now legalized at the South." Yet "our pulpits are silent." Who had ever heard this terrible truth, before the alarm was raised by "the silly women and striplings?" The whole affair was reported in the *Liberator*. Barzillai Frost huffed that Phillips must have bewitched all the women of Concord.[107]

If the women of Concord were bewitched, then Henry Thoreau lived in the very heart of the coven. Helen Thoreau was vice president of the Concord Female Anti-Slavery Society. Her earnest, intelligent, and deeply moral voice had always weighed heavily with Henry, who returned home to find a new album displayed in the family parlor: Helen had clipped and assembled a compendium of antislavery articles from abolitionism's most radical periodicals— the *Liberator*, the *Herald of Freedom*, the *National Anti-Slavery Standard*—pasting them into an old accounting ledger from Charleston, South Carolina, covering over the shameful records of slave commerce with tales of the nationwide struggle for freedom and equality. Her brother, paging through it, must have lingered appreciatively over Lydia Maria Child's "Letters from New York," for she, too, had seen the "hollow glazed life" of the city, the "discouragement, desperation, crime, and suicide" written on "the anxious, care-worn faces" of its streets.[108] There on those same streets Henry had met and measured the era's most brilliant reformers: W. H. Channing, Brisbane, Greeley, Henry James. He'd watched Alcott and Lane found their utopian society and watched it collapse; he'd crossed swords with the Fourierists as they took over Brook Farm; he'd denounced their fantasies of social engineering in the pages of the nation's leading reform periodical. It was time to speak up.

In mid-February, Emerson gave him some pointers: stand up to your audience and paint your thought "in fire." Just the week before, while giving a speech in Boston, Emerson had felt how the power of his eloquence awakened the assembly, beckoned the "Ghost" of their deep craving. But Thoreau was suspicious of rhetoric; he refused to perceive how "natural" was eloquence, and only heard "the word Art in a sinister sense." No wonder: what Emerson's lecture, "The Young American," had painted in fire was the glory of technological expansion from sea to shining sea. "The bountiful continent is ours, state on state, and territory on territory, to the waves of the Pacific sea," he had trumpeted. "Railroad iron is a magician's rod, in its power to evoke the sleeping energies of land and water." Sinister? This was a virtual paraphrase of Etzler, the same false art and triumphant industrial fantasy Thoreau had parodied in the *Democratic Review*. O'Sullivan himself would give this ideology a catchy new name: Manifest Destiny.[109]

A month later it was Thoreau's turn. He'd been invited to present a two-part lecture in Boston's Armory Hall, joining a stellar series of reformers including Garrison, Lane, Phillips, Adin Ballou (cofounder of the American Non-Resistance Society), and Emerson himself, who had just given "New England Reformers." There, Emerson mocked the two extremes of reform: proud dissenters and "solitary nullifiers" who spoke only for "this kingdom of me"; and communal members who lowered themselves "to the humble certainties of the association." For his part, Emerson had struck and stood on the middle ground by defending the individual who speaks divine truth, such as Phillips: "We exclaim, 'There's a traitor in the house!' but at last it appears that he is the true man, and I am the traitor." As Emerson added, Phillips marked the only path to true reform, which was to surrender to divine genius: "Obedience to his genius is the only liberating influence. . . . We drink water, we eat grass, we refuse the laws, we go to jail: it is all in vain."[110]

Now, for the first time in public, Thoreau drew the line: as a proud dissenter and a solitary nullifier himself, who had seen two close friends refuse the laws and go to jail, he, too, stood with the "traitor" Phillips—but he lashed out at Emerson's temperate middle ground, his insinuation that his friends' actions were "all in vain." Extremism? "I know of few radicals as yet who are radical enough," Thoreau countered; they meddle with "the roots of innocent institutions" and never their *own* roots. He had said the same thing to Helen right after meeting with William Henry Channing and his Associationist friends: "They want faith, and mistake their private ail for an infected atmosphere; but let any one of them recover hope for a moment, and right his *particular* grievance, and he will no longer train in that company."[111] Now he turned those words against his Boston audience. If anything ails a man, what does he do? He sets about reforming the world. Do ye hear it, ye Woloffs, ye Patagonians, ye Tartars, ye Nez Percés? The world is going to be reformed, formed once for all. Presto—Change! Methinks I hear the glad tidings spreading over the green prairies of the west; over the silent South American pampas, parched African deserts, and stretching Siberian versts; through the populous Indian and Chinese villages, along the Indus, the Ganges, and Hydaspes.

But turn the tables, he challenges: Do you really believe in community? Then give us actions, not mere words: deeds speak louder than rhetoric.

The audience (did he meet their eyes here?) knows full well, Thoreau continued, that "the speaker does not mean to abolish property or dissolve the family tie, or do without human governments all over the world to-night, but that simply, he has agreed to be the speaker and—they have agreed to be the audience." You all know the lecturer who speaks against money is being paid for his words—and *that's* the lesson you remember.[112] Against such hollow words, only real action—real, not symbolic or rhetorical—can produce real progress. Don't go to another committee meeting, gavel down another pointless set of resolutions, and adjourn for tea. Dig down to your own roots, and figure out how, radically, you must change your life.

This was new. Thoreau was looking not to Emerson but to Wendell Phillips and Frederick Douglass, men of moral action, as well as Nathaniel P. Rogers, the fiery editor of the New Hampshire *Herald of Freedom*. The *Dial* had just one more issue to go, and for his final contribution, Thoreau wrote an homage to Rogers, whose words flowed "like his own mountain-torrents, now clear and sparkling, now foaming and gritty, and always spiced with the essence of the fir and Norway pine." Into the timid pages of Emerson's *Dial* Thoreau threw great chunks of Rogers's righteous "war-whoop": "Slavery must be cried down, denounced down, ridiculed down, and pro-slavery with it," wrote Rogers. "Down, then, with the bloody system, out of the land with it, and out of the world with it,—into the Red Sea with it." You say this is all fanaticism? *"Wait and see."*[113] Rogers was thrilled with Thoreau's review. Where had this radical new voice come from?, he asked in the next *Herald of Freedom*. "Probably a German. He cannot have written much in this country, or his name would have reached me, from no farther off than Concord, Mass." Write more! he begged of the unknown author.[114] Alas, Rogers died in 1846, before they could meet and before he could read Thoreau's own great antislavery writings.

The end of the "felon Dial," which had stolen so much of Emerson's time, was a liberation. He had continued it for others, and it was time they went off "to write in their own names," leaving him free to finish his next book: *Essays, Second Series*.[115] Several *Dial* writers did go on to fame, if not fortune: Alcott published volumes of poetry and reflections, and Margaret Fuller expanded her groundbreaking essay "The Great Lawsuit" into the book *Woman in the Nineteenth Century*, the foundation of the women's rights movement in the United States. And Thoreau? That October he opened Emerson's new book to read "The Poet," his mentor's seminal statement on American poetry. Walt Whitman said he'd been simmering, simmering, simmering, until this essay brought him to a boil; when Emerson received his copy of *Leaves of Grass*, he dropped everything and wrote to Whitman, "I greet you at the beginning of a great career." For Thoreau there would be no such giddy annunciation. Late in life Thoreau told Franklin Sanborn that after Emerson criticized his poetry, he burned it. No ashes survive to corroborate the tale, but the story rings true. If true, the most likely date was late 1844, after the *Dial* ended and after Thoreau received his inscribed copy of Emerson's new book. There, near the close of "The Poet," he found Emerson's crushing words: "I look in vain for the poet whom I describe."[116]

→>-<+

While Emerson was finishing his new book, Thoreau was getting outdoors. April 1844 had been spectacularly warm and dry, and one fine April morning Thoreau and Edward Hoar—Samuel Hoar's son, about to graduate from Harvard—set off to follow the Concord River to its sources, camping and fishing along the way. After catching a nice mess of fish that morning, they rowed to Fairhaven Bay and landed in the northeast corner, by Well Meadow Brook, to kindle a fire on a stump and cook them up for dinner. Thoreau had built countless campfires since his childhood picnics with Cynthia, but this time the flames caught the dry grass around the stump and flared out of control. A warm, dry southwest wind fanned the fire straight up the notch behind them like a bellows. "Where will this end?" cried Hoar in dismay. "It will go to town!" wailed Thoreau as "the demonic creature to which we had given birth" raced uphill, "leaping & crackling wildly and irreclaimably toward the wood." Hoar rowed off to sound the alarm while Thoreau tore through the woods toward town. The first farmer he met refused his help— "Well, said he, it is none of my stuff"—but the next ran back to the fire with Thoreau, past a woodcutter fleeing with his axe. While the farmer ran back to town, Thoreau, exhausted, collapsed. "What could I do alone against a front of flame half a mile wide?"[117]

Thoreau would not write his account of the debacle until 1850, after he'd been helping farmers set brushfires to clear the woods. They showed him the right way to do it: "You must burn against the wind always & burn slowly." But that day back in 1844, the fire had burned with the wind, and fast. Thoreau recalled walking ahead of it to the highest rock on Fairhaven Cliff and watching it approach until it almost swallowed him. By then the town was arriving in force. For the rest of the day he fought the fire with his neighbors, surrounding the flames, cutting trenches with hoes and shovels, setting back-fires. Now, recalling this six years later, Thoreau suggested the town form a volunteer fire department of forty or fifty men who, at an alarm sounded on a drum, would cart to the scene hoes and shovels, kept specially for the purpose since neighbors refused to lend their own tools for fear of losing them, and fight fires in an orderly way directed by an experienced captain.[118] His suggestion made sense: by 1850, when Thoreau finally confronted his actions in the 1844 fire, wildfires were a constant problem, sparked by railroad engines along the tracks. Already the very land Thoreau had burned once had burned a second time. Throughout the 1850s he studied with special care the effects of fire and regrowth on Concord's pine-oak ecology, which, he discovered, was actually the product of frequent fires, some natural, some set by Native Americans who for hundreds of years had managed the forest with controlled burns.

But none of this helped Thoreau face up to the memory of that terrible day. One witness remembered that "people blamed Thoreau's carelessness but thought well of him for coming at once to say what he had done" and for helping them fight the flames.[119] But others were far less generous, calling Thoreau "a 'damned rascal,'" and for years afterward, some would taunt him by hiding and shouting "Burnt Woods" at his back. The farmer who'd said it was "none of his stuff" lost sixty cords of wood he'd cut and stacked to sell. His daughter never forgave Thoreau: "Don't talk to me about Henry Thoreau," she used to say. "Didn't I all that winter have to go to school with a smootched apron or dress because I had to pitch in and help fill the wood box with partly charred wood?" The *Concord Freeman* scolded "the thoughtlessness of two of our citizens," but also pointed out the fire was "mainly confined to the young wood, underbrush, and leaves," so it appeared "more destructive than it really was." The newspaper estimated 300 acres were burned—an exaggeration, for the woodland in that part of town was roughly 150 acres in extent, closer to Thoreau's own estimate of a hundred acres or more. And despite Thoreau's panicked exclamation, the fire could not have reached town, for the woods stopped far short of any buildings.[120]

But the damage was real and lasting. The newspaper set the financial loss at about $2,000—a huge sum—and there was talk of prosecution. Had Thoreau been alone or with anyone other than Samuel Hoar's son, he might have faced charges in court; but once again Concord's leading citizen smoothed things over by quietly paying damages to the injured. The harm to the woods was soon forgotten, but the harm to Thoreau's reputation lived on. Long after his death, when the 1850 confession buried deep in his unpublished Journal was unearthed and reprinted in the *Atlantic*, the jeers resumed: The icon of woodcraft, so careless he burned down the woods! The saint of environmental protection, scorching the earth! The town ne'er-do-well, off fishing when he should have been earning a living!

The damage to Thoreau's own psyche was also real and lasting. Not only did it take him six years to confess, but when he did, his own words convicted him of the profound remorse he denied. Watching the fire advance, perched helpless and alone on Fairhaven Cliff, he "felt like a guilty person—nothing but shame and regret." But the instant the alarm bell told him the town was on its way, he turned prickly and defensive: "Who are these men who are said to be the owners of these woods & how am I related to them? I have set fire to the forest—but I have done no wrong therein—& now it is as if the lightning had done it.... So shortly I settled it with myself & stood to watch the approaching flames. It was a glorious spectacle & I was the only one there to enjoy it." Of course this rings hollow emotionally, but there's a certain truth here. From the perspective of the woods, Thoreau's destructive agency was indeed as natural as the lightning and impersonal as the railroad, setting off a course of regeneration that was part of this forest's normal ecological cycle, clearing away dead leaves and undergrowth, releasing nutrients back into the soil and activating the cycle of regeneration known as forest succession.

From that day forward, Thoreau knew a truth few others fully understand: human beings are not separate from nature but fully involved in natural cycles, agents who trigger change and are vulnerable to the changes they trigger. That night, Thoreau wandered through "the blackened waste . . . far in the night," threading his way back to the stump where he started the fire. There were the fish, scattered over the burnt grass, perfectly broiled. For the rest of his life he returned to these same woods relentlessly, over and over again, and what he saw astounded him: "In the spring I burned over a hundred acres till the earth was sere and black—& by mid-summer this space was clad in a fresher & more luxuriant green than the surrounding even. Shall man then despair? Is he not a sproutland too after never so many searings & witherings?"[121] Thoreau could never forget that he, too, was a fallen man—he, too, was a son of

Adam. And nature, unaccountably and miraculously, forgave him, even when his neighbors would not.

+>-<+

One friend never wavered in his loyalty: Ellery Channing, still living in Concord with Ellen and their newborn baby girl. Channing had business in New York that summer and agreed to meet Thoreau afterward in Pittsfield, in western Massachusetts near the Hudson River. In mid-July, Thoreau set off alone and on foot, with a staff and a pilgrim's knapsack holding a few books and a change of clothes, to climb the weathered, rocky peak of New Hampshire's Mount Monadnock.[122] After a night on the summit, he headed southwest to Mount Greylock, or "Saddleback Mountain," eighty miles away. He tramped over the hills for days, stopping to pick berries or eat a loaf of bread purchased at a farmer's house, followed the Connecticut River south, then turned west up Deerfield River through valleys that rose higher and higher, until he crossed the Hoosac Range to drop to the valley below and ascend Greylock, tracking up the long notch called "the Bellows" for the wildness of the wind that rushed through it during storms.

Thunder rumbled at his heels as he climbed, but the storm passed off. When the trail veered right, Thoreau followed his compass straight ahead to the summit, "the shorter and more adventurous way." At one house he met a young woman who was "busily and unconcernedly combing her long black hair while she talked, [giving] her head the necessary toss with each sweep of the comb, with lively, sparkling eyes, and full of interest in that lower world from which I had come."[123] Tempted to linger, instead he followed his compass through dense undergrowth of mountain laurel, then through scraggly trees, then above the treeline to the summit. Desperate for water, he drank dry the tiny puddles pooled in horse tracks, "a pure, cold, spring-like water." He made a campsite, cooked up his supper of rice, and read scraps of newspaper by firelight into the night, which was so cold he covered himself in old boards from the ruins of the observatory tower.

Dawn found him surrounded by an ocean of mist reaching precisely to the base of the tower, "left floating on this fragment of the wreck of a world, on my carved plank in cloudland." It was, he wrote, "a favor for which to be forever silent to be shown this vision." As the sun rose and gilded the mist, he wavered: Could he return to the house of the woman with the long black hair? Instead he felt called by the summits of the yet higher mountains westward. Down he went into the clouds and drizzling rain, where Channing waited at the Pittsfield station. He looked, thought Channing, like a bum. "He had no shirt-collar perceptible, carried a small leather wallet belonging to the late Charles Emerson on his back and looked as if he had slept out in the fields, as he was unshaven & drest very poorly."[124] They spent the night "before the mast and on the deck of the world"—or more prosaically, on the open deck of a steamboat down the Hudson to Albany—Thoreau standing entranced at the prow, watching "the moonlight amid the mountains." Another passenger took him for a deckhand and elbowed him: "Come now, can't ye lend me a chaw o' baccy?" Later Channing chuckled to see him walking the deck past fine gentlemen and ladies, "eating upon a half loaf of bread, his dinner for the day."[125]

In the Catskills they passed an elegant tourist resort (famed later as the Mountain House) to spend the night at a sawmiller's by Kaaterskill Falls. Thoreau remembered not the famous falls—higher than Niagara and more wild—but the unplastered house, clean and airy with all the music of the Catskills sweeping through its aisles. He dreamed of living in just such a house, somewhere on his own high mountain tarn.[126] In the Southern Berkshires they stopped at Bash Bish Falls, then walked thirty miles to Chester, boarded the Western Railroad to Framingham, and walked north, trudging into Concord early on August first. Thoreau had been gone for weeks, measuring the land from Concord to Monadnock in the north, then to Greylock far in the west: now his feet knew the breadth of Massachusetts, step by step. It had been a test of his physical endurance, his resourcefulness alone, his inner reserves of strength, and of his literary reserves as well. Walking was becoming synonymous with writing, the measure of his steps with the measure of his prose. Thoreau's first great excursion never made it into a separate essay, but out of it came many rich and lyrical pages.

They reached Concord just in time to celebrate the tenth anniversary of the emancipation of the slaves in the British West Indies, which called for a gala event. That May, Concord's delegates to the Anti-Slavery Convention in Boston, including Cynthia, Helen, and Sophia Thoreau, had demanded the "dissolution of the Union," refusing to obey a Constitution that empowered slaveholders. Two weeks later, Frederick Douglass returned to Concord, and Helen Thoreau, as secretary, recorded the angry antislavery meeting where the town fathers, led by Rev. Barzillai Frost, condemned the Disunionists. Douglass fired back, and the women rose in defiance to sing their anthem: "no union with slaveholders you followers of the free." Hardly had the meeting ended when they were planning an even bigger one: by August 1, the railroad would be open; it could bring crowds from the city to Concord. The *Liberator* got busy imploring those crowds to come while the organizers recruited the speakers—Douglass, of course, but also, astonishingly, Emerson himself. Up to this moment he had withheld all support for organized abolitionism.[127]

When Thoreau arrived for the gala kickoff, everything was chaos. Crowds were pouring in, but there was nowhere to meet: a furious Reverend Frost had slammed shut the doors of the First Parish Church, and the Trinitarians closed theirs as well. Nathaniel and Sophia Hawthorne offered the great lawn behind the Old Manse, but a sudden summer rainstorm had everyone running for shelter. Visitors mobbed the courthouse, but who would ring the First Parish bell to call the town? The sexton refused, and five or six others milled about, afraid to touch the bellrope without permission. Thoreau, "not an hour home from his journey," pushed his way through, seized the rope "with a strong arm," and the bell "pealed forth its summons right merrily."[128] The audience assembled at the courthouse, where Emerson rose and delivered a two-and-a-half-hour speech, his first antislavery address and one of his greatest. Margaret Fuller, listening, cried for joy: Emerson had finally taken a stand. Transcendentalism's energies were reaching out into the world. Thoreau, too, took up the cause, printing and distributing Emerson's speech, signing himself "agent for the Society"—that is, the Concord Female Anti-Slavery Society.[129] More and more he aligned himself with abolitionism, not by formal membership, but by his words and deeds.

At home that night, Thoreau found a most intriguing letter waiting for him. Earlier that spring, the young religious seeker Isaac Hecker, having left Brook Farm with a pause at Fruitlands, alighted in Concord to study with fellow Brook Farmer George Bradford.[130] Hecker moved in with the Thoreaus, and over the next two months, he and Henry became friends. Indeed, Hecker wished he were studying under Thoreau instead, for he had "a better knowledge of languages," taking real "delight" in them, and more leisure, too. Like his mentor Brownson, Hecker was drawn to Catholicism; now, back home in New York on the eve of his baptism in the Roman Catholic Church, he wrote Thoreau with a grand, crazy idea: Come with me to Europe. "Let us take a walk over the fairest portion of the planet Earth and make it ours. . . . We shall prove the dollar is not almighty and the impossible moonshine. The wide world is before us beckoning us to come let us accept and embrace it."[131]

Thoreau hesitated. He knew from walking across Massachusetts that this was the way to see the world. But, he finally told Hecker, he needed something else now, not a "wanderjahr" but "a kind of Brahminical Artesian, Inner Temple, life."[132] Channing thought Thoreau was crazy to say no, and Hecker pleaded that only Thoreau could be his companion on such a heroic quest. Thoreau wavered again, stirred by the sheer romance of it. "*Far* travel very *far* travel or travail, comes near to the worth of staying at home," he replied. "If you don't go soon," he added, write me again. He literally could not bear to say no.[133] But he couldn't say yes, either, and in 1845 Hecker set off to Europe without him. Two years later he returned and founded the Paulist Order, becoming, with Brownson himself, one of the nation's great Catholic intellectuals.

When Thoreau pushed past his timid neighbors to ring the church bell, an observer concluded this man must be "the general Scapegoat" of the town. Indeed, that "damned rascal" Thoreau found alienation oddly liberating: "What demon possessed me that I behaved so well?"[134] Once, he'd been the good striving son; now he was the ragged seeker with knapsack and pilgrim's staff, the town conscience, the gadfly who would sting them into awareness. "Henry is a good substantial childe, not encumbered with himself," wrote Emerson about this time; he "lives extempore, & brings today a new proposition as radical & revolutionary as that of yesterday, but different. The only man of leisure in the town." Like all the other "grand promisers," Thoreau, too, had fizzled out, but at least he hadn't sold out. "With his practical faculty, he has declined all the kingdoms of this world. Satan has no bribe for him." For his part, Thoreau told Emerson that not this world but "the other world was all his art; that his pencils would draw no other; that his jackknife would cut nothing else."[135]

The path before him was coming clear; he knew exactly where he needed to go. All he needed now was the means.

PART TWO

THE MAKING OF WALDEN

CHAPTER FIVE

"Walden, Is It You?"

(1845–1847)

Why, here is Walden, the same woodland lake that I discovered so
many years ago. . . . I can almost say, Walden, is it you?
HENRY DAVID THOREAU, *WALDEN*

PREPARATIONS

Emerson was right: the railroad changed everything. Once passenger service opened in June 1844, running four trains daily from sunrise to dusk, Concord would forever be a Boston suburb. The tracks curved northward just enough to graze the southwest edge of Concord village, opening up a commuter rail hub centered on the new Concord Depot. Overnight the nearby farm fields were being platted and sold as house lots—new lands for the landless, including John and Cynthia Thoreau. After six years renting the Parkman House, it was time, thought Cynthia, to move into their own home.

John was skeptical, but Cynthia prevailed. She selected a three-quarter-acre lot by the tracks, in the bare fields of what everyone jokingly called "Texas," after the barren, faraway, and disputed territory dominating the headlines. Cynthia arranged to buy one of Concord's solid, well-built houses and have it moved onto the site—common practice then, which saved immense sums in labor and conserved scarce wood.[1] On September 10, John Thoreau paid $25 to the developer of the farmland. Two days later, he mortgaged the property for $500 to pay for the house and supplies.[2] Henry got to

work digging and stoning the cellar, helping the carpenter with reno-
vations, banking the house, and setting out an orchard's worth of
apples.[3] With the Irish workers moving up the line, Sam Staples was
auctioning off the vacant railroad shanties; the Thoreaus recycled a
couple into a pencil factory and shop behind the house. Early in 1849
Henry would survey for the new road out front, eventually named
Belknap Street after one of the railroad developers, but the house
would always be known as the "Texas House." The Thoreaus moved
in sometime early in 1845 and lived there until 1850. Even after they
moved back to Main Street, they held on to the Texas House, renting it to newcomers. Near the end of his life, Henry, who was always
fond of the place, boasted that he'd harvested nearly eleven barrels
of apples from the trees he'd planted there fourteen years before.[4]

Land speculators were eyeing Walden Woods, too. Late in September 1844, Emerson celebrated turning in the final proofs of *Essays:
Second Series* by taking a walk to Walden Pond. There he ran into
several men bidding on Wyman Field, an overgrown patch alongside
Walden Road with a side road running through it to Walden's shore.
One thing led to another, and Emerson walked home the owner of
eleven acres of briar patch, at $8.10 an acre. The next day his friends
pointed out the briar patch was worthless without the neighboring
pine grove, which the owner surely would cut soon, so Emerson
bought three or four more acres for $125—more expensive thanks
to the timber. Thus Emerson became "landlord & waterlord of 14
acres, more or less, on the shore of Walden," just the place to build
"a cabin or a turret there high as the tree-tops, and spend my nights
as well as days in the midst of a beauty which never fades from me."[5]
Now he had land fever: he thought of building a cottage for Lucy
Brown near his house, and buying a farm for Ellery Channing, who
was pining away in New York City working for the *New-York Tribune*,
plus buying a little more Walden for himself. A year later, Emerson
purchased another forty acres rising from Walden's farther shore to
the heights everyone took to calling "Emerson's Cliff." From there
he could see Monadnock to the north, Wachusett to the west, and
the Sudbury River below—perfect, thought Bronson Alcott, for

"a poet's lodge," where Emerson could retreat "with book and pen when good hours come."[6]

The idea was not new. Thoreau had dreamed of living in a cabin by a pond ever since his idyllic summer with Wheeler, reading and writing in a shanty overlooking Flint's Pond—a dream he shared with Margaret Fuller as far back as the autumn of 1841.[7] Summerhouses, writer's shanties, and wilderness retreats were all the rage: in December 1843, even as Thoreau was packing up on Staten Island, his city friends Giles Waldo and William Tappan were packing up to move into a log cabin deep in the upstate New York wilderness. Undeterred by December's snows, they planned to hunt and live off the land and, as Emerson optimistically wrote Fuller, "in that wild boundless country" find words for their dreams. It didn't turn out quite that way. The log cabin proved so cold and drafty they couldn't write at all. Waldo's feet were frostbitten, and Tappan huddled so close to the fire that he burned his feet and had to find a doctor. Their bold experiment collapsed after a mere six weeks.[8] No wonder, wrote Charles Lane, still stinging from the collapse of Fruitlands: "The experiment of a true wilderness life by a white person" could be nothing more than an "interesting dream. He is not born for it; he is not natured for it." For true progress to the soul, one must "look in some other, some new direction."[9]

Ellery Channing thought he had found that new direction. At the end of April 1845, tired of stewing away in New York City, he laid out six hundred dollars for a farm on Concord's Punkatasset Hill. That September, he moved in with his family. To his bachelor friend Thoreau, he suggested something similar: "I see nothing for you in this earth but that field which I once christened 'Briars'; go out upon that, build yourself a hut, & there begin the grand process of devouring yourself alive. I see no alternative, no other hope for you. Eat yourself up; you will eat nobody else, nor anything else."[10] Thoreau talked it over with Emerson. He had found a site on Flint's Pond, but Flint had denied him permission to build. Now here was another chance. Sometime early in 1845 they shook hands: Thoreau, not Emerson, would build his "poet's lodge" by Walden's shore. Thoreau—who no doubt reminded Channing that farms are more easily acquired than gotten rid of—was content to claim nothing more than squatter's rights. In exchange, he agreed to clear and plant the cultivable land and sell his house back to Emerson, who meanwhile would build his own poet's lodge high on the cliff. Thoreau obligingly drew up some plans for him, to which Alcott added his own design for a tower.[11] There was room enough in the wide woods for each of them to forge his own way.

While these schemes went forward, Thoreau labored on, finishing up the Texas House and some fresh essays, too. Once again abolitionism was roiling the town, though now the fight was getting personal. Late in November 1844, Samuel Hoar traveled to Charleston, South Carolina, as the official emissary from Massachusetts, charged with lodging a formal protest against South Carolina's practice of incarcerating free black citizens of Massachusetts who docked in Charleston's port. Anticipating a peaceful diplomatic mission, he brought his daughter Elizabeth, Thoreau's friend and a virtual sister to Emerson; she planned to visit family friends. The moment they stepped ashore, lawmakers ordered Hoar to cease his hostile actions and leave immediately. When he refused, Governor Hammond permitted mob violence to escalate until, after a terrifying week, the Hoars were forced bodily into a carriage to a northbound ship. Back home, they told and retold their story of harassment and expulsion until Concord burned with fury. Even the cool Reverend Frost erupted, penning vengeful resolutions "so fiercely redolent of disunion, independency, and Massachusetts dignity, so sadly blood and thunderous" that the committee in charge of the town meeting at first refused to read them aloud.[12] Emerson, too, flirted with disunion and darkly meditated retaliation. Though the conservative Hoar tried to tamp down the angry talk, the town's radicals were quick to seize the moment. The lyceum curators must invite Wendell Phillips for a third time, to give the town some hard truth about slavery and Texas annexation.

Curator Samuel Barrett agreed, and at the end of February he put Phillips's name forward to the lyceum. For the third time a Keyes stormed to his feet to protest—this time John Shepard Keyes, Thoreau's eternal rival and John Keyes's son, who was determined to carry on his deceased father's conservative legacy. Keyes was joined by Reverend Frost, still simmering from his humiliation at Phillips' hands the year before. Keyes and Frost were outvoted, 21 to 15. What happened next was nothing less than a coup: the conservatives—Keyes, Frost, and the lyceum president, Mr. Cheney—all resigned on the spot. The lyceum membership hastily voted in an all-progressive slate of curators: Barrett, Emerson, and Thoreau (who declined). Emerson tore off a scrap of paper and scrawled an urgent invitation to Phillips. Someone rushed it to him in Boston, and five days later, on March 11, Wendell Phillips mounted Concord's lyceum podium, this time to warn of the danger Texas annexation posed: admitting a new slave state would give proslavery forces a permanent majority in Congress, dashing all hope for the abolition of slavery by legal means. One woman, noted Thoreau, walked five miles through snow to hear Phillips speak. Emerson said he'd "not learned a better lesson in many weeks than last night in a couple of hours."[13]

Twice before, Thoreau had listened to Phillips but kept silent. This third time he spoke, preparing a long and spirited defense of Phillips, which he mailed to the *Liberator* the next morning and which Garrison published, anonymously, on March 28, 1845. How refreshing, wrote Thoreau, to hear not "'God save the Commonwealth of Massachusetts,' but God dash it into a thousand pieces," leaving not a single fragment big enough to bear a man who dares not speak his name. The man who could not speak his name was Frederick Douglass, who, as Phillips told his audience, was at that very moment "writing his life, and telling his name, and the name of his master, and the place he ran from." There in Concord, Thoreau wrote, under the very shadow of the monument to freedom ran the horrified whisper: "'He had better not!'"[14]

What Thoreau liked best in Wendell Phillips was "the freedom and steady wisdom, so rare in the reformer, with which he declared that he was not born to abolish slavery, but to do right." Back on the crowded streets of New York, Thoreau had asked when the world would learn "that a million men are of no importance compared with one man."[15] In Phillips Thoreau saw his "one man," righteous and eloquent, who, instead of collating the consensus of the million, deliberates and occupies his own solid moral ground "from which the varying tides of public opinion cannot drive him." It was easy to give one's assent to such a man—hadn't Thoreau just seen most of Concord doing so? But how could one do more? Thoreau didn't want to merely *hear* Phillips, waving his approval from the sidelines as the great leader passed by. He wanted to *be* Phillips, to stand alone before the million with just such dignity, courage, and integrity—to be, in words he would soon write, "a majority of one."[16]

Meanwhile, Thoreau had his own lyceum lecture to finish, two weeks after Phillips's. His subject, "Concord River," might seem to escape to nature rather than face the political heat, but Thoreau saw it as a turning toward his larger project, "to *do* right." In his view, slavery was not a single cause whose cure would solve everything; rather, it was one symptom of a larger sickness preying on a universe of beings, not all of them human. In the same notebook where he drafted his defenses of Phillips and Douglass, Thoreau also drafted his defense of Musketaquid's fish, driven out of their home by the Billerica Dam: "Mere shad armed only with innocence—and a just cause—I for one am with thee.—And—who knows—what may avail a crow bar against that Billerica dam!" No text survives of "Concord River," but the draft shows Thoreau's conviction that attention to the natural environment confronted the root of all political evil. In a memoir of his lecture, the local newspaper published Thoreau's words: "I had often stood on the banks of the Concord, watching the lapse of the current, an emblem of all progress, following the same law with the system, with time, and all that is made . . . and at last I resolved to launch myself on its bosom, and float whither it would bear me."[17] Douglass and Phillips told Thoreau that knowing the true "law" of the system and the right path to justice required deliberating his own moral ground. No person could tell him what that ground must be—this he had to learn alone.

It was the end of March, it was spring, and the river was flowing. It was time to launch. Henry Thoreau borrowed an axe, walked down to the woods beside Walden Pond, and began to build.

ON WALDEN POND: THE FIRST SEASON

Thoreau already knew where his house would be: nestled on a shoulder of land sloping down to the water, backed by Bigelow's pine grove and facing southeast to the morning sun, shaded by a large chestnut tree and "tall arrowy white pines." He cut down a few of those young pines and hewed them six inches square, leaving the bark on when he could, to make the timbers for his house; the studs he hewed on two sides only, and one side for the floorboards and rafters. There by the stumps he chiseled the mortises and sawed the tenons, fitting them so the joints would be tight and strong. At noon he rested amid the pine boughs strewn on the ground at his feet, eating his dinner of buttered bread spiced with the fragrance of fresh pitch on his hands and reading the newspaper wrappings with interest. When the curious came by, lured by the sound of his axe, he paused to chat over the pine chips. At first the pond was icy and the snow flurried around his strokes; but on April 1, the snow turned to fog and rain, and the last of the ice melted away. Every year from then on, Thoreau would watch and note down the date when Walden was ice free and open to the sky and wind.

Early in April Thoreau bargained with James Collins, an Irish railroad worker moving up the line, to buy his shanty. It was a hillock shanty, covered with dirt, likely one of the last remaining in the pretty Irish village between the railroad and the pond. A year later the ruins of that village, all overgrown with mullein, would strike awe in the Emerson children as they came to explore their father's land on Walden's far shore. Thoreau thought the dirt-insulated dwelling dank and "smotherish" inside, but he followed along as Mrs. Collins held her lamp high to show him that the boards were good and solid. The deal was struck. That evening he returned with their price of $4.25, and early the next morning he returned again to

take possession, meeting the Collins family on the road—one large
bundle holding their all, feather bed, silk parasol, gilt-framed mirror,
coffee mill, and hens. He dismantled the building and carted the
boards down the woodland path to the house site, where he cleaned
them and laid them to bleach in the sun.[18]

By early May, the frame was ready to be raised. Thoreau called his
friends to help. Emerson, Alcott, and Channing came, as did George
and Burrill Curtis, lately from Brook Farm, their friend Edmund
Hosmer, the "dreadful dissenter" from the farm over the hill, and
his strong sons John, Edmund, and Andrew. By then Thoreau had
dug his cellar, spading into the sandy soil through sumac and blackberry roots until he had a shelved hole six feet square and seven feet
deep—deep enough that potatoes would not freeze in any winter.[19]
For a king post, they set an entire tree into the cellar floor, reaching to the ridgepole above; with the frame raised up around it, the
house took shape. Thoreau finished the floor, with a trapdoor to the
cellar, and laid the chimney foundation on the end by the hillside,
hauling up cartloads of glacial cobblestone from the pond. Finally he
boarded and roofed his new house with Collins's good boards, planing them and feathering the edges so that, overlapped, they would
keep out the rain. The result was a light and airy house, ten feet by
fifteen, eight feet tall, and in move-in condition for summer weather.
Thoreau put off the finishing touches until fall, when he built the
chimney, shingled the roof and sides, and plastered the interior. His
weatherproof and insulated house would keep him warm in even
the coldest New England winter.

As spring advanced, Thoreau turned some of his attention to his
farm, hiring a team of oxen and a man to drive them. Together, holding the plough himself, they cut furrows into two and a half acres of
the "briar-patch" above the house near Walden Road, breaking apart
the blackberry vines, St. John's wort, and cinquefoil, "sweet wild
fruits & pleasant flowers." The ox team pulled out enough old stumps
to supply Thoreau, once he cut and stacked the wood, with most
of his fuel for two winters, fulfilling the driver's prophecy that the
stumpwood would warm him twice, once when he split it and again

when he burned it. Then he planted the light sandy soil with rows of white bush beans—seven miles in all, he calculated—mostly for the market, plus potatoes, peas, turnips, sweet corn and yellow corn, mostly for himself. Hosmer gave him the seed corn. The turnips and the yellow corn he planted too late, though he enjoyed feeding the unripe corn to the squirrels and birds. It was hard labor, he wrote, "making the earth say beans instead of grass," but "I come to love my rows—they attach me to the earth—and so I get new strength and health like Antaeus."[20] After each day's work at the pond, he walked home along the railroad tracks to the Texas House, a little over a mile away, where he was still putting in finishing touches.

This season Thoreau was writing not in words, but in deeds. The most symbolic of them approached as the calendar turned from spring to summer, when he borrowed a hayrick, loaded it with some carefully chosen books, writing supplies, and a few pieces of furniture—his green writing desk, a small table, three chairs, his cane bed—and drove to his new address on Walden Pond. "A good port and a good foundation," he would later write, from which to open trade with "the Celestial Empire."[21] It was Friday, the Fourth of July 1845—a cloudy day at first, but that afternoon, as Thoreau unpacked and arranged his new life, the sun came out and shone on his own personal declaration of independence.

The next morning Thoreau took out a fresh notebook and opened it with a flourish: "Yesterday I came here to live."[22] His "house," he continued, reminded him "of some mountain houses I have seen, which seemed to have a fresher auroral atmosphere about them"— like the miller's house at Kaaterskill Falls, high in the mountains, where he had stayed the year before. Such was his model: an airy mountaintop hall, open to the breeze, above quicksilver water where he could read the reflections of the sky or the writing of the winds. Here in this open shelter, he could reflect and write like a double of the pond, whom he addressed as a fellow: "True, our converse a stranger is to speech, / Only the practiced ear can catch the surging words, / That break and die upon thy pebbled lips." So he had written back in 1838, in his poem "Walden": it seemed all his life had directed him here, to this morning dawning on a vision he had cherished since childhood. "Walden, is it you?" he would ask in astonishment; in his notebook, his very handwriting bubbled into loops of ecstasy.[23]

Others have called the shelter on Walden's shores a cabin, hut, or shanty, but Thoreau almost always called it a house, insisting on the solidity and dignity he worked so hard to attain. As Emerson commented, "Cultivated people cannot live in a shanty."[24] Thoreau's whole experiment hinged on the distinction. Had he built only a "poet's lodge" for "the good hours," his move would have troubled no one; lots of people did that. But spending *all* his hours there made him a pioneer—not a Western one, but an inward one, "the enterprising and independent thinker, applying his discoveries to his own life." Outbuildings or vacation retreats only exercised a self already established. Thoreau wanted a house to embody a new self, so that building that house meant building that self, literally from the ground up. It was so small that "two was one too much," said Channing, after living there for two weeks that August. Really, it was a kind of "durable garment, an overcoat, he had contrived and left by Walden."[25] To Thoreau's family it looked dangerous, or at least uncomfortable. On his first night away, Cynthia and Sophia were so worried they tossed and turned until dawn. Cynthia packed up some food and Sophia brought it to her preoccupied brother. He "didn't like to receive it very well," she reported, and "the house seemed very bare of everything." They missed him at home.[26] Nevertheless, Henry's family supported him staunchly and agreed to let him carry out his "experiment" in his own way.

But why exactly did Thoreau go to Walden Pond? The question still lingers today. On one level, the answer is easy: he went there to write. As Waldo Emerson explained to his brother William, Henry had always had a room of his own, to write, to dream, "and always must." But now, instead of claiming a little space in a communal house, an alcove or attic, he would claim an entire life, and declare that writing would be not an occasional hobby but the central hub of his whole being. From now on, Thoreau would be a writer in an entirely new sense: instead of living a little, then writing about it, his life would be one single, integrated act of composition.

On his second full day at Walden, Thoreau put it to himself like this: "I wish to meet the facts of life—the vital facts . . . face to face, and so I came down here. Life! who knows what it is—what it does?"[27] This declaration of purpose has the force of a vow, a sacred commitment to confront, "face to face," the conditions of possibility for life itself. Hawthorne, that most acute of psychological analysts, had previously observed that Thoreau "morally and intellectually, seems not to have found exactly the guiding clue," putting him "physically out of health"—out, that is, of both wholeness, and holiness. Emerson, too, caught something of Thoreau's larger intent when he pondered how his friend, like his Irish gardener Hugh Whelan, was pocketing "every slip & stone & seed, & planting it." This was the true writer's vocation, he thought: "Nothing so sudden, nothing so broad, nothing so subtle, nothing so dear, but it comes therefore commended to his pen, & he will write. In his eyes a man is the faculty of reporting, & the universe is the possibility of being reported." Tell Thoreau that some things just cannot be described, and he knew better: he would "report God himself or attempt it."[28]

"Life! who knows what it is—what it does?" At the moment he wrote those words, sitting at his green writing desk by the window, the pond glinting through the pines outside, Thoreau had no guarantee that his experiment would work. He knew only that he had to try. This was literally his last move. "If I am not quite right here I am less wrong than before," he added cautiously, "—and now let us see what they will have." His purpose was profoundly religious. His house was "a temple . . . made of white pine. Seasoned and seasoning still to eternity," as natural and welcoming as the shade of a tree. Eating would be a sacred act, "a sacrament . . . sitting at the communion table of the world."[29] And writing? After the long lapse of centuries, it was time "for the written word—the *scripture*—to be heard." The trains passed by eight times a day; in two years it would be at least twenty.[30] Mass migration had housed him in an Irish laborer's recycled shanty. The world was changing. Instead of collating scriptures, now he would write one, a new sacred book for the modern age.

All time must be folded into this time. He was just turning twenty-eight years old, and ever since the age of five, Walden Pond had made the drapery of his dreams. "Well now to-night my flute awakes the echoes over this very water, but one generation of pines has fallen and with their stumps I have cooked my supper." As he wrote under the new generation of young pines rising around him, time collapsed: his communion supper simmered over the old stumps, and the notes of John's flute, bequeathed to Henry, came to life again, awakening echoes across the waters even as "the rattle of the rail-road cars" died away in the distance. "Even time has a depth," he reflected. "Self-emancipation in the West Indies of a man's thinking. . . . One emancipated heart & intellect—It would knock off the fetters from a million slaves."[31]

→>-<-

Had he ever imagined retirement to the pond would offer an escape from society, Thoreau soon learned it was the opposite: never before had he been so conspicuous. His house stood just over a low rise from the popular road to the pond, right next to a favorite fishing hole, the weedy hollow known as Wyman's Meadow, or "Pout's Nest." People took to starting conversations on the road. There was the townsman "driving a pair of cattle to market—who enquired of me how I could bring my mind to give up so many of the comforts of life—I answered that I was very sure I like it passably well.—I was not joking." A neighbor driving a load of wood to Boston complained to him of the cost of living, what with buying pork and tea and coffee, and laying up something against a sick day. "Sir I like your notions," said a passing railroad worker. "I think I shall live so myself." In his solitude, Thoreau became a sort of magnet. Most folks he welcomed, especially girls and boys who seemed glad to be in the woods, and young women who "looked in the pond and at the flowers and improved their time."[32]

Others were less kind. "How came Mrs._____ to know that

my sheets were not as clean as hers?" he exclaimed in *Walden*. Many retold the story of how Thoreau came across two "young ruffians, sons of influential parents," pursuing a terrified young woman through the woods. Thoreau protected her and testified on her behalf until the offenders were punished.[33] Travelers on the road fired barbs at him as he hoed his crops: "Beans so late!" As for the pond itself, it was hardly the private preserve of Emerson and his friends. "For one hundred years, certain, Walden has been visited at all seasons of the year by hunters, sportsmen, boys, woodchoppers, and landowners," reminisced Horace Hosmer; men would drink for long hours in a tavern in town, then, on a bet, go for a swim across the pond, "*even at midnight.*" And visitors? Hosmer, who worked at Walcott's grocery and restaurant, packed up many a picnic basket for Thoreau's visitors, "all sorts of people, at all hours"—and, he'd wink, "the baskets were generally loaded *for two.*"[34]

Nor was the pond off-limits to family. Prudence Ward notified a friend that "Henry T" has "many visitors, whom he receives with pleasure & does his best to entertain. We talk of passing the day with him soon."[35] The family made a custom of visiting him on Saturday afternoons, and Henry repaid their visits on Sundays; family friends recalled Cynthia's pleasure that her son came home every week "to eat a deliciously prepared dinner which their old family cook took pains to have as perfect as she knew how, and which he very evidently enjoyed to the full after his abstemonious days at Walden." John S. Keyes warned posterity that Thoreau dined sometimes at the Emersons', too—and at the Alcotts' and Hosmers'—"and though not intrusive was altogether too egotistic to be either shy or retiring."[36] Waldo Emerson's son Edward, still a baby during the Walden years, was astonished to learn that Thoreau was supposed to have cut off all family ties and foregone his habit "of appearing from time to time at night-fall, a welcome guest at the fireside of friends. He came for friendship, not for food."[37]

Such reports reveal the simple fact that Walden Pond was hardly wilderness; it was a familiar part of Concord's daily life, as it had been for two hundred years. Moving there hardly removed Thoreau from the circles of family, friends, and village life, and he made a point of maintaining his friendships as before. As for all those festive family dinners, how hurt Cynthia would have been had her own son refused her famously generous table! And Thoreau kept on taking jobs as the town handyman, just as he'd done for years—jobs on which he depended for his modest but still necessary income. For a dollar a day, good pay for a day laborer, he built fences, painted houses, did carpentry, bricked up at least one chimney, and performed a host of other odd jobs, often for Emerson—who was not above interrupting Henry's literary labor when he needed a fence built, a cellar floor laid, or the new schoolroom in the barn fitted up for classes. Once, when Thoreau was building a woodshed behind the Kettell house, his horse spooked and kicked him flat out on his back, spraining his stomach so badly that for some years he had trouble with heavy lifting and had to cut back on the jobs he accepted.[38] In one sense, moving to the pond at the edge of town had changed nothing, for he went about his life much as he'd always done.

Yet of course it changed everything. Never before had he been so self-sufficient or enjoyed such control over how he spent his hours. Even when he moved back to town, he never lost this new sense of independence. And never before had he attracted so much attention. As a son in the bustling Thoreau household or yet another inmate at the Emersons', Thoreau was invisible. But now, living alone on the pond in ostentatious simplicity, right in sight of a main road, he became a spectacle. It's not clear that Thoreau anticipated this. His original determination to live deliberately and confront only the essential facts of life, voiced so movingly in his earliest days at the pond, show his design to pursue an inward journey, but the accidental circumstances that made that journey possible meant it would be performed on a very public stage. His two years, two months, and two days living at Walden Pond became and would forever remain an iconic work of performance art. The surprise is how quickly and effectively Thoreau understood what was happening and pivoted his vision and goals to take advantage of it, starting with those first curious passersby drawn by the sound of his axe. After all, what good is a reporter, even of God Himself, without someone to report to? As soon as Thoreau found himself explaining himself to another, the conditions for *Walden* were laid.

But those conditions built in a certain irresistible damage that Thoreau could not control. His self-declared experiment demanded pure intentions and an integrity of purpose, which from the first he cast in religious terms as the devotional retreat of the religious hermit. Many have called his Walden house a "hermitage." But pursuing this devotional path as a middle way, not out in the wilderness but on the edge of town—"just far enough to be seen clearly," in the phrase of the philosopher Stanley Cavell—forced Thoreau, an intensely solitary introvert, to devise a public persona that could stand up to all the scrutiny and defend his private self from the glare of publicity. Paradoxically, he found himself in the very role he extolled in his essay "The Landlord," living openly on the highway with no lock on his door, offering hospitality and a good story to all who came by, no matter what their motives. But, as he remarked, the innkeeper "keeps an inn, and not a conscience."[39] Hence the bind: for since Thoreau was also the town gadfly and keeper of the public's conscience, his every act was a sermon, and his every encounter— even a casual meeting on the road—was a challenge to explain, to justify, to proselytize.

From then on, there would no casual meetings with Henry T. As word spread, circumstances he hadn't anticipated and couldn't control were turning him into a new kind of being, that product of modern commerce and communications: a celebrity. Meeting Thoreau became an Event, the kind of thing one retailed to posterity. As a consequence, all those harmless and loving dinners at home, where he dropped off his laundry, caught up on the news, packed in a good meal, and maybe carried away a pie for breakfast laid him open to endless charges of hypocrisy. No other male American writer has been so discredited for enjoying a meal with loved ones or for not doing his own laundry. But from the very beginning, such charges have been used to silence Thoreau.[40]

The immediate result of all this was that Thoreau, who went to Walden to write one book, instead wrote two. The first, the one he'd been planning all along, was *A Week on the Concord and Merrimack Rivers*, his elegy for John—and now for his younger, more innocent self, and for the world they'd shared together, which was swiftly passing away. As *A Week* grew in range and depth, so did Thoreau's understanding of the ways the Industrial Revolution was already, in less than a decade, rewriting the New England landscape, as the ribbons of railroad displaced commerce from the rivers of yore. For years Thoreau had been collecting passages for it in the "Long Book," adding paragraphs as they came to him, building it up piece by piece like a mosaic. Working steadily out at his "inkstand" by the pond,[41] his dedication and discipline were paying off. By fall 1845 he had the first draft in hand, and by spring 1847, the book was done (or so it seemed at the time), and Emerson was helping him shop it around to prospective publishers. Into *A Week*, this intensely personal and private work of his Walden days, Thoreau poured all the best of his younger self, all the passion and poetry of three decades.

The second book, *Walden*, was something else again. It was born on July 5, 1845, his first morning at the pond, when he opened a new journal by announcing why he'd come there to live. Fresh, saucy, iconic passages, now familiar to generations of readers, sparkle in its pages like gold in a Yukon riverbed. Thoreau's voice here is wholly new: bold, lyric, yearning, prophetic, confrontational. It's the voice not of a confiding poet but of a prophet, a teacher discovering how—since, it turns out, he's up on a soapbox—to speak in a way that others will hear. From then on, there were two Thoreaus: one quiet, introspective, self-questioning, intensely private, occasionally depressed, and often in poor health; the other brash, boastful, self-certain, loud, and healthy as the rooster crowing to bring in the dawn. As the second Thoreau would trumpet in the motto to *Walden*, "I do not propose to write an ode to dejection, but to brag as lustily as chanticleer in the morning, standing on his roost, if only to wake my neighbors up." Modulating between these two self-extremes would open up, in the years to come, the full resources of Thoreau's artistry. He would ever after wrestle uneasily with this new creation, "Thoreau," this outsize doppelgänger born in those first conversations over the pine timbers of a house still raw with pitch and splinters, who would grow up to narrate his creator's life to the entire world.

→-←

Taking charge of this new character meant consciously organizing his newly simplified life at the pond into widening circles of responsibility: house, neighbors, nature. There in his house would be everything needed, and nothing more. Pride of place went to the simple green-painted pine writing desk that Thoreau had used since the summer of 1838, placed front and center under the Walden-facing window, holding his notebooks. While there was no lock on the door, there was a lock on his desk, and the wear in the wood shows he used it. One chair sat at the desk, two more near a little three-legged table that held a few books; whenever he wanted company, he set one of the chairs outside his door. Extra visitors could spill over onto the sturdy little cane bed behind the door, a platform recycled from a Chinese sofa bed onto which Thoreau nailed legs and stretchers. This cot was his bed for the rest of his life. It was low enough for children to climb onto but high enough, they later remembered, that their feet didn't quite reach the floor—and just high enough for Channing, when he stayed for a fortnight that first summer, to sleep underneath, like a bunk bed.[42]

Thoreau's needs were ludicrously simple: for vanity, he kept a three-inch looking glass off the cover of a shaving box; for cleanliness, a dipper and a washbasin, and, for water, all of Walden Pond, in which he bathed every morning when he could. In summer when the lake was too warm to drink, he portaged cool water from Brister's Spring over the hill. If he had a privy, no record of it survives. As for a kitchen, that first summer he cooked in a hole in the earth lined with stones on which he built a fire: one early visitor recalled their earthen dinner of "roasted horn pout, corn, beans, bread, etc.,"; the fish were, with a little salt, "delicious." For bread Thoreau mixed meal with lake water, spreading the dough on a stone and baking it in his earth oven: unleavened flatbread. Once he had finished his chimney—built of used bricks and pond stones and mortared with white sand from the pond—he could cook on a hearth; for his second winter, he installed a stove. For kitchenware he had a kettle, a skillet, a frying pan, a jug for oil and another for molasses, three plates, two knives, two forks, one spoon, and a cup.[43] No wonder so many of his visitors brought picnic baskets.

The light and airy unfinished house was perfect for summer, but as fall approached, Thoreau weatherproofed it by buying a load of cheap shingles, planing them straight, and shingling the roof and sides. While the open rafters with the bark on and the rough brown knotty pine boards pleased his eye, inside they were too drafty for comfort. So that November he reluctantly plastered the interior, learning by trial and error and living at home with his family until it dried. Back inside in early December, with stumpwood crackling on the hearth and shadows flickering around the rafters, he felt he "first began to inhabit" his cozy house, "kitchen, chamber, parlor, and keeping-room" all at once—small, to be sure, but all the larger for being entirely his own.[44]

In one of *Walden*'s most famous one-liners, Thoreau declared he kept three chairs: "one for solitude, two for friendship, three for society." His most frequent visitors were his closest friends: the farmer Edmund Hosmer, the poet Ellery Channing, and the philosopher Bronson Alcott, who that second winter walked over every Sunday, plus the occasional call from his "landlord and waterlord" Emerson, or the French-Canadian woodchopper Alek Therien, "who made his last supper on a woodchuck which his dog caught."[45] But society didn't only come to his door; he went out and found it as well. One Saturday late in August, a sudden thunderstorm sent Thoreau running for shelter to a nearby hut, where he found the Irishman John Field with his "broad faced" boy and his wife Mary, an infant on her knee. Thoreau recorded the story of the "honest, hard working" John and his "brave" wife, who longed to catch a piece of the American dream. The owner of Baker Farm had hired John to "bog" for ten dollars an acre and the use of the land for a year. It was a hard share-cropper's life, a bad bargain, thought Thoreau. With the horizon all his own, John Field was stuck in his "boggy" Irish ways, "thinking to live by some derivative old country mode in this primitive new country," not to rise in this world until he or his posterity got wings to their feet.[46]

Those wings were hard to come by. At the far end of the pond lived Hugh Coyle, whose wife worked in town. "Colonel Quoil" had fought at Waterloo before emigrating from Ireland to America, where he, too, became a Concord ditcher. Thoreau spoke to him once and tried to show him Brister's Spring, where good water ran even in the heat of summer, but the alcoholic old man was too weak to walk that far. Soon after, he collapsed on Walden Road and died. Thoreau, troubled, spent an afternoon studying Coyle's eerie, weed-infested house before the town burned it down.[47]

These experiences turned Thoreau's attention outward to the other inhabitants of Walden woods—ruined houses, ruined lives. One had to look hard to see their traces, but Thoreau found them. Hugh Coyle was not an anomaly, but the last of a struggling community, a rural slum of outcasts, drunks, and derelicts.[48] There was Cato Ingraham, "slave of Duncan Ingraham, Esquire," an African living alone in a little house his owner built in 1795 in exchange for his labor, the last of perhaps a dozen slaves who'd moved to Walden woods. All that remained was a half-filled cellar hole, visible beyond the beanfield at the head of the path to Goose Pond. There was also John Wyman the potter, who had squatted in the house that became Hugh Coyle's, digging the clay for his pottery from the pond's silty banks. His son Thomas, also a potter, had bought the acres under Thoreau's house (hence "Wyman's field") and later sold them to Emerson.[49]

Zilpah White, enslaved until the Revolution, had declared her freedom by building her own one-room house; she lived as a "her-mitess" near Thoreau's future beanfield for over forty years, depending on the pennies she earned spinning flax into linen and making baskets, brooms, and mats. Arsonists burned down her house in

1813, killing her chickens, cats, and dog. Zilpah rebuilt and survived another seven years until her death at eighty-two. Kicking aside the leaves, Thoreau unburied a few bricks from her chimney. Brister Freeman, another of Concord's slaves, had fought in the Revolution and declared his personal independence through his surname. Eager to establish his independent identity, he bought an acre on the hill north of Walden Pond, "Brister's Hill," where he planted an orchard, kept a few pigs, and raised a family with his African wife Fenda, "who told fortunes, yet pleasantly." Every fall Thoreau crunched gratefully into a few of Freeman's "wild and ciderish" apples.[50] A few steps beyond stood the tiny house of John Breed the barber. Local boys burned it down in 1841; Thoreau raced out from Emerson's, where he was living, to watch it burn. The next night he returned to commiserate with Breed's son, a field hand, who'd come by to mourn his childhood home. Breed, like Coyle, had died drunk on Walden Road, in 1824; his wife's clothes were all from the Concord Female Charitable Society, which regularly made donations to churchgoing Zilpah White as well.[51]

As Thoreau explored the ruins and cellar holes in his neighborhood, a surprising reality emerged: not long before, this land was a little village of former slaves, day laborers, immigrants, and poor whites, nearly all squatters and all without money. Yet they'd had houses, gardens, and chickens, families and lives, dreams. Why had they lived here, rather than in town? The road behind his house had once been the Great Country Road connecting Boston to New Hampshire, one of the major arteries of New England. But after 1785, when the shortcut opened by way of Lexington and Charlestown, it was just Walden Road, leading out of town to nowhere in particular through marginal land too rocky and sterile to farm. The land's owners didn't care enough about it to evict the squatters, so Walden Woods became one of the two places where Concord tolerated the impoverished, the displaced, and the abandoned, who were left alone to scrabble out a living as best they could. The other place, the edge of the Great Field, had done better. Freed slaves would live out there for generations: Peter Hutchinson the butcher, with his family; Jack Garrison, the laborer who'd escaped from New Jersey, with his wife Susan Robbins, daughter of Caesar Robbins, and her brother Peter Robbins and his family; the Garrisons' daughters worked in town, and their son John was the gardener at the Old Manse. In Thoreau's day the neighborhood still survived, as families helped one another out, squatting on Humphrey Barrett's land.[52]

Why, Thoreau wondered, did Walden village fail while Concord village thrived? Could not "the basket, stable-broom, mat-making, corn-parching, linen-spinning, and pottery business have thrived here, making the wilderness to blossom like the rose?" There were no "water privileges," he punned, leaving the "good port" of Walden Pond "alas all unimproved." It would be up to him, now, to found the next generation, "my house raised last spring to be the oldest in the hamlet."[53] Ironically he would be right, but not in the way he envisioned. Emerson and his descendants would buy up most of the land around Walden Pond, which they deeded to future generations as a park. Long after Thoreau's house was gone, it would be honored as the foundation of a new generation of environmental thinking. Walden Pond would not be settled after all, but preserved—and not because it was valued, but because it wasn't. What Thoreau was studying at Walden was how to see, in the wastelands at the margins of commerce, the center of a new system of value.

→►◄←

To see this meant widening his sense of responsibility to the largest circle of all, beyond house, beyond neighbors, to the world of nature. Or perhaps, he realized, it was the circle of nature that extended to include himself. Either way, Thoreau felt a powerful intimacy: "What sweet and tender, the most innocent and divinely encouraging society there is in every natural object," he wrote. "I was so distinctly made aware of the presence of my *kindred*, even in scenes which we are accustomed to call wild."[54] Each night he fell asleep to the sounds of wind and wild animals, and each dawn he awoke to a world humans did not dominate. He had experienced this while camping, but now he was not merely camping, but dwelling where the "outdoors" came inside with the summer air, wafting through the chinks in the walls, carrying the scent of pine and the sounds of birds.

His first "kindred" was the mouse who built its nest under his house and, having "never seen the race of man before," did not fear him but came to pick up the crumbs at his feet, running "over my shoes and up my pantaloons inside clinging to my flesh with its sharp claws." Instead of repelling it, Thoreau invited it closer: "When I held it a piece of cheese it came and nibbled between my fingers and then cleaned its face and paws like a fly." Thoreau's new companion was still wild enough to stay hidden when Joseph Hosmer came to visit, and he had to take on faith Thoreau's report that "when he played upon the flute, it would come and listen from its hiding place," disappearing again when Thoreau changed the tune. Someone memorialized Thoreau's small friend by drawing a mouse on the back of his door.[55]

Wilder kindred turned his thoughts in a new direction: in the dead of his first winter, Thoreau found not three paces from his door one "Jean Lapin," "trembling with fear—yet unwilling to move—a poor wee thing lean & bony—with ragged ears—and sharp nose— scant tail & slender paws." He stepped toward the poor starving hare, "and lo away he scud with elastic spring over the snowy crust in to the bushes a free creature of the forest—still wild & fleet. . . . and soon put the forest between me and itself." The wild beings he became aware of were far more intensely aware of him. In time, stories would multiply of Thoreau's mystical bond with the wild creatures of Walden: how with one whistle he could summon a woodchuck, with another a pair of squirrels, with a third various birds, including two crows—one of them, as a startled witness recalled, "nestling upon his shoulder." He would feed them from his pockets with his hands, stroke them gently, and dismiss them each with their own strange, low whistle. He could reach into the water and the fish would not flinch away, but allow him to clasp them gently and bring them into the air unharmed.[56]

As such stories multiplied, legends grew of Thoreau as a modern

Orpheus, who could draw the creatures to him and charm them with music, or an American Saint Francis of Assisi, who withdrew from the world, preached to the birds, and tamed the fearsome wild wolf with his blessing. Ridiculous, thought his Yankee townsmen. When woodchucks ravaged his beans, Thoreau asked a local farmer how to trap them without injury. "Yes, shoot 'em, you damn fool," he snapped back.[57] The town giggled at Thoreau when he trapped the woodchuck and released him miles away—with a good talking to, to be sure. But despite the legends of sweet wild harmony at Walden, Thoreau was well aware there was at least as much conflict as harmony. Living simply out in the woods didn't eliminate problems; it only made them easier to see. Take, for example, shelter: building even this simple house to satisfy life's most basic needs meant negotiating permission with the landowner, chopping down thriving young trees, borrowing an axe to do so (probably from Alcott, though once that axe became famous, both Channing and Emerson laid claim to it), and caring for that axe—returning it, Thoreau declared, sharper than before. It meant securing help to raise the frame and bargaining for boards to close it up, and it meant discovering his house wasn't really "closed" at all; the field mice and ants moved in before he did, and the wasps soon after. Building a house catalyzed an army of helpers, rivals, and detractors.

Worse yet was that other obvious essential: food. Planting beans was Thoreau's way of teaching a basic fact forgotten by virtually the whole of philosophy: plant life is the foundation of all human intellection.[58] Confronting this fact meant entangling himself with seven tedious miles of beans and their many associates, starting with the brace of oxen whose strength he needed to break open the hard soil and a man to drive the oxen and provide the plow. It also meant acquiring the seed to plant, hoping for rain (but not too much) to water the ground, and deploying a hoe (an edged weapon from a plant's perspective) to drive back the weeds—all performed in view of passersby who jeered at Thoreau's refusal to add manure, which would require employing a bogger—that is, a John Field. Once the beans sprouted, the entanglements multiplied: "My auxiliaries are the dews and rains—to water this dry soil," Thoreau observed early in July. "My enemies are worms cool days—and most of all woodchucks. They have nibbled for me an eighth of an acre clean." Eventually the beans would be too tough for woodchucks, but even then, "they will go forward to meet new foes."[59]

So, what to do about the woodchucks? If they wrecked his bean crop, his experiment's economic foundation collapsed. Should he do what Alek Therien did—kill them and put the carcass in the cooking pot? Thoreau tried that: "Once I went so far as to slaughter a woodchuck which ravaged my bean-field . . . and devour him, partly for experiment's sake." He enjoyed it, too, he admitted, but even if you had "your woodchucks dressed out by the village butcher"—that is, by Peter Hutchinson—this didn't seem in the long run precisely "a good practice." Thoreau's friends noticed he ate whatever was served, even meat, rather than make a fuss over their dinner table, but when he was alone, high on his new ethical platform, Thoreau fussed plenty: How could he eat animals without worrying about the *ethics* of eating animals? How could he condemn savagery in others, when he was part predator himself? Fishing, his favorite display of the harmonious integration of humans and nature, posed a real dilemma. He loved to fish, but did his "mystic spiritual life" at the pond include killing to eat—even killing fish? Could he live on apples, nuts, and berries? Was his robust appetite for fish a sin, or a sacrament? Thoreau did not stop killing and eating fish, but he did start worrying about it. "I find I cannot fish without falling a little in my own respect," he fretted in his Journal; "always I feel that it would have been better if I had not fished."[60] Over the years, his worries evolved into the conflicted defense of vegetarianism in *Walden*'s "Higher Laws."

Then there were the arrowheads that rattled against the blade of his hoe as he worked the furrows of his beanfield. They told him that the corn he planted was seeding furrows originally opened by Indians—that in a real and literal way, his act of creation was displacing even the memory of a people who'd been violently forced off their homelands. On his breaks from hoeing beans, Thoreau meditated on the ruins and cellar holes of slaves and impoverished migrants, who tried to rise to freedom but died out instead. While researching their lives, he uncovered narratives of abuse, exploitation, arson, and theft, as well as hope, determination, heroism, and at least temporary victories, like Brister Freeman's fine orchard or Zilpah White's defiant independence. In the open and simplified setting of Walden Woods, not only was Thoreau more visible—to himself as well as to his neighbors—but his neighbors were more visible, too: *all* his neighbors, nonhuman and human, past and future as well as present. As the nature and extent of his relations dawned on him, his questions multiplied. "What are these pines & these birds about? What is this pond a-doing? I must know a little more—& be forever ready. . . . The elements are working their will with me."[61]

In short, Thoreau discovered that even this simple, stripped-down life offered no simple way to realize his utopian vision without some form of harm to others. There was no easy way to resolve the long history of conflict, struggle, and displacement evident everywhere in those woods, with their deep and entangled human and natural history. He began to imagine a new role for himself, looking after "the wild stock of the town," which, being part of the commons and owned by no one, had been neglected and ignored. And if he couldn't cure the woodchuck problem, he could at least work himself up to a state of reconciliation: "These beans have results which are not harvested by me. Do they not grow for woodchucks partly?"[62] There was no word in Thoreau's lifetime for what we now call "ecology," but his growing awareness was turning his thought— far in advance of his time—to ecological relationships in which humans participated but could not declare dominance, as well as to historical struggles and inequalities that laid the foundation for his political thinking on power and justice.

All this would go into *Walden*, starting with the moment Thoreau began a record of his life at the pond. But the gesture that crystallized *Walden* into a visionary whole occurred a few months later, in January 1846, after Walden had frozen solid enough to bear his weight safely. Thoreau brought to Walden the surveying equipment he'd used at the Concord Academy. For at least a week, maybe two, perhaps alone but probably with an assistant, Thoreau surveyed the pond in the bitter cold. This is harder than it sounds. First, he had to flag some twenty or so sighting posts along the shoreline, then haul the heavy instruments—the compass on its tripod, the metal surveying chain, an axe, a plumb line, and a round solid stone for a weight, and the graduated staff—across the ice, where he established a 925-foot baseline with two primary traverse stations. From those two stations Thoreau conducted what is known to surveyors as an "angle intersection survey" of the pond's perimeter, measuring it out, 66 feet at a time, almost 2,900 feet. Then, with axe and ice chisel, he cut well over a hundred individual holes through the ice to lower the plumb line into the water. At each point he paused to note every bearing and measure. Finally, he collated the data set and transferred it to a meticulous and extremely accurate pencil drawing.[63]

It was an extravagant thing to do, wholly impractical. No one needed the pond surveyed, and it took severe study, hard physical labor, and concentrated mathematical skill, not to mention practice with the instruments of science and technical drafting. But he did it. Thoreau used the tools of science and engineering to create a remarkable work of art, a working survey that accurately mapped Walden Pond to the inch: length, breadth, and depth. He accomplished this, he said, to prove that the pond had a bottom, for legend had it the lake was bottomless. In fact, Thoreau found it was 102 feet at the deepest point, making Walden Pond the deepest inland body of water in Massachusetts. Thank goodness, Thoreau added in *Walden*, "that this pond was made deep and pure for a symbol."[64] What, exactly, it symbolized would take the entire book to explain, but by spring 1846 he had the takeaway in a nutshell: "The line of greatest breadth intersects the line of greatest length at the point of greatest depth or height." This was a universal law, true for ethics as well as mechanics: "It is the heart in man—It is the sun in the system.... Draw lines through the length & breadth of the aggregate of a man's particular daily experiences and volumes of life into his coves and inlets—and where they intersect will be the height or depth of his character."[65]

Walden took shape here, in two key discoveries: First, that the pond had "a hard bottom and rocks in place, which we can call *reality*, and say, This is, and no mistake."[66] Thoreau's quest for the "bottom" of the pond was also his quest for a bedrock truth, that face-to-face confrontation with "actuality" that drove him to the pond to begin with. But once you found that bedrock truth, what should you do about it? This was his second discovery: each person's answer will depend upon, and will reveal, the exact height, breadth, and depth of their individual moral character. The angle intersections inscribed by our particular daily experiences, the coves and inlets of our lives, will ground the decisions we make, our actions in the world. And the sum total of all our moral actions combined will constitute the ethical character of the society we build together.

GOING TO EXTREMES I: THOREAU IN JAIL

Out on the ice in January 1846, Thoreau was drawing his first major conclusions, even as events were about to test them. Less than a year before, Wendell Phillips's angry denunciation of Texas annexation split the Concord Lyceum, but even then it was already too late: in the 1844 presidential election, the proslavery, pro-annexation James Polk prevailed over Henry Clay, who argued that annexing Texas meant war with Mexico. Polk and the outgoing President Tyler took their victory as a national mandate. Tyler pushed annexation through Congress, which ratified it soon after Polk took office. Emerson was worried—"Mexico will poison us," he predicted darkly—but Orestes Brownson spoke for the Democratic millions when he proclaimed in John O'Sullivan's *Democratic Review*, "Our new lands are exhausted."[67] America needed more territory. In July 1845, O'Sullivan himself chimed in: only expansion would fulfill America's "manifest destiny to overspread the continent allotted by

Providence for the free development of our yearly multiplying millions." Manifest Destiny was on the move. On the very day Thoreau was unpacking at Walden Pond, Texas legislators were approving annexation. By December, Jane Thoreau had collected over a hundred signatures on her petition protesting annexation, but by then it was far too late.[68] The paperwork was already under way; once it was filed, in February 1846, Texas annexation was history. As for Jane Thoreau and her fellow petitioners, in a Presidential Address of December 8, 1846, Polk declared those opposed to Texas were giving "aid and comfort" to America's enemy. It was an accusation of treason.

For on May 13, 1846, the United States of America declared war on the United Mexican States. It would be a hard and bloody war, making clear, as historians point out, that America's "destiny" was not so much "manifest" as it was a hard-fought campaign of violent aggression, brilliantly led by Zachary Taylor, the general in the field.[69] When the peace treaty was finally signed in March 1848, Mexico was forced to surrender its entire northern half, territory it had administered and settled since the 1500s, and the United States was suddenly in possession of a Spanish Catholic empire stretching from Texas north to Colorado and west to California, where gold would be discovered within months. The resulting gold rush would flood California with "forty-niners," prospectors and settlers from the Atlantic states, destabilizing the Spanish inhabitants and leading to a genocidal war against California's indigenous peoples. Back in the US capital, expansion of slave territory into the newly annexed lands upset the precarious balance of power between North and South. Step by step, roads that might have led away from civil war were closing.

One sunny afternoon toward the end of July 1846—probably on Thursday, July 23—Henry Thoreau walked into town from Walden Pond, intending to pick up a mended shoe. Toward sundown he crossed paths with Sam Staples, who was planning to step down as tax collector and needed to clear the books. Thoreau hadn't paid since 1842, and ever since Staples had arrested Alcott and Lane back in '43, he'd been nagging Henry about it. "Oh yes," he recalled in old age, "I'd spoken to him a good many times about his tax and he said he didn't believe in it and shouldn't pay." It was only the poll tax, a dollar and a half levied on every man from twenty on up, and Staples even offered to pay it for him. "But he said, 'no *sir*; don't you do it.' Well I told him then that he'd have to pay it or else go to jail. 'I'll go now,' says he. . . . 'Well come along,' says I and so I locked him up. He didn't make any fuss, he took it all right."[70]

As Thoreau later recounted in "Civil Disobedience,"[71] by then it was late, time to lock up. The prisoners had all been lounging in the prison yard, and as Sam led Henry to his upstairs cell, he could hear their footsteps echoing down the hollow rooms. He spent the evening chatting with his amiable cellmate, who'd accidentally burned down a barn when he fell asleep while smoking, and who was calmly awaiting trial while enjoying the clean whitewashed cell and the good cooking from the Middlesex Inn next door.[72] Long after his cellmate went to bed, Henry lingered at the cell's double-barred windows, watching the bustle in the tavern's kitchen, listening to dishes rattling, the town clock tolling, and the voices in the street. Legend has it Emerson saw Thoreau at the bars and exclaimed, "Henry, why are you here!" to which Thoreau replied, "Mr. Emerson, why are you not here?"[73] It couldn't have happened that way: Henry's cell was upstairs, and a ten-foot stone wall surmounted with iron pickets surrounded the jail. Yet the anecdote does reflect Thoreau's thinking: "It was a closer view of my native town. I was fairly inside of it. I never had seen its institutions before." The scales fell from his eyes; the more clearly he saw "the State in which I lived," the more dismayed he grew. His friends and neighbors were good for "summer weather only," too timid to risk themselves in the name of doing right. That he was in jail, and Emerson was not and never would be, crystallized perhaps the most important difference between them.[74]

Sometime that evening, when Thoreau was still doing window duty, a lady in a veil knocked at Sam Staples's door and handed over an envelope with the money to pay Thoreau's back taxes. No one has ever been sure who it was—Sam was away, and his daughter Ellen, too young to pass along a name, answered the knock. Sam sometimes averred it was Samuel Hoar, who'd done the same for Alcott. The Thoreau family passed down a story of Cynthia descending in alarm on Aunts Maria and Jane Thoreau, who flew about gathering the cash, which Maria delivered to the Staples' door "while the others waited near." Scholars have long agreed it was probably Aunt Maria. What is certain is that it was late, and dark, and when Sam Staples got home and found the envelope, he saw no reason to rush things. So he waited until next morning after breakfast, and when he was letting the prisoners out for their daily work details, he told Thoreau he was free to go. "Oh he took it all right," Staples told an interviewer in 1891; other times, though, he liked to embellish the story by laughing at how Henry was "mad as the devil" to have his gesture of protest undercut.[75]

No doubt Thoreau was annoyed that, in his words, "some one interfered, and paid that tax," but given that he'd seen the same thing done for both Alcott and Lane, he couldn't have been surprised. What did surprise him was the sense of estrangement he felt when he came out of jail, as his neighbors "first looked at me, and then at one another, as if I had returned from a long journey." Yet he went about his interrupted day as planned: picked up his mended shoe, then "joined a huckleberry party, who were impatient to put themselves under my conduct." If it was a typical huckleberry party, Thoreau would have driven the hayrick himself, with children and servants laughing in the back and a few adults along to watch from the shade and pick berries off the loaded branches Thoreau brought them. So it was that in half an hour, he was on Fairhaven Hill, surrounded by children and the scent of huckleberries in the warm July sun, "and the State was nowhere to be seen."[76]

"This," he concluded with a flourish, "is the whole history of 'My Prisons.'"[77] The arrest itself was trivial enough, as Thoreau well knew—the gravity of his account seems undercut by the folksy Sam Staples and his lounging fellow inmates. Yet the Middlesex County Jail was formidable: a three-story granite building, rebuilt and fortified since the Revolutionary War, when Thoreau's Tory grand-uncle had broken out and escaped; and it housed its share of thieves and murderers. Unlike Alcott, Thoreau actually did do time, even if just overnight, allowing him to glimpse America's carceral society from the "inside"; and if, like Alcott and Lane, his act of resistance was quietly neutralized by someone paying his taxes behind his back, both Alcott and Lane showed him what his next step needed to be. On the evening of his arrest and release, Alcott had sounded off at the lyceum, which, conveniently, had already gathered to hear a lecture on nonresistance; the very next day, Lane had sent a passionate defense of Alcott to the *Liberator*. Thoreau would use both approaches: first, speak out to his neighbors at the lyceum; then, publish an eloquent defense of his actions. However, it would take time. No one in town had taken the impractical Alcott or the eccentric Lane all that seriously, but Thoreau was one of Concord's own sons, and they took him seriously indeed. He found himself unexpectedly exposed and vulnerable, the subject of heated controversy.

He'd gotten the whole town talking. John S. Keyes voiced the standard view that Thoreau, Alcott, and Lane were "silly, would-be martyrs." Dr. Bartlett's fourteen-year-old son George, one of the lads who visited Thoreau at Walden, remembered how Thoreau sought counsel from his father the night of his release; it was like "seeing a Siberian exile."[78] The furious pages in Thoreau's Journal suggest what he said that night—the problem lay not with frail humanity but with "institutions," those "grim and ghostly phantoms like Moloch & Juggernaut because of the blind reverence paid to them." How ironic that the State, which should protect his freedom, robbed him of it: "When I have asserted the freedom it declared it has imprisoned me." About Staples himself, Thoreau was restrained: "The jailer or constable as a mere man and neighbor . . . may be a right worthy man." The real question was, how could a good man lend himself to evil? Staples knew Thoreau acted out of principle, not poverty, yet still he locked him up, agreeing to be a tool of the State that was committing one of the worst crimes since time began, "the present Mexican War." But who had committed this atrocity? All the people Thoreau saw around him were decent and well meaning.

Yet daily the crime continued, unhindered. The lesson was, "Any can command him who doth not command himself."[79] Men were acting not like men, but like stones, letting themselves be used as bricks in a wall.

As for Bronson Alcott, just weeks earlier Staples had threatened him, too: if Alcott didn't pay up on his back taxes, he would advertise the Alcotts' house, Hillside, for sale—hard words for the husband of Abigail Alcott and the father of four growing "little women." Bronson fumed in his journal, in words echoing Thoreau's: see how the State forces itself on the freeborn, even putting its hand right in your pocket "if it will, but I shall not put mine there on its behalf." As soon as he could, Thoreau sought out Alcott, and they talked it over. No doubt Alcott passed along Emerson's harsh judgment: when Alcott had defended Thoreau's actions as "a dignified non-compliance with the injunction of civil powers," Emerson scoffed. No, he argued back, what Thoreau did was "mean and skulking, and in bad taste."[80]

Emerson was hurt and confused. In the privacy of his journal, he struggled with his mounting anger. His first impulse was respect: "My friend Mr. Thoreau has gone to jail rather than pay his tax. On him they [the rabble in Washington] could not calculate. The abolitionists denounce the war & give much time to it, but they pay the tax." Ah, allegations of hypocrisy. As that sank in, Emerson realized that since he, too, paid that tax, Thoreau was accusing *him*. He prickled in self-defense. The State, that poor beast, meant well: "Do not refuse your pistareen." It was all right for the abolitionists to refuse, for they were single-issue agitators and only sought to redress their one grievance; they "deserve to resist and go to prison in multitudes." But not *you*, "you generalizers. You are not citizens." "Don't run amuck against the world." As he wrote on, Emerson worked himself up from indignation to cutting insult: "But you, nothing will content. No government short of a monarchy consisting of one king & one subject, will appease you. Your objection then to the state of Massachusetts is deceptive. Your true quarrel is with the state of Man." It was pointless to refuse payment—no, it was worse, hypocritical! The real hypocrite was *Thoreau*, not himself. "The state tax does not pay the Mexican War. Your coat, your sugar, your Latin & French & German book, your watch does. Yet these you do not stick at buying." Emerson ended with unmasked contempt: Thoreau was no citizen. He did not deserve to go to war alongside true citizens "as their equals. . . . This prison is one step to suicide."[81]

Four days after Thoreau was jailed, a weary Emerson wrote the local news to Elizabeth Hoar. It was a sorry chronicle of disappointments and failures: "Mr Channing has returned, after spending 16 days in Rome; Mr Thoreau has spent a night in Concord jail on his refusal to pay his taxes; Mr Lane is in Concord endeavoring to sell his farm of 'Fruitlands'; Mr E—but I spare you the rest of the weary history. It seems the very counting of threads in a beggar's coat, to tell the chronicle of nothings . . . and it is out of this sad lint & rag fair that the web of lasting life is woven."[82] Nothing, absolutely nothing, would have astonished Emerson more than to learn that Thoreau's act, which Emerson wrote off with such loathing, would be honored as the torch whose light would lead a hundred peaceful revolutions that still shape, and shake, the world.

→>-<+

Only time would tell the meaning of Thoreau's night in jail. For the time being, he kept his thoughts to himself. As for his Concord neighbors, two further acts of resistance seemed to them more consequential. Two years before, Thoreau had returned from his long walk across the state in time to ring the bell for Concord's first great antislavery gala. On August 1, 1846, just a week after his night in jail, Thoreau hosted the Concord Female Anti-Slavery Society's second gala celebration, again in honor of West Indian Emancipation. One of the event's organizers—probably the brave and outspoken Anna Whiting, Thoreau's Concord Academy classmate—wrote excitedly to the *Liberator*, "I think this the best celebration ever had any where." The weather was perfect, cooled by a few morning clouds, and Thoreau's grove in the woods "seemed the best of all groves. We had seats enough and to spare, plenty to eat, and a hogshead of good ice-water to drink."[83]

They also had a full slate of speakers, who stepped one by one to the open doorway of Thoreau's house and addressed the crowd. William Henry Channing, whom Thoreau had met in New York, solemnly announced that his doomsaying prophecies of the year before had come true. The calm and philosophical Emerson spoke, too, "closely scrutinizing, nicely adjusting the scales, so that there should be not a hair too much in the one scale or the other, telling us the need be of all things." Lewis Hayden, the escaped slave from Kentucky, "stammer[ed] out touchingly that which none has power fully to utter, what a glorious thing liberty is." Bronson Alcott was invited to defend Thoreau's arrest, but he turned down the invitation to tend to his garden instead, leaving Thoreau without his closest ally. As for Thoreau, he said not one recorded word, nor did he mention the event in his Journal, though he did mention it obliquely in *Walden*: "It is surprising how many great men and women a small house will contain. I have had twenty-five or thirty souls, with their bodies, at once under my roof, and yet we often parted without being aware that we had come very near to one another."[84] Thoreau, watching the long-planned gala unfold on his doorstep, felt very far away.

At "twenty-five or thirty," the numbers were small. Radical abolitionism was still the work of a tiny minority fighting a hard uphill battle against hostility and indifference.[85] No doubt, mocked Whiting, Concord's people are all obliged to stay home, "being so busy in providing for the wants of their new sister Texas, and her interminable offspring." Nor do they mean, she added with a nod to their silent host, "to repudiate any of their debts, but are willing to pay the last farthing." Least of all, she sallied on, could Concord people allow themselves, in these new times, a celebration of "that sacred word liberty." Shout it as loud as you can in their ears, they but "give you a look, very similar to that of some superannuated person, from whose mind the memory of all those formerly dear has passed away." But at least it was a diverse turnout: "a handsome sprinkling of women and children," plus "a very few farmers," about as many mechanics, "one merchant, one lawyer, two physicians" (which almost certainly included the sympathetic Dr. Bartlett), plus the ministers. The day's events ended with a choral concert, which, Whiting closed, was "excellent."[86]

As the music died away through the woods and the attendees packed up the leftovers, Thoreau must have pondered the length, breadth, and depth of character of each person there, not least his own. From his own doorway, the full spectrum of abolitionist positions and personalities had spoken, from Garrisonian disunionists to Emerson's balanced moderation to the raw pain in Hayden's stammering voice, recalling his first wife and firstborn child dragging out their lives "on some tyrant's plantation . . . driven all day under the lash, and then at night to be under the will of any demon or deacon that has a white face. How long shall these things be?" How long indeed? No one there—least of all Thoreau—was clear whether being jailed for nonpayment of a tax could be anything more than pointless martyrdom, irresponsible dereliction, or vulgar flirtation with criminality.[87] What was his one easy night in jail compared with Lewis Hayden's life of brutal abuse under the Southern lash? Could W. H. Channing's "No Union" platform or Alcott's "No Government" nonresistance keep the lash off Hayden's back? Emerson warned that extremists unbalanced the delicate scales of "need be," and now the whole town had heard his patronizing dismissal. Mean and skulking? Thoreau stood by his actions, but his emotions were raw and his mind was in turmoil. Before he could speak, he had to measure his thoughts, carefully and deliberately. What was bedrock here, what was "reality"? He would simmer for eighteen months before facing his fellow citizens from the podium with an epochal defense of resistance against civil government.

Lewis Hayden was the first documented fugitive slave to visit Thoreau at Walden. There may have been others: Cynthia Thoreau's household served as a secure station on the Underground Railroad, one of several in town, and Henry regularly escorted escaping slaves to the northbound train, bought them tickets, ensured they had money, and either boarded with them at Concord (sitting at a distance, keeping guard) or drove them to the whistle-stop at West Fitchburg. The legend long persisted that his Walden house was a place of refuge, which is absurd: it lacked both lock and hiding place. But reliable participants recalled escaping slaves being brought there for Thoreau to look after until dark, when he would escort them to

Cynthia's house or another safe shelter.[88] No documentation was kept—it was, after all, underground, illegal, even treasonable— but, very rarely, private journals recorded particular incidents. Late in 1846, Abigail Alcott recorded the arrival of "John," "an amiable and intelligent man just 7 weeks from the 'House of Bondage'" in Maryland. Bronson Alcott recorded a few details of John's two-week stay at Hillside, where he sawed and stacked firewood, relishing his first taste of freedom and providing "image and a name to the dire entity of slavery, and was an impressive lesson to my children, bring- ing before them the wrongs of the black man." That second winter, Bronson usually spent Sunday evenings at Walden with Henry, who recalled in *Walden* "one real runaway slave, among the rest, whom I helped to forward toward the northstar." Perhaps this was John, by Bronson's account "athletic, dexterous, sagacious, and self-relying," joining the friends one Sunday evening on Henry's third chair.[89]

Jack Garrison, Frederick Douglass, Lewis Hayden, perhaps "John," and how many unnamed others? As Thoreau wrote on, the empty cellar holes of the ruined houses around him came to stand for the emptied dreams of a lost generation. In the quiet of Walden Woods, Thoreau meditated on a new irony: a rising American gen- eration could realize their own dreams of independence only by passage out of America, toward the North Star.

GOING TO EXTREMES II: THOREAU ON KATAHDIN

"Thoreau's is a walking Muse," wrote Alcott about this time, "winged at the anklets and rhyming her steps. The ruddiest and nimblest genius that has trodden our woods, he comes amidst mists and exha- lations, his locks dripping with moisture, in the sonorous rains of an ever-lyric day." For a year, Thoreau's walking muse led him around the widening circles of Walden. "Who knows who his neighbors are," he wrote that first summer. "We seem to lead our human lives amid a concentric system of worlds of realm on realm, close bordering on each other—where dwell the unknown and the imagined races—as various in degree as our own thoughts are." Now it was time to enlarge his circles beyond Walden. Maine had been in the back of his mind since May 1838, when he went looking for a teaching position and found an Indian pointing up the Penobscot, saying, "Two or three miles up the river one beautiful country!"[90] The Penobscot were familiar to Thoreau, for groups still came south to camp on the Concord River and make baskets to sell; "Penobscots by the river are my Britons come to Rome," he'd written years before.[91] It was time the Roman made a trip north.

The Thoreaus had close ties with their Maine cousins, and were always welcome there. In 1832, Henry's cousin Rebecca Billings had married George Thatcher, a Bangor merchant who owned timber interests up the river, who knew the country and the logging business. In 1846, spring floods scoured the upper reaches of the West Branch, weakening the logging dams and strewing logs down the riverbed for many miles. Some of those logs were Thatcher's, and when he decided to travel upriver and inspect the damage for himself, he invited Henry to come along. When Henry insisted they could hardly come so close to Mount Katahdin without climbing it, an expedition was born. On August 31, Thoreau took the railroad to Portland and the steamboat to Bangor, that last great outpost of commerce on the verge of a forest that stretched clear to Canada. At 11:00 a.m. on September 1, Thatcher brought around a wagon and tossed in a carpetbag and his double-barreled shotgun; Thoreau added his knapsack, and they rattled out of "this depot of lumber—this worn Old Bangor," heading sixty miles upriver to Mattawamkeag.[92]

The Penobscot River system had been for decades a great organic machine transforming the Maine woods into commercial timber: its 250 sawmills, Thoreau read, produced two hundred million board feet annually.[93] Their journey upriver allowed Thoreau to study this great machine from port to source. A few miles out, they stopped at the fall line in Stillwater, the region's largest concentration of lumber mills, where Thoreau first saw how "the arrowy Maine for-

est" was night and day "lop[p]ed—scarified—soaked bleached—
shaved—& slit" until it came out "board, clapboards, laths, and
shingles," bound for export to Boston, New Haven, and New York
City. Farther up, they watched the watermen leap from log to log
with their "spike poles," thrusting the floating logs toward the mill
and occasionally getting a ducking. They stopped at a batteau factory in Oldtown so Henry could see how the region's distinctive
riverboats were made—long, solid, canoe-like craft whose "wildly
musical" name evoked the French *voyageurs.*[94]

From there they took the ferry upriver past Indian Island, where
the Penobscot, who once roamed freely for hundreds of miles, lived
on their island reservation. The town had a "shabby and forlorn and
cheerless look all backside and woodshed," deserted, for all Thoreau
could see, except for "a short shabby washerwoman-looking Indian"
who landed his canoe and, taking up a bundle of skins in one hand
and an empty keg in the other, headed for the tiny grocery. "Here
was his history written," Thoreau intoned, offended by the squalor
and poverty. The political history that removed this "once powerful tribe" from their lands and confined them to this tiny plot of
land was, at that moment, beyond his caring or comprehension;
all he could see was a remnant swiftly heading for "extinction."[95]
The ferry landed them in Milford, and they drove up the Houlton
Military Road along a late-summer river, all rocky shallows and rapids. Everywhere, Thoreau saw damage from the flood: houses overturned, great logs strewn like matchsticks, still unclaimed though
each bore the owner's brand. Thatcher kept an eye out for his own
brand among the rest. They stayed the night at Treat's temperance
house, the country's oldest settler's house, where Thoreau noted the
fine, healthy orchard bearing heaps of worthless wild apples.

The next day, upcountry in Lincoln, they sought out an Indian
guide, walking through the forest until they could see the Indians'
shanties on an island across the river. They borrowed a canoe, paddled over, and found Louis Neptune, "a small wiry man with a puck-
ered and wrinkled face"—a respected tribal elder who had guided
Emerson's brother-in-law Charles T. Jackson, the state geologist,

up Katahdin in 1837. Neptune said he and his friend were planning to leave the next day for Chesuncook to hunt moose. What luck! Thoreau and Thatcher hired them on the spot, agreeing to meet them at McCauslin's farm by the dam on the West Branch. Thoreau teased Neptune about Pomola, the evil genius of the mountain: maybe she wouldn't let them go up. Katahdin (or Ktaadn, as Thoreau spelled it), whose name meant "highest land," was sacred to Neptune's people. He deflected the insult with a joke: they'd have to leave a bottle of rum on the top; he'd planted a good many, and when he returned, they were always empty. Thoreau understood neither the insult nor the joke.[96]

Back in Lincoln, the cousins watered their horse and bought ammunition, and Thoreau sniffed at the "bungling" pencils they sold. After reaching the inn at Mattawamkeag, they whiled away the afternoon riding up the Military Road, Thoreau studying the settlers' way of clearing the land: they clearcut the trees and burned them where they fell, rolling the remains together and burning them again, then again, until nothing was left. Meanwhile, they planted potatoes and turnips between the smoldering ash heaps. Thoreau, something of a frontier farmer himself, pulled up a few potato vines and was impressed. It seemed so easy! Why didn't the starving immigrant in New York or Boston get some of this cheap land "and be as rich as he pleases?" Back at the inn, he traced the newest map of Maine to bring along. It turned out to be "a labyrinth of errors"; despite decades of intensive logging, most of Maine's interior had never been accurately mapped. Meanwhile, Thatcher's friends walked in: his brother-in-law Charles Lowell and Horatio P. Blood, whom they all called "Raish." Early the next morning, September 3, the four men shouldered their packs, leaped over the fence, and set off. Henceforth the river was their road, for they left all other roads behind. Thoreau was thrilled. On either hand "was a wholly uninhabited wilderness, stretching to Canada": no horses, no cows, no vehicles—nothing but river and evergreen woods. "Here, then," declared Thoreau, "one could no longer accuse institutions and society, but must front the true source of evil."[97]

The wilderness trail took them first through a smoking waste-land where the trees had been clearcut, "four or 5 deep and crossing each other in all directions all black as charcoal"—enough wood, observed Thoreau, to "keep amply warm the poor of Boston and New York for a winter," here a nuisance to be eliminated as quickly as possible. Thereafter, they ran into a surprising number of people for "uninhabited" country: they rested for a spell at the Crockers' cabin, then at the Howards' sprawling household, and then a little farther on at the Fisks', passing out books to the children and newspapers to the adults as they went. To cross the river they hunted up the ferry-man, finding him in a neat little dwelling "with plenty of books and a new wife just imported from Boston." Across the river they passed a barn filled with summer hay ready to feed the overwintering cattle, and soon they were inspecting loggers' camps—great log buildings chinked with moss, roofs shingled with cedar or spruce, and huge fireplaces; no need to conserve wood here. At the Hale farm, they hoped to get a view of Katahdin from the clearing, but the air was so smoky from the burning trees that they could see nothing. Mrs. Waite served them a generous lunch and refused their payment; conversation was all she asked. They left a picture book for her boy, who, as they left, was reading it avidly.[98]

At George McCauslin's spread, they paused to wait for the Indians. After twenty-two years as a logger and waterman, "Uncle George" had settled down, clearing several hundred acres and build-ing his farm into a business supplying the lumbermen's needs. The supper table overflowed with wheat cakes, ham, eggs, potatoes, milk, cheese, shad, salmon, cakes both sweet and hot; and for des-sert, stewed mountain cranberries and tea sweetened with molasses. There was so much butter they used it to grease their boots, and "many whole logs, 4 feet long were consumed to boil our tea-kettle." The way to their bedrooms led past a dairy "teeming with new milk and cheeses in press." Rain pounded on the roof as the men slept, and they awakened to a storm, so they waited out the day, keeping watch for their guides while looking over the farm. Why, Thoreau asked Uncle George—still thinking of those immigrant masses—

weren't there more settlers on this land? Because, he replied, the land was not for sale. The companies who owned it wanted no towns on their tax rolls, and the few individuals who'd acquired land wanted no neighbors. People brought nothing but trouble.[99]

Clearly this was not the untrammeled wilderness Thoreau had expected. The Indians disappointed him too: Neptune and his friend never showed up. So the next morning, McCauslin himself agreed to be their guide, ignoring his wife's protests that she could hardly milk their cattle by herself. He packed up supplies—a tent, a blanket, fifteen pounds of hard bread, ten pounds of pork—and four miles upriver they stopped at Thomas Fowler's place to recruit young Tom to help handle the batteau, which was a two-man job. For the batteau itself, they headed up the Millinocket to find Tom's father, Old Fowler, who agreed to lend them his. This, wrote Thoreau in his notes, was the last house, for sure. While someone ran off to catch the horses to portage the batteau over the first carry, Mrs. Fowler told them how wolves had just killed nine of their sheep, and she showed off their array of steel traps: wolf-sized, otter-sized, bear-sized. By two o'clock the horses were caught, and the travelers slogged over the rutted Indian portage trail to Quakish Lake while the horses trudged behind, hauling the quarter-ton batteau on its cart. The horses arrived just as the heavens broke into a thunderstorm; the men flipped over the batteau and waited out the deluge, whittling thole pins and singing boat songs. Outside the horses stood "sleek and shining with the rain, all drooping and crestfallen."[100]

At last a streak of blue sky promised fair weather. The six men packed up and set off, the two boatmen poling the twenty-foot craft up the rapids with a speed and skill Thoreau found exhilarating. From Quakish Lake they got their first glimpse of Mount Katahdin, still twenty miles away, its summit veiled in clouds. At the head of the lake they examined the dam—a substantial work of engineering, noted Thoreau, built to flood some sixty square miles—where a gang of men was repairing the spring damage. At the loggers' camp, the cook served tea with hotcakes and sweet cakes, and Thoreau found a well-thumbed copy of Emerson's 1844 "Address on West

Indian Emancipation"—the address for which he'd rung the bell two years before, and for which he'd overseen the printing and distribution. Thatcher, himself an antislavery activist, had left it there on an earlier trip and made, he boasted, no fewer than two converts to the Liberty Party. Even here, Thoreau must have thought, the State was everywhere to be seen. This, he promised himself again, was *truly* "the last human inhabitation of any kind in this direction."[101]

This time, he was more or less right. The sun had set but the moon was up, and by its light the men rowed five miles up North Twin Lake, "a noble sheet of water" on the high tableland between the United States and Canada. By the time McCauslin guided them into a campsite he remembered from his logging days, it was growing dark, and they hurried to gather deadwood while McCauslin felled a few trees to feed a campfire ten feet long by three or four feet high, before which they pitched their cotton tent without calculating on the sparks. When the tent caught fire, they swept it away, laying the remains on the ground for a tarp and sleeping under the overturned batteau, their chilled feet toward the flames. Thoreau awoke around midnight, put some wood on the fire, and gazed far out onto the moonlit lake, hoping to see a moose or a wolf, listening to the tinkling of the rill in the vast silence, and feeling himself at last in a new world, whose "stern yet gentle wildness" he would never forget.[102]

Before dawn the men were on their way, leaving their tremendous fire to burn itself out—common practice, noted the fire-savvy Thoreau, in this damp woods where the valuable timber was gone and no one much cared if what was left burned down. He'd been reading Melville's *Typee*, and as they rowed on, he fantasized he was in the South Pacific approaching the bay of the Typee, who were rushing into the hills to gather coconuts and breadfruit to bring to the beach. But no friendly natives met the *voyageurs* as they rowed through a chain of lakes joined by narrow passages bound by "fencing stuff"—log booms of unhewn timber lashed together for the spring drives down rapids to the hungry mills below. Every time, without fail, Thoreau was startled to see "so plain a trail of the white man" in country so beautiful and wild. After breakfast at the head of Lake Umbedegis, Henry, Tom, and Uncle George explored the overgrown remains of an old logging camp, complete with a crumbling blacksmith's forge. Even here there were ruins and antiquity. "Go where you will somebody has been there before you."[103]

On they went, mile by mile, lake by lake, carry by carry. Once, they passed an orange billboard wrapped around a tree trunk, advertising Oak Hall, a large Boston clothing store. Finally McCauslin landed them at Mount Katahdin's base, at a campsite marked with the skeleton of a dead moose, where he promised "trout enough." Groping round the loose grating of the moose's ribcage, they seized the birch poles hunters left behind; soon they were hauling in fish as fast as they could throw out hooks. After Thoreau lost his hook, he was delegated to catching the fish the men tossed ashore: they fell about him in "a perfect shower," glistening, when alive, "like the fairest flowers, and he stood over them as if in a trance unable to trust his senses—that these jewels should have swum away in that Aboljacknagesac water for so long! So many dark ages these bright flowers seen of Indians only!" McCauslin remanded the bounty to the frying pan, now sizzling with pork. After they ate their fill, Thoreau counted the fin rays and scales to identify the species: "chivin" or white trout, he noted in his Journal, *Leucisci pulchelli*. He fell asleep and dreamed of trout fishing. Awakening in disbelief, he cast a line into the water again "and found the dream to be real and the fable truth." There, under the dark outline of Katahdin, Thoreau fished until the moonlight faded into dawn.[104]

-+->-<-+-

At 6:00 a.m., sated with trout, the six men set off up the creek, following Thoreau's compass in a beeline toward what he mistakenly thought was Katahdin's highest peak, tramping through rough country, eating blueberries, and stepping around bear, moose, and rabbit droppings. By four o'clock, afraid lest there be no water above, they stopped to camp; but Thoreau couldn't stop, so he kept climbing, pulling himself up by the roots of firs and birches or scrambling across precarious gardens of treetops flattened and matted by mosses and cranberries, glimpsing through holes at his feet the dark caverns below—"the most treacherous and porous country I ever travelled." Finally he broke above treeline to a hillside "where rocks grey silent rocks of every shape & size were the flocks and herds that pastured—chewing a rocky cud at sunset. They looked hardly at me without a bleat or low." This, a mockery of the pastoral, was his limit. Darkness was falling, above was nothing but cloud. But when he turned around, he saw Maine itself, "waving, flowing, rippling down below."[105]

He found his friends huddled miserably on the edge of a ravine, one rolled up in a blanket sick, the rest sitting supperless. It was a long night with little sleep "in the very nest of a young whirlwind." After a cold breakfast of pork and hardtack, Thoreau led them up the ridge. Soon he left them far behind, pressing up relentlessly to a high tableland a few hundred feet below a summit he could not see. On he pressed through the rocks—"as if sometime it had rained rocks"—until he climbed into the skirts of cloud. Now and then the wind ripped open a moment of sunshine before wrapping him in a gray dawning light. It was a cloud factory, where "the wind turned them off from bare rocks." He groped for words: this was Caucasus, where Prometheus was bound for deathless punishment; this was Pomola, the "evil genius" of Ktaadn; this was God, angry with all who climb here. No. He tried for words of his own:

> It was vast titanic & such as man never inhabits. Some part of the beholder, even some vital part seems to escape through the loose grating of his ribs as he ascends—he is more lone than one. . . . Vast Titanic inhuman nature has got him at disadvantage caught him alone—& pilfers him She does not smile on him as in the plains— She seems to say sternly why came Ye here before your time—This ground is not prepared for. Is it not enough that I smile in the vallies I have never made this soil for thy feet, this air for thy breathing. . . . Why seek me where I have not called you and then complain that I am not your genial mother.

He couldn't stay. "For what canst thou pray here—but to be delivered from here.—And should thou freeze or starve—or shudder thy life away—here is no shrine nor altar—nor access to my ear." His friends waited below, anxious to get off the mountain, back to the river, and home. The clouds might linger for days; he could not stay. But he had to will himself to leave.[106]

He found his friends waiting for him in a treeless mountain meadow, grazing on cranberries and blueberries. After consoling one another with the view from the slope—what was a mountain without its clouds and mist?—they hurried away, down and down, leaping from log to log, uncertain where they were going. Tom climbed a tree and directed them to a clearing, where fresh tracks told them they had spooked a moose. Soon the landmarks grew familiar, and by two o'clock they were back at the batteau. They hurtled downstream, their spike pole broken, their provisions short, and the weather unpredictable, praying they wouldn't strike a rock and be swamped. That night they camped at the Oak Hall carry, setting off next morning through the long chain of lakes and carries until they reached beautiful Umbedegis Lake, where they breakfasted on the last of their pork. As they glided on, the sky cleared and Katahdin rose above them, high, serene, and cloudless. The afternoon shadows were lengthening when they arrived at Tom's house, where they found Neptune and his companion paddling their birchbark canoes upriver and inquiring, mildly, "'what we kill'"? Thoreau and his party refused to reply, presuming that Neptune, who said he wasn't well, had gone on a drunken bender. After dropping Tom off and spending the night at McCauslin's, the three Bangor men plus Thoreau kept on down the river, not reaching Bangor until 1:30 the next morning, September 11. Three hours later Thoreau boarded the steamer to Boston, and by day's end he was home on Walden Pond—not quite two weeks away, yet long enough to work a revolution in his consciousness.

What, exactly, happened to Thoreau on Katahdin's high slopes? Nothing was as he expected, not even the wilderness, which wasn't wilderness at all. Even where the road ended, the houses did not, and even after the last house, there were logging camps and black-smith forges, dams and log booms, trails rutted with use, even a billboard. The untouched forest had been logged, each tree cut and branded, its destiny not to reach for the heavens but to drop down-stream through the falls to the sawmills. He saw neither wolf nor moose—not living, anyway. The Indians he saw were neither noble nor helpful. Even Katahdin refused him, harrying him with winds and mist, then smiling on him once he'd retreated to the lowlands.

And yet, somehow, it was glorious, exhilarating. Back home at his writing desk, the pages piled high and higher through the fall; he'd never written better, and he knew it. What had happened to him? The turning point, he realized in retrospect, had not been on Katah-din's rocky, cloud-whipped heights, where he'd braced for revelation and found a sublime nature that cold-shouldered him away, exactly as he expected. It had been in the peaceful meadow just below, where something far stranger had surprised him—"I found myself traversing it familiarly like some pasture run to waste," rambling along, sampling blueberries, until the uncanny truth hit him and upended him: no man had ever farmed this land. "Only the moose browsed here, and the bear skulked—and the black partridge fed on the berries and the buds." Here, on this soft and uncanny green, the ground fell away from under him. "Here was no man's garden, but the unhandselled globe. It was not lawn, nor pasture, nor mead, nor woodland, nor lea, nor arable, nor waste-land. It was the fresh and natural surface of the planet Earth." Not "Mother Earth," either, but "Matter, vast, terrific," not humanized in any sense but "a specimen of what God saw fit to make this world."

The most pivotal and most emotional passage in all of Thoreau's work follows:

> What is it to be admitted to a museum, to see a myriad of particular things, compared with being shown some star's surface, some hard matter in its home! I stand in awe of my body, this matter to which I am bound has become so strange to me. I fear not spirits, ghosts, of which I am one,—*that* my body might,—but I fear bodies, I tremble

to meet them. What is this Titan that has possession of me? Talk of mysteries!—Think of our life in nature,—daily to be shown matter, to come in contact with it,—rocks, trees, wind on our cheeks! the *solid* earth! the *actual* world! the *common sense! Contact! Contact! Who* are we? *where* are we?

Some see in these words only terror and alienation. To be reduced to a ghost possessed by an alien body is surely terrifying—an existential terror so profound that Thoreau saw here, at last, his limit point, his bedrock truth. Without flinching, he embraced it. What possesses him *he will fully possess*: "some hard matter," "this matter to which I am bound," this "*actual* world"—"rocks, trees, wind on our cheeks!"[107] The mystery that surrounds us, that touches us, that even caresses us, *is* us, all of us, for like all bodied beings we, too, are "hard matter in its home." Thoreau's response is to reach out, touch back, body to body: "*Contact! Contact!*" He brought nothing off the mountain but his own body, which he now knew was just as material to this planet—this "star's surface"—as rocks, trees, and wind. On Katahdin, Thoreau found his truth. It was deep, even bottomless, yet deeply intimate and familiar—and utterly, unutterably wild.

This meant, of course, that he had to utter it, had to find a new language as wild as the matter that bound him to this star's surface. All that fall of 1846, Thoreau expanded the careful notes he kept in the field—scribbling notes even as the batteau was whirling up the rapids—into a long narrative, the basis for a popular lecture and then for his most successful magazine publication. There he would express the "inexpressible tenderness and immortal life of the grim forest," "home of the moose, the bear, the caribou, the wolf, the beaver, and the Indian," showing an America thinking to live by railroad and telegraph that their very houses were built of timber that "grew but yesterday where the Indian still hunts and the moose runs wild." He saw even Concord's familiar fields with new eyes: "Our fields are as old as God, and the rocks we have to show stamped with his hand." The truth he brought back from Katahdin deepened his sense of kinship with the physical world around him: as he wrote that fall,

"All material things are in some sense man's kindred, and subject to the same laws with him."[108] Standing by the pond, looking into the night sky, he saw the stars themselves as "his distant relations." To stand on some star's surface was to put the heavens under his feet. Now he saw that the circles of Walden reached beyond human limits, touched the very stars above.

LEAVING WALDEN

In *Walden*, Thoreau would dismiss his second year there as the same as the first, folding two years, two months and two days into one grand annual cycle. But in fact that second year was crucial to his experiment, for living through the cycle of seasons a second time allowed him to compare and consolidate. For instance, during the second summer, he debated whether to plant beans again, or instead "sincerity—truth—simplicity—faith—trust—innocence—and see if they will not grow in this soil."[109] He did that, but he also planted his crops a second time—beans, tomatoes, squashes, corn, and potatoes—only to see a hard frost on the night of June 12 kill them to the ground. While this deflected him from repeating his agricultural experiment, it also gave him time to tend his "wild stock" instead. One of his first acts at Walden had been to gather up boxes of wild fruits—red huckleberries and sand cherries, seeds of ironwood, hornbeam, and hackberry—for his friend Marston Watson, busy building his house in Plymouth and planting nurseries and orchards on the surrounding eighty acres. A few months later, in February 1846, Watson and Mary Russell, Thoreau's "Maiden in the East," were married. Thoreau kept up a lively interest in the fortunes of their growing orchard—a Walden writ huge.

Now, through the winter of 1846–47, his interest in wild nature was exploding. His call to "contact" the world found fresh means and methods in science: at Katahdin he'd reserved one fine trout as a specimen, counting its fin rays; a couple of months earlier, he'd measured another from the river, painted its portrait in words, and keyed it out in the report on fish he reviewed in "Natural History of Massachusetts." When the author's son wrote Thoreau from Harvard about collecting birds' eggs, Thoreau replied with happy reminiscences and invited him to Walden.[110] The questions mounted. Thoreau, curious when a crew of ice cutters arrived on the pond, hacked holes in the ice to collect water temperatures. That got him asking how fish survived in the cold—the sort of question Louis Agassiz was asking, too. That winter, crowds gathered weekly at Boston's Tremont Temple, as many as five thousand at a time, to hear Agassiz's Lowell Lectures on the "Plan of Creation in the Animal Kingdom." One of his favorite tricks was to draw a single fish scale, then—awing his audience—rapidly reconstruct more and more of the fish until it seemed to swim right off the blackboard. Thoreau was fired with enthusiasm. As soon as the ice melted, he was collecting specimens for the great man, and on May 3, Agassiz's assistant, James Elliot Cabot, expressed Agassiz's delight and thanks for three boxes of specimens Thoreau sent from Walden: a small mud turtle—"really a very rare species!"—a number of suckers, plus perch, breams, and a trout. Could Thoreau perhaps send more turtles? Cabot enclosed five dollars to cover expenses.[111]

The lively exchange of letters and specimens continued. Thoreau did not merely collect, pack, and ship; he also "took toll" in a flood of questions. Why were his Walden pickerel different from those in the river? And the pouts, too? What species were the suckers?— the perch?—the shiners? What else would Agassiz like to have? "There are also minks muskrats—frogs—lizard—tortoises, snakes caddice worms, leeches muscles [*sic*], &c &c or rather *here* they are." Would Agassiz like to come and see for himself? Near the end of May, Cabot reported that Agassiz was "surprised and pleased" at the extent of Thoreau's contributions, among which he found various species new to science. As for "the little fox" Thoreau sent, he was doing well in his new home—the professor's backyard. And the final touch: Agassiz identified Thoreau's Walden housemate as "the white-bellied mouse." It was the first specimen of that species the professor had ever seen.[112]

A whole new career for Thoreau was coming into view—so, at least, thought Emerson, who recommended Thoreau to his brother-in-law Charles T. Jackson, busy organizing a scientific expedition to survey the geology of Michigan. Thoreau was so keen to go that near the end of May he told a prospective publisher of *A Week* that the printing must be completed soon, since he was about to embark on "a journey of considerable length."[113] Jackson left for Michigan without him—competition was keen for this sort of opportunity. But what if Thoreau had been selected? Might he have gone on to join Agassiz's expedition the following summer, to Lake Superior? This would have put Thoreau at the heart of Agassiz's scientific circle, at the foundation of professional science in America—a circle that years later would include a young William James, who in 1865 joined Agassiz's expedition to Brazil.

This was not, however, to be Thoreau's career path. The "white spaces" he wished to explore were not on the map, but in the mind. These two forms of exploration, outer and inner, converged in surprising ways: it was Agassiz's assistant Cabot who shared with Emerson his excitement over the Bhagavad Gita, which Emerson knew of but had never actually seen. In June 1845 the Gita arrived in Concord; soon Thoreau was reading it. "He cannot be a Yogee, who, in his actions, hath not abandoned all intentions," he copied into his Journal the summer he was jailed.[114] The Gita became the closest thing Thoreau had to a personal Bible. That spring, the Gita open on his desk, he watched as Frederic Tudor, "king" of the New England ice industry, brought in a crew of Irish laborers to harvest ice from Walden Pond, cutting a thousand tons a day. Emerson was horrified. "If this continues," he wrote angrily, "he will spoil my lot for purposes for which I chiefly value it, & I shall be glad to sell it." Thoreau was delighted: he jested with the workers, warmed them at his house, and as he watched them build their "hoary tower—of azure tinted marble," he imagined how the "parched inhabitants" of India would soon be drinking at his well. "In the morning I bathe my intellect in the stupendous and cosmogonal philosophy of the Bhagvat Geeta," then go to the pond, "my well for water, and lo! There I meet the servant of the Brahmin . . . come to draw water for his master, and our buckets as it were grate together in the same well. The pure Walden water is mingled with the sacred water of the Ganges." Via a miracle of modern global commerce—the same miracle that had brought him the Gita to begin with—he could now hope to return the gift, uniting the sacred scripture of India with his new, modern scripture of New England. The wisdom of *Walden* would mingle with the waters of the world.[115]

Thoreau had built his house to last. It's easy to imagine him living there for the rest of his life, growing old and crotchety among the pines. Indeed, the iconic hermit of American lore lives there still. But Thoreau the living person did leave, and in later years the reason puzzled him: "Why I left the woods? I do not think that I can tell. I have often wished myself back. . . . Perhaps I wanted a change— There was a little stagnation it may be. . . . Perhaps if I lived there much longer I might live there forever—One would think twice before he accepted heaven on such terms." Perhaps, he added in *Walden*, he had "several more lives to live, and could not spare any more time for that one."[116]

More prosaically, he left because he was called away by someone he could not refuse—Lidian Emerson. Waldo was planning a year-long lecture tour in Europe, where interest in Transcendentalism and in Emerson himself was growing. As late as August 29, it still appeared that Lidian would board with a friend while her husband was away, but suddenly she invited Henry to live with her and the children instead. Thoreau's life at Walden had been Emerson's greatest gift to him; if his friends needed a favor in return, he would say yes. A week later, on September 6, 1847, Henry Thoreau loaded up his books and furniture, closed his door, and left his house on Walden Pond. There would be no going back. On September 17, Emerson bought the house and leased it to his gardener, Hugh Whelan. With that done, on October 5, Henry, Lidian, and the Alcotts saw Waldo Emerson off at Boston Harbor, sailing for his great trip to Europe. Abba Alcott wept "convulsively," but Lidian, as was her way, didn't shed a tear.[117] As Waldo's ship disappeared over the horizon, Lidian and Henry returned to Concord to take up housekeeping together. Thoreau the hermit was history. Never again would Henry live alone.

CHAPTER SIX

A Writer's Life
(1847–1849)

> But how can I communicate with the gods who am
> a pencil-maker on the earth, and not be insane?
> HENRY DAVID THOREAU, *A WEEK ON THE*
> *CONCORD AND MERRIMACK RIVERS*

"WILL YOU BE MY FATHER?":
THOREAU AT THE EMERSONS'

Although Thoreau later wondered why he had been so willing to leave Walden, in a sense he never did leave. Walden stayed with him for the rest of his life, anchoring his reborn sense of self—independent, solitary even in the midst of crowds, grounded in the splash and spring of bedrock nature. A few weeks after he moved back to town, Thoreau wrote proudly to the class of '37 that he'd lived up to the defiant ideals of his Harvard commencement speech: "I have found out a way to live without what is commonly called employment or industry.... My steadiest employment, if such it can be called, is to keep myself at the top of my condition, and ready for whatever may turn up in heaven or on earth."[1] At Walden he'd met heaven. Now it was time to meet the challenges of earth, home and society—for if what he'd found at Walden was real, it would follow him everywhere, even here.

Once again the little green writing desk stood in the "prophet's chamber" at the head of the Emersons' stairs. For the next ten

months, from October 5, 1847 through July 30, 1848, Thoreau was
not merely gardener and handyman but head of the household,
responsible for a bustling community: Lidian and the three Emerson children—eight-year-old Ellen, six-year-old Edith, and three-
year-old Edward (or Ellie, Edie, and Eddy, as they became in Henry's
letters)—plus Aunt Lucy Brown and the family's live-in servants
Abby and Almira Stevens.[2] "It is a little like joining a community—
this life—to such a hermit as I," Thoreau admitted to Emerson, but
this new experiment "was good for society, & I do not regret my
transient—nor my permanent share in it." Thoreau was in charge
of the kitchen garden and the landscaping, which meant overseeing
Emerson's gardener, Hugh Whelan. He also kept track of Emerson's
complicated financial affairs, which required endless consultations,
and he spent hours each day with the children.[3]

Letters crossed the Atlantic, chock full of news and adventures.
"Lidian and I make very good housekeepers," Thoreau reassured
Emerson; "she is a very dear sister to me—Ellen & Edith & Eddy &
Aunty Brown keep up the tragedy & comedy & tragi-comedy of life
as usual." While Ellen and Edith attended Anna Alcott's day school
at Hillside, Henry tutored little Eddy, who had taken to surveying the world from Henry's shoulders, and, hinted Henry to father
Waldo, he would know how to appreciate "any new and rare breed of
wooden or pewter horses. . . . He very seriously asked me the other
day—'Mr Thoreau—will you be my father?' I am occasionally Mr
Rough-and-Tumble with him—that I may not miss *him*, and lest
he should miss you too much." Waldo was surprised and grateful:
"Our Spartan-Buddhist Henry is a *Père* or *bon-homme malgré lui*,"
he wrote Lidian. It was a daily comfort to think of Henry there with
the family.[4]

The town's juiciest piece of gossip that fall was Sophia Foord's
marriage proposal to Henry Thoreau. "She really did wish to—I
hesitate to write—marry me—that is the way they spell it," he wrote
Emerson. Of course he said no, he added hastily: "I really had anticipated no such foe as this in my career." Emerson blushed in reply:
"You tell me in your letter one odious circumstance, which we will

dismiss from remembrance henceforward."[5] Foord (who was forty-five, half again Thoreau's age) had lived with the Alcotts before joining the Emersons as a tutor, and one of Thoreau's jobs while living out at Walden was to come into town to remodel Emerson's barn into her schoolroom and living quarters. Ill health forced Foord to resign after a year, but she left an impression: the children all liked her, recalled Ellen, and Louisa May Alcott remembered her leading the girls on a walk, disrobing and splashing along in Flint's Pond, "making the fishes run like mad before our big claws, when we got to the other side we had a funny time getting on our shoes and unmentionables, and we came tumbling home all wet and muddy... bawling and singing like crazy folks."[6]

The free-spirited Foord did strike some as eccentric. Late in 1849, Aunt Maria was horrified at a rumor that she was suicidal on account of Henry, to whom she sent "incoherent" letters, which he burned after reading. Foord kept on teaching, kept in touch with the Alcotts, and kept an eye on the Thoreaus, too: in 1869, she startled Henry's sister Sophia by approaching her at a meeting in Boston with the words "You don't know me, Miss Thoreau." After Foord's death in 1885, Louisa paid tribute to her happy lessons, with "many a flower-hunt with Thoreau for our guide," and to "her life-long desire for high thinking and holy living."[7] To the end, Foord insisted she was Thoreau's soul mate, whose spirit would join his in the afterlife, where neither age nor Victorian proprieties of marriage could come between them.

Another preoccupation that summer and fall was the building of Emerson's summerhouse. After plans for a poet's lodge on Emerson's Cliff languished, Alcott found a way to spiritualize the summer day by cutting and weaving willow wands into a twiggy tent. Thoreau and Emerson liked it, and Emerson commissioned Alcott to build a grander version in his yard. In July 1847, they all rode out to Emerson's Walden woodlot, cut down twenty young hemlocks, and carted them home for the house posts. Think of these trees, wrote Emerson, growing for so many years even as he was sleeping, "fenced, bought, & owned by other men," now to grant him their share of sun and earth, rain and frost! Neither he nor Alcott mentioned how Thoreau had to catch a tree Alcott felled toward some neighboring trees, guiding it by main strength to land on open ground.[8] Soon Alcott and Thoreau were laying the floor and raising the nine joists—one for each of the Muses, said Alcott. Instead of framing the house with timbers in the usual way, as Thoreau did at Walden, Alcott wove and lashed the whole together, branch by crooked branch, each one searched out and carried home by Thoreau. Emerson watched anxiously as it took shape, expecting the whole mess to collapse. "I think to call it Tumbledown-Hall," he joked to Lidian; to Fuller he wrote that it was "of growing—alarming—dimensions—peristyle gables, dormer windows, &c in the midst of my cornfield."[9]

Through the fall of 1847, Alcott reveled in the work—his "Sylvan" style of building, he called it, all sweeping mystic curves. After sweating over it all day, he dreamed of it all night. Thoreau found it more of a nightmare. Aunt Maria fretted that Alcott "pulls down as fast as he builds up," which was bad enough; worse, one time, the top rafter was accidentally knocked off, and Henry had to leap for his life into a nearby haystack.[10] In November Thoreau alerted Emerson that things were growing serious: Alcott's air-castle needed some foundation in the laws of physics and mathematics. "'Did you ever study geometry?'" he hollered to Alcott one day. "'The relation of straight lines to curves—the transition from the finite to the infinite? Fine things about it in Newton & Leibnitz.'—But he would hear none of it." But Alcott did hear the jibes of passersby who stopped to stare: it was odd, the strangest thing they ever saw, a whirligig. Still, it had a certain charm; even Thoreau admitted it had a "disposition to be beautiful."[11] Through the winter it sat unfinished, but next spring Alcott roofed it with thatch and moss. As a poet's lodge it proved useless, being open to rain and mosquitos, but to everyone's surprise it stood for many years, a two-story picturesque wonderment of art—at least, to some. When Emerson's mother saw it, she snorted and dubbed it "the Ruin." Emerson paid Alcott $50 for his labor, Thoreau $31.50, and for years afterward he funneled money to

Alcott for repairs—a clever way, friends suspected, to help Alcott's struggling family.[12]

By contrast, Thoreau's Walden house, built with such care and craft, met a very different fate. Three weeks after Henry moved out, Emerson rented it to his gardener, Hugh Whelan, who planned to move it up by the road, enlarge it, plant an orchard, and move in with his family. By January Hugh had moved the house, dug the cellar hole, and bought the stones to line it, but there things sat, for he quarreled with his wife and left Concord, vowing never to return, leaving the unstoned cellar to slump and swallow one end of the house. The thing was still fixable, Thoreau wrote Emerson in January—he'd envisioned his house as the first of a new and thriving Walden community, and he still hoped Emerson could manage it "to be a home for somebody."[13] Instead, Emerson let it decay until September 1849, when he sold it to a local farmer who moved it a couple of miles north as a storage shed for corn. There Thoreau's beloved house rotted slowly away, visited now and then in after years by Sophia or Ellery Channing, until the owners pulled it down in 1868, recycling the usable boards to build a shed and repair a barn, where, legend has it, a few boards linger on to this day. The rest dissolved back into the elements—sun and earth, rain and frost—of which it had been composed.[14]

The forest, too, was dissolving. Locomotives were sparking fires in Walden Woods, damaging valued timber; in November, Thoreau reported to Emerson, the woods by his Walden field had burned clear to the road on one side and to the fence rail on the other, set ablaze by "Lucifer." Years would not repair such "a great loss." Next May, that same Lucifer set fire to Emerson's own woods. Indignant, Emerson demanded the railroad pay him damages (they did), and once he was home, he sold them the burned-over acres.[15] But far worse was under way: with the railroad making cheap Maine lumber readily available, Concord landowners were converting their now useless Walden woodlots into ready cash, fuel for railroad engines and lumber for railroad ties, maybe getting a crop or two of rye or English hay out of the cutover land. For two centuries the Walden forest had been valued and sustained. Thoreau remembered how Walden Pond, in his youth, was "completely surrounded by thick and lofty pine and oak woods," with grapevines embowering the coves into deep caves through which a boat could pass. Now he watched the trees fall. By 1854, the year *Walden* was published, nearly all the woods had been clear-cut, laying waste Walden's shores: "Now for many a year there will be no more rambling through the aisles of the wood, with occasional vistas through which you see the water." Thoreau's muse was silenced; "how can you expect the birds to sing when their groves are cut down?"[16]

→>–<←

As the winter of 1848 wore on, Lidian's health began to fail, casting a cloud of worry over the household. Henry withheld the news from the lonely and overtaxed Emerson, knowing how he needed those warm and witty letters from home. In January Emerson responded with unguarded love: "Let who or what pass, there stands the dear Henry,—if indeed anybody had a right to call him so,—erect, serene, & undeceivable. So let it ever be!" The endearment broke through Henry's guard and brought a gush of gratitude: "Dear Waldo"— never before had Henry called Emerson by his familiar name— "Whatever I may *call* you, I know you better than I know your name." The sudden intimacy unleashed Henry's pent-up worry over Lidian, who, he admitted, had been bedridden for weeks without telling her husband, and was now too sick and weak with jaundice to write at all—"as yellow as saffron." All winter long, with Lidian sick in bed, Henry devoted himself to the children. Every night he read to them from the *Diadem*, a children's annual: "All the annuals and 'diadems' are in requisition, and Eddy is forward to exclaim when the hour arrives, 'Now for the dem dems!'" While Ellen offered her "wise criticisms," Edith protested that he turned the pages too soon—and thus they went through the *Penny Magazine*, too, "first from beginning to end, and then from end to beginning, and Eddy stared just as much the second time as the first."[17]

Despite Henry's reassurances, Waldo grew almost frantic with worry. He was beset with money troubles, for times were hard in England and his lectures were earning only a fraction of the promised profits. Debts at home were mounting, too, and time and again he had to instruct Lidian to borrow money from William. "I shall never dare to go from home again," he fretted, if it caused such "a crop of annoyances and pains."[18] Yet his days abroad were hugely full. Emerson was being honored as a celebrity and entertained as an equal by the British Empire's greatest names, and he had a front row view of world history: that spring he put aside his worries over the cost and ventured a side trip to Paris, walking straight into the street violence of the Revolution of 1848. Even then, Margaret Fuller was filling the front pages of the *New-York Tribune* with riveting dispatches from Rome, where she had joined the fight for the Roman Republic; fearing for her life, Emerson begged her to return home with him, not knowing she had fallen in love with an Italian rebel and given birth to their child.

Yet as world history was surging forward, the news that mattered most to Waldo came from home. Soon Lidian was writing him of her recovery: there in the brightening spring, Henry was setting out pear trees "of which you, dear husband, will gather and eat the fruit, I hope." Even as she wrote, she reported, Henry was in the midst of his nightly "go-to-bed frolic" with Eddy, who informed his mother "that Mr T. has first swallowed a book, then pulled it out of his (Eddy's) nose, then put it into his (Mr T.'s) 'pantalettes.' I tell Henry I shall send you word he is in his second childhood, a wearer of pantalettes." How strongly each loving anecdote "draws me homeward," sighed Waldo, counting the days, weary of being toasted in Britain as America's newest literary lion.[19]

What was in Henry's heart during these long and busy months as surrogate father and man of the house? He kept no surviving journal, and from the record one can surmise both a time of happy contentment and a time of deep psychic distress. As Lidian descended into the depths of her lonely illness, she wrote letters that the faraway Waldo found too appalling to keep, and to which he replied, in despair, that "a photometer cannot be a stove," that "the trick of solitariness never never can leave me."[20] Love for a distant Emerson—distant even when he was present—was one thing Lidian and Henry shared. This had drawn them together before, and it did so even more strongly now, for Henry's own love for Lidian was certainly the deepest he ever knew for a woman to whom he was not related. Yet it puzzled him to define the exact nature of their relationship.

It was, he proposed a year later, love for a "Sister," "One in whom you have—unbounded faith—whom you can—purely love." Lidian was, like young Edmund Sewall, both deeply attractive to him and profoundly unattainable, and in both cases his response was classically Platonic. "I still think of you as my sister. . . . Others are of my kindred by blood or of my acquaintance but you are mine. you are of me and & I of you I can not tell where I leave off and you begin." "I am as much thy sister as thy brother—Thou art my brother as much as my sister." It was hardly physical attraction, for to him her body was merely a "veil" that vanished utterly, leaving them both pure spirits, together: "When I love you I feel as if I were annexing another world to mine. We splice the heavens. . . . the feminine of me." Or the feminine of Waldo—embodying their united spiritual ideals better than Emerson himself. Whether this made Lidian mother instead of sister, himself son instead of brother, Henry couldn't say. What he could say was that she was life giving, and the light he saw in her eyes was creative, inceptive. She was nothing less than his morning star.[21]

This raises, without resolving, the question of Thoreau's sexuality. Here, too, his reflections are to modern ears both unsettlingly innocent and far too fluid to pin to customary gender roles. Thoreau could write, without embarrassment, "I love men with the same distinction that I love woman—as if my friend were of some third sex," he added. Those "friends" were often men: Emerson, Alcott, and Channing, of course, as well as others to come. They were also women: Lidian and Lucy, Anna Russell, Margaret Fuller, and yes, Ellen Sewall—and perhaps Sophia Foord, before she violated his ideal by proposing marriage. All had keen intellects and, with the

exception of Ellen, were married already or old enough—or, eventually, young enough—to render marriage moot. With such women
Thoreau found companionship and even, as with Lidian, something
virginal and sacred: "The end [purpose] of love is not house keeping," he hypothesized, but "the letting go of the house." Around
the time of Foord's proposal, he observed, "Considering how few
poetical friendships there are   It is astonishing how many men and
women are married," as if men yielded too easily "to nature without
consulting their genius"—an apt description of Ellery Channing's
deteriorating marriage with Ellen Fuller. "The end of nature is not
the propagation of the species," he continued, but something higher:
lovers should "incessantly stimulate each other to a loftier and purer
life." We love flowers for their blossoms, not their seeds.[22]

When Thoreau put into words his yearning for companionship,
his pronouns were often male; when he was physically attracted to
someone, they were often, though not always, men. But no evidence
exists that he acted or felt he could act on those attractions. Instead
he made himself into what Emerson called "the bachelor of thought
and nature," living an outwardly unremarkable life in a family of
unmarried aunts, uncles, and siblings, in a town where unmarried
men and women were common; Thoreau "was more unlike his
neighbors in his thought, than in his action."[23] Some of that thinking
emerged in his tortured chapter on "Higher Laws," where he battled
with his sensual, animal self: "Nature is hard to be overcome," he
concluded fiercely, "but she must be overcome." Yet he had in mind
not so much repression as sublimation. He imagined life attaining
to "purity," in which "the spirit" could "pervade and control every
member and function of the body, and transmute what in form is the
grossest sensuality into purity and devotion"—a "generative energy"
that, when controlled and contained, "invigorates and inspires us."
Why, he wondered, cannot we speak of bodily functions—eating,
drinking, voiding excrement and urine—without shame? "In a pure
society," he ventured, "the subject of copulation would not be so
often avoided from shame," hinted and winked about, "but treated
naturally and simply." For why should we be ashamed of the tem-

ple that is our body? And not be artists of our body, sculptors and builders of that "temple" instead? Until Walt Whitman published his poetry, such thoughts had no common language for expression.[24]

To a friend, Thoreau confessed, "The intercourse of the sexes, I have dreamed, is incredibly beautiful, too fair to be remembered," "an inexpressible delirium of joy" that he associated with "true marriage." But he would know it only in dreams. The flowering of passion in "beauty & art" was his true calling, which he guarded fiercely with what he called (in the language of his day) "chastity." In another day and place, his ascetic vocation might have called him to monasticism, as it did his friend Isaac Hecker, who in turn urged monkhood on Henry; a deleted phrase in Emerson's eulogy recognizes that Thoreau was nearest to "the old monks in their ascetic religion."[25] For Thoreau the deepest existential gulf between self and other was neither caused by gender difference—what greater miracle can be imagined, he wrote, than to look through each other's eyes for a moment!—nor resolved by defending sexual differences. In another place and time, he might have found his life's partner with a man. For Thoreau, however, in Victorian Concord, that door was closed. In his acute, unspeakable awareness of difference from those around him, he crafted a self of fluid but carefully guarded sensuality and intense, thwarted romantic energies, and he poured those energies, with ever-increasing passion, into his devotional life as an artist and prophet—an "azad," he wrote in *Walden*, a "religious independent" who, being fruitless, could be "a free man," as free as the evergreen cypress.[26]

"LECTURES MULTIPLY ON MY DESK": THOREAU FINDS HIS AUDIENCE

In March 1848 came an unlooked for opportunity to explore that high vocation with Harrison Gray Otis Blake, the man who became Thoreau's first real disciple. Harry Blake lived in nearby Worcester. As an 1838 Harvard Divinity School graduate, he had helped instigate and publish Emerson's breakthrough critique of conventional Christianity, "The Divinity School Address." In the ensuing firestorm, Blake had dropped out of the ministry and taken up teaching, often inviting Emerson to lecture in Worcester. Something Thoreau said caught his ear, and after reading, of all things, Thoreau's obscure "Aulus Persius Flaccus," Blake was inspired to write a fan letter: "I would know of that soul which can say 'I am nothing.' I would be roused by its words to a truer and purer life."[27]

Roused himself, Thoreau sat down at his green desk in the prophet's chamber and poured out heart and soul. "I am glad to hear that any words of mine, though spoken so long ago that I can hardly claim identity with their author, have reached you," he opened. "It is not in vain that man speaks to man. This is the value of literature." In the rest of the letter, Thoreau explored his hopes, dreams, and philosophy; gave counsel; radiated wisdom; and yearned for a higher life. Never before had anyone triggered such a generous response from him. "I need to see you," he closed. "Perhaps you have some oracles for me."[28] Blake did; he wrote back immediately. The two became lifelong friends, exchanging frequent visits and often traveling together. Many times Blake invited Thoreau to lecture in Worcester, often in his parlor, where Harry and his wife Nancy gathered their friends to listen and converse. Thoreau wrote fifty more letters to Blake, the last from his deathbed. Whenever a new one arrived, Blake would call together his circle—above all the philosophical tailor Theophilus Brown, who lived nearby—to read and weigh Thoreau's words. In after years, Blake became his friend's literary executor, and though, sadly, someone destroyed Blake's half of their correspondence, he treasured Thoreau's papers, publishing four volumes of excerpts from Thoreau's Journal and creating his first modern audience—an audience that grows to this day. Such, indeed, is the value of literature.

What's more, Blake gave Thoreau what he most needed: the conviction that he had something to say and an audience to whom he could say it. "Lectures begin to multiply on my desk," he wrote happily to Emerson.[29] He had brought away from Walden a whole stack of unfinished projects, including a complete first draft of *A Week on the Concord and Merrimack Rivers*, a nearly finished draft of *Walden*, a rough draft of "Ktaadn," and more—indeed, much of his life's work. He took up each project in turn, polishing it and turning it loose in the world. At Walden, Thoreau had learned how to live a writer's life; now at Emerson's, he was living it still, surrounded by manuscripts in various stages of composition, a different project for every mood and interest, each one finding its unique voice and stance relative to the others and all of them together composing a literary ecology.

The one project Thoreau completed at Walden Pond was, in effect, an essay on how to write. The over-the-top pyrotechnics of Emerson's Scottish friend Thomas Carlyle had intrigued Thoreau since he first encountered them at Harvard. Carlyle broke every rule Professor Channing ever prescribed and danced like the devil on the shards. In writing about Carlyle, Thoreau cared less about *what* he said than *how* he said it—that is, his "style," meaning, Thoreau explained, "the *stylus*, the pen he writes with," literally the point where a mind, in meeting the blank paper, meets the whole world. What was really at stake was Thoreau's own pen, Thoreau's own style. The essay he finally published, "Thomas Carlyle and His Works," reads like a final exam in a long, self-taught course in how to stop sounding like a Harvard graduate, how to start reaching farmers and mechanics as well as preachers and professors. Old people, wrote Thoreau, shook their heads at Carlyle's "foolishness" and "whimsical ravings," but *young* people got it: his craziness was good plain English. Defending Carlyle gave Thoreau permission to sound like himself. "Exaggeration! was ever any virtue attributed to a man without exaggeration? was ever any vice, without infinite exaggeration? Do we not exaggerate ourselves to ourselves, or do we recognize ourselves for the actual men we are? Are we not all great men? . . . The lightning is an exaggeration of the light."[30]

Best of all, Carlyle kicked philosophy out-of-doors, among the common people. Thoreau saw him as the hero of the working-man—as a workingman himself, toiling through the fog and smoke of London to earn the bread of life and share it freely with the poor, "the hero, as literary man," who would not rest until "a thousand named and nameless grievances are righted." Thoreau saw his opening here between Carlyle the literary hero and Emerson the idealist philosopher: neither one spoke to "the Man of the Age," to the life of the ordinary "working-man." That would be Thoreau's place— Thoreau the day laborer who could plow a field, swing a hammer, stone a cellar, reset a privy or plant an orchard. *Work!* said Carlyle. "*Know what thou canst work at*." But, Thoreau added—looking at Walden's calm waters—he missed in Carlyle "a calm depth, like a lake" that would still that whirligig working mind, so one could think, and reflect, and "feel the juices of the meadow." Speak of what you believe; speak out of your *experience*. "Dig up some of the earth you stand on, and show that."[31]

On February 4, 1846, Thoreau had banked his fire at Walden and walked into town to air his thoughts on Thomas Carlyle. His neighbors listened politely but protested that they wanted to hear about Henry Thoreau, not Thomas Carlyle. What was he doing out there at the pond? Was he lonely? Was he afraid? What did he eat? Thoreau wasn't ready to answer them yet. Instead he polished up his Carlyle piece and sent it to Horace Greeley in New York—the first test of Greeley's offer, made nearly three years before, to serve as Thoreau's literary agent. Greeley was as good as his word. "Carlyle" was too long, he warned, and "too solidly good" for the masses, but still, Greeley placed it almost immediately in the upscale *Graham's Magazine* after assuring the editors it was "brilliant as well as vigorous" and written by "one of the only two men in America capable of giving it." It was a good match to one of the few journals that actually paid, although *Graham's* delayed getting Thoreau's essay into print until the following spring of '47, and then forgot to pay him until Greeley, ticked, cornered the editors in person a year later with a bill for seventy-five dollars. Thoreau was overcome with gratitude to have such a champion. Emerson made sure Carlyle received a copy, which his distant friend read "with due entertainment and recognition" for Thoreau's "most admiring greathearted manner."[32]

A long, heavy essay on Carlyle would hardly put Thoreau's name in lights, but even here Greeley saw an opportunity. "Just set down and write a like article about Emerson," he prodded, then another about Hawthorne, and so on. He'd pay twenty-five dollars for each one, sell them individually, then collect them into a book. It was a great plan—for someone else. After jotting a few notes about Emerson and Alcott, Thoreau wisely stepped back from writing exposés of his friends. Indeed, he was done writing about other men. Instead he would offer what he himself wanted of any lecturer: "a more or less simple & sincere account of his life." So a year later, in February 1847, Thoreau banked his fire again, hiked into town, and stepped up to the podium to answer his neighbors' questions: "Some have wished to know what I got to eat—If I didn't feel kind o' lonesome—If I wasn't afraid—What I should do if I were taken sick—and the like. . . . After I lectured here last winter I heard that some had expected that I would answer some of these questions in my lecture."[33] It was an instant hit—"uncommonly excellent," thought Prudence Ward. Henry was asked to repeat it the following week, but instead he gave a whole second lecture. Soon he had a trio of lectures he could mix and match, or give as a series. Eventually they became the opening chapters of *Walden*.

Reactions to the new Walden material were encouraging. Even skeptics "were charmed with the witty wisdom which ran through it all," said Emerson. Abigail Alcott joked that "Mr. Alcott thinks we shall never be safe until we get a Hut on Walden Pond where with our Beans Books and Peace we shall live honest and independent"— then added, more seriously, "It is no small boon to live in the same age with so experimental and true a Man." Prudence Ward was a bit more hesitant: "Of course few would adopt his notions—I mean as they are shown forth in his life." Yet even she thought it was useful, and "much needed."[34] *Walden* was taking shape: edgy social satire, exaggerated for humor and sting, delivered neighbor to neighbor. "I trust that none of my hearers will be so uncharitable as to look into my house now," at the end of a dirty winter, with "critical house-wife's eyes"—whose eyes did he catch just then?—"for I intend to celebrate the first bright & unquestionable spring morning by scrubbing my house with sand until it is white as a lily—or, at any rate, as the washerwoman said of her clothes, as white as a 'wiolet.'"[35] When Thoreau moved away from Walden to Emerson's, he went back to work, polishing the early lectures into what he now envisioned as a second book, a sequel to *A Week*.

A winter lecture by Henry Thoreau was becoming a regular feature of Concord life. Once he was settled at the Emersons', Thoreau unpacked the manuscript of "Ktaadn" and got it ready for a test run, soon after New Year's Day 1848. This lecture, too, went well. "I read a part of my excursion to Ktaadn to quite a large audience," he reported to Emerson in England, "whom it interested. It contains many facts and some poetry." The faithful Abigail and Bronson Alcott were again in the audience, and Bronson liked the lively description of wild "Kotarden"—a misspelling that suggests how the Penobscot word sounded from Thoreau's mouth.[36] Thoreau's goal is suggested by a line from his Walden lectures: "I wanted to live deep and suck out all the marrow of life . . . to drive life into a corner, and if it proved to be mean, why then to get the whole and genuine meanness of it . . . or if it were sublime to know it by experience and be able to give a true account of it in my next excursion."[37]

Two months later, Thoreau had that true account ready. Hoping "Ktaadn" would bring in some much-needed dollars "to manure my roots," he asked James Elliot Cabot—Agassiz's assistant, now working on the new *Massachusetts Quarterly Review*—whether they paid for contributions. In the *Dial* days, Thoreau let his work go for free, but when Cabot admitted they couldn't pay, Thoreau sent "Ktaadn" to Greeley, who snapped it up with a check for twenty-five dollars: it was worth at least that much, he said, even though it was too long for the *Tribune* and "too fine for the million."[38] Once again Greeley hit the mark: two months later, in July 1848, the first of five monthly installments appeared in the *Union Magazine*. Thoreau's next letter from Greeley included *another* check, for fifty dollars. "To think that while I have been sitting comparatively idle here, you have been so active in my behalf!" Thoreau wrote back in amazement. He added a paragraph telling Greeley about life at Walden: living simply, in a house he built himself, on a dollar a day earned by manual labor. Greeley, the sharp-eyed journalist, spotted a good story. He ran the paragraph under the title "A Lesson for Young Poets" in the *New-York Daily Tribune* on May 25, 1848. The piece went viral, reprinted in newspapers across the country. Suddenly Thoreau was hot. "Don't scold," pleaded Greeley. "It will do great good," and few people would know who it was. To sweeten his apology, he enclosed yet another check, for twenty-five dollars—the balance for "Ktaadn."[39]

The way was open: Greeley knew exactly how to propel Thoreau to the top of the national marketplace. Write short pieces, he urged; follow out your thought, write an essay on "The Literary Life." And for goodness sakes, advertise! Get up some short passages from the book manuscript and get them printed around. "You must write to the magazines in order to let the public know who and what you are. . . . You may write with an angel's pen, yet your writings have no mercantile, money value till you are known and talked of as an author."[40]

Greeley's cagey business sense, plus his frank opinion that Thoreau was a major author worth real money, gave Thoreau the confidence to sass Emerson when his old mentor wrote from England to ask Thoreau to help out, for free, yet another worthy but failing literary journal—that same *Massachusetts Quarterly Review* he had already rejected. Shortly before Emerson left for England, some of the old crew had gathered to talk about reviving the *Dial*. Theodore Parker took the lead, launching a new journal in December, but by May 1848, dire reports were reaching Emerson in England: the fledgling journal was faltering. Thoreau, he urged by mail, must "fly to the rescue." But Thoreau wasn't having any of it. The problem, he tartly wrote back, wasn't getting "good things printed," but getting them *written*. Who needed more "impassable swamps of ink & paper"? "How was it with the Mass. Quart. Rev.? . . . I read it, or what I could of it," and if one man had written it, not one publisher would have printed it. "It should have been suppressed for nobody was starving for *that*." As for himself? "Greeley has sent me $100 dollars and wants more manuscript." So there. "Thank Henry for his letter," Emerson wrote Lidian. "He is always *absolutely* right, and *particularly* perverse."[41] The instant Emerson was home from Europe, he withdrew his support from Parker's magazine, which folded after three years. Thoreau never published in it.

"CIVIL DISOBEDIENCE"

Thoreau now stood at a professional crossroads. He had brought whole stacks of fresh manuscripts away from Walden, enough to keep Greeley happy for years. But if he would not follow Emerson's advice, neither would he follow Greeley's. "Ten years hence will do for publishing books," Greeley had warned, urging Thoreau to send him shorter pieces in the meantime to build up his reputation—but there on Thoreau's desk was the manuscript of *A Week on the Concord and Merrimack Rivers*, a very long book. And though he was working up a shorter piece he could have sent to Greeley, he did not: "Resistance to Civil Government." Eventually it would earn worldwide fame and notoriety under the title "Civil Disobedience."

On January 26, 1848, three weeks after entertaining the lyceum with his ascent of Katahdin, Thoreau stepped to the lyceum podium again, this time to explain, at long last, why he had gone to jail rather than pay his poll tax (the disapproving Emerson was, significantly, still away in England). Thoreau called his new lecture "The Rights and Duties of the Individual in relation to Government," and he had so much to say that three weeks later he returned to finish his remarks. Bronson Alcott, his fellow tax resister, praised Thoreau's "admirable statement" to "an attentive audience": the Mexican War, Samuel Hoar's expulsion from Carolina, Thoreau's imprisonment for refusal to pay his tax, Hoar's payment of Alcott's tax when he was taken to prison for a similar refusal, "were all pertinent, well-considered, and reasoned. I took great pleasure in this deed of Thoreau's."[42]

Only one other response to the lecture is on record: a year later, Elizabeth Peabody asked Thoreau if she might publish it in the first issue of her new journal, *Aesthetic Papers*. Yes, replied Thoreau, though he was too pressed for time to do much revising; and he stipulated it be published in the first issue only, not held over for the next. He was right to be wary, for the journal failed after the first issue and a second never materialized. Thus it was that on May 14, 1849, "Resistance to Civil Government" was published to the world, only to vanish immediately into obscurity. The few reviews were uncomprehending. The author, sniffed one, appeals to the New Testament in everything except for those ugly precepts about paying tribute and submitting to authority. Another thought Thoreau's essay the "queerest" in this collection of oddities, but still, "he writes straight on what he thinks." A third dismissed Thoreau outright "with an earnest prayer that he may become a better subject in time, or else take a trip to France, and preach his doctrine of 'Resistance to Civil Government' to the rest of the red republicans." Nevertheless, when Thoreau's essay was republished in 1866 under the new title "Civil Disobedience," it coined a phrase, started a movement, and eventually earned Thoreau international fame.[43]

In the interval between his arrest in July 1846 and his two-part lecture in winter 1848, Thoreau's sense of injury at the hands of people he trusted had simmered into a question at the heart of democracy: How can the individual assert the right to live a virtuous life in a society that refuses to permit that right, or worse, actively destroys it? As Alcott's reaction to the lecture shows, in winter 1848 Thoreau spoke directly to his friends and located his protest in the specifics of Concord politics. The lecture itself has been lost, but the essay of May 1849 shows that at some point, Thoreau universalized his arguments even as he kept them grounded in the events and personalities of the moment, speaking and writing from all the contradictory impulses, mixed reactions, and delayed responses of lived experience.

Thoreau opens with an allusion to the red-meat motto of O'Sullivan's *Democratic Review*: "That government is best which governs least." Or, as Thoreau presses, "That government is best which governs not at all"—a nod to his instructors in peaceful protest, Alcott and Lane, followers of Garrison's "No-Government" movement. But then he takes a startling turn: Thoreau *rejects* their rejection of government. "But to speak practically and as a citizen, unlike those who call themselves no-government men, I ask for, not at once no government, but at once a better government. Let every man make known what kind of government would command his respect, and that will be one step toward obtaining it."[44] Here he looks over to Emerson, who had scoffed that a person who resisted civil government could hardly claim to be a citizen of it. Thoreau's reply is carefully considered: it is precisely "as a citizen" that he recognizes the need for government, and in turn is recognized by the government whenever it hands him a tax bill. Therefore, it is *as a citizen* that he has the right—indeed, the moral obligation—to speak out. This is why taxes are the proper point of protest: taxes are the sign of citizenship. And given that every tax bill presents the citizen with precisely two choices—pay, or refuse to pay—both choices have to be deliberate actions; that is, the product not of unthinking habit but of conscious thought—of *conscience*.

Thoreau's conscience was clean on the highway tax, which he paid willingly, but not on the poll tax: since only those who paid could vote, it was not merely the sign of citizenship, but also the *instrument* of citizenship. That's why Emerson's quarrel, that payment was relatively harmless since only a tiny fraction of the tax dollar went for "mischief," misses the point: "I do not care to trace the course of my dollar, if I could, till it buys a man, or a musket to shoot one with,—the dollar is innocent,—but I am concerned to trace the effects of my allegiance." It is an allegiance Thoreau refuses: "I cannot for an instant recognize that political organization as my government which is the slave's government also."[45] For his allegiance could only abet the same government that enslaves men, shoots Mexicans, and robs Indians of their land: these are the three abuses specified by Thoreau, each a distinct form of state-sponsored violence, and each a violation not merely of his personal moral conscience, but also of the ethical conscience of the larger community. Action from conscience therefore requires effectual withdrawal from the State, at least until the State ends its abuse.

Up to this point, Alcott would have nodded agreement, but titling the published essay "*Resistance* to Civil Government" defied Alcott as well. Alcott's philosophy of "nonresistance" required submitting to the law, returning forced coercion with holy love. On this point, Thoreau listened instead to Frederick Douglass, whose narrative of self-transformation from slavery to freedom hinged on his refusal to submit to a beating by the slave master Covey: "My resistance was so entirely unexpected, that . . . [h]e trembled like a leaf. . . . He asked me if I meant to persist in my resistance. I told him I did, come what might."[46] In support of Douglass's action, Thoreau served up William Paley's essay "On the Duty of *Submission* to Civil Government"—required reading at Harvard. By using Douglass to subvert Paley, Thoreau pinpointed the error foisted onto every Harvard student and spread by all of Concord's elite: that the ultimate social good was a smooth-running social machine. Thoreau's very title states his counterargument. When the smooth-running machine of civil government causes injustice, the citizen's moral duty is not submission but resistance: "If I have unjustly wrested a plank from a drowning man, I must restore it to him though I drown myself. This, according to Paley, would be inconvenient. But he that would save his life, in such a case, shall lose it. This people must cease to hold slaves, and to make war on Mexico, though it cost them their existence as a people."[47]

And it would cost. Perhaps the most telling aspect of "Resistance to Civil Government" is Thoreau's sensitivity to the pain of those subjected to systemic violence. This included, remarkably, his Concord friends and neighbors. What held them back, he recognized, was neither stupidity nor cowardice, but fear for both themselves and their families: "They cannot spare the protection of the existing government, and they dread the consequences of disobedience to it to their property and families." Thoreau acknowledged their vulnerability and his own privilege: with no property and no dependents, he risked only his body, which meant he, in particular, was *obligated* to assume that risk. Unlike his neighbors, he could "afford to refuse

allegiance to Massachusetts, and her right to my property and life."
Ironically, poverty made him worth more, since disobedience cost
him less. Yet why risk it at all? Why (Thoreau imagines someone
asking him) "expose yourself to this overwhelming brute force?"
Emerson's answer was to assume Thoreau's act was a step toward
suicide. Thoreau replied it was not "wholly a brute force, but partly
a human force," and therefore "appeal is possible." Exposing his body
to violence (in the form of forced incarceration), in plain view of his
neighbors, revealed a hidden violence exercised by the State, making everyone's secret fear visible and hence actionable. Thoreau told
his neighbors that their revulsion, directed at him, was misdirected;
their target should be not the jailed, but the jailer. But in their very
revulsion, *rightly* directed, Thoreau found hope: this force was not
brute, but human, and humans could make moral choices. Humans
could, as Douglass did, resist.[48]

And so, finally, can those who inflict violence. Here Thoreau
turns to "my civil neighbor, the tax-gatherer," his old friend Sam
Staples, and puts him on the spot. "If the tax-gatherer, or any other
public officer, asks me, as one has done, 'But what shall I do?' my
answer is, 'If you really wish to do any thing, resign your office.'
When the subject has refused allegiance, and the officer has resigned
his office, then the revolution is accomplished." Now the fork in the
road is faced not by the citizen, but by the public official in a position
of authority, who, in turn, must make his own moral choice between
two options—to enforce an unjust law, or to resist it. He, too, must
choose with his conscience, as a *human*, not unconsciously as a cog
in a machine. Here is Thoreau's most pointed injunction, in an essay
filled with them: "If the injustice . . . is of such a nature that it requires
you to be the agent of injustice to another, then, I say, break the law.
Let your life be a counter friction to stop the machine. What I have to
do is to see, at any rate, that I do not lend myself to the wrong which
I condemn."[49] The inventor who dreamed of wheels and gears knew
how to build machines—and how to break them, too.

Alcott had used his own life as counterfriction to the machine,
and Thoreau had seen what it cost his family. Part of that cost was

the fear implanted in all their neighbors, who, watching the Alcotts as well as Henry Thoreau, came to dread the consequences of even the mildest acts of civil disobedience. This, finally, was the point: government is necessary after all, not to inflict punishment upon such civil dissenters as Alcott and Thoreau, but to value them and protect their right, along with the right of all citizens, to live ethical lives. Thoreau ends by imagining a truly just State "which can afford to be just to all men, and to treat the individual with respect as a neighbor; which even would not think it inconsistent with its own repose, if a few were to live aloof from it," neither meddling with it nor embraced by it. "A State which bore this kind of fruit, and suffered it to drop off as fast as it ripened, would prepare the way for a still more perfect and glorious State, which also I have imagined, but not yet anywhere seen."[50]

Here at the essay's end appears the utopian "better government" Thoreau calls for in his opening, one that would not merely tolerate but actually bear fruit in such dissenters as Alcott and himself, that would allow them to ripen and bear seed—*wild* fruits, like those in the fields where he led the huckleberry pickers upon his release from jail. Thoreau's essay thus suggests a range of possible actions, from his own huckleberry excursions and his mother's refusal to serve slave-grown sugar at her dinner table all the way to the heroic sacrifice of Christ himself, the ultimate martyr to the violence of the imperial State. Few citizens are called upon to be or are capable of being martyrs—but some are, and Thoreau holds that when such heroic dissenters arise, they must be recognized not as madmen but as redeemers. The seeds of Thoreau's fierce public support for John Brown are already visible here, ready to germinate.

Here, too, are the seeds of Thoreau's most remarkable innovation. "Resistance" means not just self-defense, defense of one's fellow citizens, or even of one's own nation, but defense of all those lives entangled with our own: slaves, upon whose labor even "free" Massachusetts depended economically; Mexicans, the declared enemies of the State; and Indians, the declared enemies of civilization itself. But Thoreau was not finished even here. Life at Walden

Pond helped him understand how deeply humans are related to nonhumans as well, whether animals used for labor or food, trees used for lumber, wild fishes destroyed by dams, or whole ecosystems, forests and river meadows. In the same weeks he was finishing "Resistance to Civil Government," Thoreau put the final touches on *A Week on the Concord and Merrimack Rivers*. "Who hears the fishes when they cry?" he asked in its opening pages. "It will not be forgotten by some memory that we were contemporaries." Their lives, thrown into the hydraulic machinery of the Billerica Dam, "armed only with innocence and a just cause," were lost, but "I for one am with thee, and who knows what may avail a crow-bar against that Billerica dam?"[51] Extending one's ethical community to the nonhuman world was, in 1849, novel, shocking, ridiculous. But Thoreau would give the rest of his life to this revolutionary insight. What he worked out in writing "Resistance to Civil Government" became not only the foundation of his political philosophy but also the gateway to his environmental ethics.

A BASKET OF DELICATE TEXTURE: WEAVING THOREAU'S *WEEK*

Through these years, as Thoreau grew from Emerson's apprentice to his assistant, friend, and rival, his most treasured project, *A Week on the Concord and Merrimack Rivers*, was always at his elbow, growing slowly and steadily. Years later he would tell readers of *Walden* that he had once created "a kind of basket of a delicate texture," a fitting image for his first book. Into the narrative of his 1839 river trip with John, Henry had woven everything he ever felt, thought, and experienced: Concord fishes, the feel of dew in the river dawn, the look of a cooked passenger pigeon, nonpayment of taxes, Indian names, the philosophy of friendship, Hindu scripture, bad dreams, old poems, mountain walks. "From all points of the compass from the earth beneath and the heavens above have come these inspirations," each inspiration duly entered in his Journal to be "winnowed" into lectures and then into essays that would stand at last "like statues on their pedestals," lovely to look at. But "the statues rarely take hold of hands."[52] *A Week* would, he hoped, be better than this: not a stiff and formal gallery of statues but an organic and flowing whole, its multitudinous parts held together and watered into life by the river.

John and Henry's river trip during that blessed, charged summer of 1839 had been planned as a boyish adventure, not a literary excursion. But from the start, the fledgling writer couldn't help but see its literary and symbolic overtones, though what they might mean didn't become clear until after John's death in January 1842. By the following fall, Henry had begun to reimagine the river voyage as an elegy for his lost brother. Into the pages of his big new notebook, the "long book," he sowed passages at intervals like seeds in furrows, giving each one room to germinate and grow.[53] Around the time his Walden plans were solidifying, he began to organize the notebook's entries, imagining a book like nothing Emerson had ever written— not a series of self-contained essays, each one a beautiful statue on a pedestal divorced from context, but a living book, a travel narrative, enriched with reflection and literature and history.

Margaret Fuller had shown him how to do it. When she had visited him on Staten Island in the fall of 1843, she was bubbling over with memories of her summer trip to the Great Lakes and plans for turning that trip into her first book: a travel narrative that would be "a kind of letter box" for the thoughts, observations, poems, commentaries, and extracts inspired by all she experienced along the way. *Summer on the Lakes in 1843* was published just a year later, in summer 1844, and as Thoreau read it, he saw how to pull together his own book.[54] He would fold their two weeks' journey into one, a seven-days' creation story from Saturday launch to Friday return, a journey of discovery climaxing in their climb to the summit of Mount Washington. Thoreau tested out the concept at the Concord Lyceum in March 1845, just before he built his Walden house, and on his first day at Walden he had begun the first draft. A year later he read some of it aloud to Emerson, sitting under an oak tree on the riverbank. An invigorated Emerson blessed it: "pastoral as Isaak

Walton, spicy as flagroot, broad & deep as Menu."[55] Thoreau knew he was on his way.

A year after that, March 1847, he read it aloud to an ecstatic Alcott, who called it "picturesque and flowing as the streams he sails on," with "a toughness too, and a sinewy vigor, as of roots" and "wild meats" and "the moist lustres of the fishes in the bed below." This was *American* literature at last, with "the sod and sap and fibre and flavor of New England." Emerson was still excited about it, too: in a letter to Evert Duyckinck, the editor of Wiley and Putnam's *Literary World*, he declared this book of "extraordinary merit" would attract lovers of nature, scholars of literature, and thoughtful readers of all kinds "for its originality and profoundness." He hoped Wiley and Putnam would publish it in their Library of American Books series, alongside Hawthorne, Poe, and Melville—even though Emerson's critical eye already spotted trouble ahead: the narrative of the little voyage "is a very slender thread for such big beads & ingots as are strung on it."[56]

Duyckinck might have been skeptical—after all, Hawthorne had warned him there was but "one chance in a thousand" Thoreau would produce a good book—but Emerson convinced him something promising was afoot, so he announced Thoreau's forthcoming book in *Literary World*. But Emerson had jumped the gun. Thoreau wasn't quite ready. A month, then two went by while he polished the manuscript. By the time he finally sent it off to Duyckinck at the end of May, it was too late: Duyckinck liked it, but he'd just been fired. After two anxious months, it became clear that Wiley and Putnam had said no. Emerson tried again, sending another enthusiastic letter to the Philadelphia publisher W. H. Furness, but his firm was too overwhelmed with submissions to bother with an unknown writer. William Emerson sent feelers to the Harpers in New York City, but they, too, said no. All through September Thoreau persisted, even after Emerson set off to England, but by November he'd given up. Four different publishers, he wrote Emerson, had turned it down, though Wiley and Putnam had agreed to publish it—if Thoreau would pay the costs. "If I liked the book well enough, I should not delay; but for the present I am indifferent. I believe this is, after all, the course you advised—to let it lie."[57]

Emerson had advised no such course. Don't delay even a month, he fired back from England: "I should print it at once, nor do I think that you would incur any risk in doing so that you cannot well afford. It is very certain to have readers & debtors here as well as there." Henry delayed a month, and then another. An impatient Emerson wrote to Lidian: "If Henry Thoreau means one day to come to England let him not delay another day to print his book. Or if he do not, let him print it."[58] But how could he? Emerson's assurances that Thoreau could "well afford" to incur the "risk" would hardly pay the printer. Four years before, Emerson's financial backing had gotten Ellery Channing's first book into print, but to Thoreau Emerson made no such offer. Boxed in, unable to afford publishing costs, Thoreau concluded that his book would not be published until it was simply too good to turn down. So he took it off the market and set himself to making it even better. In the meantime, to raise money he polished up "Ktaadn" and sent it off to Greeley—hence his fervent gratitude when, in mere months, Greeley had not only placed "Ktaadn" but paid handsomely and begged for more.

But what Greeley begged for was more *short* pieces. What Thoreau had was a book. "My book is swelling again under my hands," he replied, "but as soon as I have leisure I shall see to those shorter articles. So look out."[59] Nothing Greeley said could dissuade him from making A *Week* his highest priority. Thoreau was certain only a big, new book would get him out from under Emerson's shadow; and besides, before anything else must come his memorial to John.

→>-<+

Emerson returned from Europe at last, steaming into Boston on July 27, 1848, and heading straight home to Concord "in good health and spirits." "He has seen the elephant," said Thoreau, "or perhaps I should say the British lion now, and was made a lion of himself." After three days of unpacking, Emerson was ready to take over the household, so on July 30, Thoreau left the newly anointed literary lion alone with his family and moved back into the Texas House. From then on, remembered Ellen, the Emersons lived "as a regular family" without boarders or live-in guests;[60] and from then on, Henry Thoreau never left his family.

Emerson was preoccupied for months, putting his household, garden, family, and strained finances back in order. Thoreau continued to come by to see the children, to help finish Aunt Lucy's new house, to help Alcott put the final touches on Emerson's grand new summerhouse—working on it felt like being "nowhere, doing nothing," he snapped—but the tide of warmth that had filled the two men's letters was receding. "As for taking Thoreau's arm, I should as soon take the arm of an elm tree," Emerson jotted, again, in his journal. He was full of praise for England's high civility, and suspected Thoreau of flirting with a kind of insanity: "Henry Thoreau is like the wood god who solicits the wandering poet" and draws him away, leaving him "naked, plaiting vines & with twigs in his hand. Very seductive are the first steps from the town to the woods, but the End is want & madness."[61] Now Channing, not Thoreau, was Emerson's regular walking companion, their relaxed and happy days together a welcome relief from long hours laboring on his next book, *Representative Men*, which was urgently needed to offset those steep travel expenses.

Money was on Thoreau's mind, too; his family needed all the help he could give them. In May, the Concord Steam Mill Company, where the Thoreaus' wooden pencil casings were manufactured, burned to the ground in a spectacular blaze that lit up the rivers and meadows. Some suspected arson. The owners were insured, but the renters weren't, and the Thoreaus suffered the most: they lost, Henry estimated, $400 to $500. The instant he was home, he set about earning money with odd jobs—gardening, carpentry, papering, and whitewashing—lending sums to his mother, paying monthly rent to his father, putting in extra hours at the pencil shop.[62]

Moving in with the Emersons had cost him his summer excursions; in the summer of 1848 he'd hoped to get away to Maine, but late in August he called it off. All he could manage was a long walk with Channing, setting out on September fourth up the Merrimack River into New Hampshire by way of Dunstable to climb Mount Uncanoonuc, and returning by way of Hooksett and Hampstead. It was partly a research trip: the route allowed Thoreau to measure changes to the country he had traveled nine years before and enter them in his growing book. It also allowed him to procure a copy of Dunstable's town history by asking a young woman at the finest house in town if they owned the book, and "whether she 'would not *sell* it to him.'" (She did.)[63] They were home in four days, having walked over a hundred miles. Aunt Maria was unimpressed. "I wish he could find something better to do than walking off every now and then," she sniffed.[64]

That fall, Thoreau started looking for "something better to do" to contribute to the family income. He had two good possibilities: surveying and lecturing. Thanks to the railroad, Concord was growing, and surveyors were much in demand. Thoreau already knew the basics, and over the years he'd completed a handful of jobs. Given his love of outdoor work and his talent for mathematics and machinery, it seemed a good fit. That fall he prepared a long list of books to study and noted he'd need to fix his compass and buy some supplies—a new journal for surveying notes, some drawing paper, new shoes, a hat.[65] The next spring he borrowed a compass from the town's longtime surveyor, Cyrus Hubbard, and took on a few jobs, starting with the road his father wanted the town to lay out in front of the Texas house.

On April 2, 1849, the Concord Town Board accepted Thoreau's survey, approved "Belknap Street," and hired Thoreau to help build it. Then he surveyed Emerson's land on Walden Pond, about eighty acres; in May he surveyed a woodlot near Flint's Pond, which he persuaded Emerson to buy for the sake of its rare flowers and beautiful waterfall. He began a new journal, "Field-Notes of Surveys"; the first entry was a large woodlot surveyed for an owner who logged it off and subdivided it into house lots. Over the next eleven years, Thoreau would complete more than 150 additional surveying jobs, each requiring days or weeks of hard work, as far away as New Jersey:

house lots, woodlots, farms and orchards, town boundaries, Concord's Middle Street and New Bedford Road, even, late in life, the
length of Concord River. In a very real way, Thoreau's work carved
the map of Concord, incised on the ground in yards, fence lines,
and roadways.[66]

As for lecturing, so far he'd given all his lectures for free. That
changed in October 1848, when Hawthorne, who'd moved away
three years before to work in the Salem Customhouse, offered
twenty dollars for a lecture at the Salem Lyceum. "Ktaadn" was
even then appearing in monthly installments in the *Union Magazine*.
"Resistance" was nearly finished, and Greeley had just whipped up
a national controversy with his preview of *Walden*. And here was a
paying engagement in the cosmopolitan port of Salem. The literary life, it seemed, was finally turning a profit. Thoreau decided to
refine his trio of Walden lectures, take *Walden* on the road, make a
little money, drum up some publicity, and try out his new material
before fresh audiences. At this rate, soon he'd have to his name not
one book, but two.

An annoying setback came out of the blue late that October,
when Thoreau's old Harvard nemesis, James Russell Lowell, published a satiric pamphlet, "A Fable for Critics," skewering America's
literary lights in phrases too delicious to resist. Of Emerson: "All
admire, and yet scarcely six converts he's got / To I don't (nor they
either) exactly know what." Of Alcott: "When he talks he is great,
but goes out like a taper, / If you shut him up closely with pen, ink,
and paper." Emerson could afford to ignore him, and Alcott had
long been a national laughingstock, but the arrow Lowell reserved
for Thoreau went deep:

> There comes ——, for instance; to see him's rare sport,
> Tread in Emerson's tracks with legs painfully short;
> How he jumps, how he strains, and gets red in the face,
> To keep step with the mystagogue's natural pace!

It was the same snicker from a decade before: "Fie, for shame, brother bard, with good fruit of your own, / Can't you let Neighbor Emerson's orchards alone?" Lowell's clever slur, echoed endlessly by generations of reviewers, would dog Thoreau for the rest of his life. His response was to keep writing. He knew "Ktaadn" was like nothing Emerson had ever written, and that "Resistance to Civil Government" defied Emerson's patronage, even if it took shape under Emerson's roof. But the old wound was unhealed, and Lowell's barb left its mark.

Thoreau gave nine lectures from *Walden* in six towns over the next six months, earning him over a hundred dollars in fees and invaluable publicity.[67] Reviews were always opinionated and often positive, though most reviewers took their cue from Lowell and pegged Thoreau as an Emerson imitator. But the publicity stoked curiosity, and Thoreau was catching on to how the marketplace worked: when a Gloucester newspaper panned him, he shrugged it off as good advertising. Getting out into the world helped him strengthen ties with old friends, too, starting with the Hawthornes. Nathaniel tipped off his Salem friends that his guest was Greeley's mystery man, the poet on the pond, and on November 22, 1848, Thoreau created "quite a sensation" in Salem with his Walden lecture's "exquisite humor" and "delicate satire against the follies of the times." Sophia Hawthorne was enchanted and wrote her sister Mary that Thoreau had risen quite above his old arrogance and was "as gentle, simple, ruddy, and meek as all geniuses should be"—even "his great blue eyes" outshined and "put into shade a nose which I once thought must make him uncomely forever."[68] After catching up with the Hawthornes, Henry traveled with Nathaniel to Cambridge, to dine with Henry Wadsworth Longfellow. Hawthorne had alerted Longfellow to Thoreau's wearisome "iron-pokerishness," but also praised him as a man of thought and originality. Longfellow, who had dined with Thoreau at the Emersons' the week before, proved receptive: some months later he pronounced "Resistance to Civil Government" to be "extremely good."[69]

Thoreau, in short, was a hit. Aunt Maria was finally pleased: Salem seemed to be "wonderfully taken" with him; they had invited him back. Soon he would be lecturing in Portland, Maine, too—good paying engagements!—and "he is preparing his book for the press, and the title is to be Waldien (I don't know how to spell it) or life in the woods. I think the title will take if the Book don't."[70] After Salem and the somewhat chilly reception in Gloucester around Christmas, he tried out his third Walden lecture in Concord, before a friendly audience, just after New Year's. Then he was back in Salem in February and Lincoln early in March. Two weeks later he spoke in Portland as an equinoctial rainstorm pounded the rooftop. The audience listened "wide awake" for a good two hours to his "unique, original, comical, and high-falutin" thoughts.[71] Portland's praise caught Greeley's ear, and in April 1849 he penned a sprightly publicity paragraph on Thoreau at Walden that was reprinted in newspapers across the country. A week later Greeley printed a rejoinder by a so-called Timothy Thorough who, baffled, asked his wife what *she* thought of such goings-on. Well, she answered, this foolish fellow must be "a good-for-nothing, selfish, crab-like sort of chap" shirking his duties as a *man*. Greeley further stoked the controversy by penning an indignant reply, and the affair ricocheted around the nation, unhindered by anything Thoreau actually wrote. Greeley's publicity stunt tapped into something deep, and the resulting caricature of Thoreau persists to this day.[72]

Thoreau capped his first season as a professional lecturer by presenting all three Walden lectures in Worcester, spaced a week apart, to an audience that included H. G. O. Blake and his circle of friends. The local newspapers scoffed—"A wheel-barrow, with an Irishman for its vitals, renders the world a far better service," said one—but some in the audience connected with the "sylvan philosopher" and his message.[73] Blake and his circle, who probably organized the series, would invite Thoreau back so many times that Worcester became a testing ground second only to Concord in importance. And the method Thoreau established of developing his writings by watching his words miss or hit home with a living audience stayed with him; behind his pages are the faces of thousands of men and women, often opinionated and always unpredictable, who laughed, argued, and, sometimes, rolled their eyes.

All this was wonderful publicity—for the wrong book. Just as the national audience was itching for an argument over *Walden's* biting social commentary, Thoreau was about to publish *A Week on the Concord and Merrimack Rivers*—something very different. In the eighteen months since he took it off the market, it had nearly doubled in size. The great beads and ingots that worried Emerson had swelled alarmingly. Early in 1849, Thoreau sent it to Longfellow's publishers, the Boston firm Ticknor and Company, who replied that they would take *Walden*—but not *A Week*. Then they relented: they would take *A Week* if Thoreau paid the printing costs up front, $450 for a thousand copies, half to be bound.

They might as well have asked him for the moon. Thoreau turned back to James Munroe, whose terms were still terrible, but not strictly impossible—instead of asking for money up front, Munroe offered to print a thousand copies, paying costs out of the sales of the book. If the book didn't sell, Thoreau would guarantee reimbursement in full. Henry's family was worried. "How he will pay for it I don't know, for I fear it will not sell well," Maria fretted; she thought parts of it sounded "very much like blasphemy." Cynthia agreed that Henry put things into his book "that never ought to be put there," and even Helen was uneasy. But Henry stood firm.[74] After all, Emerson had published with Munroe under the same terms and done just fine. And Emerson had repeatedly urged him to take the plunge and print it at his own risk, assuring him it would sell. Alcott loved *A Week*, and when he told Hawthorne that Thoreau had his book in press, Hawthorne—assuming he meant *Walden*—rejoiced at the news and assured Thoreau of success. "I have thought of you as a reader while writing it," Thoreau replied gratefully,[75] and dived into correcting the proof sheets as they rolled off the press.

Spring 1849 was tense. Thoreau's handwriting was terrible, and the proof sheets were riddled with errors. He was busy with many lectures and his first wave of surveying jobs. When Elizabeth Peabody asked him for "Resistance to Civil Government," he gamely added it to the pile, warning her he had no time for revisions. Worst of all, his sister Helen was dying. She'd long dreamed of a career in teaching and social activism, but poor health had kept her from it.

Now it was painfully clear that her time was short. Henry hurried home from his lecture trip to Maine, canceling his engagement in Bangor and putting off, once again, his dreamed-of second excursion with Thatcher. By May 1, Helen was insisting there should be "not the least gloom" attached to her funeral. Henry brought a visiting daguerreotypist home, knowing that the Emersons' one consolation in their grief had been a portrait John Thoreau arranged of young Waldo just weeks before they both died.[76] Now Henry would do the same for his sisters. A delicate and ethereally composed Helen looks out from her portrait with luminous unflinching eyes, a trace of a smile playing about her lips. Sophia—who hated her first portrait so much that she had it retaken—looks out earnestly, as if arrested by the camera, impatient to leap up out of the frame and get on with her day. Henry had none taken of himself. Tense, busy, expectant, in a household shadowed by cares, he labored on.

→>·<←

There's nothing quite like an author's excitement upon beholding his first book. On May 26, 1849, Henry Thoreau took the train to Boston to pick up his author's copies of *A Week on the Concord and Merrimack River*: a thick, plain, brown-bound volume. He left one copy to be mailed to Blake in Worcester and stopped off to give another to Bronson Alcott in person. Alcott sat down and read it through in two days straight: "An American book," he admired, "worthy to stand beside Emerson's Essays on my shelves."[77] Other responses were slower in coming. The first major public notice, and the most nationally prominent, appeared two weeks later on the front page of Greeley's *New-York Tribune*—and it set a deeply damaging tone. *A Week*, it opened, if not *quite* a "fresh, original, thoughtful work," was very nearly so, and Thoreau's nature descriptions had an "Aeolian sweetness." But his verse was "halting" and his philosophy execrable, "a bad specimen of a dubious and dangerous school." Worst of all was the blasphemy. Mr. Thoreau dared to assert that the sacred books of the Brahmins were "nothing inferior to the Christian Bible"—a "revolting" attack on good sense, good taste, and all received opinion, which the author should humble himself by using the pages of the *Tribune* to retract.[78]

Thoreau was deeply hurt, for he assumed the anonymous reviewer was Greeley himself, his trusted friend—perhaps in an attempt to whip up another controversy. Sadly, his anger and blame were misplaced, for the review was written by someone else, probably George Ripley.[79] As for Emerson, he said nothing—except once, in a letter to an English friend, to whom he complained four days before Thoreau picked up his author's copies that "there is nothing very good to tell you of the people here, no books, no poets, no artists." He mentioned Thoreau's book only as an afterthought. When Theodore Parker asked him to review it in the *Massachusetts Quarterly Review*, Emerson pointedly refused: "I am not the man to write the Notice of Thoreau's book. I am of the same clan and parish." Such qualms had not prevented him from writing helpful reviews of other friends' work, but for Thoreau he offered instead a list of names of potential reviewers. Parker, long wary of Thoreau, found to his surprise that he rather liked the book, which he sent not to any of those whom Emerson had suggested but to that emerging arbiter of literary good taste: James Russell Lowell.[80]

It could have been worse. Lowell procrastinated for six months, but when he finally got around to writing his review, it was surprisingly balanced. He found much to praise in the book's tasteful parts, particularly in Thoreau's enchanting nature descriptions. The worst he could say, aside from dismissing Thoreau's verses as "worsification," was that the book's many digressions hit "like snags, jolting us headforemost out of our places as we are rowing placidly up stream or drifting down." Out of proportion and out of place, they "mar our Merrimacking dreadfully. We were bid to a river-party, not to be preached at." Aunt Maria thought Lowell's review was "beautiful," "so just, and pleasant and some parts of it so laughable that I enjoyed reading it very much."[81] But by the time Lowell had his say, it was December 1849, and much too late. The book was dead.

The problem was not the number of reviews: Emerson helped Thoreau mail seventy-five copies to friends and possible review-

ers, and it was widely reviewed in the United States and England.
Nor was it the nature of the reviews—many were favorable, and
even the negative ones could have excited interest. The problem
was Munroe. He didn't publish books; he only printed them. He
refused to advertise, and he had no distribution network. One could
purchase Thoreau's book only by visiting Munroe's shop in Boston
or by ordering it from Munroe by mail. This business model had
worked for Emerson, who was already well known and whose fame
was centered in Boston. But for a first book by an unknown author
seeking a national audience, it was a disaster. Hawthorne had also
taken a hit from Munroe; three years after Munroe printed his *Twice-
Told Tales* in 1841, six hundred copies remained in storage, unsold.
Emerson tried to steer Fuller's first book to Munroe, too, and a naive
Thoreau had urged her to publish it at her own expense—but Fuller,
wisely, took *Summer on the Lakes* to a publisher who spared her from
assuming the risk for books they could not, or would not, market.
Thoreau, by contrast, was in real trouble. His book sold barely over
two hundred copies. The man who took pride in building a house
for $28.12½ owed his publisher $290—a year's ordinary wages. It
would take him four years to pay it off, dollar by hard-earned dollar.

Perhaps the saddest irony of Thoreau's life is that the book he
went to Walden to write, an elegy to his brother and closest friend,
became an elegy to so many other losses: his sister Helen; his friendship with Emerson; his hopes for a literary career. Helen died of
tuberculosis on June 14, 1849, just two weeks after her brother's book
became a reality—long enough to share the family's pride and joy,
for surely there was some, despite the misgivings. Of the four children, only Henry and Sophia remained. The women of the family
laid Helen out in state in the family parlor, as was the custom. Four
days later, in a gesture of deep respect, both the town's ministers,
the Unitarians' Barzillai Frost and the Trinitarians' William Mather,
performed her funeral in the Thoreaus' parlor, honoring Helen's
refusal to attend their churches since she found their doors open to
slaveholders but closed to the defenders of the enslaved.

Reverend Mather's wife remembered how Henry, who also never

went to church, sat seemingly unmoved until the service was concluded. As they were about to lift the bier, he stood to wind a music
box to a tune "of the *sweetest tenderest* minor strains that seemed
like no earthly tune. All sat quietly till it was through."[82] William
Lloyd Garrison printed a passionate remembrance of Helen's years
of service to the abolitionist movement in the *Liberator*, honoring
her patient investigation of the truth, her candor in acknowledging
it, and her moral courage in acting on her convictions. In his farewell
poem, Henry said that "regret doth bind / Me faster to thee now /
Than neighborhood confined." What he regretted, he did not say.
He may not have been as close to the cerebral Helen as he was to
the plucky Sophia, but she was his moral lodestar. The minister's
wife was not alone in suspecting Helen had "more sympathy in his
peculiar ways perhaps than any other."[83]

By fall 1849, it was painfully clear to Thoreau that the book he
wrote to prove himself to Emerson had failed to please him. Worse,
by following Emerson's advice to print it no matter the risk, Thoreau precipitated himself into ruinous financial debt. Tension built
through the spring and summer. Even as Emerson complained of
Thoreau's elm-tree stiffness, a distressed Thoreau stammered in his
Journal, "(I was never so near my friend when he was bodily present
as when he was absent) and yet I am And yet I am indirectly accused
by this friend of coldness and disingenuousness— When I cannot
speak for warmth—& sincerity." The crisis broke in September. In
private Thoreau spat with cold and bitter fury:

> I had a friend, I wrote a book, I asked my friend's criticism, I never
> got but praise for what was good in it—my friend became estranged
> from me and then I got blame for all that was bad,—& so I got at last
> the criticism which I wanted.
>
> While my friend was my friend he flattered me, and I never heard
> the truth from him, but when he became my enemy he shot it to me
> on a poisoned arrow
>
> There is as much hatred as love in the world. Hate is a good
> critic.[84]

Again and again, for years afterward, Thoreau's Journal would be disfigured by eruptions of raw pain and tortured declarations that his friendship with Emerson had, at last, finally and irrevocably ended. Yet somehow, despite his unrelenting bereavement, it never quite ended. As Thoreau already understood, "Ours is a tragedy of more than 5 acts—this is not the fifth act in our tragedy no, no!"[85]

Emerson, in his own journal, seemed unconscious of anything unusual. He had handled Thoreau gingerly for years, without realizing what turmoil he stirred under his friend's prickly exterior. The one thing neither could bear was leaving the other alone. So although they never entirely trusted each other again, they went on, outwardly pretty much as before: taking walks together; Henry doing odd jobs and Emerson paying him; Henry wandering into the house to rummage through the library, entertain guests, visit with Lidian, romp with the children. Even as tensions built, Thoreau wrote a delightful letter to Ellen, away on Staten Island, filling her in on Eddy's fifth birthday party: Henry supplied them with "onion and squash pipes, and rhubarb whistles," and "Little Sammy Hoar blowed them most successfully, and made the loudest noise, though it almost strained his eyes out to do it."[86] If their personalities set each other on edge, if their impossible Platonic ideal of friendship pushed them apart, that very distance bound them together, walking, talking, provoking each other—a provocation that Emerson, who saw his own self-reliance mirrored in Thoreau's nay-saying, could not resist. They met sometimes "with malice prepense, & take the bull by the horns," as Emerson remarked in 1850, but they met, always, intellectual sparring partners to the end.[87]

--><--

The failure of *A Week on the Concord and Merrimack Rivers* was the most consequential event in Thoreau's life as a writer. It is doubly sad that while the book is a flawed masterpiece, it is still a masterpiece. Had it been truly published, rather than printed and laid into storage, it would have taken its place next to Hawthorne's *Mosses from an Old Manse* and Melville's *Typee* as the culmination of the national quest for a distinctive American voice, heralding the breakthrough works of the 1850s—Hawthorne's *Scarlet Letter*, Melville's *Moby-Dick*, his own *Walden*, Walt Whitman's *Leaves of Grass*.[88] Thoreau kept faith with his first book: looking back in 1851, he was proud to call it "hypaethral or unroofed," open to the sky and to all weathers, smelling of "the fields & woods" rather than the study or library. And though he had tossed into it too many of his oldest and dustiest pages—unread *Dial* essays, musty poems, dry extracts from colonial histories—the pages written at Walden Pond breathe a fresh, wild, outdoors air.

In *Walden* he called *A Week* a "basket of a delicate texture," giving the clue to his method: baskets are woven warp and woof. Here, the structuring warp is the brothers' two-week river journey, the narrative thread; onto it the artist has woven the woof of reading and reflection, crosswise strands giving strength and texture, making the journey not a vacation from thought, as Lowell wanted, but an occasion for thinking more deeply. River and book move forward together, fusing progress and accident, purpose and randomness. Existential conflict becomes the key to the book's design: a rhythm of motion and rest, purpose and chance, the spark of a moment and the long shimmer of memory. What holds it all together is the dynamic bond of brother and brother, river and boat, the long flowing lapse of linear time and the free-floating self who lives both in time and out of it, flowing with the lapse of the river or stepping aside onto the solid ground of shore. As the pages turn, days pass and time deepens—as the brothers discover when their many days of upward voyaging are "unraveled" on their final day's rapid passage downward and home.[89]

The poet inscribes this dance of dualism on the first page by announcing the river has two names: "Concord" and "Musketaquid, or Grass-ground." Only one name is permanent: "It will be Grass-ground River as long as grass grows and water runs here; it will be Concord River only while men lead peaceable lives on its banks."[90] Through the Indian name runs the eternal river of grass and water, Thoreau's axis of nature and poetry; through the English name runs the transient river of farms and canals, Thoreau's axis of history and politics. At every place along the river, Thoreau plays off the two names to signal two sets of concerns: an eternal world of natural growth and harmonic rhythms, and a human world of historical change, where peace is precarious and harmonies soon end as the river of time sweeps the brothers' world ever deeper into the past. *A Week* is a complicated, many-folded book because even as Thoreau was writing it, adding layer upon layer over ten years, it kept shifting. His research into colonial and Native American history complicated his sense of time. His updates on the landscape showed it disappearing as the factories grew, the dams rose, and the railroads lengthened; his insertions of current events, such as the Mexican War and his jailing for nonpayment of taxes, tangled a peaceful and idyllic past with a troubled and challenging future. Time shifted as Thoreau wrote the book; it shifts constantly as one reads it.

The boat is the vehicle—that sturdy homemade fisherman's dory, the *Musketaquid*. Its very name flags the brothers' wistful identification with the Indians, people who are, like them, out-of-doors and out-of-time. It's an amphibious craft, Thoreau tells us with a wink, "a creature of two elements," all fish below with wooden keel, all bird above with cotton sail, and painted two colors, green below for the land and blue above for the water and sky.[91] In this amphibious craft, the two brothers—one present, one remote—navigate all the multiplying dualisms, weaving them together into a new and higher wisdom: real and ideal, surface and depth, holy and profane. Thoreau's "week" announces his book as a seven-days' creation story, a genesis of knowledge. So each weekday on the water gives back its own reflections, day by day, while the whole journey circles out and back—out to the misty mountain, the anticipated climax. But the older Thoreau who had also written "Ktaadn" can no longer bear to include his juvenile ascent with John. So time shifts even beyond the pages of this book: forces from outside its pages ripple inward and leave puzzling gaps and omissions. Every reader expects the narrative to climax on the top of Mount Washington. Instead, in its place, there is nothing but a single, Indian name—

"AGIOCOCHOOK"—and a blank quarter-page. On this mythical terrain, Thoreau will honor not the heroic quest of Western tradition but the sacred silence evoked by the Algonquin name.[92]

As it turns out, the mountain climax happened two days earlier, in a digression about awakening alone on the summit of Mount Saddleback to a world sealed off by clouds. The seventh-day return sweeps us swiftly home, to a world that is familiar and yet not: as the keel of the boat "recognized" the Concord mud, "we leaped gladly on shore, drawing it up, and fastening it to the wild apple-tree, whose stem still bore the mark which its chain had worn in the chafing of the spring freshets."[93] That enchained wild apple tree points to the source of this book's strangeness: Thoreau's tree of knowledge, in his retelling of Genesis, turns out to be a tough, resilient domestic tree gone feral. And those apple trees, common everywhere in Thoreau's home landscape, were, like so many other things he loved, swiftly disappearing. At the end of his life, Thoreau would give this title to his only autobiography: "Wild Apples."

Reviewers found this meandering binary structure—or this "Musketaquidding" structure, as Thoreau joked—maddening. But Lowell's disgust at being invited to a river party only to be preached at points to a more serious problem: Thoreau had broken all bounds of good taste by writing not merely poetry, but what he called "SCRIPTURE" for a modern age. It was one thing to edit "Ethnical Scriptures" for the *Dial*, but now Thoreau was playing with fire, putting the Christian New Testament on a level with other world religious writings: "It is necessary not to be Christian, to appreciate the beauty and significance of the life of Christ," he ventured. "I would say to the readers of Scriptures, if they wish for a good book to read, read the Bhagvat-Geeta. . . . It deserves to be read with reverence even by Yankees, as a part of the sacred writings of a devout people."[94] Whoosh! In a stroke, Thoreau swept the modern world away for a new world infinitely deeper and wider. As a child trapped indoors during all those Sabbaths, bookless except for the one Book, he had stared out the window, scanning the clouds, hoping to see a hawk cutting open the sky. Now he sailed on its wings:

"I know of no book that has so few readers. There is none so truly strange, and heretical, and unpopular. . . . 'Seek first the kingdom of heaven.'—'Lay not up for yourself treasures on earth.'" "Think of this, Yankees!," he mocks. "Let but one of these sentences be rightly read from any pulpit in the land, and there would not be left one stone of that meeting-house upon another."[95] The horrified George Ripley was right: this was revolting, a revolt.

Even had it sold well, *A Week* would never have found a wide audience. Thoreau had been instructed by the era's most deeply radical thinkers: Orestes Brownson, Ralph Waldo Emerson, Bronson Alcott, Theodore Parker, Margaret Fuller, Frederick Douglass. He was experimenting wildly with form, dangerously in thought, assuming he was on solid ground—taking the next step, following the logic of his elders' critiques of social convention and historical Christianity to offer a new moral framework strong enough to bear the weight of modern science, eloquent enough to assert that preacher and poet were one, and sharp enough to address the ethical challenges of slavery, industrialization, and wars of conquest. Aunt Maria had hoped no editor would print her nephew's blasphemy, but self-publishing with Munroe meant Henry's words went straight from his manuscript pages into print. Genius, to be heard, must not outrun its audience—but Thoreau had left his audience far behind. Yet his fundamental insight never wavered: "Your scheme must be the frame-work of the universe; all other schemes will soon be ruins."[96] He had gone to Walden to see through the matrix to the bedrock. He had gotten a glimpse of it on Katahdin and confirmed it under the skies of Walden Pond. He had spent ten years trying to find the best words to share all he'd found, only to fail.

Thoreau had written two good books and published one; the other he put away. His only choice was to start over.

CHAPTER SEVEN

From Concord to Cosmos: Thoreau's Turn to Science

(1849–1851)

The man of genius knows what he is aiming at; nobody else knows.

HENRY DAVID THOREAU, DECEMBER 27, 1858

"THE LAW WHICH REVEALS": CAPE COD

The summer of 1849 was so hot that the children were cooped up indoors and Emerson's gardener had to pump water to keep his new pear trees alive. In the fields, the corn rolled and withered, and by the end of July the farmers were cutting it down, salvaging what they could. Despite the heat, Thoreau was on the move. That September, when the acorns were still green but the poke stems were ripening purple, he inventoried all the places within a day's walk: "the great meadows—The Baker Farm—Conantum—Beck-Stows swamp— the Great Fields," Nagog Hill, "famous for huckleberries where I have seen hundreds of bushels at once—Nashoba—of Indian memory—from which you see Uncanunuc Mt well," Strawberry Hill, Annursnuck, Ponkawtasset, Walden Pond, Sandy Pond, White Pond—which needed a better name, perhaps "God's Drop."[1] It was an inventory of possibility. Transitions are hard to mark, but one can take this list as the moment when Thoreau began to reinvent himself as the writer of world fame.

Thoreau had always walked; it was how a man without means got from here to there. But in the previous year, he realized, "my walks have extended themselves," and after his morning work, almost every afternoon, he visited "some new hill or pond or wood many miles distant." In another year, these long walks would no longer be a diversion from work; they would be the work itself, his major literary project. He was, for the first time, really free: free of Emerson's expectations, free of the literary marketplace, free of all hopes for travel abroad. With roads to a conventional literary career closed, Thoreau veered off-road, learning to see familiar landscapes with a traveler's eye—an "advancing eye," wrote Emerson, that saw "rivers, & which way they run . . . that like the heavens journeys too & sojourns not." Thoreau's long years writing *A Week on the Concord and Merrimack Rivers* helped him craft that insider's outside view of American history and society. Now he hungered for a wider view of the universe—not "that old Jewish scheme" taught on Sundays, but the true geography of "heaven's topography."[2] Such blasphemy outraged his readers even as they admired his limpid nature descriptions. For Thoreau, though, preaching and river parties were not two things but one—not a vague religious pantheism, but a serious attempt to reach beyond the traps of unthinking social convention to true "geo-graphy," earth-writing, inscribed not in the leaves of dusty books but in the strata of the planet itself.

"Obey the law which reveals and not the law revealed," he wrote.[3] He meant the laws outlined in such books of science as Charles Lyell's *Principles of Geology* (1830–33), a foundational work and the first book of modern science he read, slipping it off Emerson's shelves in 1840. The opening was irresistible: Lyell reached beyond Genesis to the Hindu "Great Year," citing the *Institutes of Menu* to show how the world's most ancient religions—Hindu, Egyptian, and Greek—all recognized, in the fossils buried in the earth, the cyclical creation and destruction of worlds across unimaginable time scales. Lyell's vision of deep time showed that Earth's strata were the leaves of a great book of creation, overturning orthodox biblical chronologies and allying the most ancient scriptures with the deepest insights of modern science. Anyone could see this: a simple telescope turned to the heavens revealed astronomical distances measured in millions of light-years and entire world systems in every stage of creation and collapse; geology revealed that those heavens are literally under one's feet. For as Lyell demonstrated, the greatest of revolutions were caused by the smallest of changes, accumulating through eons to transform the planet: mountains uplifted inch by inch by earthquakes, worn away grain by grain by raindrops. Over and over Thoreau inscribed Lyell's fundamental insight into his Journal: "We discover the causes of all past change in the present invariable order of the universe." The present is the key to the past, and to the future as well; the pulse of the universe is beating still.[4]

Reading Lyell had changed how Thoreau understood the world. He extended Lyell's insight to the human world as well: "As in geology, so in social institutions, we may discover the causes of all past change in the present invariable order of society. The greatest appreciable physical revolutions are the work of the light-footed air—the stealthy-paced water—and the subterranean fire."[5] While one cannot, in a day, see mountains rising or wearing away, one can in a day see the creative processes at work; imagination does the rest. Thoreau longed to understand the workings of things, and, like Emerson, he believed this was poet's work: "The poet uses the results of science and philosophy, and generalizes their widest deductions." But unlike Emerson, Thoreau calibrated those insights with the instruments of science and engineering. "How many new relations a foot-rule alone will reveal, and to how many things still this has not been applied! What wonderful discoveries have been, and may still be, made, with a plumb line, a level, a surveyor's compass, a thermometer, or a barometer! Where there is an observatory and a telescope, we expect that any eyes will see new worlds at once." This hymn to science shows Thoreau cashing out the discovery he had made surveying Walden Pond with plumb line and compass. Early in 1851 he repeated the experiment on White Pond, "God's Drop," and he entered the confirming data into *Walden*.[6] As his eye searched out causes and processes, his hand grasped with equal ease pencil and foot rule, compass and thermometer, earth and world.

This didn't mean giving up on Transcendentalism, but it did mean giving Transcendentalism a fresh spin. In *Nature*, Emerson announced that "nature is the symbol of spirit," and natural facts are the materialization of preexisting "Ideas in the mind of God." When Thoreau first read these words, they cracked the shell of Harvard open: every least object in nature signified a hidden life and a final cause. For years it was all he needed. But now, at the end of *A Week*, he turned on Emerson with an anguished plea: "May we not *see* God? Are we to be put off and amused in this life, as it were with a mere allegory? Is not Nature, rightly read, that of which she is commonly taken to be the symbol merely?"[7] On the high cold tablelands of Katahdin, Thoreau had cried out for "*Contact! Contact!*" He meant literally: body to body, savors and tastes, odors rank and sweet, rainwashed, sun-beaten, melted by the song of the wood thrush, absorbed into the muck of the meadows. After sketching his list of wild places that he could walk to any day of the week, Thoreau added his reason why: "How near to good is what is wild. There is the marrow of nature—there her divine liquors—that is the wine I love. . . . A town is saved not by any righteous men in it but by the woods & swamps that surround it."[8] At the far end of this, thought Emerson, was madness. Thoreau, with nothing more to lose, would defy Emerson and pursue his madness to the end of wisdom.

→>◅-

In October 1849, Thoreau followed his new path to the shore of the wild ocean. After two summers with no excursions, he was ready for a good long walk, and a glance at the map of Massachusetts told him where to go: Cape Cod. Just look at it! There must be a good thirty miles of uninterrupted beach along Cape Cod's outermost shore. Early on the morning of October 9, he and Ellery Channing boarded the train to Boston, planning to ferry across the bay to Provincetown and walk south, or "up," the Cape toward its connection with the mainland. But when they got to the harbor, they found the ocean roiling with a violent storm that kept the ship in port. And posted in the streets were fresh handbills: "Death! 145 lives lost at

Cohasset!" Three days before, the brig *St. John,* sailing from Galway, Ireland, had foundered in the high winds and heavy seas, breaking up on the treacherous rocks just south of Boston. Of 120 souls on board, only 23 were rescued. Bodies were washing ashore as far south as Scituate. The *St. John* was a "famine ship," packed with desperate Irish refugees fleeing mass starvation. Thoreau and Channing hopped the cars to Cohasset, squeezing in among hundreds of Irish heading down for the funeral.

Chance and contingency: who was conducting that funeral but the Reverend Joseph Osgood, the man Ellen Sewall—Thoreau's one romance—had married. Thoreau and Channing stopped at the parsonage to visit with Ellen and Joseph, and Joseph walked with them to the nearby beach, where the three men fell in step with the crowd, the Irish seeking lost relatives and the curious seeking a souvenir, all streaming over the sand past the fresh-dug open grave, "a large hole, like a cellar," while farm wagons rumbled up from the beach hauling rough board coffins stacked three each. The fence was lined for a mile or more with carriages. The friends stepped through to the beach beyond, walking slowly, pausing to study bodies still uncovered or fragments of wrecked ship, watching families watch the waves or peer into one coffin after another, hoping, dreading, to find a sister, a cousin, a brother.

Thoreau was appalled. The scene was grotesque beyond all reason or calculation. Yet no one else seemed disturbed; he witnessed no signs of grief. He did see "many marble feet and matted heads . . . and one livid, swollen and mangled body of a drowned girl—who probably had intended to go out to service in some American family," a family like his own, which included two live-in Irish servants, one who had arrived on a famine ship like this one. A practiced journalist trained in the virtues of restraint, Thoreau conveyed his shock and rage through facts on the ground—"a woman's scarf, a gown, a straw bonnet" blowing on the beach; waves that cracked the ship's iron braces "like an egg-shell on the rocks"; ship's timbers so rotten he could thrust his umbrella almost through; men pulling seaweed away from the corpses, more interested in the weed than the bodies. "Drown who might, they did not forget that this weed was a valuable manure. This shipwreck had not produced a visible vibration in the fabric of society."[9]

Cape Cod opens with this surreal scene. Thoreau might have skipped it altogether—it had nothing to do with "Cape Cod" proper. Instead, he opened his book with it. Contact? Nature's blithe willingness to toss and mangle so many human bodies haunted everything that followed. The uncanny wildness he had encountered on Katahdin followed him to Cohasset, triggering again his brooding unease at the body's precarity before wild nature. Late in 1857, when he was revising *Cape Cod*, he wrote Blake: "You must ascend a mountain to learn your relation to matter, and so to your own body, for *it* is at home there, though *you* are not." Here was the paradox: without matter, soul is without life; but to be a soul, embodied, means that only through a mortal body can soul "contact" the world. This experience should be the source of your writing, he told Blake: return to it again and again, until your essay contains all that is important, nothing that is not. This can be done only afterward, at home—for what do we do when we actually reach the mountaintop? We sit down and eat our lunches. "It is after we get home that we really go over the mountain, if ever. What did the mountain say? What did the mountain do?"[10] It would take Thoreau the rest of his life to "go over" this particular mountain, to put on paper what it said and what it did. For a decade he kept returning to *Cape Cod*. It would be published only after his death.

Meanwhile, the two travelers were on the beach, still minding about lunches and where to spend the night. They turned inland to overnight in Bridgewater; next morning they took the railroad to the base of the Cape. The storm was still raging, so they crammed into a narrow, crowded stagecoach, which drew them over sandy wet roads, through bare flats and scrubby hills, to Orleans on the "elbow" where the Cape turns north. It felt like being stranded "on a sand-bar in the ocean," and in the mist they wondered whether the inn looked out on land or water. Next morning, the rain pounded on. But they had planned a walk, so walk they did, bracing their open umbrellas behind them, letting the south wind drive them north. As they crossed the desolate Plains of Nauset, they heard the Atlantic's dull roar raging beyond Nauset Harbor. Finally they reached a bluff overlooking the beach. Down they scrambled to the ocean's edge, letting their umbrella-sails push them north again in the blowing rain under a dark sky while the breakers beat time on the sand. The one person: a Cape Cod wrecker who showed them a cleft in the sandbank opening to the barren bank above. And so they walked on, alternating between bank above and beach below. Thoreau was finally satisfied: "There I had got the Cape under me," riding it bareback, looking out upon "that sea-shore where man's works are wrecks."[11]

That afternoon the showers cleared into rainbows, and the two walkers, wet and cold, tried the door of a "charity house" erected to shelter the shipwrecked. But the door was nailed shut, and, peering through a knot-hole, they could see nothing but cold stones and a few wads of wool. Shivering on, they turned inland, where they came across a house and, knocking on the door, found themselves face-to-face with John Young Newcomb, who as a boy had heard the gunfire at Bunker Hill and still remembered George Washington. Newcomb joshed them along, judging the character of the two drenched vagrants who claimed to be from Concord, until they passed the test: "'Well, walk in, we'll leave it to the women,' said he." All evening they entertained one another with stories and conversation, while "the women" served meals and the crazy son muttered away in the background: "Damn book-peddlers,—all the time talking about books. Better do something. Damn 'em. I'll shoot 'em." Thoreau would visit Newcomb again the following year, when he learned he and Channing had been suspected as the two thieves who, a few days later, robbed a Provincetown bank.[12] Later he would memorialize Newcomb as "The Wellfleet Oysterman," the greatest and funniest of his many character sketches.

October 12 dawned clear and bright, and after a memorable breakfast the travelers kept on northwestward to the Highland Light. Sailing vessels dotted the horizon on an ocean now smooth and gentle as a lake. "Yet this same placid Ocean," mused Thoreau, "will toss and tear the rag of a man's body like the father of mad bulls." After arranging to stay the night at the lighthouse, they rambled over the Cape's spine to investigate Truro on the Bay, returning in time to receive their first lesson in lamplighting from the keeper, "a man of singular patience and intelligence."[13] The next morning Thoreau rose to watch the sun emerge from the ocean and the mackerel fleet set sail in the sparkling dawn. This was their last day hiking, all the way around the wrist of the Cape and down into Provincetown, where they stayed two nights at Fuller's Hotel. On Sunday they pottered around the nearby swamps and sandhills in wind and cold. On Monday, after a final tour of the town, they took the steamer *Naushon* back across the bay, reaching Boston that evening.

Thoreau turned this accidental itinerary into the armature for a book. He took three more trips to Cape Cod and began a whole new research campaign: Cape Cod struck him as the key to how New England became both "new" and "English" instead of ancient and indigenous. In the summer of 1849 he had prepared for his first trip there by opening a new notebook and copying into it the words of Captain Bartholomew Gosnold, the English voyager who had named Cape Cod in 1602 and described the Indians they encountered there: "The coast was full of people that ran along the shore."[14] But who were they? Thoreau's notebook became the first of twelve "Indian Books"—"a library by themselves," said Channing—in which he amassed nearly three thousand pages of information gleaned from hundreds of sources: explorers, settlers, missionaries, ethnographers, and Native American accounts and self-descriptions, at a time when Native writers were just breaking into print. That September, after exhausting local libraries, Thoreau wrote to Harvard's President Jared Sparks, requesting permission to check out books and bring them home to Concord. "*I have chosen letters for my profession,*" he argued, so this privilege, normally reserved for clergy, should be extended to him as well. "One year," Sparks penciled on the letter.[15] Thoreau returned in November, letter in hand, to continue his research. He was met by his old friend, the naturalist Thaddeus Harris, now Harvard's full-time librarian. Harris never questioned Thoreau's right to check out all the books he needed.

As soon as he'd shaken the sand out of his shoes, Thoreau got busy. Soon he had three lectures for the 1849–50 lyceum season. Aunt Maria pronounced a practice run "very entertaining, and much liked." Concord booked him for January, but only for two nights, so he made a few cuts before taking his audience through the shipwreck and up the beach to meet the Wellfleet Oysterman. Some were puzzled by the eerie first lecture, but at the second they "laughed till they cried."[16] Emerson tipped off South Danvers that Thoreau had a crowd-pleaser, and they invited him to speak on February 18—for only one night, so Thoreau rolled the two into one. This streamlined version pulled in several more invitations. Altogether things were looking up, thought Alcott. Just a few years before, he and his friends had been not merely unpopular, but "obnoxious"; now, even Thoreau read lectures "with a decided acceptance." For the following year, Thoreau freshened up "Cape Cod" with material from his second visit, including the delicious tidbit about their being suspected bank robbers, and delivered it three more times. These lecture trips opened up new windows on local histories: in December 1850, after giving "Cape Cod" at Newburyport's Market Hall, Thoreau was entertained by a local naturalist, who gave him a microscope's view of the circulation of fluids in plant cells. Three weeks later, when he repeated "Cape Cod" at the Bigelow Mechanics Institute in Clinton, Massachusetts, his host gave him an insider's tour of the cotton mills.[17]

Not all these audiences were friendly. The earnest Clinton millworkers thought "Cape Cod" was "one of those trifles, light as air," that whiled away the hour pleasantly, but one didn't *learn* anything; lectures should be for self-improvement, not mere poetic whimsy. One grumpy auditor in Portland complained—through his laughter—that the lyceum committee should "pay him for the time lost in listening to such trash!" And another dressed Thoreau down for quoting profanity, huffing that "such language is in bad taste." But in Portland Thoreau was blessed with one reviewer who sketched a rare portrait of him as a lecturer: "He bewilders you in the mists of transcendentalism, delights you with brilliant imagery, shocks you by his apparent irreverence, and sets you in a roar by his sallies of wit," all without any apparent effort. Thoreau's style, voice, manner, were all "a part of himself," along with the "peculiar look which prepares you for something quaint, and adds its effect far more than words." It was all too much to transfer to paper; one had to hear him in person. Sure, slow plodders were bewildered, but anyone with any imagination found him "a rich treat," quaint, infinitely amusing—a true American original.[18]

Slow plodders still miss the deadpan wit in Thoreau, a master of the humorous story in the tradition of Mark Twain. But *Cape Cod* came to life before audiences that laughed through their tears: whimsical, irreverent, knowing, mischievous and lyrical, a macabre dance with darkness. As Thoreau worked it up for publication, deepening the dark undertones and calibrating his historical research to undermine America's smug narratives of Manifest Destiny, a second front opened to the north, in the Maine Woods and French Canada. All through the 1850s Thoreau pressed forward on both fronts, filling one Indian notebook after another—by 1851 he was already at work on his fifth volume—and pursuing fieldwork whenever he could. As his vision clarified, he returned to the Cape alone, from June 25 through July 1, starting from Provincetown and retracing his original steps backward, interviewing the new lighthouse keeper, visiting John Newcomb, spending more time on the harbor side. The first trip had been a lark; the second was a research trip, notebook in hand, book in mind. Back home he wrote on, tearing the evolving drafts out of the Journal, leaving nothing in it but shreds and patches. "Seeds beginning to expand in me," reads one fragment, "which propitious circumstances may bring to the light & to perfection."[19]

"EVEN THIS MAY BE THE YEAR": 1850

The drought of 1849 gave way in spring 1850 to rains that flooded the meadows and raised Walden Pond to heights not seen for many years—"quite into the bushes, excluding all walkers from its shores" and killing back the pines. Thoreau, out walking in the rain, was exhilarated. "The life in us is like the water in the river," rising to unknown heights, flooding the uplands—why, "even this may be the eventful year—& drown out all our muskrats."[20] It was. By the end of 1850 Henry Thoreau had found his groove, setting his life and his writing into a new pattern.

His family's support enabled this new direction. The Thoreaus were proven market leaders in the pencil business, but late in 1849, profits starting coming in from an unexpected source. Thoreau pencils earned their market share by the high quality of the ground graphite, or "plumbago," which thanks to Henry's milling process was finer and smoother than their competitors'. When orders for their ground plumbago arrived from the Boston printing firm Smith & McDougal, the Thoreaus feared a competitor was edging in. But after swearing the family to secrecy, the firm explained: they needed great quantities of the finest plumbago for a new print process, electrotyping. They would buy it exclusively from the Thoreaus if the Thoreaus, in turn, protected their trade secret. Thus Henry Thoreau's graphite mill not only made possible the highest-quality American pencils; it also fostered the fledgling technology of mass printing. Many times Henry carted ground graphite home from various mills to refine, package, and ship to Boston and, eventually, around the nation. As the new business grew, the Thoreaus made fewer and fewer pencils. In 1853, about the time German pencil-makers in New York flooded the market, they gave up making pencils altogether. Henry, to put off friends who asked why, was said to have answered, "Why should I? I would not do again what I have done once." Profits stayed high even as prices plunged from ten dollars to two dollars a pound; the Thoreaus shipped up to six hundred pounds a year of the precious commodity. But friends noted how the fine, slick graphite dust covered everything in the house. Breathing it must have shortened Henry's life, which might have been shorter still had he not been taking vigorous daily walks outdoors.[21]

Henry had always liked the Texas House, on the edge of town surrounded by his thriving orchard. From his window he could see cows grazing on Fairhaven Hill, and he could walk to Walden or the river without going through town. But Cynthia was restless again, and with their new prosperity they could afford to look at some of the finest houses in town. The "Yellow House" on Main Street caught their eye, just down from the Parkman house they had rented for so many years. The storekeeper Josiah Davis had built it in his heyday, but lost it to bankruptcy during the Panic of 1837. After bouncing from owner to owner, it had come to the shopkeeper Daniel Shattuck, who was happy to sell. So it was that John Thoreau bought the Yellow House on September 29, 1849, for $1,450. Cynthia drew up a long list of repairs and renovations: raise the entire house so the ceilings would be nine feet high; put in new partitions and doors, new window glass, new sinks, new shingles; and on and on. They hired a carpenter, and Henry helped attach the pencil shop (moved from the Texas House) to the back corner. It would be nearly a year until renovations were complete and the family could move in, on August 29, 1850. Henry, who didn't want to move "at all," found himself despite his protests living once again on Main Street, near the heart of town in one of Concord's finest neighborhoods.[22]

Even he had to admit his new quarters were splendid: the entire attic, a slope-ceilinged room stretching the length of the house, with a staircase opening in the middle and windows overlooking the town on one end, where he put his desk, and the river on the other, where he put his bed so he could look out on the weather before rising. The attic was so hot in summers that for weeks at a time he spent evenings downstairs with the family, but it was roomy enough to hold his cane bed, his writing desk, and his driftwood bookshelves. It also had ingenious nooks and crannies to hide his rolled-up canvas camping tent and display his arrowheads, Indian relics, herbarium, mosses, lichens, birds' nests, birds' eggs, mineral cabinet, insect collection, hatching turtles, and whatever else he dragged home. The Yellow House attic became his bedroom, parlor, workshop, nature museum, and window on the world. As Sophia apologized once, escorting a friend up the stairs, Henry regarded the dust on his furniture "like the bloom on fruits, not to be swept off."[23] For a crowning glory, the Concord River was right across the street, in Ellery Channing's backyard. For in June 1849, his old friend had sold his Ponkawtasset farm and bought the house on the riverbank, where Thoreau could moor his boat; in years to come, John Thoreau enlarged their backyard by purchasing the adjoining lot, where Henry planted a splendid orchard, transplanting one of his beloved "Texas" Baldwin apple trees. This would be his home for the rest of his life—his busiest, happiest, and most productive years.

Thoreau was used to earning his keep, and between paying his father for room and board, paying off the debt to Munroe, and funding his books and travels, bringing in a steady income was a priority. Lecturing paid little—most out-of-town lectures earned twenty dollars or so, less travel expenses—and so did manual labor; once he even considered speculating in cranberries.[24] Far more reliable was the income he earned from surveying. In 1850, Thoreau became a fully professional civil engineer: he invested in his own equipment, including a surveyor's chain and a set of ten chaining pins, a measuring tape, drafting paper, tools—protractors, triangles, a T square, and various rulers and straightedges—and, most glorious of all, a top-of-the-line fifteen-inch compass made of lacquered brass with a silvered five-inch dial. He even printed up a handbill advertising his warrant of accuracy "within almost any degree of exactness, and the Variations of the Compass given, so that the lines can be run again."[25]

Thoreau's claims of accuracy were not hyperbolic. After his death, his Concord surveys were deposited with the town library, where for decades they provided invaluable documentation of town property boundaries. Later measurements have shown Thoreau's work was fastidious: he even took the unusual step of ascertaining the "True Meridian," or true north, rather than using simple magnetic bearings—a complex two-day procedure that he performed early in 1851, in front of the Yellow House.[26] His first full season brought a wave of jobs: a survey of the Yellow House lot, a commission from Emerson to resolve a long-festering boundary dispute, sixty house lots up in Haverill on the Merrimack River, the town's new court-house grounds, and a new road to the depot. Thoreau was earning a reputation as a careful and resourceful civil engineer. One client told how, when darkness fell before they could finish surveying his ten-acre woodlot, Thoreau finished the job by lighting a candle and sighting to the flame.[27] All in all, he completed at least fifteen surveys in 1850 and another eighteen in 1851—making, as Alcott remarked, "the compass pay for his book."[28]

It was not lost on Thoreau that, though the work suited him, surveying made him complicit in destroying the forests he loved. In November 1850, he walked over land he had surveyed the year before, which the owner had clearcut and subdivided into fifty-two house lots. As a child he'd played in those woods, but, he consoled himself, cutting the trees opened a fine view of the distant blue mountains. Still, he was pestered with guilt. "To day I was aware that I walked in a pitch pine wood which erelong—perchance I may survey and lot off for wood auction and see the choppers at their work." Surely the trees would grow back? After all, a grassy field he remembered from his youth was now pleasant woods. But two days later he couldn't forgive himself: "I saw the fences half consumed . . . and some worldly misers with a surveyor looking after their bounds," ignoring the angels singing all around him, "looking for an old post-hole in the midst of paradise. I looked again and saw him standing in the middle of a boggy stygian fen surrounded by devils . . . and looking nearer I saw that the prince of darkness was his surveyor." Had he sold his soul to the devil? "Trade curses everything it handles," he muttered darkly.[29] A particularly diffi-cult survey, the perambulation of the Concord town boundaries in September 1851, left him feeling he had "committed suicide in a sense."[30] Long stretches spent surveying always left him grouchy and snappish.

But surveying also gave Thoreau a respected professional identity, and he took pride in his high standards, his resourcefulness, his
ability to hack through swamps and briars in all weather, and his precise and exacting drawings, always finished with a flourish. Townspeople who mocked him before now called on him for a valuable
service, and his Journal began to fill with the homespun observations of landowners, farmers, and laborers. Thanks to his voracious
curiosity, what might have narrowed his field of view and blinded
his vision had the opposite effect: a surveyor's eyes were open eyes,
and as his surveying journal filled with professional notes, his private
journal filled with scientific and poetic observations of all he could
see with what he called "the side of his eye." If his profession forced
him to step aside from his chosen path, it also helped him to see
the world around him anew: "I wanted to know the name of every
shrub," he declared, even as he hacked through the underbrush.[31]

Back in 1847, when Thoreau had dreamed of going on a scientific
exploring expedition, he had written gleefully to Emerson that Harvard at last was "really beginning to wake up" and "overtake the age":
its new telescope was the most powerful in the United States, and
its new Lawrence Scientific School had just hired Professor Hors-
ford in chemistry and Professor Agassiz in zoology. Just down the
road, Concord's amateur astronomer, Perez Blood, had invested in
a telescope powerful enough for serious astronomy, strong enough
to show Thoreau the rings of Saturn and the mountains in the
moon.[32] Astronomy was not his calling—he was gratified when
Harvard's new professor of astronomy, William Cranch Bond, told
him the naked eye was still of service to science—but he was making good on his vow to learn the name of every shrub. Even on the
way to look through Bond's telescope, Thoreau studied plants out
the window, amazed to see that Concord and Cambridge, so close
together, were clearly different botanical regions—which reading
Asa Gray, Harvard's new (and world-class) botanist, helped him
see. In January 1848, after collecting so many specimens for Louis
Agassiz, he had finally met the great scientist in person during Agassiz's second course of Lowell Lectures. Thoreau tried to lure him to

Bangor for a lecture series, and though the perennially overworked Agassiz turned him down, they remained on cordial terms through the 1850s, thanks in part to their mutual friendships with Emerson and James Elliot Cabot.[33]

This was what science and engineering meant for Thoreau: local, hands-on, immediate. And urgent, too: "It should be a part of every man's education today to understand the Steam Engine," he wrote his cousin George Thatcher, whose teenage son was interested in engineering. "What right does a man have to ride in the cars who does not know by what means he is moved?" Young George should visit every machine shop, mill, and factory within reach. Thoreau himself—who could never pass a manufactory without stopping for a tour—had just spent a day at Hinckley and Drury's, the largest manufacturer of locomotives, and he now "saw and understood the use of every wheel & screw, so that I can build an engine myself when I am ready." When lecturing had taken him to Clinton, Massachusetts, where he toured the huge gingham mills to see exactly how cloth was made, he not only detailed the process carefully in his Journal, he applied it to his own craft as a writer: "The arts teach us a thousand lessons. Not a yard of cloth can be woven without the most thorough fidelity in the weaver. The ship must be made *absolutely* tight before it is launched." Part of the lesson was the deliberate pun on his own name: "thorough fidelity" to process, to craft, was becoming his watchword.[34]

Later generations would lose touch with Thoreau's immediate, visceral feeling for science and technology, as "science" receded to a specialized profession practiced by an elite corps of intellectuals and "technology" was black-boxed into machines powered as if by magic. By contrast, in Thoreau's world, the coupling of man and nature through machine could still be a thing of wonder. One Sunday afternoon during the spring rains of 1850, Thoreau heard from over the meadow "a faint tink-tink, tink-tink, as of a cow bell amidst the birches and huckleberry bushes." As he approached, the mystery grew, sounding up from the ground as if the open meadow spoke. Perhaps this was some unknown frog or muskrat, some discovery in natural history? Then he found it: a boy's toy waterwheel engineered to tap a small hammer on a tongueless cowbell nailed to a board. "The little rill itself seemed delighted with the din & rushed over the miniature dam & fell on the water wheel eagerly as if delighted at & proud of this loud tinkling"—which Thoreau could hear, he realized that night, all the way from home. He called the family to the window, and they all marveled to hear the sweet sound from so far away. This became another figure for Thoreau's own artistry: if he arranged his materials just so, nature would speak through him in a voice that carried to town, where even people in the streets would stop to listen, to hear something higher, beyond themselves.[35]

Thoreau needed this breakthrough insight for his own kind of Transcendentalism. Science showed him how to see the Cosmos in a grain of sand or the ocean in a woodland pond, a mountain range in Fairhaven Cliff, a glacier in the cobblestones of Walden Pond. Poetry gave him a voice to show the world why this mattered. Late in 1849, Thoreau plunged into a new course of reading: he worked his way through Alexander von Humboldt's volumes of exploration science and the scores of books by scientists and explorers whom Humboldt had inspired to see the world—up the Orinoco, down the Andes to Tierra del Fuego, out to the Rocky Mountains and the far Northwest, south to Antarctica, north to the Arctic, beyond to the steppes of Asia or the African savannah. As he read his way around the globe, Thoreau imagined his own travels as one-person exploring expeditions. What the world explorers of his day were doing writ large, he could do in microcosm, traveling and writing about the earth as a planet whose smallest and most local features illuminated, and were illuminated by, the Cosmos itself. To the leading edge of science, Thoreau could add his own "home-cosmography." By November 1850 he had caught hold of the method, and by September 1851 he captured it in a phrase: "A writer a man writing is the scribe of all nature—he is the corn & the grass & the atmosphere writing."[36]

But first, there was a chasm to cross. Nearly ten years before, Margaret Fuller advised Thoreau that nature "is not yours till you have been more hers." He in turn appreciated Fuller deeply, calling "The Great Lawsuit," her pioneering essay in women's rights, "a noble piece, rich extempore writing—talking with pen in hand" that showed how "in writing conversation should be folded many times thick."[37] *A Week*, his own attempt to fold conversation many times thick, owed much to Fuller's example. In the years since, Fuller's path had taken her from Boston to New York, where she reported on a wide range of social issues as a correspondent for Greeley's *Tribune*, then to Europe, where she became Greeley's foreign correspondent.

Fuller settled in Rome, and as the Revolution of 1848 broke over Italy she became a revolutionary herself, a fierce partisan for the Roman Republic who enthralled and alarmed American readers with harrowing eyewitness reports from the front lines. And though she told no one about it, she married—so it was implied—her lover Giovanni the Marquis d'Ossoli, an Italian revolutionary, and gave birth to their son Angelo, or "Nino." As the Republic collapsed, Fuller fled to England, where she drafted a first-person history of the Italian Revolution.[38] Determined to see it through the American press herself, she booked passage for her family, their nursemaid Celesta Pardena, and their friend Horace Sumner on the *Elizabeth*, a British sailing ship. They left Italy on May 17, 1850, bound for New York with a reliable crew, pleasant friends, and a hold filled with luxury goods: silk, almonds, olive oil, castile soap, hats and straw bonnets, a gallery's worth of fine paintings, a statue of John Calhoun for South Carolina, and 150 tons of Carrera marble.[39]

Ill fortune began when the ship's captain died of smallpox just as they reached Gibraltar, where they laid over in quarantine before proceeding under the command of the inexperienced first mate, Henry P. Bangs. As they neared New York in mid-July, they did not know that a historic hurricane was sweeping up the Atlantic coast. Nor did they know quite where they were: Captain Bangs thought they were safely off New Jersey in deep water, but actually they were sixty miles east, dangerously close to Fire Island. Just before four in the morning on Friday, July 19, a thunderous crash awoke the passengers: the *Elizabeth* had struck a sandbar head-on. A great wave struck the brig broadside, driving her onto the bar with a force that smashed the marble through the hold. The seas broke over the ship and poured through the cabin, tearing away sails, masts, and life-boats, sending the terrified passengers, still in their nightclothes, to the deck, where they could see the shore was only three hundred yards away. The tide was falling, and already in the dawn there were scores, hundreds, of people on the beach. Rescue seemed sure. But as they watched in mounting horror and disbelief, the crowds ignored them, swarming over the trunks and boxes washing ashore, smashing them open and bearing away in cartloads clothing, possessions, and merchandise.

The abandoned passengers tried to save themselves. Some dived into the water and made it ashore, battered by the wave-tossed timbers but alive. Others, including Horace Sumner, sank out of sight and drowned. The Ossolis huddled together, refusing to be separated, protecting their terrified child and waiting for the lifeboat—which never came. The furious first mate later told Thoreau, "The men on shore had not courage enough to launch the lifeboat." All they did was sit and watch, now and then snatching up "a hat that came ashore."[40] Finally, at flood tide, well into the afternoon, with the last of the ship breaking up around them, the ship's steward took Nino in his arms and jumped overboard. Both were borne under by the waves and drowned. Then Celesta and Giovanni were washed away, while Margaret, as Thoreau would later write, "sat with her back to the foremast with her hands over her knees—her husband & child already drowned—a great wave came & washed her off."[41] Nino's small naked body was carried ashore and buried in the sand in a sailor's chest. The bodies of his parents were never recovered.

Not until three days later, on the evening of July 22, did the calamitous news reach Concord. All through the night, Emerson agonized whether he should go himself, but in the morning he delegated Thoreau—"the most competent person that could be selected"—to go at once to Fire Island "on all our parts, and obtain on the wrecking ground all the intelligence &, if possible, any fragments of manuscript or other property."[42] Thoreau left immediately, with a seventy-dollar advance from Emerson, and on Wednesday morning, July 24, he stopped in New York long enough to leave a note for the absent Greeley before joining William Henry Channing on the 9:00 a.m. cars to Fire Island. They reached Fire Island at noon; Margaret's brother Arthur Fuller and Horace Sumner's brother Charles reached the beach later that night. Back in Concord, Margaret's sister Ellen was so devastated her friends feared for her sanity. Her husband Ellery Channing traveled to Fire Island to add his own efforts to the futile search for something, anything, of Margaret's.

If Thoreau had expected horror, what he found was worse: nothing. Or nearly nothing. Wreckers had scavenged the beach for days—three days earlier, one eyewitness counted nearly a thousand persons walking the miles of sand, over half of them "secreting and carrying off everything that seemed to be of value." Thoreau coursed up and down the beach, hunting for any scrap, interviewing with the intensity of a police investigator every witness he could find, trying to make sense of chaotic and conflicting reports. What became terribly clear was that everything of any possible worth had been plundered. No one denied it. "There are some proper pirates among them but most do not deserve this name—they are rather low thieves & pilferers," who divvied up the spoils among themselves, even as friends of the dead sought any remains: "This will do for your child & that for your wife—these were the expressions which they themselves quoted. I found the young men playing at dominoes with their hats decked out with the spoils of the drowned"—Fuller's own tassels and ribbons.[43]

On Thursday morning Thoreau wrote his sad report to Emerson from Smith Oakes's nearby house—"a perfect pirate's house" filled with wreckage and stolen goods, where the survivors had gathered and the bodies had been collected. Of Giovanni Ossoli there was an empty carpetbag and one shoe, possibly his. Of Margaret Fuller Ossoli there was a black leather trunk with a wrenched-off lock, and inside nothing left but twenty or thirty books and a few papers— only enough to cover a small table. Margaret's writing desk, in a blue calico bag, was broken, and inside were a few letters. Of her manuscript, there was nothing. The second mate told Thoreau he had seen a man open a bundle of handwritten papers, which he threw down on the beach as of no value.

There were a few more leads, so Thoreau lingered until Saturday morning, walking the sands, kicking apart heaps of almonds and juniper berries from the hold. Something more might yet wash ashore. He posted advertisements and searched houses all the way to Patchogue and Sayville on Long Island. The results could not have helped his view of humanity. "Some had heard that there were 3,000 doll[ar]s in rings on the fingers of the Marchioness," he noted grimly. "They stole from one another—what some had hid in the bushes others stole again." After poling to Patchogue in an oyster boat full of drunken, snoring fishermen wallowing in their own vomit, he found the dresses of the drowned—Fuller's dresses—worn by the wives of men who had stolen them; the women refused to give them up.[44] No trace of Margaret's or Giovanni's bodies was ever found. Rumors persisted that they had washed ashore, been plundered of clothes, jewels, and money, and were secretly buried to hide the robbery.[45]

Thoreau himself took one keepsake: out on the beach he found the skirt of a gentleman's coat, from which he ripped a single button. At the Oakes' he compared it with those on a coat known to be Ossoli's; it was a match. On Friday, the lighthouse keeper reported a body four or five miles west of the wreck. Next morning Thoreau walked out to it: "a portion of a human skeleton," he wrote to the grieving Charles Sumner, perhaps the remains of his brother Horace, though Thoreau could not be sure whether it was male or female. Thoreau ordered the lighthouse keeper to bury it and mark the gravesite, pending a "trustworthy examination." Sumner sadly agreed that the remains must be impossible to identify—another futile search.[46] But his thanks to Thoreau were profound. Less than a year later, Sumner was elected to the US Senate, replacing the disgraced Daniel Webster, and ever after he repaid the favor by sending Thoreau all the government scientific reports he thought Thoreau might find useful.

One button and some bones on the beach: for all the lives lost and all the hopes, this was what remained. Back home in Concord, Thoreau fingered the button and brooded. "Held up it intercepts the light & casts a shadow, an actual button so called—And yet all the life it is connected with is less substantial to me than my faintest dreams." True, our bodies float on the stream of the "actual" and "we have sympathy with it through them"—but then he added, overcome with nausea, "I do not think much of the actual. . . . It is a sort of vomit in which the unclean love to wallow." A few days later, a calmer Thoreau wrote to H. G. O. Blake: "Our thoughts are the epochs in our lives; all else is but as a journal of the winds that blew while we were here."[47]

The bones disturbed Thoreau in a very different way. They were unremarkable, "simply some bones lying on the beach." But months later they haunted him still, not because they were nauseating but because they weren't—they seemed "singularly inoffensive," even possessing a "certain majesty": "They were alone with the beach and the sea, whose hollow roar seemed addressed to them, and I was impressed as if there was an understanding between them and the ocean which necessarily left me out, with my sniveling sympathies."[48] The beach of Fire Island brought Thoreau back to the mystery of Katahdin, where he'd first divined the uncanny nature of the body: "for *it* is at home there, though *you* are not." The bones and the ocean understood something his mind struggled to grasp— not merely the blunt fact that all things pass, but the further insight, which he'd come to after John's death, that only the passing of the body gave passage to spirit. Once again harrowed by tragedy, Thoreau turned not away from the things of nature, but toward them, voicing again his awe before the fundamental strangeness of materiality. Nature is not yours until you are more hers: that sympathy had been part of Fuller's legacy to him.

Ellery Channing, in his own grief, wrote that Fuller drew forth from her friends, by some "secret magnetism . . . the cherished secret, which now runs like a vein of fire through all the meshes of each one's correspondence. To each she answered in some one part, was an answer to some one question, & accomplished some one desire."

Turning to his own most cherished correspondent, Thoreau tried to pass forward Fuller's gift: after fingering the button one more time, he put it down, picked up his pen, and wrote to Blake, "I say to myself, Do a little more of that work which you have confessed to be good. . . . If there is an experiment which you would like to try, try it. . . . Do what nobody else can do for you. Omit to do anything else." To himself he was even more expansive: "If you can drive a nail & have any nails to drive, drive them. If you have any experiments you would like to try—try them—now's your chance. . . . Be native to the universe."[49]

—>—<—

Two months after returning from Fire Island, Thoreau and Ellery Channing had a chance to drive one of those nails. All summer long, Boston had been talking about William Burr's "Moving Mirror," a "Seven-Mile Panorama" that unscrolled a painted moving-picture show scripted to narrative and music, which took viewers on the waterway from the Great Lakes to Niagara Falls and down the St. Lawrence River. Thoreau was one of perhaps a million people to see it.[50] As a publicity stunt, Burr arranged three railroad excursions from Boston to Montreal, for five dollars round trip; an optional boat ride down the St. Lawrence River to Quebec cost only two dollars more. European travel was out of the question for Thoreau, but this opportunity for foreign travel was irresistible. Purchasers had to return within ten days; nonetheless, 1,346 subscribers bought tickets for the first excursion, Thoreau and Channing among them. It would be a lightning-quick trip, and Thoreau set himself to making the most of it. All year he'd been walking daily—often nightly, too, exploring the woods and fields by moonlight despite many raised eyebrows.[51] The thought of taking such a walk in the heart of French Canada, along the greatest river in North America, was tantalizing, and after helping the family move into the Yellow House that August, he was ready for a break. So a month later, Thoreau bundled up his few travel necessities, put on his "bad weather clothes," seized his ever-present umbrella, and set off for Canada with Channing.

At 7:40 a.m. Wednesday, September 25, 1850, the two self-styled "knights of the umbrella and the bundle" stepped from the Concord Depot onto the northbound train. They must have drawn some looks: while the other excursionists were decked out in their finest clothes, Thoreau wore his oldest leather shoes, well greased to keep off the rain, with a cheap brown linen duster over his second-best coat and a palm-leaf travel hat.[52] The train reached Burlington, Vermont, at six in the evening. It was too dark to see the great reaches of Lake Champlain, but after a night's delay, they boarded a steamboat in time for dawn to reveal the long narrow lake threaded between two blue ranges of mountains. Steaming north on the Richelieu River, they crossed the invisible border into Canada—and Thoreau, for the first time in his life, was in a foreign country. His quick eye immediately picked up differences in the houses and the pirogues on the shore and in the strangeness of dual-language signs on the frontier at St. Johns, aka Saint-Jean-sur-Richelieu.

After three hours of watching earnest red-coated soldiers at their drills and Canadians driving past in dust-colored homespun, the excursionists rolled overland to La Prairie, where Thoreau and Channing pushed ahead to be first in line for the ferry crossing the Saint Lawrence—a river nine miles wide! Across the river, Thoreau thought Montreal looked like a New York in the making. In early afternoon they stepped onto the wharf, pushing through crowds hurrahing welcome to the Yankees, to walk straight to Notre Dame, the heart of French Catholicism and the gateway to all that was new and strange. Thoreau the Yankee Puritan boggled at the cool silence of the cathedral, worth any thousand Protestant churches, a sanctum "where the universe preaches to you and can be heard"—almost as grand and sacred as a Concord forest. "I am not sure but this Catholic religion would be an admirable one if the priest were quite omitted," he quipped. Coming from him, it was a compliment.[53]

What most moved Thoreau, again and again, was the French language. The very street names evoked a whole French Revolution—should the omnipresent soldiers ever put their heads and hearts together for "cooperation and harmony" instead of war. At the mar-

ket he stumbled through his rusty Harvard French to bargain for
pears and apples, which they munched on the steamer's deck while
watching the last Yankees being ferried over in the dusk. As they
steamed through the night down the St. Lawrence to Quebec, 180
miles away, Thoreau pored over the map, sounding out the poetry
of such place-names as Point aux Trembles, for the aspen leaves that
once trembled there: "For there is all the poetry in the world in a
name. It is a poem which the mass of men hear and read. . . . all the
world reiterating this slender truth, that aspens once grew there."[54]

Dawn found them nearing Quebec's imposing cliffs. The moment
they stepped ashore, they headed as far away from the crowd as they
could get, up a narrow road, then up a set of stairs to the stone citadel
at the top, back in time to the Middle Ages of Sir Walter Scott. They
wandered over the stones, admiring the view and picking flowers
among the guns before setting off northeast with the immense St.
Lawrence on their right. On their left, an uninhabited and largely
unexplored wilderness stretched clear to Hudson's Bay. The miracle
of it dazzled them utterly: only two days before they had been in
Concord, and here they were, rambling not to Flint's Pond or Sudbury Meadows but "taking a walk in Canada, in the Seigniory of
Beauport, a foreign country" that seemed "almost as far off as England and France." "Well," thought Thoreau, "here I am in a foreign
country, let me have my eyes about me and take it all in."[55]

They took in a long band of narrow farms that ran along the
riverbank, with neat whitewashed stone houses every few feet—a
continuous village one street wide, with no front doors and no front
yards, where women worked in the fields alongside the men, digging
potatoes or bundling grain. About sundown they reached Beauport near the Falls of Montmorenci, where the two Yankees asked
for directions to the nearest tavern. To their shock, not one person
could answer them in English. The very dogs barked in French, they
fancied. So in broken schoolboy French, they finally made out that
here, in this country, there were no taverns, because there were no
travelers. House after house turned them away for lack of a spare
bed, until they found lodgings with the master of the sawmills at the

falls, where, with the roar of the falls in the background, the Yankees "talked or murdered French" all evening to everyone's amusement before tucking in under homespun linen sheets.

The next morning, they found the mill owner's private grounds blocked the Falls of Montmorenci from view. Natural wonders, grumbled Thoreau as he trespassed over the fences, should be kept sacred from the intrusions of private ownership. Of the falls themselves, a hundred feet higher than Niagara, he said little. Soon they were slogging through rain down a muddy clay road toward the Falls of St. Anne, twenty-two miles farther, noting the humble houses, the people washing and cooking outdoors, the wooden crosses and shrines, and the ubiquitous red woolen caps and sashes (which Thoreau, chilled in his thin duster and straw hat, began to envy). Everywhere they were greeted with the universal salutation "*Bon jour*" and everywhere the great feature was the Great River of Canada, which looked, even 325 miles from the mouth, as if it were opening into an ocean. Near the house they lodged at that night stood a church whose walls were adorned by crutches left behind by the miraculously cured. To Thoreau, it looked as though the village carpenter turned them off new-made. They breakfasted on bread and butter, tea and maple sugar, and potage, the local dish of boiled potatoes and meat. Then they spent their Sunday in this "thoroughly Catholic country," self-consciously aware of being the only Protestants in sight.

At the Falls of St. Anne, a three-mile bushwhack "by guess and by compass," Thoreau made a grand scramble deep into the gorge, a "most wild and rugged and stupendous chasm." This was the limit of their walk. The travelers retraced their steps. The country looked, Thoreau thought, "as old as Normandy itself, and realized much that I had heard of Europe and the Middle Ages," including saintly names that made him "dream of Provence and the Troubadours" and feudal patterns of land tenure that challenged his sense of modernity—especially when he learned that a higher percentage of people could vote in Canada than in the United States.[56] That night they lodged at a farmhouse where they warmed themselves in the great kitchen and parleyed their murdered French to a merry family, who swept clean the oiled tablecloth so they could chalk it over with local geography and French vocabulary, spreading it with local plants and produce, plums and *senelles* (or hawthorns) and hard glossy apples, Thoreau scribbling notes all the while. Back in Quebec, eager to see yet another waterfall, they hired a calèche to take them nine miles southwest to the Falls of Chaudière. By then Thoreau was tired of waterfalls, but the rainbow they made so entranced him that they missed the ferryboat and had to stay the night at a pension, where their obliging hostess sewed a warm woolen lining into Thoreau's straw hat.[57]

By October first they were back in Quebec, but Thoreau was coming down with a cold, so they cut their trip short and booked passage back to Montreal. They rambled through the Upper Town while they waited, visiting the memorial to Wolfe and Montcalm and counting cannon—twenty-four thirty-two-pounders arrayed against American invaders. Thoreau, inspired, mapped gates and noted positions as if he were on a secret reconnaissance mission. Back at the market stalls in the city below, he bargained for cake and fruit and searched for souvenirs that weren't imported from elsewhere. To his disgust, even the genuine Canada crookneck squash seeds were from Boston. With an hour or so to kill before the steamer raised anchor, he dashed back to a restaurant and stood on their mahogany table to copy the great map of Canada on their wall. That night Thoreau nursed his cold in a berth on the steamer.

Back in Montreal, he felt well enough to climb the city's namesake Mount Royal, following in the footsteps of Jacques Cartier himself, who had climbed it in 1535, nearly a hundred years before the English set foot on Plymouth Rock. Where Cartier had looked down upon "an Indian town in the interior of a new world," Thoreau looked down upon "a splendid and bustling stone-built city of white men," with only a few "squalid" Indians left to sell them baskets.[58] Late that afternoon they rejoined their boisterous Yankee countrymen. For a night and a day, they retraced their steps by railroad and steamer, reaching Concord on the evening of October 3. They had been gone exactly a week and two days, traveled eleven hundred miles, and spent, in Thoreau's case, $12.75, including $1.12 for two guidebooks and a map.

Had he seen Canada? Hardly, and he knew it. But he had learned something: "The Canada which I saw, was not merely a place for railroads to terminate in, and for criminals to run to." Thoreau longed to see more, and he signed off from "A Yankee in Canada," the travel essay he eventually published, with his hope for "a longer excursion on foot through the wilder parts of Canada."[59] For while writing up the excursion, Thoreau began to envision something wider and deeper than a mere traveler's tale; he plunged into a new course of research, sketching a kind of sweeping, cosmopolitan, *longue durée* history, a "Seven-mile Panorama" of greater New England conceived across deep time and planetary space. Canada had shown him puzzles to unriddle: What accounted for the contrasts between familiar New England and alien New France? Why had the French been explorers while the English were settlers? Why had the French joined with the Indians and become so much like them, while the English and Americans cut themselves off from the Indians and destroyed them? How had the land's rivers and mountains shaped the lifeways of nations, and how had those nations—English, French, and Indian—shaped the lands they lived on? Thoreau's notes and observations convinced him that the great era of New World exploration, settlement, and industrialization had produced a historic shift to the modern world. He knew he was a child of this world, even as he seemed born to stand outside it and resist it; perhaps, with his learning, energy, and deep gift for languages, he could understand the causes of the changes happening around him.

His grand and unifying vision pointed to that deeper, wider reality he'd called "the frame-work of the universe." When one surveys the dozens of research notebooks, scores of meticulous Journal volumes, the maps and surveys and thousands of pages of natural history notes and unpublished manuscripts, one begins to comprehend the scope of his vision; but to see the full picture, one must also examine the hundreds of books he annotated and the hundreds of charts and graphs where he pooled and organized his growing data. It was a staggeringly ambitious vision—impossible, really—but Thoreau embarked on it with ferocious energy. Nearly all of this activity dates from 1850. Out of this vast front, particular nodes crystallized into a series of books and projects: "Cape Cod" and "The Maine Woods," taken together, explore the two ultimate poles of wilderness, ocean and mountain and the rivers that connect them. A third node took shape in the Indian Books, Thoreau's attempt to document indigenous alternatives to European narratives of social and economic life. Connecting them all was natural history, the basic environmental framework on which he could weave his portraits of social and historical change—rather as the Concord and Merrimack Rivers had given, in *A Week*, a unifying natural baseline, the thread for his golden ingots of study and reflection. Had Thoreau lived long enough to make that western journey through "the wilds of Canada," it would be easier to see how his brief excursion to Canada fit—even precipitated—his larger vision.[60]

Greeley admonished him to publish the Canada trip while it was still fresh, but to Greeley's annoyance, Thoreau plunged into his ambitious research program instead, using his new library privileges to check out stacks of history books and copy reams of information into his new "Canada" notebook. Instead of working up the Canada journey for the lecture season of 1850–51, he made do with the updated "Cape Cod." Not until the 1851–52 season loomed, with its demand for an absolutely new lecture, did he turn to the Canada material, premiering "Excursion to Canada" at the Lincoln Lyceum at on December 30, 1851,—well over a year after their return. He repeated it in Concord in two parts on January 7 and March 17, 1852. By then he knew the whole mess was a failure, a mere potboiler. Don't expect too much, he warned his audience, for he "visited" Canada only "as the bullet visits the wall at which it is fired & from which it rebounds as quickly & flattened." Being forced to travel so fast, he had little to say: "What I got from going to Canada was a cold."[61]

He might have shelved the whole thing, but, again desperate for money, he shipped it to Greeley. "It looks unmanageable," Greeley groaned, too long and, let's face it, outdated. By then plenty of others had traveled to Canada—and published, too. After a discouraging run of rejections, Greeley placed it with the new *Putnam's Monthly*, whose editor, George Curtis, had helped Thoreau raise his Walden house. Curtis broke Thoreau's "unmanageable" narrative, "An Excursion to Canada," into five parts, starting with the magazine's inaugural issue of January 1853. Trouble flared immediately: Curtis, though an old friend, knew enough not to publish heresy. He deleted Thoreau's ironic and absurdly offensive sentences about Montreal's Cathedral of Notre Dame: "I am not sure but this Catholic religion would be an admirable one if the priest were quite omitted. I think that I might go to church myself sometimes, some Monday, if I lived in a city where there was such a one to go to." When Thoreau discovered the bowdlerization, his fury almost ended their friendship. A distraught Greeley begged Thoreau to calm down: "Don't you see," he reasoned, that since *Putnam's* conceals the names of its authors, "the elimination of very flagrant heresies (like your defiant Pantheism) becomes a necessity?" No, Thoreau did not see. The quarrel continued, and *Putnam's* pulled the series after the third installment—because, as Thoreau fulminated to Blake, "the editor Curtis requires the liberty to omit the heresies without consulting me—a privilege California is not rich enough to bid for."[62]

No other publisher would touch the aborted series. "Excursion to Canada" was a flop. Nor would this be the last time an adversarial Thoreau crossed pens with an editor too afraid of public outrage to print his words unexpurgated: "Cape Cod" and "Chesuncook" would meet the same fate, with similar results. The more Thoreau knew his own mind and spoke it aloud, the more the era's outraged guardians of public morality sought to cut off his tongue. Even a potboiler like "A Yankee in Canada," as it was eventually retitled, proved inflammatory. But in Thoreau's defiant mind, the closed-door Sunday Cosmos had exploded, which meant that if God was anywhere, God was everywhere, including right underfoot at home in Concord. Call it pantheism, call it heresy, but the question remained: how to *live* this truth, there on Main Street in full view of everyone, as well as how to write it—and in living it and writing it, to show it forth to others.

→>—<-

What Thoreau did just after returning from Canada defies calculation or explanation. For three more weeks he continued to use the Journal, as he had for nearly ten years, as a writer's workbook. But on November 8, 1850, he wrote up everything he noticed and thought during his daily walk as one long entry. Remarkable, he opened, how quiet everything is this time of year, as if it were waiting for winter. The next day he did the same, this time concentrating on seeing the landscape through layers of memory, as if to look around were to look back into time. Then two days later—writing all this up must have taken the intervening day—he did it a third time: "I am attracted by a fence made of white pine roots," he opened, filling pages with a stream-of-consciousness flow of words as if he were writing while walking: "I pluck," "I heard," "I saw yesterday," "I notice."[63] Again on the fourteenth, the fifteenth, the sixteenth— when he wrote a huge entry on how to see the smallest rill as if it were the Orinoco or the Mississippi, and how to write about seeing in this odd new way. Thoreau's new experiment made the very act of writing visible on the page—as if I were to tell you about the warmth of a May afternoon seeping through my open window as I type these words—even interruptions: "Somebody shut the cat's tail in the door just now & she made such a catewaul [*sic*] as has driven two whole worlds out of my mind."[64] But soon Thoreau had his "two whole worlds" back, for he continued for more pages. The next day, he did it again. Two days later, again. And again. And again.

And this is what truly staggers the mind: from this point, Thoreau did not stop doing this, ever—not until, dying and almost too weak to hold a pen, he crafted one final entry. Until November 7, 1850, he had treated the date as incidental. Starting on November 8, 1850, he treated the day and the date as essential to his artistry. The date, and what he can write of his life on that one day, is no longer incidental to some larger quest—it *is* the quest. Virtually every day from then through the end of his life, with few exceptions, Thoreau wrote a dated entry that explored whatever caught his mind that day. Whereas before he had scissored out entire chunks of his journal, sometimes leaving little behind but ribbons and fragments, from then on he cut out very little, and soon, he would cut out nothing at all, carefully preserving each Journal volume intact. In short, without announcing it, Thoreau simply stopped using his Journal as the means to the "real" work of art somewhere else, and started treating the Journal *itself* as the work of art, with all the integrity that art demands.[65] Or, perhaps all the integrity that *science* demands: in this new mode, his Journal volumes were something like scientific notebooks, laboratory records whose value lay precisely in their regularity and completeness.

Reorienting his writing required reorienting the pattern of his daily life. Thoreau's new protocol required a high degree of focus and discipline, for its value depended on consistency: going out every day, and every day pressing language to find something new to see, making studies, noted an early biographer, "as carefully and habitually as he noted the angles and distances in surveying a Concord farm."[66] Thoreau developed the practice of walking with pencil and paper and scribbling notes on the spot, brief names and phrases that he wrote up the following morning in long, often lyrical Journal entries—sometimes, when he got backed up, writing out two or three days' worth at a time—then setting out that afternoon for another three- or four-hour walk. "In the forenoon commonly I see nature only through a window—in the afternoon—my study or apartment in which I sit is a vale," he wrote in October 1851, after the experiment had become routine. Sometimes he varied it, walking abroad in the morning and writing in the afternoon; sometimes he unsettled his senses by walking before dawn or staying out well past midnight. But he must go out, he told Channing, every day, to see what he had caught in his traps set for facts; as Emerson remarked, "The length of his walk uniformly made the length of his writing."[67]

Thoreau usually walked alone, but often Channing came along, though Thoreau could be impatient: "In our walks C. takes out his note-book some times & tries to write as I do—but all in vain. He soon puts it up again—or contents himself with scrawling some sketch of the landscape. Observing me still scribbling he will say that *he* confines himself to the ideal—purely ideal remarks—he leaves the facts to me." Channing's criticism pushed Thoreau to articulate what he wanted with those heaps of "facts": not mere data, but "material to the mythology which I am writing"—or, more largely, "facts which the mind perceived—thoughts which the body thought with these I deal." Thoreau's walks became a form of meditation, a spiritual as well as physical discipline. He worried about walking bodily into the woods without getting there in spirit, some piece of business in his mind literally blinding his eyes. "I am not where my body is—I am out of my senses. In my walks I would return to my senses like a bird or beast. What business have I in the woods if I am thinking of something out of the woods." Animal minds became a model for him; he strove to walk like a fox, mind and senses wholly open. As he said of a muskrat: "While I am looking at him I am thinking what he is thinking of me. He is a different sort of man, that is all."[68]

On November 26, Thoreau walked through the drizzle and mist melting an early snow to sit down with a group of Penobscot Indians, camped in tents on the river. Just as he had done with the French Canadian family a few weeks before, in their farmhouse on the banks of the St. Lawrence River, so now did he sit with this family in their home on the banks of the Concord, asking them questions and recording their answers: How do you live? he asked. How do you hunt, cook, make canoes, boil water, cradle your children? As they showed him, he wrote down their words: "Kee-nong-gun or pappoose cradle," "Jeborgon or Jebongon?" or sled—where we get our word *toboggan*. And, for the first time, he drew the things they showed him on the Journal page. "The pencil is the best of eyes," said Louis Agassiz, who drew at the blackboard during his popular lectures. The books on Indians Thoreau was taking notes from were full of drawings, too, and Thoreau had started to copy them. Now, sitting down with the Penobscot, their tents holding off the

November drizzle, he was seeing not just with his eyes, but with his ears and hands as well.[69]

What Thoreau couldn't carry away in his notebook, he often carried away in his pockets. Thus it was that the Yellow House attic became a kind of material memory, the place that held and preserved his expanding mental universe: notebooks, journal volumes, books, maps, charts, tables, natural history specimens, and curiosities. The townspeople started to bring him things, too. In December 1849, a neighbor, annoyed by a large hawk killing his hens, shot it out of the sky—but instead of tossing the carcass into the woods to rot, he brought it to Thoreau. What Thoreau did next was also remarkable: he brought it to the Boston Society of Natural History, to show Samuel Cabot (brother of James Elliot Cabot), their curator of birds. Remarkable indeed, agreed Cabot—it was a rare and beautiful American goshawk. Thoreau's donation allowed Cabot to settle a controversy, for it was clearly a new species, unique to America, and not, as Audubon had claimed, the same as the European goshawk. Cabot skinned the bird, now officially a scientific specimen, dissected and measured it, preserved the remains in alcohol, and stuffed the skin. It occurred to Emerson that Thoreau was providing a real service to the town; indeed, every town needed someone like Thoreau, a practical naturalist on a par with the village doctor or lawyer, who could be provided with microscope and telescope and who in return would answer questions—"What bird is this? What hyla? What caterpillar?"—rather like a park ranger.[70]

Thoreau also caught a useful lesson. "Science applies a finite rule to the infinite.—   & is what you can weigh & measure and bring away," he journalized after bringing the goshawk to Cabot. "Its sun no longer dazzles us and fills the universe with light." The second lesson came a year later, when Cabot notified Thoreau that in honor of his goshawk, the BSNH had elected him a corresponding member, "with all the *honores, privilegia, etc., ad gradum tuum pertinentia*" (or pertaining to the grade of membership), without having to pay an annual subscription. In return, Thoreau was "to advance the interests of the Society by communication or otherwise, as shall seem good."[71] From then on, Thoreau's trips to Boston meant at least two stops: one at the Harvard Library, where he and Thaddeus Harris could talk nature over the history books, and one at the rooms of the BSNH, the center of science in Boston, where he could conduct research in the collections and talk over his findings with some of the era's leading naturalists.

Word spread to Washington, DC, and early in 1853 Thoreau was elected to membership in the American Association for the Advancement of Science. He accepted the invitation and returned their questionnaire promptly, listing as his particular interest the "Manners & Customs of the Indians of the Algonquin Group previous to contact with the Civilized Man"—"that poor part of me which alone they can understand," he qualified in his Journal. In fact, he declared proudly to himself, "I am a mystic—a transcendentalist—& a natural philosopher to boot," a combination he didn't expect the AAAS to understand. At year's end, he wrote again to decline the renewal of his membership, explaining that he could not attend the meetings.[72] For Thoreau, science made the most sense on the local level, among friends who would accept that he was the scientist among poets, and the poet among scientists—the one person in America who could make poetry and science not two things but one.

"THE CAPTAIN OF A HUCKLEBERRY PARTY"

Thoreau was now living his life on two tracks, one visible and one hidden. The visible Thoreau was the busy town surveyor, village naturalist, active lecturer, and publishing writer who helped out with the family business. "The independent of independents," Alcott proclaimed him, "indeed, the sole signer of the Declaration, and a Revolution in himself."[73] Emerson, though, was disappointed to see his friend, now well into middle age, making so little of himself. He "will not stick," he complained. "Pounding beans is good to the end of pounding Empires, but not, if at the end of years, it is only beans." Into his notebook Emerson scored the bitter words his eulogy would pound home: "I cannot help counting it a fault in him that he had no ambition. Wanting this, instead of engineering for all America, he was the captain of a huckleberry party."[74] Not until after his death would Emerson, reading Thoreau's Journal, glimpse the breathtaking ambition of the hidden Thoreau, whose "oaken strength" and "field-laborer's" hands performed intellectual feats that were, acknowledged Emerson, beyond his own, like seeing his own "initial grapplings & jumps" continued by a gymnasium full of youths who "leap, climb, & swing with a force unapproachable."[75]

Cultivating that force unapproachable was Thoreau's primary task all through 1851. His published *Journal* for that single year fills 446 pages, which sparkle and dance with a giddy sense of expanding power. Back in November 1850, just two weeks into his experiment, he had what might be described as a mystical vision: low sunlight falling on a distant angle of the woods affected him singularly, "a place far away—yet actual and where we have been . . . like looking into a dream land—It is one of the avenues to my future." Suddenly a flash like "hazy lightning" flooded all the world "with a tremulous serene light which it is difficult to see long at a time." He could see two hawks sailing over the water perfectly still and smooth, yet "I do not see what these things can be. I begin to see such an object when I cease to *understand* it." "But I get no further than this," he added in frustration.[76] The paradox simmers through the winter and spring: to "get further" means knowing, but also letting go of what one knows. Only then does one reach true knowledge, what Thoreau defined as "a novel & grand surprise on a sudden revelation of the insufficiency of all that we had called knowledge before. An indefinite sense of the grandeur & glory of the Universe. It is the lighting up of the mist by the sun."[77]

The first step to true knowledge was learning everything he could. Through 1851 Thoreau continued to read voraciously in the sciences, above all Asa Gray's botanies, the scientific explorers Humboldt and Michaux, and Charles Darwin's *Voyage of the Beagle*. Seeing through their eyes turned his world into a "faery land." "I wonder that I even get 5 miles on my way—the walk is so crowded with events—&

phenomena. How many questions there are which I have not put to the inhabitants!"[78] When his eyes were exhausted, he walked by moonlight and navigated by touch, hearing, and odor, startling small creatures in the dark who startled him back. Or he plunged into the river, trying "to get *wet* through," lying on the sandy bottom amid the weeds, drowning all thought, letting the air and water plant seeds in him which he brooded and hatched.[79] How much was in the germ! "Here I am 34 years old, and yet my life is almost wholly unexpanded," he exclaimed. The scale was too great for human life, but so what? "I am—contented. . . . Let a man step to the music which he hears however measured." His ultimate question: "With all your science can you tell how it is—& whence it is, that light comes into the soul?" Impatient as he was to find an answer, the scale of his inquiry was too great to waste any of his time in hurry. Urgency warred with ecstasy: "But this habit of close observation—In Humboldt—Darwin & others. Is it to be kept up long—this science—Do not tread on the heels of your experience   Be impressed without making a minute of it. Poetry puts an interval between the impression & the expression—waits till the seed germinates naturally."[80]

His only excursion that year was local, and alone. Though it produced no essay, it was unusually satisfying. On Friday, July 25, Thoreau set off to Plymouth Harbor, intending to see for himself where the Pilgrims landed to found New England's first colony. From Boston he ferried to Hull and walked down the South Shore, practicing his explorer's eyes, noting down everything—weather, local customs, buildings, flora, the shapes of eroding islands—a Darwin turned loose on the way to Duxbury. At Cohasset he lingered for a day, studying sea and shore, bewildered that no trace remained of the *St. John* wreck two years before. He called again on Joseph and Ellen Sewall Osgood, and on Captain Snow, who still remembered how fishermen "fitted out at Thoreau's."[81] On Sunday, Jean Thoreau's grandson continued to Scituate, visiting Ellen Sewall's father—such significant memories in that home—and reaching Duxbury that afternoon through sunbreaks and thundershowers. Legend has it that Thoreau, too much the landsman to know the dangers of tides, was confident he could reach Clark's Island, three miles away over the tideflats, with a bit of wading. Just as the treacherous Plymouth tide was about to sweep him away forever, a passing fisherman plucked him out of the waves and landed him on the island. Or perhaps this is apocryphal: with more poetry and less embarrassment, Thoreau told of setting sail at sunset in a mackerel schooner, which obligingly dropped him off.[82]

There, where the Pilgrims had first anchored the *Mayflower* in the bleak December of 1620, Thoreau was met by "Uncle Ned" Watson, sailor, farmer, poet, and philosopher, born on Clark's Island and third in line to own it since it was deeded to his family in 1690.[83] Uncle Ned rarely left the eighty-six-acre island, and for four days they explored it together while Thoreau scribbled his copious notes. Ned one-upped Thoreau's old Harvard professor Benjamin Peirce by giving Henry his first lessons in ocean navigation—first taking a turn down the harbor, then sailing over to Plymouth so that Henry might step ashore onto Plymouth Rock, just as the Pilgrims had done 231 years before. After taking Thoreau bass fishing in the ocean, Ned dropped him off in Plymouth, where Thoreau walked the mile or so to "Hillside," the famed home of Ned's nephew Marston Watson and his wife Mary, partners in creating Old Colony Nurseries, one of the century's great orchards and arboretums.

Plymouth had long been a virtual Concord-on-the-Coast: Emerson lectured there in 1834 and was drawn back by the stately Lydia Jackson, whose name he changed to "Lidian" (for the sake of euphony) upon their marriage in 1835. Lidian's sister Lucy lived in Plymouth when she wasn't in Concord, and her brother, the scientist Charles T. Jackson, made his home there, too. Mary Russell, Lidian's childhood friend and now Marston Watson's wife, lived there still. Marston heard Emerson lecture at Plymouth in 1835 and proudly counted himself one of the world's first true Transcendentalists, and he'd been a dedicated naturalist ever since he and Henry helped found Professor Harris's Harvard Natural History Club. One of Henry's first acts at Walden had been to send Marston native berries and seeds for his thriving center of horticulture. But despite these numerous ties, this was Thoreau's first visit. Over the next decade he returned often, sometimes with a lecture and once with his compass for a full-scale formal survey of the Watsons' eighty-acre estate. That first afternoon they dug through the earliest Pilgrim records at the courthouse and inspected relics in Pilgrim Hall; at tea, Mary's father reminisced about seeing as a child Ebenezer Cobb, who in turn had remembered seeing as a child Peregrine White, the first child born to the Pilgrims in New England. History, for Thoreau, was not dead in books but alive in people and places. From evening tea to the Pilgrim founders was but the span of three human lives.[84]

On his return to Concord, Thoreau made one more stop, at the BSNH, where the newly elected member pumped his new colleagues for information on jellyfish and the causes of sea fog. This was the pattern of his travel now: focused and intense field trips, taken with purpose in mind and notebook in hand, with guidebooks at his fingertips together with his map of Massachusetts, divided into four parts so he could take only the section he needed—why, he grumbled, did no one print a decent pocket map for the convenience of travelers?—plus his plant press and measuring tape, all tucked away in his custom-made waterproof backpack with pockets designed for easy storage.[85] Home or abroad, from now on, his philosophy was the same: "Why not begin his travels at home—!" Imagine a traveler who began "with all the knowledge of a native—& add thereto the knowledge of a traveller ... the world would be absolutely benefited. It takes a man of genius to travel in his own country—in his native village." What he said in *Walden* was literal truth: "I have travelled a good deal in Concord."[86]

-+->-<+-

One night late in October 1851, Thoreau had the strangest dream: he was learning to sail, dragging his anchor far into the sea—he saw buttons off the coats of drowned men—he quoted poetry he didn't know to Alcott—and he awoke to the thought that his body itself was a musical instrument, "the organ and channel of melody as a flute is of the music that is breathed through it. My flesh sounded

& vibrated still to the strain—& my nerves were the chords of the lyre." With "infinite regret" he recollected his body was "but a scuttle full of dirt after all"—but he knew the music would come again.[87]

Six weeks later, on November 30, 1851, Thoreau felt "a transient gladness" at something he saw without quite knowing what it was—perhaps the stratified tier upon tier of white pines before him, or the squirrel who frisked in the tree behind him. It seemed he was asking nature to give him a sign. He was standing, he realized suddenly, on the site of his Walden house. "Where is my home? It is indistinct as an old cellar hole now a faint indentation merely in a farmer's field . . . and I sit by the old site on the stump of an oak which once grew there. Such is the nature where we have lived."[88] The old manuscript he had put away two years before, discouraged and defeated, had been a book *about* nature. Now he was ready to write a book that would *be* nature, would *be* "the corn & the grass & the atmosphere writing."

He had his sign. Soon after finding himself sitting on the oak stump by his Walden home, Thoreau got out the old pages, shook off the dust, and set to work.

CHAPTER EIGHT

The Beauty of Nature, the Baseness of Men

(1851–1854)

I walk toward one of our ponds, but what signifies the
beauty of nature when men are base?
HENRY DAVID THOREAU, "SLAVERY IN MASSACHUSETTS"

ABOLITION AND REFORM
AFTER THE FUGITIVE SLAVE LAW

On the Fourth of July 1854, at one of the era's largest and angriest antislavery rallies, the professed hermit of Walden Pond stepped onto a high lecture platform under a black-draped American flag hung upside down. In the blistering heat, before a crowd of some two thousand souls, the retiring philosopher opened his heart. "I walk toward one of our ponds"—by then, they all knew which one— "but what signifies the beauty of nature when men are base?" This question had tormented Thoreau for nearly four years, since passage of the Fugitive Slave Act in 1850 had brought slavery to his own backyard. Even as his creative springs were blossoming, even as he had completed the masterwork of his career—that very week, his publisher was binding the printed pages of *Walden*—he felt everything he stood for was being destroyed. "The remembrance of my country spoils my walk," he confessed to the crowd. "My thoughts are murder to the State, and involuntarily go plotting against her."[1]

Thoreau's move to Walden Pond nine years earlier had been a declaration of freedom in full view of an America enslaved. Weeks before he began building there, he learned Frederick Douglass was writing about his escape, "telling his name and the name of his master and the place he ran from." "He had better not!" the audience had murmured.[2] What were the chains that bound Douglass compared with the chains that bound everyone in that Concord meetinghouse? *Walden* grew in the shadow of that question, for Walden was not where one escaped it—but where one confronted it head-on. Leaving Walden pressed upon Thoreau a still harder question: In a world of chains and fetters, was it enough to live a free and principled life? On good days, he knew the answer was yes. On bad days, when the world looked shallow and corrupt, he believed he was seeing not its true state, but merely his own blindness: as he wrote, "The perception of beauty is a moral test."[3] His conviction that justice and beauty were the very framework of the Cosmos drove him daily to the woods and his writing desk. During peace, that would have sufficed. But all around him, America warred with itself and with nature, and he feared that more was asked of him. Ever and again some event, some "moral earthquake" would shatter his faith, and the struggle to renew his faith would infuse his walks with added purpose and his writing with added urgency. Out of that struggle, *Walden* was born.

Ironically, the Fugitive Slave Law of 1850, which tipped the nation to civil war, was part of a compromise designed to keep the peace. "Mexico will poison us," Emerson had predicted, and he was right: in 1848, when a victorious United States annexed the northern half of Mexico, the states clashed over whether it would be slave or free. The Compromise of 1850 split the difference: California was admitted as a free state; the territories of Utah and New Mexico would decide the question for themselves; and the slave trade—but not slavery itself—was banned from the nation's capital. In exchange, Southern states got something they dearly wanted: a strengthened Fugitive Slave Law. Their "valuable property" had been escaping north, draining away Southern capital, so the new law required all federal and state officials and all ordinary citizens to return fugitive slaves. Any person suspected of being a fugitive slave was to be arrested, jailed, and tried, with no right to testify in his or her own defense, even if he or she were free. Every United States citizen was required to assist in the capture, custody, and return of all persons who might be property. Resistance was punishable by six months in jail and a thousand-dollar fine. No state, not even Massachusetts, had the right to protect its people of color. Slavery was no longer a Southern institution; it was the law of the land, and every citizen was bound to obey it. If you weren't a slave catcher, you were a criminal.

When Massachusetts' own Senator Daniel Webster threw his support to the Fugitive Slave Law, he ensured its passage. "Mr. Webster decided for slavery," hissed Emerson, debauching moral law by agreeing to treat human beings as "a species of money."[4] Most of Massachusetts agreed with Emerson, and Webster was forced to resign in disgrace, opening the Senate seat filled by Thoreau's friend Charles Sumner, an outspoken abolitionist who took office in 1851. Nevertheless, the law that Webster's treachery helped to pass went into effect on September 18, 1850. Barely three weeks later, Boston put it to the test when two Georgia slave catchers arrived to arrest William and Ellen Craft, who for two years had been giving popular lectures telling the powerful story of their daring escape. The Boston Vigilance Committee swung into high gear, moving the Crafts from house to house and harassing the Georgia men until they finally gave up and returned home. Lewis Hayden, the escaped slave who had told his story standing in the doorway of Thoreau's Walden house, sheltered the Crafts in his Boston brownstone, vowing he would blow it up before he gave them up. Once the threat passed, the Crafts fled to England, but Boston's complacency had been shattered: slavery had arrived. Rallies mobilized thousands who vowed to defend their freedom at any cost.[5]

Concord's first test came a few months later. On February 15, 1851, Shadrach Minkins, an escaped slave who had been waiting tables in Boston, was arrested. At his hearing, hundreds of protesters stormed the Boston courthouse and, galvanized by Lewis Hayden, broke through the guards and spirited Minkins out of the clutches of the federal justice system. That night, Hayden bundled Minkins into a wagon and rushed him through a storm over muddy roads straight to Concord, where at 3:00 a.m. he knocked on the door of Ann and Francis Bigelow, neighbors of the Thoreaus. While the travelers dried out and breakfasted in front of the fire, the Bigelows arranged to drive Minkins thirty miles west, to Leominster. That morning, after hearing what had gone down in the night, Henry Thoreau stormed in his Journal: "What is it to be free from King Geo the IV. and continue the slaves of prejudice? . . . What is the value of any political freedom, but as a means to moral freedom."[6] Minkins was soon safe in Canada, and the identity of the Concord conspirators remained secret for many years. Hayden was arrested and tried for his open defiance, but the Boston jury refused to convict him. He went on to aid scores of fugitives, sending many more through Concord, unrecorded.

When the fugitive slave Thomas Sims was arrested on April 4, Boston authorities were ready: instead of an open courtroom, Sims was confined to a third-floor cell with iron bars across the windows. Vigilance Committee members plotted in secret while thousands of supporters rallied in public, raising hopes that Sims would be freed. Surely this time the courts would try not just Sims but the constitutionality of the law imprisoning him. But the Boston court affirmed the law, and in the predawn darkness of April 12, to the dismay of over a hundred abolitionists keeping vigil, four hundred police armed with sabers escorted Sims out of the "Boston Bastille" and marched him down State Street to a waiting ship bound for Savannah and slavery. Should anyone resist, "draw your sabres & cut him down" were their orders. Protesters—including Concord's new Trinitarian minister Daniel Foster—followed the police with cries of indignation and shame. As the ship cast off, the minister led the grieving company in prayer and song, earning Thoreau's deep respect: "When I read . . . that the man who made the prayer on the wharf was Daniel Foster of Concord I could not help feeling a slight degree of pride." Foster opened his ministry to Concord's most radical abolitionists, preaching in the town hall and reaching the town's "best men," farmers and laborers like Thoreau whom Concord's churches had rejected as "infidels."[7]

But where, fretted Thoreau, was the *rest* of Concord? For the first time in history, Boston had bound and fettered a black man and returned him to bondage. On April 19, as Concord was celebrating the battle that ignited the Revolution, Sims was landed in Georgia, jailed, and publicly flogged. The contradiction, the sheer moral blindness of it, was too much for Thoreau, who poured out his anger in his Journal: "As if *those* 3 millions had fought for the right to be free themselves—but to hold in slavery 3 million others." Some spoke of "trampling this law under foot—why one need not go out of his way to do that" since the law's "natural habitat" was the gutter. "Let your life be a counter friction to stop the machine," he'd asserted two years before—but now, injustice was not merely a by-product; a whole new government machine had been erected to grind men into "sausages." Cannibalism was the order of the day. For page after page Thoreau sputtered on, but he did not make a public statement. Instead it was Emerson who spoke, two weeks later: "The last year has forced us all into politics," he lamented. The infamy "robs the landscape of beauty, and takes the sunshine out of every hour," and ends all the nonsense about freedom, Christian religion, and divine law echoed every April nineteenth and July fourth. Now even Emerson took a page from Thoreau's "Resistance to Civil Government": "An immoral law makes it a man's duty to break it, at every hazard."[8]

Thoreau was scheduled to speak at the lyceum on April 23, four days after Concord's annual celebration. For months he'd been working on his new lecture, "Walking, or, The Wild," his declaration of what Emerson was calling the *higher law*—a supreme moral law nullifying any civil statutes that contradict it. New York Senator William Seward had popularized the phrase in a speech opposing Daniel Webster, four days after Webster spoke in support of the Compromise Act of 1850. There is, declared Seward, "a higher law than the Constitution." Emerson used the phrase in his 1851 speech protesting the Fugitive Slave Law, and it became a touchstone for Transcendentalists. This was the crucible in which Thoreau's posthumous essay "Walking" was originally written and delivered. Overwhelmed with dismay at a society that could ring the bell of freedom with one hand and grasp the manacles of slavery with the other, Thoreau argued for a space of true freedom and a way of life that could take us to that space daily.⁹

To explain to his audience why he spoke on that "older and wider union" instead of the infamy of the moment, Thoreau rewrote his introduction: "I feel that I owe my audience an apology for speaking to them tonight on any other subject than the Fugitive Slave Law on which every man is bound to express a distinct opinion,—but I had prepared myself to speak a word now for Nature—for absolute freedom & wildness, as contrasted with a freedom and culture simply civil—to regard man as an inhabitant, or a part and parcel of nature—rather than a member of society." "Walking" became one of Thoreau's most popular lectures, given many times and not finished until his deathbed. Over the years it grew into the single greatest statement of his philosophy of life, for walking—away from the village, away from politics, into the "Wild" for spiritual regeneration—was not, Thoreau asserted, a form of retreat, but "a sort of crusade . . . to go forth and reconquer this holy land from the hands of the Infidels." Higher law was not a court of appeal in which sins might be tried; it was a land where freedom was not a state of exception, where freedom was a home in which one could dwell.¹⁰

For the time being, Thoreau enacted his antislavery principles in private—even in secret. The Thoreau household had long been a trusted station on the Underground Railroad, but under the new federal regime, this was riskier than ever. Thoreau did let his caution slip once: on October 1, 1851, he noted, "Just put a fugitive slave who has taken the name of Henry Williams into the cars for Canada." Williams had escaped from Virginia and taken refuge in Boston. When he learned a deputy was on his trail, Williams fled on foot to Concord with a letter to the Thoreaus, where he stayed while they gathered funds for his journey to Canada. Henry went to the depot, money in hand, to buy Williams's ticket to Burlington,

Vermont, but when he saw a man who looked suspiciously like a Boston policeman, he backed away and made alternate plans, probably driving Williams ahead to West Fitchburg. How, he asked Williams, do escaping slaves navigate in the dark? By following the stars, Williams answered, including the North Star; also by following the telegraph lines—with "a turf in their hats," a bit of the green earth, for good luck.[11]

After this incriminating entry, Thoreau mostly kept his Journal silent. "To night a free colored woman is lodging at our house," he mentioned late in 1853; she was on her way to Canada to earn money to buy her husband, a Virginia slave purchased for six hundred dollars by a man who wouldn't sell him to his wife for less than eight hundred.[12] By chance one other portrait survives. On July 26, 1853, the Virginia abolitionist Moncure Conway arrived for a visit and found Thoreau caring for a fugitive slave who had knocked on the door that morning. "I observed the tender and lowly devotion of Thoreau to the African. He now and then drew near to the trembling man, and with a cheerful voice bade him feel at home, and have no fear that any power should again wrong him. That whole day he mounted guard over the fugitive, for it was a slave-hunting time."[13] Conway's account of the family's skill and ease with the situation shows they sheltered and forwarded many others, but how many, or who they were, will never be known. One person they helped—legend says it was Henry Williams—gave Thoreau a Staffordshire ceramic figurine of Uncle Tom and Eva, which thereafter stood proudly on the family mantelpiece, advertising the Thoreaus' home as an abolitionist safe house.[14]

Yet Henry avoided *organized* abolitionism. He probably enjoyed the visit of Conway's Quaker friend William Henry Farquhar, a Maryland abolitionist likely vetting Thoreau for future service on the Underground Railroad.[15] But when three agents for the Massachusetts Anti-Slavery Society descended upon the family in June 1853, Henry loathed the way they "rubbed you continually with the greasy cheeks of their kindness," cuddling up with you "spoon fashion," licking you "as a cow her calf." The instant Thoreau opened his mouth, one said "with drawling sultry sympathy Henry,—I know all you would say—I understand you perfectly—you need not explain anything to me." "I am going to dive into *Henry's* inmost depths," he oozed to the others. "I trust you will not strike your head against the bottom," Henry snapped back.[16]

→>–◅-

Abolitionism and women's rights were twinned causes: as Margaret Fuller had said years before, it was "the champion of the enslaved Africans" who made "the warmest appeal on behalf of woman," partly out of principle, but also because women, not men, were the leaders of abolitionism at the grass-roots level. Fuller's own writings were laying the foundation for women's rights. As she proclaimed, "We would have every arbitrary barrier thrown down. We would have every path laid open to woman as freely as to man." Men, she added scornfully, were too much under the "slavery of habit" to help with women's liberation.[17] It's true that her friend Henry Thoreau did not fight for women's rights, but he did praise Fuller's foundational women's rights essay, and about that same time he went to a Quaker church in New York to hear Lucretia Mott speak on "Slavery and the Degradation of Woman." "It was a good speech," he had told Helen, "transcendentalism in its mildest form," and he liked the Quakers' plain-style ways.[18]

Five years later, Mott had helped organize the 1848 Seneca Falls Convention—the first public meeting in the United State in support of women's rights. In 1850, Elizabeth Oakes Smith ran a ten-part series on women's rights in the *New-York Tribune*, then set off to become the first woman to lecture on the lyceum circuit. As Thoreau noted late in 1851, when she spoke in Concord, "The most important fact about the lecture was that a woman said it"—for women were forbidden from public speaking. Smith long remembered how Thoreau, "that gentle Arcadian of the nineteenth century, gave me his hand gravely, and said with solemn emphasis, 'You have spoken!'"—which her host, Bronson Alcott, translated to her as "'You have brought an oracle!'" Thoreau was less chivalrous in his Journal, where he complained that "she was a woman in the too common sense after all"—the pocket in which he'd carried her lecture for her reeked of perfume, and it annoyed him that "the championess of woman's rights still asks you to be a ladies' man."[19]

Mary Moody Emerson, though, did not. "The wittiest and most vivacious woman that I know," Thoreau wrote in November 1851, the "least frivolous" and the surest to provoke you to "good conversation"—the tough, chewy, intellectual kind he valued above all else. Mary enjoyed his company and Henry admired her genius; she confirmed his opinion by holding that women were "frivolous almost without exception" and that wherever she went, it was the men with whom she most often found society, for they were more likely to have opinions of their own. "Be still," Mary shushed one young woman; "I want to hear the men talk."[20] In short, Thoreau respected women who threw down the barriers and set out on their own paths—women he could meet on "the ascending path," he wrote, women like Fuller, who thought that gender was fluid and that women, too, could be masculine.[21] But "frivolous" women who merely followed the dictates of fashion or the commands of convention earned Thoreau's instant scorn and undying contempt. He preferred the company of women who took on leadership roles, like his own mother and sisters—all bold, smart, well read, and outspoken.

THE HERMIT AT HOME

Through these years, Henry Thoreau's outward life was quiet and industrious. Though he went out virtually every day, he rarely went farther than Boston, where he would head out to Long Wharf to gaze on the ocean before making the rounds to Harvard Library and the Boston Society of Natural History. With rare exceptions, from May 1852 until fall 1854 he even kept his schedule clear of lectures. Yet these quiet years were the most creative of his life. For 1852 and 1853, his Journal alone fills 1,253 rich and provocative pages. He also wrote something over five hundred pages of notes in his Indian Books and two new drafts of *Walden*, which doubled in size. These pages show his inner life was as extravagant and inventive as his outer life was steady and disciplined. Indeed, his contented homelife provided the stability Thoreau needed to pursue his career the way that he did. Against Emerson the patriarch, Hawthorne the political appointee, Channing the occasionally loveable misanthrope, or Alcott, whose flights to the Ideal were anchored by the hard work of Abigail and their daughters, Thoreau bought his freedom by keeping his needs simple and his account books balanced to the half cent.

Yet Thoreau in these years was no hermit, though Emerson thought so, or worse. "Emerson is too grand for me," Thoreau muttered. "He belongs to the nobility & wears their cloak & manners," and even his praise felt patronizing. The low point came in spring of 1852: "He finds fault with me that I walk alone, when I pine for want of a companion," and he "curses my practice even," accusing Thoreau of committing his thoughts selfishly to a journal instead of sharing them. Wounded, Thoreau called Emerson's "awful" curse down upon himself: "I pray that if I am the cold intellectual skeptic who he rebukes his curse may take effect—& wither & dry up those sources of my life—and my journal no longer yield me pleasure or life."[22] Meanwhile, Emerson had his own complaints: Thoreau's new project of endless journalizing looked like empty procrastination, a way to postpone real accomplishment. "But all this old song I have trolled a hundred times already," he sighed. "Only, last night, Henry Thoreau insisted much on 'expansions,' & it sounded new." Well, maybe it *was* new. Emerson was always willing to listen, even push back, knowing it took some opposition, "a little sense of victory, a roll of the drums," to call up his friend's highest powers.[23] So they stumbled on together in their mutual misunderstandings, friends yoked in opposition.

Yet when Emerson needed a steady and capable hand, he called on Henry. When his elderly mother died, in November 1853, Henry handled the arrangements, and when distinguished lecturers needed a host or an escort, Emerson counted on Henry's "courtesy & counsel" to smooth the way. Still, the distance between the two did not close. Thoreau wrote into *Walden* a sad epitaph for their friendship: "There was one other with whom I had 'solid seasons,' long to be remembered, at his house in the village, and who looked in upon me from time to time; but I had no more for society there."[24] For society they both turned to Ellery Channing, who had made the Walden house ring with boisterous mirth and resound with sober talk.

Walks with Channing must have been fun. "'What a fine day this is! Nothing about immortality here!'" he exclaimed once to Emerson, who dubbed him "Professor of the Art of Walking." Thoreau said Channing was the only one he could really walk with, for only Channing could stay in the present moment "& vary exactly with the scene & events & the contour of the ground."[25] While his poems may have been too Ideal—"sublimo-slipshod," Thoreau called them— Emerson noticed that Channing started to imitate Thoreau, carrying around a little pocket notebook in which he wrote down the name of every new plant or the date of every first flower.[26] Sometime around January 1852, Channing showed up with a big black Newfoundland puppy—for company, he said, "to stir up the air of the room" and break his "awful solitudes." Soon the town dubbed the faithful dog who followed him everywhere "the Professor," as the smarter of the two. For years thereafter, Thoreau recorded the antics of "this great calf of a dog" as he muddied the clear brook, or stood in the water snapping at each wave as if it were alive, or barked ridiculously at an oddly shaped stump, or piddled on upright objects—watering and manuring the plants, smiled Thoreau, no doubt contributing to nature's economy.[27]

Ellery had his dark side, too—"the moodiest person perhaps that I ever saw," Thoreau called him, as brindled as a cow with gentle and rough. Channing's boorishness made his friend wince, as when two boys to whom Thoreau had lent his boat were returning quietly through Channing's yard, whereupon Channing stalked out in shirtsleeves and closed the gate behind them "as if to shut them out." He could be cruel, too: one evening Thoreau saw him punch his cat with a poker because she purred too loud.[28] Such comments make one fear for his family, and indeed, calamity came shortly after Ellen gave birth to their fourth child, Giovanni (named for his uncle, the Marquis d'Ossoli). Tired of living in penury with her moody and unemployable husband, she called in the help of her brother-in-law, Thomas Wentworth Higginson. On November 18, 1853, Higginson arrived, packed up Ellen and the children, and swept them out of the house for good. Ellery, miserable, never left his room. The scandal rocked Concord: a shocked Mrs. Barzillai Frost gossiped indignantly that the very next night, Henry Thoreau and Ellery Channing "had a jubilee in the front parlor"—an uncharitable interpretation of what must have been, for Thoreau at least, an awkward and difficult situation. The storekeeper Horace Hosmer, who adored Ellen, admitted that "I should have enjoyed lynching Channing at that time." Channing thereafter reverted to his best behavior, and he continued to be welcomed at the Emersons' home and at least once at Cynthia Thoreau's dinner table. But he remained mercurial as ever: "Who can predict his comings and goings," said Thoreau in *Walden*.[29]

Bronson Alcott was another regular in Thoreau's social world. Henry called him "perhaps the sanest man" of any he knew, with no creed to defend, pledged to no institution, a peddler of philosophy whose talk put the world behind them.[30] But the world, despite Alcott's serene indifference to it—not to mention the unflagging work and steely economies of his wife and daughters—was nipping at his heels. In November 1848, his happy years tending Hillside's beloved gardens came to an end when the money ran out and the family was once again in crisis. Alcott put Hillside on the market and moved the family to Boston, where the women sought work while Bronson sought a paying audience for his "Conversations."

Hillside, that once-proud showcase, had deteriorated considerably by the time Nathaniel Hawthorne returned to Concord, hoping to settle down and write. After being forced to vacate the Old Manse in October 1845, the Hawthornes had decamped to Salem, where Nathaniel took up his famous, lucrative, and soul-killing political appointment as surveyor of the Salem Custom House; there Thoreau had found them in 1848. As it happened, both Thoreau's and

Hawthorne's fortunes had collapsed soon afterward and in synchrony: at the very moment the failure of *A Week* put Thoreau into a tailspin, the loss of Hawthorne's plum position propelled him into crisis. Faced with poverty, he turned to his pen and completed in quick succession *The Scarlet Letter*, *The House of the Seven Gables*, and *The Blithedale Romance*. None were best-sellers, but all were well received, and they put enough money into Nathaniel's pocket that when he looked over Alcott's dilapidated old house—still on the market in February 1852—he had the funds to buy it. In June 1852 the Hawthornes returned to Concord in triumph, moving into a refurbished Hillside, which they promptly renamed "the Wayside"—the name the famous house still bears.

For the next year (until the Hawthornes moved yet again, to England), Thoreau's steps often turned up the walkway to the Wayside's front door. Their son Julian recalled a day in 1852, when he was not yet seven: Thoreau showed up with his surveying equipment on his shoulder. The curious boy followed "the short, dark, unbeautiful man with interest" while the property survey went on, not missing a move and not uttering a word. Hours later, the work done, Thoreau turned to his father: "Good boy! Sharp eyes, and no tongue!" Julian became another of Thoreau's walking companions: "In our walks about the country, Thoreau saw everything, and would indicate the invisible to me with a silent nod of the head." Once, when they stood on the bank of the Concord River, Thoreau told the boy how the water lilies closed their petals at sunset, but at the first touch of morning sun "stirred and awoke, and, from green buds, became glorious blooms. 'Worth seeing!' said Thoreau, turning upon me his 'terrible blue eyes.' . . . All the strange man said was gospel to me, and I silently resolved to get up early some morning, and witness that exquisite drama."[31]

Meanwhile, the Alcotts, having been evicted to Boston, were trying to find their way. To earn some money, Bronson set about peddling "his brains . . . like the nut its kernel"—indeed, Thoreau elaborated, given that Alcott could talk to anyone—"children, beggars, insane, and scholars"—he should "keep a caravansary on the world's highway, where philosophers of all nations might put up."[32] So Alcott rented rooms next to Elizabeth Peabody's West Street bookstore to hold his Conversations, which Thoreau attended whenever he could. In February 1849, Alcott started a monthly symposium called the Town and Country Club, gathering a select company of gentlemen for "the study and diffusion of the Ideas and Tendencies proper to the nineteenth century."[33] Thoreau was invited, duly attended the first meeting, and promptly dropped out. Channing scoffed at the impossible alliance between Boston lawyers and country ministers, and it dissolved after a year. Not long afterward, Emerson tried the concept himself, helping found the far more successful Saturday Club, whose forward-looking magazine, the *Atlantic*, would eventually give Thoreau a place to publish some of his best work.

Alcott kept his caravansary rolling, passing through Concord from time to time, venturing west on long lecture tours or circulating around Boston, organizing lectures and Conversations wherever he thought Ideas and Tendencies might find a hospitable reception. Thoreau was always on his short list, and once Alcott learned *Walden* was again under way, in March 1852, he invited Thoreau to his Conversation rooms to read his lecture on "The Sylvan Life." (Alcott was nudging his friend to title his book *Sylvania*.) He rounded up an audience of sixty or so, who heard Thoreau's lecture with "great delight."[34] When the audience clamored for more, their old friend Higginson stepped in and arranged a second lecture for two weeks later. Thoreau hesitated, fearing his meditative second lecture was too "transcendental" to "*entertain* a large audience," but he needed the money and hated to turn down a friend. It turned out his worst nightmare. Decades later, Higginson still cringed at the memory: a blizzard had blocked the entry, and once he and Thoreau forced their way in, they found only Alcott and four or five others. Alcott decided they should enlarge the audience by enlightening the young men in the adjacent reading room. Thoreau read into the echoing silence while his auditors shuffled their newspapers in boredom or fell asleep. Afterward he heard one ask another, "What does he lecture for?" "It made me quake in my shoes," Thoreau added.[35]

Thoreau had one more lecture scheduled that spring of 1852: Marston and Mary Watson invited him to Plymouth to give his Walden lectures to the Leyden Hall Congregation—secular Sunday sermons exploring the day's social and moral questions for those who refused to attend church. Each Sunday a different speaker would hold forth, once in the morning and again in the evening, for ten dollars and expenses—half the going rate, but the Watsons had pull. Emerson, Channing, and Alcott all spoke, plus Garrison, Phillips, Greeley, and Higginson. Thoreau's was a double invitation: on February 22 he preached from *Walden* and on May 23 from "Walking, or The Wild." The next morning one admirer, James Spooner, rushed out at dawn to see Thoreau off on the morning train. When Thoreau didn't show, Spooner hunted him up and tagged along, playing Boswell to Thoreau's Johnson, recording everything he said and did. They saw the graveyard, visited the scientist Charles T. Jackson, and rummaged around at Pilgrim Hall, where Thoreau read the letters of the Wampanoag warrior King Philip. Then they set off to the depot again, Thoreau talking a blue streak all the way while carrying a bunch of flowers from Marston's garden for Mrs. Alcott in Boston. As they walked, Thoreau philosophized about missing trains, books, the ocean, the weather, and the gossip about Channing, Emerson, Alcott, Hawthorne, and himself. They shook hands before Thoreau boarded the train: come again, said Spooner. Next time, stay longer.[36]

"It is astonishing how much information is to be got out of very unpromising witnesses," Thoreau remarked; "a wise man will avail himself of the observation of all." Spooner paints a rare portrait of Thoreau at work, perpetually in motion, covering miles before others had poured their second cup of morning coffee—seeking, looking, asking, carrying. He was courteous, generous, alert, purposeful, occasionally curt. He spent much of every day out on his "springy & unwearable" legs, as Channing called them, interrogating farmers, children, laborers, woodchoppers, shopkeepers, Indians, railroad workers, hunters, fishermen—in short, everyone except the loafers

and "bar-room idlers" with nothing to do and with whom he had
no patience. When Channing asked him why he was so endlessly
curious about everything, Thoreau answered, "What else is there in
life?"[37] Only one man rebuffed him totally—Concord's true hermit,
Oliver B. Trask, who lived in the woods on the Acton town line.
"Poor and crazy," said Channing, with his rocking chair under a pine,
some herbs and winter rye on a patch of cleared land, a padlocked
door, and a sign on the roof: "Any pirson who shall Burn or distroy
this bilding is liable to 15 years inprisonment." It looked sad, thought
Thoreau: "Is he insane or of sound serene mind?" If he knew it were
the latter, "how rejoiced I should be to see his shanty!"—but the
signs were worrisome.[38]

The Irish, too, continued to intrigue Thoreau, as growing numbers of refugees settled in Concord. In 1850, when three generations
of the Riordan family moved into a shanty near the Deep Cut, at
first he was horrified by their dirt-floor poverty. But as he came to
know them, he wondered if the Irish weren't realizing his ideals better than he was, living independent lives close to the land without
being seduced by Yankee markers of success. He especially admired
young Johnny Riordan, leaping "lively as a cricket" from snowbank
to snowbank on his way to school while the worthies of Concord
waddled past encased in furs.[39] In January 1852, when he saw Johnny
with no jacket and snow melting on his bare toes, Henry rushed to
tell Cynthia, who set the Charitable Society to sewing. A week later
Henry brought Johnny's new coat to the shanty, which he found
"warmed by the simple social relations of the Irish. . . . What if there
is less fire on the hearth, if there is more in the heart." There he
learned that Johnny's uncle had moved to town and took the Irish
newspaper, the Flag of Our Union; and it was "musical news" to hear
that Johnny, one of the school's best students, "does not love to be
kept at home from school in deep snows."[40]

The Thoreaus, like their neighbors, employed young Irish servants, who went out on their own once they had learned the American way of life. The 1850 census lists as members of Thoreau's own
family a Margaret Doland, eleven, and Catherine Riordan, thir-

teen, born in Ireland—likely Johnny's big sister. Concord's farmers employed Irish laborers, too. When Michael Flannery, an immigrant from Kerry County, won the spading contest at the Middlesex County Fair only to see his employer claim the four-dollar prize for himself, an outraged Thoreau drafted a petition collecting money to make up the theft; he also carried a subscription door-to-door to raise the fifty dollars needed to bring Flannery's wife and children over from Ireland, lending much of the money himself. In March 1854, money in hand, Thoreau helped Flannery write home to bring them over. Perhaps thinking of the *St. John*, he was moved when Flannery dictated the words, "Don't mind the rocking of the vessel, but take care of the children that they be not lost overboard." The Flannery family made the crossing safely and lived with the Thoreaus until they were settled.[41]

Without such a stable and contented homelife, Thoreau could not possibly have pursued his career in the way that he did. His attic chamber in the Yellow House became Walden-on-Main, a room of his own in an equitable and interdependent household in which everyone helped out. There was wood to chop and fires to stoke, water to pump and chamber pots to empty, floors to sweep and carpets to beat, clothes to wash and bedding to air, food to purchase, gardens to plant and weed, meals to cook, dishes to clean, and trips to the post office twice daily (this increasingly became Henry's job). Cynthia was the household manager, and Henry generally referred to his home as "her" house: growing up working in a tavern, then on a farm, taught her plenty of New England faculty, which included keeping a sharp eye on the servants—a necessity, in those labor-intensive days, for every middle-class household.

None of this was in any way remarkable, except that Thoreau did, often, remark on it, up in his attic where he noticed that melody carried farther than noise. He loved "those strains of the piano which reach me here in my attic," where only "what is sweet & musical" could find him; the sound was sure to draw him downstairs to join the family. To Thoreau even the most ordinary sounds were music, and his journal records the many "melodies" that reached him, little vignettes of ambience: warm summer evenings when neighbors and farmers "come a-shopping after their day's haying are chatting in the streets and I hear the sound of many musical instruments and of singing from various houses"; the mild October night when he heard boys at play in the street and his neighbor playing his flute; the morning after the first snow when he found "miniature drifts against the panes" and a little conical peak in the fireplace under the chimney, while outside the neighbors' snow shovels scraped on the doorsteps. One morning, roused by the train whistle, he glanced out his window to see "shooting through the town 2 enormous pine sticks stripped of their bark, just from the north west and going to Portsmouth navy yard they say. Before I could call Sophia they had got round the curve & only showed their ends on their way to the deep cut."[42]

Whenever he saw something rare or interesting, he called Sophia, and he thought of his family whenever he found an especially beautiful flower, bringing it home in the sewn-in compartment of his special "botany hat": "How fitting to have every day in a vase of water on your table the wild flowers of the season—which are just blossoming—can any house said to be furnished without them?"[43] When waterlilies were in bloom, Henry brought them home in armfuls to brighten and scent the house. The cook gamely baked his serviceberries into a pudding ("rather dry" was the family's verdict), and he brought asters home by the pail so Sophia could sort the species by their beauty.[44] Years later a family friend recalled the home's "undisturbed orderliness, the restful sitting-room where the sun lay all day" illuminating Sophia's glorious window-plants, which she could always conjure into "luxuriant bloom." There were evenings of reading aloud, playing the piano and singing together, games of chess and backgammon, tea parties, distinguished guests and lyceum lectures on cold winter nights, followed by hours of talk—a regular, steady drumbeat of social interaction that supported Henry's explorations in nature and literature.[45]

Sometimes he revealed snatches of that talk: one Sunday, after refusing to read a certain religious tome, he heard Aunt Maria shout through the wall to Aunt Jane, "Think of it, he stood half an hour today to hear the frogs croak, and he would'nt read the life of Chalmers!" One night, after talking with Uncle Charles about who, among the nation's worthies, was a true genius, the door opened long after they'd gone to bed and Uncle Charles "called out in an earnest stentorian voice loud enough to wake the whole house— 'Henry! Was John Quincy Adams a genius'? '—No, I think not' was my reply—   Well I did n't think he was" answered Charles.[46]

The question of genius was on Henry's mind. Was it was something one *had*? "Men commonly talk as if genius were something proper to an individual. I esteem it but a common privilege & if one does not enjoy it now—he may congratulate his neighbor that *he* does."[47] No, one didn't possess genius—but if you lived right, genius might possess you.

→>-<←

Under the surface of Thoreau's placid homelife was a mind on fire. The quieter his days, the more extravagant his pages. The key to creativity, he thought, was to keep writing and not judge or edit too soon: "You must try a thousand themes before you find the right one—as nature makes a thousand acorns to get one oak." And stay close to the earth, away from books: "Antaeus like be not long absent from the ground," so sentences could be "like so many little resiliencies from the spring floor of our life."[48] In January 1852, Thoreau dusted off the manuscript of *Walden* and reimagined the book he wanted to write. Outside his window he saw farmers carting peat and muck over the frozen meadows to fertilize the soil. Didn't scholars do the same?—muck out in winter the fertile soil thrown up in summer? "My barn-yard is my journal," he joked, and "decayed literature makes the best soil."[49] Once, he had dreamed of buying a farm, and despite his condescension to farmers in *Walden*, he always felt a kinship with them. They lived on the land; he, too, should "live in each season as it passes—breathe the air, drink the drink, taste the fruit," give himself to it wholly. *Walden* must live in season, it must be an agrarian book, close to the earth. To write it, he would dig deep into the muck: "It is rare that we use our thinking faculty as resolutely as an Irishman his spade."[50]

The *Walden* Thoreau had put away in 1849 was a spring-and-summer book, recalling the bright days when he built his house and set off to find reality beneath the shams and delusions of society. But starting in 1852, *Walden* encompassed fall and winter as well, recalling the closing of the house against the winter cold, and the visitors, both human and animal, who brought society in dark days. The great cycle of seasons seemed to be not merely weather, but the deep metaphysical framework for a spiritual life: "Would you see your mind,—look at the sky. Would you know your own moods, be weather-wise." This new *Walden* would be about watching through the long night to announce the break of day, bragging like chanticleer at the dawn.[51] Politics and war had drawn Thoreau deep into the newspapers, but now he set them aside: "You cannot serve two masters. It requires more than a day's devotion to know & to possess the wealth of a day." So he wrote instead the story of another war, between "the red republicans & the black despots or imperialists" at Walden, mortal enemies engaged in deadly combat—reaching beyond the headlines to the wider world "of thought & of the soul." Thus was born the Ant War, Thoreau's famous mock-heroic parable. Afterward he paused: Why had he left Walden, anyway? Why did he feel compelled now to return, if only in his imagination? Perhaps "the contemplation of the unfinished picture may suggest its harmonious completion." It was time at last to "make wholes of parts."[52]

THE HIGHER LAW
FROM CHESUNCOOK TO *WALDEN*

The question now, with *Walden* under way again, was how to buy enough time to finish it. The few dollars he'd earned in Plymouth wouldn't go far. Thoreau wrote Greeley asking for a slot in the popular "People's Course" lectures in New York, but Greeley doused that idea: Thoreau was neither good enough nor famous enough.

FIGURE 1: Herbert W. Gleason, "Autumn view down river from Fair Haven Hill, Concord, Mass. October 15, 1903." Courtesy of the Concord Free Public Library.

FIGURE 3: Henry Thoreau's mother, Cynthia Dunbar Thoreau (1787–1872); this silhouette is the only known image of her. Courtesy of the Concord Museum.

FIGURE 2: Henry Thoreau's father, John Thoreau Sr. (1787–1859). Courtesy of the Concord Free Public Library.

FIGURE 4: Helen Thoreau (1812–49), shortly before her death. No known authenticated portrait exists of John Thoreau Jr. (1815–42). Courtesy of the Concord Free Public Library.

FIGURE 5: Henry David Thoreau (1854), crayon portrait by Samuel Worcester Rowse. Courtesy of the Concord Free Public Library.

FIGURE 6: Sophia Thoreau (1819–76), in 1849. Courtesy of the Concord Free Public Library.

FIGURE 7: Ralph Waldo Emerson (1803–1882), photograph by J. W. Black.
Courtesy of the Concord Free Public Library.

FIGURE 8: Lidian Jackson Emerson (1802–92), holding the Emersons' young son Edward, ca. 1847. Edward, the Emerson's only surviving son and a particular favorite of Henry Thoreau, grew up to defend Thoreau's reputation to the world. Courtesy of the Concord Free Public Library.

FIGURE 9: "Central Part of Concord, Mass." (engraving, 1839). This view
from the front porch of the Thoreau family's town square house shows, from left to right,
the Courthouse, the top of the Old Hill Burying Ground, the Reverend Ezra Ripley's
First Parish (Unitarian) Church, and the Middlesex Hotel. Courtesy of the
Concord Free Public Library.

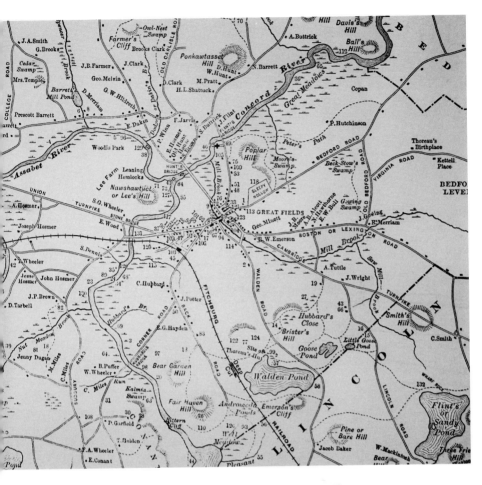

FIGURE 10: "Map of Concord, Massachusetts," by Herbert W. Gleason, 1906; detail showing Concord Center and immediate environs, including Walden Pond and the Fitchburg Railroad.

FIGURE 11: The Wheeler-Minott farmhouse, 341 Virginia Road, in which Henry Thoreau was born. This photograph by Alfred Winslow Hosmer was taken after the house was moved down the road from its original site; the building, which still stands, is now the headquarters of the Thoreau Farm. Courtesy of the Concord Free Public Library.

FIGURE 12: The original Thoreau House on Concord's town square (the building on the right); once a popular boardinghouse run by Henry Thoreau's aunts Elizabeth and Sarah Thoreau, the building is now part of Concord's Colonial Inn. Photograph by Alfred Winslow Hosmer. Courtesy of the Concord Free Public Library.

FIGURE 13: The Texas House, on Belknap Road by the railroad tracks, in which Henry Thoreau's family lived from 1845 to 1850; Henry planted the apple trees still visible in this undated photograph. This house no longer exists. Courtesy of the Concord Free Public Library.

FIGURE 14: The Thoreau family's "Yellow House" on Main Street, in which Henry Thoreau lived from 1850 until his death. Photograph by Alfred Winslow Hosmer. Courtesy Concord Free Public Library.

FIGURE 15: Two of the elegant blue boxes in which "Thoreau Superior Graduated Drawing Pencils" were sold and displayed, with a sampling of Thoreau pencils showing various labels, kinds, and grades. Courtesy of the Concord Museum.

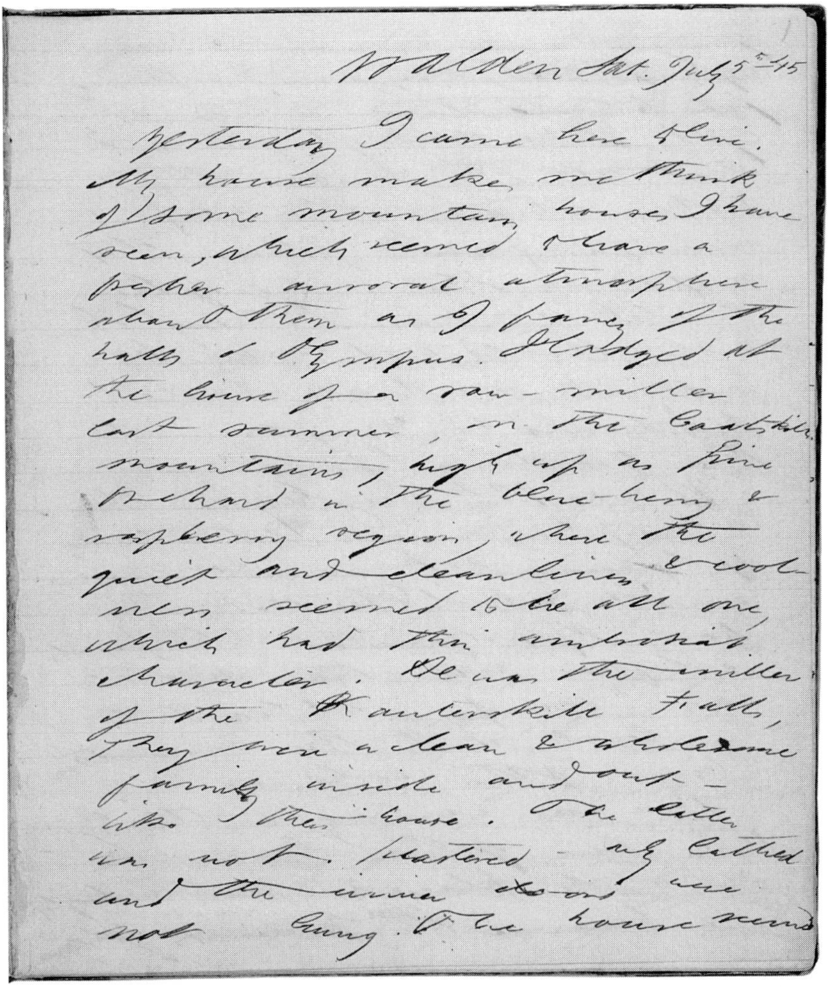

Walden Sat. July 5th 45

Yesterday I came here to live. My house makes me think of some mountain houses I have seen, which seemed to have a fresher auroral atmosphere about them as I fancy of the halls of Olympus. I lodged at the house of a saw-miller last summer, on the Caatskill mountains, high up as Pine orchard in the blue-berry & raspberry region, where the quiet and cleanliness & coolness seemed to be all one which had their ambrosial character. He was the miller of the Kaaterskill Falls, they were a clean & wholesome family inside and out—like their house. The latter was not plastered—only lathed and the inner doors were not hung. The house seemed

FIGURE 16: A page from Thoreau's Journal, written on Saturday, July 5, 1845—his first full day on Walden Pond: "Yesterday I came here to live . . ." Courtesy of the Pierpont Morgan Library, New York. MA 1302.8. Purchased by Pierpont Morgan with the Wakeman Collection, 1909.

FIGURE 17: Three of Thoreau's Journal volumes, with a bundle of the Thoreau pencils that allowed him to write in the field. Courtesy of the Pierpont Morgan Library, New York. MA 6069.

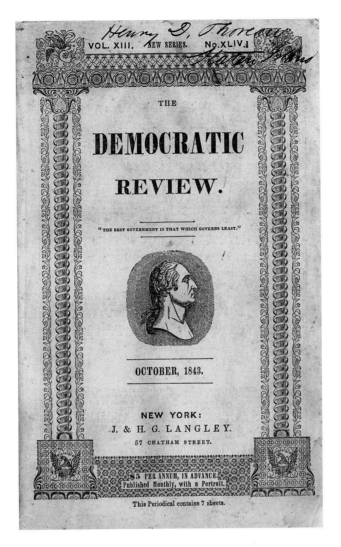

FIGURE 18: *United States Magazine and Democratic Review* of October 1843, with Thoreau's signature from Staten Island; the November issue featured his essay "Paradise (To Be) Regained." The journal's motto, "The best government is that which governs least," prompted the opening to his essay "Civil Disobedience." Courtesy of the Concord Free Public Library.

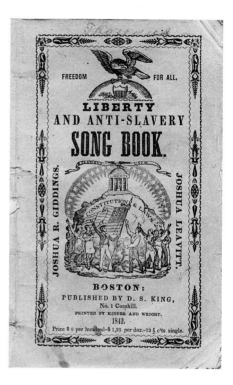

FIGURE 19: The Thoreau family's copy of the *Liberty and Anti-Slavery Song Book* (1842). Courtesy of the Concord Museum.

FIGURE 20: Herbert W. Gleason, "Fitchburg Railroad Train with Walden Pond in Background"; this photograph was taken from the shore closest to Thoreau's house. Courtesy of the Concord Free Public Library.

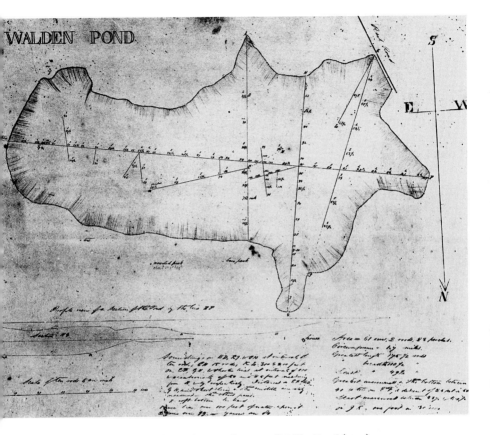

FIGURE 21: Henry Thoreau's original survey of Walden Pond (1846).
Courtesy of the Concord Free Public Library.

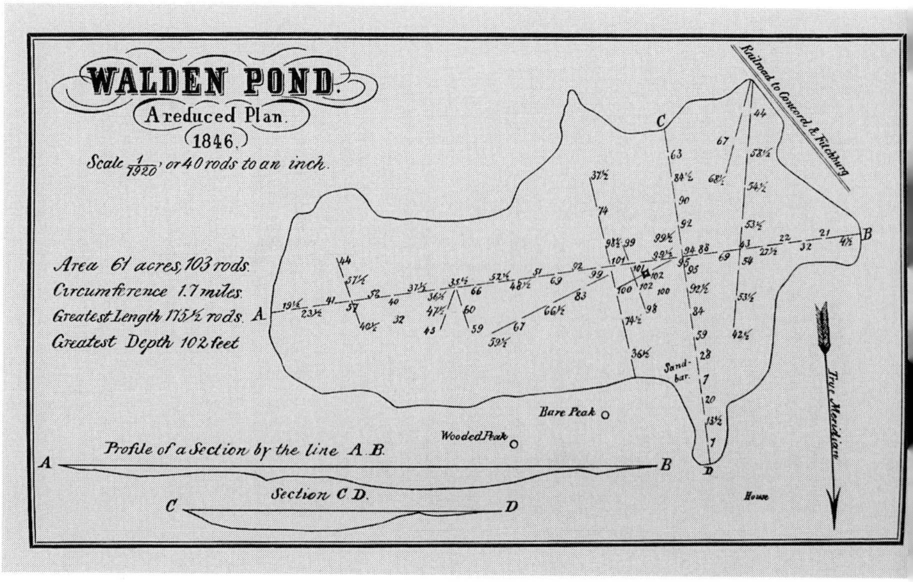

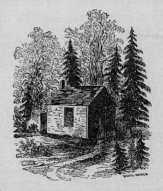

FIGURE 22:
"Walden Pond: A reduced Plan" (1846) as Thoreau published it in "The Pond in Winter," *Walden* (1854).

WALDEN;

OR,

LIFE IN THE WOODS.

BY HENRY D. THOREAU,

AUTHOR OF "A WEEK ON THE CONCORD AND MERRIMACK RIVERS."

I do not propose to write an ode to dejection, but to brag as lustily as chanticleer in the morning, standing on his roost, if only to wake my neighbors up. — Page 92.

BOSTON:

TICKNOR AND FIELDS.

M DCCC LIV.

FIGURE 23:
The title page of *Walden*, showing the drawing by Sophia Thoreau of her brother's house together with his motto: "I do not propose to write an ode to dejection . . ." Wiki Open Source.

FIGURE 24: Henry David Thoreau (1856), daguerreotype taken in Worcester, Massachusetts, by Benjamin D. Maxham; this is the copy Thoreau gave to his friend Theo Brown. Courtesy of the Thoreau Society and the Walden Woods Project.

FIGURE 27: W. Ellery Channing
(1817–1901), the Transcendentalist poet, was
Thoreau's close friend and first biographer.
Courtesy of the Concord Free Public Library.

FIGURE 28: Ellen Sewall Osgood
(1822–92), the only woman to whom Henry
Thoreau proposed marriage. Courtesy of the
American Antiquarian Society.

FIGURE 29: Harrison Gray Otis Blake
(1816–98), Thoreau's Worcester friend, lifelong
correspondent, and literary executor. Courtesy
of the Concord Free Public Library.

FIGURE 30:
Daniel Ricketson
(1813–96), a Quaker from
New Bedford who had built
his own "Shanty" before
reading *Walden*; Ricketson
immediately sought out
Thoreau and became a close
friend. Courtesy of the
Concord Free Public Library.

FIGURE 31:
Ricketson's sketch of Henry
Thoreau on their first
meeting, December 1854: "In
my imagination I had figured
[him] as a stout and robust
person, instead of the small
and rather inferior looking
man before me." From *Daniel
Ricketson and His Friends*
(Boston, 1902), facing p. 12.

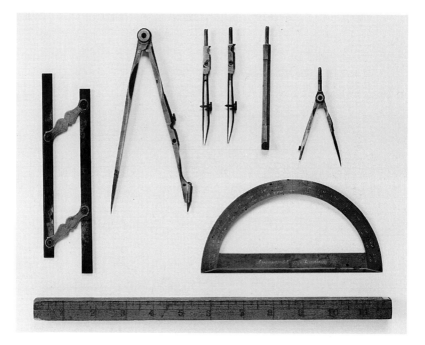

FIGURE 33: A selection of Thoreau's surveying instruments. The accuracy of his surveys and the exacting precision of his work as a draftsman became his hallmark. Courtesy of the Concord Museum.

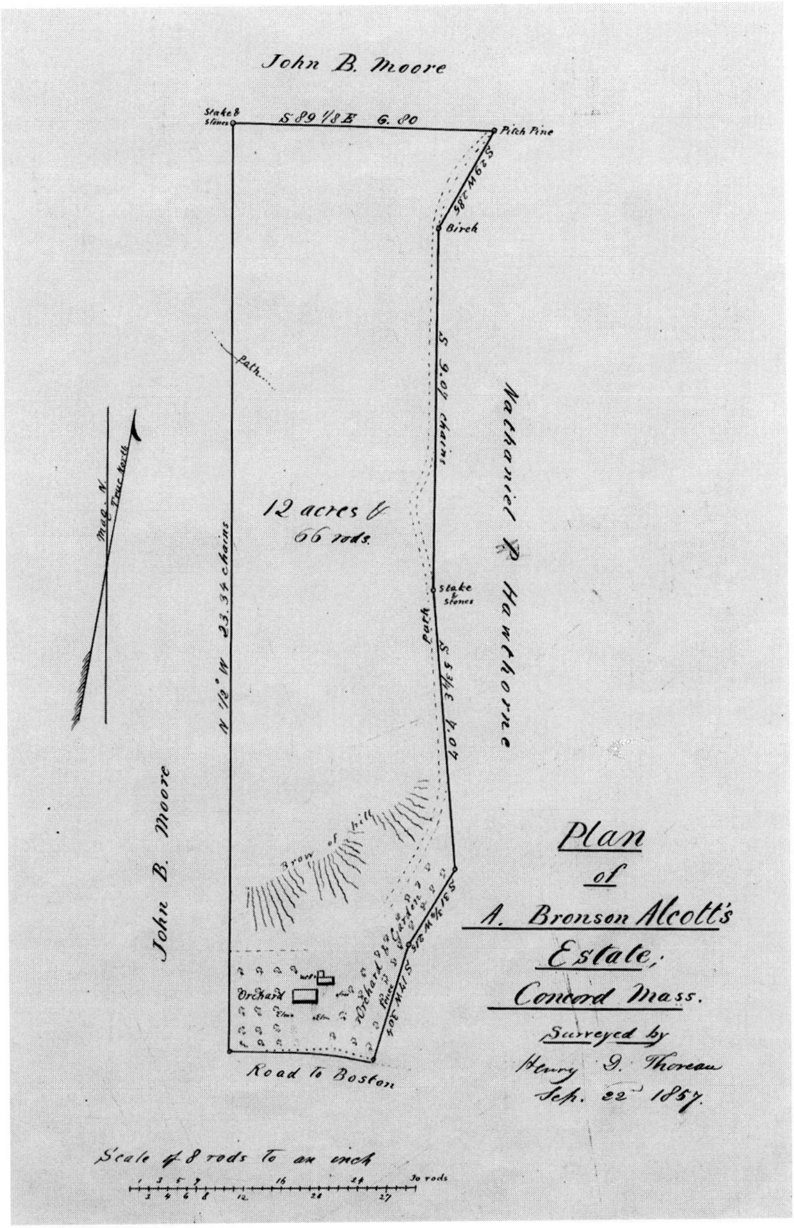

FIGURE 34: "Plan of A. Bronson Alcott's Estate," Thoreau's survey of
September 22, 1857, when Alcott was in the process of purchasing it; soon the Alcotts
were calling this property, which they liked for its many apple trees, "Orchard House."
Courtesy of the Concord Free Public Library.

FIGURE 35:
Thoreau's furniture: In the
summer of 1838, Thoreau
had a carpenter make this
green desk for his use as a
schoolteacher; he used it
for the rest of his life. The
rockers on the chair were his
addition, though he likely
did not make them himself.
He did make his bed, by
adding legs and stretchers
to a cane frame recycled
from a Chinese sofa bed. All
three items were with him
at Walden. Courtesy of the
Concord Museum.

FIGURE 36: Thoreau as natural historian: In March 1856, Thoreau began experimenting with collecting tree saps and boiling them up into sugar; he whittled this birch tree tap from a sumac branch. Thoreau's skill with woodworking is evident from this box he made to hold geological specimens, a gift to Ellen Sewall Osgood's husband Joseph Osgood. He purchased the spyglass (not without misgivings) for eight dollars on March 15, 1854; thereafter he carried it constantly. Courtesy of the Concord Museum.

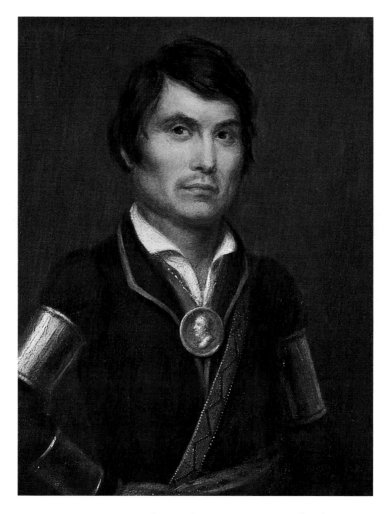

FIGURE 37: "Joseph Polis (or Porus)," by Charles Bird King (1842). Polis, a Penobscot elder, was Thoreau's guide on his 1857 excursion to Maine. From the collection of Gilcrease Museum, Tulsa, Oklahoma.

FIGURE 38: "Mt. Ktaadn" (1853), by Frederic Edwin Church. In 1846 Thoreau nearly summited Mount "Ktaadn," as it was then spelled; in 1857, his hopes to climb it a second time were defeated. Courtesy of the Yale University Art Gallery.

FIGURE 39: "Tuckerman's Ravine from Hermit's Lake," from William Cullen Bryant, ed., *Picturesque America* (New York, 1872). Thoreau, Ed Hoar, H. G. O. Blake, and Theo Brown camped in Tuckerman's Ravine, below the summit of Mount Washington, for four nights in July 1858; it had a rim, wrote Thoreau, "somewhat like that of the crater of a volcano" (*J*, 11:33).

FIGURE 40:
Horace Mann Jr. (1844–
68), the son of Horace and
Mary Peabody Mann, who
accompanied Thoreau to
Minnesota; upon his return,
Mann studied botany with
Asa Gray, although his life
was cut short by tuberculosis.
Courtesy of the Concord Free
Public Library.

FIGURE 41: "At the Mouth of the Wisconsin," from William Cullen Bryant, ed.,
Picturesque America (New York, 1872). Thoreau and Mann passed this spot, just below
Prairie du Chien, on May 24, 1861.

FIGURE 42: Henry David Thoreau (1861), by E. S. Dunshee. Daniel Ricketson
had two ambrotypes taken after Thoreau returned from Minnesota; the second, which
Ricketson gave to Sophia Thoreau as the better of the two, was stolen in 1910 and has
never been seen again. Courtesy of the Concord Museum.

FIGURE 43: In April 1859, Thoreau replanted his old Walden beanfield
with four hundred young pines; his pine forest lasted until it was largely destroyed by the
Great New England Hurricane of 1938. Photograph by Alfred Winslow Hosmer.
Courtesy of the Concord Free Public Library.

FIGURE 44: "On the spot in the woods where Thoreau had his solitary house is now quite a cairn of stones, to mark the place; I too carried one and deposited on the heap." Walt Whitman, *Specimen Days*, September 1881. Photograph ca. 1895 by Alfred Winslow Hosmer. Courtesy of the Concord Free Public Library.

Perhaps he could swap some of his "wood-notes wild" for dollars? Thoreau sent him two excerpts from *Walden*—"The Iron Horse" and "A Poet Buying a Farm"—plus the Canada manuscript. While the latter made the rounds, Greeley quickly placed the former with *Sartain's Union Magazine*, where they ran in July and August 1852. But the magazine went bankrupt and Thoreau went without pay, again. Write something that will sell, begged Greeley: a profile of Emerson, "calm, searching, and impartial" along the lines of that Carlyle essay. For that he'd pay fifty dollars out of pocket. For a second time, Thoreau declined to exploit his friendships for money, asking instead if Greeley would loan him seventy-five dollars—a sign of real distress.[53] In March 1853, *Putnam's* finally paid the fifty-nine dollars for the aborted "Excursion to Canada," allowing Thoreau to repay Greeley's loan. Fiasco though it was, the Canada essay bought him enough time to complete a fresh draft of *Walden*. Meanwhile, he took Greeley's advice and concentrated on writing, excusing himself from the Plymouth circle's December lecture invitation by claiming his current work was too "profane," if not downright "unholy"—"for, finding the air of the temple too close, I sat outside."[54] The new *Walden* was not ready to share.

When lecturing and writing both failed, surveying must pay. Lecturing "has not offered to pay for that book which I printed," he grumbled, but though a hundred others could do it just as well, "I can get surveying enough." The summer of 1853 he landed a big job surveying the new Bedford Road and the adjacent farms, where the town was building the Sleepy Hollow Cemetery, the innovative new garden cemetery inspired by Emerson's writings. It was sweaty work: by June Concord felt like "the black-hole of Calcutta," and by August it was "sultry mosquitoey nights with both windows & door open—& scarcely a sheet to be endured." The heat was so intense that in New York, hundreds died of it.[55] By February 1854, though, workers were cutting into ground frozen a foot deep and carting off the icy lumps, turning Thoreau's abstract lines into reality. By then he was laying out the cemetery grounds, which meant cutting down more than nine acres of woods—oak and pine worth $767.25, he wrote Thatcher.[56] Altogether, it was a good time to stay home, he told Blake. Let others wheel and deal; the whole westward enterprise "toward Oregon, California Japan &c, is totally devoid of interest to me," nothing but "a filibustiering [sic] *toward* heaven by the great western route. No, they may go their way to their manifest destiny which I trust is not mine." Thank goodness, he told himself, poverty had nailed him to "this my native region so long and steadily—and made to study & love this spot of earth more & more."[57]

Yet Thoreau also longed "for wildness—a nature which I cannot put my foot through." Drafting a new chapter, "Higher Laws," reminded him that even as he asserted that hunting and fishing introduced young men to the wild, he himself had never hunted anything bigger than a woodchuck.[58] So when George Thatcher invited him on a late-summer hunting trip to Lake Chesuncook, Thoreau said yes in a heartbeat. On Tuesday, September 13, 1853, when the steamer *Penobscot* left Boston Harbor bound for Bangor, Thoreau was leaning on the rail in the warm night, watching the lake-smooth seas glide past. By noon the next day he was walking up to the Thatchers, where he learned that George had gone to Oldtown to hire an Indian guide—just what Henry had hoped. For if George's goal was to hunt moose with a gun, Henry's was to hunt the Indian with a pen. He was not disappointed: George returned having hired Joe Aitteon, son of the Penobscot Governor John Aitteon, who had already planned to go moose hunting at Chesuncook and was happy to adjust his plans for a little extra money.

Joe Aitteon arrived punctually that evening, and next morning he loaded his birch-bark canoe onto the stagecoach to Moosehead Lake while George and Henry followed behind in a wagon loaded with enough provisions to feed "a regiment": hard bread, pork, smoked beef, tea, and sugar. While Henry groused at the seven-dollar fare for Joe and his canoe—better to have hired a canoe and an Indian up ahead at the lake—Joe spent the long day riding outside in a driving rain, having given up his inside seat to the ladies. Fifty miles up, Thoreau and Thatcher stopped overnight at a tavern in Monson, getting under way before dawn to meet the little steamer *Moosehead* at the foot of the wild and shaggy Moosehead Lake. There they joined a soaking-wet Aitteon, who had hoped to dry out before setting off. But it would be four days before the steamer's next trip, so when the whistle summoned them, they piled aboard, bound for the northeast carry at the head of the lake—thirty-eight miles over rough stormy waters.

Once Henry had a chance to size up Joe, his doubts vanished: "He was a good-looking Indian—short and stout with a broad face and reddish complexion," eyes turned up at the outer corners. Aitteon was an experienced lumberman, and he wore the river-driver's practical clothing: wool pants, cotton undershirt, red flannel overshirt and a black Kossuth hat, with an India rubber raincoat (the only one of them equipped for the weather). At half past noon they reached the carry, and the cousins walked on ahead, Henry with his eye out for plants, George with his gun out for partridges, while the little railway drew the baggage on behind to the West Branch of the Penobscot River. At the log camp at the north end of the carry, the cousins lit a fire and boiled tea for dinner while Aitteon pitched his canoe—carefully blowing a small flame from a firebrand onto the birch bark to soften and spread the mix of rosin and grease, testing it for leaks by setting the canoe on crossed stakes and pouring water into it. "I narrowly watched his motions," noted Thoreau, "and listened attentively to his observations, for we had employed an Indian mainly that I might have an opportunity to study his ways." He observed that Aitteon swore once—"Damn it, my knife is dull as a hoe"—but what Aitteon thought of being put under such close inspection is not recorded.[59]

Soon they were in the canoe: baggage in the middle, Aitteon on a crossbar in the stern, the cousins in the bow, complaining. No matter how he sat, grumbled Thoreau, the position was unendurable. While they paddled on looking for moose sign, he pressed Aitteon for Penobscot names: *kecunnilessu* for chickadee, *wassus* for bear, *upahsis* for mountain ash, words that Thoreau thought had possibly never been spelled before, but he pronounced them carefully until his informant said it would do. The only moose they saw that day was the rotting carcass left behind by hunters at their campsite that night, which gave Thoreau pause. But, he reminded himself, he was "not sorry to learn how the Indian managed to kill one." His role would be innocent, "as reporter or chaplain." That evening, they pitched their tent and went out hunting, Aitteon calling again and again through his birch-bark horn, but all they heard in response were the nearby timber cruisers, and, once, in the twilight, "a dull dry rushing sound, with a solid core to it," a bit like the shutting of the door to the "damp and shaggy wilderness." What was that? they whispered to Aitteon. "Tree fall."[60] Thoreau never forgot the beauty of the moonlight on the treetops, and he went to sleep watching sparks from their campfire ascend through the firs.

The next day they got their moose. Thoreau had begun to lose faith in their Indian guide, who disconcerted him by saying "Yes siree" and "sartain" and whistling "Oh! Susannah," but in midafternoon, when Henry called his attention to the crackling of some twigs, Joe back-paddled a few feet and there they were: a cow moose and her half-grown calf, looking around the alders at them like "great frightened rabbits." George fired his first barrel at the mother, who spooked away; then, as she paused to look back at her shivering young, he leveled his second barrel at the calf, which fled up the hill. Joe landed the canoe to track their victims. Now Henry was impressed: "He proceeded rapidly up the bank & through the woods with a peculiar elastic—noiseless & stealthy tread—looking to right & left on the ground & stepping in the faint tracks of the wounded moose—now and then pointing in silence to a single drop of blood."[61] After a half hour—too soon, Henry thought—Joe gave up, and they pushed on upstream until suddenly there she was, the mother, lying warm and dead in the water. Henry grabbed her by her ears while Joe pushed the canoe ashore, where, with Joe's assistance, Henry measured her with the canoe's painter cord: seven and a half feet tall (inaccurate, he later concluded), and eight feet two inches long, a "grotesque and awkward" animal, the true "kind of man" at home in this wilderness.

And then began the butchery. "Joe now proceeded to skin her—

with a pocket knife—while I looked on—& a tragical business it was—to see that still warm & palpitating body pierced with a knife—to see the warm milk stream from the rent udder (There were 4 teats) —& the ghastly naked red carcass appearing within its seemly robe—Some of the muscles continued to twitch even after the skin was stripped off." The hunters were not sated. They sampled a little moose meat for supper—rather like veal, thought Henry—and then were off again, thrashing upstream through bushes and drift logs, Henry in a dream state. By the time they returned to camp, he had had enough. While Aitteon and Thatcher hunted on downstream, Thoreau stayed behind and, by the light of the campfire, filled pages with his visceral shock and horror: "The afternoon's tragedy and my share in it—as it affected the innocence—destroyed the pleasure of my adventure." Hunting for subsistence was one thing, but "this hunting of the moose merely for the satisfaction of killing him—not even for the sake of his hide ... is too much like going out by night to some woodside pasture & shooting your neighbor's horses—They are God's & my own horses." Late that night the hunters returned, having seen no more moose. On Henry's insistence they hauled up a quarter of the meat, a great weight for the small canoe.[62] At least some of it would not go to waste, rotting pointlessly in the wilderness.

The next day, a Sunday, there was no hunting. Instead they paddled to Ansell Smith's logging camp at the head of Lake Chesuncook, where friends of Aitteon's walked in and reported on moose hunting up north: lousy, so bad that Thatcher, though eager for more, gave up his plan to hunt up that way. Thoreau had stepped out for a walk and was sorry to learn he had missed the Indians camped nearby. But it was too late to visit them, so he made do with inspecting the logging camp—buildings, batteau, farm, livestock, blacksmith, and a cool cellar where they left the moose meat to feed the loggers. Thoreau and Thatcher stayed the night in a comfortable bedroom at the lodge, while Aitteon stayed at the Indian camp. The next day they backtracked up the Penobscot to the north end of the carry. Henry stayed near Joe the whole way, closely observing how he paddled so powerfully and walked so noiselessly. He wrote down more Penobscot names for everything, and tasted all the berries Joe sampled. When they reached the carry, three Indians were camped there, smoking moose meat and curing moose hides. They shared their cooked moose tongue (tough, they apologized, there not being time to cook it properly) and boiled cranberries—delicious after days of pork and hard bread. While Thatcher fixed supper, Thoreau watched Aitteon cure the moose hide, which he could use even though Thatcher's duckshot had damaged it.

Then came an interesting moment. Thatcher wanted to continue hunting up the Penobscot. But, "somehow," that plan "was given up." Then Thatcher wanted to spend the night with the white lumbermen at the nearby log camp, though the Indians had invited them to stay. Thatcher seems to have prevailed, for the cousins headed to the log camp—which Thoreau found disgusting, "close & dirty," with an "ill smell." He'd rather spend the night with the Indians, who were "more agreeable & even more refined company." So back they went. Joe said something about heading out after midnight to do a little hunting, so the cousins spread their blankets over the moose hides on the ground and settled in to talk with the Indians, who included Joe's friend Sebattis Dana, also Penobscot, and Tahmunt Swasen, a St. Francis River Abenaki from Quebec, who wrote out his name for Henry.[63]

This was a pivotal night in Thoreau's life. Until that night, "the Indian" had been a figure casually encountered on the margins of his own world, or a remote and vanishing legend from books of history and romance. After that night, they were, for Thoreau, far more— just what, he spent his last years trying to understand. All night long the Wabanaki talked, for "they were very sociable," sometimes with the white men in English and sometimes with each other in their own language. Thoreau took pages of notes, trying to recall every word they said: about hunting moose and the many uses of moose hide; about the meaning of Indian words—*penobscot*, said Tahmunt, meant "rocky river," and Moosehead Lake, said Joe, was *sebamook*, though "Tahmunt pronounced it Sebemook." What does it mean? asked Henry. Tahmunt explained the concept in English with difficulty, until Henry caught the meaning: "reservoir," where water runs in and does not run away. On it went: what does *musketaquid* mean? It's *musketicook*, they corrected him, and it means "dead water." And other Concord names—*Ponkawtasset? Annursnack?* They shook their heads: these names were in another language. And Quebec? asked Thatcher. It means "Go back!" answered Tahmunt mischievously.[64] It's not clear if either George or Henry got the joke.

That night there was no hunting. Somehow Joe forgot, and no one reminded him. As darkness deepened, Henry lay back on his blanket and listened, in awe, as the Wabanaki friends talked on with each other: "There can be no more startling evidence of their being a distinct & comparatively aboriginal race—than to hear this unaltered Indian language spoken—which the white man cannot speak nor understand." Here, living in their own world, they were complete and whole, utterly themselves, and utterly "unintelligible to us." Weeks later, he was still thinking about that night: hearing their language had convinced him that Indians were real, "not the invention of poets"—more so than all the arrowheads he had ever found. "I sat & heard Penobscots gossip & laugh & jest in the language in which Elliots Indian Bible is written—The language which has been spoken in New England who shall say how long? This sound these accents...." He liked to fancy himself the last man in nature. But here were the true men in nature, as present to the world of 1853 as he, speaking a copious and living language entirely their own. The reckoning begun here would force Thoreau to rethink everything he knew.[65]

Next morning they awoke to drizzle and the sounds of red squirrels and peeping hyla. The cousins dawdled, deciding what to do, until the rain thickened and decided for them: time to go home. Thatcher lent his gun to Aitteon in exchange for a pair of moose antlers, which duly appeared, serving as a hat rack. Thoreau walked ahead, botanizing, waiting for a thoughtful hour on the lonely lakeshore while the railcar with Thatcher and the baggage caught up. At half past noon the steamer carried them down the lake to Greenville, where Thatcher reclaimed his horse and wagon. Three hours later they reached the Monson tavern, and Thoreau, disgusted at the "dirtiness," went straight to bed. All the next day it rained, cutting off hoped-for views of Katahdin. Tension lingers in Thoreau's account: ever since Thatcher had killed the moose, the cousins had been at cross-purposes. Even if Thoreau had managed to keep his mouth shut, his moral outrage surely ruined the fun of their great adventure. Not until they reached Bangor did the mood lift, when they traveled to Indian Island and called on Governor John Neptune, a living link to the past at eighty-six years old. Neptune sat on his bed in stocking feet, entertaining his visitors with stories about moose hunting until his son-in-law turned the conversation to local politics, including the Penobscots' battle to bring a school to their town. As he said, "If Indians got learning they would keep their money." Education was the path to reestablishing sovereignty and, amid the encroaching white society, staking out a future and a place for themselves.[66]

Thoreau found that, unlike the lumber camp or the country tavern, the Penobscots' village was clean: composed of neat white-painted two-story houses and enlivened by cheerful boys who ran to Thoreau, bows and arrows in hand, teasing him for a penny. "The Indians appeared to live very happily at the Island and to be well treated by the inhabitants of Old town," he noted.[67] One man was busy building canoes, and Thoreau interviewed him closely, making long and careful notes—for "the process deserves to be minutely described," at least as much as "the white man's arts, accounts of which now fill the journals." Then they toured a sawmill and a batteau manufactory; Thoreau barely bothered to take notes at all. He lingered on for three more days before returning to Concord on September 27, bringing one souvenir: a fine pair of Penobscot snowshoes for which he paid five dollars—five days' wages.[68] Deep snows would no longer keep him from exploring the heart of the winter woods.

→>–<←

It was a relief, Thoreau wrote in the account he eventually published, to get back to the "smooth but still varied landscape" of home, where woods and fields were "the common which each village possesses, its true paradise," dwelling halfway between the wilderness and the city's "wealth-constructed" parks and gardens. Nevertheless, he concluded, we must protect the wilderness. Why not, he asks, "have our national preserves, where no villages need be destroyed, in which the bear and the panther, and even some of the hunter race, may still exist, and not be 'civilized off the face of the earth'"? Will we save our forests "for inspiration and true recreation? Or shall we, like villains, grub them all up, poaching on our own national domains?" Thoreau's dream of a national park system began there on the Penobscot River, where he listened as Joe Aitteon and his friends and relatives spoke a language he never had ears to hear before. Earlier he called for local parks and preservation; now he called for "national preserves" to protect our "national domains"—which, in his vision, included indigenous peoples, whose right to continue living on their land would thus be protected as well.[69]

"In October the man is ripe even to his stalk & leaves," Thoreau wrote that fall; "he is pervaded by his genius."[70] He worked on "Chesuncook" well into October, and in late November, when he was invited to contribute to a new magazine, he sent in his new essay. Nothing came of it—the plan folded—but years later, the Saturday Club would revive the plan as the *Atlantic*, and Thoreau would indeed publish "Chesuncook" in one of its first issues. Meanwhile, he now had a brand-new lecture ready for the Concord Lyceum, where he'd again been elected curator and again resigned—this time protesting there weren't enough good lecturers available to fill the season. Emerson took his place, and, knowing exactly where to find good lecturers, turned right around and scheduled Thoreau for December 14. Emerson's daughter Edith immediately put Thoreau on the spot: would his lecture be "a nice interesting story, such as she wanted to hear, or . . . one of those old philosophical things that she did not care about?" Thoreau turned to the twelve-year-old girl and "bethought himself." "Chesuncook" met her challenge: the children enjoyed it, said Lidian, even little Eddy, allowed to sit up for the occasion.[71]

Edith's opinion mattered to Thoreau: she was growing up into a helpful ally, often bringing him flowers and specimens. It was a beautiful fair-weather fall, and suddenly Thoreau was busy again in the social world. He took Ellen, Edith, and Edward "a-barberrying" at Conantum, took Ellery Channing sailing, then took Sophia boating on Fairhaven Bay, where she made a sketch; he paddled Elizabeth Hoar and her friend up the Assabet and Sophia and Cynthia down the Concord. All the while he took notes on autumn leaves, which moved him as never before. "How beautifully they go to their graves—how gently lay themselves down—& turn to mould!" They "stoop to rise—to mount higher in coming years," the year's great crop. "They teach us how to die."[72] *Walden*, with its powerful emphasis on spring and regeneration, was not the place for these darker reflections. He set them aside, to become the seeds of "Autumnal Tints."

The busy social season rolled on into winter. Cynthia's friend Caroline Brooks Hoar, wife of Judge Ebenezer Rockwood Hoar, had an idea: the Christmas of 1853 should be a true community celebration. Every child in town, rich or poor, would have a gift chosen especially for them. Organizers compiled a list of every child through age sixteen—seven hundred in all—and for weeks the women of Concord prepared a present for each one, collecting money and sewing clothes for the poorest families. Henry agreed to provide the Christmas tree, and on December 22, he walked out to a swamp in Lincoln and cut a small black spruce, which he delivered to the town hall. Inside, the little tree was suddenly huge, filling the stage, so tall that its topmost spire had to be cut off. At six o'clock on Christmas Eve, the doors were thrown open and hundreds of children rushed into the hall, lit by the candles decorating the great spruce—perfectly splendid (though Thoreau, true to character, said the starlit December sky was more splendid still). Around the tree were piled hundreds of presents, and Saint Nicholas himself bounded onto the stage, tossing sweets to waiting hands as names were called and packages distributed.[73]

It was a festive start to a real New England winter, so cold it nearly froze the Thoreaus' water pump, followed by a grand snowstorm that blocked all the roads and closed the schools. Henry tried out his new snowshoes in a wind so strong that in just twenty minutes it wiped away his great snowshoe tracks. The streets were desolate and the snow banked high against the doors and windows, but inside, Thoreau found everyone merrier than ever. At the post office, every traveler was pressed for news of the railroad cars and the depths of the snow out their way—from fourteen to twenty-four inches, Thoreau calculated, out and about with his two-foot ruler. Then, as suddenly, it thawed and the eaves ran with water: "We too have our thaws," he reflected. "They come to our January moods.... Thought that was frozen up under stern experience gushes forth in feeling & expression."[74]

Thoreau had indeed thawed; his busy social life continued into the new year, 1854. William Tappan, the New York acquaintance who ten years before had tried life in a wilderness cabin in New York, visited in early January, saying little but running through the snow, lifting his knees in delight like a child.[75] Reluctantly Thoreau got himself fitted for a new coat, and though he hated it—"who am I that should wear this coat? It was fitted upon one of the Devil's angels about my size"—it decked him out suitably for a court appearance in Cambridge on January 19, 1854, as an expert witness in a property dispute. His client lost, but the day gave him occasion to visit with Thaddeus Harris, who identified his mysterious cocoons as the magnificent emperor moth. Clad in his warm new coat, he set off late that January for a long-anticipated visit with Blake and the Worcester disciples, including a long walk with them all in the bitter cold.[76]

But the news that season—the *real* news—had been the arrival on October 28, 1853, of 706 unsold copies of *A Week*, which Thoreau hefted up two flights of stairs and stacked in his attic bedroom, half as high as his head. "I have now a library of nearly 900 volumes over 700 of which I wrote myself," he joked mordantly.[77] Then followed the bittersweet moment, exactly a month later, when he walked into the office of James Munroe and Company and paid off, to the last penny, the debt of $290 for publication of *A Week*. It had taken him four years and seven months. He opened a new account with Munroe, placing twelve copies of *A Week* for sale—"How can a poet afford to keep an account with a bookseller?" he moaned—noting glumly that his first book had earned, all told, the grand sum of fifteen dollars.[78]

At long last, however, he was free of debt. Thoreau celebrated his release by plunging into the final round of revisions to *Walden*, working in new material from his 1853 Journal and intensifying the incandescent coming of "Spring" by adding, in real time, a giddy passage from the sudden wonderful thaw: "That sand foliage! It convinces me that nature is still in her youth," the earth not "a mere fragment of dead history . . . but living poetry like the leaves of a tree."[79] A week later, Walden Pond was thundering with the weather and Thoreau was marveling how alive it was, though "so large & cold & thick-skinned a thing to be so sensitive." Even in the dead of winter, everything was pulsing with life, attuned to changes no human being could register. "For the earth is all alive & covered with feelers of sensation.—*papillae*. The hardest & largest rock—the broadest ocean—is as sensitive to atmospheric changes as the globule of mercury in its tube. Though you may perceive no difference in the weather—the pond does."[80]

Walden was finished. Near the end of February 1854, Thoreau was writing out the fair copy for the printers. By mid-March he'd contracted with Ticknor and Fields, Boston's finest publishing house, for an edition of two thousand copies. Greeley congratulated Thoreau and announced the book immediately. After nine long years, everything was accelerating: on March 28, the first proof sheets arrived, and for two months Thoreau was busy correcting them (promising an annoyed printer to write more legibly), polishing for clarity and force, coherence and accuracy.[81] He was so preoccupied he missed the first skunk cabbage and the ice-out date on Walden Pond, but whenever he could break away, he was richly alive to the world around him. "The earth is all fragrant as one flower," he wrote on May 16; "Nature is now perfectly genial to man."[82] On May 24, he walked to Emerson's Cliff before dawn. As the sun raked across the eastward expanse of ground fog, he thought the effect gave a new aspect to the world: "The sun is eating up the fog." He waded into Beck Stow's swamp, observed frogs and andromeda flowers, and late in the day drew up a long list of the leafing times of shrubs and trees, casting up the true accounts that had gone into arrears, what with all the proofreading.[83] He did not know that in Boston that same day, federal marshals arrested and imprisoned Anthony Burns, an escaped slave working quietly in a Boston clothing store.

Two days later, an angry crowd led by several of Thoreau's friends—Higginson, Alcott, Theodore Parker, and Wendell Phillips—mobbed the courthouse where Burns was held, but failed to free him. In the trial that followed, Judge Edward G. Loring ruled that, as property, Burns must be returned to his owner. On June 2, Bostonians shrouded their streets in black and watched as Burns was marched in chains to the harbor, where a ship waited to take him south. The procession was guarded by police with guns drawn, armed federal marshals, an artillery regiment, and three platoons of marines, one armed with cannon. The birthplace of the American Revolution was effectively under martial law.[84]

-+><+-

In the wake of Burns's arrest, Thoreau kept walking and journalizing, but soon an uneasy note emerged. "Is our life innocent enough?" he wondered. "Do we live inhumanely—toward man or beast—in thought or act?" The least needless injury to any creature was to that extent "a suicide. What peace—or life—can a murderer have?" He had himself in mind; he'd been collecting specimens for Agassiz again. While killing for science had not worried him in 1847, now it did: "The inhumanity of science concerns me as when I am tempted to kill a rare snake that I may ascertain its species—I feel that this is not the means of acquiring true knowledge." Next day, the storm broke. "I see the court house full of armed men holding prisoner & trying a Man to find out if he is not really a Slave. . . . It is really the trial of Massachusetts—every moment that she hesitates to set this man free—she is convicted."[85]

From now through the end of June, the heat of politics scorched and withered his customary spring roll call of shadflies and eagles, hylodes and snipes, gooseberries, rhodoras, and rainbow showers. Three years before, when Thomas Sims was arrested, Thoreau pounded out pages of outrage but kept silent. Now he was again possessed, tucking a pencil under his pillow so he could vent the rage keeping him awake at night. This time he was ready to speak. All that June, Thoreau stoked the fires he had banked after Sims's arrest, pouring onto the pages the fresh fuel of his fury, and pounding it all together into his inflammatory address "Slavery in Massachusetts."[86] Thus on July 4, 1854, even as the printed sheets of *Walden* were being gathered and bound at Ticknor and Fields, Thoreau was standing under that black-draped, upside-down American flag in the Harmony Grove amphitheater in South Framingham, joining Sojourner Truth, Wendell Phillips, Moncure Conway, and William Lloyd Garrison, who set the tone at the end of his opening speech by holding up a copy of the United States Constitution, "that covenant with death and agreement with hell," and lighting it on fire. To jeers, hisses, groans, and howls of anger Garrison held the burning Constitution aloft, until the ashes singed his fingers.[87]

Thoreau was one of the last to speak. "Words That Burn," one newspaper called his speech: "Again it happens that the Boston Court House is full of armed men, holding prisoner and trying a MAN, to find out if he is not really a SLAVE. Does any one think that Justice or God awaits Mr. Loring's decision?" The choice was clear: serve the law of the United States Constitution—on whose ashes Thoreau was treading as he spoke—or the higher law of God, "not Edward G. God, but simple God." Thoreau spoke, said one observer, with such "serene unconsciousness" of anything shocking in his words that he could say the unspeakable: since majority rule had produced such an obscenity, the moral path was clear. "Let the State dissolve her union with the slaveholder. . . . Let each inhabitant of the State dissolve his union with her, as long as she delays to do her duty." For a month, he told the crowd, he had lived with a profound sense of having suffered "a vast and indefinite loss." What was it? "At last it occurred to me that what I had lost was a country." In a nation that could send an innocent man, Anthony Burns, to slavery, all lives, life itself, was devalued; unfreedom undoes and subverts everything. We dwell not in a state somewhere between heaven and hell, but now "wholly within hell," in a landscape covered with ashes and cinders.[88]

At the end of this address, Thoreau asked himself that terrible question: "I walk toward one of our ponds, but what signifies the beauty of nature when men are base?" Thoreau did not ask rhetorical questions. This crisis realized his deepest fear, and his words expressed his deepest betrayal. They indict not merely his walks to Walden Pond, but his entire career as an artist, including *Walden* itself—the culminating work of his life. What signified the beauty of his book now? *Walden*, too, lay in ashes. Politics had turned nature into ruin. "The remembrance of my country spoils my walk. My thoughts are murder to the State, and involuntarily go plotting against her." But Thoreau could not, would not, go forward into night. In an extraordinary final turn, he willed himself toward hope: "But it chanced the other day that I scented a white water-lily, and a season I had waited for had arrived. It is the emblem of purity." Pure to the eye, sweet to the scent, yet rooted in "the slime and muck of earth," the lily became his emblem for "the purity and courage" that may yet—that *must* yet—be born of "the sloth and vice of man, the decay of humanity."[89] In offering his audience this American lotus flower, the sacred Buddhist emblem of enlightenment he had found lighting his path of Concord, Thoreau was offering them the core of his own being and belief, and the story of his own redemption.[90]

The "moral earthquake" of Anthony Burns forced Thoreau to a moral reckoning: since his success and his serenity both demanded that he "be at one with the universe," he must recognize that people live humanely only insofar as they injure no other—not man, not moose, not snake. Thoreau turned this ethical imperative first to science, according to whose dictates he must kill the animals he wished to know; then to politics, according to whose laws he must turn a person into a slave, a human into a thing. His resolve bound science, politics, and nature together: the test of human virtue was allowing all beings, human and nonhuman alike, to flourish in their own ways. But tried by this severe test, no one wholly escapes indictment. We all have roots in the mud. The redemption Thoreau offered in the lily was his deepest belief: purity and courage may be compounded of the foulest filth, even of "sewer" muck—the shit (though he used the word only in private) that spawned the Fugitive Slave Act. We must "ask ourselves weekly—Is our life innocent enough? Do we live *inhumanely*—toward man or beast—in thought or act?" The answer, if honest, can never be unqualified; humanity can never be innocent. But we can strive to be innocent *enough*. As for "slavery and servility," they were not life at all; they could only decay and stink. Let the living bury them, he concluded; "even they are good for manure."[91]

Thoreau's address propelled him into the most militant ranks of radical abolitionists. William Lloyd Garrison printed "Slavery in Massachusetts" in the *Liberator* on July 21, and on August 2, Horace Greeley reprinted it in the *New-York Daily Tribune*, calling it "a *genuine* Higher Law Speech" with lightning bolts of dark humor. Many will blame us for printing it, said Greeley, "but our back is broad and can bear censure."[92] The *National Anti-Slavery Standard* picked it up on August 12 under the headline "Words That Burn," pronouncing the old imputation that Thoreau was a mere imitator of Emerson "little better than profanity." As for Thoreau, his Journal notes only: "A sultry night the last—bear no covering—all windows open—8 Am—To Framingham." He checks off a few flowers, and closes: "A very hot day."[93]

Over the next several weeks the heat deepened, turning his attic chamber into an oven and forcing him to spend his evenings downstairs with the family. Thoreau felt close and dissipated, "cheap and vulgar," "invaded and overrun." Suddenly his name was everywhere. In May, the New York publisher Charles Scribner wrote asking him, as one of the "American authors of importance," for information for an entry in his new *Cyclopaedia of American Literature*.[94] On June 7, his publisher James T. Fields embarked for England with proof sheets of *Walden* in hand, to publish it there and so secure copyright. Ticknor and Fields were working hard for *Walden*, which they believed was one of the highlights of the season: as Fields wrote to his English contacts, "*Walden* is no common book and is sure to succeed." Alas, he became so seasick that he had to leave the ship at Halifax and return to Boston; in his absence, no English publisher would take on the radical American book.[95] Greeley fired up his publicity machine, and by July, advance notices of *Walden*, complete with excerpts, were breaking into the newspapers even as word of Thoreau's Framingham protest speech spread. Thoreau was being styled as the "Massachusetts Hermit" who had stepped boldly into the glare of radical abolitionism—the glare in which *Walden* was published to the world.

Though the official publication date was not until August 9, copies were leaking out: the first was sold on August 1, Thoreau received his on August 2, and soon orders were coming in from Virginia to Maine, New Orleans to San Francisco. On August 8 Thoreau wrote Blake, affecting disdain for all the attention, "Methinks I have spent a rather unprofitable summer thus far. I have been too much with the world." On August 9, his Journal entry reads in its entirety:

Wednesday Aug 9th To Boston
Walden Published. Elder berries XXX. Waxwork yellowing X.[96]

That Wednesday in Boston, carrying his author's copies, Thoreau dined with Bronson Alcott and left one with him; the rest he carried to Concord. He was having his chanticleer's crow at last. Would anybody hear him?

READING *WALDEN*

Walden was born in face-to-face conversation with friends and neighbors who freely asked "impertinent" questions and expected honest answers in return. As Thoreau stood before them early in

1847, his house could authenticate his every word: come and see! But by 1854, Walden was no longer. Of course the pond was still there, but most of the trees were cut, and his house was gone. Nothing marked the site but a weedy cellar hole. If the meaning of his years there were to live on, Thoreau needed to recreate his performance as a book, convert the material place—the wooden-floored house reeking of woodsmoke and damp wool, pine needles tracked underfoot, the mouse drawn on the door—into a space of words. His other difficulty was to locate his readers. Thoreau knew plenty of town scoffers sneered at him behind his back, but he also knew that dreamers and "poor students" like him too often lived in quiet desperation. To all the others—not just the scoffers but the "strong and valiant" natures who relish things as they are—he asked only that, should they try on the coat that is *Walden*, they not "stretch the seams" lest they ruin it for those whom it fits.[97]

A *Week* imagines life flowing irretrievably down the river of time, but *Walden* imagines life lit by passion and pain into a single, many-faceted diamond. Robert Frost was impressed by this: "Think of the success of a man's pulling himself together all under one one-word title."[98] Yet despite its aura of timelessness, *Walden* insists on literal, historical reality. It needs the rough edges: the railroad's whistle, the woodchucks gnawing his beans, Zilpha muttering curses over her pot. This insistence on materiality reverberates through the ideational content of *Walden*, especially drawing our attention to how personal and social identities depend on material facts and actions. The long opening chapter, "Economy," makes us feel how building that house is (re)building a self, literally from the ground up; but *this* time the choices will be made "deliberately," with full consciousness of their costs. When Thoreau moves in on Independence Day, as the narrator tells us three times, we recall America itself was founded as a nation of citizens who did not inherit the conditions of their lives, but built them.

After hearing Frederick Douglass indict the Declaration of Independence as a lie, Thoreau turned Douglass's anger toward his own moral outrage: his elders' contentedness to prosper commercially on the backs of slaves, rather than working to finish the promise of America's great Revolution, gave the lie to their every ideal. Thoreau's anger and contempt can make us squirm today, when those who ride still ignore the many who are ridden upon—inexcusable in a democracy, constituted as it is by the daily decisions made by every citizen. Hence emancipation must begin with self-examination: "What a man thinks of himself, that it is which determines, or rather indicates, his fate." Or as Saint Augustine wrote in his *Confessions*: "I was held back not by the fetters put on me by someone else, but by the iron bondage of my own will." What Wilberforce, Thoreau asked, will emancipate the self?

The original *Walden* put Thoreau front and center, building his own world, pounding nails, plowing beans, walking the rails to Concord, and accounting for every halfpenny: a solid warm house, he proclaimed with a Yankee flourish, for $28.12½. Top that! It's a story riddled with moral lessons piled on until even the most sympathetic reader tires. Young Thoreau, yearning for truth, high on his soapbox needling his elders for their follies, defending himself from their catcalls with his own implacable wit, and making them wince through their laughter: that was the book he put away in 1849 and did not publish.

The Thoreau of 1852 was a very different man, chastened by failure and mellowed by family life. Had Walden prepared him to meet the challenges of Main Street? If not, his achievement there had been pure, but limited: it meant one could attain virtue only by leaving society. A utopia of one? The Thoreau who dusted off the old manuscript, hoping at last to make wholes of parts, could imagine himself as more than a preacher haranguing his audience—he could imagine himself as an agent of change. This required him to reorient his book. Nearly the entire second half was written not by the hermit at the pond but by the walker on Main Street, brimful of discovery— the practical surveyor training his moral compass on people and their doings. His new pages turned outward to what would later be called "the environment." Before, he told us what he thought; now he will show us how he sees. These chapters founded the genre of "nature writing," but Thoreau did not understand nature as other, existing outside the self or beyond town boundaries. Instead, Thoreau understood nature as a higher truth encompassing the self and society, a dynamic truth shot through with all the forms of life swirling around and collecting themselves into a whole with Walden, not Thoreau, at the center.[99] In these pages, *Walden* blossoms as a holograph of the planet and of one human life, lived as a prism refracting the sunlight onto the page.

To pivot from the old material to the new, from philosophy to poetry, Thoreau crafted a dramatic device that has cost him many readers.[100] In "Baker Farm" he staged John Field, the impoverished Irish bogger who had sheltered him during a thunderstorm, as the embodiment of failure, the deserving victim of the narrator's aggression. But the failure is the narrator's as well: Thoreau staged himself as a pedantic meddler who hectors the family with a pile of proverbs, then turns away in disgust when the poor Irish immigrants gape at him uncomprehending instead of magically mutating on the spot into "philosophers" like himself. Many have found Thoreau's ethnic slurs here unforgiveable. But the Fields are the vehicle of a central metaphor, even though that metaphor is problematic. The Fields stand in for readers who, bogged down in old ways, make the same tragic mistake of assuming a better life means working harder to earn more money to buy more stuff—tea, coffee, meat—thus buying into the very economy that feeds off slave labor, and fueling the machine *Atropos*, "Fate," the destroyer of worlds and consumer of souls.

Thoreau, the person, really did want to change our lives, or at least make us confront the conditions of our lives and, if we cannot change those conditions, realize the extent to which the fault is our own. But by the midpoint of *Walden*, Thoreau, the narrator, has, thus far, changed nothing. The reader, just like the Fields, gapes at him in uncomprehending rapture—then goes on exactly as before, selling their life to buy a few consumer trinkets. If Thoreau cannot persuade the desperate and hungry Fields face-to-face, with his house at his back and all Walden before, how can he hope to persuade the reader, so far in the future, his house a ruin and Walden gone? At this moment, Thoreau's great book is, by his own account, a failure.

Thoreau's charity consisted literally of trying to teach John Fields to fish. But as *Walden's* narrator returns home with his own string of fish, he is filled with shame for craving animal food. What follows is "Higher Laws," a queasy self-examination of the killing his appetite demands; this is the chapter that sent Thoreau to Chesuncook to witness George Thatcher's moose hunt. He anatomized the reality of this violence in "Chesuncook," but in *Walden*, he wrote instead as a tortured Puritan compelled to put down beastly appetites: "Nature is hard to be overcome, but she must be overcome." Those very words made Thoreau pull back from his prudery in dismay, ashamed of his own shame. If we truly revered human nature, would we not, like the Hindu lawgivers, speak simply and openly of our bodily functions, of "how to eat, drink, cohabit, void excrement and urine and the like"? Instead of fighting to "overcome" our bodily nature, we should accept and redeem it.

And so Thoreau closed this chapter, the turning point of his book, by staging himself a second time, this time as "John Farmer" sitting on the threshold one September evening. That is, what we are seeing when we see Thoreau within the pages of *Walden* is not the author who so carefully staged the book, but the book's protagonist, who, in the course of the year and a day, is utterly changed by the experience. John Farmer, the next stage in this metamorphosis, yearns for rest while his mind natters on with plans and contrivances for the next day's work. The notes of a distant flute reach his ears, but half-heard and dismissed, "out of a different sphere from that he worked in," until gently they do away with street and village and state, asking him to come out of this "mean moiling life." But how? "All that he could think of was to practice some new austerity, to let his mind descend into his body and redeem it, and treat himself with ever increasing respect."[101] It is, at least, a beginning.

"Brute Neighbors" completes the turn: Thoreau opened it with yet a third mocking self-portrait, this time as the navel-gazing "Hermit" interrupted by the "Poet"—a sprightly Ellery Channing with his faithful dog, who jollies the Hermit out of his involuted thoughts to come along fishing. In a flash, the hectoring and self-consumed philosopher transforms into a lyric poet himself, the neighborhood Orpheus who asks as he sets off for the river, fishing pole in hand, "Why do precisely these objects which we behold make a world?" The beholding that follows begins with the little wild mouse who sits on his palm nibbling cheese from his fingers, and extends ever outward, peopling Walden Woods with life not his own, most of it not even human: an unseen world conjured into being. As Thoreau reminded himself, "Poetry *implies* the whole truth. Philosophy *expresses* a part of it."[102]

Bending *Walden* toward the cycle of rebirth meant opening it to seasonal change and the ways that living "in season" alters the rhythm of living and thinking. As winter drives life "into a corner," it proves not "mean" but rich and warm. The narrator surrounds his hearth with visitors, including the freed slaves and impoverished laborers whose circle he has joined and the "brute neighbors" who shelter beside him, like the wasps he accepts until they disappear into the cracks. The human "economy" of his first chapter thus enlarges to a new concept—not "eco-*nomia*," or management of the household, but "eco-*logia*," ecology, the *speaking* of the household, composed of a thousand voices: mice and wasps, rabbits and squirrels, jays and chickadees, and also his human friends, Bronson Alcott, Ellery Channing, Edmund Hosmer and (with a chill) Ralph Waldo Emerson—the closest Thoreau came to meeting Greeley's request for sketches of his famous friends. Walden Pond itself, iced over now, catches his surveyor's eye, so the narrator literally takes the measure of this personality, too, finding the long-lost bottom of the pond that will turn out, in the end, to be bottomless after all.

Walden opens in spring with a fractured and furious narrator who can diagnose despair in others because he knows it so well in himself: an Ishmael casting off into the world ocean of Walden. By the second spring, the narrator is remade, and ready; healed, whole, and strong. The man who railed at the Fields to change has instead changed himself, proceeded through a cycle of rebirths from philosopher through farmer and hermit to poet. The payoff of that initial uncomfortable encounter with the Fields has finally begun, the conceit finally completed, with the poet integrating all that came before. As the raw wound of the railroad's "deep cut" thaws and flows, he sees in the flowing sands the canvas of creation, revealing the great truth that we live not on the surface of a dead planet but in and through a living earth, like a leaf unfolding. As the pond whoops and thaws into quick and shimmering life, he sees the coming of Cosmos out of Chaos, a spiritual understanding so deep that he can even accept the grossness of a dead and rotting horse, death and sacrifice not as the betrayal of Nature's beauty but the sign of a "universal innocence" that transgresses the limits of our life, sublime, intimate, and terrible. The man who embraced the dying body of his brother admits the terrible truth that bodies, too, melt and flow like sand on the beach of Fire Island.

The fables of rebirth Thoreau offered in his "Conclusion" include his own Walden experiment: time swept it away, to be resurrected by art. For more than two years Thoreau dedicated himself to perfecting *Walden*, putting off everything else, refusing to compromise with Time; and as he added the finishing strokes, it "suddenly expanded before the eyes of the astonished artist into the fairest of all the creations of Brahma." On his title page he emblazoned his motto: "I do not propose to write an ode to dejection, but to brag as lustily as chanticleer in the morning, standing on his roost, if only to wake my neighbors up." And on his final page, he greeted the eternal dawn with a chanticleer call: "The light which puts out our eyes is darkness to us. Only that day dawns to which we are awake. There is more day to dawn. The sun is but a morning star." He who, midway through *Walden*, had been arrested on the threshold of life, is now himself the player on the flute, whose notes reach the ears of those who, hearing, might be released to begin their own journey toward the dawn. The ceremony enacted at Walden, and in *Walden*, creates a kind of miracle: scripture written, as Emerson imagined, in our own time, by a man both in and out of time itself.

PART THREE

SUCCESSIONS

CHAPTER NINE

Walden-on-Main
(1854–1857)

For what shall it profit a man, if he shall gain the
whole world, and lose his own soul?

MARK 8:36

"WHAT SHALL IT PROFIT?":
THOREAU AFTER *WALDEN*

"We account Henry the undoubted King of all American lions," said
Emerson; "He is walking up & down Concord, firm-looking, but in
a tremble of great expectation." *Walden* was barely three weeks old,
but already the reviews were putting a spring in Henry's step. Alcott,
to whom he'd given the first copy, read it straight through that very
night, reread it the next day, and predicted it would "find readers and
fame as years passed by."[1] Higginson wrote from Worcester to thank
Thoreau for "Slavery in Massachusetts," which he thought surpassed
everything else published in that terrible week, and added that after
peeking at *Walden*'s proof sheets, he'd snapped up two copies.[2] It's a
"hit," raved Richard Fuller—full of faith and nobility, a fruit sure to
"keep and grow more golden mellow and fragrant with the years."
"You have made a contribution to the permanent literature of our
mother tongue," declared Senator Charles Sumner; Emerson added
that it was "cheerful, sparkling, readable, with all kinds of merits,
& rising sometimes to very great heights."[3] Not everyone was so
admiring—the monastic Hecker warned Brownson of its "pride,

pretension, and infidelity," and Hawthorne, even as he bought two copies as gifts, groaned that few readers would have the "resolution" to get to the end of it—but at last Thoreau had good reason to hope (or fear) that he stood on the brink of literary fame and fortune.[4]

The print reviews were plentiful and mostly warm, even effusive. "Get the book," advised the Boston *Daily Bee*. "You will like it. It is original and refreshing; and from the brain of a *live* man." "A fresh bouquet from the wilds, fragrant and inspiring," said a New Jersey newspaper. The New Bedford *Mercury* was "enchanted" with its freshness and charm, and rejoiced that its seeds of moral truth would "spring up and flourish and beautify new homes." One New York reviewer marveled at Thoreau's "great mastery of language"; another called it "half mad, but never silly." The *Christian Register* delighted in its "acute and wise criticisms upon modern life" as well as its "playful humor and sparkling thought," though one Boston critic fretted at Thoreau's "selfish philosophy," and the offended *New York Times* carped that "Mr. Thoreau denounces everything that indicates progress." British reviewers were also kind. *Walden* was "a brave book, one in a million, an honour to America, a gift to men," wrote one, "worth reading and re-reading"; George Eliot, in the widely read *Westminster Review*, praised Thoreau's "deep poetic sensibility" and the "sturdy sense mingled with his unworldliness."[5] Thoreau could hardly ask for more. *Walden* was finding its readers. The lowering fear that he had failed his friends and disappointed his family finally lifted; from now on, Henry Thoreau could face the future knowing that he had written a great and lasting book.

Managing success—perhaps even celebrity—was a new and disconcerting prospect. That fall the *New-York Daily Tribune* published Thoreau's name in a list of lecturers for the upcoming season, which they expected to be "more brilliant" than ever. Thoreau geared up, bravely announcing to Blake that he had a lecture planned in Plymouth, a second in Philadelphia, "and thereafter to the West, *if they shall want me.*" Yet the prospect filled him with qualms. In "obscurity and poverty" he was free to live as he wished, free to spend two whole years with the flowers alone and an entire fall observing the changing tints of the foliage. "Ah, how I have thriven on solitude and poverty! I cannot overstate this advantage." What if the public demanded him? "If I go abroad lecturing, how shall I ever recover the lost winter?" Perhaps he owed his very success to his vices, including his willingness to make "enormous sacrifices" to gain his ends.[6] Nevertheless, Thoreau pushed aside his fears and resolved to go on the lecture circuit, plunging into the most active social season of his life.

Thoreau sat for his portrait only three times in his life, the first just after *Walden*'s publication.[7] One of Boston's most important illustrators, Samuel Worcester Rowse, had been commissioned to paint a formal portrait of Emerson, and while boarding with the Thoreaus he became intrigued with Henry's features. A family friend recorded Rowse's process: for two or three weeks he studied Thoreau's face without putting pencil to paper, until "one morning at breakfast, he suddenly jumped up from the table, asked to be excused and disappeared for the rest of the day." A certain expression had crossed Henry's face, and Rowse wished to capture it. The following morning he brought down a sensitive rendering in chalk and charcoal of a young and gentle poet. It pleased most of Henry's family—Sophia treasured it for the rest of her days—although Aunt Maria scoffed it was a poor likeness, and Henry's friends were unconvinced. Blake thought it "very unsatisfactory," Franklin Sanborn judged it "rather weak," and Alcott complained it made his friend "too much of a gentleman." That, no doubt, was exactly the intent. Rowse sought to capture artistic impressions rather than render factual accuracy; in an age when the camera was turning the art world upside down, he earned his fame by transforming his sitters into idealized, sentimental images of middle-class Victorian gentility. Henry's reaction to his bland and dreamy avatar does not survive, but after his death, it would become the nineteenth century's iconic image of Thoreau.[8]

Another visitor that August was the Salem botanist John Lewis Russell. For two days they walked and boated while Thoreau peppered him with questions. Russell was in quest of Concord's rarest and most treasured plant, the beautiful and delicate climbing fern that, alone of all the ferns of New England, twines up other plants like a vine. It grew in only one place, a thicket deep in the woods, where Thoreau discovered it late in November 1851—a secret he shared with only his most trusted friends. Elizabeth Hoar was one; in August 1854 he helped her gather a little for a garland, unwinding the delicate and lacy fronds with care and patience. Two days later, on the bright morning of August 16, Thoreau took Russell to gather a specimen of the rare and elegant treasure for his own collection. From then on, the two remained friends. The following March, Russell published a graceful essay on their "tour of discovery into unknown regions of fairy land."[9] Russell returned two years later for a second ramble in the field, and in September 1858 they explored Cape Ann together, botanizing cheerfully in the estuaries and boiling their dinnertime tea over fires kindled from dead bayberry bushes.[10]

Walden soon brought Thoreau fan letters and new friendships. One came from Adrien Rouquette, a French Catholic priest in New Orleans who spotted a review of the book and hurried out to buy a copy. Rouquette, an ardent abolitionist who admired Orestes Brownson and Isaac Hecker, would soon remove from the city to live with the Choctaw Indians as a missionary and protector, adopting their clothing, their language, and the Choctaw name "Chahta-Ima." Writing in his native French, he expressed immense admiration for Walden, beseeched Thoreau for a copy of A Week on the Concord and Merrimack Rivers, and enclosed his own books of sacred poetry and reflections on his life as a religious hermit. Thoreau was gratified to receive so cordial a greeting in French, "the language of my paternal Grandfather." As he added gracefully, "I assure you it is not a little affecting to be thus reminded of the breadth & the destiny of our common country."[11] His sense of kinship with the French in North America, ignited by his brief excursion to Canada, had not abated.

Then there was an odd missive from New Bedford, which opened with a stiff "Dear Sir," then warmed up quick as a teakettle to rattle on for pages as the writer bubbled over with his own love for nature, his beloved Middleboro Ponds, his rural retreat—but he had a wife and four children and being in his forty second year had "got a *little* too far along" to undertake a new mode of life; but still, he was writing from his own "rough board Shanty 12x14 three miles from New Bedford in a quiet & secluded spot." Pages later, the effusion abruptly ends: "Dear Mr Walden good bye for the present. Daniel Ricketson." Thoreau penned a courteous but cautious reply that included kind wishes, a book recommendation, and a mild joke: "Much as you have told me of yourself, you have still I think the advantage of me in this correspondence, for I have told you still more in my book. You have therefore the broadest mark to fire at." "Letter hastily written and hardly satisfactory," Ricketson scrawled in his journal before seizing a new sheet of paper and inviting Thoreau to come visit—an invitation he did not send. Impulsive, querulous, quick to sense insult, a restless chatterbox, Ricketson had, it would seem, no future with "Mr Walden."[12]

While Ricketson's cheeky letter lay on his desk unanswered, Thoreau was busy on his rounds, watching the summer drought finally break and the turtle eggs he'd buried in the garden that spring hatch. He was moved to see the earth could nurse such fragile seeds of creaturely life. Often he walked with friends, such as Minot Pratt, a Brook Farmer who bought a farm in Concord and was learning about beekeeping and native plants, or Rowse, who was teaching Thoreau to see with an artist's eye, or Channing, still tormented and lonely, rattling around his empty house across the street. Or his latest visitor, a lanky Shropshire gentleman named Thomas Cholmondeley—"pronounced *Chumly*"—who showed up at Emerson's door in August and was now boarding with the Thoreaus through the fall. The Oxford-educated Cholmondeley had just published *Ultima Thule*, a study of New Zealand's political and social economy based on his years as a New Zealand sheep farmer; now he wanted to see what the English Commonwealth had done in the New World. Thoreau praised him as "an English country gentleman of simple habits and truly liberal mind, who may one day take part in the government of his country."[13] Somehow they took to each other. Just after New Year's Day, about to board a ship home to England, Cholmondeley stopped by Concord to talk Thoreau into coming along. Their friendship must have been warm indeed: Emerson feared Thoreau might go.[14]

Thoreau's fall campaign to cut a figure on the lecture circuit had gotten off to a good start. His first invitation came from Marston Watson in Plymouth, who raised ten dollars with James Spooner and a few others for an encore.[15] Alcott was there, scouting out a possible new home for his family, and Watson hoped Thoreau would survey his extensive gardens and orchards as well. Thoreau cheerfully packed both compass and lecture and set off for Plymouth on October 7, though Watson's invitation put him in a bit of a bind: they requested two lectures, but Thoreau had only one on hand, which they had already heard. Pressed for time, he expanded sections of "Walking" into a suite of lectures suitable for his planned Western tour. In Plymouth, he began with "Moonlight," a rhapsody on walking by the moon's ethereal light, which revealed that we "are not of the earth earthy, but of the earth spiritual."[16] The audience was tiny: the Watsons, the devoted Spooner, Alcott—supportive as ever, pronouncing the new lecture "admirable"—plus a few others, barely more than a "sewing circle." Thoreau kept no record of the trip; the writer who loved wide margins in his life had, this autumn, no margins at all. He roomed with Alcott, the two talking until bedtime, and spent three days surveying Hillside's eighty acres—Watson showing the way and Alcott carrying the chains—before returning by way of Boston and a visit with the Alcott family on October 13.[17]

The instant he was home, Thoreau wrote to Blake to arrange their excursion to Mount Wachusett—not much of a trip, but all he could manage. At least it would show Cholmondeley, eager to climb an American mountain, a bit of the countryside. By the time they set off on October 19, the drought-stricken trees had already shed their leaves and the uplands were sugared with early snow. From Westminster they walked to Daniel Foster's home; after a year as Concord's Trinitarian minister, Foster had settled on a farm in East Princeton. Daniel was away lecturing, but his wife Dora, a close friend of Sophia Thoreau, welcomed them warmly. It was only a two-mile jaunt to the top of Wachusett, so off they went, meeting Blake at the summit, where they marveled to see the ships docked at Boston Harbor through Henry's telescope.[18]

After a few hours' sleep at the Fosters', they were back on the summit by sunrise, looking east into "misty and gilded obscurity." To the west, Wachusett's shadow touched the Hoosac Mountains in the farthest horizon before contracting steadily into a sharp pyramid on the farmlands below. They were home by day's end. Daniel Foster wrote regretting his absence and hoping Thoreau would soon return, for he had been reading *Walden* to the family, slowly, with plenty of pauses for discussion, and wanted Thoreau to know that his fellowship "has been uncommonly useful in aiding & strengthening my own best purpose."[19] That purpose was to "seek truth and immortal living" in a happy home on a bit of his own land. A poignant wish—the ardent Foster would pursue his ideals to the Kansas frontier to join John Brown's insurrection, and later would die in the Civil War, captain of the 37th Regiment of US Colored Troops.

-+->-<+-

As soon as he was home from Wachusett, Thoreau plunged back into writing. He had landed a major lecture engagement as the second speaker in a series at Philadelphia's prestigious Spring Garden Mechanics Institute—his first appearance outside New England—and it weighed on his mind. His topic, he announced, would be "The Wild," the second in his planned suite of lectures carved out of the ballooning pages of "Walking." But plans for the big Western tour were not going well. He'd received only two nibbles, one from Akron, Ohio, and another from Hamilton, Ontario. In a flurry of letters, he tried to schedule them both for early January while angling for more—two would hardly pay expenses—plus juggling dates for appearances in Providence and Nantucket and trying to pin down yet another nibble, from the Boston area, that never materialized.[20] His plans were still up in the air when he set off for Philadelphia on November 20, a long day's journey: the early train to Boston, the express train to New York, connecting by candlelight to a third train across New Jersey to the Camden Ferry across the Delaware River to Philadelphia, arriving at 10:00 p.m. Fifteen hours, Thoreau noted, from Concord.[21]

Thoreau stayed in America's first capital for just one day. First thing in the morning, he headed to the Statehouse, where the Declaration of Independence had been signed, and climbed to the top of the cupola to look over the city (though he preferred the squirrels bustling around his feet to the great historical sights). Emerson had written ahead to ask a college friend, Philadelphia's Unitarian minister William Henry Furness, to show Thoreau around. Furness got Thoreau admitted to the National Academy of Sciences, where carpenters were adding four more stories to house the growing collections. Thoreau lingered over Morton's infamous collection of human skulls, whose crania measured the immutable scale of intelligence—the bigger the skull, the smarter the person, putting white men at the top. Of the American Philosophical Society, Thoreau noted that it was described "as a company of old women." Of his lecture itself, he noted nothing. Yet "The Wild" was of the deepest importance to him: as he scrawled across the title page, "I regard this as a sort of introduction to all I may write hereafter." Furness, who could not attend, told Emerson that a parishioner's daughter said "the audience was stupid & did not appreciate him," although Thoreau himself was "full of interesting talk," in the most "amusing" intonations. To illustrate, Furness sketched a goofy Thoreau with staring eyes, pouting lips, a vanishing chin, scraggly hair, and an absurdly drooping nose, like a tapir.[22]

Any discouragement Thoreau may have felt in Philadelphia was dispersed the next day in New York, where the ebullient and ever-supportive Greeley treated his newly published client like a celebrity. Thoreau was dazzled by the Crystal Palace, with its displays of everything from a column of solid coal fifty feet thick to iron and copper ores, sculptures and paintings innumerable, and eighth-century armor from the Tower of London. At Barnum's Museum he paused over Indian artifacts dug out of the mounds, towering "camelopards," or giraffes—not nearly so tall as Barnum claimed, scoffed Thoreau the surveyor—and Barnum's diorama of the world, which told the builder of a house at Walden that houses were pretty much the same the world over. Greeley introduced Thoreau to the *Tribune* staff before sweeping him off to the opera, Bellini's *I Puritani* (The Puritans), all the rage in Paris and Queen Victoria's favorite. As the page ushered them around the opera house to meet this group and that, Thoreau lost track of the social whirl: "Greeley appeared to know and be known by everybody."[23]

Back home, there was no time to rest. In two weeks he was due in Provincetown, where he had promised to deliver an entirely new lecture, "What Shall It Profit?"—the debut of what became his most frequently delivered lecture and eventually his great polemic, "Life without Principle." This, too, like "Moonlight" and "The Wild," was a spin-off from "Walking": this third segment expanded on the failure to walk with a redemptive "saunterer's" eye. Alone of all his lectures, Thoreau reserved these two, "Walking, or The Wild" and "What Shall It Profit?", to remain lectures, not moving them to publication until he was on his deathbed. They were designed as a complementary pair—nature and humanity—which, taken together, gave voice to Thoreau's leading principles. Once he had asked, in the aftershock of Shadrach Minkin's escape, "What is the value of any political freedom, but as a means of moral freedom?" These two lectures were his answer. "Walking" advanced the freedom to step away from the demands of earning a living, to shape one's day as a dwelling wholly within the higher law. This new lecture advanced the freedom to earn that living honestly, even poetically—to make the higher law one's daily bread. As his biblical title asked his audience, "For what shall it profit a man, if he shall gain the whole world, and lose his own soul?"[24]

The irony of it all pierced Thoreau to the quick. He was earning a living telling audiences to "get your living by loving," but hated what he was doing; it cost him everything he loved. On December 6, after days of writing and a whirl of engagements, he collapsed into a window seat on the train to Providence and brooded on the landscape: "I see thick ice and boys skating all the way to Providence, but know not when it froze, I have been so busy writing my lecture." It was as he feared in September: "If I go abroad lecturing, how shall I ever recover the lost winter?"[25] But he soldiered on. The Providence organizers specified that, given the "outrages of slavery," their speakers must emphasize reform. They'd invited Theodore Parker, Wendell Phillips, William Lloyd Garrison, and T. W. Higginson, ranking Thoreau with the era's greatest reform speakers. The audience would have loved that great barnburner "Slavery in Massachusetts," but Thoreau, who did not repeat published material, gave them "What Shall It Profit?" instead—less fire, more philosophy. Their reaction was cool, and Thoreau left deeply unhappy. "I fail to get even the attention of the mass. I should suit them better if I suited myself less." They wanted not the original, but the familiar: "You cannot interest them except as you are like them and sympathize with them." The only saving grace was the "providential" appearance of H. G. O. Blake's best friend, Theo Brown. Knowing there was some "Worcester soil there" saved his words from falling on "stony ground."[26]

Even stony ground might yield a little fruit, though. In Providence that meant meeting Emerson's protégé Charles King Newcomb, he of "The Two Dolons," who took Thoreau to see Roger Williams' Rock and the old fort on Narragansett Bay. But Thoreau couldn't get rid of the bad taste in his mouth. He had cheapened himself, exhausted himself trying to become a popular lecturer, and for what? Twice now, audiences in major cities had yawned at his best new material. The whole enterprise was a failure. Worse, it took away what he treasured above all else, his freedom to walk daily into nature, to see what each new day brought forth. "Winter has come unnoticed by me," he sulked again, on his return from Providence. Better to write books. Let his audience be sifted that way; better they come to him than he go to them.[27] And with that resolution, his plans for a big Western lecture tour evaporated. Such grand tours worked for Emerson, who made them annually, but this was the last time Thoreau sought a lecture engagement outside New England. Meanwhile, he honored the commitments he'd already made, giving "What Shall It Profit?" to the New Bedford Lyceum the day after

Christmas and to the Nantucket Atheneum two days later. Fortunately, given his despairing mood, both places gave him good reason not to give up altogether.

New Bedford was Daniel Ricketson's neighborhood, and sure enough, the instant Ricketson heard Thoreau was coming, he whipped out the letter he'd shelved back in October, added a note inviting Thoreau to stay with him, and dropped it in the mail. Thoreau promptly accepted, and by return mail Ricketson sent instructions to take the evening train on Christmas Day—instructions that Ricketson promptly forgot.[28] On Christmas morning, 1854, he rushed to meet the noon train, only to return home, disappointed. Thoreau, meanwhile, arrived on the evening train as instructed and found no one there to meet him. Ricketson was just clearing the snow off his front steps when he saw "a man walking up the carriage road carrying a portmanteau in one hand and an umbrella in the other—He was dressed in a long overcoat of dark color, and wore a dark soft hat." A peddler of small wares, he assumed, but the peddler walked up to him and stopped. "You do not know me," said the stranger. "It at once flashed on my mind that the person before me was my correspondent whom I had expected in the morning, and who in my imagination I had figured as a stout and robust person, instead of the small and rather inferior looking man before me. However I concealed my disappointment and at once replied, 'I presume this is Mr. Thoreau.'"[29]

Out of this ludicrous series of miscues was born a remarkable friendship. Ricketson was a wealthy Quaker who had given up a career in law to live on the fortune his great-grandfather had made in the whaling industry. He was a perennial student and well-meaning dilettante dabbling in a dozen pastimes—writer, poet, local historian, naturalist, reformer, and abolitionist—and a nervous hypochondriac who spent most of his waking hours in his "Shanty," a writer's cabin warmed by an open fire and filled with books and papers. A few feet away stood Brooklawn, the fine large family home presided over by his wife, Louisa Ricketson, and made lively by their four children, Arthur, Walton (who became a well-known sculptor),

Anna, and Emma. As he and Thoreau talked into the night, Daniel's disappointment melted away. The effect on Henry was instantaneous: "I went to walk in the woods with R. It was wonderfully warm and pleasant. . . . I felt the winter breaking up in me, and if I had been at home I should have tried to write poetry."[30] "Dear Walden," a cheery Ricketson saluted Henry a week later, already inviting a return visit; Thoreau bounced back a sunny reply. In a flash the two were old friends, intimate, open, and relaxed, teasing each other in one moment, in the next fondly laughing off their frequent and mutual annoyances.

After a day's ramble through the woods and a drive around the area, the overstimulated Ricketson did not feel well enough to attend Thoreau's lecture, so Walton stayed with his father while Louisa and the "young folks" went to the New Bedford Lyceum. Thoreau's audience was large and, once again, baffled. "I think he puzzled them a little," admitted one listener; the lecture was thoughtful, agreed the local newspaper, but "decidedly peculiar." Ricketson assured his new friend that several "sensible" people liked it.[31] What else could Thoreau have expected? New Bedford was a seaport boomtown riding high on the whale-oil industry, and the lecture hall was filled with wealthy merchants, captains, carpenters, coopers, and sailors on shore leave, all dedicating their lives to reaping the ocean for huge profits. What sense could they have made of Thoreau's warning that the pursuit of profit would cost them their souls?

The next day the small man who looked like a peddler of small wares pocketed "What Shall It Profit?" once again and set out in a misty rain over rough seas to Nantucket, thirty miles offshore, his head "hanging over the side all the way." The seasick Thoreau spent the evening recovering at the home of an old whaling captain, Edward W. Gardiner, who regaled him with whaling stories: in this land a man must go a-whaling before he could marry, and have struck a whale before he could dance; Gardiner's own relative had been drowned, like Ahab, by a whale. Nantucket had long since been stripped of trees, and the sea captain's mission in retirement was to replant new pine forests. Thoreau listened closely while Gardiner drove him to Siasconset on the outer shore, pointing out his tree plantations and discoursing on the costs and sources of bulk pine seed. "These plantations must very soon change the aspect of the land," Thoreau noted. Concord, too, was stripping the land of its trees. Would this be a way to hasten the land's regeneration? He filed away the thought. At the Nantucket Athenaeum they showed him curious artifacts brought by sailors from the South Pacific, but when he asked about the local Native Americans, he was shown only a photograph of the last Indian on the island, a basket of huckleberries in his hand. Thoreau was too late; the man had died less than a month ago.[32]

Thoreau's notoriety drew a large audience who traipsed through the rain and mud to hear "What Shall It Profit?". Three times before it had bombed, but the worldly Nantucketers loved it. "This is the very audience for me," Thoreau crowed. The next morning his ship set out in the morning mist, only to get lost in the fog off Hyannis (once, said Captain Gardiner, it took five weeks for the mail ship to land), guided in by careful soundings and, at last, "the locomotive's whistle & the life boat bell."[33] Thoreau was back in Concord by evening. Two days later, New Year's Eve, he walked on the frozen river to Fairhaven Bay. "How glorious the perfect stillness and peace of the winter landscape," he exulted. He was free; the winter was all his. Thoreau carried "What Shall It Profit?" to audiences twice more that season, but only close to home. Four days later he had a splendid time with his old friends at Worcester, where he rambled around Quinsigamond Pond, pausing to interview a Wabanaki making baskets and a Mr. Washburn making telegraph wire. Six weeks later, on February 14, 1855, he concluded the season by reading the now-battered pages of "What Shall It Profit?" one more time, to the Concord Lyceum. Nothing happened there to make him regret his decision to cancel his lecture tour. It would be nearly two years before Thoreau stepped onto the lecture podium again.

ILLNESS AND RECOVERY

In December Thoreau had fretted at missing winter; now he was out in it daily. Far from envying the boys skating, now he was one of them—thirty miles in a few hours! This was truly "the winter of skating." On February 4, he and William Tappan spread their coattails to the wind like birds and sailed down Pantry Meadow on the ice "like a graceful demon in the midst of the broad meadow all covered and lit with the curling snow-steam," leaping over the foul places to save their necks. Everyone marveled at the cold. The ice came so close to the town center one could step from the rear of the bank "and set sail on skates for any part of the Concord River valley."[34] In February the cold stopped the clock, bedsheets froze about their faces as people slept, and fingers were so numb they "must leave many buttons unbuttoned." The cat mewed to have the door opened, then was disinclined to go out, returning hours later from some barn smelling of meadow hay; "we all took her up and smelled of her, it was so fragrant." Indoors, Thoreau thawed his ink and wrote. Outdoors, he traced what mice, partridges, and foxes had written on the snow. He watched Therien the woodchopper cut down the great chestnuts that had shaded his Walden house: seventy-five tree rings, and the axe broke, it was so cold. Sophia's plants froze in the house. It was important, thought Thoreau, to describe the weather, for "it affects our feelings. That which was so important at the time cannot be unimportant to remember."[35]

Near the end of a cold, blustery March—so raw that even Thoreau's patience was fraying—he met his future biographer: Franklin Benjamin Sanborn. The ambitious Harvard senior had dropped in on Emerson the previous fall, and Emerson, impressed, invited Sanborn to open a school in Concord, right away—they needed one badly. Thoreau and Sanborn almost crossed paths in January, when Thoreau dropped off a copy of *A Week* at Harvard for a student who had written a kind essay on him for the *Harvard Magazine*. Sanborn took the book without recognizing its author and duly passed it along. Only hours later did he put two and two together, when he saw Thoreau deep in conversation with Thaddeus Harris—too late to introduce himself. So he wrote an unctuous letter spiced with an undergraduate's careless contempt—"ask me what I think of your philosophy, I should be apt to answer that it is not worth a straw"— —a put-down that Thoreau's reply diplomatically ignored.[36]

Sanborn moved fast: on March 13 Emerson offered him the schoolhouse rent free, twenty pupils, and a salary of $850. Two days later he and his sister Sarah arrived in Concord, arranging to rent Ellery Channing's upstairs rooms and take their meals across the street with the Thoreaus. Later Sanborn sketched a typical dinner: a deaf Mr. Thoreau presiding silently while Henry led the conversation, pausing patiently when interrupted by the "loquacious" Cynthia, taking up his train of talk exactly where he'd left off the instant she was done, Sophia joining in energetically all the while. When Thoreau paid his new neighbors a formal call, Sanborn judged him to be "a sort of pocket edition of Emerson," plainly dressed in unfitted clothes, ruddy and weather-beaten like "some shrewd and honest animal—some retired, philosophic woodchuck or magnanimous fox."[37] There was talk of Thoreau's coming on as a teacher, which he declined, although he often led the students—including various young Emersons, Alcotts, and Hawthornes together with Henry James's sons Wilkie and Bob and a daughter of John Brown—out on Saturday excursions.[38] On May 12, two of Sanborn's Harvard friends brought his furniture up from Cambridge in a wagon, and the three men borrowed Thoreau's boat (moored, as it was, in their own backyard) for a leisurely float down the Concord River. Sanborn was home.

Well into 1855, Thoreau's Journal simmered happily along. It was spring, and everywhere the work of killing was going on. Through his telescope he watched Garfield shoot a red-tailed hawk out of the sky and hunters boat through the meadows, shooting muskrats. He dodged bullets to retrieve a beautiful duck floating dead in the water, and found it was a rare merganser. Jacob Farmer said he trapped a hundred mink a year, and Goodwin the hunter took twenty-five pouts and one perch at Walden. Hunting with his telescope instead, Thoreau watched a herring gull "stroking the air with his wings." He hunted with his hands, too, reaching into a stump and clasping a flying squirrel on a guess. It struggled and bit his fingers; Thoreau tied it up in a handkerchief and brought it home. He spent the evening watching it fail to fly, leaping pathetically from the furniture, only to plop ridiculously onto the floor. Next day he returned the defeated little being to the same stump, where, eyeing him closely, it skimmed down and away from him, up a nearby maple, then "away it went in admirable style, more like a bird than any quadruped I had dreamed of," steering around the trees like a hawk.[39] Finding a screech owl in a knothole, he reached in and stroked it. Like a cat, the little owl "reclined its head a little lower and closed its eye entirely." One day, when a few loafers jeered at him, he was ready: "Halloo, Thoreau, and don't you ever shoot a bird then when you want to study it?" "Do you think that I should shoot you if I wanted to study you?"[40]

But that May, something started to go terribly wrong. Thoreau's Journal entries thinned and frayed; the sparkle dimmed. By June 17, Emerson was deeply worried. "Henry Thoreau is feeble, & languishes this season, to our alarm," he wrote his brother William. "We have tried to persuade him to come & spend a week with us for a change." Ten days later, in a letter to Blake, Thoreau finally admitted the truth: "I have been sick and good for nothing but to lie on my back and wait for something to turn up, for two or three months." He wrote to cancel their plans for a summer excursion. Nearly three months later, he interrupted his Journal to confess to "four or five months of invalidity and worthlessness."[41] The weakness had started in his knees and spread from there, leaving him, at its worst, barely able to walk.

The cause was uncertain. Dr. Bartlett was at a loss. Was it psychosomatic—depression following the completion of *Walden*, brought on when Thoreau realized he could never again come up to his lifetime's achievement? The notion is plausible, given the unyielding press of ambition that had driven him so hard all through 1854. Yet what of the sheer exuberance through the winter, the joy radiating from the Journal, the tireless energy of long days skating in the bitter subzero cold, tracking in the deep snow, sailing in the raw and blustery spring? More likely Thoreau was leveled by a flareup of his chronic tuberculosis, caused when a lesion in his lungs ruptured and sent the virulent bacilli coursing through his body to lodge in his knees and hips, inflaming the bone and degrading the muscle. By April he had known something was up, and he was taking all the recommended precautions. At their first meeting, Sanborn had noted that he wore a beard on his throat. This was not a fashion statement: "Galway whiskers," worn from ear to ear below the chin, were thought to prevent consumption by warming the throat, keeping cold air away from delicate lungs. Growing throat whiskers, together with taking plenty of exercise in the fresh outdoor air, were understood to be the best defense against the mysterious, wasting disease. Everything Thoreau did would have been approved as a reasonable precaution.

By the time Thoreau wrote his sad letter to Blake, he was bracing for a long recovery. He was supposed to be deep in the Maine woods by then, paddling a canoe. Instead he was an invalid, heartsick and deeply lonely. "I walk alone," he confided to his Journal. "My heart is full. Feelings impede the current of my thoughts. I knock on the earth for my friend. . . . but no friend appears, and perhaps none is dreaming of me." The more his misery mounted, the lonelier he got, until in the midst of writing Blake to cancel their plans for a visit, he couldn't bear it. Come now!—he added impulsively to his Worcester friends; come to Concord. You can attend our antislavery meeting, and next morning we'll head out to Cape Cod together. I can manage only short walks, but we can have *long* talks.[42] Blake and Brown were both too busy to break away, but the wayward Channing was willing—indeed, lounging on the beach had been his idea in the first place. The Cape it would be.

→>◦<←

The beach had been on Thoreau's mind since April: for three years his manuscript about Cape Cod had been gathering dust on George Curtis's desk at *Putnam's*, stalled since Thoreau had withdrawn "A

Yankee in Canada" midway through publication after Curtis censored his remarks on religion. Greeley had begged Thoreau not to break with the valuable and well-placed Curtis, and now his advice was paying off: on the heels of *Walden's* success, Curtis dug out the old manuscript, dusted it off, and decided to run it as *Putnam's* summer travel series. By April Thoreau was correcting the proofs for the first monthly installment, and on July fourth, even as he and Channing were boarding the holiday train to Boston bound for Cape Cod, the July issue was hitting the booksellers with the second installment. Thoreau and Channing, those knights of the umbrella and bundle, might have looked like tramps before, but now they would return as celebrities.

After rushing to meet the steamer, they arrived at the wharf, only to be told the captain had decided to lay over for the holiday. They spent the day visiting the galleries of the Boston Athenaeum, where Thoreau studied Frederic Church's sublime sun-washed canvas "The Andes of Ecuador," then watching a regatta. They overnighted with the obliging Alcotts, who were packing to move to a rent-free house in Walpole, New Hampshire. Next morning they sailed to Provincetown and the following morning they took the first stage to North Truro, arriving at 6:00 a.m. and walking a mile through the fog to the Highland Lighthouse. Since Thoreau's last stay there in June 1850, the lighthouse keeper, James Small, had added a boardinghouse for $3.50 a week, and they settled in for the next two weeks. It's still not too late to join us, Thoreau urged Blake; the table was "not so clean as could be desired," but it was better than Provincetown, and Small was intelligent, a good man to deal with. "Come by all means," he pleaded. His Worcester friends still couldn't come, but Thoreau enjoyed himself anyway, relishing the sea fog and a bracing nor'easter, bathing in the ocean, botanizing here and there, talking with the locals, and filling pages of his neglected Journal with notes. He and Channing left early on July 18, sailing back with so little wind that they did not reach Boston Harbor until candlelight. "Methinks I am beginning to be better," Thoreau reassured Blake.[43]

Then came bad news. Just as *Putnam's* was running the third installment of *Cape Cod*, "The Beach," in August, even as Thoreau was thanking them for payment and sending revisions for the September installment, Curtis canceled the rest of the series. Why? Thoreau surmised they heard he planned to expand the series into a book, which was, he wrote back to Curtis, news to him. But Curtis equivocated. The real problem wasn't Thoreau's future publication plans—it was his tone. Curtis had already cut the more indelicate passages, which bowdlerization Thoreau astonishingly accepted in silence. But when Curtis got down to reading the next installment, "The Wellfleet Oysterman," he must have choked in dismay. Irreverent and profane, this was the chapter that had made the Concord audience "laugh 'till they cried." Worse still, even the cleaned-up versions of the previous chapters had already offended the Cape's residents, who were complaining in the newspapers. Better, reasoned Curtis, to feed the prickly Thoreau a fake excuse than be honest and ignite his wrath. As Curtis wrote his publisher, just send it all back to Thoreau. "He has an overweening conceit . . . and it will deplete him grandly." It did. Thoreau, sick and defeated, glumly asked Curtis to return the remainder. Once again, he had been burned by America's timid and censorious press. "It costs so much to publish," he sighed in his Journal, "would it not be better for the author to put his manuscripts in a safe?"[44]

Walden was supposed to have been his breakout book, buoying the rest of his work. That April, with *Putnam's* reviving the dormant *Cape Cod*, an encouraged Thoreau had prodded his publishers: wasn't it time, with *Walden* leading the way and *Cape Cod* in press, to reissue *A Week*? After all, he still had those 700-plus copies boxed in the attic. But there they would stay. Late in September, Ticknor and Fields reported back that *Walden* was selling, but not selling well. They still had 256 copies of the initial print run of 2,000; after a promising start, sales had plummeted. They were very sorry, "for your sake as well as ours."[45] Sales would stay slow. By February 1857, only sixteen copies were left, but by December 1858 they calculated even the tiny handful of copies remaining were enough for the foreseeable future.[46]

→>─<←

Thoreau was too ill to write, but he wasn't totally housebound. There was bathing in the river, boating with Channing, and, though it was a bad year for berries, a-berrying as usual with the Emerson children. He even managed a little surveying: sometime that August he hauled his tripod and compass (or had someone haul them for him) out to Sleepy Hollow, where he leveled for a new artificial pond in a meadow behind what would be known as Author's Ridge.[47] Workers began to dig out the new pond soon after, gradually deepening it over the years. By mid-September, as cool fall weather approached, Thoreau was reporting that "after four or five months of invalidity and worthlessness, I begin to feel some stirrings of life in me."[48]

What he yearned for was not nature but society, and his friends rallied around him. Ricketson arrived on September 21 and was instantly thrilled with all things Concord: "How charmingly you, Channing, & I dove-tailed together," he bubbled, and Edmund "Solon" Hosmer was the "real 'feelosopher.'" Though his headaches cut short his stay, Ricketson had barely returned home when he invited Thoreau for a visit, enclosing railroad fare. "You are the only 'millionaire' among my acquaintance," he assured him, covering for the handout. "*Cars* sound like *cares* to me," sighed Thoreau as he started to say no—until suddenly, once again, he changed his mind. "Perhaps your sea air will be good for me." For all was not well. As he wrote Blake, "I do not see how strength is to be got into my legs again." The night before, he added poignantly, he had dreamed "that I could vault over any height it pleased me. That was *something*."[49]

On September 29, when the rest of Concord was dedicating Sleepy Hollow Cemetery, Thoreau was on his way to the Ricketsons'. Life was good there: the boys, Arthur and Walton, met him at the railroad station with a string of fish they'd just caught. There were rambles along the river, rides to the ponds or to New Bedford, hours perusing the boys' collection of shells and Indian artifacts or their father's library. There was "feelosophy" in the Shanty and piano in the parlor, with violin and flageolet. One day Ricketson drove Thoreau to see "the old Indian burying-place" and meet the widow of his friend John Rozier, who'd been part Indian and part black. While nosing along the shore, they noticed an old Indian couple fishing. Ricketson called them over: "Don't be afraid; I ain't a-going to hurt you"; he and Henry were "interested in those of the old stock, now they were so few." "Yes," the "squaw" shot back, "and you'd be glad if they were all gone." On their last day, the friends drove to Plymouth, where Thoreau introduced Ricketson to the Watsons over tea. Next morning Thoreau returned to Concord to rest, while Ricketson, "much fatigued," rode home to revise his original impression of Thoreau: "He improves, unlike most people, upon an intimate acquaintance—modest and gentle in his manner, the best read and most intelligent man I ever knew. . . . My respect for his character and talents is greater than for any man I know."[50]

Back home, two letters awaited Thoreau's attention. One was from his old Harvard classmate William Allen, to whom he had given his copy of Emerson's *Nature* as a graduation present and who had taken over the Concord School classroom after Thoreau resigned. Allen was coming to Concord for a Sunday school convention and wanted to board with the Thoreaus and revisit his old haunts. When Allen arrived, Thoreau was disgusted that he didn't want to call on any of his former students, but only walk around Concord's New Burying Ground and pore over the epitaphs. Thoreau waited for him at the gate, muttering that "that ground did not smell good."[51] His schoolboy friend was growing old in all the wrong ways, living in the past, prying into graveyards—the very last place Thoreau, so hungry now for life and health, wanted to be. Far better was the second letter, from Thomas Cholmondeley: he had enlisted as a soldier in the Crimean War and was settling his affairs before going into battle. In the interim he had busied himself collecting "a nest of Indian books" for Thoreau, a token of their deep friendship. Keep an eye out for them; meanwhile, Cholmondeley added, should he survive the war, he was going to buy a Waldenesque cottage on the south coast of England and lure Thoreau away to join him there, where a room would always be his for the asking.[52]

-➤-➤-◄-◄-

Thoreau told Ricketson he needed to rest, but in truth, he was waking up: "I am planning to get seriously to work after these long months of inefficiency and idleness."[53] He watched the workers at Sleepy Hollow dig out the pond he had leveled for that summer; on the ridge overlooking it was the new Emerson family plot, "rudely staked on the pine-grove mound." Alcott, seeing it, had decided on the spot that he, too, must be buried there, in calm repose near his benefactor and friend.[54] All around the pine needles fell, laying a new mold for future soil. "How much beauty in decay!" Thoreau marveled, holding an oak leaf up to the light. Surely the leaves were not dead, only ripe. He brought a few home, birch and maple; laid them on white paper; and passed them around the supper table, where everyone admired their colors, beautiful beyond anything any artist ever painted. He brought home chestnuts, too, knocking them down by casting a stone into the branches, then shamed himself for his violence to the tree. "Old trees are our parents. . . . If you would learn the secrets of Nature, you must practice more humanity than others."[55] He took to gleaning driftwood from the river, rowing each piece home and recalling its history when he set it on the fire; he built driftwood bookshelves to hold Cholmondeley's books. He filled his pockets with wild apples—in the October wind they tasted spirited and racy, but at home so harsh and crabbed he spat them out; they should be labeled "To be eaten in the wind." His thoughts, too, should be wild apples, food for walkers—not warranted "to be palatable if tasted in the house."[56]

It was a triumph merely to eat, that fall of 1855, and every walk was a celebration: "When the leaves fall, the whole earth is a cemetery to walk in." *Here* were no vain or lying epitaphs. "I buy no lot in the cemetery which my townsmen have just *consecrate* with a poem and an auction, paying so much for a choice. *Here* is room enough for me."[57] As the days shortened and the leaves fell, a new Thoreau emerged: pensive and sadder, slower, deeper. As he fought to regain strength, fighting the grave, he turned to the most common activities and the most mundane needs with intentionality and deliberation. *Walden* had been his book of spring and summer. Now, willing his recovery, he was learning a mind of autumn. In these darkening and haunted pages of his Journal, Thoreau began to trace the outlines of *Walden*'s sequel: he would call it *Wild Fruits*, and it would be his final harvest.

In his deepening sense of worldly poverty, too ill even to write, Thoreau renewed his commitment to getting his living "in a simple, primitive fashion," elevating his life as much as possible. But what worked at Walden proved a challenge on Main Street. What use was it here to raise one's own food, build one's own house, glean one's own firewood, when the people to whom one was yoked "insanely want and will have a thousand other things"? Every child's birthday was a crisis: Thoreau wanted to make them presents, but given their luxurious museums of expensive gifts, it would cost him a year's income "to buy them something which would not be beneath their notice." Yet he delighted in the ingenuity of making do. One day, late in November, he found a solid pine log in the river; he hauled it in, sawed off two stout rounds for wheels, and fitted them to an axle—also reclaimed from the river—to make a cart with which to roll his boat around. Three days later, when the river iced up, he proudly rolled his boat home for the winter. He chuckled, remembering how he'd flummoxed the tax assessor when he was called in for an inventory of his taxable property. Any real estate? No. Stocks or bonds? No. *Any* taxable property? "None that I know of"—except his boat. Well, they thought, perhaps that was taxable as a pleasure carriage. Now that he had it up on wheels, perhaps they were right![58]

Cholmondeley's books arrived that very evening. A month earlier the mail had brought a packing list "half long as my arm," and on the spot Thoreau had started an overwhelmed letter of gratitude to his distant friend, still fighting in the Crimean War. Now here they were! The family made a festive evening of it as Thoreau unwrapped each volume, drew it forth from a growing heap of papers, and handed it around for everyone's admiration, spreading his treasures on the carpet and "wading knee deep in Indian philosophy and poetry":

the *Institutes of Menù*, the Upanishads, the Rig Veda, the Vishnu Purana, and crowning all like Cotapaxi's cone seen against the sun in Church's painting *The Andes of Ecuador*—the Bhagavad Gita! Cholmondeley had sent not just a few books but an entire library, probably the best of its kind in America at that moment: twenty-one works, in English, French, Latin, Greek, and Sanskrit, forty-four volumes in all.[59]

Thoreau placed them lovingly in the driftwood bookcase he had built for them, and when he awoke the next morning, childlike in his joy, he could hardly believe they were real until he "peeped out and saw their bright backs." He read relatively little in them, partly because his interests had moved on to colonial history, exploration, and the literature of Native Americans, but also because he had long since read and reread many of them, absorbing Hindu philosophy and poetry so deeply that *Walden* reads, at times, like a successor in the same tradition. As he wrote to Ricketson, "I am familiar with many of them & know how to prize them"—which included lending them out to his friends. Ricketson himself had little use for such "namby-pamby," so Thoreau, writing on Christmas Day, explained it to him this way: "I send you information of this as I might of the birth of a child."[60]

What mattered most about Cholmondeley's gift, together with the steady friendships of such men as Blake and Brown, the Watsons, Ricketson and Russell, was the affirmation they all gave Thoreau in these months of illness and disappointment. Amid all the reminders that he was leading an anomalous life against the grain of modern society, the fact that he had the respect and admiration of such people helped Thoreau move past his moments of self-doubt. As he wrote to Calvin Greene, a new disciple from Michigan, "I am gratified to hear of the interest you take in my books; it is additional encouragement to write more of them."[61]

Thoreau greeted the winter of 1856 with zest, reveling in the deep snows and notching his walking stick in inches so he could keep track of snow depths wherever he went. After watching a frozen pickerel revive, he took to measuring water temperatures under the ice, and when the great elm at the center of town was cut down, he mourned the loss of this vital link to the past—then measured it and counted the tree rings: 127 years at nine and a half feet. Few of the sidewalk spectators guessing its age wanted to hear his science—"Surely men love darkness rather than light," he sighed—but he went on measuring other fallen trees. He drew pictures of crow and mouse tracks in the snow, and untangled the cryptic stories they told. He collected old birds' nests and, teasing them apart, marveled at the precision with which they were engineered.[62] When Min, a Maltese kitten, joined the household, her wild freaks delighted him and he played with her by the half hour, pausing to shake his head in his Journal: "What sort of philosophers are we, who know nothing of the origin and destiny of cats?"[63] With the same zest, he recorded the voices of men and women, stopping nearly every day at the post office to get the mail and the gossip, talking with anyone with something interesting to say. Only a great talker himself could have generated so much material. Sometimes he reported friction, too. When he started collecting tree sap and boiling it up in the kitchen to make sugar, his father had had enough. What's the use of making sugar, he quarreled, when one could buy it cheaper at the grocer's? "He said it took me from my studies. I said I made it my study; I felt as if I had been to a university."[64]

Thoreau was also looking back, recording family history as if aware he might someday have biographers: a list of all the houses they had lived in, family stories of his childhood in Chelmsford and Concord, the Jones family genealogy. Then, on March 27, 1856, Uncle Charles, the beloved family eccentric, died in the night at age seventy-six. In this winter of deep snows beyond living memory, the snow still lay thick on the ground. It fell to Henry to make burial arrangements, and together with the sexton he located a site in the New Burying Ground where the earth was not frozen. There, the next day, they buried Charles Dunbar. In his Journal Thoreau recorded a brief eulogy: "He was born in February, 1780, the winter of the Great Snow, and he dies in the winter of another great snow,—a life bounded by great snows."[65] As the old-timers traded stories about his uncle—his card tricks and hat tricks, the way he could "burst" any man at wrestling, or run up a twelve-foot ladder and down the other side—Thoreau remarked how many old people died that winter, just as spring was approaching. It seemed to prove the old adage: as the sap begins to flow, "diseases become more violent."[66]

The sap was flowing and the river was running, and it was time to roll his boat back down to the riverbank. As Thoreau eased it into the water, it occurred to him, with some surprise, that despite all, he was still *alive*. Why? "To perform what great deeds? Do we detect the reason why we also did not die on the approach of spring?"[67]

"THE INFINITE EXTENT OF OUR RELATIONS"

The first hint of an answer came on a warm afternoon late in April, when Thoreau was surveying a farm by the Old Marlborough Road. Isn't it interesting, pointed out his assistant, that when a pine wood is cut down, young oaks spring up? Indeed it is, agreed Thoreau; sure enough, where a white pine wood had recently been cut down, "the ground was all covered with young oaks." "*Mem.—*" he jotted: go look at some logged-off woods, and take note of what has sprung up. Two weeks later he had worked out a hypothesis: on the forest floor of even the thickest pine woods, one could observe many little oaks, sprouted from acorns planted by squirrels. They struggled in the deep shade, and most would die, but log off the pines, and *voila!*— the infant oaks, "having got just the start they want," would spring up into an oak forest. Though no one credited the agency of birds and squirrels in spreading seeds, it must be that all the while, they were planting the forests of the future.[68] The fall before, he had seen the earth as a cemetery. Now he saw it as a nursery as well.

The odd fact of pine/oak succession had puzzled Concord farmers for years—indeed, it was just the sort of question they had formed the Concord Farmers' Club to discuss. Every year during the off-season, they held weekly seminars to compare notes, trade ideas, and ask how Concord's gardens and farms could be improved. At every meeting, one of the fifty-odd members would present a formal paper on an assigned topic, which was inevitably followed by a long and spirited discussion. Their minutes recorded (often verbatim) the practical concerns on the minds of Thoreau's friends and neighbors: how to care for pigs and cattle; how to grow corn and hay, apples and peaches, grapes and cranberries; how to plant gardens, manure the land, get crops to market. Also how to educate children so they would stay on the farm instead of leaving for the cities or the West—education, they agreed, was the key—and how to educate themselves so they could incorporate the latest advances in mathematics, chemistry, geology, plant breeding, and agricultural science. In part they wanted to learn how to adapt Concord's colonial-era farms to modern industrial agriculture, but they were also eager to care for the land and make Concord a place of great natural beauty, from its gracious yards, treelined streets, and innovative new garden cemetery to its farms, fields, rivers, meadows, and forests.[69]

On certain questions, they all agreed, the person to ask was Henry Thoreau. Though not a member, he was friends with many who were: their founder and first president, Jacob Farmer; their dedicated secretary, Minot Pratt from Brook Farm; his childhood friends Joseph Hosmer and John S. Keyes; the town printer and librarian, Albert Stacy; Ephraim Bull, who developed the Concord grape out of the sweet wild grapes Thoreau gathered every fall; Ebenezer Hubbard, who owned the fine pine-oak woods near Walden Pond. While these men kept the town's *live*stock, it became Thoreau's job, as he had punned in *Walden*, to keep the town's "*wild* stock." Emerson noticed that local farmers who once remarked on Thoreau as an oddity came to admire his deep knowledge of their land.[70] When the Concord Farmers' Club wanted to know where to find native wildflowers to grace Concord's gardens or native trees to shade its yards and streets, they asked Thoreau. In the late 1850s, as their attention turned to healing Concord's damaged forests, Thoreau showed them the way.

Thoreau's quick solution to the puzzle of pine-oak succession only opened more questions. Right away, one longtime farmer asked: How do you know that the seeds haven't been there all along, lying dormant? Others argued that one didn't need seeds at all; the new plants were generated spontaneously, right out of the ground.[71] Thoreau felt that had to be false, but proving it meant figuring out exactly where the seeds had come from, and how they had been carried, or "dispersed"—by squirrels? Birds? Wind, or water? Humans and other animals? How had they had been planted—or had they planted themselves? How had they managed to survive, if in fact they had survived at all? As answers multiplied, they cascaded into more questions. Thoreau's new studies took him deeper and deeper into the field. Emerson noticed that Thoreau read "less in books lately, & more in nature."[72] With good reason: books held no answers for the questions he had started to ask. There wasn't even a name for this new kind of science. Later generations would call it "plant succession" and honor Thoreau as a pioneer working in the fields of forest management and plant ecology.[73]

→>⋅<⋅←

Spring of 1856 settled into a hot summer—of course, summers in Concord were always hot, but this was hot with a difference, terrifically wet and damp. It made for a bumper crop of berries and a panoply of wild mushrooms, whose fabulous colors and bizarre shapes fascinated Thoreau—even the disgusting stinkhorn, shaped like "a perfect phallus" and smelling so strongly like a dead rat that when he brought one home, the household howled in protest and Thoreau couldn't sleep until the attic had been aired out. What on earth was Nature thinking? "She almost puts herself on a level with those who draw in privies." Despite the heat, he worked at his studies like a man obsessed. "I am drawing a rather long bow," he wrote Calvin Greene; "I pray that the archer may receive new strength before the arrow is shot." "When the arrow has flown, please post me," Greene replied gracefully.[74] He put off Greene's invitation to Michigan, and Blake's request for a lecture, and Greeley's plan for a job—after giving it some thought; Greeley wanted Thoreau to move in with his family on their New York farm for a year or so, to tutor their two young children. Too young, Thoreau finally decided, and the Greeleys amiably agreed to call it off. "It is not that we love to be alone," Thoreau wrote to Blake, "but that we love to soar." Very few could follow him to the heights he craved.[75]

Emerson was one of those few. Channing had left Concord to join Ellen in Dorchester, hoping to reconcile, and in his absence the two old friends attempted a thaw. It was bumpy. Emerson grumbled that Thoreau would drop in, deliver his thought "in lump," and stalk out again, while Thoreau feared to open his mouth lest he make the "long tragedy" of their friendship even worse.[76] But by May 1856 they were walking together as in old times. Emerson chuckled that Thoreau kept account of the plants "as a banker when his notes fall due," but when Thoreau boasted he could tell by the flowers what day of the month it was, Emerson was dazzled; this was truly telling time by the sundial. And when Henry went off soaring, Emerson glowed with pleasure. One day he warned Thoreau against finding a long-sought bird, "lest life should have nothing more to show him. He said, 'What you seek in vain for half your life, one day you come full upon all the family at dinner.—You seek him like a dream, and as soon as you find him, you become his prey.'" In his journal Emerson fondly sketched his friend: "There came Henry with music-book under his arm, to press flowers in; with telescope in his pocket, to see the birds, & microscope to count stamens; with a diary, jackknife, & twine, in stout shoes, & strong grey trowsers, ready to brave the shrub oaks & smilax, & to climb the tree for a hawk's nest. His strong legs when he wades were no insignificant part of his armour."[77]

The iconic photograph of Thoreau dates from this summer. Henry, Sophia, and the Aunts Thoreau were visiting family in Worcester; on their last day, June 18, Harry Blake and Theo Brown induced Henry to sit before a photographer, something he'd always resisted. At Benjamin D. Maxham's studio on 16 Harrington Street, for sixteen cents apiece, Thoreau had three daguerreotypes taken. He promptly gave one to Blake and one to Brown, and sent one to Greene, who had written fervently from Michigan that he longed to see the author of *Walden*. "I am not worth seeing personally—the stuttering, blundering, clod-hopper that I am," Thoreau replied, but he went along with his friends' desire for a memento, facing the camera with calm directness and the merest hint of amusement. Most sitters selected their finest clothes, straightened their collars, combed their hair neatly. Not he: hair rumpled and wild, bowtie slightly askew, Galway whiskers a-scraggle, Thoreau presented himself to the camera as he was, take it or leave it. Sophia hated the image, preferring Rowse's gentle and dreamy poet. Alcott disliked it, detecting Thoreau's illness lingering in the shadows. Thoreau mailed it to Greene with a rueful blessing: "My friends think [it] is pretty good—though better looking than I."[78] But Horace Hosmer loved it: "That Photo shows Thoreau at meridian. . . . He looked like this when he removed his hat and showed me the climbing fern in it, making a real crown or chaplet for its discoverer. I never saw him look so happy and human, as he did that day."[79]

The social season continued: even as Thoreau was sitting in Worcester for his portrait, Ricketson was sitting in Concord awaiting his return. Having set off on a whim, Ricketson was disappointed to find his friend away, but instead of returning home, he took tea with Henry's parents, listening patiently as Cynthia gave him a long and loving account of her son's many virtues. He befriended Henry's quiet father as well, walking with him to the cemetery the next morning. "A fine specimen of the gentleman of the old school," Ricketson said of him; "a character of honesty illumines his countenance. Few men have impressed me so favorably." Once Henry returned home that afternoon, Ricketson finally had his friend all to himself, and they went off boating together. For four more days he lingered in Concord, walking and talking, rowing and sailing, meeting other Concord luminaries, including Emerson, whom Ricketson, a professed collector of characters, found kind and intelligent but not "warm-hearted" and, though "a blessing to the age," a little limited in power.[80]

Thoreau then accompanied Ricketson back to Brooklawn to continue their rambles. On Naushon Island they explored the deep forest of grand old trees long protected from the axe—great beeches, large and spreading oaks, tupelos three feet in diameter—and startled two deer, creatures long since hunted out of Concord.[81] They visited old Martha Simonds, the last "pure-blooded" Indian in New Bedford, at her hut on the tiny scrap of Indian land that remained hers. "She had half an acre of the real tawny Indian face," wrote Thoreau, but he found her vacant and listless, answering his questions in monosyllables. Though born on that spot, she knew not a word of her native language and nothing of her race, having gone out to whites as a servant early in childhood. But she lit up when Thoreau asked what she called a certain plant: "That's husk-root. It's good to put into bitters for a weak stomach." Ah, if only he'd had a hat full of plants. To cap it off, "a conceited old Quaker minister, her neighbor, told me with a sanctified air, 'I think that the Indians were human beings; dost thee not think so?'"[82]

After a week, Ellery Channing dropped in, anxious to see Thoreau. The two camped out in the Shanty that night, and early next morning Ricketson drove Thoreau to the train station while Channing walked back to town. It was not a chance visit and could not have been pleasant. The previous fall, Ellen had infuriated her family by reconciling with Ellery, and for a while they got on well enough. Just after Christmas, Ellery, resolving to turn over a new leaf, asked Ricketson for help setting them up in New Bedford. Ricketson must have put a word in, for Ellery landed a job as assistant editor for the New Bedford *Mercury*, but then he started avoiding his family, working long hours on weekdays and hanging out at Ricketson's all weekend. Bewildered, Ricketson wrote Thoreau for help: Channing was clearly miserable, but he would reveal nothing of his private life. Was there something . . . wrong with him? Could he be trusted? Thoreau hastened to reassure him: Channing is exactly what you see, both good and bad. He had long been a problem for his Concord friends, and now—oh dear—he was Ricketson's problem, too; "perhaps it is left for you to solve it." Daniel and Louisa Ricketson did what they could for Ellery and, behind his back, for Ellen.[83] But by mid-May, Daniel was losing patience and feeling "oppressed" by Ellery's "black mood." When Daniel dropped in unannounced on the Thoreaus a month later, it was partly to inquire about Channing. The blunt-speaking Cynthia gave Daniel a "long and particular" account, and once Henry returned, they, too, took up the Channing Problem.[84]

When Channing himself materialized that afternoon to shut himself up with Thoreau for the night, their conversation must have been grim. Thoreau, caught in the middle, had tried for years to distance himself from the "problem" of Channing, who in his "obtuseness" had made any emotional closeness impossible.[85] But that night he had to listen when Channing told him, as he must surely have done, that Ellen had just given birth to their fifth child, whom they named Henry (later changed to Edward), and that, weakened by childbirth and ill with consumption, she was not expected to live. Three months later, on September 22, Ellen Fuller Channing died. Arthur and Richard Fuller buried their sister and distributed the five children among various Fullers, while Ellery stayed away in New Bedford, boarding alone, working at the *Mercury*, and walking to the Shanty on weekends to sit by the fire and smoke. For hours, Ricketson would sit at his table by the window, writing in his journal, ignoring the guest he could not bear to turn away.[86]

→-→-◄-

Back home in Concord, Thoreau watched the "dog days" of mid-summer come in, writing in his own Journal every morning and panting in the hot afternoons through sproutlands and copses as the mercury climbed to 98 in the shade. It was so damp that his pressed flowers all mildewed and the family washing wouldn't dry, but he loved the moist hot air and drew it deep into his lungs like a vapor bath. The berries were so thick they blackened the hillsides, "five or six species deep"; on August 4 he led the annual berry party to Conantum, where they picked blackberries big as thumbs and huckleberries big as bullets.[87] Storms broke on August 8, and that day, just as Henry was about to rise from the dinner table to inspect the flooding river, a servant burst through the door and exclaimed (in the words of a witness), "Faith! th' pig's out o' th' pin, an' th' way he's tearin' roun' Jege Hoore's fluer-bids es enuf ter scare er budy." While Henry, John, and Michael Flannery ran to pursue the marauder, the ladies "flew to the windows to see the fray." Afterward Thoreau wrote up "The Capture of the Pig" as a shaggy-dog comedy worthy of Mark Twain.[88]

As his energy returned, Thoreau grew restless. He wanted to see September, and he decided that a look at the Connecticut River would help him see September on the Concord. On September 5, he took the cars to Brattleboro, Vermont, shouldering his valise and walking the tracks from Fitchburg to Westminster rather than waiting for the next train. The Connecticut was disappointing, narrow and shallow even at high water—"The Concord is worth a hundred of it for my purposes," he sniffed—but the botanizing was grand and the welcome warm. For four days he tramped the mountains, woods and fields with Rev. Addison Brown, who ran a local girls' school; his wife Ann, who had a flair for botany and astronomy; their daughters Frances and Mary; and their botanist friend Charles Christopher Frost, who made shoes.[89] The Brown girls led Thoreau up the local mountain, which Frances called by the indigenous name, Wantastiquet; Mary recalled how their guest, who seemed to know everything, kept asking her all sorts of questions she couldn't answer—as if a fourteen-year-old girl could know more than he did! The following March, Thoreau sent her a sample of the climbing fern and a letter explaining how it grew, adding gracefully, "The Climbing Fern would have been a pretty name for some delicate Indian maiden."[90] It was the first of three letters he would send her, all of which she said were among her most cherished possessions.

His next stop was Walpole, New Hampshire, to spend a day with Bronson Alcott. To get there he took the railroad north to Bellows Falls and walked south over Falls Mountain, slipping and sliding all the way down on his smooth-soled leather shoes, swimming in the Connecticut to wash up, then hitching the last mile into Walpole with a lumberer who said he'd helped get four million logs out of Bellows Falls, including some of the very masts Thoreau had seen carried through Concord on the railroad. The visit did Alcott good. It had been over a year since the family had moved to Walpole, and the people, he felt, were still strangers. After a morning talking politics—"Frémont, Garrison, Emerson, and the rest"—and an afternoon's walk to view the Connecticut Valley, Alcott penned in his journal: "Seldom has a scholar's study circumscribed so much of the Cosmos as that of this footed intelligence of ours."[91] In his own Journal Thoreau happily listed all the new plants he had gathered, and congratulated himself: the Concord River was in every way richer and more various than the Connecticut, "the most fertile in every sense." The real advantage of circumscribing the Cosmos was how clearly it enabled him to see home.

After his long illness, Thoreau felt anxious to write and pressed for time, but instead his perennial need for income took him away from Concord for a hard month of surveying in New Jersey. Alcott had set it up: after their day together in Walpole, he had walked off to New York City, stopping at the Eagleswood Colony on Raritan Bay, east of Perth Amboy, to scout a possible new home for his family. The colony was the brainchild of Marcus and Rebecca Spring, liberal Quakers and ardent social reformers. In 1846, they had brought Margaret Fuller along on their European grand tour, whence Fuller had ventured off to become an Italian Revolutionary. In 1852, the Springs had tried to help the future along by founding their own utopian community, the Raritan Bay Union, modeled on Brook Farm. But it was a financial failure. By the time Alcott arrived, they were subdividing the land into estates to sell to New York City commuters who would be drawn, they hoped, to life in a planned community rich with cultural amenities.[92] When they mentioned they needed a surveyor, Alcott suggested Thoreau, who not only needed the work but could bring along some culture, too. So on October 24, 1856, Henry Thoreau packed up all his available lectures plus compass and tripod and set off for New Jersey.

"This is a queer place," Thoreau wrote home; it consisted of a huge stone phalanstery, the Springs' residence (where he stayed), a few shops, an office, and the school. He had arrived on a Saturday afternoon, riding in with Elizabeth Peabody, just in time for the regular Saturday evening dance, which *everyone*, even he, was expected to attend—"They take it for granted that you want *society*!" Sunday morning was Quaker meeting, and when someone warned him they all expected him to be moved by the spirit, he prepared a few words, "just enough to set them a little by the ear & make it lively." That night he read "Moosehunting" to the collective—composed mostly, he discovered, of children—and on Monday morning he set to work. And hard work it was: two hundred acres, "through woods ravines marshes & along the shore, dodging the tide—through cat briar mud and beggar ticks—having no time to look up or think where I am." And as he worked, the job got bigger: the Springs decided he should set out an orchard and vineyards as well, and some of the new owners asked him to survey their plots.[93]

"I am sold for the time,—am merely Thoreau the surveyor here," he wrote wearily to Blake. But it wasn't all work. On Saturday, November first, Alcott arrived from New York to ask some tough questions about the struggling community's future and whether his family might find a place in it. After spending the evening with Thoreau and the morning leading a Conversation on "Liberty and Responsibility," Alcott listened approvingly that night as Thoreau read "Walking," which he thought the children particularly enjoyed.[94] Alcott was full of plans: next Saturday he brought Thoreau out to see Greeley's Westchester farm, the same farm where Greeley had hoped Thoreau would live for a year or two. What Thoreau thought is not recorded, but Alcott thought the whole affair—acres and ditches, barn and crops, man, wife, and children—a disaster in the making. After a night in the city, they crossed on the Brooklyn Ferry to hear Henry Ward Beecher's Sunday sermon. The church was jammed to the rafters, and Alcott was awed with the sheer spectacle of it, the congregation weeping and laughing and devout under the great evangelical's powerful magnetism. Thoreau "called it pagan, and was restive under it."[95]

Then they dropped in on Walt Whitman. The poet was out, but his mother was in, and she fed them with cakes hot from the oven and loving praise for her son, so good and wise, always for the weak against the strong. Her son would be home the next morning, she assured them—after all, he had nothing to do in life but "eat, drink, write, and sleep"—and he would be glad to see them. Alcott was eager to introduce Thoreau to Whitman; he had visited the strange new poet a few weeks before, and found him full of "brute power," genius, and audacity. Emerson already knew all this, but especially the audacity. The year before, when Whitman published *Leaves of Grass*, he had mailed a copy straight to Emerson, who, seeing yet again a brilliant new poet to mentor, had written him one of his thrilling trademark letters of support. The buoyed Whitman seized on the letter's most quotable line and, to Emerson's horror, blazoned it right across the spine of his next edition: "I greet you at the beginning of a great career." In one stroke Whitman had given birth to the modern cover blurb, quite without Emerson's permission.

Now at last it was Thoreau's turn. Thoreau was deeply interested in Whitman, but still unsure what to make of him. Their meeting did not go particularly well. Alcott brought along Sarah Tyndale—"a solid walrus of a woman," he called her, "the kindliest piece of cumbrous candour and common sense." It is unclear whether her candor eased the conversation. Whitman met them at the door and escorted them up two flights of stairs to the attic, where the chamberpot stood visible and the unmade bed still showed the imprint of his body and that of his "feeble brother," with whom he shared the room. After some small talk, they removed to the parlor downstairs, where Alcott contrived to set Thoreau and Whitman into direct communication. But the great men sat eyeing each other "like two beasts, each wondering what the other would do, whether to snap or run." Thoreau feared he got off to a bad start by retorting to Whitman, who declared he represented America, "that I did not think much of America or of politics & so on—which may have been somewhat of a damper to him." Then someone raised the issue of the Emerson letter, which put Whitman on the defensive. It was "a simple thing," he apologized weakly, suggesting the blame rested partly on Emerson. After two hours, Alcott ended the interview, leaving Mrs. Tyndale "to have him all to herself."[96] A week later, Thoreau told Blake he was "still in a quandary," still not sure what to make of Whitman—a man so coarse and rough yet so gentle and sweet, who loved "to ride up and down Broadway all day," sitting beside the omnibus driver and declaiming Homer at the top of his lungs.[97]

Before he left, Whitman gave Thoreau a copy of the 1856 second edition of *Leaves of Grass*—the one with Emerson's greeting on the spine—and as soon as he was back in Concord, Thoreau read it through with deep attention. He liked what he saw. "It has done me more good than any reading for a long time," he wrote Blake; he especially liked "The Sundown Poem" (soon retitled "Crossing Brooklyn Ferry") and "Song of Myself." As for Whitman's brag, Thoreau declared he had a right to it—a tip of the hat from one chanticleer to another. And as for Whitman's notorious eroticism, Thoreau wrote simply, "It is as if the beasts spoke," a complex comment from one who had studied the beasts with such closeness and empathy that some said the same of himself. Thoreau wished, he finally decided, not that Whitman had not written such profanity, "as that men & women were so pure that they could read it without harm."[98] To make his point, Thoreau carried his new copy of *Leaves of Grass* around Concord "like a red flag, defiantly," as Emerson later told Whitman. As for Whitman, late in life he praised Thoreau's "lawlessness—his dissent—his going his own absolute road let hell blaze all it chooses." Emerson's eulogy asserted that three people had profoundly impressed Thoreau, and one of them, he told Sanborn, was Whitman—whose name he later withheld from the eulogy, at Sophia's request.[99]

Two weeks after his sit-down with Whitman, Thoreau finally finished his labors at Eagleswood. On his last Sunday there, he read one more lecture, "What Shall It Profit?", "unexpectedly with some success." This seemed to be a lecture only eccentrics could appreciate. Blake, who had missed Thoreau on the way down, urged him to stop at Worcester on his return and give another lecture, but the exhausted Thoreau literally couldn't wait to get home. On Monday, November 24, he washed the red New Jersey clay off his hands, packed up his surveying equipment, and headed north. When the train deposited him in Worcester at 3:30 a.m. with several hours to kill before the connection to Concord, he wandered Main Street in a daze of fatigue, alarming the night watchman as he cruised past Theo Brown's tailor shop, halfway tempted to rouse his friends out of bed.[100] Relief washed over him the moment he was back on New England's "sandy, wholesome land" of scrub oaks, birches, and pines, now "all in their russet dress." As he walked in the door, he laughed to see how in a month, Min the cat had suddenly turned all grown up and stately, cheeks "puffed out like a regular grimalkin" with thick new winter fur.[101]

He, too, must get ready for the winter. Merely carting his boat home through the snow was enough to make him break out into a sweat. Time for some real work! Thoreau turned some of his New Jersey profits into a new pair of cowhide boots, waterproofed against all slush and snow, and that night he gazed at them happily, "dreaming of far woods and woodpaths, of frost-bound or sloshy roads."[102] After the stifling air of Eagleswood, everything his eyes touched turned to gold. "How I love the simple, reserved countrymen, my neighbors, who mind their own business and let me alone!" he gushed; "Friends! Society! It seems to me I have an abundance of it, there is so much that I rejoice and sympathize with." Everything, he told a friend, is "made for happiness": "Wood, earth, mould, etc., exist for joy. Do you think that Concord River would have continued to flow these millions of years by Clamshell Hill and round Hunt's Island, if it had not been happy?" And here, to top it off, was "that grand old poem called Winter" come round again. "I have never got over my surprise that I should have been born into the most estimable place in all the world, and in the very nick of time, too."[103]

→>⋅<⋅

Through the winter of 1856–57, Thoreau stayed strong enough to lecture, but not too much: he was grateful that lecture invitations were so few. "I cannot afford to be telling my experience, especially to those who perhaps will take no interest in it. I wish to be getting experience."[104] Now that he was writing again, new material was accumulating fast, but the old lectures would serve for another year. On December 18—"a snapper" of a day, said the newspaper, with the mercury at 20 below—he hired a horse and sleigh to deliver "Walking" in Amherst, New Hampshire. For the last eleven miles, he warmed one hand against his body while the other held the reins, until it went numb with the cold and he switched. He spoke in the basement of the Amherst Congregational Church, which perhaps, he joked, he'd helped to undermine. No one spoke to him afterward, but they listened, and anymore that was all he expected. He spent the night at a desolate country tavern, where the noise from a dance kept him awake and the staff disgusted him by blowing their noses with their fingers and wiping them on their boots. Deep in the night the ground cracked and startled him awake. It shook the house "like the explosion of a powder-mill" and split the road open a quarter-inch. On the way home the next morning, he paused to walk on the frozen Merrimack River, and that afternoon he walked to Walden Pond. Sure enough, it froze over in the night, with ice so clear he felt he was walking on water.[105]

Six weeks later, on February 3, 1857, he delivered "Walking" again, at the Fitchburg Athenaeum. Given that his topic was walking, he was bemused to observe that no one did: the snow crust was unbroken for miles around, showing not one of the town's thousands had even once stepped off its narrow and crowded streets. Their minds, he feared, were just as circumscribed as their feet, and sure enough, his audience stared up at him, there at the podium going through the motions, "as if they were the antics of a rope-dancer or mountebank pretending to walk on air" or playing kittly-benders on thin ice. But one, at least, cheered him on: "This lecture contains more genuine wit, wisdom, and poetry, than can be found in whole courses of Lyceum lectures," declared the local newspaper.[106] The author was almost certainly none other than the devoted Blake, who in his fit of enthusiasm invited Thoreau to repeat the performance in Worcester. Thoreau did, giving "Walking" one more time, on February 13 at Worcester's fine newly renovated Brinley Hall, thus keeping the promise he made to Blake in November when he hastened through Worcester too tired to stop.

The extreme cold was this winter's grand feature, breaking all records. The ground was cracking all over New England—because, reasoned Thoreau, there was too little snow to insulate it. On Christmas Day he pushed the snow aside under Lee's Cliff and got some fresh green catnip for Min.[107] Around New Year's Day he surveyed Lee's Farm on Nawshawtuct Hill, the same farm staked out in 1635 by Simon Willard for his trading post at the junction of Concord's three rivers. How old do you think this house is? asked the new owner. Thoreau rummaged around in Shattuck's *History of Concord* and guessed it was the oldest house in Concord, dating back to the 1650s. Only weeks later it burned down in the night, leaving nothing standing but the chimneys. Thoreau laid a board across the embers and examined the ancient chimney, copying out the inscription in the crumbling old mortar: "Concord Made—October 1650." Given that the mortar had been laid over bricks already blackened with soot, the house must have been older still. He brought a brick home as a keepsake.[108]

As winter deepened and the cold intensified, Thoreau realized that here in Concord, too, no one but himself was abroad in the woods and fields. Nothing, he realized, marked so strongly the difference between himself and everyone else he knew. He tried to put into words why he felt impelled each day to enter the cold heart of winter: it was like coming home to the homesick, or like prayer to the religious, or water to a fish, or opening a window in a suffocating room. "I must have a true *skylight* . . . . It chances that the sociable, the town and country, or the farmers' club does not prove a skylight to me. . . . They bore me." But in the wildness of winter solitude, he met "some grand, serene, immortal, infinitely encouraging, though invisible, companion, and walked with him"—steadying his nerves, recovering his senses. He recalled a recurring dream from his childhood, which he named "Rough and Smooth"—tossing on "a horrible, a fatal surface," then suddenly "lying on a delicious smooth surface, as of a summer sea": "My waking experience *always* has been and is such an alternate Rough and Smooth. In other words it is Insanity and Sanity."[109] It was only in his "sane" state that he could be "a witness with unprejudiced senses to the order of the universe," or address "the problem of existence," the problem winter presented in its starkest terms.

The pith of winter was reached in the depths of January: Boston Harbor froze on the eighteenth. On the nineteenth neither butcher nor milkman could make it to the house. On the twentieth, Eddy Emerson proudly showed Henry his deep and marvelous snow cave: a single lamp lit the interior like reflectors in a lighthouse, but when Eddy shouted at the top of his lungs, he could barely be heard. All the children and Henry took turns crawling inside and trying the experiment, the snow drinking up all the sound. On the twenty-third, Thoreau's ink froze; on the twenty-fourth, the thermometer dropped into the bulb, which made it, he guessed, 26 below. He, too, had dropped into the bulb, solidified and crystallized like ice: "in my solitude I have woven for myself a silken web or chrysalis, and, nymph-like, shall ere long burst forth a more perfect creature, fitted for a higher society. By simplicity, commonly called poverty, my life is concentrated and so becomes organized, or a Κόσμοσ, which before was inorganic and lumpish."[110] Thoreau would be Walt Whitman, inverted: "I, Walt Whitman, a Kosmos, of Manhattan the son," who barreled down the streets of New York bellowing Homer to the crowds, had conjured Thoreau, a Kosmos, of Concord the son, a chrysalis deep in a crystal cave.

→>–<–

He'd reached his limit. First, with Emerson: "And now another friendship is ended," he wrote that same Kosmos day, February 8, 1857. This, he was certain, was the final, ultimate and irrevocable break with his oldest and deepest friend. "I could better have the earth taken away from under my feet, than the thought of you from my mind," he agonized. Day and night he suffered "a physical pain, an aching of the breast which unfits me for my tasks." What had happened? Emerson offers no clue. Just returned from his Midwestern lecture tour, he was harassed for time; Thoreau, at this moment of his deepest spiritual intensity, felt cruelly rebuffed. But then the traveler's cough Emerson brought home worsened into an acute illness. As he lay in bed, ill and feverish, a frantic Thoreau finally understood that Emerson, his deepest spiritual friend, would never change. Thoreau could not live with him, but life without him was unthinkable: "At the instant that I seem to be saying farewell forever to one who has been my friend, I find myself unexpectedly near to him, and it is our very nearness and dearness to each other that gives depth and significance to that forever. Thus I am a helpless prisoner, and these chains I have no skill to break. While I think I have broken one link, I have been forging another."[111] The crisis passed, and soon Thoreau was dining at the Emersons', where he argued cheerfully with Louis Agassiz. By May first, they were again taking long companionable walks together. Thoreau's emotional storm cleared the air between them. Never again did he question his love for Emerson, or Emerson's love for him.[112]

For emotional balance and sanity, Thoreau needed the "skylight" of Nature. But the very image illustrates that he lived in a richly peopled social space, tied to those around him with a network of unbreakable chains. Ironically, just then Cholmondeley sent a shrewd evaluation of his character that verified the insight. Thoreau had written Cholmondeley, fighting in the Crimea, back in October, confessing his run-down health. He received no word back. Finally, in December, Cholmondeley found Thoreau's letter in Rome and, exhilarated to be alive, wrote a magnificent reply, many pages long, brimful with his experiences and impressions of war, people, landscapes, nations, and destinies—including his own and Thoreau's. For himself, he prescribed a dose of Thoreauvian medicine: a cottage in Kent with a few acres and plenty of room for Thoreau to visit. For his friend, he prescribed the opposite: "You are not living altogether as I could wish. You ought to have society. . . . Without this you will be liable to moulder away as you get older. *Forgive my English plainness of speech.*" In words echoing Fuller's from many years before, Cholmondeley told Thoreau that his love for Nature "is ancillary for some affection which you have not yet discovered." Let your retirement be not too lonely, he warned: "Take up every man as you take up a leaf, and look attentively at him." Try writing a history of Massachusetts, or Concord. "It would be a great labor and a grand achievement,—one for which you are singularly qualified."[113]

It was excellent advice, and by the time Thoreau received it— Cholmondeley did not mail his missive until February, after he reached the secure postal services of England—Thoreau had, for all his glacial meditations on solitude, been filling his Journal with canny studies of his friends and neighbors, taking them up quite like leaves. Having made up his mind to like Whitman, he sent off a copy of *Leaves of Grass* to Cholmondeley (along with *Walden* and Emerson's *Poems*), then on April 2 he set off for a nice long fireside vacation at the Ricketsons. Could fish, once frozen, revive? That was what he and Agassiz had been arguing over. Fish remained an open question. What about frogs? On the way to Brooklawn, Thoreau pocketed a frog frozen stiff; no, he concluded. Frogs, once frozen, could not revive.

He, however, could: for two weeks Thoreau, melted into jollity, took his ease among friends. Alcott was staying there, too, and sometimes Channing, who struck Alcott as "saner, & sounder than heretofore," walked down to smoke his pipe. One evening, as Daniel and Ellery were holed up in the Shanty, Louisa Ricketson struck up the lively Scottish air "The Campbells Are Coming" on the piano in the parlor. Their daughter Anna, laughing, called to the Shanty: Come see! Thoreau had burst into dance, pirouetting and taking mad "Indian" leaps over the furniture, delighting the children. When a disapproving Alcott squirmed deeper into the sofa, Thoreau danced his way over to tread on his toes.[114] When Louisa, holding the sheet music for "Tom Bowling"—Henry's favorite song, in memory of John—sat down at the piano and begged him to sing along, he protested, "Oh, I fear if I do I shall take the roof of the house off!" Then he belted out the sea chanty with "spirit and feeling," and Louisa copied out the music and mailed it to Concord. "It has been sung & encored several times," Thoreau thanked her, "& is duly made over to my sister & her piano."[115]

He even waxed romantic: on April 13, Thoreau and Ricketson stopped on a ride around Quinsigamond Pond to take dinner with Kate Brady. Part Irish and part Yankee, Kate had once been a maid in the Ricketson household. She grew up on the farm, riding the horse to plow, fishing, keeping sheep, learning to spin, weave, and sew. She had read *Walden*, and now was keeping school for a living. Kate had big plans, as she confessed to Henry during their long walk together. Despite the jeers of her female friends, she would return, alone, to the abandoned family farm to "'live free'" and make it bloom again. "I never heard a girl or woman express so strong a love for nature," wrote Thoreau, deeply affected. He was forty years old, twice her age, and had long since closed the door on marriage—"All nature is my bride," he reminded himself—but there is a sparkle of glee in his portrait of Kate as one of the "Children of the Golden Age," a strong soul with a love for good books who would make "a true home in nature, a hearth in the fields and woods."[116]

Thoreau returned home ready for more company. The instant he learned he had missed a visit from Blake, he wrote inviting his Worcester friends to return, adding, with a grin, his wickedest pun: "Come one & all. . . . Come & be Concord, as I have been Worcestered."[117] Meanwhile, he was busy planting: his father had bought the plot of land next door, and Henry set out new apple trees, built a new fence, and spaded the garden, amused as their neighbor Riordan's handsome cock followed his every move. At "Texas" he dropped beans in the garden, and he spent three May days in shirtsleeves building a new arbor for Emerson. When Ricketson came for a visit, the Emersons held a family party for him at Emerson's Cliff. That evening at supper, when Ricketson confessed his terror of thunderstorms and divine retribution, Thoreau, to Emerson's delight, insisted that fearing God's judgment was a false theology, while a new pear tree was the real religion: "No ecstasy was ever interrupted," declared Thoreau, "nor its fruit blasted."[118] Next morning, when Ricketson complained, as he so often did, of headache, Thoreau lured him out of the house and cured him with a swim and a boating excursion—for now it was Henry, "suddenly become much stronger than for the last 2 years," cajoling such "notional nervous invalids."[119]

While bounding through forest and field with renewed energy, Thoreau was struck by the leaps that the young pines had taken in just a year. Barren fields had burst overnight into thrifty young forests, little trees stretching to the sky, grown three feet in a single season. Back on Nantucket, he had seen how Captain Gardiner was reforesting even that bleak landscape; now, walking with Emerson, Thoreau proposed to do the same at Walden: one could run a plow over Wyman's field, follow the plow with a planter supplied with pine seed, and reseed that way a whole forest. Everywhere Thoreau saw a season of regeneration. On a walk to Lee's Cliff, he stopped to talk with a farmer's son on his way to graft apples, then, sizing up a small dark cloud low to the northwest, walked on under a serene blue sky to Fairhaven, where the raindrops started to spatter. As the storm broke out of ash-dark clouds, he rushed to Lee's Cliff, and there in the rock cleft, sheltering amid lightning and thunder, Thoreau sang out "Tom Bowling" in the rain.[120]

Two days later he was again surprised by joy, out on a hillside, by a bobolink's song. At first, "one or two notes globe themselves and fall in liquid bubbles from his teeming throat," a vase full of melody. "Oh never advance farther in your art, never let us hear your full strain sir. But away he launches, and the meadow is all bespattered with melody."[121] For three long years, Henry Thoreau had held back his full strain, had advanced no farther in his art. Now, released into the spring of 1857, he was ready to go full-throat, all the way to the end.

CHAPTER TEN

Wild Fruits

(1857–1859)

A State which bore this kind of fruit, and suffered it to drop off as fast
as it ripened, would prepare the way for a still more perfect and glorious State.
HENRY DAVID THOREAU, "CIVIL DISOBEDIENCE"

THE LAST EXCURSIONS TO CAPE COD
AND THE MAINE WOODS

"It is time now to bring our philosophy out of doors." It was June
1857, and as the softening air brought out the earth-song of the crick-
ets, Thoreau longed for a good long walk. When Channing said
he was game, Thoreau cleared his calendar—and when Channing
backed out, he went anyway, setting off on the bright Friday morning of June 12 for the broad, bleak sands of Cape Cod. In Plymouth,
Marston and Mary Watson brought him along on a Sunday sail to
Clark's Island to investigate lobster pots and grackle nests with
Uncle Ned.[1] Monday morning, after a visit with James Spooner at
his farm amid the woods, the Watsons drove Henry to Manomet
and, with a twinge, watched him shoulder his knapsack and head
down the beach alone.[2]

For the next week Thoreau followed the bay shore, turned east to
cross the peninsula to the outer banks, then trekked north to Provincetown—a good eighty miles navigating by map and compass.[3]
By the time he hit the outer banks, the wind and drizzly fog had
soaked him through and plastered his legs with a carapace of sand.
After shivering in a cold "Humane House" for a spell, he walked on

to visit John Newcomb, the Wellfleet Oysterman—until a neighbor told him Newcomb died the previous winter, ninety-five years old. It must have been a strange conversation: Thoreau had just found a dead storm petrel which, with perfect Thoreauvian logic, he tied to his umbrella to measure once he found shelter. "They may have taken me for a crazy man," he admitted. That afternoon he reached the Highland Lighthouse for three delicious days of rambling over the dunes, visiting the new telegraph station, and chatting with the lighthouse keeper, the neighbors, and the carpenters repairing the lighthouse. One of them remarked that the Cape Ann beach had no equal for grandeur. Thoreau took note. Sunday he headed to Provincetown, drinking in the dunes' solitude like medicine, "sweet to me as a flower." After a night in the Pilgrim's House, scratching at bedbugs while listening to feral cats, he boarded the steamer to Boston on June 22 and made it home in time for supper.[4]

It had been a good trip, restful and invigorating. Thoreau took more than fifty pages of notes, almost none of which made it into *Cape Cod.* Though he tinkered with the book's final chapter, for the most part the manuscript had tucked in its corners and declared itself finished. So he let other projects claim his attention; not until spring 1865, nearly three years after his death, would *Cape Cod* be published. Interestingly, his long-alienated Catholic friend Isaac Hecker gave one of its strongest reviews, acknowledging Thoreau's "deep religious feeling" despite his skepticism toward all organized religions: "Had he lived in the fifth century he would have been a father of the desert."[5] Hecker catches something of the strangeness of *Cape Cod, Walden*'s dark twin. Into the one Thoreau confessed all the metaphysical terrors that the other would allay. He never altered the narrative structure given him by chance on his first trip there: the long, tedious approach by stagecoach; the astonishments of the beach, strangely disorienting, populated with anomalous creatures shaped by the rough chaos of the littoral zone; the mordant hilarity of the Wellfleet Oysterman; the earnest labors of the lighthouse keeper, keeping his lamps "trimmed and burning to the last";[6] the searching inquiry into history, until the shifting sands of the Cape and the shifting forces of time nibble at the foundation of all certainties.

Most important of all, Thoreau kept his narrative embedded in his shocking opening, the ghoulish shipwreck of the *St. John* wrenched through the unspeakable pain of Fire Island. He did not dispel the existential darkness of this opening but held it in view, right through the cosmic wreck of humanity in the locked-up "humane house" to the bitterness of "naked Nature" turning the carcasses of men and beasts alike in their beds, tucking fresh sand under them, "inhumanly sincere."[7] *Cape Cod* is a work of late-century naturalism, as dark as anything by Stephen Crane: "The annals of this voracious beach! who could write them, unless it were a shipwrecked sailor?" Like Crane, Thoreau leavened his nightmare with touches of weird beauty, but unlike Crane, he relished it with a visceral joy, making this book of darkness blaze with light. *Cape Cod* was Thoreau's own Highland Lighthouse, beaming from the edge of chaos across "the spring of springs, the waterfall of waterfalls," a beacon to reach all humanity at sea. "A man may stand there," he ended, "and put all America behind him."[8]

Ready for more, on July 11 Thoreau wrote George Thatcher that he was strong again and "bent on making a leisurely and economical excursion" by canoe with perhaps two companions—say, up Moosehead Lake to the Allagash River and beyond to French Canada, some hundreds of miles, a good month's trip. Would his son George, who had grown up on these waters, be willing to come along? When George declined, Thoreau decided to hire an Indian guide instead. He wrote Eben Loomis, too: would he care to join a party of three on a "leisurely" trip? Loomis came to visit, and they boated the Assabet together where, at the outflow from Barrett's sawmill, Thoreau lit the methane fumes belched from the sawdust shoals with a match, and they heard it flash—but no, Loomis could not go, either.[9] Next on his list was Edward Hoar, who long ago had been his partner in setting Walden Woods ablaze, and who had just returned to Concord: Ed's wanderlust had taken him to California to practice law and pan for gold, then to Peru, where he learned of his father's death. Back home to help his family, the prodigal son was proving a thoughtful man and skilled naturalist who respected Thoreau's way of doing things. Years later Hoar recalled what that meant: "To walk long & far; to have wet feet, & go so for hours; to pull a boat all day; to come home late at night after many miles. . . . If you flinched at anything he had no more use for you." Thoreau knew few of his friends were rugged enough to be true "wayfaring" outdoorsmen.[10] Blake, though he longed to go, was not. But the quiet and capable Ed Hoar was.

They set off for Bangor on Monday, July 20, 1857. The cars to Portland were hot and cindery, but Maine was springlike, cool and fresh, and the steamer into Bangor was delayed by fog. By early afternoon they reached the Thatchers' house. The locals warned Thoreau not to hire an Indian guide—insisting they were dirty, obstinate, prone to drunkenness, and hard to understand—but Thoreau "was bent on having an Indian at any rate."[11] So next morning, the cousins drove to Oldtown and ferried over to Indian Island, where they found the village almost deserted. Whoever wasn't off hunting, gathering shellfish, or canoeing the waterways of New England selling baskets had evacuated to other Indian settlements in fear of smallpox, which had broken out in Oldtown. Thatcher and Thoreau walked up to the first person they saw, a sturdy man dressing a deerskin in the yard of his solid two-story frame house amid a garden and fruit trees. It turned out to be Joe Polis, whom Thatcher greeted as an old friend; they'd grown up together, and Polis's brother had been Thatcher's guide the year before. Would Polis like to take them up to the Allagash? "Yes me want to get some moose," he answered, still scraping the deer skin. Thatcher bargained Polis down from $2 to $1.50 a day—Thoreau had a very limited budget—and they shook on it.[12]

They were lucky, reported Thoreau—Polis was known to be "a particularly steady and reliable man."[13] Just how very lucky, time would reveal. Thanks to Polis, what could have been another boy's adventure would be an adult's exploration, a mutual encounter along a vexed cultural frontier. Polis was a tribal leader equally at home in New York and Philadelphia as in the deep woods. He had represented his people before the governments of Maine and the United States and helped secure the Penobscot a permanent place in the white world, whose own leaders had leveraged away nearly all of the Penobscots' immense lands. By treaty they retained possession of Indian Island, one of their ancestral homes. From this small but protected sovereign base, the Penobscot people were fighting to establish their niche in a rapidly modernizing economy: expanding their traditional gardens into market farms, their subsistence hunting into a commercial economy, their crafts and technologies—above all, basketry and birch-bark canoes—into products they themselves marketed across commercial networks extending into the Northeast's urban centers.

Thoreau had some awareness of this, for he habitually struck up conversations with the Penobscot camped along the Concord River or on the riverbanks near Harvard. Ed Hoar knew this, too, for he recalled from childhood how the Penobscot Indians would canoe down the coast from Maine outside the surf, carry their boats around Lowell, and continue up the Concord River, where they would put up their cone-shaped bark shelters and "sell those fragrant baskets they make."[14] But Thoreau did not realize the Penobscot were fighting for cultural sovereignty as well. On this front, too, Polis was a leader, honored by his people as a *meteoulin*, a teacher and shaman. As a guide for white adventurers, Polis was responsible for educating white society about the Penobscot world. Saying yes to Thatcher meant taking Thoreau in hand. Perhaps he could teach this New English villager a thing or two about the Penobscot way of life in their ancestral lands.

→>-<+-

The process began that evening, when Polis and his birch-bark canoe (which he had made himself) arrived at the Bangor train station. Thoreau led him up to the Thatchers', chattering all the way in his eagerness to break the ice. Polis, who was carrying a hundred-pound canoe over his head and who, as Thoreau editorialized, "above all, was an Indian," puffed along, only grunting once or twice. As he would later exclaim to Ed Hoar, Why do you keep asking pointless questions? "May be your way of talking—may be all right—no Indian way."[15] The next morning, Polis studied how to pack his two guests and their mountain of gear into his small canoe. Then they boarded the stage together, lashing the canoe securely on top. Thoreau marveled that Polis himself carried nothing but the clothes he wore, a blanket, an axe, and a gun—all he needed. The stagecoach was crowded, the weather stormy, and all the way to Moosehead Lake, Polis sat stolid and wordless, even when the gibes of one rude passenger made his eyes "glisten a little." The light began to dawn on Thoreau when "a tipsy Canadian" asked Polis, "You smoke?" "Yes." "Wont you lend me your pipe a little while?" "Me *got* no pipe," said Polis with his trademark "far horizon" stare. But you do! thought Thoreau, who that very morning had watched Polis carefully pocket his pipe and a good supply of tobacco.[16]

The raging storm quashed their plans to start that day. Instead they pushed past the crowds to an inn near the shore. Early next morning, they stepped gingerly into the canoe under Polis's watchful eye (lest they tip it or put a foot through the bottom) and launched into the cloudy dawn twilight. As they paddled toward Mount Kineo, Thoreau soaked up the scenery and watched Polis narrowly. I'd like to go to school with you, he ventured, and learn your language. How long would it take? A week, Polis answered: plenty of time. Thoreau started writing down all the names Polis gave them, for ducks, songbirds, loons—and places as well. He was pleased Polis knew the meaning of *Musketaquid*, or *Muskéeticook*, as Polis preferred;[17] it proved that Massachusetts and Maine were two poles of one world, linked by the Indian. Encouraged, Polis pointed to Mount Kineo and related his people's tradition that it was a great moose killed by a mighty hunter—whose name Thoreau ignored, dismissing the tale as Indian superstition, related with longwinded "dumb wonder." This was a serious mistake. Polis had offered one of his people's deepest creation stories, central to their cosmography. While Thoreau could readily see the poetic and symbolic dimensions of, say, the artist of Kouroo, he was utterly deaf to Polis when he spoke in the same mythic register—showing the distance Thoreau had yet to travel in shedding nineteenth-century stereotypes. Unfortunately Thoreau's ridicule was instructive to Polis, who recalibrated accordingly. From then on, Polis offered no more cosmologies, only names and histories. Thoreau never realized what his rudeness cost him.[18]

That afternoon the group camped at the base of Mount Kineo, where Polis showed Thoreau and Hoar how to build a fire in the driving rain with wet wood. While Polis fished, Thoreau and Hoar climbed the mountain, looking down on the buildings and grounds of the Kineo House hotel far below. The mountain was made, Thoreau discovered to his delight, of the same unique hornstone as the arrowheads he was forever pocketing in Concord. There under his feet was the very rock, the source and raw material, of Tahatawan's arrowhead. It was yet another link in the widening network that bound his Walden world to the Penobscot world of Joe Polis—and a hint, had he listened, to the deeper meaning of Polis's Kineo story. That night, as they sat around the campfire looking into the dusky woods, Polis told them of his hay and potato farming, and pressed Hoar, the lawyer, with questions about white property law. He also identified a snake by its call—Thoreau was startled to learn that snakes had calls, but there it was—and sang them to sleep with songs he learned in childhood from Jesuit priests.[19] The pages of the *Jesuit Relations*, which Thoreau had been reading for years, were coming alive.

So was the wood itself. Around midnight, Thoreau awoke to stoke the dying fire and found something that moved him profoundly: the unburned end of a stick of firewood was glowing not hot with flame, but cold and brilliant white. Years later Hoar remembered how Thoreau shook him awake to show him the cold white coals of wild wood burning in his palm, lighting up his hands like fire. This was *Artoosoqu'*, explained Polis, and his people had seen fires like this passing by as high as the trees, making a noise. This time Thoreau was prepared to believe him. Polis's people had been abroad in nature at all times, in all seasons, and "Nature must have made a thousand revelations to them which she still keeps secret to us."[20] Here he wanted not science, but sheer wonder—suddenly the woods were "not an empty chamber, in which chemistry was left to work alone but an inhabited house,—and for a few moments I enjoyed fellowship with them."[21]

Now Polis had his full attention. Early the next morning, as they paddled to reach the Northeast Carry before the wind rose, Thoreau questioned him hard: How do you find your way in the woods? The more he asked, the vaguer Polis's replies became. To Polis, the real puzzle was how Thoreau, or any white man, could *fail* to know such things. Pathfinding in the deep woods was simply too obvious to put into words. As a guide, Polis knew how easily white men got themselves turned around and hopelessly lost, and every time, laughing, he would lead them straight back to camp. But how do you *do* that? pressed Thoreau. "Oh I can't tell *you*—Great difference between me & white man."[22]

At the Penobscot River end of the Northeast Carry, they found a group of St. Francis River Abenaki camped where Thoreau had lain awake four years before, listening as another group regaled one another with stories of which he had understood not a word. Canoes, though, he did understand, and since they were building one, he stopped for another lesson, sorry to think the art of making birch-bark canoes would someday be lost. At least he could record it, perhaps learn enough to build one himself. That night they camped early to beat another storm, cursing the mosquitoes hatching in the wet woods. The next day Thoreau was anxious to move on. Not so fast, objected Polis: How can you not honor the Sabbath?[23] They compromised, perhaps encouraged by the mosquitoes, on a short day's work, paddling to a nearby camp on the river junction above.

Polis knew the place well—just how well, Thoreau began to realize when he saw Polis's blaze on a tree, a bear paddling a canoe, with his name, "Niasoseb Polis / We alone Joseph Polis," and the dates he had been there. As Polis added a new date, July 26, 1857, Thoreau realized "this was one of his homes"—in fact, every square rod of this alleged wilderness was his home. The lessons continued: Polis showed them how to tell black spruce from white and how to dig up spruce roots, strip their bark, and split them into a tough, flexible string for lashing canoes together. He made it look easy, but Thoreau found it impossible to imitate. When Polis showed them how to make a different herbal tea for every day of the week, using plants within easy reach, Thoreau's head began to spin. Tell me all you know, he begged, and I'll tell you all I know.[24] Polis agreed: the teaching would continue.

As the Concord men learned the next day, it wouldn't be quite that easy. Reaching the Allagash Lakes meant crossing Mud Pond Carry, then canoeing to Chamberlain Lake. Mud Pond was the wettest carry in Maine, and that summer was the wettest in years. The Concord men took a deep breath as Polis gave them careful instructions before setting off with the canoe. They gathered up their own loads—Thoreau calculated his pack weighed sixty pounds, while Hoar divided his to make two trips—and set off in Polis's footsteps. But they could not make out Polis's tracks on the mossy forest floor. After two miles, Thoreau knew they were lost, but a sign ahead pointed to Chamberlain Lake. How hard could it be? They pushed on. Soon they were sinking into mud up to their knees. Thoreau dropped his pack onto a tussock and waited while Hoar backtracked for his second load. After a very long time, Hoar returned with his load and a very surprised Polis, who could not comprehend how they could possibly had gotten themselves onto the tote road to Chamberlain Lake—twice the distance—instead of the carry path to Mud Pond, which his own footsteps had made perfectly obvious. He "evidently thought little of our woodcraft," observed Thoreau in chagrin. But it was too far to turn back. On they went, while Polis returned to move the canoe and the rest of the gear on up to Chamberlain Lake.[25]

It got worse. Thoreau and Hoar slogged themselves into a second swamp, this one clotted on all sides by dead and fallen trees high as their heads—trees killed when Chamberlain Lake had been dammed a few years before, reversing the flow of the Allagash to carry commercial log traffic south to Bangor. The two men scrambled miserably from pool to pool, over tree after tree, as the sun sank behind them. To make it still worse, Hoar's boots (which, unlike Thoreau's thinner shoes, held in the water) had rubbed his feet raw. Every step was torture, and Hoar was reaching the outermost limit of physical exhaustion. Darkness was falling and they were growing desperate until, once again, Polis reappeared and led them to the lakeshore. Too exhausted to pitch their tent, they ate a late supper and stretched out on the stones for the night. As they stared up at the night sky, Polis named the stars for Thoreau, and a loon called from far over the lake: the very voice of the wilderness, thought Thoreau. Brutal as the day had been, he "would not have missed that walk for a good deal."[26]

They began the next day by washing up in the lake before paddling across to the outlet of the Allagash River. Polis, paddling at the stern, had to prod poor Hoar, who kept threatening to tip the canoe by falling asleep. They portaged over a pair of dams to Eagle Lake, part of the Allagash itself, and landed on Heron Island. There they munched an early dinner while they weighed their options. Originally Thoreau had planned to continue north from this point, on into French Canada and back by way of the St. John River. This was perfectly feasible, said Polis, as he pointed to the various camps they would use; he knew the way well. And it was easier than going around on the rugged Penobscot, which was full of dangerous rapids. But which way was *wilder*? asked Thoreau. The Penobscot, replied Polis: the Canadian route took them through well-settled country. In this land, *north* did not mean "wild." That settled it: Heron Island, almost 110 miles from Bangor, marked their northernmost point. From there they turned south and east, following the "lumberer's road" that every spring carried Maine's trees downriver to Bangor's sawmills. It was faster, too. That meant there would be time for a side trip to the summit of Mount Katahdin, which beckoned in the distance.

By then the clouds had rolled in again, and for the rest of the day they hurried between thunderstorms, relieved to reach Chamberlain Farm by nightfall. Thoreau ran up to the main house to buy supplies, then Polis ran up for a visit—it was bad form, he explained, to pass a house without stopping to exchange the news. Thoreau and Hoar waved him off with a laugh. They wanted wilderness, not gossip at every cabin along the way. While Polis sat visiting, the weary Concord adventurers snugged into their tent, lulled by the rain into deep sleep.

Thoreau would need it, for the next day brought his severest test. They skipped breakfast to cross Chamberlain Lake in the early morning, coasting along while Polis scoped out the hillsides with an eye to purchasing a few hundred acres—commercial success meant that the dispossessed Polis could buy back some of the Penobscots' former lands.[27] Their route led them through Telos Lake, the original head of the Allagash–St. John watershed, and down the artificial canal to Webster Lake, the head of the Penobscot watershed. When the northbound drainage had been reversed, it released rushing waters that carved this connecting canal into a fast, rocky waterway, "somewhat like navigating a thunder-spout"—far too dangerous, judged Polis, for his inexperienced clients. So while Polis ran the birch-bark canoe down the rapids, his clients portaged the baggage and rejoined Polis at Webster Lake. During an exhilarating coast down the lake's smooth-slanting water, Polis reminisced about stopping by Daniel Webster's home in Boston to pay his respects. The great lawyer kept Polis waiting so long that he gave up and left. Being patient, Polis returned the next day, and was again ignored. Seeing Webster walking back and forth past the open door, still ignoring him, Polis approached. "What do you want?" challenged Webster, raising a hand as if to strike. The architect of Manifest Destiny was not open to diplomacy, let alone common courtesy. Polis left disgusted. No Indian would have been so rude.[28]

The trouble started at the next rapids. The water was high and violent, and again Polis asked the white men to lighten the canoe and walk alongside, keeping him in sight to make sure he was all right. Some ways down, as Thoreau paused to help Polis lift the canoe over a rock, Ed Hoar quite unaccountably disappeared. The last Thoreau had seen him, he was rounding a precipice, picking his way down toward shore. Thoreau knew his friend was very nearsighted, and that his mangled feet disabled him from walking far—that Hoar was, in fact, struggling badly. One more carry, he had confessed to Thoreau, and "we should see a dead man." "It was as if he had sunk into the earth," wrote Thoreau, who bolted along the precipice looking for him, then in mounting panic coursed back and forth at the base, fearing to find Ed's broken body in the rocks.[29]

Polis, meanwhile, was searching down the river, but by the time he returned to tell Thoreau he found Hoar's tracks, Thoreau was in a full-blown anxiety attack: What if Hoar were not found? How could he face Ed's family if he returned without him—the same family that had smoothed over the damage when Henry and Ed set fire to the woods? Polis struggled to calm the hyperventilating Thoreau, who tried to listen. The sun was setting, and they could not possibly continue down the rapids in the dark. Hoar had surely found his way downriver, and nothing in these woods offered him the slightest danger. A night alone would hardly kill him. But all night Henry tossed and turned, hearing Ed's voice calling him, and he darkly distrusted Polis. Perhaps the Indian had deceived him; perhaps he'd only pretended to find Ed's tracks, in order to placate Thoreau and excuse his own Indian laziness. In short, Thoreau was a wreck and he knew it, but he couldn't control his emotions.

The awful night was barely over when Thoreau shook Polis awake, insisting they leave before breakfast. Polis obliged, and they managed the rest of the difficult carry together, Thoreau constantly hallooing Ed's name until, joy of joys, Ed answered, just after Polis and Thoreau reached calmer waters and launched the canoe. Again and again Thoreau shouted back until Polis, exasperated, snapped, "He hears you"—"as if once was enough," recollected Thoreau drily. And there, just below the mouth of Webster Stream, was Ed Hoar, sitting by his campfire smoking his pipe. He had done exactly as Polis said. The reunited three cooked their breakfast over Hoar's campfire, and ate it, Thoreau remarked, with "good appetites."[30]

Their intense relief carried them down the beautiful Grand

Lake Matagamon, calm, serene, and smooth as glass—a halcyon moment. Suddenly Polis exclaimed: "Moose! Moose!" His own goal for the trip had been to shoot a moose, and here she was, watching unafraid from the shallows as they approached, then stepping warily to higher ground. Polis fired and missed; she moved off, without haste, while he reloaded and fired two more shots. Polis was as excited as a fifteen-year-old boy, said Hoar, who saw his hand trembling, but his shots were true: the moose dropped where she stood, "perfectly dead." Despite all his objections at Chesuncook, Thoreau had just witnessed his second moose kill.[31]

Polis skinned and butchered the moose with swift and practiced efficiency while Thoreau noodled about looking for fish in the muddy shallows. Polis wrapped a large sirloin neatly in the folded skin, which he packed in the bottom of the canoe—a hundred pounds or, as he said, "one man" more, in a canoe already heavily loaded with two clients and their massive gear. If they waited, Polis offered, her calf would come by, and he would get it for them. Thoreau, revolted, picked an argument with him. It was a sore subject: killing moose for the market had allowed Polis to maintain his traditional culture and buy back his land, but when he insisted that he had to kill to support his family, Thoreau charged this was "the common white man's argument." While Thoreau had protested that economy in *Walden*, in Maine neither Thoreau's philosophy nor his example could help Polis and his people survive. But, finally, there by the river, the whole argument was academic. They were all sick of cured pork, and Thoreau admitted that the moose meat, fried up over the campfire, was "very sweet & tender."[32]

The rest of the journey was far easier. As they coursed down the Penobscot in their overloaded canoe, Polis lightened the load a bit at every stop by cutting away more fur from the moose skin, which he stretched one night in camp. The teaching continued: Polis showed them how to write on birch bark with a black spruce twig—a form of literacy long known to his people—and when he noticed Thoreau having trouble reading in the firelight, he showed him how to make a birch-bark candle. When Hoar lost his pipe, Polis made him another from birch bark. By August first, two days after killing the moose, they had nearly reached the Hunts' house, the last on the journey upstream before the road turned to Katahdin. Thoreau hoped to complete the ascent he had attempted in 1846—a chance to reckon again with the mountain that still troubled his dreams. But it was not to be. Ed Hoar could barely walk; his feet were still raw from sloshing for miles in the swamps around Chamberlain Lake. Polis offered to run up to Hunt's for a pair of soft moccasins, swearing that with a few pairs of socks, they would allow Hoar to walk, and that, being porous, they would keep his feet dry. But the men went down the river nevertheless. Getting seriously lost was deeply instructive for Thoreau, but it cost him his longed-for rematch with the primal mountain of his imagination. And Polis had his own cause for sorrow: had he known they were heading straight home, he would have taken all the moose meat to his family, not just one sirloin—a waste he regretted deeply.[33]

As they approached the settlements, Polis took care to lighten the mood. At the carry around Whetstone Falls, he challenged Thoreau to a race: "I take canoe & you take the rest—suppose you can keep along with me?" Thoreau took the bet and started packing up ("gun—axe—paddle—kettles—frying pan—plates, dippers—carpets &c") whereupon Polis tossed him his cowhide boots. "These *too*?" gasped Thoreau. "O yer," called Polis as he disappeared in bare feet over the hill with the canoe on his head. Thoreau scraped his load together and pounded off, soon passing him, but suddenly the plates and dippers "took to themselves wings," and while Thoreau grabbed them up, Polis passed him again. So Thoreau hugged the sooty kettle and rattled off again, passing Polis, for good this time. "Where've you been?" Thoreau teased him at the finish. "Rocks cut my feet," laughed Polis. "O me love to play sometimes—often race at carries—see who get over first." "I carried the sign of the kettle the rest of the voyage," added Thoreau.[34]

On down the river, whole villages appeared where in 1846 Thoreau had seen only a house or two. Once, a mother held her child up to the window to see the motley voyagers pass by. On their second-to-last day, Polis woke up sick, forcing them to lay over just above Lincoln. An annoyed Thoreau thought Polis was moaning for show and considered leaving him to take the stage to Bangor, but when Polis objected, Thoreau stayed with him. The next morning Polis was well again—having cured himself with a decoction of gunpowder! He knew, he told Thoreau, the medicinal uses of all the plants in the woods. And as they approached their last rapids, Polis finally taught Thoreau how to paddle a canoe properly. Puzzled, Thoreau went along, recalling that Polis had earlier praised him, even given him a name that meant, he said, "Great Paddler." But that was then, and this was serious: Polis genuinely needed Thoreau's help. He showed Thoreau where to place his hands, and how to use the side of the canoe as a fulcrum. Thoreau was astonished at the improvement and proud to pass his first test: as they reached the rapids, Polis shouted, "Paddle!" and paddle he did, getting them through without splashing a single drop into the boat.[35]

In the 325 miles and nearly two weeks they traveled together, Polis shared with Thoreau many stories of his own life, each one revealing something of the Penobscot world. Now, on their last day, he shared some of his tribe's history, including the ruse Polis used to prevent a Catholic priest from cutting down their liberty pole, which for Polis and his followers signified their belief in modern schools. Polis believed education was essential as a way to protect Penobscot sovereignty. As he told Thoreau, if you had been to college and learned to calculate, you could "keep 'em property,—no other way." He was proud of his son, the best scholar at the white school at Oldtown. As for himself, when Thoreau asked if he wasn't glad to get home, Polis answered, "It makes no difference to me where I am." Thoreau was impressed: "There was no relenting to his wildness." They lingered for an hour at Polis's "roomy & neat" house, and Thoreau saw Mrs. Polis, though without being introduced. When he and Hoar inquired about the next train to Bangor, Polis's son brought in the Bangor newspaper, which Thoreau noticed was addressed to "Joseph Polis."[36] They took the last train, reaching Bangor that night, and lingered for three more days, resting, healing, and regaling Thoreau's cousins with stories as they hunted ducks or poked around the sites of old Indian villages. On Friday, August seventh, they headed home. Thoreau was back the next day in time for breakfast.

Through the fall, Thoreau worked on "The Allegash [*sic*] and the East Branch," wrestling with the meaning of his encounter with the Penobscot world. Once upon a time he and John had played Indian, Thoreau pretending to be the long-vanished Tahatawan mocking the "council chambers" of white America. But Polis had been inside those very chambers, playing for real and for keeps for the future of his people as a living and vital nation. Polis confounded everything Thoreau knew. He lived in a neat and roomy frame house and took the daily newspaper, even while stretching animal hides in his front yard. He was at home on the streets of Philadelphia, calling on Senator Daniel Webster, purchasing a few hundred acres of real estate, or managing his fifty-acre hay and potato farm. He was also at home, "Niasoseb / We alone Joseph," from the high Allagash to the slopes of Katahdin to the inland seas of Millinocket, "places where he might live and die and never hear of the United States . . . never hear of America, so called from the name of a European gentleman."[37]

From then on, Thoreau never missed a chance to praise Indians and defend them against the prejudices of his friends. In a sentence he wrote for *The Maine Woods* (which someone eventually deleted), he asserted that his Indian guides were as reliable as white men, "far more instructive companions," and "*first-rate fellows*" to boot.[38] "He begins where we leave off," he gushed to Blake a few days after his return. "The Indian, who can find his way so wonderfully in the woods, possesses so much intelligence which the white man does not,—and it increases my own capacity, as well as faith, to observe it. I rejoice to find that intelligence flows in other channels than I knew."[39]

At Harvard, he startled the new librarian, John Langdon Sibley, by insisting on the mistake of science "in not giving more attention to the Indians & their languages and habits." They have much to teach: for instance, what must they know of the cedar, they who have "more than fifty names" for it? His guide had located a snake by its call—what naturalist knew that fact? Polis could call animals to him, and knew more of the habits of fish than Agassiz had even dreamed.[40] George Curtis was astonished at such talk, so entirely unlike that in novels or the theater, "untouched by romance or sentimentality." Thoreau told Curtis the Indian was not doomed, but "damned, because his enemies were his historians; and he could only say, 'Ah, if we lions had painted the picture!'" He startled Alcott and Emerson, too, by defending "the Indian from the doctrine of being lost or exterminated," and asserting "he holds a place between civilized man and nature and must hold it." Alcott dismissed the notion; like the woods and the beasts, "the savage succumbs to the superiority of the white man," for savages "all are brute largely still." As Emerson said with a fond smile, "Henry avoids commonplace, & talks birch bark to all comers."[41]

Throughout 1857, Thoreau added to his Indian Books, finishing volume 10 early in 1858. Only in April 1861 did he set aside the twelfth and final volume. His thousands of pages of notes documented the damnation he saw visited upon Indians by their so-called historians and recorded all he could glean of their lives and customs. Most of his sources were by white authors, since few Native Americans had yet broken into print. But when Thoreau could find books by Native authors, he read them avidly—such as the history of the Ojibwe of western Lake Superior by George Copway, or Kah-ge-ga-gah-bowh, the first book by a Canadian First Nations author. Thoreau, who could rarely afford books, purchased a copy for his personal library and annotated it heavily.

What were his intentions for this tremendous project? He may have planned to write a book on "the Indian," but if so, this plan ended with Joe Polis.[42] Even so, his interest in Indians continued. He worked *The Maine Woods* into a counter-ethnography of living Indians as well as a revealing account of his own evolution from prejudice and disgust in "Ktaadn," to his awed recognition of their humanity in "Chesuncook," to a flawed and challenging exploration of cultural boundaries in "The Allegash and East Branch." After this journey, Thoreau's goals shifted: his next book would weave Indian names and practices together with the seasonal ripening and communal enjoyment of "wild fruits," imagining a turn to nature not as a return to primitivism, but as a contemporary renewal of the deep communal intertwining of nature and culture. The idea had been percolating for years. Now, having been tutored by Polis, he could see how it might be focused and organized. From the fall of 1857 on, Thoreau's Journal explored some of his most luminous insights before honing them into his next book: *Wild Fruits*.

As usual, Thoreau took his new material out on the road. His annual advertisement in the *New-York Tribune* yielded, that year, only one lecture engagement, but it was a good one, in Lynn, just northeast of Boston, on January 13, 1858. There he read "The Allegash and East Branch" to a gathering in the parlor of John B. Alley, a Massachusetts state senator, Quaker abolitionist, and friend of Charles Sumner. No one kept notes, but when Alcott spoke to the same group a few weeks later, he found them a good company, "thoughtful, catholic," and receptive. They liked what they heard so much they invited Thoreau back a year later. John Russell had invited him back, too, for a visit in nearby Salem; once he was home, Thoreau had to write Russell an apology. Later, he pleaded—more than one visit at a time made him feel rushed.[43]

A few weeks later, on February 25, Thoreau repeated his new Maine Woods lecture at the Concord Lyceum. In the normal course of events, the next step would have been publication, but curiously, when his old nemesis James Russell Lowell wanted the new Maine essay for the *Atlantic*, Thoreau held back. The "fatal objection," he insisted, "is that my Indian guide, whose words & deeds I report very faithfully,—and they are the most interesting part of the story,—knows how to read, and takes a newspaper, so that I could not face him again." Nothing could more clearly signal Thoreau's shift in thought. His subject was no longer the Indian, that mythic generalization, but Joe Polis, a specific person who would most certainly read Thoreau's frank portrait. But he still had the earlier, unpublished "Chesuncook" on hand. Would that do? Though it was a bit outdated, Lowell accepted it, and Thoreau got down to revisions.

Yes, he assured Lowell late in February, in this case he would name names. On March 5 Thoreau posted "Chesuncook" to Lowell, asking to see the proofs so he could check the spellings of the Indian names and reserving the right to publish it in a future book.[44] *The Maine Woods* was now, in Thoreau's eye, a future reality.

Lowell broke "Chesuncook" into three parts to run as the summer travel feature over June, July, and August 1858. In June he gave Thoreau pride of place: "Chesuncook," his first publication in three years, opened the issue. The Boston *Transcript* sniped that Thoreau was washed up as a writer, merely repeating himself. This was hardly fair: July's installment hit readers with Thoreau's powerful indictment of hunting, dramatized by the lurid butchery of the nursing mother, and August's concluded with his clarion call: "Why should not we, who have renounced the king's authority, have our national preserves, where no villages need be destroyed, in which the bear and panther, and some even of the hunter race, may still exist, and not be 'civilized off the face of the earth' . . . ? or shall we," he ended, "like villains, grub them all up, poaching on our own national domains?" His vision of a national commons would help to inspire America's unique system of national parks and forest and wilderness reserves.[45]

Over and over Thoreau entrusted his words to print only to find them censored. While reviewing proofs on June 22, he discovered Lowell had ignored his instructions and deleted a key sentence. "A pine cut down, a dead pine, is no more a pine than a dead human carcass is a man," he had written, before concluding that honoring the living tree was a sacred commitment: "It is immortal as I am, and perchance will go to as high a heaven, there to tower above me still." Lowell deleted that final sentence, turning Thoreau's statement of religious principle into a poet's mere personal preference. Furious, Thoreau fired off a letter protesting Lowell's "very mean and cowardly" action, so "bigoted and timid" that he could hardly believe Lowell himself was responsible. It broke the fundamental contract between author and editor: "I do not ask anybody to adopt my opinions, but I do expect that when they ask for them to print, they will print them. . . . I should not read many books if I thought that they had been thus *expurgated*." Worse, it was "an insult" to presume "that I can be hired to suppress my opinions." No reply from Lowell survives. This time the series was not aborted, but Lowell deepened the insult with injury, withholding Thoreau's $198 until Thoreau begged for it, twice, in ice-cold letters.[46] Thoreau wouldn't touch the *Atlantic*—America's leading literary magazine—until Lowell resigned the editorship, and *The Maine Woods* be not be published until 1864, two years after Thoreau's death. Thus Thoreau never had the satisfaction of seeing in print either of the books he completed after *Walden*.

LIFE IN THE COMMONS: VILLAGE, MOUNTAIN, RIVER

A raft of letters awaited Thoreau's return from Maine. Marston Watson had mailed him a "glowing communication," literally: six glowworms, rare and beautiful as precious gems. Soon the Watsons came to visit, and they puzzled over glowworms together. Meanwhile, Thoreau issued an apology to Ricketson for postponing a visit to New Bedford, and another—ticklish, this one—to Blake for not inviting him to Maine. Blake was deeply hurt, so Thoreau tried to explain, without coming right out and saying Blake wasn't up to the physical challenge: it would have been "imprudent"; he had left so suddenly; the trip had been so difficult even the sturdy Ed Hoar "suffered considerably." It rained all the time, the mosquitos were terrible, they never even made it up Katahdin.[47] He would have to make it up to Blake later. For now there was a round of social calls: to Natick to examine Indian sites and landmark trees with a local naturalist; up the Assabet with Ed Hoar (from now on, one of Thoreau's steadiest friends) and the old Brook Farmer George P. Bradford; walks with Emerson; and, best of all, long conversations with Bronson Alcott.[48]

Ever since poverty had forced him to sell Hillside, Bronson had been looking for a home. The Alcotts hated the isolation of Walpole, and their daughter Elizabeth's lingering illness—she never recovered from scarlet fever—made his search more urgent. They finally settled back in Concord, next door to their old home on Lexington Road: twelve acres with woodlands and a fine apple orchard that would supplement the family income. Soon they were calling it "Orchard House." On September 22, 1857, Alcott closed the deal while Thoreau surveyed the grounds, and the family moved into rented rooms in their old house next door, the Hawthornes being still abroad.[49] In July 1858, repairs finally completed, the Alcotts moved into the home Louisa would make famous with *Little Women*. Thoreau found it good having them back in his daily life. When Elizabeth passed in March 1858, he attended her funeral and burial; when Anna married his friend Minot Pratt's son, Thoreau danced at the wedding.[50] When Louisa directed a theatrical fundraiser for the antislavery cause—she had "Slavery," in clerical dress, take swigs out of a bottle in the form of a Bible while "Manifest Destiny" staggered on stage "whining for a bolt of whiskey"—he was there. Returning through the village afterward, Thoreau noticed the clouds were "distinctly pink or reddish, somewhat as if reflecting a distant fire."[51] It was the aurora borealis, but by then, everyone saw fire on the horizon.

Throughout his years of village life, Thoreau had always enjoyed the annual "Cattle Show," known more formally as the Middlesex County Agricultural Fair; but in the fall of 1857, he was more than a spectator. That spring he had planted six seeds from the patent office labelled "*Poitrine jaune grosse*"—large yellow squash—and two of them sprouted, one yielding four huge squashes and the other a single squash that tipped the scales at 123½ pounds and captured the Cattle Show premium. The man who bought Thoreau's prize-winning squash planned to sell the seeds for ten cents apiece, but it was so coarse it was inedible—exactly the kind of artificial forcing that turned the most simple and wholesome garden plants into rank weeds, wrote Thoreau, foul products of human "vileness and luxuriance."[52]

His pessimism fit everyone's mood, for that year the talk at the Cattle-Show was the Panic of 1857. "Nobody seems to know the cause of all this trouble," Thoreau's neighbor Fanny Prichard wrote her mother from New York. "The hard times is all we hear of—every body has failed—there is the fear of great suffering and a great deal of crime."[53] The causes were many. Wheat prices plunged as the Crimean War ended and Russia reentered the global market. Western railroads were failing, banks were collapsing, and even the SS *Central America* sank in a hurricane, sending four hundred souls and thirty thousand pounds of California gold (worth half a billion dollars today) to the bottom of the ocean. Businesses all over the North went bankrupt, causing mass unemployment and urban riots. The depression spread around the globe and lasted into the Civil War. It was all utterly bewildering. Thoreau was exuberant: the Panic vindicated everything he ever said. "If thousands are thrown out of employment," he wrote sagely to Blake, "it suggests that they were not well employed. Why don't they take the hint?" For decades men of wealth and power had stood on the Roman porticos of banks built of granite atop safes of iron and mocked his Transcendental moonshine. Now they were all toppling away—Concord's own bank among them—and lo! "there is the moonshine still, serene, beneficent, and unchanged."[54] "How grandly your philosophy sits now in these *trying* times," exulted Ricketson. When a merchant friend failed, Ricketson offered him his copy of *Walden*.[55]

Despite the collapse, Thoreau had all the surveying work he could handle. All fall, his Journal thinned under the strain. He hated seeing his dear Walden woods mapped so meticulously: rummaging in crumbling old deeds reminded him that his "wilderness" was really just "some villager's familiar wood-lot from which his ancestors have sledded their fuel for generations, or some widow's thirds, minutely described in some old deed." In one of those old deeds he found a flicker of redemption: it turned out that in 1797, his Walden beanfield had belonged to George Minott, brother of his grandfather-in-law Jonas Minott, descended from Thomas Minott in Essex who had been the Abbot of Walden.[56] Thoreau's family history was inscribed deep into those Walden woods, even into Walden Pond's very name.

To compensate, Thoreau read all five volumes of John Ruskin's

Modern Painters, though in the end he was disappointed. Where he wanted to see Nature, Ruskin wanted to see Nature through Art. But Ruskin showed him how to see autumn through an artist's eye, and he painted in words a Red Walden of color fields and abstract form—like Indian tattoos. For everywhere Thoreau looked that fall, Walden spoke of Indians. They may have been swept away, but their Kineo arrowheads remained. "Such are our antiquities. These were our predecessors. Why, then, make so great ado about the Roman and the Greek, and neglect the Indian?"[57] The insight grew: "The man of science makes this mistake, and the mass of mankind along with him: that you should coolly give your chief attention to the phenomenon which excites you as something independent on you, and not as it is related to you." How, then, was he *related* to Maine's pines? To build Concord's new houses, people turned beaver: damming streams, raising lakes, turning nature against itself to float their spoils out of the country. Like ten thousand mice they nibbled at the base of the noblest trees, toppling them and dragging them off, then scampering away "to ransack some other wilderness." For what? To build the hollow wealth destroyed by the Panic of 1857. The four hundred who drowned in the SS *Central America* were like men gasping out "I am worth a hundred thousand dollars" as the weight of their gold bore them to the bottom.[58]

His new writing gave him a surge of joy. The Romantics were mistaken "that writing poetry was for youths only." Youth obtained the vision, but real poetry took a lifetime of "steady corresponding endeavor thitherward"—not just seeing the road, but traveling it. Which took real resolve, he reflected that Thanksgiving, as he hauled his boat out of the river and braced for winter. To further protect his throat from the coming cold, he grew his Galway whiskers into (as Ricketson teased) a "terrible long beard." But winter soured. The January air warmed, the snow didn't fall, the river didn't freeze, and one hardly needed gloves. "What is winter without snow and ice in this latitude? The bare earth is unsightly. This winter is but unburied summer."[59] In a foul mood, Thoreau even lashed out at "the *Indian*, inevitably & resignedly passing away—in spite of all our efforts to christianize and educate them. . . . The fact is the history of the white man is a history of improvement—that of the Red man—a history of fixed habits—stagnation."[60] It was as if he'd never gone to Maine, never met Joe Polis. Yet on that very day, he offered "Chesuncook" to the *Atlantic*, insisting on withholding "The Allegash and East Branch" because Polis (that Christianized and educated Indian) would read it. Fatalism was rare for Thoreau. Perhaps he was lashing out at Polis for being too literate to subdue, or at Lowell for enforcing the same old gloomy savagism.

There were other sources of tension. His father, the family's quiet and steady anchor, was gravely ill. In November the family alerted his father's sisters Jane and Maria to come up from Cambridgeport. By New Year's his ominous cough had worsened, and the family knew he was dying. Henry had to shoulder the family business, even as the Panic of 1857 was hitting home. Their customers were often unable to pay, or paid in IOUs that Henry feared were worthless. He pushed to increase his surveying income, and when Thatcher came to visit, he pumped him for business advice. One obvious solution was to hire outside help, and in May 1858 Henry did just that, traveling to New York City to find an agent for their graphite business. As his father wrote to Thatcher, Henry succeeded, but not until he cut their price in half; their old rivals the Munroes had cut their prices, too, and the depression was still squeezing business.[61]

His glum mood started to lift as spring approached. On March 5, he put "Chesuncook" in the mail to Lowell, while still riding a high from reading Father Rasles's dictionary of the Abenaki language, "a very concentrated and trustworthy natural history of that people." Indians were back to being thrilling and generative. That very evening Thoreau was riveted by the performance of "a Chippeway Indian, a Doctor Mung-somebody." Maungwudaus, or George Henry, was a Mississauga Ojibwe from Canada and a friend of George Copway, whose book Thoreau owned—an accomplished speaker, tall, commanding and at ease with his audience, who had led his performance troupe on tour across England to Europe. After smallpox took his wife and three children, Maungwudaus toured the United States on his own, selling herbal medicines—hence "Doctor." Thoreau listened closely as Maungwudaus, draped in the theatrical "Indian" garb his audiences demanded (a buffalo-skin robe decorated with porcupine quills, an eagle-feather headdress) explained his people's origins over the Bering Strait from Asia, showed how they cradled their children, detailed their marriage customs, displayed their inscribed birch-bark basketry, and blow-darted arrows straight through an apple at twenty feet. He was aided by a Penobscot friend—none other than Joe Polis's brother Pielpole (or Peter) Polis.[62]

When the Concord audience laughed at Maungwudaus's speaking voice—like Polis and the Penobscot generally, he ended his words with "um" or "em"—Thoreau righteously defended his "unsubdued Indian accent," the real "bow-arrow tang!" And he was deeply moved by what he saw: "How little I know of that *arbor-vitae* when I have learned only what science can tell me! It is but a word. It is not a *tree* of *life*. But there are twenty words for the tree and its different parts which the Indian gave, which are not in our botanies, which imply a more practical and vital science." In the light of the Abenaki words, he saw the world "from a new point of view," revealing "a life within a life . . . threading the woods between our towns still." A few days later, Thoreau came across an Indian fishtrap made of willow wands and full of fish—a cunning art that filled him with regret: had his father stayed on the farm with an Indian for his hired man, "how many aboriginal ways we children should have learned from them!" He drew it carefully, thinking how the Indians' words were objects, and their objects, words. The man who wove that fish-trap basket "was meditating a small poem in his way. It was equal to a successful stanza whose subject was spring."[63]

Soon Thoreau was weaving his own spring stanzas. His subject this year was frogs, and his theme was patience: "He must take his position, and then wait and watch." He brought frog and fish eggs home and watched them hatch; the little frogs woke him up at night with their jostling and peeping. He noticed how closely frog song registered the temperature: "perfect thermometers, hygrometers, and barometers" who expressed with their voices "the very feelings of the earth."[64] Emerson was fascinated by Thoreau's ability to sit still for hours, becoming "a log among the logs," until the birds and frogs came to him, but he also thought his friend carried his studies to extreme. "My dear Henry," he wrote, "A frog was made to live in a swamp, but a man was not made to live in a swamp. Yours ever, R." But young people loved to enter Thoreau's charmed circle, and their numbers were growing: Edith Emerson was cultivating a wild garden; Dr. Bartlett's son Edward had an aquarium full of snails, bugs, and salamanders, which everyone envied; and Ellen Emerson wrote her cousin that "we are, as usual at this season, interested especially in flowers and birds, and Mr. Thoreau is in great demand."[65] And there were others: Mary Brown sent more flowers from Vermont, the Worcester circle sent a hummingbird's nest, Marston Watson sent pear trees from Hillside. "This looks like fairy housekeeping," a pleased Thoreau wrote back.[66]

-+>-<+-

"Ktaadn is there still," Thoreau had written to Blake once he returned from Maine, just as "the *truth* is still *true*." The mountain had haunted him all through the fall of 1857; late in October he had climbed it in his dreams, wandering lost and thrilled over "the bare and pathless rock" of the misty summit, feeling "purified and sublimed." As he later wrote to Blake, "You must ascend a mountain to learn your relation to matter, and so to your own body, for *it* is at home there, though *you* are not. . . . It is after we get home that we really go over the mountain, if ever."[67] Going "over the mountain" became his next project—not to look *from* the mountain but to look *at* it—and for this the best companion was Blake the philosopher. On June 2, 1858, the two met at the Troy railroad station and hiked the four miles to the rocky summit of Mount Monadnock, barren of soil ever since farmers had set fire to the mountaintop to destroy wolf habitat.[68]

They were hardly alone. Climbing Monadnock was all the rage, and that very year a local entrepreneur had opened the "Halfway House" hotel on its slopes. Thoreau and Blake picked their way not over a pathless summit but through a litter of newspapers and eggshells among graffiti-covered rocks. After setting up camp in a sheltered spot, they spent the next day tracing a circle a mile in diameter with two transepts over the summit itself—an ecological survey, Thoreau noting everything he could see: the alpine plants and birds; the worn, rounded rocks scratched by glaciers; the wee wet bogs tucked into the hollows. The frogs, high up in a barren rocky cistern, baffled him. How had they gotten there? It boggled belief to think they had hopped up. "Agassiz might say that they had originated on the top," yet it seemed about as likely that they had rained down from the clouds. And how did they survive? Thoreau pondered the puzzle as they walked down the next day to where, right by the railroad, stood some of the grandest white pines he had ever seen, old-growth timber that would long since have been logged out of Maine. He stopped to gape at their straight, tall, polished perpendicularity.[69]

Thoreau still had mountains on the mind. A month later, on July 2, Ed Hoar hired a horse and wagon, Thoreau tossed his knapsack aboard, and the two rattled off, intending to circumnavigate the entire range of the White Mountains and live "like gipsies" along the way, meeting Blake and Brown on Mount Washington. Walking, complained Thoreau, would have been better: "You have to sacrifice so much to the horse," which confined them to good roads, dreary roadside campsites, or "trivial" inns, "pestered by flies and tavern loungers."[70] Three days later, mountains came into view and his mood lifted. In Tamworth, New Hampshire, the innkeeper captivated them with bear stories; the next night they camped near the home of one Wentworth, who told them of killing bears and rearing the orphaned cubs at home. They hired Wentworth as their guide up Mount Washington, and next morning, July 7, they rode through Pinkham Notch to Glen House, where they sent the horses back to Wentworth's and spent the night with two merry colliers, busy making coal for the two hotels on the summit. While the wind shook the shanty, the five men sat up drinking goats' milk and eating boiled beef tongue.

Thoreau was out at first light, anxious to reach the summit before the clouds rolled in. Hoar and Wentworth followed behind with the colliers herding their goats. There on the summit of Mount Washington, the highest peak in New England, Thoreau again had no epiphany. The clouds and mist arrived with the men and the goats. They chatted with an artist taking the view, and with Spaulding and Hall, landlords of the Summit and Tiptop Houses who competed for the tourists, who arrived by the scores. By 8:30 a.m. Thoreau had had enough of summit society. He led them over the rocks into Tuckerman's Ravine, the fog so dense they navigated by compass. The ground was so rough they stopped short of their goal and camped amid the dwarf firs. Wentworth, ignoring Thoreau's advice, kindled a fire that the wind whipped into the firs. Soon the whole ridge was on fire. No harm done, said Wentworth—the more trees that burned, the better. As the fire raged up the mountainside, the three men waded downstream to a small lake, where they set up Thoreau's white canvas tent. A faint "Halloo!" from above alerted Thoreau that Blake and Brown had arrived, and he scrambled up to meet them, "wet, ragged, and bloody with black flies." Thoreau noted ruefully that he'd told Blake "to look out for a smoke and a white tent, and we had made a smoke sure enough."[71]

Somehow the five men cozied up into Thoreau's tent, there in the soaking rain. It would be their home for four nights. Not the original plan, but Thoreau sprained his ankle the next day, costing him several days' walking. He made the best of it, studying all he could see, hear, and reach from camp, stoking the campfire to keep off the flies while the others pottered around in the mizzling weather. Finally, on Monday, July 12—Thoreau's forty-first birthday—they packed up and walked off the mountain, picking up the horse and wagon at Wentworth's, then jouncing off toward Mount Lafayette, their next goal, arcing west then south around the base of the range. Heavy rains shuttered the scenery until Tuesday evening, when a short walk above Jefferson Hill brought the whole Presidential Range into glorious view, the fogs rolling beneath and the sun glimmering off the peaks: "the grandest mountain view I ever got," exulted Thoreau.

Two days later he stood on the summit of Mount Lafayette, behold-ing shaggy forest to the south and west, and to the north and east, half-cleared woods: "the leopard-spotted land." While they ate din-ner, he cut some dwarf spruces and firs and counted their tree rings. The tiny trees were, Thoreau realized with a shock, hundreds of years old—the largest perhaps over a thousand. The fire Wentworth sent blazing up Tuckerman's Ravine had killed an ancient forest.[72]

The return trip took four more nights, heading due south through Plymouth, where Thoreau said farewell to the mountains, through Franklin and Weare, then over the state line and home by noon on Monday, July 19. Thoreau wrote a long, detailed account in his Journal, suggesting an essay in the making, but neither of these two mountain excursions took on a life beyond the Journal. Monadnock had promise, and in 1860 he would return, but the White Mountains were a bust; the wagon trip had not been "simple and adventurous enough."[73] It seemed about on par with Emerson's adventure later that summer to the Adirondacks with a hunting party, where he, Louis Agassiz, and some friends "broke some dozens of ale-bottles, one after another, with their bullets." Emerson did manage to shoot a peetweet for Agassiz—"the first game he ever bagged," snorted Tho-reau, who'd been a crack shot in his youth before he swore off guns. "Think of Emerson shooting a peetweet . . . for Agassiz, and cracking an ale-bottle (after emptying it) with his rifle at six rods!"[74] Wilder-ness just wasn't what it used to be. Indeed, the whole world was turning into something Thoreau disliked intensely. While scouting out huckleberry fields for the annual berry party, he was horrified to find stakes set up with "No Trespassing" notices. The "evil days" had come: pickers had to pay for the privilege of gathering wild fruits; huckleberries were being butchered and sold like beefsteak.[75]

But no one cared. All that mattered was the trans-Atlantic tele-graph. It arrived in Concord on August 5, and on August 16, when Queen Victoria used it to congratulate President Buchanan, towns all across America erupted in celebration. In Concord bells pealed merrily, pillars were wreathed, banners were hung, houses were lit up for block parties—one neighbor even fired off a cannon—and the fireworks were splendid. It was perfectly sublime, inspiring, an emanation from the Deity—unless you were Thoreau.[76] Of course the telegraph was important, he snarled, but what was the real *meaning* of it? Not how many blasted guns were fired or what each and every little town had done to celebrate. The world was ruled by cliques who filled the news with "a tissue of trifles and crudities," ignoring what really mattered. Things had reached a tipping point, but no one else seemed to notice. It even got personal: when someone shot the summer ducks he had befriended, Thoreau took it hard. Those ducks had belonged to everyone, to Thoreau just as much as her, "but it was considered of more importance that Mrs. _____ should taste the flavor of them dead than that I should enjoy the beauty of them alive."[77] Wherever Thoreau looked that summer, from village to mountain to river, he saw the commons under assault.

He made one more excursion, for he had not forgotten the Cape Cod carpenter's remark that no beach equaled the outer banks of Cape Ann. So he reconvened the "knights of umbrella and bundle": on September 21, Thoreau and Ellery Channing visited John Russell in Salem, who took them botanizing in Marblehead. The next day the knights walked from Russell's house to Gloucester, sounding out the "musical" sands near Manchester—the beach indeed squeaked, like waxing a table—and dined on ship bread and herring in a salt marsh while watching the stars come out. Next morning they cut south to the beach and followed it all the way around the Cape in a long day's circle back to Gloucester, nooning on the outermost point of Cape Ann facing the rocky reefs of the "Salvages," by which, reasoned Thoreau, early navigators must have set their course. At sundown they boiled tea over a bayberry fire in a field of big round boulders and watched the moonrise—"she was the biggest boulder of them all"—then got lost in the moonlight on their way back to Gloucester. Next day Thoreau examined the curiosities in Salem's East India Marine Hall—lynx pelts, a fossil turtle, a British sword abandoned during the Concord fight. It had been an "interesting" walk, but no more. At least he had reconnected with the elusive Channing, that troublesome "creature of moods."[78]

It was time to reconnect with Ricketson, too, who was pining for a visit. Late in November 1858, the peripatetic Cholmondeley wrote out of the blue that he was in Montreal and heading south, planning to winter in the West Indies and hoping Thoreau would come along. On December 7, Thoreau brought the English gentleman-adventurer along for a visit with Ricketson. The three sat up late in the Shanty talking of English poetry—Gray, Tennyson, Wordsworth—and for two days alternated walks in the dull, cold drizzle with fireside talks "of mankind and his relationship here and hereafter" before returning to Concord on December 10.[79] Later that winter Cholmondeley indeed headed south, but without Thoreau. He made it no farther than Virginia, where he abandoned his plans to travel—anywhere, ever again, he told Thoreau on his return. Though their correspondence continued, it was their last conversation. "He is a good soul," Thoreau wrote to Ricketson. "I am afraid that I did not sufficiently recognize him."[80]

Thoreau recorded none of these visits in his Journal. There the hidden, interior Thoreau was busy writing the first canto of "Wild Fruits": "Autumnal Tints," his passionate meditation on the creation and perception of beauty in the shared human and natural world. While few could claim material wealth, this spiritual wealth was open to all, "equally distributed on the Common," an October festival in which every tree was a liberty pole of a thousand bright flags—a gala instituted by the town's fathers, who had planted those straggling bean-pole saplings up and down the streets. A generation later, they had grown up to give the people a festival of beauty, a living institution.[81] Once the leaves had fallen, Thoreau sketched notes for a second essay, "November Lights," on "the hundred silvery lights" reflected from twigs, from leather-brown leaves, from water and windows. *Every* season brought its unique phases of beauty. What others overlooked, Thoreau reclaimed: "Brown is the color for me," he exulted, "the color of our coats and our daily lives, the color of the poor man's loaf," the color of earth, "the great leopard mother," lying with "her flanks to the sun."[82]

Channing complained this fall of Thoreau's new pedantry, a "dry rot" consuming him.[83] But in this hidden molten core Thoreau was fusing and transforming his accumulated years of scientific study into a new kind of instrument, a musical instrument, where every object was a key that, struck, resonated across hidden chambers of memory and meaning. He called it his "Kalendar," but it was far more: a symphonic rotation capable of fusing and igniting a lifetime's immersion in a single, beloved, deeply known New England village. In his youth Thoreau had imagined writing "a poem to be called Concord"; now, on his worn green writing desk, that great poem was taking shape.[84]

The problem was how to be heard when nearly everything he wrote had been rejected, ignored, or censored. While his outer self was professional—dry and workmanlike—in private he was incandescent, phosphorescing in the dark like a stick of Maine foxfire. When he identified a new species of fish, in public he proudly presented it to his scientific colleagues, who duly recognized him while they argued over its taxonomy. But in private he wrote in awe of "those little striped breams poised in Walden's glaucous water," unseen since Tahatawan paddled his canoe on those same waters. Walden was wild again, and America was young again. But how could he get beyond mere description? He must poise his thought "there by its side and try to think like a bream for a moment." He thought of jewels, music, poetry, beauty, the mystery of life: "The bream, appreciated, floats in the pond as the centre of the system, another image of God." He must convey what mattered most: the bream as "a living contemporary, a provoking mystery."[85]

Thus when Lowell deleted his attribution of souls to trees, Thoreau felt it as nothing less than an existential threat. "Freedom of speech!" he howled in his Journal. "It hath not entered into your hearts to conceive what those words mean." The alleged freedom of church, state, school, magazine, was "the freedom of a prison-yard." Look at the popular magazines—"I have dealt with two or three the most liberal of them. They are afraid to print a whole sentence, a *round* sentence, a free-spoken sentence."[86] Amid the Panic of 1857, the graffiti and the litter, hotels erected on sacred mountaintops, laughter that mocked Polis and Maungwudaus, "No Trespassing" signs on the town's ancient commons, newspapers trivializing the most historical events—where and how could Thoreau communicate his urgent call to true freedom?

-+->-<-+-

The night of January 10, 1859, a cold snap cracked the ground open with explosions that jarred the house. Next morning, Henry checked the thermometer on his way out the door: twenty below at 6:00 a.m. He was en route to Cambridge, having been summoned to attest to Barzillai Frost's will. The train was full of talk about the strange cracking of the ground. Henry took note. His thoughts must have been somber: three years before, Henry and his father had witnessed Frost's last will and testament. Now the reverend had succumbed to consumption, and Henry was doing this work alone because consumption was taking his father, too. Two days later, he wrote Harry Blake to postpone his lecture in Worcester: John Thoreau was too weak to join the family downstairs. Even a brief trip was out of the question, as Henry dedicated himself to nursing his father. For a time John hoped to see another spring, but toward the end of January, when it became clear his hope was vain, he reconciled himself to death and took leave of his family—several times, it turned out, until he was expressing impatience at the delay. When the end finally came, they were clustered around his bed, attending closely, and he was gone "almost before we were aware of it." His surviving son mounted the stairs to the attic, turned to a clean page in his Journal, and wrote across the center:

Feb. 3   Five minutes before 3 p.m., Father died.[87]

Of all Henry's friends, the only one who had taken the time to know his father was Daniel Ricketson. Henry mailed him a copy of his father's obituary, and Ricketson immediately returned warm words of consolation. John Thoreau had been "a real embodiment of honest virtue, as well as a true gentleman of the old school" who

reminded him of his own father: "Both bore upon their counte-
nances the impress of care and sorrow, a revelation of the experiences of life, written in the most legible characters."[88] Thoreau
responded with a eulogy: his father had been an artisan—almost an
artist—who always studied how to make a good article rather than
sell a poorer one for ready gain, "as if he labored for a higher end."
No one, he added in his Journal, knew Concord's history and people
better than his father, who had been part of it for more than fifty
years. "He belonged in a peculiar sense to the village street; loved
to sit in the shops or at the post-office and read the daily papers."
Everyone else had come later, or kept more aloof. It occurred to
Henry that of the four who had signed Reverend Frost's will, he
alone was still alive. "How swiftly, at last, but unnoticed, a generation passes away!"[89]

With this thought, Henry's letter to Ricketson drew to a close,
but in his Journal he wrote on, for by some obscure link his father's
death called up the deaths of American Indians. Henry rose up in
indignation, bemoaning the California gold diggers who shot an
Indian "as a wild beast" and the inhumanity of historians who were
every bit as lethal, only wielding "a pen instead of a rifle." These
intertwined losses felt deeply personal. "I perceive that we partially
die ourselves through sympathy at the death of each of our friends
or near relatives," he continued. "Each such experience is an assault
on our vital source." His only defense was to write and keep writing: sentences might lie "dead" at first, but "when all are arranged,
some life and color will be reflected on them from the mature and
successful lines," the lines that "pulsate with fresh life." Slowly the
writer breathes life into the "rubblestone and foundation" of his first
gropings, finds his way to his theme to "make one pertinent and just
observation." His writing must awaken the dying, give them voice,
call the sleepers awake. In March he picked up the usual late-winter
crop of "stone fruit"— newly exposed arrowheads—"humanity
inscribed on the face of the earth," footprints—no, he corrected
himself, "rather a mindprint,—left everywhere" of the oldest man.[90]

Objects as mindprints. Thoreau's observations were linking

up. In April he drafted a ringing condemnation of the fur trade, a
"pitiful business" run by "famous companies which enjoy a profit-
able monopoly and control a large portion of the earth's surface,"
ferreting out small animals for fashionable hats and the luxurious
trimmings of judicial robes, leaving their "bare red carcasses on the
banks of the streams throughout all *British* America." Tahatawan
and Polis, Maine's woods and Concord's plowed fields, the trade in
tortoiseshell and animal skins—"in such a snarl and contamination
do we live that it is almost impossible to keep one's skirts clean."
Why, even "our sugar and cotton are stolen from the slave." When
he took up a handful of soil, he found it ash-colored from Indian
fires with pieces of campfire coal still visible: "We do literally plow
up the hearths of a people and plant in their ashes."[91] Thoreau was
a haunted man. He and everyone he knew were all implicated: the
evil of slavery, the damnation of the Indian, the global traffic in animal parts, the debasement of nature, the enclosure of the ancient
commons—the threads of the modern global economy were spinning him and everyone around him into a dehumanizing web of
destruction. Tahatawan's arrow, planted in his pocket twenty-two
years before, was bearing fruit, in the most ominous way.

→>⋅<⋅

How did Thoreau find time to write at all? His father's death meant
he was now head of the household. The man without property suddenly had a net worth of $5,500, with legal responsibility for his
mother, her sisters Louisa and Sophia Dunbar, and his sister Sophia.
He was also in charge of the family graphite business: submitting
bills, dunning for late payments, paying employees and contrac-
tors, managing a constant flow of orders, inquiries, and bills, which
he flipped over to scribble drafts of *Wild Fruits*. He purchased and
studied *The Business Man's Assistant and Legal Guide*, and he sought
improvements to the industrial process. Following his assistant Warren Miles's suggestion, he walked the woods in Acton searching for
a millstone. Stones, thought Miles, would be better than the iron
balls they used. Thoreau found a good one, tried it out, and agreed.[92]

Affairs multiplied: in May he helped Emerson organize his brother Bulkeley's funeral; in August he readied the Yellow House for the September muster of six thousand Massachusetts militiamen, which packed all the boardinghouses and clogged Main Street with troops, camp followers, ragtags, and pickpockets. On his way to buy a lock for the front door, he was told the governor was coming, too: "Then I must buy a second lock for the back door," he quipped.[93] In October he was called to court to testify in a lawsuit against Aunt Maria's neighbor who, claiming right-of-way through Maria's yard, tore down her fence and erected a "spite fence" of her own eighteen inches from Maria's front door and windows. (Maria won.)[94] Throughout the year, he felt pressed and anxious. That fall he told Blake—starved for a good, long philosophical letter—that he was "too much like a business man" to write, besieged by "irksome" family concerns. "I have many affairs to attend to, and feel hurried these days," he fretted to his Journal. It felt fatal. To create art, time must stand still; "the artist cannot be in hurry," he scribbled hurriedly.[95]

Affairs beyond his family multiplied as well. On March 28, 1859, the president of Harvard appointed Thoreau to the Harvard Committee for Examination in Natural History. This put him in a select company of New England naturalists who met annually in mid-July, under the direction of Asa Gray, to conduct the final examination of Harvard's sophomores in botany. Thoreau was now officially part of the scientific establishment.[96] In April he performed his own practical lesson in applied botany: for two and a half days, with the help of two men and a horse and cart, he planted four hundred young pines, each carefully selected from sunny pastures, dug up with a good root ball and set in the ground with his own hand on two acres of land where his house once stood. A week later he returned and set out, for good measure, a hundred more trees, two-year-old English larches.[97] His little trees grew into a fine forest of colonnaded trunks, an evergreen memorial that survived well into the twentieth century.

Thoreau worked on lecturing as well. By January 1859, "Autumnal Tints" was nearly finished. On February 22 he broke away from his grieving family long enough to read it to the Worcester circle, hold-ing up as illustration a large, handsome scarlet oak leaf displayed on a board. Their initial reaction disappointed him—someone remarked he had seen plenty of autumn leaves, thank you very much—but Higginson told a friend he missed "one of the best lectures" of the season. Caroline Healey Dall thought the lecture was charming, though Thoreau was not—an impression she modified that Decem-ber, when she delivered "Lives of Noted Women" at the Concord Lyceum. A literary lecture by a woman was a novelty, and Emerson laughed that Thoreau, who thought women never had anything to say, would certainly not come. Soon after she began, Dall saw a work-ingman in a green jacket enter and sit on the back bench by the door. As she continued, he "edged nearer and nearer" until she lost sight of him. It was, of course, Thoreau. "But this woman has something to say!" he replied to Emerson's ribbing, before inviting Dall to stay an extra day with the Thoreaus. It was, she wrote years later, a day "filled to the brim with charming talk." Her admiration for Thoreau reads like an Emily Dickinson poem: "His tongue—like a Damascus blade—was hardly fit for ordinary use, but it shaped or severed at a blow—the substances, which most weapons—do only tear."[98]

After staying overnight with Blake in Worcester, he read "The Allegash and East Branch" to the same gathering. Thoreau's new work was finding an audience: a week later, on March 2, he repeated "Autumnal Tints" at the Concord Lyceum to "constant spontaneous bursts of laughter" and applause. Their energy encouraged him. As he wrote the next day, "The lecturer will read best those parts of his lecture which are best heard."[99] A week later he read it again at the Emersons' to his circle of young people, where Alcott, as usual, was one of his best hearers: "A leaf becomes a Cosmos, a Genesis, and Paradise preserved," he marveled. He read it one last time that season, on April 26, returning to Lynn as a last-minute substitute for a lecturer who had canceled; the local newspaper reported his audience listened with "deep attention." He would read this hymn to life in the face of death one last time, in December 1860, in what would be his last lecture.[100]

Thoreau's multiplying responsibilities did not free him from surveying. On the contrary, he spent much of 1859 in the field, and for every hour in the field there were more hours at his desk, drawing his painstakingly accurate plans: "It is the hardest work I can do," he wrote Thatcher that August. "While following it, I need to go to Moosehead every afternoon, & camp out every night." To Blake—another dreamer with a family to provide for—he commiserated that worlds don't run by themselves but must be constantly oiled and goaded along. "In short, you've got to carry on two farms at once,—the farm on the earth and the farm in your mind." Maintaining a family or a state was easy compared with maintaining the children of your brain, yet that was the only way to keep up the power of original thought. "Keep up the fires of thought, and all will go well."[101]

Only once before had those "two farms" folded together into a single survey—back in January 1846, when Thoreau had sounded the depths of Walden Pond. In the summer of 1859 he would again make those two farms one, when his friends in the Concord Farmers' Club approached him with the biggest commission he would ever undertake: a survey of the Concord River from East Sudbury all the way to the dam at Billerica Mills, over twenty-two miles in all. At stake was the future of Concord itself. For generations the Concord River's grassy meadows had been the heart of the valley's agricultural economy. Kept fertile by spring floods, in summers the meadows grew into lush grasslands that cured into hay so rich that cows would turn away from the finest English hay whenever they heard its distinctive rustle. Manure from those cows fertilized the croplands, leaving the wooded uplands free for fuel and timber—an elegant sustainable economy that had kept Concord Valley green for two centuries.

But something was going wrong. Spring floods were rising too high, lingering too long, and returning in the fall. Thousands of acres of valuable grasslands had degenerated into immense reeking, stagnant bogs of decaying vegetation—"one uniform Dead Sea," as the farmers' petitions put it. The cause of this calamity was, they felt

sure, the Middlesex Canal Company, which had built the dam in Billerica to power the Lowell textile mills. Recently the company added
a three-foot riser, making a serious problem worse. The valley's farmers had had enough. In spring 1859 they formed the River Meadow
Association and prepared to bring a lawsuit. Among them were most
of Thoreau's closest Concord friends: Warren Miles, Simon Brown,
Jacob Farmer, Sam Staples, Albert Stacy, Franklin Sanborn, Minot
Pratt, Edmund Hosmer—townsmen of the land.[102] They needed an
expert witness, someone who knew the river intimately, who had
witnessed and recorded the changes, and who understood what was
at stake. Someone who could draw a map. They called on Henry
Thoreau.

On June 4, 1859, Simon Brown and three other men commissioned Thoreau to study and measure all the bridges from Wayland
to the Billerica dam. Soon Thoreau was hard at work, often assisted
by Channing, who had resigned from the New Bedford *Mercury*.
He paddled to every bridge, studied and measured it, looked up its
history in town records, and interviewed and corresponded with
local informants. On June 24, the Concord Township hired him to
survey the entire riverbed. Thoreau paddled every inch of the river's
twenty-two miles, measuring depths and breadths, noting sandbars
and shallows and potential obstructions, charting the river's every
meander, recording vegetation and noting flood zones, piling up
scores of pages of notes and calculations. Emerson was bemused:
"Henry T. occupies himself with the history of the river," he wrote
Elizabeth Hoar: "measure[s] it, weighs it, & strains it through a col-
ander to all eternity."[103]

The more Thoreau worked, the more the data spoke to him of
the river as a grand human-natural system. He could tell the day of
the week by the height of the water, which rose and fell as the millers
upstream went to work, left off for the night, or kept the Sabbath. As
he measured depths with his foot rule, he watched a heron measure
them with its legs. He thought about erosion patterns and stream
flow, the gradual deposition of sand, the slow movements of sand
bars and the abrupt reshaping of shoreline and riverbed by heaving

blocks of melting ice. He weighed the human history spoken by the stone bridges, and studied the way the river wriggled itself into meanders and the way willows and bulrushes found the places they liked best. He drew up a huge chart of all the bridges, and he glued together heavy sheets of surveyor's cloth to make a roll nearly seven feet long, upon which he enlarged an 1834 map of the river. On this base he recorded the grand sum of his findings, including an elevation of the Billerica Dam showing the new flashboard that raised it another three feet, blocking the river's flow. In twenty-two miles, he measured, the river dropped just over four feet, barely enough to keep it from reverting into one huge inland lake, as it had been back in glacial times.[104]

The lawsuit went to trial in January 1860. One farmer testified the river was "dammed at both ends and cursed in the middle."[105] The Massachusetts legislature agreed, ordering the dam removed and damages paid. The next year, a state commission with an army of laborers and a budget of $10,000 repeated Thoreau's work, producing a map much like his own but far more detailed, plus a massive report that concluded the dam was only one of many causes. Restoring the Concord River would require a massive reengineering project. In 1862, the legislature reversed their earlier decision: it was too late to do anything. The farmers had lost. The flooding, which kept getting worse, was a fact of life. Today the Great Meadows, where Thoreau timed his summers by the hay harvest, is a great sheet of water fringed by cattails and crossed by dikes, a wildlife sanctuary for waterfowl. Only by orienting himself to the surrounding hills could Thoreau tell, today, where he was. No one knew then that the farmers' own actions, clearcutting the forested hillsides and draining the swamps and bogs for croplands, had helped destroy the river meadows. Denuded hillsides could not hold runoff, and with no bogs to sponge it up, rainwater ran straight into the river. The more the river flooded and killed off the grasslands, the more farmers logged off the uplands to plant English hay and drained wetlands for new crops. In Thoreau's short lifetime, this vicious circle rewrote the Concord landscape.[106]

On October 14, with the river survey nearly completed, Thoreau took an afternoon to visit his transplanted pines and larches. The little trees made sturdy green rows in the withered autumn grasses, boding well for the future. The next day he walked up a hill to overlook the Great Meadows. As he watched the sun light up the red banners of distant forests, he returned to an old idea: "Each town should have a park, or rather a primitive forest, of five hundred or a thousand acres, where a stick should never be cut for fuel, a common possession forever, for instruction and recreation. . . . All Walden Wood might have been preserved for our park forever, with Walden in its midst." In *Wild Fruits* he developed this idea into a proposal: each town should have "a committee appointed to see that the beauty of the town received no detriment," to preserve its rivers and forests, hills and cliffs, for a higher use than "dollars and cents." The town planners "should have made the river available as a common possession forever," opening its banks to public walks and parks instead of lotting them off into private hands.[107]

Over the Maine Woods Thoreau had no influence, but in Concord, his voice carried weight. On March 6, 1862, his friend Albert Stacy, the printer, bookseller, and occasional postmaster, stood up in front of the Concord Farmers' Club with Thoreau's proposal: "Why should not every village have its public park of from 50 or 100 acres in extent supported at public expense . . . Suppose we had such a park in Concord of 100 acres in extent, comprising hill and dale and water scenery, beautifully laid out in walks and drives; a perfect arboretum of all the trees and shrubs that will grow in this vicinity. . . . Would it not be the resort of the whole town; would it not have its silent influence upon everyone, making us more social and genial; bringing out all the finer traits which are inert in the human character?"[108] Thoreau was heard. His friends in the Concord Farmers' Club put his ideas into practice, and soon his words reached beyond Concord as well, leaving traces in every American public park—places protected as a "common possession forever," so that the commons might survive.

"A TRANSCENDENTALIST ABOVE ALL": THOREAU AND JOHN BROWN

Ever since the turmoil of 1854, Thoreau had watched his world slip deeper and deeper into the "hell" he had denounced in "Slavery in Massachusetts." On May 19, 1856, his friend Senator Charles Sumner delivered to the Senate a scathing speech condemning Southern aid to proslavery insurgents who were forcibly taking control of the government of Kansas. Two days later, a proslavery militia of several hundred men attacked the free-state town of Lawrence, Kansas, founded two years before by New England immigrants. The raiders sacked, looted, and burned the town, killing most of its male population, as many as two hundred men and boys. The next day, while Sumner sat alone writing at his desk on the Senate floor, Representative Preston Brooks of South Carolina attacked him with a heavy cane, beating him on the head with its gold tip until Sumner, covered in blood, collapsed unconscious. Brooks kept beating Sumner's bleeding body while his South Carolina colleague, Representative Laurence Keitt, held off horrified spectators with a pistol. Finally the cane broke. Brooks threw it down and walked away. For this act he was levied a $300 fine and given neither jail time nor reprimand.

Sumner survived, but it took three years to recover from the brain damage. The proxy war being fought in Kansas had come home to the seat of American power. While South Carolinians gloated, brandishing pieces of the True Cane in murderous glee, Emerson told a rally of his townsmen that "we must get rid of slavery, or we must get rid of freedom."[109] Just two nights before, May 24 and 25, 1856, on the front lines of Kansas, a sheepherder-surveyor had gathered his followers and, in retribution for the sacking of Lawrence, dragged five proslavery householders out of their cabins along Pottawatomie Creek and murdered them, one by one. He was now a wanted man. His name was John Brown.

Seven months later, in early January 1857, John Brown found his way to the dingy office of the State Kansas Committee in Boston,

Massachusetts, where Thoreau's friend and neighbor Franklin Sanborn, the Concord schoolmaster, was working as secretary. Sanborn
had injected fresh radicalism into Concord's long-standing community of antislavery activists, and the atrocities in Kansas allowed
him to bring even Concord's moderates into the alliance: in June
1856 his fundraiser for Kansas relief won the support of jailer Sam
Staples and county sheriff John S. Keyes. On July 4, when Sanborn
carried a petition around Concord calling on the Governor of Massachusetts to investigate the seizure and imprisonment of several
Massachusetts citizens by Missouri border raiders, Simon Brown,
lieutenant governor, signed first with a John Hancock flourish, followed by Emerson, Henry and John Thoreau, John S. Keyes, and
Albert Stacy.[110] Thus when John Brown sat down in Sanborn's office
and explained that he was touring the Northeast to raise funds for
an army to save Kansas, Sanborn was ready to listen. There were
deep pockets in Concord, he told him; Brown should come and
make his case there.

Brown arrived in Concord in March 1857. He lodged with Sanborn, still living in Channing's house, and at noon they crossed the
street to dine with the Thoreaus. Henry was fascinated by Brown,
and after Sanborn left to tend school, Thoreau and Brown sat in the
parlor talking Kansas. When Emerson dropped by, Thoreau introduced them to each other. Emerson, too, was interested, enough to
invite Brown to spend the night at his home. His children remembered how Brown spoke to them only of "peaceful" things, such as
how every sheep had its own unique face, and out of a flock of five
hundred, Brown could pick out any one.[111] But at the town meeting, Brown was not peaceful. He spoke of the crimes of the Missouri
Ruffians and the Kansas proslavery forces, and of the penance due
from a nation that countenanced slavery; he said it was better a
generation should pass away than that a single word of the Bible or
the Declaration of Independence be violated. He claimed to abhor
violence, but vowed to commit it at God's will. He showed them
the heavy chains proslavery forces used to bind his son John, and
he showed them the bowie knife he had captured at the Battle of

Black Jack, kept sheathed under his trousers on his right leg. Brown would use this same knife as the model for the pikes he ordered with money raised through talks like this one.[112]

Rapt as he held the people of Concord, they gave little. Emerson thought Brown had given "a good account of himself," and pledged fifty dollars; John Thoreau Sr. had donated ten dollars. Henry, suspicious of what Brown would do with the funds, tossed in "a trifle."[113] When Brown returned to Kansas later that spring, he had raised less money than he'd hoped, but he'd made vital connections that would soon pay hugely. Out of this web of contacts would crystalize the "Secret Six," who continued to raise funds for Brown's army. Thoreau knew them all, some of them as close friends: Franklin Sanborn, T. W. Higginson, Theodore Parker, George Luther Stearns, Gerrit Smith, and Samuel Gridley Howe. He also knew Lewis Hayden and Frederick Douglass, two of Brown's truly secret supporters, and he likely knew the third, Harriet Tubman, who came to Concord in May and June of 1859.[114]

Amid the escalating massacres, the raw violence, and the unfathomable brutalization—by their own government—of millions of enslaved Americans, Thoreau and his circle longed for a hero. For the calamities did not cease. On March 6, 1857, the eve of Brown's first visit to Concord, the US Supreme Court handed down the infamous Dred Scott decision, declaring that under the Constitution, no black person, free or enslaved, was in fact a person, let alone a citizen, for slaves were property and therefore had no rights of personhood whatsoever. That meant any regulation of slavery was beyond the purview of the US government, which did not control or regulate property. The decision immediately revoked any protection from slave power in the disputed territories of Kansas and Nebraska.

The resulting specter of the entire West dissolving into a region-wide "Bleeding Kansas" destroyed the east-west railroad lines, helping trigger the financial Panic of 1857. The nation had been polarized repeatedly: by the Fugitive Slave Act, by Bleeding Kansas, by the presidential election of 1856—when the free-soil John C. Frémont carried every state in the North while the proslavery James

Buchanan carried every state in the South, and therefore the nation, which the South controlled. War was already breaking out, Thoreau wrote to Cholmondeley. Concord was mad for Frémont, but he doubted Frémont had a chance. Out in Kansas, free men were being forged into heroes, while in the North, men dithered. "I only wish," confessed Thoreau to his English friend, "that I for one had more skill to deal with them." Six months later, in April 1857, he watched the Reverend Daniel Foster, his friend, leave his family and his lovely Wachusett farm to join Brown's men in Kansas.[115]

The circle of hell drew tighter in 1858 as the incoming President Buchanan moved forward with plans to admit Kansas to the Union as a slave state. John Brown, defeated in Kansas, returned east with a new battle plan: the war must be brought to the heart of the nation, to "Virginia, the queen of the slave states." On January 10, 1859, as his father lay dying, Thoreau joined Emerson and one of Brown's Secret Six, George Luther Stearns, a sober, wealthy Boston entrepreneur who vowed he would mortgage all he owned to see the end of slavery. As they skated on Walden Pond in the bitter cold, Stearns convinced Thoreau that Brown was a hero to be trusted.[116] By March, even the gentle Quaker Daniel Ricketson felt "as though a crisis was approaching," as he wrote Thoreau, "when the use of every means that 'God and nature affords' will be required to oppose tyranny." When John Brown returned to Concord in May, speaking for the second time at the town hall on May 8, Alcott, the soul of nonviolent resistance, found himself deeply moved. The imposing, steel-eyed, square-shouldered man was charged with power and graced with an apostle's long, flowing beard. "Our best people listen to his words—Emerson, Thoreau, Judge Hoar, my wife—and some of them contribute something in aid of his plans without asking particulars, such confidence does he inspire with his integrity and abilities."[117] They had found their hero.

On October 9, 1859, Thoreau was attempting once again to awaken the North from their "drunken somnolence."[118] Sanborn had earlier heard "Autumnal Tints," and liked it well enough to recommend it to Theodore Parker for his Twenty-Eighth Congregational Society, the independent church whose Sunday services were held at the Boston Music Hall, the only venue large enough for the two thousand or more who gathered weekly to hear Parker's sermons. Recently Parker's health had collapsed under the strain of overwork, and he had traveled to Italy to recover his strength. Church leaders were looking for substitutes. Thoreau agreed to speak, but informed them he would read not "Autumnal Tints" but "Life Misspent"—a revised version of his difficult lecture "What Shall It Profit?". Audiences had rejected this lecture time and again, but Parker's liberal congregation listened to it with respect and approval. Emerson was pleased and relieved to hear that Thoreau had prospered. It was an "original, racy, and erratic" address, said one reviewer; it was given in "a fine voice, and a prompt, effective style of oratory," said another—though a third was disgusted to see the audience approve Thoreau's "fanaticism."[119] Thoreau was at the top of his game, confident in his ideas, confident in his ability to deliver them. Good thing, too: what came next called on everything he had.

News of John Brown's failed raid on the federal arsenal at Harpers Ferry reached Thoreau on October 19, 1859, while he and Alcott were visiting at Emerson's house. On hearing the news of Brown's imprisonment, Thoreau's response was immediate, visceral, and profound: "When a government puts forth its strength on the side of injustice, as ours (especially to-day) to maintain slavery and kill the liberators of the slave, what a merely brute, or worse than brute, force it is seen to be! A demoniacal force!" Tyranny ruled—not merely in the government, but in the hearts and heads of his neighbors, who disparaged Brown "because he resorted to violence, resisted the government, threw his life away!—what way have they thrown their lives, pray?" For his own neighbors preserved the so-called peace by deeds of violence: the policeman's club and handcuffs, the jail and the gallows, all sanctioned by the State.[120]

But Brown had split open the skies to reveal another order, a higher law that transcended the State to render judgement on the State's own criminality: "High treason which is resistance to tyranny here below has its origin in, and is first committed by, the power that makes and forever re-creates man." Thoreau grasped immediately what no one else could yet see: Brown was neither madman nor mere criminal, but something far more uncanny, a singularity that rent open the founding logic of a State that declared itself free and holy by virtue of its right to enslave and brutalize its own subjects. Brown's capture had opened an existential trap: The United States could return his violence with violence of its own, executing Brown to protect itself; or refuse violence, pardon him, and thereby confess its own cosmic criminality. It could destroy Brown to save itself, or destroy itself to save justice. Either way, Thoreau realized, Brown's turn to violence had precipitated a crisis of historic proportions. Brown would, as Thoreau immediately foresaw, live forever: "There sits a tyrant holding fettered four millions of slaves. Here comes their heroic liberator; if he falls, will he not still live?"[121]

Over the next three days, Thoreau kept writing at white heat, finding words for the fury he had pent up for years. The transcendent nature of the sacrificial logic Brown had triggered was the same, Thoreau realized, as the sacrifice that had founded the Christian church: "A government that pretends to be Christian and crucifies a million Christs every day!" he wrote. "Some eighteen hundred years ago Christ was crucified; this morning, perhaps, John Brown was hung. These are the two ends of a chain which I rejoice to know is not without its links." Could a new, redeemed America be founded on Brown's sacrifice? The political crisis was upon them, poised, but the future was in doubt. Nothing, absolutely no providence whatsoever, guaranteed redemption. The nation's fate was in their hands: "I regard this event as a touchstone designed to bring out with glaring distinctness the character of this government."[122] Kairos was upon them—the moment of sacred time when past, present, and future collapse together and await decision. Whatever happened next would reveal the true America, for all time, indelibly.

As this realization sank in, Thoreau began thinking historically, placing Harpers Ferry in the arc of liberation history stretching from Christ to Cromwell, 1776, and John Brown. As he read the sacred and historical portents, he choked with rage at the trivializing pointlessness of every newspaper account.[123] He had to speak out. No one else was. He must find a way to defend Brown—"a Transcendentalist above all"—to the world. With this, two days after hearing the news, Thoreau envisioned an audience. An effective defense required thinking biographically, so he framed Brown's character through a narrative of his deeds and words. He was shaken to realize that two years before, he had doubted Brown. Worse, entering Brown's life forced him to confront the unimaginable: "I do not wish to kill or to be killed, but I can foresee circumstances in which both of these things would be by me unavoidable."[124] Thoreau wrote constantly, keeping paper and pencil under his pillow. By Sunday, October 30, he was ready. That morning he walked the town, spreading word he would speak that evening on John Brown. His family was divided; his friends counseled silence. Sanborn—who had helped orchestrate the raid, though Thoreau did not know this—had fled to Canada in a panic, forcing himself to return days later and face events. He in particular begged Thoreau to be silent. Thoreau, unmoved, replied: "I did not send to you for advice but to announce that I am to speak."[125]

→►◄←

The church was full. The occasion was momentous, and the moment Thoreau had seized carried far, far beyond Concord. Until that evening, not one person in the nation had stood up in public to defend John Brown. Even as Thoreau stood to speak, Brown was on trial for treason in a Virginia courthouse, and everywhere the newspaper headlines pitched hysteria against him. For Thoreau to stand and speak, a minority of one in this explosive atmosphere, took great moral courage. It also took moral courage for the people of Concord to assemble and listen, as they did, with courtesy and respect. Few, if any, came out of sympathy for Brown. Many came expecting to scoff; more came in pain and confusion, uncertain what to think. To them all, Thoreau read his "Plea for Captain John Brown," quietly and with "no oratory, as if it burned him." To Edward Emerson, "It was as if he spoke for his own brother, so deeply stirred was he, so

searching and brave his speech." Minot Pratt was astonished at Thoreau's extravagance for Brown, and further astonished to discover
Thoreau's sympathies "were so strong in favor of the poor slave"; he
finally judged Thoreau's speech was "full of noble, manly ideas." As
Edward Emerson summarized, "Many of those who came to scoff
remained to pray."[126]

The next day Thoreau received an urgent telegram: "Thoreau
must lecture for Fraternity, Tuesday evening—Douglass fails—
Letter mailed." Frederick Douglass had been scheduled to speak at
Boston's Tremont Temple as part of the popular "Fraternity Course"
lectures sponsored by Theodore Parker's congregation, secular lectures held on Tuesday evenings for the public. Douglass had long
worked with Brown but had refused to join, or support, the Harpers
Ferry raid. But when Brown was captured, his pocket held a letter
from Douglass, evidence implicating him directly. A warrant went
out for his arrest, and Douglass fled to Canada, leaving the Fraternity Course without a speaker, whereupon Emerson wrote to the
organizers recommending Thoreau's "Plea for Captain Brown" as
a replacement: "every man in the Republic" needed to hear what
Thoreau had to say. Thoreau had read it in Concord "with great force
& effect" to an audience of "widely different parties" who heard him
"without a murmur of dissent."[127]

The recommendation did its work. On November 1, Thoreau
carried his "Plea" to Boston's Tremont Temple, where 2,500 people
gathered to hear him. Thoreau stepped to the podium and calmly
faced the sea of faces. "The reason why Frederick Douglass is not
here is the reason why *I* am," he opened. For an hour and a half he
held his audience enthralled, an audience that broke in, time and
again, with spontaneous applause. Caroline Healey Dall listened in
amazement—"I had thought Mr. Thoreau *only* a philosopher"—
and in some discomfort, for many of his sharpest lines were, she
thought, "in very bad taste." Nevertheless, she found "the whole a
grand tribute to the truest American who has lived since George
Washington." A young William Dean Howells thought Thoreau had
caught something important: that "Brown has become an *idea*," not

a mere criminal.[128] There, under Thoreau's gaze, it seemed the tide of history was turning. Blasphemy and fanaticism!—spat the proslavery newspapers. But the wave of Brown's supporters was growing. By now Wendell Phillips had also stood up in defense of Brown, and Emerson agreed that Brown had made "the gallows as sacred as the cross."[129] Newspapers reprinted Thoreau's speech, spreading his words across the nation. "Just *the* words I so longed to have some living voice speak, *loud,* so that the world might hear," one reader wrote Thoreau.[130]

He gave his plea for Captain Brown once more, on November 3, to an enthusiastic audience Blake assembled in Worcester's Mechanics Hall. History was moving fast: only the day before, the Virginia court had condemned Brown to die in a month, on December 2, 1859. In his lecture Thoreau grimly noted the date. Next day he called on Alcott, busy sorting his Baldwin apples for the market. "The men have much in common," reflected Alcott: Thoreau comprehended Brown's virtues so well because he so largely owned them himself. But where Brown drove "straight at institutions . . . Thoreau contents himself with railing at them and letting them otherwise alone." Was there nothing to be done? Thoreau thought someone—Emerson?—should write the governor of Virginia for mercy; he still held out hope for a pardon, for the work a pardon could do to save the soul of the nation. Sanborn thought Alcott might go and intercede, or at least learn whether Brown would accept a rescue attempt. Neither letter nor meeting materialized. Thoreau tried to get his speech printed as a pamphlet, to reach the public directly. He planned to donate the proceeds to Brown's widowed wife and orphaned children. But no Boston publisher would touch it; his words would be carried only in the newspapers' abridged and distorted reports.[131] Again his voice was stilled before he had finished speaking.

In the coming weeks Thoreau was obsessed and despondent. In 1854, the white water lily had given him a vision of hope, but after the condemnation of John Brown, nature offered no comfort. It seemed strange that the "little dipper" grebe was still diving in the river as of yore, and that people were still going about their affairs indifferently. Blinded by anger, he stood and watched a sunset and he could see it was beautiful, could even describe its beauty, but he could not *see* it. "So great a wrong" as Brown's fate "overshadowed all beauty in the world."[132]

Thoreau turned his attention to the least he could do: organize a memorial to mark the hour of Brown's execution, set for 2:00 p.m. on Friday, December 2.[133] He carried the idea around town, and on Monday, November 28, 150 Concord citizens gathered at the town hall to approve the memorial and appoint Thoreau, Emerson, Simon Brown, and John S. Keyes to arrange the program. They also voted to toll the church bell at the fated hour Brown was to hang, and someone—perhaps Thoreau—proposed the American flag be raised to half-mast, union down. The next day Thoreau formally asked permission of the Concord Selectmen to toll the First Parish bell during the memorial, but they recoiled at the prospect and refused. Concord was hardly united in Brown's support. Dr. Bartlett warned Thoreau that he had heard "'five hundred' (!) damn me for it," and threaten a counterdemonstration —involving guns. Much of Concord, Thoreau concluded, was in the same condition as Virginia, "afraid of their own shadows." But, as he reminded himself, "fear creates danger, and courage dispels it," and so plans went forward.[134] Keyes insisted they must not read any speeches, as "there was too much danger of our giving way to treasonable utterances if we allowed ourselves to speak our own sentiments." Instead they agreed to read selections of poetry, scripture, and Brown's own words. Thoreau had a piano moved into the town hall to accompany the hymns.[135]

December 2 dawned warm and oppressively humid under low and looming clouds. Sometime in the night, the opposition hung a life-size effigy of Brown on the elm tree in front of the town hall. Attached to it was John Brown's "Last Will and Testament," which included the line: "I bequeath to H. D. Thoreau, Esq., my body and soul, he having eulogized my character and actions at Harper's Ferry above the Saints in Heaven."[136] Thoreau's supporters cut the effigy down and destroyed it. By 2:00 p.m. the town hall was full, including many from neighboring towns. Simon Brown chaired the program, and after piano music quieted the crowd, Rev. Edmund Sears from nearby Wayland offered a prayer, and a hymn was sung by all assembled. Then Thoreau rose and spoke. To Keyes's immense annoyance he did not stick with the plan but added some "rambling and incoherent sentences."[137] If true, then perhaps Thoreau extemporized: his script, "The Martyrdom of John Brown," is succinct, ceremonial, and pointed. Emerson, Keyes, and Alcott read their selections without editorializing. At the end, the audience stood to sing a dirge Sanborn had composed for the occasion. Afterward Alcott thought it was good the bells had not been rung. Better than "any clamor of steeples and the awakening of angry feelings" were the subdued tones of grief, and silence.[138]

Thoreau's work with John Brown was not done. Late that night, Sanborn knocked on his door: before first light, Thoreau must retrieve a horse and wagon from Emerson's, drive Mr. "X" from Sanborn's to the South Acton depot, and put him aboard the next train to Canada, at all costs. The lowering clouds of the day before had brought in winter overnight, and Thoreau's breath frosted in the predawn air as he directed Emerson's wagon through the center of town to Sanborn's house. The frantic Mr. X would not stay seated and would not stop babbling about invading the South, about finishing the work John Brown had begun. "I know I am insane," he chattered. He didn't trust the unknown driver and demanded to be taken to Emerson immediately. The unswerving Thoreau unnerved him. "I don't know but *you* are Emerson; are you? You look somewhat like him." "No, I am not," answered Thoreau, steadily urging Emerson's horse on. In Acton, the agitated Mr. X flung himself out of the wagon. Somehow Thoreau reassured him, perhaps with some "judicious force," and got Mr. X onto the northbound train, which delivered him safely to Montreal. Not until Thoreau was on his deathbed did Sanborn tell him that Mr. X was Francis Jackson Merriam, a member of Brown's band who had financed the Harpers Ferry raid with $600 in gold, escaped from the melee, and fled to Canada, whereupon he seized on the resolution to return and carry on Brown's mission. That morning, Merriam was perhaps the most wanted man in America, with a steep price on his head. Thoreau was therefore a criminal conspirator of the first order.[139]

Thoreau's "Plea for Captain John Brown" was finally published when James Redpath, a Scottish immigrant who worked for Horace Greeley as an undercover correspondent in the South, requested it as the opening entry in his collection *Echoes of Harper's Ferry*, with the profits to go to the families of the "colored men" who died at Harpers Ferry. Redpath had interviewed Thoreau for his biography of Brown, which he wrote at lightning speed and published on January 5, 1860. "I hope the contents of the third page will not offend you," he wrote Thoreau on the day of its publication.[140] Thoreau opened his author's copy and read: "To Wendell Phillips, Ralph Waldo Emerson, and Henry D. Thoreau, Defenders of the Faithful, Who, when the mob shouted, 'Madman!' said, 'Saint!' I humbly and gratefully dedicate this work."

Redpath's collection was published in May 1860, and its hundreds of pages documented the immense and mounting wave of Northern support for John Brown, a tidal wave of ink that can be traced to the first drop from Thoreau's pen, deep in his Journal, on October 19, 1859. Alcott was correct in saying that, where Brown went straight for the institution, Thoreau only railed at it from the sidelines; but without the words of Thoreau, Phillips, Emerson, and all who followed, Brown's swords and rifles would have been nothing more—mere weapons of bodily harm, tools of violence used against a State able in a moment to crush Brown with tools just the same. John Brown's sword was impressive, but without the word, it was just a sword. At the end of "Civil Disobedience," Thoreau hoped to be a kind of wild fruit, born of democracy but living aloof from it, preparing the way "for a still more perfect and glorious State, which also I have imagined, but not yet anywhere seen." The Transcendentalist philosopher-poet had helped turn Brown's sword into an idea powerful enough to blow slavery apart—and with slavery would go every part of the nation that was all Thoreau had ever known, and all that he had ever loved.

CHAPTER ELEVEN

A Constant New Creation
(1860–1862)

The country knows not yet, or in the least part, how great a son it has lost.

RALPH WALDO EMERSON, "THOREAU"

THE YEAR OF DARWIN

"Awake to winter," Thoreau noted. It was December 4, 1859, the morning after he had smuggled Mr. X to safety. All week he had been reflecting on the changes he was witnessing: "The North is suddenly all Transcendental," able to recognize justice and glory in Brown's apparent failure. Even little children were asking their parents why God didn't save John Brown. Now that the work of translating Brown to sainthood was going forward all around him, Thoreau's mind was clarified and at peace. It struck him that the recent death of Washington Irving, that giant of American literature, had passed unremarked; real literature, literature that mattered, wasn't conned like Irving's from the dictionaries but fired like a bullet from a rifle. "If I were a professor of rhetoric I should insist on this": the writer must *"speak the truth*. This first, this second, this third." With that settled, Thoreau swapped his summer shoes for his winter boots and set off on a winter walk.[1]

Thoreau was forty-two, old enough to have watched forests fall, but also old enough to see new forests spring up from barren fields. At Walden, the snow set off his rows of sturdy little trees. "What a change there will be in a few years, this little forest of goldenrod giving place to a forest of pines!" As winter deepened, he found new life everywhere. The gardener at Sleepy Hollow Cemetery told him they caught pouts and some hefty pickerel in the pond Thoreau designed, just months after workmen finished it. With no outlet and only a faint inlet, the fish found their way; the artificial pond was full of life. It was all about *seeds*, he reflected; every new tree must come from a seed. Take care of your seeds, and you will have woods again. So where did the seeds come from? The new-fallen snow was already covered with them, fine seeds of birches and alders, blown everywhere by the wind. One day he came across bits of frozen-thawed apple on the snow, under an oak tree. How? Ah—crow tracks. Crows liked the sweet cidery buzz as much as he; by dropping the seeds on the snow, they were planting wild apples for the future. Everywhere Thoreau looked, he saw tracks. Even in the heart of winter, the earth below, the skies above, and the woods around throbbed with life. He could even hear it: "The crow, flying high, touches the tympanum of the sky for us, and reveals the tone of it."[2]

On New Year's Day 1860, Thoreau walked to Sanborn's for a dinner party with Bronson Alcott and Sanborn's reformist friend Charles Loring Brace, a Unitarian minister and ardent abolitionist in town to lecture on his Children's Aid Society, which he'd founded in New York City to give orphans and street children free schooling, medical care, homes, and jobs. Brace had just been visiting his aunt and uncle, Professor and Mrs. Asa Gray, in Cambridge, where the renowned botanist had just finished reading a new book by an old friend: Charles Darwin's *On the Origin of Species*, published in London five weeks before. Darwin had posted an advance copy to Gray, who lent it to Brace, who showed it to Sanborn, Alcott, and Thoreau. All afternoon the four friends read *Origin of Species* aloud to one another and discussed Darwin's extraordinary principle of "Natural Selection": Darwin, declared Brace, had just exploded the scientific basis for slavery. Louis Agassiz, who hadn't seen the book yet but hated it when he did, held that all natural species were separately created by God, unchanged through eternity. The frogs Thoreau found atop Monadnock were indeed, Agassiz would insist, created by God right there among the rocks. The same was true for humankind: God had separately created each race as an unchanging natural species, not to be mixed. Of them all, only one, the white race, was fully human. All others were lesser creations, some of them—he named the African race—closer to chimpanzees.[3]

Darwin barely mentioned human beings in *Origin*, lest the resulting controversy prevent a fair hearing of his theory of evolution. But the four men in Sanborn's parlor that day understood exactly what Darwin's breakthrough meant for human beings; as Sanborn put it in an excited letter to Theodore Parker, Darwin showed "that one race can be derived from another."[4] Which meant, to this gathering of abolitionists and John Brown supporters, not only that all animals were related by common descent—but so were all human beings. Darwin knocked away the scientific foundation of racism, for if all human races were interrelated, then slavery was a moral abomination. All races, everywhere in the world, were biologically human; and humans of all shapes, sizes, and colors were a unity in diversity, one single family.

Darwin's revolutionary book would take on many meanings over the years, but on this New Year's Day, for the four radicals in Sanborn's parlor, *Origin of Species* was first and foremost an argument debunking the so-called scientific basis for slavery. Brace went on to write his own book, using Darwin's theory to refute the American racial science promoted by proslavery apologists such as Agassiz.[5] Thoreau, too, would use Darwin to further his own work. Over the next month he read *Origin* carefully, copying several pages of extracts into a notebook, making Thoreau one of the very first Americans to read Darwin's *Origin* from cover to cover on American soil.[6] The passages Thoreau copied show he followed Darwin's argument closely, noting specific instances he could verify for himself: evidence that common domestic animals had wild origins, plus several facts showing the explanatory power of natural selection.

"Why do precisely these objects we behold make a world?" he had asked in *Walden*. Ever since, Thoreau had studied patterns of growth and destruction, regrowth and adaptation. Though early in *Walden* he had celebrated the economic freedom of the seedless cypress, his interests shifted to the ecological freedom of generation and creation: all the objects he beheld—herons, owls, and chickadees; woodchucks, frogs and flying squirrels; bulrushes and willows; pines and oaks—lived precisely *there* because, somehow, a "seed" had found that place and flourished. The key was to study how seeds moved around, like those birch and alder seeds carried by the wind, the apple seeds carried by cider-drunk crows, the acorns buried by squirrels—even the annoying "beggar tick" seeds that hitched a ride on his pants legs, landing wherever he sat down to pick them off. Thoreau copied out Darwin's point that the plants and animals found on ocean islands always resembled those on the neighboring mainland: "Hence not created there," Thoreau added triumphantly. Take that, Louis Agassiz! Darwin told Thoreau he was on the right path. There was *always* a seed; there were *always* tracks, there on the ground, or in the water or the air, to be followed. "A man receives only what he is ready to receive," he wrote three days after his Darwin dinner. "We hear and apprehend only what we already half know. . . . Every man thus tracks himself through life."[7]

With John Brown behind him and "Autumnal Tints" done, Thoreau turned to "Wild Apples." Ever since 1855 he'd been writing of his relish for the crabbed scabby apples on feral trees or in abandoned orchards. On February 8, 1860, he stepped to the podium at the Concord Lyceum to celebrate, in Alcott's words, "the infinity of Nature," from the apple in Eden to the wildlings in Concord's woods. Sanborn called the lecture "full of juice and queer wit," and one Concord schoolboy thought it the best of the season. The audience long applauded the man who, though the lyceum had nurtured his career for three decades, only now stood revealed to them all.[8] "Wild Apples" is quintessential Thoreau, a puckish autobiography told in apples "wild only like myself, who belong not to the aboriginal race here, but have strayed into the woods from the cultivated stock." The shrubby little trees, browsed by cattle in their youth, put out stiff thorny branches to fence themselves from harm until, after twenty years or more, "some interior shoot, which their foes cannot reach, darts upward with joy: for it has not forgotten its high calling, and bears its own peculiar fruit in triumph." Thoreau repeated his spicy autumn brew of wit, wisdom, and sorrow on February 14 at the Bedford Lyceum. The audience of two hundred was "pleased and surprised by it."[9] It was a good lecture, a lecture with legs, but he never got a chance to deliver it again.

The winter of 1860 served up plenty of the cold, glittering days Thoreau liked best for river walking—"a solid crystalline sky under our feet"—and he filled his Journal with sketches of ice forms. Even after all these years, there was no end to wonder: "Thought breeds thought. It grows under your hands."[10] He turned from reading Darwin, the cutting edge of science, to reading the oldest naturalists—Aristotle, Topsell, Gessner, Gerard's *Herball*—seeking the roots of ideas in words pungent as wild apples. Early in March, he met a group of Indians setting up camp on Brister's Hill, who asked him where to find the rare black ash they needed for their baskets. Six days later they had their distinctive splint-wood baskets hanging out on the trees for sale, including a solid bushel basket with, he noticed, a white oak rim. Were not baskets of that size and style an Indian invention?[11] Everywhere he looked, he saw invention and adaptation, artistry and resilience.

He saw this in his Concord friends as well. Ed Hoar had not, as his friends feared, been lured back to the California gold fields, but stayed to marry the learned and quick-witted Elizabeth Prichard, Henry's friend since childhood—literally, the girl next door. Ed, who hankered for a country life, bought a nearby farm, which Henry surveyed for him at the end of March. From then on, visits with Ed and Lizzie Hoar were a regular part of Henry's life. Bronson Alcott, too, found new life: in 1859, the Town of Concord had hired the old educational reformer to be the superintendent of the Concord School District. The rejuvenated Alcott plunged into the work, converting a routine appointment into his chance to create a model public school system. Alcott's first annual report announced an important collaboration: Henry Thoreau had agreed to prepare "a small text book, for the schools, comprising the geography, history, and antiquities of Concord." By 1860 he was calling this the "Atlas of Concord" and was urging community support: "happily we have a sort of resident Surveyor-General" whose "illustrated Atlas for the citizens" would be a model for outdoor education, a gift to our children and to us all. "The town should find ways of using its best men," editorialized the new superintendent.[12]

That May, when Thoreau joined the wedding dance around Anna Alcott and John Pratt, he must have known that Anna's sister Louisa planned to be a writer, but he may not have known that she was already drafting her novel *Moods*, in which her heroine must choose between two lovers—one a serene and kindly minister who teaches her the wisdom of self-governance, the other a dashing naturalist-explorer who liberates her deepest desires. Her thinly disguised portraits of Emerson and Thoreau hint at layers of feeling hidden beneath the few surviving anecdotes, letters, and fragmentary journals. When Louisa saw Emerson kissing the bride, she thought "the honor would make even matrimony endurable, for he is the god of my idolatry." As for Thoreau, he was, she wrote, already married—to "swallow and aster, lake and pine."[13]

Hawthorne, too, had transfigured Thoreau into fiction: the title character of his novel *The Marble Faun*, published early in 1860, incarnated the half-wild qualities Hawthorne had seen in Thoreau years before. In June 1860, seven years after they had left Concord for Europe, the Hawthornes returned. The day they had arrived, Abba and Bronson Alcott, their new neighbors, dropped in to say hello amid the chaos of trunks and suitcases, and the next afternoon the Emersons threw a welcome-home party, where over strawberries and cream the Hawthornes were greeted by friends old and new. Thoreau, ignoring Nathaniel's silvered hair, wrote his sister that his old friend had not altered beyond a suntan from the steamship voyage home, "as simple & childlike as ever." The newcomer Sanborn was awestruck: nothing had prepared him for the famous novelist's "remarkable personal beauty," which made him by far "the most distinguished" in appearance of all the Concord authors.[14] Sophia Hawthorne quickly made herself at home: her sister Mary Peabody Mann had moved into the Wayside after the death of her husband, the renowned educator Horace Mann; upon the Hawthornes' return, Mary moved into her own house on Sudbury Road, conveniently next door to Sanborn's school, which enrolled both her son Horace Jr. and Julian Hawthorne.

Nathaniel, though, found no place in Concord life. Concord had changed, and despite Henry's assurance, so had he. His old friends had wound themselves tightly into crises of American democracy that a newly cosmopolitan Hawthorne found repugnant. Bronson Alcott observed sadly how the "coy genius" never called on anyone, never attended any lectures, seldom left the improbable Italianate tower he added onto the sober New England house—keeping "his moats wide and deep, his drawbridges all up on all sides." Thoreau breached those moats at least a few times. On August 20 he surveyed Hawthorne's twenty-acre property, startling nine-year-old Rose with his "enormous" eyes, wild as an animal's and "grey as autumn pools lit by a rift in the clouds."[15] Thoreau's eyes haunted Nathaniel, too. As he struggled in his "sky parlor" to draft his next novel, he hit on a story of Concord's own (fictional) Septimius Felton, "a hermit-like scholar with Indian blood in his veins" who killed a British soldier hand-to-hand in the heat of the Concord Battle. Hawthorne never completed the sketch of Thoreau he planned for the preface, perhaps because his fictional description said it all: ever "brooding, brooding, with his eyes fixed on some chip, some stone, some common plant ... as if it were the clue and index to some mystery." When he lifted his eyes, "there would be a kind of perplexity, a dissatisfied, wild look in them, as if, of his speculations, he found no end."[16] Thoreau was working his way into the minds of the writers around him, already finding his biographers.

Given Hawthorne's horror at the shrill and toxic turn in American politics, it was fortunate he returned just as the worst aftershocks of John Brown's insurrection were subsiding. After Brown's execution, Sanborn opened his school free of charge to Brown's daughters Annie and Sarah. When they arrived in February, Cynthia and Sophia held a welcoming party for them at the Thoreaus, where Annie, a precocious sixteen-year old, told Alcott that Henry Thoreau "reminded her of her father." (What Henry thought of Annie doesn't survive, but she must have made an impression: during preparations for the Harpers Ferry raid, she ran the nearby farm her father had purchased as cover for his conspiratorial meetings.) The Thoreaus, Emersons, Alcotts, and others pitched in to provide clothing and lodging for Brown's daughters, and Sophia Thoreau organized a quilting bee at which the women of the town made a comforter for their mother, Mary Brown, each square embroidered with a telling quotation.[17]

Such aid and comfort to John Brown's family was an act of militant defiance. Even as his daughters were being welcomed to Concord, a Senate Investigating Committee issued a summons to anyone suspected of complicity with John Brown. James Redpath refused his summons and went into hiding, sending Thoreau his address in secret to pass along to Sanborn—who had also ignored his summons, and who was living in daily fear of a knock on the door. A few minutes after nine in the evening on Tuesday, April 3, just as Sanborn had put on his slippers and settled in at his desk, the knock came. When the unshod Sanborn opened his door and extended a hand to greet the stranger on his threshold, the stranger slapped on handcuffs while four burly assistants burst in to wrestle him to a waiting carriage, the tall and gangly Sanborn kicking and spluttering protests all the way about warrants and authority while his sister Sarah howled loud enough to raise the neighbors, then jumped the federal marshal, kicking, screaming, and pulling his beard so hard he dropped her brother to the ground, while their neighbor Mary Brooks rushed up and down the street crying bloody murder.[18]

Soon everyone on Sudbury Road was pouring out of their houses. Someone ran to the First Parish and started the church bell tolling, which roused Thoreau to what he at first thought was a fire—yes indeed, he later said, "the hottest fire he ever witnessed in Concord." While Sanborn was kicking in the side of the carriage, a dozen people held back the horses. Others pelted the carriage with rocks, and Anna Whiting squeezed inside to wale on the driver while her father Colonel Whiting tried to whip the horses on. John S. Keyes ran to the melee, sized it up, and tore off to the home of Judge Hoar, who scribbled out a writ of habeas corpus, which Keyes thrust into the face of the marshals, who refused to recognize it until the county deputy sheriff explained to them that if they did not release Sanborn, he, personally, would call on the citizens of Concord—by now numbering well over a hundred—to take back their schoolmaster by force. That persuaded the five marshals to unhand Sanborn, and the riot wound down before anyone was seriously injured. Sanborn armed himself with a six-shooter and decamped to a neighbor's, while Henry Thoreau took up watch at the Sanborns' lest the federal marshals return in the night.[19]

The next morning, Sanborn and Keyes appeared before the state Supreme Court in Boston, where Judge Lemuel Shaw voided the federal arrest warrant. Word got back to Concord, where a cheering crowd of hundreds met Sanborn and Keyes as they stepped off the train to a cannon salute, Sanborn holding his manacled hands high in triumph. The crowd filed into the town hall for a boisterous "indignation meeting" on the theme of resistance to tyranny—embodied, now, by the beloved schoolmaster's manacled hands, which he again held high. Sanborn spoke, of course, and so did Reverend Reynolds, Emerson, Higginson—and Thoreau, to be sure, whose concluding words had them all roaring: Concord was being congratulated in the newspapers for conducting this affair in "a lawful and orderly manner." No! He could not agree. "The Concord people didn't ring the alarm bells according to law—they didn't cheer according to law—they didn't groan according to law—(loud applause)—and as he didn't talk according to law, he thought he would stop and give way to some other speaker."[20] Fifteen years ago, Concord had jailed Thoreau for resistance to civil law; now they hailed him as a leader of their united civil disobedience.

Sanborn was not off the hook—a new warrant was issued for his arrest for assaulting federal officers—and for several days he avoided his house, rotating among his neighbors for shelter, including a night at Mary Mann's next door and another at the Thoreaus' around the corner. For a year his case roiled through the Senate, until the secession of South Carolina rendered it moot. Meanwhile, Brown continued to be a flash point of resistance, and Thoreau continued to feed the fire. John Brown's body had been buried at his home in North Elba, New York, and on July 4, 1860, supporters planned to dedicate a memorial for his grave. They invited Thoreau to speak, and he wrote out an address, "The Last Days of John Brown." But in the end, instead of traveling to upstate New York, he passed it along to the organizer to read aloud in his absence, and the *Liberator* printed it on July 27.[21] This was Thoreau's last word on John Brown's meteoric career. That the North had gone "suddenly all Transcendental" gave Thoreau hope in the power of words that "*speak the truth.*" Brown's victory was won not by force of arms but by "the sword of the spirit," which meant Brown could no longer be confined to Kansas or North Elba, and he no longer worked in secret: "He works in public, and in the clearest light that shines on this land."[22]

There was at least one more invitation to speak, at the annual picnic of Theodore Parker's congregation on July 11, which, as Thoreau wrote Sophia, his famous allergy to picnics gave him a reason to avoid. But he was happy to speak at political meetings where he didn't have to make small talk, such as the Middlesex Anti-Slavery Society meeting four days later in Concord. Parker Pillsbury opened by praying God would raise up others to complete the work begun by John Brown, then launched a series of resolutions affirming the duty and virtue of "treason and rebellion against such a government as ours," which had destroyed the rights and assaulted the liberty of one of our very own, at our very doors, even while aiding in the enslavement of others. After Thoreau, Alcott, and a few other spoke their minds, the "very spicy" resolutions were unanimously adopted. Pillsbury made a point of condemning Senator Sumner for his support of Abraham Lincoln (by then running for president on a platform too moderate for the radicals), so Thoreau made a point of smoothing the waters with his old friend, writing Sumner the next day with thanks for his speech "on the Barbarism of Slavery," which addressed the issue from a broadly ethical rather than narrowly partisan point of view. For the truth, of course, belongs to no party, and should never be used "to perfume the wheel-grease of party or national politics."[23]

It was hard, in this climate, for Thoreau to talk about anything else. That August, when a callow William Dean Howells turned up at his door, the young man's glowing admiration for his hero barely survived Thoreau's appearance—"a quaint, stump figure of a man" in unfashionable clothes, with a noble face, "tossed hair, a distraught eye," and a nose that failed, despite its aquilinity, to redeem "his unfortunate short stature." Thoreau once remarked that he didn't know how to entertain a visitor who didn't walk, and unfortunately Howells planted himself in the parlor, seated. Worse, he turned the conversation to John Brown, triggering Thoreau's now well-worn platitudes about "a sort of John Brown type, a John Brown ideal, a John Brown principle, which we were somehow (with long pauses between the vague, orphic phrases) to cherish, and nourish ourselves on." Howells had just come from an hour with Hawthorne, who, similarly tongue-tied before the young idolizer, hit on the solution of escorting his guest up the hillside for a meditative smoke. It's too bad Thoreau didn't jolly the timid youth out for an hour on the river. As it was, their interview "was not merely a defeat of my hopes, it was a rout"—and Howells's "demigod" did not outlive the afternoon.[24]

About this time, Thoreau took a stack of leftover programs he had printed for Concord's John Brown memorial, flipped them over, and drafted on the backs a few pages of *Wild Fruits*. For months he'd been searching for a structure. Late in March he tried out one idea, "The Story of March," from the moment when sleigh bells give way to horse carts in the slush to the "brown season" when the earth is "the color of a teamster's coat" or his own worn coat, brown with a little green to it, that concealed him from landowners and allowed him to approach wild animals.[25] He gave it up. There is no "the" story of March—every March tells a *similar* story, but no two tell the *same* story. He realized the solution was there in his Journal: a whole decade of Marches, each one similar but different, with every phenomenon carefully noted and dated. Thoreau went to

work, paging back through a decade of Journal volumes and drawing up massive charts of phenomena for each month, year by year:
leafing, flowering, leaf fall, fruits and seeds, when fingers are cold,
when fires are lit, when windows are opened, when washing is hung
outside to dry. The result arrayed a near infinity of data points across
scores of pages.[26]

These charts were working tools allowing Thoreau to visual-
ize every least event in the broadest context, the grand cycle of
the seasons in pointillist detail. Alcott had commissioned him to
write the "Atlas of Concord," and Thoreau's lists mapped an atlas
of details normally overlooked. In the context of larger patterns,
the least observation could yield astonishing results. On June 4 he
tossed a piece of wood against a pitch pine in bloom and watched
a cloud of pollen float away, still visible at fifty feet. Weeks later
Thoreau noticed pine pollen skimming the surfaces of lakes and
pools—"*pollinometers*," he called them—even far away from the
nearest pine tree. How far did pine pollen travel? He found a pond
as far away as possible from the nearest pine, and even there, after
a rain, at the end of the season, he detected yellow pine pollen in
the water. This meant pollen, in season, was everywhere in the air.
Was this what caused those peculiar seasonal diseases? Moreover,
beauty itself, like pine pollen, was everywhere, unseen even by the
landscape artist who paints only shades of lighter and darker green;
whereas the botanist knows each green is a particular species of
grass and finds "another and different beauty" so deep it goes to the
core formative processes of being. The more one knows, the more
beauty one sees. Thoreau's charts were telescopes, instruments of
vision—drafts, in names, of poems written by the earth.[27]

In Darwin Thoreau read how plants and animals were "bound
together by a web of complex relations."[28] Now he was finding
cycles within cycles, wheels within wheels. Darwin untangled a
bit of that web on ocean islands like the Galapagos. This summer,
Thoreau decided, he would go back to the bare rocky summit of
Mount Monadnock, a kind of alpine island in the sky, and camp out
long enough to study *everything*, get the whole big alpine picture

in one place. On Saturday morning, August 4, 1860, Thoreau led the every-ready Channing, who had never been camping before, slogging straight through a rainstorm to the very same hollow on Monadnock's summit where he and Blake had camped two years before. Once they got their spruce hut built and their fire going—rotating before it like roasting meat—they were dry and positively radiant with glee: the genius of the mountain had driven off all the summer tourists to welcome these two pilgrims from Concord. The storm cleared that night, and shreds of cloud chased the stars; overhead the nighthawks hunted while firelight glimmered off the wet rocks and the green boughs that tucked them in. Thoreau was in his heaven.

He wanted time, lots of it—time enough to allow the mountain to sink in. He would happily have stayed for weeks, but after five nights Channing declared he'd put in a week's work and was ready to leave. After two nights at the first camp they found an even better one, where they could lie and gaze out over the world without lifting their heads. Thoreau was up by four every morning to set his watch by the sunrise, followed by breakfasts of blueberries and wild mountain cranberries. They watched sunsets over suppers of bread and salt beef. In between, for four long days, Thoreau roamed and inspected, took notes and gazed into the distance, thinking. They were hardly alone—at least a hundred people a day whooped and hallooed from the summit, squinted through spyglasses, chipped their names in the rocks, and gathered berries, covering the peak "with men, women, and children in dresses of all colors, like an observatory on a muster-field."[29]

Thoreau's notes go on for more than twenty-five pages: scores of plants, from trees to grasses to lichens; birds, both visiting and resident; mammals (only two, rabbit droppings and a porcupine skull); insects, frogs—and people, of course, and their ways of making the mountain their own. Thoreau mapped the summit, studied the bogs, and decided which rivers drained out of each. He sketched the rocks and described their glacial grooves, aligned so precisely northwest to southeast they could have steered him in a fog. He studied the clouds and the fogs below, the way the light changed, the feel of the air, the way that, up there, distance defied judgment and sound carried far. Had he owned one of Humboldt's cyanometers to measure the blue of the sky, he would surely have used it.

At the end of his notes, Thoreau added memos—what to pack next time (no eggs, more sweet cake), what to observe next time. He had found his laboratory, "an example of what the earth was before it was finished." Here on this alpine island, he could trace to their origin the threads of Concord's bewildering maze of landscapes. This mountain would be his Galapagos. His Journal shivers with excitement: not only was Monadnock a laboratory of ecological science, it was also a spiritual center and a magnet for ordinary people, local mechanics and farmers' boys and girls. This was a place of beauty and paradox, one that people cared about. He would go back. So enthralled were the Emerson children by his stories of rocks and berries that they all clamored to set off for Monadnock at once, with Henry as their guide.[30]

All he needed, this man who set his watch by the mountain sunrise—all he needed was a little more time.

Thoreau returned from Monadnock ready to write. The Concord Farmers' Club had devoted its last spring meeting to "Forest Trees," and in the lively discussion that followed, they agreed they needed a more accurate knowledge of trees. Some questions were easy, like how to tell the different species of pines and maples apart, but there were harder questions, too: "We find a succession of different trees grow on the same soil. If we cut off pines, oaks will come up. If we cut off oaks, pines will follow"—except on some soils, when *oaks* follow instead. Odd, that. They argued: Should one prune forest trees? Replant the forests, or let them seed in naturally? Such questions were so ubiquitous that Darwin could confidently state, "Everyone has heard that when an American forest is cut down, a very different vegetation springs up."[31] But why? Reading Darwin, then hearing the question resurface at the Farmers' Club, put Thoreau on the alert. He knew why—he'd figured it out back in 1856. On September 1, he wrote it up: the missing piece was the *seed*. Since we don't associate great trees with little seeds, we hardly bother to think about them. But the time will come "when this regular succession will cease and we shall be obliged to plant," as in England and Germany. The organizers of the Middlesex County Agricultural Fair announced their annual honorary speaker would be Henry Thoreau, and his topic would be "The Succession of Forest Trees."

Thursday, September 20, 1860, turned out wet and stormy, a terrible day for the county fair, which raised everyone's general hilarity and made the damp, slightly inebriated crowds all the happier to elbow their way into the town hall to listen to the afternoon's "excellent address" by one of Concord's own. "Ladies and Gentlemen," he quipped, "every man is entitled to come to Cattle-show, even a transcendentalist"—and with that good laugh at his own expense, Thoreau was off, leading them straight out into their familiar woodlots with wit and charm, guiding them through his own story of puzzlement, discovery, and widening understanding. He closed with the six wonderful patent office seeds that grew 310 pounds of prizewinning squash for him. "I do not believe that a plant will spring up where no seed has been," he told this audience of planters, but "I have great faith in a seed." Give me a seed, and I shall expect wonders—even the millennium itself, once the people begin to plant the seeds of "the reign of justice."[32]

Thoreau's old professor Cornelius Felton, now president of Harvard, stood up to applaud his former student, who he'd once said was too pertinaciously odd to amount to much, and to urge upon them all "a higher culture as a means of still greater advancement." The society's president, George S. Boutwell—the former governor of Massachusetts and the current secretary of the state's Board of Education—congratulated them all on hearing an address "so plain and practical" yet showing such close observation. Thoreau, he admonished, was a model they all should follow. "If they would exhibit a little of the spirit shown by Mr. Thoreau in his experiments and researches, they could greatly benefit themselves and the whole community."[33] Thoreau, come down from the mountaintop, had found his new audience.

More people read "The Succession of Forest Trees" in Thoreau's lifetime than anything else he ever published. Horace Greeley printed it immediately in the *New-York Weekly Tribune*, and it was reprinted widely across the country. No doubt Greeley cocked an eyebrow when the author asked him to return the manuscript: "It is a part of a chapter on the Dispersion of Seeds."[34] A new book by Thoreau! Greeley, a weekend farmer himself, got ready to give it the same publicity bump he'd arranged for *Walden*. He wrote Thoreau a long, lively letter arguing he must be wrong: only spontaneous generation could account for the sudden appearance of, say, fireweed on burned-over land, where no fireweed grew for miles. Thoreau wrote a detailed and pointed reply, and Greeley ran them both in his newspaper, stoking the fire of a good national controversy—for in the roil over Darwin's *Origin of Species*, this debate was terrific copy. Better still, at the very moment when the fact of mass deforestation was troubling landowners, farmers, and the general public from Maine to Minnesota, Thoreau's new work not only answered their "plain and practical" concerns, but turned such matters of concern toward the "higher culture" called for by President Felton.[35]

Now Thoreau had not just one new book in the offing, but two. Writing "Succession" had sent him paging through his old Journal volumes, which he began to reread in the new light of Darwin's *Origin of Species*—and suddenly Darwin's ideas came to life. Thoreau hurried back to the woods with new sets of questions. Farmers were making a botch of their forests, and they knew it, but now Thoreau realized they didn't mean to damage their woodlots; they simply needed more knowledge. For instance, take the mess on Smith's Hill—a textbook case of a bare, eroded hillside. If Smith would just stop hacking down the little hickories seeding in and keep his cattle out for a few seasons, he would soon have a dense and valuable hickory wood.[36] As for oaks, 1860 was an astonishing year: no one had ever seen the white oaks so prolific. Their acorns covered the forest floor solid—enough to feed the squirrels, busy planting future oak forests under the pines, with plenty left over for farmers to reseed new oak plantations all over Concord. Emerson gathered some up for his own planting. It was all so elegant: everywhere, it seemed, Nature's design was playing into humanity's benign stewardship of the land.

Then something strange happened. On September 28, a "black frost" hit, lasting nearly a week. By October third, all Thoreau saw were shriveled, hoary leaves, dead before they could ripen into their fall colors. The stench of decay permeated the woods. Ten days later, still pleased with the bumper crop of acorns, he opened a few and found them decaying inside. Yet there were plenty left, so he gathered more, still rejoicing in Nature's plenitude. His Journal snowballed as he followed the track of seeds and woods, woodlots and old fields, coursing across boundary lines, examining stumps and seedlings, marveling at the seed's significance and the forest's tender nursery.[37] It all came together on October 18: the frogs on Monadnock, the fish in Sleepy Hollow, the water plants in Beck Stow's swamp, where there was no inlet stream—"How did they get there?" The point, he wrote, was how did *anything* get *anywhere*? "We are not to suppose as many creations as pools." Greeley and Louis Agassiz were both wrong; everything came from an actual, material seed, which meant Darwin was right: all seeds came originally from one seed, which had multiplied, spread, and evolved into new varieties, from the fossil lilies of geologists to the white lilies we carry to church. All were dispersed by seeds, all were evolving new forms and new lives. "The development theory implies a greater vital force in nature, because it is more flexible and accommodating, and equivalent to a sort of constant *new* creation."[38]

But still, there was a problem. Thoreau went back out to reexamine those white oaks. There were acorns still on the tree, a bad sign; by then they should all have ripened and fallen. Thoreau pulled a few off the tree, cut them open. Dead! Black within, or sour and soft, every one—*all* of them, on the ground, too. Baffled and dismayed, he stopped short: what kind of nursery kills off all its infants in their cradle? He'd been so certain he held the key in his hand, but here was "a glaring imperfection in Nature, that the labor of the oaks for the year should be lost to this extent." All woodland creatures—pigeons, jays, squirrels—were "impoverished" by this unaccountable loss. "It is hard to say what great purpose is served by this seeming waste."[39]

Darwin's breakthrough came when he realized natural selection had not one key but two: the fecundity of nature and the pressure of mortality. Darwin's theory of evolution was driven by differential survival, or "survival of the fittest." Thoreau understood that most seeds died, but he reasoned that since they were eaten, they still supported life: design still ruled the great beneficent cycle of the universe. But this spectacle, an entire year's bumper crop pointlessly destroyed, meant other forces were in play, random contingencies and strange cruelties. Thoreau knew he was at the cutting edge of science, one of the first to apply Darwin's theories in the field. Now he knew something even more powerful: there was more to learn, more he did not understand. He was finding answers to questions that puzzled even Darwin himself.

Virtually every day Thoreau was back outside, scouting fresh sites, observing, questioning, counting, gathering. His Journal exploded, from 28 pages in September to 104 in October and another 81 in November. When he heard of Inches Woods in Boxborough, an old-growth forest about to be logged, he took the train to see it, walking in awe under the tremendous spreading oak trees. Here he could study forest succession in a New England forest that had never seen an axe, glimpse the whole panorama rolling forward from its origins. Once, he had begged the farmers to leave a few trees standing, lest New England's forests exist only on the crumbling paper of old property deeds. Now he saw that the forest itself, dating back before the first English settlement, was writing its *own* deeds—deeds he now could read: "Thus you can unroll the rotten papyrus on which the history of the Concord forest is written."[40]

"My own destiny made & mended here"—that should be his signboard, he joked with Blake.[41] The year after his father's death had been riddled with challenges and pressures, leaving him hurried, even embattled. Somehow this year he had, indeed, mended his destiny: rebalanced his life, rededicated himself to walking and writing, reoriented to a deeper social purpose. He was connecting better than ever with his audiences, from the town hall, to the Concord classroom, to readers far beyond the reach of his voice— audiences so moved by his words that he could feel he'd changed the course of history. On Thanksgiving Day, November 29, 1860, Thoreau had a lifetime of thanks to give. At 7:00 a.m. he walked to the riverbank and pulled in his boat for the winter; that afternoon he inspected the woods on Fairhaven Hill, where a field of seedling hickories begged for his attention. There are never any hard times for poets or philosophers, he reflected at day's end, for they deal not with moonshine but with "permanent values."[42]

Around noon Alcott dropped by to firm up their plans for the commemoration of John Brown's death on December 2. Perhaps, as they put their heads together over the program, Alcott apologized for the cold he had caught earlier in the week, attending the crowded Teachers' Association Meeting in the drafty town hall. The next day Alcott couldn't leave the house. The day after, he took to his bed, so wracked with fever, sore throat, and a bad cough that for a week he couldn't even write in his journal. Not till Sunday, December 9, did he feel a little better, though still hoarse and "choked full."[43]

Four days after his meeting with Alcott, Thoreau, too, came down with a cold. It was just a cold, he must have thought, annoyed as he went about his day: back out to Fairhaven Hill for more work with the hickories, stopping off on his way home for a vigorous argument with neighbors about—what else?—John Brown. Despite the sniffles, work went on: next day he stormed on about a fugitive slave who had been tracked to Toronto (in free Canada!) by his "kidnappers." Then he finished drawing up his survey of a house lot on Monument Road.

It would be his last survey. Thoreau's Journal stops here. It would sputter back to life weeks later, for a few more pages. Never again would Thoreau walk across Concord's hillsides, tramp through its swamps, or seek out oak seedlings among the pines. It was just a cold, maybe the flu—but for a man with lurking tuberculosis, it was the beginning of the end.

"THE WEST OF WHICH I SPEAK":
THOREAU'S LAST JOURNEY

It was obvious to no one yet, including Thoreau, that this was no ordinary cold. At first he soldiered on: anxious to extend his lecture circuit, he had expanded his advertising, and while engagements in Rochester and Buffalo fell through, he had read two lectures in September before a group of spiritualists in Lowell, probably "Walking" in the morning and "Life Misspent" that afternoon. He'd also arranged to lecture before the Young Men's Institute in Waterbury, Connecticut, on December 11. By then he'd been ill for a week, but on December 10, in the teeth of a nor'easter spitting snow and rain, Thoreau boarded the train to Worcester anyway for a social evening with old friends: the Blakes, Browns, and a handful of others, including Harry's friend E. Harlow Russell, who in 1893 would inherit Thoreau's manuscripts from Blake and determine their fate. Russell never forgot this evening, the only time they met. While taking off his overcoat, he heard Thoreau's "deep musical voice" from within. As he entered the parlor, Thoreau leaped to his feet, extending a hand with a friendly "I am glad to see you, Mr. Russell." Russell noted that Thoreau spoke with a certain deliberation: "The emphatic words seemed to hang fire or to be held back for an instant as if to gather force and weight"—something Emerson did as well, though Russell saw not imitation but a way of "looking at his thought" before speaking. He also noted Thoreau's hoarseness and cough. Only later did he realize their significance.[44]

By the time Thoreau reached Waterbury the next day, he was exhausted. He had brought along "Autumnal Tints," his crowd-pleaser, and a good-sized audience bundled through the season's coldest night yet to hear him—only to be bitterly disappointed. The lecture was "dull, commonplace and unsatisfactory," neither practical nor poetic, delivered in a "monotonous" style that kept anyone from detecting any merits it had. All in all the worst lecture, the reviewer cruelly concluded, not merely in that year's season but in the entire history of the institute.[45] Thoreau returned from this debacle a very sick man. He'd had his share of colds, but something sent this one deeper, deep enough to ignite the slow-burning tuberculosis that slumbered in his lungs. It's entirely possible that his fervent desire to connect with audiences—especially audiences of young people—was his undoing.

By Christmas Day the flu symptoms had abated, and Thoreau was up to a holiday visit at the Alcotts, where he laid into Emerson's latest book, *The Conduct of Life*, charging that it lacked the "fire and force" of the earlier works. A cocky thing to say, but back at his own writing desk he was working again, using the downtime to explore his new ideas, and he was writing brilliantly. With two book projects on hand, *Wild Fruits* and the emerging *Dispersion of Seeds*, he reopened his Journal and drafted chunks of both, starting with "Huckleberries," his next lecture. For days he relived golden moments picking blueberries, reviewing his books to place blueberries, as he had placed apples, within the great narrative of human history, infusing poetry with polemics. By mid-January he was back to seeds, which were, in his revision of Darwin, "the origins of *things.*"[46]

Reaching from his youthful reading of Lyell all the way to October's frost-killed acorns, Thoreau began to lift his new vision into place: there has not been a sudden new creation of the world, "but a steady progress, according to existing laws." Seeds were a material way to trace the workings of those laws. It was easy to see destruction, which is sudden and spectacular: everyone hears the crash of a falling tree. But who hears the growth of a tree, the constant, slow work of creation? "Nature is slow but sure." She wins the race by perseverance; she knows that seeds have many uses, not just to reproduce their kind. "If every acorn of this year's crop is destroyed, never fear! She has more years to come."[47] Here was his solution to the baffling waste of the white oak crop: what made no sense on a human scale could be understood by lengthening the measure of time to the scale of the planet. The man who was running out of time now thought as if he had all the time, literally, in the world.

Channing worried and Alcott sympathized, knowing how hard

it was for Thoreau, who so loved to live outdoors, to be cooped up in the house. But spring would come with its good medicine, and meanwhile Thoreau was busy and happy, spreading out his Journals, arranging new subjects by topic, "as if he had a new book in mind."[48] Perhaps, nudged Alcott, it would be that atlas of Concord? "But he must work in his own ways and times," and whatever it turned out to be would surprise, and be worth the wait. Alcott added Thoreau to the program for the upcoming Concord School exhibit; Channing came by with new data to update Thoreau's seasonal charts; Emerson came by to stretch his thoughts. "All the music, Henry T. says, is in the strain, the tune don't signify, 'tis all one vibration of the string. He says, people sing a song, or play a tune, only for one strain that is in it." Waldo didn't agree, and he challenged his friend, but he stayed with Thoreau's thinking long enough to draw him out, and afterward kept considering the idea until he caught something in it he liked.[49]

Channing fretted the most, posting worried letters alerting Mary Russell Watson that their dear friend was coughing heavily and losing weight.[50] By late February, he was escorting Thoreau outside for a stroll or two in town—Was that a bluebird? thrilled Thoreau one mild afternoon—and on March first, Blake and Brown walked all the way from Worcester on a pilgrimage to see him. Alcott thought walking all that way in the slush was a bit extreme, but still, their gesture impressed him. "I know of nothing more creditable to Thoreau than this thoughtful regard and constancy" shown him by "some of the best persons of his time."[51] When the school exhibition came, on March 14, Thoreau was too ill to attend, but he wrote Ricketson proudly that Alcott was now "perhaps the most successful man in the town," aglow in the universal praise for his work in their schools. As for himself, he insisted to everyone that while the house kept him prisoner, still he was happy, working hard, and hopeful, ever hopeful, that spring's mild air would bring an end to his cough.[52]

What spring brought was civil war. Thoreau kept up with politics: in March he fulminated to Thatcher against the cowardice of Lincoln's presidency—just a month old—for being "no government at all." It had punished not one Southerner for "treason—stealing from the public treasury—or murdering on political accounts," and the North must know there could be "no *Union* between freemen & slaveholders, & vote & act accordingly."[53] The "purgatory" ended two weeks later, on April 12, 1861, when South Carolina fired on the federal garrison at Fort Sumter in Charleston Harbor. It had been coming for months. Lincoln's election galvanized the South, and South Carolina seceded just before Christmas. Six more Southern states followed, and on February 4, 1861, the seven seceders formed the Confederate States of America, electing Jefferson Davis their president. Lincoln, in his inaugural address, called their actions void. Since he did not recognize their rebellion, he would fire no shots. Hence Thoreau's fury: all this, and still no action! But the attack on Fort Sumter changed everything, crystallizing years of seething anger. When Lincoln called for 75,000 volunteers to retake the fort, Concord ignited. "Everyone is boiling over with excitement," wrote Louisa May Alcott. Young men and boys "drill with all their might," women and girls sew uniforms, old folks "settle the fate of the Nation in groves of newspapers, & the children make the streets hideous with distracted drums & fifes."[54]

But on April 19, as Concord's forty-man militia marched to war, Thoreau's Journal recorded only the specimens and observations brought him by friends—mostly young Horace Mann, Mary's oldest boy, who had lately become Thoreau's eyes, ears, and hands. As for war, Thoreau could not bear to acknowledge it. "What anyone can want to read your 'battle of the Pissmires' for, at a time like this, is past finding out," spluttered a furious Parker Pillsbury, who'd begun his letter by calmly asking for a copy of *Walden* for a friend. But good lord! "Who wants to read how you can play with a 'bream' in the water, when the Leviathan of Slavery is hourly threatening to swallow 'Old Abe' like Jonah?" In one thrust, Thoreau's life's work was swept into the dust, worthless, pointless. From his imprisonment, he nevertheless held firm: "I hope that he ignores Fort Sumpter [*sic*], & Old Abe, & all that, for that is just the most fatal and indeed the only fatal, weapon you can direct against evil, ever." What business had an "angel of light" to be pondering the deeds of darkness? "I do not so much regret the present condition of things in this country (provided I regret it at all) as I do that I ever heard of it."[55]

Lincoln had miscalculated; Southern secession was not a local rebellion to be put down in a mere police action. But the terrible truth and cataclysmic costs that unfolded over the coming months and years shaped a course of events that Thoreau would not witness. In the midst of spring's war fever, Dr. Bartlett told him his lungs might not heal in time for another New England winter. He must "clear out" somewhere healthful, perhaps the West Indies. Too muggy, thought Thoreau; he settled instead on Minnesota. Today it seems an odd choice, but then the Upper Midwest was touted as a uniquely healthful climate for consumptives. For Thoreau there were other, still more telling reasons: he had always wanted to see the West. "West *I* must go, at all accounts," he had pleaded with John in his youth. "The West has many attractions for me, particularly the lake country & the Indians," he had told Calvin Greene, tempted by his invitation to Michigan.[56] Margaret Fuller had gone West to restart her career, and her book on that trip provided the model for *A Week*. Emerson toured the West regularly, and with many contacts there, Thoreau would never be far from friends. He also had family out there: Samuel Thatcher Jr., George Thatcher's brother, had moved from Maine to St. Anthony, Minnesota, where his own lung disease had cleared up; he'd lived there happily ever since. The Thatchers could provide a home base and local contacts. Minnesota it would be.

But with whom? Channing was Thoreau's first choice, but Channing waffled. So he turned to Blake, the kind, wise, and ever-devoted disciple: they would have to go slow and take it easy, he warned; he'd need perhaps three months, and would come back by a different route, say, through Mackinaw and Montreal. His romance with Canada pulled him still. "I have no right to offer myself as a companion to anybody," he apologized, in his invalid condition—but perhaps Blake could make a part of this journey with him?[57] Blake, though, had to say no. But the seventeen-year-old Horace Mann Jr., Thoreau's attentive young friend, said yes. Horace had grown up in

Ohio, where his famous father founded and was the first president of Antioch, and he had visited Michigan, so he knew something of the West already. Best of all, he wanted to enroll at Harvard's Lawrence Scientific School, study with Agassiz and Gray, and become a natural scientist. Thoreau with his many Harvard connections would make a perfect tutor. And the boy had a pesky cough, too— Minnesota might be just what he needed. Young Horace was shy, amiable, eager to please, and naively unabashed by the responsibility; as for his mother—a teacher herself, sister to Sophia Hawthorne and to Elizabeth Peabody who had published the *Dial* and "Civil Disobedience"—well, of course she said yes. Henry Thoreau was practically a member of the family.

"It is all a mistake," protested Emerson. Thoreau should stay home, buy "Mr. Minot's piece" instead. That's what he told Ellen, when she came back from bringing Thoreau a map the day before they were set to leave. Ellen invited Henry over to dinner, where the two old friends divided their discussion between natural history and politics, and Emerson did not persuade Thoreau to call it off. Next morning Emerson sent over a farewell note and a list of names of "good men" that an invalid traveler could call on for aid and comfort.[58]

And with that, on Saturday afternoon, May 11, 1861, Henry Thoreau and Horace Mann Jr. boarded the train, gaining speed as they passed Damon's Mills in West Concord, busy cranking out blue Union uniforms.[59] They stayed two nights in Worcester, where Harry Blake took them riding to Quinsigamond Pond; it would be Thoreau's last visit. From there they took the great Western Railroad to Niagara Falls. Passing Pittsfield, Thoreau might have craned his head to see Mount Greylock on the horizon. In Albany they overnighted at the Delavan Hotel, said to be the best in town: "Not so good as costly," grumbled Thoreau, worried about finances. Horace assured his mother that Thoreau "has got along very well, only he is pretty tired." They would rest in Niagara Falls, where they put up for the night at a tourist stop before seeking a boardinghouse next morning, only to find them all full—they had arrived on May 15, the opening day of tourist season. Finally the American House took them in for a dollar a day, and Horace sat down dutifully and again wrote home: Thoreau is better already; he can hear the Falls even as he writes.[60]

Thoreau, too, was writing home: the world-famous falls sounded like "a train coming or a locomotive letting off steam," a sound so familiar he'd hardly noticed it. It was, he jotted in his notes, the "most imposing sight as yet," like the sea off Cape Cod.[61] They botanized around Goat Island, where Thoreau collected his first specimens of the trip, tucking them into his plant press and listing them by the dozen. When they crossed over to Canada for the best view of the falls, they, like everyone else, fell victim to a tourist scam that cost a painful five dollars. He poked around all the little wild spaces he could find. It was cold and wet, and Thoreau felt it. He bought some "trochees," or throat lozenges, to help with his cough.

From Niagara they headed to Chicago on Monday, May 20, taking the train through Lower Ontario, or Canada West, the very country Thoreau had always meant to explore. He liked what he saw out the window—"agreeably diversified"—and Lake Ontario to the north, "quite sea like." But there would be no exploration. At Windsor they ferried across the river to Detroit. Thoreau's correspondent Calvin Greene lived just a few miles north, but a social call was beyond his strength. Instead he let the train carry him through Michigan hardwood forests, bearing west to Lake Michigan, then down through the high sand dunes along the Indiana shoreline into Illinois, reaching Chicago by suppertime. They splurged for two nights at the celebrated Metropolitan Hotel, $1.50 a night, for next day they had urgent business: Horace must convert their Massachusetts bank draft to gold coin. But Chicago was in financial chaos. The city's banks were backed with Southern securities, which now, in wartime, were all failing. Mann worked his connections, finding a family friend who exchanged their Massachusetts bank draft for a check for $100, which, in a small miracle, Thoreau's devoted correspondent Benjamin Wiley, now a banker, converted to $100 of scarce gold coin.

Thoreau had his own round of visits to perform: first to the comfortable sofa of the Reverend Robert Collyer, a fiery abolitionist and Unitarian minister who talked of the war, and the West, and literature, and who long remembered the musicality of Thoreau's low voice, the way he hesitated for the right word or paused with "a pathetic patience to master the trouble in his chest," continuing with words "as distinct and true to the ear as those of a great singer" in sentences perfect and entire.[62] That evening Collyer wrote Thoreau a note: we hope you write your great book about the West, the one "that will be to us what your other books are"—a wish with special poignancy for all Thoreau's Western fans. That afternoon, Horace and Henry toured the town with a family friend, William Hull Clarke, brother to the Transcendentalist James Freeman Clarke, an engineer helping lay out Chicago's 223 miles of sewer lines and a man after Thoreau's own heart: "Sewers or main drains fall but 2 feet in a mile," noted the surveyor who had spent a summer calculating the fall of the Concord River. Next morning Horace made a dash to the post office to mail his update: all was well. Thoreau was "getting along very well," except for "a little trouble with his bowels" due to the lime in the drinking water.[63] Their next mail stop would be St. Anthony, Minnesota.

It would take another three days. They spent a long day riding across the Illinois prairie, passing near the 160-acre homestead Ellery Channing had tried to farm in 1839. From the speeding cars Thoreau, frustrated, craned his neck to see a pink-blooming tree: Was it the wild crabapple? There was no way to tell. At the Mississippi River, in East Dubuque, the line ended; from there they traveled by riverboat. Next morning they were chugging up the Mississippi aboard the *Itasca*, reaching Prairie du Chien, Wisconsin, that afternoon, passing Red Wing, Minnesota, the next evening, and docking at St. Paul early Sunday morning, May 26. Years before, Thoreau had seen a moving panorama of the Mississippi scrolling past, and celebrated it as a picture of the golden age of America. Real life on the Mississippi seemed less heroic. Immense stacks of wheat straw overshadowed wheatfields, houses, and people like "mice nesting in a wheatstack which is their wealth." The river journey fascinated him: each little one-street village was a drama in itself, the stately approach of the steamboat, the whistles and bells, the postmaster running down with his bag, the passengers hustling off and on, the dogs and pigs rushing to the commotion, the great silent bluffs beyond.[64] After breakfasting in St. Paul, they rode nine miles by stage through a rainstorm to St. Anthony. After two long weeks, they had arrived. Now for a warm welcome by the Thatchers and a long healing rest.

Instead they found the Thatcher household in crisis. Samuel Thatcher had been thrown from a carriage, and his injuries were life threatening. Soon he would die of them. Of course Thoreau and Horace could not stay, but before they left, Thatcher managed to pen a note recommending the wayfarers to his friend Dr. Charles L. Anderson, a local physician who lived across the river in Minneapolis. From a room in the Tremont House overlooking the river, Henry wrote Sophia of their relative's plight while Horace wrote his mother another reassuring letter. For nine days they explored the area around St. Anthony. Horace, the budding naturalist, bought a five-gallon keg at the local drugstore that he filled with alcohol, and which the obliging owner allowed him to keep in the store, so each day Horace could deposit into it whatever he had shot. When it was full, he'd seal it up and ship it home for dissection and study. Gleefully Horace went to work with his gun, blasting away at birds and small animals, while Henry—who had long ago put his gun away—nosed around collecting plants and observing prairie birds. He must have explained his philosophy to Horace, for over the course of their weeks together the young man began to shoot less and botanize more. In fact, at Harvard, Horace Mann would grow into the era's most promising young botanist, the very man Asa Gray himself picked to be his successor. Thoreau had made another convert.

On Tuesday they looked up Dr. Anderson, who happened to be the Minnesota state geologist. The moment he read Thatcher's note, he invited them home to dinner, and that afternoon he drove them out in his buggy to see Lake Calhoun. The next day he drove them down to Minnehaha Falls—a name made famous by Longfellow's *Hiawatha*, but which, Thoreau noted testily, was entirely fictitious—

then out to Fort Snelling, whence three hundred men had just left for the Civil War. Anderson was a generous host: later he drove them into the great woods to the northwest and opened his library to them as well, so when the weather turned cold and wet, Henry could curl up by the fireside with copies of the *Transactions of the Wisconsin State Agricultural Society* or the *Annals of the Minnesota Historical Society*. He took pages of notes: when the last bison was seen in Wisconsin (1832) and the last beaver (1819), the Indians' culture of wild rice, the best books to follow up for further studies.

For Thoreau was still thinking ahead. Here in the western prairie was a fascinating new landscape, a whole new laboratory to test his ideas. Every plant he listed was a fresh bundle of relations, facts that keyed to a changing landscape of flowers and seeds, new suites of animals, deep histories of Native land uses, settlement, destruction, regeneration. Thoreau was particularly curious about the distinctive "oak openings," clusters of oaks kept open by fire such that the scattered trees each developed full and rounded crowns. The University of Minnesota, he found, was set "in the midst of such an oak opening," which looked strangely artificial. Did he think back to Inches Woods and the Indians' use of fire to keep the forest open? He roamed and rested, studied and took notes, working intensely, filling his field notebook, laying a foundation for future work. It was his usual method: dense, elliptical jottings in the field for expansion in his Journal, revision into lectures, essays, books. This was meant to be the start of a new chapter on the West.

Lake Calhoun, four miles southwest of Minneapolis, proved too enticing to merely visit. On Wednesday, June 5, they rode to the lakefront boardinghouse run by one of the region's first settlers, the widowed Mrs. Hamilton, and for nine idyllic days at the edge of the prairie they ate fish, went swimming, and explored. When Thoreau ran into some local lumberers, he was full of questions; Minnesota was nothing, they told him, compared to the Penobscot. And here, Thoreau finally found the wild crabapple. The Hamiltons had tried to transplant a few trees, but they were tricky to manage and had not survived; neither had those planted by their horticulturalist neighbor, Jonathan Grimes. But Grimes led Thoreau toward a few living trees in his pasture, and finally Thoreau had the pleasure of finding the wild apple for himself, and securing "a lingering corymb of flowers for my herbarium."[65]

But something broke into this idyll. Thoreau had planned to stay for a couple of months, but after three weeks he was ready to leave. Did his health defeat his hopes for recovery? Were their funds running low? Perhaps it was the news from the war front: the first major engagement, the Battle of Big Bethel on June 10, flooded the newspapers with alarming reports of Union incompetence and Confederate victory, the first clear signal that this would be no brief skirmish but a long and bloody campaign. Northern troops were dying, and Confederate forces were advancing. Thoreau had tried to avoid the war, but at Lake Calhoun his closest contacts, Dr. Anderson and Jonathan Grimes, were both Virginians. Talk of the war infected everything. "Our faces are already set for home," he wrote in a letter to Sanborn.[66]

But first there was an opportunity Thoreau could not resist: the newspaper announced a special excursion, only ten dollars round-trip, for a two-hundred-mile riverboat journey up the Minnesota River to the Lower Sioux Agency in Redwood, where five thousand Indians had gathered to receive the government's annual annuity payments, promised by treaty to the Sioux (known today as the Dakota) in exchange for the southern half of what, since 1858, was the new state of Minnesota. It would be the perfect climax. On Friday, June 14, they returned to St. Anthony so Horace could ship home his keg full of critters, then moved to St. Paul for the weekend. On Monday they boarded the side-wheeled steamboat *Frank Steele*— named, Thoreau noted, after "the first white man who flashed his axe in the unbroken wilderness." That afternoon they embarked on the "Grand Pleasure Excursion to the Sioux Agency" up the meandering Minnesota (or "sky-tinted") River. [67]

It was late in the season and the water was low, making for a slow trip as the boat ran aground and backed astern to swing around tight, winding turns. There was lots of time to watch the shore slide past, so close they could reach out a hand and sample the plant life. On board, a hundred boisterous partygoers tripped to the tunes of two different German dance bands. Also on board were twenty-five soldiers bound for Fort Ridgely to train for the Civil War, Minnesota Governor Alexander Ramsey and his wife, the new Indian agent Thomas Galbraith, a few other officials, and by coincidence, Joseph May, a cousin of the Alcotts and a Harvard classmate of Sanborn's. About half the people they met in Minnesota, Thoreau calculated, had come there from Massachusetts. Henry and Horace had a stateroom, giving them some privacy against the crowds that piled aboard and slept on chairs, decks, or sprawled over trunks.

They arrived in Red Wing four days later, at 9:00 a.m. on June 20. Henry and Horace had just enough time to walk a few miles south to overlook the Great Plains. Henry longed for more time, to walk farther, far enough to see the bison herds said to be grazing twenty or thirty miles away. Instead they turned back to witness the council meeting at one o'clock. The annuity payments, $100 to each "chief" and $20 to each "brave," would not, it was announced, be made that day after all. But there were plenty of speeches. Governor Ramsey assured the Indians that the new Fort Ridgely offered no threat, only protection against the bad white men, and Galbraith promised to look after them "as a father should care for his children." Thoreau, dipping his pen in irony, noted the Dakota looked "hungry, not sleek & round faced" like children well cared-for. Their spokesman was Red Owl, a dark and sinewy Mdewakanton with an intelligent face from Wabash's band, a vigorous and eloquent orator. His complaints were many and bitter: stingy payments, promised food and supplies diverted and lost, promised schools unbuilt. Altogether they were quite dissatisfied, noted Thoreau, "and probably have reason to be so," adding that the Indians, as usual, had "the advantage in point of truth and earnestness, and therefore of eloquence."[68]

The speeches over, two beef oxen were presented, and one of them was butchered and cooked for a general feast. The dance followed: thirty men, Thoreau counted, half-naked, dancing to twelve musicians. Some were blowing flutes; others struck their bows with arrows. They kept good time, moving "feet & shoulders, one or both." What he saw and thought of the Dakota was never made public, but another onlooker published his report in the newspaper: the Indians' dance was nothing but "the rudest hoppings" with wild howls and vehement gesticulations, "a pitiable, disgusting spectacle" that proved these "poor childish creatures" could never be elevated unless such barbarism were stamped out.[69]

The dance over, the boatload of inebriated tourists headed back toward St. Paul. The band made them howl with laughter by stomping around in moccasins, draped in quilts and chanting "ugh" to each of the governor's pompous pronouncements. Apparently Henry and Horace were sheltering in their stateroom and spared the spectacle. Thoreau noted many had purchased souvenirs for fifty cents or a dollar or two, elaborate ceremonial pipes carved of the distinctive red Catlinite pipestone. Thoreau himself had acquired not tourist art but functional clothing. Many of the Dakota were being forced to exchange their Native attire for proper European trousers and jackets and dresses; he may have bargained with some for their clothing, or he may have picked a few items out of the discard pile: a man's handsome fringed deerskin jacket and leggings; a woman's deerskin dress, beautifully fringed and beaded; a fine working saddle, elaborately beaded, with stamped leather stirrups. He also noted that "the most prominent chief was named Little Crow," the future leader of the Dakota War.[70] Red Owl would not survive the harsh winter to come; Little Crow, who lived nearby, would take his place.

The annuity payments were eventually made, but they were the last the Dakota ever saw. That summer, cutworm destroyed their corn crops, and the winter that followed was unusually bitter. By the following summer they were starving. Galbraith proved incompetent; time and again the desperately needed annuity payments were unaccountably delayed. Without money, the Dakota were refused the food stored for them in the warehouse. Tensions exploded in August, when four young Dakota killed five white settlers. In the war that followed, hundreds of whites and unknown numbers of Dakota were killed. Governor Ramsey vowed that all the Sioux Indians of Minnesota must be "exterminated or driven forever beyond the borders of the State."[71] The treaties were nullified, the reservations disbanded, and the surviving Dakota forced under armed guard to Fort Snelling or pushed westward out of the state. Three hundred and three Dakota men were condemned to be hanged. President Lincoln commuted the sentences of all but thirty-eight, who were hanged in a public spectacle, the largest mass execution in US history.

Some of them were likely men Thoreau had seen, perhaps had spoken with. Little Crow fled west. In July 1863 he was shot by a white settler while picking blueberries with his son; his grave, if any, is unknown. His head and arms were put on public display at the Minnesota Historical Society, until they were removed and eventually returned to his descendants in 1971, who buried them in a private ceremony. What words would Thoreau, the defender of John Brown, have written had he lived to hear of Little Crow's desperate battle? How would Thoreau have reacted to the government's abrogation of the treaties, to the forced removal of the Dakota—the very people he had seen and met—to the hanging of thirty-eight Dakota men for defending their treaty rights and ancestral lands, or to the public display, in a historical museum, of Little Crow's decapitated head? Here, too, Thoreau's life reads like a prelude to an alternative history that died in the cradle.

Two days after the *Frank Steele* left the Lower Sioux, Henry and Horace were back in St. Paul. They stayed overnight before heading downriver to Red Wing on Sunday, June 23. There they stopped for three nights, picking up their mail, swimming in the Mississippi, exploring the steep-sided Barn Bluff, viewing the grave of Chief Red Wing at the summit, and visiting with Professor Horace Wilson at Hamline University. On June 26 they continued down the Mississippi on the steamboat *War Eagle*, disembarking the next morning at Prairie du Chien to board the railroad straight across Wisconsin to Milwaukee. They passed through Madison on June 27, where the university had just let out for the year, and a twenty-three-year-old John Muir was, that very day, walking north to his home in Portage.

Muir, a student of geology, botany, and chemistry, had just finished his first term. Not until he quit school for "the University of the Wilderness" would he hear of Thoreau, who would become one of his heroes; in Muir's work, Thoreau's emerging environmental activism would mature into a national politics.

Thoreau and Mann arrived in Milwaukee to find the city under martial law after the banks had failed and riots had broken out. Next morning, after a night under guard at the Lake House, Thoreau posted a letter of thanks to Dr. Anderson, and they boarded the *Edith*, outward bound across the northern length of Lake Michigan with a cargo of flour and three safes. Horace had fond memories of his summer on Mackinaw Island, and when they docked there at 2:00 a.m. on June 30, he led Thoreau down Main Street to the Mackinac House, their home for the next four days. Minnesota had become uncomfortably hot—102 in the shade, someone read off the *Frank Steele*'s thermometer—but here it was so cool that Thoreau found himself, on July 2, sitting by the fire. The list of plants he found on Mackinaw runs for pages, showing him active and curious still.[72]

On July 4, they cadged a ride on a freight ship for the long trip across Lake Huron, arriving at Goderich, Ontario the next evening and boarding the train for Toronto in the morning. Even in Canada they could not escape the turmoil of war: the escalating violence led Canadians to call for garrisons on the border, lest the war spill north into the nation where so many fugitive slaves had found new lives. They also feared Union blockades of Southern ports would cut off Southern cotton bound for British mills and destabilize the Canadian economy. Special elections were held to install a new government to cope with the threats. The polls closed late in the afternoon of Sunday July 7, just as Henry and Horace stepped off the railroad platform. As they made their way to the Rossin House downtown, the victors were being announced. Even here, the world was in an uproar.

The next day they retreated to the grounds of Toronto College before boarding the Grand Trunk Railway, which they rode east along Lake Ontario, then up the St. Lawrence River. At Prescott

Junction they ferried to Ogdensburg, New York. It was morning, July 9, and they had many hours to wait until the next train to Boston, at 4:00 a.m. What they did is unknown. Henry's notes stop here, and Horace had already posted his last letter home. The tired travelers finished with a long, weary ride through northernmost New York, across Vermont and New Hampshire, and down into Massachusetts along the Merrimack River. Gazing at the once-familiar landscape, Thoreau could see the changes wrought by two decades of industrialization. They arrived in Boston too late to catch the last train for Concord. They had friends in the city and could have sought them out, but instead they waited through the night for the first train home. It was Thursday morning, July 11, when they walked the last couple of blocks from Concord station: to Horace Mann's home on Sudbury Road, where his mother greeted her son; a bit farther on to Henry's home on Main Street, where his mother, sister, and aunts were relieved to see him home again, safe, after a long two months away.

It was a bittersweet homecoming. Thoreau had set off still hopeful, still venturing, still planning future work. He came back knowing that he had, at best, a few months to live. It was a hard blow to family and friends. His letters home had told of views and adventures without a word about his health, and Horace had always insisted his charge was "pretty well," always just about to get better. About his own cough Horace said nothing, but it is all the more heartbreaking that he, too, would die of consumption, at age twenty-six, on the verge of a major career in science. When Alcott read the reports they sent home, he dared to hope that Thoreau's trip West had been "predestined from the beginning," his "lassitude" merely the sign that he had exhausted Concord and was ready for a new field of observation. But now the truth was evident to all. Moncure Conway visited Thoreau shortly after the Battle of Bull Run on July 21—the first pivotal battle of the Civil War, another Union rout. Conway found his old friend was the only happy man in Concord, "in a state of exaltation about the moral regeneration of the nation"—but also "sadly out of health." Perhaps it was he who wrote the note, published soon after in the *New-York Tribune,* alerting the world that the celebrated naturalist and poet was in "poor health."[73] The season of goodbyes had begun.

"THE LEAVES TEACH US HOW TO DIE"

Back in October 1860, Thoreau had opened his latest letter from Daniel Ricketson to find his old friend was seriously annoyed: "Friend Thoreau, Am I to infer from your silence that you decline any further correspondence and intercourse with me?" An embarrassed Thoreau replied he meant no neglect, but was merely busy; then in March 1861 he had to tell the anxious Ricketson that "bronchitis" kept him indoors. Now, back from Minnesota, Thoreau found waiting a most extraordinary letter announcing the old Quaker's born-again conversion to Christianity. "I hardly know what to say," he wrote back; "I must see you before I can judge." Of course!— responded Ricketson. Come visit; all you need is rest and mild occupation, the perfect Ricketson cure.[74] On August 19, the old friends met at the depot, and Ricketson began administering treatment: long fireside talks in the Shanty, slow buggy rides around the lake. But seeing Thoreau put him in a tailspin. Thoreau's case was critical, his cough nasty, his body emaciated. But his spirits were good— reason to keep fighting.

Two days later, on a clear warm morning, Ricketson drove Thoreau to the studio of E. S. Dunshee, photographer, where his friend obligingly sat for two ambrotypes. One was lighter, and Ricketson kept it for himself, leaving the other image, darker and stronger, at the studio. The photograph delighted his family—an excellent likeness, they agreed, scarcely showing Henry's loss of health. From its oval frame, an aging Thoreau looks out soberly, in formal attire, full beard trimmed, mustache grizzled, hair as ever dressed by a pine cone. His gaze holds ours: gray eyes steady, deep and sad as a requiem. Alcott saw in the portrait the pallor of disease, and Emerson thought the beard disfigured his friend's face, but when Ricketson sent Sophia the second copy, she could not hold back her tears at seeing "her own lost brother again," just a "slight shade about the eyes expressive of weariness."[75] It was the last image of Thoreau, and his last trip away from home.

Ricketson could not bear to see his friend so ill. He persuaded his personal physician, Dr. Denniston, to visit Thoreau. The two arrived together on September 2. Thoreau listened to the doctor's prescription, a course of water treatments starting with a two-week stay at his spa, and politely declined. Ricketson returned home convinced Thoreau was improving. Others thought so, too: Channing wrote Mary Russell Watson that another month of such recovery would see Thoreau well again. Judge Hoar lent him a horse and carriage, and in the fine autumn days Henry took Sophia out riding.[76] Sometime that September they rode to Walden Pond together, where she sketched as he sat and gazed out on the pond, tossing grapes from a vine overhead into its clear waters—his last visit to the pond that, since childhood, had been the drapery of his dreams.[77] In October he assured Ricketson that, on the whole, his health was better. But, as he admitted, "It is easy to talk, but hard to write."[78] It was his last letter to Ricketson. They did not see each other again.

On November 3, Thoreau took his Journal out one last time. He had abandoned regular entries since he first caught cold, and after Minnesota he had brought it out only a few times, mostly to capture his fond observations of the family's several cats and newest kittens. Then, at noon on November 3, 1861, he looked outdoors: a violent storm was just clearing, and what he saw gave him the conclusion he wanted. The wind-driven rain had carved ruler-straight ridges behind each pebble, from which he could read the precise direction of the storm. "All this is perfectly distinct to an observant eye," he wrote, "and yet could easily pass unnoticed by most. Thus each wind is self-registering."[79] With this he closed his Journal, his great monument to self-registration, forever.

The cold of winter undermined all his apparent progress. Writing was impossible; but talking, as Thoreau had said to Ricketson, was easy, and with his writing voice stilled, his speaking voice became his lifeline. A family friend recalled how, that last winter, toward evening a flush would come to his cheeks and "an ominous brightness and beauty to his eyes, painful to behold." His conversation was "brilliant," and he held them charmed, talking "until his weak voice could no longer articulate." At a family dinner in December, Alcott found the feeble Thoreau expansive on books, men, and the nation's "civil troubles," impatient as ever with the politicians' "temporizing" and the people's "indifferency" to the true issues at stake. He sat up with the family at the dinner table as long as he possibly could, telling Channing, "It would not be social to take my meals alone."[80] When he grew too weak to manage the stairs, Sophia had his cane bed brought down to the front parlor overlooking the river, where she surrounded her brother with plants and flowers. At bedtime she arranged the furniture so the lamplight would make fantastical shadows on the walls to entertain him on sleepless nights. Sophia Hawthorne sent over their "sweet old musicbox" so he could lie back and rest as it dreamed forth its tunes, and neighbors brought more flowers, dropping by daily with tempting treats—a dish of jelly, fresh-caught game, sweet apples and bottles of cider.[81]

At first the town's children stayed away, fearing to disturb the sick man. "Why don't they come to see me?" Thoreau cried to Sophia, watching them pass by. "I love them as if they were my own." Sophia told Lidian, who told Edith, who spread the word, and after that, children came often. Ever the teacher, Thoreau once asked some lads who had been robbing birds' nests if they knew what a wail of anguish their cruelty sent over the fields and through the woods.[82] The universal kindness brought out the side of Henry he hid from all but his most trusted friends. While Emerson said the stoic Henry was "with difficulty sweet," Ed Hoar explained that Henry was "very affectionate," but had gotten it in his head that people didn't mean what they said. But now, with all the visits and flowers, "he came to feel very differently toward people, and said if he had known he wouldn't have been so offish."[83]

Formal callers found him in an easy chair, dressed in a handsome black suit instead of his raffish dun corduroys. Intimate friends found him surrounded by masses of books and manuscripts, busy and cheerful, delighting them with his bon mots. One day in January, Blake and Brown skated through a snowstorm all the way from Framingham to spend a few hours. "You have been skating on the river," Thoreau told them; "perhaps I am going to skate on some other." Perhaps that was when the conversation turned to gray hair. He'd never had any trouble in his life, teased Thoreau, at least not since about age fourteen, when for a little while he felt bad on account of his sins—"but no trouble since that I know of. That must be the reason my hair doesn't turn gray faster. But there is Blake; he is as gray as a rat."[84] When his orthodox Aunt Louisa asked, "Henry, have you made your peace with God?" he answered pleasantly, "I did not know we had ever quarreled, Aunt." By the time Parker Pillsbury called, Thoreau's voice was reduced to a whisper. "I suppose this is the best you can do now," Pillsbury said as he grasped Thoreau's hand. "The outworks seem almost ready to give way." "Yes," whispered Thoreau with a smile, "but as long as she cracks she holds"— the saying of boys playing kittlybenders on the vanished millpond ice. Pillsbury kept on: "You seem so near the brink of the dark river, that I almost wonder how the opposite shore may appear to you." "One world at a time," quipped Thoreau.[85]

When his speaking voice failed, Thoreau took command of his literary voice. "You know it's respectable to leave an estate to one's friends," he whispered to Reverend Reynolds, who found him sitting up amid a sea of manuscripts. There could be no new work. Mary Stearns sorrowed that Thoreau would not write the biography of John Brown, leaving it to be written by "the winds of heaven."[86] There would be no *Wild Fruits* or *Dispersion of Seeds*, either. After working through the fall, accumulating hundreds of pages, that winter Thoreau arranged the pages carefully, wrapped the thick bundles, and tied them with string, putting them away for posterity.[87] Then he turned to the rest of his literary legacy. Sometime that winter, James Fields, the publisher of *Walden*, offered to publish Thoreau's lectures in the *Atlantic*, which he had just taken over from Thoreau's nemesis, James Russell Lowell. On February 11, 1862, too weak to hold a quill pen, Thoreau penciled a reply for Sophia to copy and mail: Yes, the *Atlantic* could publish them—on two conditions. Fields must alter no "sentence or sentiment" without Thoreau's consent, and Thoreau must keep the copyright.

The deal was struck. Sophia added amanuensis and assistant editor to her other roles of caretaker, companion, and, eventually, literary executor: one by one she passed the pages through Henry's hands. She read his drafts aloud when his eyes failed, entered his corrections, made fair copies when pages became too muddled with changes, took his letters by dictation, and sent essay after essay to the *Atlantic*'s owners, Ticknor and Fields.[88] "Autumnal Tints" was the first and most urgent. Thoreau had it ready in a week, and sent it with his carefully chosen scarlet oak leaf to be engraved. The autumn leaves "teach us how to die," he affirmed on his deathbed. "One wonders if the time will ever come when men . . . will lie down as gracefully and as ripe,—with such an Indian-summer serenity will shed their bodies, as they do their hair and nails."[89]

Next was *Walden*: they settled on terms for a new edition, and Thoreau made one change, dropping the subtitle "Life in the Woods." *Walden* was, of course, about far more than that. Then came "Higher Law," his latest title for the much-reworked lecture he wrote in *Walden*'s wake under the title "What Shall It Profit?". When Fields objected to the new title, Thoreau changed it again, and the great polemic "Life without Principle" at last took its final form. By now it was March, and Thoreau was polishing its companion essay, "Walking, or The Wild": "The West of which I speak is but another name for the Wild," wrote the man who had returned from the West with dying eyes; "and what I have been preparing to say is, that in Wildness is the preservation of the world." Through the rest of March, between reading page proofs, Henry and Sophia tied off "Wild Apples," and Sophia recruited Elizabeth Hoar to assist.

Now Henry was racing the clock. Would they take on his stored copies of *A Week*, and reissue the book? Yes, they agreed, though their terms were not attractive. No matter. Thoreau had no time to dicker. *The Maine Woods* urgently needed his attention, especially the unfinished third section on Joe Polis. Thoreau had originally entitled it "The Allegash and Webster Stream," but no book of his would do honor to the name of Daniel Webster, certainly no book with Polis's account of Webster's rudeness to the Indian. Thoreau struck out the offending words and wrote above them, "East Branch." In the somber mood of these weeks, he was also striking out all the sentences that pained him with their mirthfulness.[90] Perhaps that was why he deleted his convivial defense of Indians as "good fellows." But an ending still eluded him: "It is a knot I cannot untie," he sighed to Sanborn, and he left it unfinished, forever suspended in the act of saying goodbye to Polis on Indian Island. He had worried how Polis would react to reading his portrait of him. By the time *The Maine Woods* was published in 1864, the omnicompetent Polis was fighting for the Union in the Civil War, where he lost an arm. What he thought of Thoreau's portrait of him was not recorded.[91]

Thoreau's friends were captured by the deep deliberation of his dying. As early as January, Theo Brown found him in an "exalted" state of mind, insisting "it was as good to be sick as to be well." To an admiring correspondent, Thoreau replied in March that he *supposed* he had not long to live, but "I am enjoying existence as much as ever, and regret nothing."[92] A few days later, Sam Staples came away from Henry's deathbed declaring, "Never saw a man dying with so much pleasure & peace." In fact, Staples told Emerson, very few in Concord really knew Mr. Thoreau. Sophia, wrestling with her own grief, wrote Ricketson of her sainted brother's "child like trust" in his fate, "as if he were being translated rather than dying in the ordinary way of most mortals." Come, Henry chided his distraught friend, come *soon*, "and be cheered."[93] From then on, Ricketson sent a succession of bubbly letters, but still he could not bear to come in person. By contrast, Channing rarely left Thoreau's side. He was profoundly moved that his dearest friend refused all opiates, "declaring uniformly that he preferred to endure with a clear mind the worst penalties of suffering, rather than be plunged in a turbid dream by narcotics." Sleep, Thoreau told Channing, had its own terrors. One night he dreamed he was the railroad cut, and they were digging through and laying down the rails, right through his lungs.[94]

On Sunday May 4, Alcott came by and, finding Channing already there, they went in together to see their friend. Alcott feared for Channing, knowing the "great desolation" Thoreau's death would be to him. And Channing never forgot how Alcott, that day, bent down and kissed Henry's brow "when the damps and sweat of death lay upon it, even if Henry knew it not." It seemed "an extreme unction," with Alcott the best priest. Perhaps it was then he heard Thoreau murmur the words "moose" and "Indians." The next day the mail brought Ricketson's last letter, and Sophia read it aloud to Henry: "I hope this may find you *mending*," wrote the incurable optimist to his "dear and fellow pilgrim."[95] Later that afternoon, Sophia caught one of the Hosmer sisters passing the house, and told her Henry was asking for her brother to come sit with him through the night. Edmund, the "long-headed" farmer-philosopher who had helped raise the house at Walden, came, telling Henry he'd heard the robins sing as he walked along. "This is a beautiful world," whispered Henry, "but soon I shall see one that is fairer. I have so loved nature. . . ." At his request, Sophia brought down Henry's personal copy of *A Week*, the one in which he kept a lock of John's hair, and Henry pressed it into the hands of his oldest surviving friend.[96]

At 7:00 a.m. Tuesday morning, May 6, Judge Hoar called from across the street with a spring bouquet of hyacinths, which Henry smelled, and liked. He began to grow restless, and at eight he asked to be raised sitting up. Sophia, Cynthia, and Aunt Louisa all watched as his breath grew faint, then fainter, until at nine o'clock in the morning he was still. Her brother's mind was clear to the last, said Sophia; as she read to him from his river voyage with John, she heard him say, "Now comes good sailing."[97] At forty-four years of age, Henry Thoreau had lived just long enough to see one last spring, and one more dawn.

→-⋅-←

Word went out quickly. Channing brought the news to the Alcotts, Emerson wrote to Blake and James Fields, and someone brought the news to the Old Manse, where Sarah Ripley wrote a friend: "This fine morning is sad for those of us who sympathize with the friends of Henry Thoreau, the philosopher and the woodman." They agreed that Alcott would plan the funeral, to be held at the First Parish Church. Alcott modeled it on the memorial Thoreau designed for John Brown: a public event, a town ceremony. As school superintendent, he ordered the town's teachers to dismiss classes early that day so the children could attend. By three o'clock on Friday, May 9, the church where Thoreau had stood to defend John Brown was again filled: Anna Alcott Pratt and Louisa May Alcott came early with their father, and saw to it that Henry Thoreau lay in state, covered in wildflowers and forest boughs. While the church bell tolled, according to tradition, forty-four times, once for each year of Thoreau's life, the company filed in: the Thoreau family with George Thatcher from Maine; the Emerson family; Harry Blake and Theo Brown from Worcester; James and Annie Fields from Boston; Nathaniel and Sophia Hawthorne with Una, Julian, and Rose; and untold others. Sophia Hawthorne told a friend she would have preferred to mourn in private, but attended to show others "her deep respect and value" for the man whose death made "a very large vacuum" in Concord.[98]

With Thoreau's voice stilled, other voices took over. Reverend Reynolds opened the funeral with a few verses from the Bible, and the choir sang a hymn written by Ellery Channing: "His perfect trust shall keep the fire, / His glorious peace disarm all loss!" Bronson Alcott rose and read Thoreau's early poem "Sic Vita" and passages from *A Week*: "May we not *see* God?" he had Thoreau ask.[99] Emerson's sermon had grown so long that it filled the lengthening afternoon. As he said near the end of this eulogy to his closest lifelong friend, "The scale on which his studies proceeded was so large as to require longevity, and we were the less prepared for his sudden disappearance. The country knows not yet, or in the least part, how great a son it has lost." After Reverend Reynolds ended with a prayer, six of Thoreau's friends lifted his coffin to their shoulders and carried it across Bedford Road to his grave in the New Burying Ground, followed by the procession of his friends and over three hundred of Concord's schoolchildren. There, among the violets and under the pines, they laid him between his brother and his father. There went, thought Sophia Hawthorne, "Concord itself in one man."[100]

Years later—no one thought to record exactly when—the graves of Henry Thoreau and his family were moved from the slope behind Bedford Road to the edge of the glacial ridge overlooking Sleepy Hollow, where they joined the Emersons, the Alcotts, and the Hawthornes on what folks took to calling "Authors' Ridge." Thoreau had been no fan of Sleepy Hollow when it opened, and had made a point of boycotting the dedication ceremony, but when the architects called for a new pond in the meadow behind the ridge, Thoreau leveled for it—the only job he accepted during the summer of 1855, when his illness first threatened his life. Thoreau had often visited the place since, watching skeptically as workmen shoveled the artificial pond out of the meadow, finally finishing it in the summer of 1859.

What happened next had stunned him: only months later, the cemetery gardeners were hauling in good-sized fish—bream!—and pickerel!—and then not a year later, in October 1860, he found it graced with great yellow pond lilies, and little kalmiana lilies too. Where had they come from, these unplanned, undesigned wild settlers? It was a revelation: "You will no sooner have your pond dug than nature will begin to stock it," he marveled. "Thus in the midst of death we are in life."[101] The insight had jolted him awake, as awake as he had ever been at Walden Pond, and sent him back outdoors day after day throughout the fall of 1860, writing in a kind of ecstasy of nature's bottomless vitality. How fitting that from his grave on Author's Ridge, Thoreau looks down upon the pond he helped create, the spring of wild life there in the midst of death—a constant new creation.

As for Tahatawan's arrowhead, Thoreau never found its maker. But his final advice to Edward Emerson, about to leave on his own journey West to the Rocky Mountains, was to carry an arrowhead in his pocket and hold it up to every Indian he met, until he found the one who could tell him the secret of how it was made.[102] The charge Henry had been given, back in September 1837 on the banks of the Musketaquid, was now in the hands of his heirs.

Acknowledgments

It has been a very long journey since the day I walked into Island Books, on Mercer Island, Washington, and found *Walden* on its shelves; I'm happy to report that this fine independent bookseller continues to thrive. In the decades since, I have accumulated a literal lifetime of debts, far too many to acknowledge properly. I'm deeply grateful to all my friends, colleagues, students, and audiences who have so patiently borne with my Thoreau obsession, and even fostered it through lively questions and discussions. At the University of Washington, Martha Banta and Robert Abrams first showed me how to turn passion into scholarship. At the University of Iowa, Robert Sayre introduced me to Transcendentalism with the stunning news that some of Thoreau's best writing had never been published. Nearly a decade later, at Indiana University, Lee Sterrenburg introduced me to science studies and turned me loose to explore Thoreau's writings, with the aid of Kenneth Johnston, Jim Justus, Christoph Lohmann, and Cary Wolfe; the encouragement of Scott Russell Sanders and Christoph Irmscher; and the inspiration of Richard Nash and my cohorts in the Science and Literature Affinity Group—special thanks to Donna Haraway and Bruno Latour for giving us, in those heady days, the pluriverse. Those rich exchanges became the foundation for my *Seeing New Worlds: Henry David Thoreau and Nineteenth-Century Natural Science*, which George Levine generously helped shepherd into print. During those years, I was teaching at Lafayette College, where I have too many debts to list—but a tip of the hat to James Woolley, who, when I said my first book had paid my debt to Thoreau, replied, Don't be too sure about that. He was right.

I was introduced to Thoreau studies in the best possible way: at the Thoreau Society Golden Jubilee of 1991. I will always honor Edmund Schofield for putting me, an unknown graduate student, onto a panel, and my fellow panelists Bob Sattelmeyer and Bill Rossi for their generosity then and many, many times thereafter. The Thoreau Society offers a home for Thoreauvians of all kinds, and I have been deeply grateful, through all the years and meetings since, to my many friends and colleagues there. Among them—too many to name!—I must thank Walter Harding for bringing Thoreau into our time; Walter Brain for Thrush Alley; Tom Potter for holding us all together; Joe Wheeler for preserving Thoreau's Birth House; and Beth Witherell for steadfastly anchoring Princeton's Thoreau Edition, bringing new revelations with every volume. I owe special thanks to Mike Berger, Shirley Blancke, Ron Bosco, Kristen Case, Patrick Chura, James Finley, Mike Frederick, Jayne Gordon, Ron Hoag, Samantha Harvey, Bob Hudspeth, Rochelle Johnson, Linck Johnson, John Kucich, John and Lorna Mack, Dan Malachuk, Ian Marshall, Andrew Menard, Austin Meredith, Wes Mott, Dan Peck, Nikita Pokrovsky, David Robinson, Dick Schneider, Corinne Hosfeld Smith, Richard Smith, Robert Thorson, and all of you who have so cheerfully sweated with us through hot summer days in Concord's Masonic Temple and cooled off with drinks at Concord's Colonial Inn: may it long continue. Above all, to Francois Specq, for France; to Sandy Petrulionis, for comradeship; and, finally and forever, to Brad Dean. Everyone who knew Brad knew that Thoreau lived on in him.

To Larry Buell, who has supported me in innumerable ways, I offer the most profound thanks; to Bob Richardson, I owe more than I can ever say; to Bob Gross, I owe thanks for showing how the highest scholarship and the deepest generosity go hand in hand. I thank Wai Chee Dimock for her aid and insight on so many occasions, and Phyllis Cole and Jana Arbersinger for their solidarity: Exaltadas! My understanding of all things Thoreau would be far poorer were it not for the ongoing aid and inspiration of Joel Myerson; this biography was born in our conversations at the University of South Carolina. In my years there I benefitted immensely from the steady wisdom of Paula Feldman, the wry wit of David Shields, John Muckelbauer's nonstop intellectual fireworks, Jerry Wallulis's deep grace, and Ed Madden's unswerving solidarity. My South Carolina graduate students put me on my toes and kept me there; my thanks especially to Jessie Bray for keeping the faith, and to John Higgins, Brad King, Jeffrey Makala, and my research assistant Michael Weisenburg.

This biography could not have been completed without the generosity of the University of Notre Dame, and of the William P. and Hazel B. White Foundation. My deepest thanks to John McGreevy, Dean of the College of Arts and Letters, who opened the door; John Sitter, who lights up the path; and Valerie Sayers, in whom the moral urgency of Transcendentalism lives on. Notre Dame has proven the most exciting of intellectual homes: my thanks to all my colleagues in the English Department, particularly Steve Fallon and Jesse Lander for their support, and to Kate Marshall, Steve Fredman, and Steve and Maria Tomasula for making literature, art, and science alive in our time. My colleagues in the History and Philosophy of Science Program have opened a wealth of interdisciplinary insights: of them all, particular thanks to Katherine Brading, Anjan Chakravartty, Chris Hamlin, Don Howard, and Philip Sloan. My friends in the Sustainability Program remind me daily why Thoreau matters today: of them all, special thanks to Phil Sakimoto, Rachel Novick, and Celia Deane-Drummond. Finally, I honor my dear friend and colleague Jacque Brogan, for her poetry, her intellectual passion, and not least for her brave reading of this manuscript when it was still a raw draft. My Notre Dame graduate students persuade me that we have a future worth fighting for: Erik Larsen, Joel Duncan, Aleksandra Hernandez, Margaret McMillan, Tyler Gardner, Caitlin Smith, Justin Saxby, Jay Miller: you all, singly and together, make Thoreau and Transcendentalism matter. And for making this book better, additional thanks to Erik, Joel, and Aleks, my ever-patient research assistants.

Without the financial support of major foundations, we teachers would spend our lives dreaming of books we never have time to write. I owe deepest thanks to the Guggenheim Foundation, whose fellowship allowed me to begin this book, and to the National Endowment for the Humanities, whose fellowship granted me time to finish it. Publication costs were supported in part by the Institute for Scholarship in the Liberal Arts, College of Arts and Letters, University of Notre Dame; I offer a special note of gratitude to Ken Garcia, the Institute's Associate Director, for his absolutely peerless assistance with all aspects of grant proposals and administration.

This biography could not have been completed without the help of Leslie Perrin Wilson, who so generously opened to me the rich archives of the Concord Free Public Library, and Conni Manoli, who assembled the bulk of the images. At the invaluable Concord Museum, Carol Haines helped me think about outreach, and David Wood helped me grasp Thoreau's words—literally, putting some of Thoreau's most precious possessions into my hands. My thanks to Kathi Anderson and the Walden Woods Project for working to protect Thoreau's landscape and legacy, and to Jeff Cramer at the Thoreau Institute at Walden Woods for so generously sharing his knowledge and the Thoreau archives. My deep thanks to Christine Nelson and the staff of the Morgan Library for their careful stewardship of some of Thoreau's most precious papers; to the Boston Public Library and the New York Public Library's Berg Collection, where the staff so kindly brought out treasure after treasure; and to Paul Schacht, Alan Harding, and the dedicated curators of the Harding Collection at SUNY-Geneseo. My journey would have been incomplete without the guidance and inspiration of Huey, the filmmaker (James Coleman); working with him on his documentary film, *Henry David Thoreau: Surveyor of the Soul*, sharpened my sense of plot and narrative. Thoreau's crucial journeys in the Maine Woods would have been mere tourist excursions had it not been for the Penobscot elders of Indian Island, who welcomed him and opened his eyes. For helping me see how fully the Penobscot Nation lives on today, I offer my humble thanks to the members of the Penobscot Nation, particularly James Francis and Chris Socka-lexis of the Penobscot Nation Cultural and Historic Preservation

Department; Charlie Brown (Chris Francis), Penobscot guide; and James Neptune, Coordinator of the Penobscot Nation Museum on Indian Island.

The University of Chicago Press has been at every stage a model of professionalism. Christie Henry opened the way with her support and encouragement. Kerry Wendt's editorial good sense helped lift this book from clotted printouts to readable pages; Johanna Rosenbohm smoothed them still further, and the book's designer, Jill Shimabukuro, made them beautiful to behold; Levi Stahl enthusiastically ushered those pages into the world; Randy Petilos and Jenni Fry kept it all on track. At every stage, everyone on the staff has made the process of publication a pleasure. Above all, I am forever grateful to Alan Thomas for his shrewd advice and continuing guidance: whatever reach this book attains beyond the Ivory Tower is thanks largely to him. Randall Conrad provided the index, and much more. My anonymous readers smoothed many snags and repaired many errors; those that remain are, of course, my own, which I hope a second edition may someday correct.

My parents, John and Ethel Dassow, made sure their child had a Walden Pond nearby; my godparents, John and Polly Dyer, fought hard to protect the wild places on Seattle's horizon. Finally, above, behind, and through it all, my deepest and most loving thanks to Bob Walls, who has walked this long journey always by my side, no matter where we were.

Abbreviations

ABAJ *The Journals of Amos Bronson Alcott.* Edited by Odell Shepard. Boston: Little, Brown, 1938.

ABAL The Letters of Amos Bronson Alcott. Edited by Richard L. Herrnstadt. Ames: Iowa State University Press, 1969.

CC Henry David Thoreau. *Cape Cod.* Edited by Joseph J. Moldenhauer. Princeton, NJ: Princeton University Press, 1988.

CEP Henry David Thoreau. *Collected Essays and Poems.* Edited by Elizabeth Hall Witherell. New York: Library of America, 2001.

CFPL Concord Free Public Library

CHDT *The Correspondence of Henry David Thoreau.* Edited by Walter Harding and Carl Bode. New York: New York University Press, 1968.

***Corr.,* 1** Henry David Thoreau. *The Correspondence, Volume 1: 1834–1848.* Edited by Robert N. Hudspeth. Princeton, NJ: Princeton University Press, 2013.

***Corr.,* 2** Henry David Thoreau. *The Correspondence, Volume 2: 1849–1856.* Edited by Robert N. Hudspeth. Princeton, NJ: Princeton University Press, forthcoming.

***Corr.,* 3** Henry David Thoreau. *The Correspondence, Volume 3: 1857–1862.* Edited by Robert N. Hudspeth. Princeton, NJ: Princeton University Press, forthcoming.

Days of HT Walter Harding. *The Days of Henry Thoreau: A Biography.* 1965. New York: Dover, 1982.

E&L Ralph Waldo Emerson. *Essays and Lectures.* Edited by Joel Porte. New York: Library of America, 1983.

EEM Henry David Thoreau. *Early Essays and Miscellanies.* Edited by

Joseph J. Moldenhauer et al. Princeton, NJ: Princeton University Press, 1975.

Exc Henry David Thoreau. *Excursions*. Edited by Joseph J. Moldenhauer. Princeton, NJ: Princeton University Press, 2007.

J Henry David Thoreau. *The Journal of Henry David Thoreau*. Edited by Bradford Torrey and Francis Allen. 14 vols. Boston: Houghton Mifflin, 1906; New York: Dover, 1962.

JMN *The Journals and Miscellaneous Notebooks of Ralph Waldo Emerson*. Edited by William Gilman et al. 16 vols. Cambridge, MA: Harvard University Press, 1960–1982.

LRWE *The Letters of Ralph Waldo Emerson*. Edited by Ralph L. Rusk and Eleanor M. Tilton. 10 vols. New York: Columbia University Press, 1939–91.

MW Henry David Thoreau. *The Maine Woods*. Edited by Joseph J. Moldenhauer. Princeton, NJ: Princeton University Press, 1972.

PEJ Henry David Thoreau. *The Journal of Henry D. Thoreau* (Princeton edition *Journal*). 8 vols. to date. Princeton, NJ: Princeton University Press, 1981–.

RP Henry David Thoreau. *Reform Papers*. Edited by Wendell Glick. Princeton, NJ: Princeton University Press, 1973.

Thoreau as Seen William Harding, ed. *Thoreau as Seen by His Contemporaries*. New York: Holt, Rinehart and Winston, 1960; New York: Dover, 1989.

Thoreau Log Raymond R. Borst. *The Thoreau Log: A Documentary Life of Henry David Thoreau, 1817–1862*. New York: G. K. Hall, 1992.

THOT Sandra Harbert Petrulionis, ed. *Thoreau in His Own Time*. Iowa City: University of Iowa Press, 2012.

TL I Bradley P. Dean and Ronald Wesley Hoag. "Thoreau's Lectures before *Walden*: An Annotated Calendar." *Studies in the American Renaissance* (1995): 127–228.

TL II Bradley P. Dean and Ronald Wesley Hoag. "Thoreau's Lectures after *Walden*: An Annotated Calendar." *Studies in the American Renaissance* (1996): 241–362.

To Set This World Sandra Harbert Petrulionis. *To Set This World Right:*

The Antislavery Movement in Thoreau's Concord. Ithaca, NY: Cornell University Press, 2006.

Translations Henry David Thoreau. *Translations*. Edited by Kevin P. Van Anglen. Princeton, NJ: Princeton University Press, 1986.

TSB *Thoreau Society Bulletin.*

Walden Henry David Thoreau. *Walden*. Edited by J. Lyndon Shanley. Princeton, NJ: Princeton University Press, 1971.

Week Henry David Thoreau. *A Week on the Concord and Merrimack Rivers*. Edited by Carl F. Hovde et al. Princeton, NJ: Princeton University Press, 1980.

Notes

PREFACE

1. Ralph Waldo Emerson, "History," opening paragraph (*E&L*, 237); *Walden*, 9.
2. Emerson, "History," in *E&L*, 254.
3. *Walden*, 82; Ellery Channing quoted in Henry S. Salt, *The Life of Henry David Thoreau* (London: Richard Bentley, 1890; revised version of 1908, edited by George Hendrick, Willene Hendrick, and Fritz Oehlschlaeger. Urbana: University of Illinois Press, 1993, 2000), 55. See Alan D. Hodder, *Thoreau's Ecstatic Witness* (New Haven, CT: Yale University Press, 2001), 190; see also Philip Cafaro's *Thoreau's Living Ethics: Walden and the Pursuit of Virtue* (Athens: University of Georgia Press, 2005), an excellent introduction to Thoreau's ethics of simplicity.
4. *Exc.*, 202. For Thoreau and climate science, see the work of Richard B. Primack, starting with *Walden Warming: Climate Change Comes to Thoreau's Woods* (Chicago: University of Chicago Press, 2014). The word *ecology* was coined by the German scientist-artist Ernst Haeckel in 1866, four years after Thoreau's death. Donald Worster, *Nature's Economy: A History of Ecological Ideas* (Cambridge: Cambridge University Press, 1977), 191–93.
5. Henry Seidel Canby, *Thoreau* (Boston: Houghton Mifflin, 1939), xvi–xx.
6. As Sophia Thoreau wrote to Ellen Sewall Osgood, May 23 [1875?]: "By accident one letter alone of dear John's has escaped the flames. I will enclose it at y'r request. I have found it a painful task to destroy my family letters—many sad duties fall to the lot of the last of a race." Thoreau-Sewall-Ward Papers, IVJ: Ellen Sewall Papers, letter #70, Thoreau Society Archives, Henley Library.
7. Many fine collections offer excellent and wide-ranging introductions to the best current work on Thoreau's life and thought in a range of disciplines. Good general introductions include Kevin P. Van Anglen and Kristen Case, eds. *Thoreau at 200: Essays and Reassessments*. Cambridge: Cambridge University Press, 2016; Joel Myerson, ed., *The Cambridge Companion to Henry David Thoreau* (Cambridge: Cambridge University Press, 1995); William E. Cain, ed., *A Historical Guide to Henry David Thoreau* (Oxford: Oxford University Press, 2000); François Specq, Laura Dassow Walls, and Michel Granger, eds., *Thoreauvian Modernities: Transatlantic Conversations on an American Icon* (Athens: University of Georgia Press, 2013); and Henry David Thoreau, *Walden, Civil Disobedience, and Other Writings*, ed. William Rossi (New York: Norton Critical Edition, 3rd ed., 2008). *Walden* is reconsidered in Sandra Harbert Petrulionis and

Laura Dassow Walls, eds. *More Day to Dawn: Thoreau's "Walden" for the Twenty-First Century* (Amherst: University of Massachusetts Press, 2007); environmental writing is represented in Schneider, ed., *Thoreau's Sense of Place* (Iowa City: University of Iowa Press, 2000); politics and philosophy are introduced in Jack Turner, ed., *A Political Companion to Henry David Thoreau* (Lexington: University Press of Kentucky, 2009) and Rick Anthony Furtak, Jonathan Ellsworth, and James D. Reid, eds., *Thoreau's Importance for Philosophy* (New York: Fordham University Press, 2013). In addition, the historical introductions to the many volumes of the Princeton edition of the Writings of Henry D. Thoreau offer troves of authoritative information and informed perspectives.

8. Richard M. Lebeaux, "From Canby to Richardson: The Last Half-Century of Thoreau Biography," in *Thoreau's World and Ours: A Natural Legacy*, ed. Edmund A. Schofield and Robert C. Baron (Golden, CO: North American Press, 1993), 127.

9. In 1977, Harding himself said he was "astonished" to see that no one had yet built on his armature of facts the kind of narrative he envisioned but did not write himself: "I very definitely did not intend or even hope to say the last word on the subject" (Walter Harding, "Thoreau Scholarship Today," *TSB* 139 [Spring 1977]: 1). I thank Walter for his generosity, and second his words on my own account!

INTRODUCTION

1. PEJ, 1:9 (October 29, 1837). "Musketaquid" was the name of the river, the valley it ran through, and the people who lived upon it.

2. PEJ, 1:5 (October 22, 1837).

3. Lemuel Shattuck, *A History of the Town of Concord* (Boston: Russell, Odiorne; Concord, MA: John Stacy, 1835), 50–51; Ruth R. Wheeler, *Concord: Climate for Freedom* (Concord, MA: Concord Antiquarian Society, 1967), 49–54.

4. Shattuck, *History of Concord*, 32; Jean O'Brien, *Firsting and Lasting: Writing Indians Out of Existence in New England* (Minneapolis: University of Minnesota Press, 2010), xi–xii; see also her *Dispossession by Degrees: Indian Land and Identity in Natick, Massachusetts, 1650–1790* (Cambridge: Cambridge University Press, 1997). Wolverton points out that practicing Native crafts as a form of livelihood was a kind of economic resistance: see Nan Wolverton, "'A Precarious Living': Basket-Making and Related Crafts among New England Indians," in *Reinterpreting New England Indians and the Colonial Experience*, ed. Colin G. Calloway and Neal Salisbury (Boston: Colonial Society of Massachusetts and the University of Virginia Press, 2003), 360.

5. PEJ, 3:130–31; Richard D. Brown, "'No Harm to Kill Indians': Equal Rights in a Time of War." *New England Quarterly* 81.1 (March 2008): 34–62.

6. J, 7:132–37 (January 24, 1855), in William Wood, *New England's Prospect* (1633).

7. Brian Donahue, *The Great Meadow: Farmers and the Land in Colonial Concord* (New Haven, CT: Yale University Press, 2004), 61, 69, 111–12; Shattuck, *History of Concord*, 379; *Walden*, 183.

8. Donahue, *Great Meadow*, 79 and passim, 107; *Walden*, 195.

9. Brian Donahue documented this collapse in "Henry David Thoreau and the Environment of Concord," in *Thoreau's World and Ours: A Natural Legacy*, ed. Edmund A. Schofield and Robert C. Baron (Golden, CO: North American Press, 1993), 181–89.

10. PEJ, 4:166–69. On this "poetic symbiosis" between Thoreau and his home landscape, see J. Walter Brain, "Thoreau's Poetic Vision and the Concord Landscape," in *Thoreau's World and Ours: A Natural Legacy*, ed. Edmund A. Schofield and Robert C. Baron (Golden, CO: North American Press, 1993), 281–97.

11. *Walden*, 182.

12. Robert M. Thorson, *Walden's Shore: Henry David Thoreau and Nineteenth-Century Science* (Cambridge, MA: Harvard University Press, 2014); see especially 96–99, 106–11, 135–48. As Thorson details, Walden Pond is more precisely "a coalesced lake created by the filling of four separate kettle basins with groundwater" (144).

13. Shirley Blancke and Barbara Robinson, *From Musketaquid to Concord: The Native and European Experience* (Concord, MA: Concord Antiquarian Museum, 1985); Jean O'Brien, *Firsting and Lasting*, 3. Clamshell Hill is now the site of Emerson Hospital.

14. Donahue, *Great Meadow*, 34; see also William Cronon, *Changes in the Land: Indians, Colonists, and the Ecology of New England* (New York: Hill and Wang, 1983), ch. 3.

15. Shattuck, *History of Concord*, 2.

16. R. Wheeler, *Concord*, 19; Shattuck, *History of Concord*, 4; Donahue, *Great Meadow*, 75.

17. Cronon, *Changes in the Land*, 58–66.

18. Shattuck, *History of Concord*, 20–24; 28–31.

19. Ibid., 76–87.

20. *J*, 9:160.

CHAPTER ONE

1. Maria Thoreau to Jennie M. LeBrun, Bangor, Maine, January 17, 1878, Thoreau Family Correspondence, vault 35, unit 3, Concord Free Public Library (hereafter CFPL); Franklin Benjamin Sanborn, *Henry D. Thoreau* (Boston: Houghton Mifflin, 1882), 6; *Days of HT*, 6. Sanborn's great-uncle, Levi Melcher, was a clerk in Jean Thoreau's store. Sanborn, *The Life of Henry David Thoreau* (Boston: Houghton Mifflin, 1917), 5.

2. Jean, or possibly Philippe.

3. *J*, 7:325–27. The letters from HDT's great-uncle Peter/Pierre Thoreau (addressed to Elizabeth Thoreau in reply to her letter telling of Jean's death in 1801) give the Concord Thoreaus the family news from Jersey. HDT copied them into his Journal on April 21, 1855, and noted Aunt Maria's theory that the letters ceased at Peter/Pierre's death in 1810 because he was the only Jersey Thoreau who could write in English. See Wendell Glick, "The Jersey Thoreaus," *TSB* 148 (Summer 1979): 1–5.

4. *EEM*, 113; *CC*, 183; William Ellery Channing II, *Thoreau: The Poet-Naturalist*, ed. F. B. Sanborn (Boston: Charles E. Goodspeed, 1902), 2.

5. *J*, 9:132–33.

6. Jayne E. Triber, *A True Republican: The Life of Paul Revere* (Amherst: University of Massachusetts Press, 1998), 133; *Days of HT*, 4–5.

7. PEJ, 6:194–95. A skeptical Henry turned to the diary of John Adams to confirm this family narrative.

8. Ibid., 3:337.

9. Annie Russell Marble, *Thoreau: His Home, Friends, and Books* (New York: Thomas Y. Crowell, 1902), 35–36; Maria Thoreau to Harriet Lincoln Wheeler, Bangor, December 5, 1876, Thoreau Family Papers, vault 35, unit 3, CFPL.

10. John Thoreau once recollected that he, as well as all his sisters except for Elizabeth, had been born on Richmond Street between Salem and Hanover Streets; this would be the street in back of Prince Street, in North Boston near Paul Revere's House and the Old North Church (*J*, 11:381). The children of Jean Thoreau and Jane "Jennie" Burns Thoreau were Elizabeth or "Betsy" (1782–1839), John (1783–84), Jane (1784–1864), Mary (1786–1812), John (HDT's father, 1787–1859), Nancy (1786–1815), Sarah (1790–1829), David (July 15, 1792–December 1792), Maria (1794–1881), and David (1796–1817).

11. *J*, 11:381, 131, 9:132.

12. Ibid., 10:252, 275; 278–79 (the neighbor was Mrs. William Munroe).

13. Maria Thoreau to Harriet Lincoln Wheeler, December 5, 1856, Thoreau Family Correspondence, vault 35, unit 3, CFPL.

14. Robert A. Gross, "Faith in the Boardinghouse: New Views of Thoreau Family Religion," *TSB* 250 (Winter 2005): 1.

15. Gross, "Faith in the Boardinghouse," 1; Marble, *Thoreau: Home, Friends, Books,* 35.

16. Sanborn writes that Isaac Hurd, son of Dr. Isaac Hurd and nephew of Joseph Hurd (who profited so handsomely from Jean Thoreau's estate), involved his father in his debts and "was for a while a prisoner for debt in the Concord jail," implying it was Hurd rather than John who had incurred some of John Thoreau's early debts (Sanborn, *Life of Thoreau*, 43).

17. *J*, 11:436; Robert A. Gross, *The Transcendentalists and Their World* (New York: Farrar, Straus and Giroux, forthcoming), ch. 5, mss. pp. 5–8.

18. Anne McGrath, "Cynthia Dunbar Thoreau," *Concord Saunterer* 14.4 (Winter 1979): 9.

19. Edmond Hudson, "The Wide Spreading Jones Family" (1917), *TSB* 221 (Fall 1997): 6. Eventually the British government, recognizing this family's extraordinary sacrifice and service to the Crown, awarded four of the surviving Jones brothers a modest grant of £100 each. Mary and the four brothers who remained in the United States received nothing (ibid., 11).

20. PEJ, 4:445–46 (April 14, 1852), 3:15. Contrary to Thoreau's account, the escapee was not Simeon but Josiah Jones; Simeon was then imprisoned for his role in Josiah's escape. Thoreau lists Mary's brothers as best the family recollected them; four had escaped to Nova Scotia across the bay from Bangor, Maine. In 1795, when Mary brought her daughters Sophia, Louisa, and Cynthia to visit them, they were nearly shipwrecked—a dramatic story whose ending was lost when pages were torn out of Thoreau's Journal (ibid., 3:15–16).

21. See Sanborn, *Life of Thoreau*, 18–19, 534; and E. Harlow Russell, "Thoreau's Maternal Grandfather Asa Dunbar: Fragments from His Diary and Commonplace Book," *Proceedings of the American Antiquarian Society*, April 19, 1908, 66–76.

22. Mary Jones Dunbar's children were Polly, born in Salem in 1773; William, born in

Weston in 1776; Charles, born in Harvard in 1780; Sophia, born in Harvard in 1781; Louisa, born in Keene, 1785; and Cynthia (HDT's mother), born in Keene, 1787; see S. G. Griffin, *A History of the Town of Keene* (Keene, NH: N.p., 1904), 586–87.

23. Joseph C. Wheeler, "Where Thoreau Was Born," *Concord Saunterer*, n.s., 7 (1999): 8; Robert A. Gross, *The Minutemen and Their World* (1976; New York: Hill and Wang, 2001), 59, 63.

24. *J*, 9:381; Marble, *Thoreau: Home, Friends, Books*, 55–56; W. E. Channing II, *Poet-Naturalist* (1902), 3; J. Wheeler, "Where Thoreau Was Born." Thoreau's Birth House is the center of Thoreau Farm, an educational institution; see http://thoreaufarm.org/thoreau-birth-house/ (accessed March 17, 2016).

25. *J*, 9:213.

26. George Hendrick, ed., *Remembrances of Concord and the Thoreaus: Letters of Horace Hosmer to Dr. S. A. Jones* (Urbana: University of Illinois Press, 1977), 4, 10–11. Daniel Ricketson noted Cynthia's "rare intellectual power" and "unusual vivacity," attributing Henry's "fine gift for conversation" to her influence (Marble, *Thoreau: Home, Friends, Books*, 42).

27. *Days of HT*, 8.

28. *J*, 14:329–30; Leslie Perrin Wilson, *In History's Embrace: Past and Present in Concord, Massachusetts* (Concord, MA: Concord Free Public Library, 2007), 39–42.

29. *J*, 11:436; Wilson, *In History's Embrace*, 42.

30. T. D. Seymour Bassett, "The Cold Summer of 1816 in Vermont: Fact and Folklore," *New England Galaxy* 15.1 (Summer 1973): 16.

31. *Middlesex Gazette*, July 19, 1817; William R. Baron, "1816 in Perspective: The View from the Northeastern United States," in C. R. Harrington, ed. *The Year without a Summer? World Climate in 1816* (Ottawa: Canadian Museum of Nature, 1992), 125–26; Bassett, "Cold Summer" 19.

32. *J*, 9:411, 8:64. David Henry reversed his first two names around the time he graduated from Harvard.

33. W. E. Channing II, *Poet-Naturalist* (1902), 3.

34. *J*, 8:65; Marble, *Thoreau: Home, Friends, Books*, 36.

35. Hendrick, *Remembrances*, 20; Sanborn, *Life of Thoreau*, 33.

36. *J*, 8:93–94.

37. Ralph L. Rusk, *The Life of Ralph Waldo Emerson* (New York: Charles Scribner's Sons, 1949), 84–86; Gay Wilson Allen, *Waldo Emerson: A Biography* (New York: Viking, 1981), 113–14; *JMN*, 14:327–28, September 1859.

38. *J*, 8:23.

39. *PEJ*, 2:173–74.

40. *Days of HT*, 15; *J*, 8:245–46, 12:38.

41. John Farmer and Jacob P. Moore, eds., *Collections, Historical and Miscellaneous; and Monthly Literary Journal* (Concord, NH: Jacob B. Moore, 1823), 30–31; *Middlesex Observer*, November 9, 1822, 3.

42. For the history of pencil-making in Concord, see Robert A. Gross's definitive exposition in *Transcendentalists and Their World*, ch. 5, mss. pp. 28–42; "Memoir of William Munroe," *Memoirs of the Members of the Concord Social Club*, 2nd series (Cambridge, MA: N.p., 1888): 145–56; Hendrick, *Remembrances* 23–25; Lemuel Shattuck, *A History*

of the Town of Concord (Boston: Russell, Odiorne; Concord, MA: John Stacy, 1835), 218. See also Henry Petroski, *The Pencil: A History of Design and Circumstance* (New York: Knopf, 1990), ch. 9.

43. Gross, *Transcendentalists and Their World*, ch. 5, mss. pp. 11, 42. Harding reproduces the October 1825 notice in Milton Meltzer and Walter Harding, *A Thoreau Profile* (New York: Thomas Y. Crowell, 1962), 138; see also *Days of HT*, 16–17. Harding states that John Thoreau learned the process of making pencils in 1820 from Joseph Dixon in Salem (Meltzer and Harding, *Profile*, 136), but I have been unable to confirm this. Dixon is widely credited with introducing the first wood and graphite pencil in the United States, but since he did not start manufacturing pencils until 1829 (at the Joseph Dixon Crucible Company in Jersey City), this seems unlikely.

44. Edward Waldo Emerson, *Henry Thoreau as Remembered by a Young Friend* (1917; Concord, MA: Thoreau Foundation, 1968), 32.

45. *J*, 11: 437; *CHDT*, 543 (Daniel Ricketson to HDT, February 9, 1859), 546 (HDT to Daniel Ricketson, February 12, 1859).

46. Marble, *Thoreau: Home, Friends, Books*, 39; Hendrick, *Remembrances*, 93; records of the Ornamental Tree Society, CFPL.

47. Sanborn, *Henry D. Thoreau*, 24; *JMN*, 15:489; Edward Emerson, *Thoreau as Remembered*, 14, 13; Jean Munro LeBrun, neighbor to the Thoreaus, in Meltzer and Harding, *Profile*, 3; *J*, 12:38 ("*chattable* society").

48. Hendrick, *Remembrances*, 77, 15; Alfred Munroe, quoted in *Thoreau as Seen*, 49.

49. [Joseph Hosmer?], "J. H.," "A Rare Reminiscence of Thoreau as a Child," *TSB* 245 (Fall 2003): 1–2; W. E. Channing II, *Poet-Naturalist* (1902), 5.

50. *J*, 8:94; *EEM*, 15; Edward Emerson, *Thoreau as Remembered*, 14–15.

51. *EEM*, 15–16; W. E. Channing II, *Poet-Naturalist* (1902), 5–6; Sanborn, *Life of Thoreau*, 39.

52. *Autobiography of Hon. John S. Keyes* (CFPL online), 6; Gross, *Transcendentalists and Their World*, ch. 4, p. 7; *Walden*, 330.

53. Tom Blanding, "Beans, Baked and Half-Baked (6)," *Concord Saunterer* 12.4 (Winter 1977): 14.

54. *Autobiography of Hon. John S. Keyes* (CFPL online), 31.

55. Ann Bigelow quoted in McGrath, "Cynthia Dunbar Thoreau," 12–13; Hendrick, *Remembrances*, 92–93. Henry remembered helping boil up a kettle of chowder on Walden's sandbar when he was seven years old (*Walden*, 180).

56. Sanborn, *Life of Thoreau*, 39; JoAnn Early Levin, "Schools and Schooling in Concord: A Cultural History," in *Concord: The Social History of a New England Town, 1750–1850*, ed. David Hackett Fischer (Waltham, MA: Brandeis University, 1983), 366–68; *Autobiography of Hon. John S. Keyes* (CFPL online), 5; *J*, 8:94–95.

57. Details of the Mill Dam are taken from Gross, *Transcendentalists and Their World*, ch. 4, pp. 3–7, and from *Autobiography of Hon. John S. Keyes* (CFPL online), 7–9.

58. Edward Jarvis, *Traditions and Reminiscences of Concord, Massachusetts, 1779–1878*, ed. Sarah Chapin (Amherst: University of Massachusetts Press, 1993), 41.

59. Gross, *Transcendentalists and Their World*, ch. 1, pp. 30–48; *Autobiography of Hon. John S. Keyes* (CFPL online), 7; Jarvis, *Traditions and Reminiscences*, 39–41.

60. The following discussion is deeply indebted to Gross, "Faith in the Boardinghouse."

61. PEJ, 4:458–59; J, 8:270–71; Gross, "Faith in the Boardinghouse," 3–4.

62. *Week*, 72–73; *Walden*, 98.

CHAPTER TWO

1. Edward Jarvis, *Traditions and Reminiscences of Concord, Massachusetts, 1779–1878*, ed. Sarah Chapin (Amherst: University of Massachusetts Press, 1993), 109–18.

2. Robert A. Gross, "Men and Women of Fairest Promise: Transcendentalism in Concord," *Concord Saunterer*, n.s., 2.1 (Fall 1994): 7. The citizens were William Whiting (whose son had returned from the Concord Grammar School black and blue from a beating by his schoolmates), Samuel Hoar, Josiah Davis, Abiel Heywood, and Nathan Brooks. They purchased land and built the school on what is now Academy Lane, and their policy of welcoming Concord's daughters as well as its sons was seen as progressive for its time.

3. Allen boarded with the Thoreaus for his first few months in Concord, and Cynthia enrolled John for two terms in 1828, Henry from fall 1828 until graduation in 1833, and Sophia in 1833 (although Allen's rolls are incomplete). See Kenneth Walter Cameron, "Young Henry Thoreau in the Annals of the Concord Academy (1829–1833)," *Emerson Society Quarterly* 9.4 (1957): 19; Hubert H. Hoeltje, "Thoreau and the Concord Academy," *New England Quarterly* 21.1 (March 1948): 103–9.

4. *Autobiography of Hon. John S. Keyes* (CFPL online), 10, 30; *Corr.*, 1:308 (HDT to Henry Williams Jr., September 30, 1847).

5. Phineas Allen, letter to the editor, *Concord Freeman*, September 21, 1838; reproduced in *TSB* 193 (Fall 1990): 4–5; Gladys Hosmer, "Phineas Allen, Thoreau's Preceptor," *TSB* 59 (Spring 1957): 1, 3.

6. *Autobiography of Hon. John S. Keyes* (CFPL online), 10, 33–34; Thomas Blanding, "Beans, Baked and Half-Baked (6)," *Concord Saunterer* 12.4 (Winter 1977): 14. Leslie Perrin Wilson edits the diary of one of these young women in "'Treasure in My Own Mind': The Diary of Martha Lawrence Prescott, 1834–1836," *Concord Saunterer*, n.s., 11 (2003): 92–152; see also George Moore's diary, transcribed in K. W. Cameron, "Young Henry," 5–14.

7. Gross, "Men and Women of Fairest Promise," 7–9, 15.

8. K. W. Cameron, "Young Henry," 3–8 (no records of this society survive); Dorothy Nyren, "The Concord Academic Debating Society," *Massachusetts Review* 4.1 (Autumn 1962): 81–84.

9. Holbrook's manifesto quoted in Carl Bode, *The American Lyceum* (New York: Oxford University Press, 1956), 12. The lecturer who so inspired Holbrook was Benjamin Silliman, founder of the *American Journal of Science*.

10. Robert A. Gross, "Talk of the Town," *American Scholar* (Summer 2015), 34–35; *Yeoman's Gazette*, January 17, 1829; records of the Concord Lyceum, CFPL. With the Concord Debating Club rendered moot, its members disbanded and joined the lyceum.

11. K. W. Cameron, "Young Henry," 10; Ruth R. Wheeler, *Concord: Climate for Freedom* (Concord, MA: Concord Antiquarian Society, 1967), 152.

12. William Ellery Channing II, *Thoreau: The Poet-Naturalist*, ed. F. B. Sanborn (Boston: Charles E. Goodspeed, 1902), 13.

13. George Frisbie Hoar, *Autobiography of Seventy Years*, 2 vols. (New York: Charles Scribner's Sons, 1903), 1:86; K. W. Cameron, "Young Henry," 7, 14.

14. W. E. Channing II, *Poet-Naturalist* (1902), 13; Thoreau, "Class Autobiography," *EEM*, 114.

15. Hoar, *Autobiography*, 1:82.

16. Edmund A. Schofield, "Further Particulars on Thoreau's Harvard Scholarship Awards," *TSB* 264 (Fall 2008): 4–6. The monetary amounts are not recorded. Both William and Ralph Waldo Emerson received funds from the James Penn legacy as well, which, unlike Harvard's end-of-year "exhibition" prizes, were not distributed by the Harvard Corporation but by the elders of Boston's First Church of Christ.

17. *Autobiography of Hon. John S. Keyes* (CFPL online), 53; Henry Williams, ed., *Memorials of the Class of 1837 of Harvard University* (Boston: George H. Ellis, 1887), 23–24.

18. Andrew Preston Peabody, *Harvard Reminiscences* (Boston: Ticknor, 1888): 196–97; Hoar, *Autobiography* 1:119.

19. Franklin Benjamin Sanborn, *The Life of Henry David Thoreau* (Boston: Houghton Mifflin, 1917), 154.

20. Their visit home was on Saturday, October 6. John Thoreau, letter to George Stearns, Concord, October 18, 1833, in K. W. Cameron, "Young Thoreau," 15–16.

21. *Autobiography of Hon. John S. Keyes* (CFPL online), 55; Harriet Martineau (who visited Harvard when Thoreau was there), in *Retrospect of Western Travel* (1838), in William Bentinck-Smith, *The Harvard Book: Selections from Three Centuries* (Cambridge, MA: Harvard University Press, 1960): 338–40. George Ticknor, who had studied in Germany before becoming the Smith Professor of French and Spanish, quit in disgust just as Thoreau arrived, complaining bitterly that after thirteen years of pushing for reforms, he'd given up hope: "In my own department I have succeeded entirely, but I can get these changes carried no further." George Ticknor to C. S. Daveis, January 5, 1835, in *Life, Letters and Journals of George Ticknor*, 2 vols. (Boston: James R. Osgood, 1876, 1:400.

22. Peabody, *Harvard Reminiscences*, 200; Hoar, *Autobiography*, 1:127; James Freeman Clarke, *Autobiography, Diary, and Correspondence*, ed. Edward Everett Hale (Boston: Houghton Mifflin, 1891), 43.

23. Charles W. Eliot, *Harvard Memories* (Cambridge, MA: Harvard University Press, 1923), 53–54.

24. *Corr.*, 1:287–88 (HDT to Horatio Robinson Storer, February 15, 1847); Edward Waldo Emerson, *Henry Thoreau as Remembered by a Young Friend* (1917; Concord, MA: Thoreau Foundation, 1968), 18; John Weiss, "Thoreau," *Christian Examiner*, July 1865, 96.

25. *Thoreau as Seen*, 204; Weiss, "Thoreau," 97.

26. *Autobiography of Hon. John S. Keyes* (CFPL online), 50.

27. Frederick T. McGill Jr., "Thoreau and College Discipline," *New England Quarterly* 15.2 (June 1942): 349–50.

28. Marshall Tufts, *A Tour through College* (Boston: Marsh, Capen, and Lyon, 1832), 40. Tufts printed his book anonymously; Thoreau's classmates circulated it underground, inspiring their petition. Reproduced in Kenneth Walter Cameron, *Transcendental Ap-

prenticeship: Notes on Young Henry Thoreau's Reading (Hartford, CT: Transcendental Books, 1976), 270–99.

29. Students could be reinstated the following year only if they passed a new set of examinations and presented certificates of good conduct. K. W. Cameron, *Transcendental Apprenticeship*, 268; Weiss, "Thoreau," 101; *Days of HT*, 41–43.

30. McGill, "Thoreau and College Discipline," 349–53.

31. Weiss, "Thoreau," 101–2.

32. Peabody, *Harvard Reminiscences*, 201–2; Clarke, *Autobiography*, 38.

33. Tufts, *Tour through College*, 5.

34. Robert D. Richardson Jr., *Henry David Thoreau: A Life of the Mind* (Berkeley: University of California Press, 1986), 14; Hoar, *Autobiography*, 1:103.

35. Horatio Hale, *Remarks on the Language of the St. John's, or Wlastukweek Indians with a Penobscot Vocabulary* (Boston: N.p., 1834).

36. Hoar, *Autobiography*, 1:100–102; *Walden*, 52.

37. Hoar, *Autobiography*, 1:101.

38. Clark A. Elliott, *Thaddeus William Harris (1795–1856): Nature, Science, and Society in the Life of an American Naturalist* (Bethlehem, PA: Lehigh University Press, 2008), 178–79, 194; T. W. Higginson quoted on 191.

39. See Caroline Winterer, *The Culture of Classicism: Ancient Greece and Rome in American Intellectual Life, 1780–1910* (Baltimore: Johns Hopkins University Press, 2002), 2, 60, 77–83.

40. *Walden*, 144.

41. For a full accounting of Thoreau's reading at Harvard, see Robert Sattelmeyer, *Thoreau's Reading: A Study in Intellectual History with Bibliographical Catalogue* (Princeton, NJ: Princeton University Press, 1988), 3–24.

42. Thoreau's friends published a literary journal, *Harvardiana*, from 1835 to 1838; Thoreau does not appear in it.

43. Henry Seidel Canby, *Thoreau* (Boston: Houghton Mifflin, 1939), 50. Only one essay survives from Thoreau's years with Phineas Allen, "The Seasons," written when Thoreau was twelve. While childish in tone, it is alert to sensual impressions and structured on a Waldenesque seasonal cycle—just like thousands of others.

44. *E&L*, 59; Hoar, *Autobiography*, 1:87.

45. Sandra M Gustafson, *Imagining Deliberative Democracy in the Early American Republic* (Chicago: University of Chicago Press, 2011), 22–23; Peabody, *Harvard Reminiscences*, 87–88.

46. *EEM*, 110.

47. The Institute of 1770 library consisted of about 1,400 volumes when Thoreau arrived, but by 1836 it was big enough to be moved to 2 Holsworthy; see Kenneth Walter Cameron, *Thoreau and His Harvard Classmates* (Hartford, CT: Transcendental Books, 1965), 106–13.

48. Quincy misread his own handwriting, counting what should have been 4,068 as 4,668; the error was never detected. Had it been, Thoreau would still have managed a place in his 1837 commencement exercises, but he would have been twenty-first instead of nineteeth.

49. McGill, "Thoreau and College Discipline," 350.

50. On July 13, 1835, "David H. Thoreau" played Cato defending the Roman Republic against Caesar; Thoreau's text is reproduced in *Translations*, ed. Kevin P. Van Anglen, 145-47 (in Greek), 279-80 (translated into English); for Thoreau's source in Addison, see Ethel Seybold, "The Source of Thoreau's 'Cato-Decius Dialogue,'" *Studies in the American Renaissance* (1994): 245-50.

51. W. E. Channing II, *Poet-Naturalist*, 32.

52. Orestes Brownson, "Independence Day Address at Dedham, Massachusetts," *Works in Political Philosophy, Vol. 2: 1828-1841*, ed. Gregory S. Butler (Wilmington, DE: ISI Books, 2007), 120, 115, 121; *RP*, 64.

53. *EEM*, 60-61.

54. *Corr.*, 1:30 (HDT to Orestes Brownson, December 30, 1837); *Days of HT*, 46 (John Thoreau to Helen Thoreau, June 24, 1836); Brownson, "Independence Day Address," 124.

55. *Corr.*, 1:2-4 (Augustus Peabody to HDT, May 30, 1836), 7-8 (HDT to Henry Vose, July 5, 1836), 12-14 (HDT to Charles Wyatt Rice, August 5, 1836).

56. *Walden*, 50; *J*, 8:66.

57. Philip Gura, *American Transcendentalism* (New York: Hill and Wang, 2007), 69.

58. William Simmons, "Report to the Overseers," in K. W. Cameron, *Thoreau's Harvard Years*, 8-9; *Days of HT*, 47.

59. *Autobiography of Hon. John S. Keyes* (CFPL online), 48-49.

60. Charles Hayward Jr., who died weeks later of typhoid fever during his first term at Harvard's Divinity School; quoted in Charles Stearns Wheeler's obituary of Hayward, in K. W. Cameron, *Transcendental Apprenticeship*, 257.

61. Morton Berkowitz, "Thoreau, Rice and Vose on the Commercial Spirit," *TSB* 141 (Fall 1977): 1-5.

62. *EEM*, 115-18; 115.

CHAPTER THREE

1. *E&L*, 65.

2. *Corr.*, 1:16 (James Richardson to HDT, September 7, 1837); *EEM*, 103; PJ 1:36, March 14, 1838.

3. "Sic Vita," in *CEP*, 542-43.

4. *Thoreau as Seen*, 153, 71.

5. See Dick O'Connor, "Thoreau in the Town School, 1837," *Concord Saunterer*, n.s., 4 (Fall 1996): 150-72.

6. The building, which still stands, is now in use as the Masonic Lodge and has for many years been the site of the annual meetings of the Thoreau Society.

7. William Ellery Channing II, *Thoreau: The Poet-Naturalist* (Boston: Roberts Brothers, 1873), 24; Edward Waldo Emerson, *Henry Thoreau as Remembered by a Young Friend* (1917; Concord, MA: Thoreau Foundation, 1968), 20-21.

8. Edward Waldo Emerson interview notes, box 1, folder 14, CFPL; *Thoreau as Seen*, 216;

Martin Bickman, *Uncommon Learning: Henry David Thoreau on Education* (Boston: Houghton Mifflin, 1999), xvii. O'Connor suggests, based on other evidence, that Durant may have been a genuine discipline problem ("Thoreau in the Town School," 161–63).

9. *Corr.*, 1:19–20 (HDT to Henry Vose, October 13, 1837); Prudence Ward to Caroline Ward Sewall, September 25, 1837, Thoreau-Sewall-Ward Letters, letter #14, Thoreau Society Archives, Henley Library.

10. Sanborn, *The Life of Henry David Thoreau* (Boston: Houghton Mifflin, 1917), 128–29; *JMN*, 5:349 (August 2, 1837). The line from Emerson found its way into "Self-Reliance." Harmon Smith puts their first meeting in April 1837; see *My Friend, My Friend: The Story of Thoreau's Relationship with Emerson* (Amherst: University of Massachusetts Press, 1999), 6–8.

11. PEJ, 1:5.

12. Ibid.; Ralph Waldo Emerson, *The Early Lectures of Ralph Waldo Emerson, 1833–1842,* ed. Stephen E. Whicher, Robert E. Spiller, and Wallace E. Williams, 3 vols. (Cambridge, MA: Harvard University Press, 1959–1972), 2:261; *EEM*, 8–9.

13. "Likeness to God," in William Ellery Channing I, *The Works of William E. Channing,* 6 vols., 8th ed. (Boston: James Munroe, 1848), 3:235. Rev. William Ellery Channing, Boston's leading Unitarian minister, and Harvard's Edward Tyrrel Channing were brothers; Ellery Channing, who became Thoreau's closest friend, was their nephew, as was the reformer William Henry Channing.

14. "Nature," in *E&L*, 7; Emerson, *Early Lectures*, 2:215.

15. Ralph L. Rusk, *The Life of Ralph Waldo Emerson* (New York: Charles Scribner's Sons, 1949), 266. After Lydia Jackson and Ralph Waldo Emerson were married in September 1835, he started calling her "Lidian," presumably for the sake of euphony—a change that Lidian Emerson accepted (ibid., 213).

16. Emerson, *Early Lectures*, 2:215–16; *LRWE*, 7:22.

17. *JMN*, 5:452, 453, 460. Henry endeared himself to Lidian about this time by making "some neat little cowhide shoes" for her hens, to keep them from scratching up her garden seeds. Ellen Tucker Emerson, *The Life of Lidian Jackson Emerson* (East Lansing: Michigan State University Press, 1992), 68.

18. James Russell Lowell quoted in *Thoreau as Seen*, 180, Ednah Littlehale Cheney quoted in ibid., 120. See also Henry S. Salt, *The Life of Henry David Thoreau* (London: Richard Bentley, 1890; revised version of 1908, edited by George Hendrick, Willene Hendrick, and Fritz Oehlschlaeger. Urbana: University of Illinois Press, 1993, 2000), 29–30, for David Haskins's similar observation, in which he remarked the identical effect of Emerson's magnetism on himself. The resemblance between Emerson and Thoreau became "a quiet joke in Concord," said Moncure Conway, who thought it wholly superficial. Moncure Daniel Conway, *Autobiography, Memories and Experiences*, 2 vols. (Boston: Houghton Mifflin, 1904), 1:143.

19. James Russell Lowell, "Fable for Critics," in *Thoreau as Seen*, 4; W. E. Channing, *Works,* 3:381.

20. PEJ, 1:73–74.

21. Ibid., 38. All that survives of the lecture "Society" are "Scraps" in Thoreau's Journal (ibid., 35–39).

22. Ibid., 31–32 (March 4, 1838); *Corr.,* 1:36–37 (HDT to John Thoreau, March 17, 1838).

23. Priscilla Rice Edes quoted in *Thoreau as Seen,* 180–81; Sophia, John and Henry D. Thoreau, "Nature and Bird Notes," Berg Collection, New York Public Library. The plants have been removed and preserved in separate envelopes; it is unclear when they were added or how they were positioned.

24. *Translations,* 148, 281. Note that *cenotaph* is, as Thoreau knew, Greek for "empty (*kenos*) tomb (*taphos*)."

25. *Corr.,* 1:27–30 (HDT to John Thoreau, November 11 and 14, 1837). By April 1838, as the Ward letters show, the Thoreau household was in an uproar over the Cherokee removals; Emerson wrote his letter of protest on April 23, 1838. Interestingly, "Hopewell" evokes the 1785 Treaty of Hopewell between the United States and the Cherokee Indians, named for a site in South Carolina, which had originally protected the Cherokee by establishing the western border of the United States; the treaty was, as history shows, ignored.

26. Kenneth Walter Cameron, *Thoreau and His Harvard Classmates* (Hartford, CT: Transcendental Books, 1965), 91–93.

27. *To Set This World,* 11, 16–19; Michael Sims, *The Adventures of Henry Thoreau: A Young Man's Unlikely Path to Walden Pond* (New York: Bloomsbury, 2014), 91.

28. Henry Petroski, *The Pencil: A History of Design and Circumstance* (New York: Knopf, 1990), 110–14; Edward Waldo Emerson Papers, series 1, box 1, folder 11 (interview of EWE with Warren Miles), CFPL. For the story about the encyclopedia article, see Edward Waldo Emerson, *Thoreau as Remembered,* 32.

29. Finding high-quality graphite was a continuing problem: after they used up their Bristol graphite, the Thoreaus bought graphite from the Tudor Mine in Sturbridge, then imported it from Canada.

30. *Corr.,* 1:31–32 (HDT to Orestes Brownson, December 30, 1837), 34–35 (HDT to David Haskins, February 9, 1838).

31. Ibid., 37 (HDT to John Thoreau, March 17, 1838.

32. PEJ, 1:46 (May 10, 1838).

33. W. E. Channing II, *Poet-Naturalist* (1873), 2.

34. Advertisement in *Yeoman's Gazette* (Milton Meltzer and Walter Harding, *A Thoreau Profile* [New York: Thomas Y. Crowell, 1962], 38). They would admit students for free if they could not pay (*Days of HT,* 76). At full enrollment, with all students at full pay, the annual gross income for both brothers would have totaled $600, less any outlay for books and supplies. For comparison, Henry Thoreau had been offered $500 annually as teacher of the Concord Center School.

35. On Transcendentalism and educational reform, see Wesley T. Mott, "Education," in *The Oxford Handbook of Transcendentalism,* ed. Joel Myerson, Sandra H. Petrulionis, and Laura Dassow Walls (Oxford: University of Oxford Press, 2010), 153–71; and Martin Bickman, *Minding American Education: Reclaiming the Tradition of Active Learning* (New York: Teacher's College Press, 2003).

36. *E&L,* 67, 70.

37. Sanborn, *Life of Thoreau,* 204; Edward Waldo Emerson, *Thoreau as Remembered* 22; George Hendrick, ed., *Remembrances of Concord and the Thoreaus: Letters of Horace*

Hosmer to Dr. S. A. Jones (Urbana: University of Illinois Press, 1977), 73; *Thoreau as Seen*, 109.

38. Sanborn, *Life of Thoreau*, 205–6; in his Journal, Thoreau recorded obtaining the surveying equipment, "a leveling instrument and circumferentor combined" (PEJ, 1:197).

39. Edward Waldo Emerson Papers, series 1, box 1, folder 8 (interview of EWE with Thomas Hosmer), CFPL.

40. *Corr.,* 1:49 (HDT to Helen Thoreau, October 6, 1838); diary of Edmund Sewall for March 28, 1840, American Antiquarian Society; Hendrick, *Remembrances*, 73–74.

41. Hendrick, *Remembrances*, 74–76.

42. Edward Waldo Emerson, interview notes with Benjamin Lee, series 1, box 1, folder 10, and with Benjamin Tolman, box 1, folder 18, CFPL; John S. Keyes quoted in *Thoreau as Seen*, 206.

43. Edward Waldo Emerson Papers, series 1, box 1, folder 8 (interview of EWE with Thomas Hosmer), CFPL.

44. *Walden*, 109–10.

45. ABAJ, 127; PEJ, 1:172, 194; *Thoreau Log*, 59–60.

46. PEJ, 1:38–39, 69–70.

47. Ibid., 74 (June 22, 1839); "Sympathy," *J*, 1:76–77 (June 24, 1839) and *CEP*, 524–25.

48. *Days of HT*, 78–79; *JMN*, 7:230–31; Ralph Waldo Emerson, and Thomas Carlyle, *The Correspondence of Emerson and Carlyle*, ed. Joseph Slater, 2 vols (New York: Columbia University Press, 1964), 1:246; *LRWE*, 2:244.

49. Clayton Hoagland, "The Diary of Thoreau's 'Gentle Boy,'" *New England Quarterly* 28.4 (December 1955): 488.

50. PEJ, 1:79–81. See also Shawn Stewart, "Transcendental Romance Meets the Ministry of Pain: The Thoreau Brothers, Ellen Sewall, and Her Father," *Concord Saunterer*, n.s., 14 (2006): 4–21.

51. Thoreau-Sewall-Ward Letters, IVJ: Ellen Sewall Papers, Thoreau Society Archives, Henley Library.

52. Two biographers who have famously explored this tension are Henry Seidel Canby, *Thoreau* (Boston: Houghton Mifflin, 1939), ch. 9, and Richard M. Lebeaux, *Young Man Thoreau* (1975; New York: Harper, 1978), esp. ch. 4 and 6.

53. *Thoreau Log*, 47–48; *Thoreau as Seen*, 218; Elizabeth Hoar, undated letter to the Bowles family of Springfield, Massachussetts, *TSB* 138 (Winter 1977): 5.

54. *Week*, 116.

55. Ibid., 196.

56. Ibid., 296.

57. Ibid., 303; *Days of HT*, 92.

58. *Week*, 215; *Days of HT*, 92.

59. *Week*, 334.

60. Ibid., 393.

61. PEJ, 1:124–26, 134–37 (June 11–21, 1840).

62. *JMN*, 7:238.

63. Joel Myerson, *The New England Transcendentalists and the "Dial": A History of the Magazine and Its Contributors* (Cranbury, NJ: Associated University Presses, 1980), 30–32.

64. PEJ, 1:100; cf 1:209. Very was dismissed in 1838 and confined for a month at McLean Asylum; after his release, Emerson collected Very's writings into *Essays and Poems* (1839).

65. PEJ, 1:132; joint statement by Elizabeth Osgood Davenport and Louise Osgood Koopman, Thoreau-Sewall-Ward Letters, Thoreau Society Archives, Henley Library; PEJ, 1:158.

66. Tom Blanding, "Passages from John Thoreau, Jr.'s Journal," *TSB* 136 (Summer 1976): 4–6. Very little of John Thoreau's journal survives.

67. PEJ, 1:193.

68. Ellen Sewall to Prudence Ward, November 18, 1840, #28 in IVJ: Ellen Sewall Papers, Thoreau-Sewall-Ward Letters, Thoreau Society Archives, Henley Library.

69. Diary of Ellen Sewall, March 8, 1841, #29 in IVJ: Ellen Sewall Papers, Thoreau-Sewall-Ward Letters, Thoreau Society Archives, Henley Library.

70. The romance seems to have been, in Henry Seidel Canby's words, "an experiment in the philosophy of love," with little if any physical attraction (*Thoreau*, 121–22). Sophia's oft-quoted statement comes down to us from Ellen's granddaughter by way of her grandmother, by way of her mother—a long chain indeed! Louise Osgood Koopman, "The Thoreau Romance," *Massachusetts Quarterly* 4.1 (Autumn 1962): 66; cf. *Days of HT*, 104.

71. *Autobiography of Hon. John S. Keyes* (CFPL online), 69–70; Hendrick, *Remembrances*, 72; PEJ, 1:149–50. "Van" referred to the Democratic incumbent, Martin Van Buren, who was widely blamed for the Panic of '37 and lost his bid for reelection.

72. *LRWE*, 2:311, 290.

73. Joel Myerson, "A Calendar of Transcendental Club Meetings," *American Literature* 44.2 (May 1972): 205.

74. *LRWE*, 2:323–24n326, 315, 322.

75. See Joel Myerson, Sandra Harbert Petrulionis, and Laura Dassow Walls, eds., *The Oxford Handbook of Transcendentalism*, ed. (Oxford: Oxford University Press, 2010), s.v. "The Dial," by Susan Belasco, 373–79.

76. *Corr.*, 1:70 (Margaret Fuller to HDT, December 1, 1840), 1:93, (Margaret Fuller to HDT, October 18, 1841).

77. "Sic Vita" appeared in the *Dial* 2.1, July 1841; "Friendship" appeared in the *Dial* 2.2, October 1841.

78. *Corr.*, 1:70 (Margaret Fuller to HDT, December 1, 1840).

79. Ibid., 72 (HDT to "Mr Clerk," January 6, 1841). The letter reads, in full: "Sir / I do not wish to be considered a member of the First Parish in this town. / Henry. D. Thoreau." Since religious disestablishment in 1833, many others had also signed off.

80. Hendrick, *Remembrances*, 131.

81. PEJ, 1:277 (March 3, 1841); *Corr.*, 1:72–73 (HDT to Samuel Gridley Howe, March 9, 1841).

82. PEJ, 1:263, 291, 297; Ellen Sewall Diary, April 8, 1841, Thoreau-Ward-Sewall Letters, #29 in IVJ Ellen Sewall Papers, Thoreau Society Archives, Henley Library. The farm was the thirty-acre Hollowell place. Ellen's entry for April 25 shows that, despite Henry's bravado in *Walden*, the family recognized it was a genuine disappointment.

83. PEJ, 1:301, 265, 273.

84. Ibid., 295, 302.
85. *The Letters of Nathaniel Hawthorne, 1813–1843,* ed. Thomas Woodson, L. Neal Smith, and Norman Holmes Pearson (Columbus: Ohio State University Press, 1984), 528–29 (Hawthorne to Sophia Peabody, April 13, 1841).
86. *LRWE,* 2:389 (RWE to William Emerson, March 30, 1841).
87. Ibid., 394 (RWE to Margaret Fuller, April 22, 1841).
88. PEJ, 1:304 (April 26, 1841).
89. *E&L,* 275; cf. *JMN,* 7:201, where the draft of this passage describes "my brave Henry."
90. Emerson and Carlyle, *Correspondence,* 1:300 (RWE to Thomas Carlyle, May 30, 1841); *JMN,* 7:454.
91. PEJ, 1:311, 320; *Letters of Margaret Fuller,* ed. Robert N. Hudspeth, 6 vols. (Ithaca, NY: Cornell University Press, 1983–), 2:210 (Margaret Fuller to Richard Fuller, May 25, 1841).
92. *Corr.,* 1:75 (RWE to HDT, June 7, 1841); "To the Maiden in the East," *Dial* 3.2 (October 1842), 222–24; cf. *CEP,* 550–51.
93. Charles Capper, *Margaret Fuller: An American Romantic Life, the Private Years* (Oxford University Press, 1992), 170.
94. *Corr.,* 1:94–95 (Margaret Fuller to HDT, October 18, 1841). The "*good week*" Fuller mentions in this letter (emphasis in the original) cannot have referred to Thoreau's book, for he hadn't yet outlined his plans to turn the voyage with John into *A Week.* Fuller's tantalizing reference elsewhere in the letter to some great and unspoken shared "crisis" also remains mysterious.
95. *Corr.,* 1:79 (HDT to Lucy Jackson Brown, September 8, 1841); Elizabeth Hall Witherell, "Thoreau as Poet," in *Cambridge Companion to Henry David Thoreau,* ed. Joel Myerson, (Cambridge: Cambridge University Press, 1995), 57–70.
96. The publisher, Rufus Griswold, never replied, and his volume made no mention of Thoreau. See Robert Sattelmeyer, "Thoreau's Projected Work on the English Poets," *Studies in the American Renaissance* (1980): 239–57. Thoreau was at Harvard from November 29 until December 10, 1841; as a "Resident Graduate" he had Harvard library privileges.
97. PEJ, 1:337–38, 321.
98. Ibid., 347, 354.

CHAPTER FOUR

1. Ellen Sewall Diary, April 27, 1841, Thoreau-Sewall-Ward Letters, #29 in IVJ: Ellen Sewall Papers (transcript is misdated April 25), Thoreau Society Archives, Henley Library; PEJ, 1:354–55.
2. Letter to W. S. Robinson from an unknown correspondent, printed in Max Cosman, "Apropos of John Thoreau," *American Literature* 12.2 (May 1940): 242; PEJ, 1:362 (January 8, 1842); *THOT,* 2.
3. Cosman, "Apropos," 242. Even today, there is no cure for tetanus; treatment involves the administration of muscle relaxants to control the convulsions, and the nerve damage may be permanent.

4. *Corr.*, 1:107 (HDT to Isaiah Williams, March 14, 1842); *THOT*, 2, letter, Lidian Jackson Emerson to Lucy Jackson Brown, January 11–12, 1842.

5. "Mr. Frost's Sermon on the Death of John Thoreau Jr.," Thoreau-Sewall-Ward Letters, Thoreau Society Archives, Henley Library.

6. *LRWE*, 3:4 (RWE to William Emerson, January 24, 1842); Edward Waldo Emerson, *Henry Thoreau as Remembered by a Young Friend* (1917; Concord, MA: Thoreau Foundation, 1968), 26; PEJ, 1:237.

7. *LRWE*, 3:6–8; 9 (RWE to Margaret Fuller, February 2, 1842).

8. *JMN*, 8:165–66.

9. PEJ, 1:364–66 (February 20–21, 1842).

10. Ibid., 365, 369 (February 20, 1842).

11. CEP, 595–96; *The Collected Poems of Henry Thoreau*, ed. Carl Bode (Baltimore: Johns Hopkins University Press, 1965), 316. Thoreau sent the mournful version to Helen soon after he moved to Staten Island, making it disturbingly self-referential.

12. *Corr.*, 1:102 (HDT to Lucy Jackson Brown, March 2, 1842), 105–6 (HDT to RWE, March 11, 1842).

13. *E&L*, 473; *Corr.*, 1:107 (HDT to Isaiah Williams, March 14, 1842). See also PEJ 1:369.

14. *JMN*, 8:375 (1843). Emerson chose to immortalize this comment in "Thoreau," in *The Collected Works of Ralph Waldo Emerson*, ed. Ronald A. Bosco and Joel Myerson, 10 vols. (Cambridge, MA: Harvard University Press, 2013), 416.

15. PEJ, 1:368, 393.

16. *LRWE*, 3:47 (RWE to Margaret Fuller, April 10, 1842), 75 (RWE to Margaret Fuller, July 19, 1842).

17. *Exc.*, 3–28. Fink details Thoreau's natural history writing as the way he reached a broader audience. Steven Fink, *Prophet in the Marketplace: Thoreau's Development as a Professional Writer* (Princeton, NJ: Princeton University Press, 1992), allusion to p. 43. For a penetrating analysis of this essay as a pivotal moment in Thoreau's struggle for cultural power, see Kevin P. Van Anglen, "True Pulpit Power: 'Natural History of Massachusetts' and the Problem of Cultural Authority," *Studies in the American Renaissance* (1990): 119–47.

18. ABAL, 88; Nathaniel Hawthorne, *The American Notebooks*. Columbus: Ohio State University Press, 1932, 1960, 1972, 355.

19. Ellen Tucker Emerson, *The Life of Lidian Emerson* (East Lansing: Michigan State University Press, 1992), 71, 79–80. Emerson reveled in all the company; as he wrote to Newcomb, urging him to move from Brook Farm to Concord, "Those of us who do not believe in Communities, believe in neighborhoods & that the kingdom of heaven may consist of such" (*LRWE*, 3:51).

20. "The Old Manse," in Nathaniel Hawthorne, *Tales and Sketches* (New York: Library of America, 1982), 1145–47.

21. *Days of HT*, 137; Hawthorne, *American Notebooks*, 353–54.

22. Hawthorne, *American Notebooks*, 356–57; *Thoreau as Seen*, 88–89; William Ellery Channing II, *Thoreau: The Poet-Naturalist* (Boston: Roberts Brothers, 1873), 257.

23. Richard Fuller, "Visit to the Wachusett, July 1842," *TSB* 129 (Fall 1972): 2.

24. *Corr.*, 1:94 (Margaret Fuller to HDT, October 18, 1841).

25. *Exc.*, 29–46.

26. Sophia, John, and Henry D. Thoreau, "Nature and Bird Notes," Berg Collection, New York Public Library. Robinson remarks, tellingly, that Thoreau reacted to the physical universe as "a creative mind at work, expressing itself in the events and physical details of nature" (David N. Robinson, *Natural Life: Thoreau's Worldly Transcendentalism* [Ithaca, NY: Cornell University Press, 2004], 26); here one sees the dawning of that powerful insight.

27. PEJ, 2:378; *Exc.*, 405. See Kevin P. Van Anglen, "Thoreau's Epic Ambition: 'A Walk to Wachusett' and the Persistence of the Classics in an Age of Science," in *The Call of Classical Literature in the Romantic Age*, ed. Kevin P. Van Anglen and James Engell (Edinburgh: Edinburgh University Press, forthcoming).

28. *LRWE*, 2:253; Emerson, "New Poetry," *Dial* 1.2 (October 1840): 222.

29. *LRWE*, 3:41, 571; *Corr.*, 1:153–54 (Ellery Channing to HDT, April 6, 1843), 157 (Ellery Channing to HDT, May 1, 1843).

30. *JMN*, 8:352; Robert N. Hudspeth, "Dear Friend: Letter Writing in Concord," *Concord Saunterer*, n.s., 11 (2003): 84.

31. Hawthorne, *Tales and Sketches*, 1141; Hawthorne, *American Notebooks*, 357.

32. Robert N. Hudspeth, *Ellery Channing* (New York: Twayne, 1973), 139.

33. ABAJ, 164.

34. *LRWE*, 3:96, 7:517; Ward quoted in Franklin Benjamin Sanborn, *The Life of Henry David Thoreau* (Boston: Houghton Mifflin, 1917), 470–71.

35. *Liberator*, September 28, 1838; Edson L. Whitney, *American Peace Society: A Centennial History*, 3rd ed. (Washington, DC: American Peace Society, 1929), 44; *Days of HT*, 142.

36. *Corr.*, 1:124 (HDT to RWE, January 24, 1843); ABAJ, 151. Staples's saying made the rounds: see Caroline Ward Sewall to Edmund Sewall [Sr.], January 25, 1843, Thoreau-Ward-Sewall Letters; and Edward Emerson interview notes with Sam Staples, box 1, folder 17, CFPL.

37. *Corr.*, 1:125 (HDT to RWE, January 24, 1843); Barry Kritzberg, "The Mr. Spear Who Ought to Have Been Beaten into a Ploughshare," *TSB* 183 (Spring 1988): 4–5. Pellico's book *My Prisons* detailed the Italian patriot's imprisonment in Austria for ten years. Charles M. Spear was a founding member of Garrison's New England Non-Resistance Society and would become a fierce opponent of capital punishment and an advocate of prison reform.

38. Charles Lane, "State Slavery—Imprisonment of A. Bronson Alcott—Dawn of Liberty," *Liberator*, January 27, 1843, 16.

39. *LRWE*, 3:230 (RWE to Margaret Fuller, December 17, 1843).

40. For an annual fee of $2.50, members could read such local, national, and international newspapers and journals as the *London Phalanx*, the *New-York Tribune*, the *Dial*, the *National Anti-Slavery Standard*, and the *Boston Miscellany*, all of which Thoreau and Emerson donated together: see Keith Walter Cameron, *Transcendentalists and Minerva*, 3 vols. (Hartford, CT: Transcendental Books, 1958), 1:290–95.

41. Quoted in *Days of HT*, 143; Walter Harding, "Thoreau and the Concord Lyceum," *TSB* 30 (January 1950): 2.

42. *LRWE*, 3:129; *Days of HT*, 143–44; *THOT*, 3; *Corr.*, 1:135 (HDT to RWE, February 10, 1843).

43. For further details, see *To Set This World*, 26–30.

44. Ibid., 30–32.

45. *LRWE*, 3:39; Hawthorne, *American Notebooks*, 361–62; *LRWE*, 3:90–93.

46. *LRWE*, 3:90–91n334; *JMN*, 8:257.

47. *Corr.*, 1:272 (Daniel Waldo Stevens to HDT, May 24, 1845); Kevin P. Van Anglen, introduction to *Translations*, 218; *PEJ*, 1:436 ("the sweetness of sugar merely").

48. Ralph Waldo Emerson, "Veeshnoo Sarma," *Dial* 3.1 (July 1842), 82–85. See Arthur Versluis, *American Transcendentalism and Asian Religions* (New York: Oxford University Press, 1993), ch. 2 and 3; Alan D. Hodder, *Thoreau's Ecstatic Witness* (New Haven, CT: Yale University Press, 2001), ch. 5; and Robert D. Richardson Jr., *Henry David Thoreau: A Life of the Mind* (Berkeley: University of California Press, 1986), esp. 106–9, 204–7.

49. Richardson, *HDT: Life of the Mind*, 107; *EEM*, 128–29, 130, 139; *PEJ*, 1:427. *The Laws of Menu* was Thoreau's shorthand for Manu, *Institutes of Hindu Law, or The Ordinances of Menu, According to the Gloss of Culluca*, trans. Sir William Jones, new edition, collated with the Sanscrit text, by Graves Chamney Haughton, 2 vols. (London: Rivingtons and Cochran, 1825).

50. *EEM*, 141, 148; *PEJ*, 1:426.

51. *Corr.*, 1:245 (HDT to RWE, October 17, 1843), 2:43 (HDT to H. G. O. Blake, November 20, 1849).

52. *PEJ*, 1:447; *Corr.*, 1:117–18 (HDT to Richard Fuller, January 16, 1843); Lidian Emerson in *THOT*, 3.

53. *Corr.*, 1:123–14 (HDT to RWE, January 24, 1843); *LRWE*, 3:75; Ellen Tucker Emerson, *Life of Lidian Emerson*, xlv; *Corr.*, 1:126n6.

54. *Corr.*, 1:145–46n6; 120 (HDT to Lucy Jackson Brown, January 24, 1943).

55. *Corr.*, 1:138–39 (RWE to HDT, February 12, 1843), 141 (HDT to RWE, February 15, 1843).

56. Joel Myerson, *The New England Transcendentalists and the "Dial": A History of the Magazine and Its Contributors* (Cranbury, NJ: Associated University Presses, 1980), 83; *Corr.*, 1:147 (Elizabeth Peabody to HDT, February 26, 1843); *LRWE*, 3:165. Emerson changed publishers, moving from Peabody to James Munroe in hopes of better distribution; see Myerson, *New England Transcendentalists*, 90.

57. *Corr.*, 1:149 (HDT to RWE, March 1, 1843); *LRWE*, 3:158.

58. *Days of HT*, 10 (the editor was Epes Sargent); *Corr.*, 1:124 (HDT to RWE, January 24, 1843).

59. *Corr.*, 1:152 (HDT to Richard Fuller, April 2, 1843); Hawthorne, *American Notebooks*, 369, 371.

60. *Corr.*, 1:158–59 (Elizabeth Hoar to HDT, May 2, 1843); *LRWE*, 3:172.

61. *Corr.*, 1:159–61 (HDT to Cynthia Thoreau, May 11, 1843).

62. The Snuggery burned down in 1855, and no sign of it remains; the neighborhood is still called Emerson Hill.

63. *Week*, 181; Fuller quoted in Ronald A. Bosco and Joel Myerson, *The Emerson Brothers: A Fraternal Biography in Letters* (Oxford: Oxford University Press, 2006), 343.

64. *Corr.*, 1:184 (HDT to John and Cynthia Thoreau, June 8, 1843); *LRWE*, 3:182, 162–63.

65. *Corr.*, 1:174 (HDT to RWE, May 23, 1843), 170 (HDT to Sophia Thoreau, May 22, 1843), 198 (HDT to Cynthia Thoreau, July 7, 1843).

66. Ibid., 174–75 (HDT to RWE, May 23, 1843).

67. Ibid., 181, 185 (HDT to RWE, June 8, 1843), 210 (HDT to Helen Thoreau, July 21, 1843).

68. Ibid., 184. Emerson complained of this, too: "The tyranny of Space I feel in this long long city: three or four *calls* will consume a day unless one is a skilled geographer" (*LRWE*, 3:27, emphasis in the original).

69. *Corr.*, 1:171–72 (HDT to Sophia Thoreau, May 22, 1843), 175 (HDT to RWE, May 23, 1843).

70. Ibid., 174 (HDT to RWE, May 23, 1843), 180–81 (HDT to RWE, June 8, 1843).

71. Ibid., 181–82 (HDT to RWE, June 8, 1843); 198 (HDT to Cynthia Thoreau, July 7, 1843); William Emerson quoted in Bosco and Myerson, *Emerson Brothers*, 343.

72. *LRWE*, 7:542–43; *Corr.*, 1:163 (Henry James Sr. to HDT, May 12, 1843), 179 (HDT to RWE, June 8, 1843); 252 (RWE to HDT, October 25, 1843); *LRWE*, 7:566–67.

73. *Corr.*, 1:225 (HDT to Cynthia Thoreau, August 29, 1843), 238 (HDT to Cynthia Thoreau, October 1, 1843), 210 (HDT to Helen Thoreau, July 21, 1843), 180. Henry McKean had also done editorial work for Emerson.

74. Ibid., 211 (HDT to Helen Thoreau, July 21, 1843).

75. *RP*, 35, 42. Thoreau's review bears comparison with Hawthorne's "The Celestial Railroad," which Emerson praised to Thoreau about this time; see *Corr.*, 1:192 (RWE to HDT, June 10, 1843).

76. *Corr.*, 1:214 (John O'Sullivan to HDT, July 28, 1843), 250 (HDT to Helen Thoreau, October 18, 1843).

77. Ibid., 185 (HDT to John and Cynthia Thoreau, June 8, 1843), 238 (HDT to Cynthia Thoreau, October 1, 1843).

78. Ibid., 224 (HDT to Cynthia Thoreau, August 29, 1843), 233–34 (HDT to RWE, September 14, 1843), 238 (HDT to Cynthia Thoreau, October 1, 1843).

79. Ibid., 199 (HDT to Cynthia Thoreau, July 7, 1843), 218–19 (HDT to Cynthia Thoreau, August 6, 1843), 221 (HDT to RWE, August 7, 1843).

80. Ibid., 164 (RWE to HDT, May 21, 1843), 174 (HDT to RWE, May 23, 1843), 203 (HDT to RWE and LJE, July 8, 1843).

81. *JMN*, 9:9–10. But Channing liked this essay, which Greeley excerpted in the *New-York Daily Tribune* for October 27, 1843, and the *New-York Weekly Tribune* for November 4, 1843.

82. *Corr.*, 1:229 (RWE to HDT, September 8, 1843), 245 (HDT to RWE, October 17, 1843). Emerson normalized Thoreau's prose, muting his meaning; see Francis B. Dedmond, "'Pretty Free Omissions': Emerson Edits a Thoreau Manuscript for the *Dial*," *TSB* 227 (Spring 1999): 8.

83. *Corr.*, 1:208, 222, 229, 252 (Emerson prompting Thoreau), 216 (HDT to O'Sullivan, August 1, 1843), 234 (HDT to RWE, September 14, 1843).

84. Ibid., 164–65 (RWE to HDT, May 21, 1843), 192 (RWE to HDT, June 10, 1843). It helped that Channing himself sustained his friendship with Thoreau, roundly defending "Winter Walk" to Emerson's face, and that Thoreau genuinely admired Channing's

book of poems, just published: "I have read his poems two or three times over" with growing appreciation; "tell him I saw a man buying a copy at Little and Brown's" (ibid., 175).

85. *Thoreau Log*, 94; *Corr.*, 1:164 (RWE to HDT, May 21, 1843); *JMN*, 8:399.

86. *LRWE*, 3:149, 137, 183. On Emerson, Waldo and Tappan, see Harmon Smith, "Henry Thoreau and Emerson's 'Noble Youths,'" *Concord Saunterer* 17.3 (December 1984): 4– 12; see also Smith, *My Friend, My Friend: The Story of Thoreau's Relationship with Emerson* (Amherst: University of Massachusetts Press, 1999), 78–94.

87. Giles Waldo quoted in Harmon, "Henry Thoreau and Emerson's 'Noble Youths,'" 5; *Corr.*, 1:180 (HDT to RWE, June 8, 1843), 207 (RWE to HDT, July 20, 1843).

88. *Corr.*, 1:187 (Charles Lane to HDT, June 9, 1843).

89. Ibid., 199 (HDT to Cynthia Thoreau, July 7, 1843), 208 (RWE to HDT, July 20, 1843), 211–12 (HDT to Helen Thoreau, July 21, 1843).

90. Ibid., 224 (HDT to Cynthia Thoreau, August 29, 1843); 228 (RWE to HDT, September 8, 1843).

91. Ibid., 218 (HDT to Cynthia Thoreau, August 6, 1843); 240 (HDT to Cynthia Thoreau, October 1, 1843).

92. *PEJ*, 1:465 (September 24, 1843), 478 (October 21, 1843).

93. For details, see Sterling F. Delano, "Thoreau's Visit to Brook Farm," *TSB* 221/222 (Fall 1997/Spring 1998): 1–2; and Edmund A. Schofield, "The Date(s) and Context of Thoreau's Visit to Brook Farm," *TSB* 258 (Spring 2007): 8–10.

94. Delano, "Thoreau's Visit," 221–22.

95. *JMN*, 8:433; *Corr.*, 1:258 (Charles Lane to HDT, December 3, 1843).

96. *Corr.*, 1:202 (HDT to RWE and LJE, July 8, 1843); *PJ* 1:495.

97. *LRWE*, 3:4, 168; *Corr.*, 1:191 (RWE to HDT, June 10, 1843), 228 (RWE to HDT, September 8, 1843).

98. *JMN*, 9:7; *Corr.*, 1:229 (RWE to HDT, September 8, 1843), 171 (HDT to Sophia Thoreau, May 22, 1843).

99. *Corr.*, 1:239 (HDT to Cynthia Thoreau, October 1, 1843), 246 (HDT to RWE, October 17, 1843).

100. Hawthorne, *American Notebooks*, 395–96; *Corr.*, 1:236 (Margaret Fuller to HDT, September 25, 1843); *JMN*, 7:590.

101. Edward Emerson interview notes with Marshall Miles, series 1, box 1, folder 11, CFPL.

102. *PEJ*, 2:289; *JMN*, 9:77.

103. *LRWE*, 7:597; the artist was Caroline Sturgis. The old-style writing pencils were graded numerically from one to four, while the new, highest-quality drafting pencils were graded alphabetically with S for "soft" and H for "hard." Both systems are still used today today—hence the ubiquitous "number 2" pencil, although today artists' pencils are graded B for "soft," instead of S.

104. *Days of HT*, 157–59; Henry Petroski, "H. D. Thoreau, Engineer," *Invention and Technology* 5.2 (Fall 1989): 8–16.

105. *JMN*, 9:45.

106. "Homer. Ossian. Chaucer," in *EEM*, 154–55, 173; *PEJ*, 2:59. For Thoreau on making arrowheads, see *PEJ*, 2:58–60.

107. *To Set This World*, 36–40.

108. Helen Thoreau's Scrapbook, CFPL; Robert A. Gross, "Helen Thoreau's Anti-slavery Scrapbook," *Yale Review* 100.1 (January 2012): 103–20.

109. *JMN*, 9:70–71; "Young American," in *Collected Works of Emerson*, 1:226. O'Sullivan's *Democratic Review* coined the phrase in July–August 1845, in regard to the annexation of Texas, and used it famously that December—echoing Emerson's language.

110. Thoreau spoke on March 10, 1844, at 10:30 a.m. and 7:30 p.m. The afternoon featured a discussion of "Non-Resistance"; it is likely, but not certain, that Thoreau participated; see TL I, 143; *E&L*, 593, 598, 607, 608. See also Linck C. Johnson, "Reforming the Reformers: Emerson, Thoreau, and the Sunday Lectures at Amory Hall, Boston," *ESQ* [*Emerson Society Quarterly*] 37.4 (1991): 235–89.

111. *RP*, 182–83; *Corr.*, 1:250–51 (HDT to Helen Thoreau, October 18, 1843).

112. *RP*, 183–185.

113. Rogers quoted in ibid., 49–51. Thoreau's early lecture has apparently never been published, but his notes survive: see ibid., 379–92.

114. Rogers quoted in *To Set This World*, 39–40.

115. *LRWE*, 3:243, 7:595.

116. David S. Reynolds, *Walt Whitman's America: A Cultural Biography* (New York: Knopf, 1995), 82; Sanborn, *Life of Thoreau*, 129; *E&L*, 465; Elizabeth Hall Witherell, "Thoreau as Poet," in *The Cambridge Companion to Henry David Thoreau*, edited by Joel Myerson. (Cambridge: Cambridge University Press, 1995), 60, 68n10.

117. PEJ, 3:75–76.

118. Ibid., 80, 85.

119. Daniel F. Potter (whom Thoreau had feruled at school, now a grown man), in Edward Emerson interview notes, series 1, box 1, folder 14, CFPL.

120. The daughter of A. H. Wheeler, quoted in *Days of HT*, 161; Edmund A. Schofield, "'Burnt Woods': Ecological Insights into Thoreau's Unhappy Encounter with Fire," *Thoreau Research Newsletter* 2.3 (July 1991): 3.

121. PEJ, 3:76–78, 4:68–69.

122. He may have shortened his journey by taking the train and/or the stage part of the way; see Thomas Woodson, "Thoreau's Excursion to the Berkshires and Catskills," *Emerson Society Quarterly* 21.1 (1975): 82–92; see also *Week*, 202–9.

123. *Week*, 182. The woman has been tentatively identified as Rebecca Darling Eddy; Thoreau writes that she reminded him of his cousin—likely Rebecca Thatcher, whom he'd met in 1838 while seeking a teaching position in Bangor, Maine. See Donald Murray and Susan Denault, "Thoreau's Dark Lady Was Probably a Darling," *TSB* 165 (Fall 1983): 1–3.

124. *Week*, 183–90; Channing quoted in Bernard A. Drew, "Thoreau's Tarn Identified: Guilder Pond," *Concord Saunterer*, n.s., 9 (2001): 128.

125. *Walden*, 323; W. E. Channing II, *Poet-Naturalist* (1902), 34.

126. PEJ, 2:155. Drew, "Thoreau's Tarn Identified," identifies this tarn as Guilder Pond.

127. *To Set This World*, 40–43.

128. Anna Whiting and George Curtis both witnessed the event and told this story; for George Curtis's account, see Sterling Delano and Joel Myerson, "'The General Scape-

goat': Thoreau and Concord in 1844," *TSB* 264 (Fall 2008): 1–2; for Anna Whiting's report to the *Herald of Freedom*, see *To Set This World*, 44.

129. *Corr.*, 1:267 (HDT to James Munroe and Company, October 14, 1844), 275 (James Munroe and Company to HDT, September 17, 1844); see Richardson, *HDT: Life of the Mind*, 146.

130. *Corr.*, 1:257 (Charles Lane to HDT, December 3, 1843). Hecker had, like Thoreau, experienced his first *Lebenstag* with Orestes Brownson; Charles Lane had encouraged Hecker and Thoreau to meet.

131. *Thoreau Log*, 106; *Corr.*, 1:259 (Isaac Hecker to HDT, July 31, 1844).

132. *Corr.*, 1:261–62 (HDT to Hecker, August 14, 1844).

133. Ibid., 264 (Isaac Hecker to HDT, August 15, 1844), 266 (HDT to Hecker, after August 15, 1844).

134. George Curtis quoted in Delano and Myerson, "General Scapegoat," 2; *Walden*, 10.

135. *JMN*, 9:103.

CHAPTER FIVE

1. It has been assumed that Henry Thoreau built this house with the help of his father and a carpenter, though how such a significant expenditure of time and hard labor could have been completed in a few months over a New England winter, without leaving significant documentation, is unclear. A newly discovered letter by Frances Jane Hallett Prichard states that the building was purchased and moved from another site: "Building houses and moving them seems to be the rage now—Mrs Thoreau has bought that house Mrs. Marshall lives in & is to move it onto a piece of land Mr Loring gave them. . . . Tis nothing to our enterprising citizens to carry a house from one spot to another—I cannot say where you may find us" (Frances Jane Hallett Prichard to her mother Jane Hallett Prichard, April 16, 1844, Prichard, Hoar, and Related Family Papers, vault A45, Prichard unit 2, box 2, folder 4, CFPL). Sadly, the house burned in 1938, along with troves of Thoreau pencils and other artifacts, and the ruins were bulldozed away in 1959.

2. The deed was filed on September 14, 1844, and was witnessed by John, Cynthia, Helen, and Henry Thoreau; see *TSB* 191 (Spring 1990): 5–6. John Thoreau paid off the mortgage on the Texas House in September 1855. *Thoreau Log*, 363.

3. Annie Russell Marble, *Thoreau: His Home, Friends, and Books* (New York: Thomas Y. Crowell, 1902), 265.

4. *J*, 14:99, October 3, 1860.

5. *LRWE*, 3:262–63; Ralph Waldo Emerson and Thomas Carlyle, *The Correspondence of Emerson and Carlyle*, ed. Joseph Slater, 2 vols (New York: Columbia University Press, 1964), 2:369. For details, including previous ownership by Thomas Wyman, see W. Barksdale Maynard, "Emerson's 'Wyman Lot': Forgotten Context for Thoreau's House at Walden," *Concord Saunterer*, n.s., 12/13 (2004–5): 63–68.

6. *LRWE*, 3:263; *CCE*, 2:101–02; *ABAJ*, 178. See also Raymond Adams, "Emerson's House at Walden," *TSB* 24 (July 1948): 1–5.

7. *Corr.,* 1:94 (HDT to Margaret Fuller, October 18, 1843), PEJ, 1:347. On the contemporary rage for rural and suburban retreats and Thoreau's ongoing conversation with their various conventions and ideals, see W. Barksdale Maynard, "Thoreau's House at Walden," *Art Bulletin* 81.2 (1999): 303–25.

8. *LRWE,* 3:231; Harmon Smith, "Henry Thoreau and Emerson's 'Noble Youths,'" *Concord Saunterer* 17.3 (December 1984): 4–12.

9. Charles Lane, "Life in the Woods," *Dial* 4.4 (April 1844): 422, 424. Lane's essay gave Thoreau his original subtitle for *Walden, or Life in the Woods,* which was dropped in the second edition.

10. Robert N. Hudspeth, *Ellery Channing* (New York: Twayne, 1973), 31; *Corr.,* 1:268 (Ellery Channing to HDT, March 5, 1845).

11. ABAJ, 178–79; Adams, "Emerson's House." Neither lodge nor tower was ever built.

12. Francis B. Dedmond, "George William Curtis to Christopher Pearse Cranch: Three Unpublished Letters from Concord," *Concord Saunterer* 12.4 (Winter 1977): 6.

13. *LRWE,* 8:13, 15–16 (RWE to Samuel Gray Ward, March 13?, 1845).

14. "Wendell Phillips before Concord Lyceum," in *RP,* 60–61. *Narrative of the Life of Frederick Douglass, an American Slave,* featuring prefaces by Garrison and Phillips, was published months later.

15. *RP,* 61; *Corr.,* 1:181 (HDT to RWE, June 8, 1843).

16. PEJ, 2:121, 124; *RP,* 74.

17. PEJ, 2:107; "Reminiscences of Thoreau," *Concord Freeman* (September 1, 1882), quoted in TL I, 146.

18. PEJ, 2:134–35; *Walden,* 43–44. Emerson described the shanty ruins to Carlyle: see *Correspondence of Emerson and Carlyle,* 1:399 (May 14, 1846).

19. *Walden,* 42; PEJ, 2:140; ABAJ, 317 ("dreadful dissenter"); "a bit of life as Arcadian as any at Brook Farm," said George Curtis of the house-raising (Dedmond, "Three Unpublished Letters," 8).

20. *Walden,* 54–55, 251, 155; PEJ, 2:129, 158–59. On the location of the beanfield, which for many decades was mistakenly said to be on the flat land just above Thoreau's house, see Bradley P. Dean, "Rediscovery at Walden: The History of Thoreau's Bean-Field," *Concord Saunterer,* n.s., 12/13 (2004–5): 86–137.

21. *Walden,* 20–21; cf. PEJ, 2:132–33.

22. PEJ, 2:155.

23. "Walden," in *CEP,* 516; *Walden,* 193.

24. *JMN,* 9:195, 1845. Roland Robbins, who excavated the original house site, noted that of Thoreau's nearly one hundred references to his house in *Walden,* "eighty odd of the number are 'house.' He says 'lodge' three times, 'dwelling' twice, 'apartment' twice, 'homestead' once; and on only one occasion does he use the word 'hut'" (Roland Wells Robbins, *Discovery at Walden* (1972; Lincoln, MA: Thoreau Society, 1999), 10.

25. *RP,* 193; William Ellery Channing II, *Thoreau: The Poet-Naturalist,* ed. F. B. Sanborn (Boston: Charles E. Goodspeed, 1902), 7–8. Emerson was astonished: "Ellery lives with H. T. at the pond, in these days, in the absence of his wife!" (*LRWE,* 8:52).

26. Edward Emerson interview notes, Mrs. White, box 1, folder 20, CFPL.

27. PEJ, 2:156.

28. Nathaniel Hawthorne, *The American Notebooks* (Columbus: Ohio State University Press, 1932, 1960, 1972), 369; *JMN*, 9:121.

29. PEJ, 2:156–57, 165.

30. Brad Dean calculated, from timetables in the *Boston Daily Evening Transcript*, that by 1846 ten trains passed Walden daily, eight passenger and two freight; by 1847 that number had at least doubled (personal communication).

31. PEJ, 2:170–74, 156.

32. Ibid., 148, 160–61, 151–52.

33. *Walden*, 153; *Thoreau as Seen*, 94, 106.

34. *Walden*, 157; George Hendrick, ed., *Remembrances of Concord and the Thoreaus: Letters of Horace Hosmer to Dr. S. A. Jones* (Urbana: University of Illinois Press, 1977), 53.

35. Quoted in Henry Seidel Canby, *Thoreau* (Boston: Houghton Mifflin, 1939), 216 (January 20, 1846).

36. Mabel Loomis Todd quoted in *Thoreau as Seen*, 187; Marble, *Thoreau: Home, Friends, Books*, 129; John S. Keyes quoted in *Thoreau as Seen*, 174.

37. Edward Waldo Emerson, *Henry Thoreau as Remembered by a Young Friend* (1917; Concord, MA: Thoreau Foundation, 1968), 61–62.

38. *Corr.*, 1:276 (RWE to HDT, October 8, 1845), 282 (RWE to HDT, late September 1846); *J*, 10:61–62. Emerson's payments are recorded in Walter Harding, "Thoreau in Emerson's Account Books," *TSB* 159 (Spring 1982): 1–3.

39. Stanley Cavell, *The Senses of Walden: An Expanded Edition* (Chicago: University of Chicago Press, 1992), 11; *Exc.*, 47, 54.

40. Rebecca Solnit opens with this point in her essay "Mysteries of Thoreau, Unsolved: On the Dirtiness of Laundry and the Strength of Sisters," *Orion*, May–June 2013, 18–23. At the Thoreau boardinghouse, laundry was done by live-in servants, as was then standard; very few in the American middle classes did their own laundry.

41. *Days of HT*, 182.

42. David Wood, *An Observant Eye: The Thoreau Collection at the Concord Museum* (Concord, MA: Concord Museum, 2006), 10–13, 57–59; Mary Hosmer Brown, *Memories of Concord* (Boston: Four Seas, 1926), 95, 98.

43. Joseph Hosmer, in Hendrick, *Remembrances*, 140–42; PEJ, 3:22.

44. *Walden*, 242–43.

45. Ibid., 140; PEJ, 2:160.

46. PEJ, 2:176–77, 210–11.

47. Ibid., 207–9, 414–16; *Walden*, 261–62. Coyle died on October 1, 1845, on Walden Road at the foot of Brister's Hill. Two days later, the *Concord Freeman* ran his obituary: "Mr. Hugh Coyle, a man of intemperate habits, residing in the vicinity of Walden pond, in this town, was found dead on the road near his house on Wednesday afternoon last. As he was seen on his way home a short time before he was found dead, with his features very much distorted and in a feeble state, he is supposed to have died in a fit of *delirium tremens*. He was an old campaigner and fought at the Battle of Waterloo." Henry David Thoreau, *Walden: A Fully Annotated Edition*, ed. Jeffrey S. Cramer (New Haven, CT: Yale University Press, 2004), 255

48. See Elise Lemire, *Black Walden: Slavery and Its Aftermath in Concord, Massachusetts*

(Philadelphia: University of Pennsylvania Press, 2009), 122–27.

49. Lemire, *Black Walden*, 162–63.

50. For the obituary of Zilpah White, see Thoreau, *Walden: A Fully Annotated Edition*, 248n15; Thoreau spelled her name "Zilpha" (*Walden*, 257). On the Freeman family, see Lemire, *Black Walden*, 163–71. John Freeman, Brister's Freeman's grandson and the family's last survivor, died in 1822 of fever at the age of eight, "the last descendent of local slaves to reside in Walden Woods" (ibid., 181).

51. *Walden*, 258–61; Lemire, *Black Walden*, 162–63.

52. Lemire, *Black Walden*, 157.

53. *Walden*, 264.

54. PEJ, 2:159, 235–36 (emphasis in the original).

55. Ibid., 2:162; Joseph Hosmer repr. in Hendrick, *Remembrances*, 142; Marble, *Thoreau: Home, Friends, Books*, 120. See also Prudence Ward's charming children's story, "The Story of the Little Field Mouse," in the Thoreau-Ward-Sewall Papers, Thoreau Society Archives, Henley Library.

56. PEJ, 2:225–26 ("Jean Lapin"); cf. *Walden*, 281. The most extensive version is by Frederick L. H. Willis (the boyhood friend of Louisa May Alcott, memorialized as "Laurie" in *Little Women*): see *Thoreau as Seen*, 134, 150.

57. *Thoreau as Seen*, 183.

58. See John Hartigan Jr., *Aesop's Anthropology: A Multispecies Approach* (Minneapolis: University of Minnesota Press, 2014), 25.

59. PEJ, 2:159.

60. *Walden*, 59; PEJ, 2:177, 241.

61. PEJ, 2:242.

62. Ibid., 2:227, 166.

63. Patrick Chura, *Thoreau the Land Surveyor* (Gainesville, FL: University Press of Florida, 2010), 30–44. When Thoreau prepared the original 1846 survey for publication, he simplified, or "reduced," it by eliminating many of the soundings, reducing the scale, and reorienting his compass from magnetic north to his "True Meridian," a significant reorientation to the North Pole, which took him several day's painstaking work to ascertain; it was this "reduced plan" of 1854 that the engraver reproduced in professional style and formal lettering (ibid., 114–20).

64. JMN, 9:329, *Walden*, 287.

65. PEJ, 2:240; written between April 18 and May 3, 1846.

66. *Walden*, 98.

67. JMN, 9:430–31; Daniel Walker Howe, *What Hath God Wrought: The Transformation of America, 1815–1848* (Oxford: Oxford University Press, 2007), 686.

68. Howe, *What Hath God Wrought*, 703; *To Set This World*, 52, 178n37.

69. Howe, *What Hath God Wrought*, 752. Estados Unidos Mexicanos, or the "United Mexican States," was (and to the date of writing, remains) the nation's formal name.

70. Edward Waldo Emerson interview with Sam Staples, Edward Waldo Emerson Papers, series 1, box 1, folder 17, CFPL. For a helpful article on the poll tax, see John C. Broderick, "Thoreau, Alcott, and the Poll Tax," *Studies in Philology* 53.4 (October 1956): 612–26.

71. Initially published as "Resistance to Civil Government" (1849).

72. He was later found not guilty and released; *Days of HT*, 204. Jailer Sam Staples had been, for a time, manager of the Middlesex Hotel.

73. Fritz Oehlschlaeger and George Hendrick, eds., *Toward the Making of Thoreau's Modern Reputation* (Urbana: University of Illinois, 1979), 199–201.

74. *RP*, 82–83; cf. PEJ, 2:262–64.

75. Oehlschlaeger and Hendrick, *Thoreau's Modern Reputation*, 201; Edward Waldo Emerson interview notes with Sam Staples, box 1, folder 17, CFPL.

76. *RP*, 83–84. The description of a typical huckleberry party is taken from Ellen Tucker Emerson, *The Life of Lidian Jackson Emerson* (East Lansing: Michigan State University Press, 1992), 107.

77. *RP*, 84. Thoreau refers to Silvio Pellico's memoir (above, ch. 4, n. 37).

78. Quoted in *To Set This World*, 59; Edward Emerson interview notes with George Bartlett, box 1, folder 1, CFPL.

79. PEJ, 2:262–64.

80. ABAJ, 179 (May 4, 1846), 183.

81. *JMN*, 9:445–47.

82. *LRWE*, 3:340.

83. I am indebted to the excellent and detailed descriptions of this event in *To Set This World*, 60–62, and Randall Conrad, "Realizing Resistance: Thoreau and the First of August, 1846, at Walden," *Concord Saunterer* 12/13 (2004–5): 165–93. There were other picnics at Walden as well (but Thoreau kept no records); for instance, Emerson mentions a "Young Concord" levee at Walden, held on July 5, 1847 (*LRWE*, 3:403).

84. *Walden*, 140.

85. See *To Set This World*, 61. Harding also points out that the antislavery movement was not respectable until *after* the Civil War—once the need for it no longer existed (*Days of HT*, 201).

86. Anna Whiting, "First of August in Concord," *Liberator*, August 7, 1846.

87. Hayden's address in Concord was not recorded; these words are from his address a year later to the American Anti-Slavery Society. See Conrad, "Realizing Resistance," 181, 177–78.

88. Oehlschlaeger and Hendrick, *Thoreau's Modern Reputation*, 143; Edward Emerson interview with Bigelow, box 1, folder 2, CFPL; *To Set This World*, 63–65, 18n59.

89. ABAJ, 190; *Walden*, 152; *To Set This World*, 62–63.

90. ABAJ, 193 (March 1847); PEJ, 2:167, 1:46.

91. PEJ, 1:172, 418. Emerson reported one such group in Concord in 1843: "Hither come in summer the Penobscot Indians, & make baskets for us on the river bank" (*JMN*, 8:385.) A group camped near Harvard in 1834 inspired Thoreau's classmate Horatio Hale to write his short monograph on their language.

92. PEJ, 2:281. See Richard S. Sprague, "Companions to Katahdin: Henry David Thoreau and George A. Thatcher of Bangor," in *Thoreau Journal Quarterly* 12.1 (January 1980): 41–65.

93. *MW*, 4; Thoreau's source was Charles T. Jackson, the state geologist and Emerson's brother-in-law, who had explored the Penobscot and climbed Mount Katahdin in 1837. Thoreau spells the name "Ktaadn."

94. PEJ, 2:281–83, *MW*, 6.

95. PEJ, 2:284.

96. Ibid., 286–88.

97. Ibid., 289; *MW*, 14–16; PEJ, 2:293–94.

98. PEJ, 2:294–98; *MW*, 16–21.

99. PEJ, 2:298–302; *MW*, 21–26.

100. PEJ, 2:302–7; *MW*, 26–31.

101. PEJ, 2:307–10; *MW*, 31–35.

102. PEJ, 2:311–15; *MW*, 35–41.

103. PEJ, 2:315–20; *MW*, 41–45.

104. PEJ, 2:330–32, 278; *MW*, 53–55.

105. PEJ, 2:332–37; *MW*, 56–62. Katahdin's true summit, Baxter Peak, was not visible from the river below; Thoreau sighted to South Peak instead.

106. PEJ, 2:338–40; cf. *MW*, 64–65.

107. PEJ, 2:278; *MW*, 70–71.

108. *MW*, 81–82; PEJ, 2:352–54.

109. PEJ, 2:175.

110. Ibid., 249–51; *Corr.*, 1:284–88 (Horatio Storer and HDT, January 17 and February 15, 1847); the report's author was Horatio's father, David Humphreys Storer.

111. Christoph Irmscher, *Louis Agassiz: Creator of American Science* (Boston: Houghton Mifflin, 2013), 92–93; *Corr.*, 1:290–91 (James Elliot Cabot to HDT, May 3, 1847).

112. *Corr.*, 1:292–94 (HDT to James Elliot Cabot, May 8, 1847), 299–300 (Cabot to HDT, May 27, 1847), 303–4 (Cabot to HDT, June 1, 1847).

113. *LRWE*, 3:397 (May 4, 1847); *Corr.*, 1:301n11.

114. *LRWE*, 3:288, 290, 293; PEJ, 2:256–57.

115. *LRWE*, 3:383; PEJ, 2:370–71, *Walden*, 297–98. See Wai Chee Dimock, *Through Other Continents: American Literature across Deep Time* (Princeton, NJ: Princeton University Press, 2003), 9–22; and Alan D. Hodder, *Thoreau's Ecstatic Witness* (New Haven, CT: Yale University Press, 2001), 212–13. Both scholars stress that the traffic Thoreau envisioned between India and Concord is not one-way but circular and reciprocal, a point Dimock makes in her analysis of Gandhi's indebtedness to Thoreau (*Through Other Continents*, 20–22). As Stanley Cavell points out, "Like *Walden*, the *Bhagavad Gita* is a scripture in eighteen parts" that begins with the hero in despair and ends with the hero resolved in the way of action. Cavell, *Senses of Walden*, 117–18.

116. PEJ 4:275, 276; *Walden*, 323.

117. *LRWE*, 3:413, 415; Ellen Tucker Emerson, *Life of Lidian Jackson Emerson*, 108. For Thoreau's description of Emerson's cramped stateroom, see *Corr.*, 1:310 (HDT to Sophia Thoreau, October 24, 1847).

CHAPTER SIX

1. ABAJ, 194; *Corr.*, 1:308 (HDT to Henry Williams, September 30, 1847).

2. Ellen Tucker Emerson, *The Life of Lidian Jackson Emerson* (East Lansing: Michigan

State University Press, 1992), 108 ("prophet's chamber"); *Corr.*, 1:316 (HDT to RWE, November 14, 1847). Lucy Jackson Brown was living in the main house while her new house next door was being built.

3. *Corr.*, 1:313. Thoreau puns on Theodore Parker's 1841 "Discourse of the Transient and Permanent in Christianity." Thoreau frequently consulted the Emersons' financial manager, Abel Adams.

4. Ibid., 313–14; *LRWE*, 3:455 (i.e., a father or a nice fellow in spite of himself).

5. *Corr.*, 1:316, 325 (RWE to HDT, December 2, 1847).

6. Ellen Tucker Emerson, *Life of Lidian Jackson Emerson* 105, 107; *Days of HT*, 224–26.

7. Maria reported Henry receiving an "incoherent" letter from the reformer Sophia Foord asking him, interestingly, to join a society to ascertain the cause of shipwrecks; Thoreau had recently returned from witnessing the shipwreck of the *St. John*. Maria Thoreau to Prudence Ward, November 15, 1849, Thoreau-Sewall Papers, 1790–1917, HM 64936, Huntington Library, San Marino, California. See also *Days of HT*, 224–26; Milton Meltzer and Walter Harding, *A Thoreau Profile* (New York: Thomas Y. Crowell, 1962), 66.

8. *JMN*, 10:116–17; *Days of HT*, 217.

9. *LRWE*, 3:411, 413.

10. *ABAJ*, 196–97; Maria Thoreau to Prudence Ward, September 25, 1847 ("I hope they will find as soft a landing place, one and all when they drop from the clouds," she added). Thoreau-Sewall-Ward Letters, Thoreau Society Archives, Henley Library.

11. *Corr.*, 1:314; *ABAJ*, 197.

12. *Days of HT*, 219; Franklin Benjamin Sanborn, *The Life of Henry David Thoreau* (Boston: Houghton Mifflin, 1917), 300–301; *LRWE*, 3:411n; Walter Harding, "Thoreau in Emerson's Account Books," *TSB* 159 (Spring 1982): 1–3 [hereafter EAB]. Marston Watson liked Alcott's summerhouse so much that in 1854 he commissioned Alcott to build one on his Plymouth property.

13. EAB, September 28, 1847; *Corr.*, 1:338–39 (HDT to RWE, January 12, 1848). The farmer who bought Thoreau's damaged house was James Clark, on the old Carlisle Road. For additional details, see Bradley P. Dean, "Rediscovery at Walden: The History of Thoreau's Bean-Field," *Concord Saunterer*, n.s., 12/13 (2004–5): 97–102.

14. David Wood, *An Observant Eye: The Thoreau Collection at the Concord Museum* (Concord, MA: Concord Museum, 2006), 125; Walton Ricketson, visiting the ruin with Channing later in 1868, brought away a few fragments that are preserved in the Concord Museum. *Days of HT*, 224, has a somewhat different story.

15. *Corr.*, 1:317 (HDT to RWE, November 14, 1847), 325 (RWE to HDT, December 2, 1847); *LRWE*, 4:110; *Corr.*, 1:378 (HDT to RWE, May 21, 1848). On August 31, 1848, the Fitchburg Railroad Company paid Emerson fifty dollars in compensation. *Corr.*, 1:381n5.

16. *Walden*, 191–92. By 1854, little more than 10 percent of the forest surrounding Walden Pond was still standing. Lawrence Buell, "Thoreau and the Natural Environment," in *The Cambridge Companion to Henry David Thoreau*, ed. Joel Myerson (Cambridge: Cambridge University Press, 1995), 173.

17. *Corr.*, 1:345 (HDT to RWE, February 23, 1848), 2:27 (HDT to Ellen Emerson, July 31, 1849). The *Penny Magazine of the Society for the Diffusion of Useful Knowledge* was a vehicle for popular natural history.

18. *LRWE*, 4:40–41.
19. Lidian Emerson to RWE (May 17, 1848), in *THOT*, 3; *LRWE*, 4:80–81.
20. *LRWE*, 4:33.
21. PEJ, 3:17–18, 125–26; see also 44–46.
22. Ibid., 2:245–46, 3:7; *EEM*, 275. Thoreau echoes Margaret Fuller's description of the highest, or "religious," kind of marriage in her essay "The Great Lawsuit": the couple will attain "more and more glorious prospects that open as we advance" (32–33). See also PEJ, 3:211, where Thoreau imagines a love "quite transcending marriage," and most interestingly, Thoreau's essays "Love" and "Chastity & Sexuality," which he composed and sent to H. G. O. Blake in September 1852 (*EEM*, 268–73, 274–78).
23. Emerson, "Thoreau," 415, 416–17.
24. *Walden*, 219–21; *EEM*, 274.
25. *EEM*, 277; Emerson, "Thoreau" 767n5.
26. *Walden*, 79 (Thoreau is quoting the classic Persian poet Saadi). Walter Harding lays out the extensive evidence for Thoreau's same-sex attraction in "Thoreau's Sexuality," *Journal of Homosexuality* 21.3 (1991): 23–45. Harding concludes, as had others whom he cites, that Thoreau's creativity sprang from a sublimated homoeroticism. Discussions of Thoreau's (homo)sexuality were quite active for some years, starting in the late 1970s; the subject is today ripe for reexamination. See George Whitmore, "Friendship in New England: Henry Thoreau. I.," *Gai Saber* 1.2 (Summer 1977): 104–11; Whitmore, "Friendship in New England: Henry Thoreau. II.," *Gai Saber* 1.3–4 (Summer 1978): 188–202; Michael Warner, "Walden's Erotic Economy," in *Comparative American Identities: Race, Sex, and Nationality in the American Text*, ed. Hortense Spillers (New York: Routledge, 1991), 157–74; Warner, "Thoreau's Bottom," *Raritan* 11.3 (Winter 1992): 53–79; and Henry Abelove, "From Thoreau to Queer Politics," *Yale Journal of Criticism* 6.3 (1993): 17–27.
27. *Corr.*, 1:357 (H. G. O. Blake to HDT, before March 27, 1848).
28. *Corr.*, 1:359–62 (HDT to H. G. O. Blake, March 27, 1848). For the complete Thoreau-Blake correspondence in a single volume, see Henry David Thoreau, *Letters to a Spiritual Seeker*, ed. Bradley P. Dean (New York: Norton, 2004).
29. *Corr.*, 1:332 (HDT to RWE, December 29, 1847).
30. *EEM*, 232, 224, 264–65.
31. Ibid., 243, 250–51, 254, 257 (emphases in the original).
32. *Corr.*, 1:365–66 (Horace Greeley to HDT, April 17, 1848), 372–73 (Greeley to HDT, May 17, 1848); Ralph Waldo Emerson, and Thomas Carlyle, *The Correspondence of Emerson and Carlyle*, ed. Joseph Slater, 2 vols (New York: Columbia University Press, 1964), 1:422 (Carlyle to Emerson, May 18, 1847).
33. *Corr.*, 1:286 (Greeley to HDT, February 5, 1847); J. Lyndon Shanley, *The Making of "Walden," with the Text of the First Version* (Chicago: University of Chicago Press, 1957), 106; cf. PEJ, 2:142. Thoreau apparently gave this lecture first in Lincoln, on January 19, 1847; see TL I, 148–50.
34. *LRWE*, 3:378; *THOT*, 5; *Days of HT*, 187–88.
35. Shanley, *Making of "Walden,"* 153.
36. *Corr.*, 1:339 (HDT to RWE, January 12, 1848); Alcott quoted in TL I, 153.
37. Shanley, *Making of "Walden,"* 141.

38. *Corr.*, 1:350 (HDT to James Elliot Cabot, March 8, 1848), 366 (Greeley to HDT, April 17, 1848).

39. Ibid., 373, 375, 383 (Greeley to HDT, May 17 to May 25, 1848).

40. Ibid., 388–90 (Greeley to HDT, October 28 and November 19, 1848).

41. *LRWE*, 4:56; *Corr.*, 1:378–80 (HDT to RWE, May 21, 1848); *LRWE*, 4:81.

42. ABAJ, 201.

43. Quoted in *Thoreau Log*, 157, 160, 153. In England, the feminist and freethinker Sophia Dobson Collet, herself on the fringes of the "red republicans," called attention to Thoreau's essay in the London *People's Review* (*Days of HT*, 207). Since the essay's working manuscripts have been lost, how much the published essay changed from the original lecture cannot be known. The title of the second printing, "Civil Disobedience," is probably Thoreau's, but the evidence is not definitive; this explains why, confusingly, the identical essay appears under two different titles. Good starting points are Lawrence Rosenwald, "The Theory, Practice, and Influence of Thoreau's Civil Disobedience," in *A Historical Guide to Henry David Thoreau*, ed. William E. Cain (Oxford: Oxford University Press, 2000), 153–79; and Anthony J. Parel, "Thoreau, Gandhi, and Comparative Political Thought," in *A Political Companion to Henry David Thoreau*, ed. Jack Turner (Lexington: University Press of Kentucky, 2009), 372–92.

44. *RP*, 63–64.

45. *JMN*, 9:446; *RP*, 84, 67.

46. Frederick Douglass, *Narrative of the Life of Frederick Douglass, an American Slave*, in *Autobiographies* (New York: Library of America, 1994), 64.

47. *RP*, 68. In resisting Covey, then, Douglass was asserting himself as a free *citizen*.

48. Ibid., 78–79, 85.

49. Ibid., 73–77.

50. Ibid., 89–90.

51. *Week*, 77.

52. PEJ, 2:205–6.

53. *Week*, "Historical Introduction" 453.

54. Ibid, 451. For more on Fuller's and Thoreau's influence on each other, see Marie Urbanski, "Henry David Thoreau and Margaret Fuller," *Thoreau Journal Quarterly* 8.4 (1976): 24–30.

55. *LRWE*, 3:338 (RWE to Charles Newcomb).

56. ABAJ , 213-14; *LRWE*, 3:384.

57. *The Letters of Nathaniel Hawthorne, 1843-1853*, edited by Thomas Woodson, L. Neal Smith, and Norman Holmes Pearson (Columbus: Ohio State University Press, 1985), 106 (Hawthorne to E. A. Duyckinck, July 1, 1845); *Corr.*, 1:316 (HDT to RWE, November 14, 1847).

58. *Corr.*, 1:325 (RWE to HDT, December 2, 1847); *LRWE*, 4:16.

59. *Corr.*, 1:376 (HDT to Greeley, May 19, 1848).

60. Ibid., 376; 384 (HDT to George Thatcher, August 24, 1848); Ellen Tucker Emerson, *Life of Lidian Jackson Emerson*, 109.

61. *JMN*, 10:347, 343, 344.

62. *Corr.*, 1:377 (HDT to RWE, May 21, 1848); PEJ, 3:3. Sanborn printed a typical page of

Thoreau's record of debts to his father, scribbled on the back of a poem: "Dec. 8, 1840, Owe Father $41.73," and so on (Sanborn, *Life of Thoreau*, 241).

63. William Ellery Channing II, *Thoreau: The Poet-Naturalist* (Boston: Roberts Brothers, 1873), 26–27; *Days of HT*, 233–34. The Uncanoonuc Mountains are, as Thoreau notes, a pair, as the name (meaning "breasts") makes clear; which of the two they climbed is unclear.

64. Maria Thoreau to unknown correspondent, September 7, 1848. "Thoreau Memorial Scrap Book," item #17, Thoreau-Ward-Sewall Papers, Thoreau Society Archives, Henley Library.

65. Keith Walter Cameron, *Transcendentalists and Minerva*, 3 vols. (Hartford, CT: Transcendental Books, 1958), 2:374–76.

66. CFPL has Thoreau's surveys online, under Special Collections (http://www.concordlibrary.org/scollect/Thoreau_surveys/Thoreau_surveys.htm). See also Marcia E. Moss, *A Catalog of Thoreau's Surveys in the Concord Free Public Library*, Thoreau Society Booklet 28 (Geneseo, NY: Thoreau Society, 1976); and Patrick Chura, *Thoreau the Land Surveyor* (Gainesville: University Press of Florida, 2010). Thoreau surveyed Emerson's Walden holdings three times over many years to settle a boundary dispute dating back to colonial days; see *LRWE*, 8:210–11n34.

67. The complete schedule of Thoreau's Walden lectures this season, with supporting details, is given in TL I, 155–84.

68. *Corr.*, 1:391 (HDT to George Thatcher, December 26, 1848); TL I, 157–59.

69. *Thoreau as Seen*, 117; *Thoreau Log*, 153.

70. TL I, 165–66; Maria Thoreau to Prudence Ward, February 28, 1849, Thoreau-Sewall Papers, 1790–1917, HM 64932, Huntington Library, San Marino, California.

71. TL I, 169–70.

72. *Thoreau Log*, 145.

73. TL I, 177.

74. Maria Thoreau to Prudence Ward, February 28, 1849, Thoreau-Sewall Papers, 1790–1917, HM 64932, Huntington Library, San Marino, California; Maria Thoreau to Prudence Ward, March 15, 1849, Thoreau-Sewall Papers, 1790–1917, HM 64933, Huntington Library, San Marino, California.

75. *Corr.*, 2:12 (HDT to Nathaniel Hawthorne, February 20, 1849).

76. Maria Thoreau to Prudence Ward, May 1, 1849, Thoreau-Sewall Papers, 1790–1917, HM 64935, Huntington Library, San Marino, California; *JMN*, 15:165.

77. ABAJ, 209. For a synopsis of the major reviews, see "Historical Introduction," in *Week*, 472–77.

78. Anon., "H. D. Thoreau's Book," *New-York Daily Tribune*, June 13, 1849; reprinted in Myerson, ed. *Emerson and Thoreau: The Contemporary Reviews* (Cambridge: Cambridge University Press, 1992), 341–43.

79. PEJ, 4:310; *Week*, "Historical Introduction," 472.

80. *LRWE*, 4:145, 151.

81. Myerson, *Emerson and Thoreau: Reviews*, 352–59; Maria Thoreau to Prudence Ward, December 17, 1849, Thoreau-Sewall Papers, 1790–1917, HM 64937, Huntington Library, San Marino, California; *Days of HT*, 251.

82. Walter Harding, "Amanda Mather's Recollections of Thoreau," *TSB* 188 (Summer 1989): 2.

83. *Liberator,* June 22, 1849 (it is unclear whether the author was Garrison or Mary Brooks); "Farewell," in *CEP,* 622–23; Harding, "Mather's Recollections," 2.

84. PEJ, 3:19, 26.

85. Ibid., 3:29.

86. *Corr.,* 2:27 (HDT to Ellen Emerson, July 31, 1849); see also Emerson's letter to Ellen, giving her fatherly advice on how to write a letter to Thoreau (*LRWE,* 4:154, July 4, 1849).

87. *JMN,* 11:283. For searching discussions of the collapse and partial recovery of this famous, and famously difficult, friendship, see Robert Sattelmeyer, "'When He Became My Enemy': Emerson and Thoreau, 1848–49," *New England Quarterly* 62.2 (June 1989): 187–204; and William Rossi, "Performing Loss, Elegy, and Transcendental Friendship," *New England Quarterly* 81.2 (June 2008): 252–77.

88. Linck C. Johnson, *Thoreau's Complex Weave: The Writing of "A Week on the Concord and Merrimack Rivers," with the Text of the First Draft* (Charlottesville: University Press of Virginia, 1986), 252, 259–60; Johnson's book provides the single best and most exhaustive analysis of Thoreau's important first book. See also Steven Fink, *Prophet in the Marketplace: Thoreau's Development as a Professional Writer* (Princeton, NJ: Princeton University Press, 1992), especially ch. 8.

89. *Walden,* 19; *Week,* 353.

90. *Week,* 5.

91. Ibid., 15–16.

92. See Alan D. Hodder, *Thoreau's Ecstatic Witness* (New Haven, CT: Yale University Press, 2001), 123.

93. *Week,* 393.

94. *EEM,* 238; *Week,* 67, 142. Note that on April 16, 1846, when Elizabeth Hoar hosted Alcott's "Conversation" on Jesus as "the genius of modern culture," Thoreau dissented "with some vehemence" (ABAJ, 175–76).

95. *Week,* 72–73.

96. Ibid., 140, 70.

CHAPTER SEVEN

1. *LRWE,* 4:156–57; PEJ, 3:23–24.

2. *Corr.,* 2:42 (HDT to H. G. O. Blake, November 20, 1849); *JMN,* 11:240; *Week,* 70.

3. PEJ, 3:201.

4. Ibid., 1:191 (October 18, 1840), 411–12 (transcribed 1842). For Thoreau's use of Lyell to open a channel between poetry and science, see William Rossi, "Poetry and Progress: Thoreau, Lyell, and the Geological Principles of *A Week,*" *American Literature* 66.2 (June 1994): 275–300; and Laura Dassow Walls, *Seeing New Worlds: Henry David Thoreau and Nineteenth-Century Natural Science* (Madison: University of Wisconsin Press, 1995), 42–45.

5. *Week,* 128.

6. Ibid., 363; PEJ, 4:385; *Walden,* 290.

7. *E&L,* 20, 25; *Week,* 382.

8. PEJ, 3:27.

9. *CC,* 5–7.

10. *CHDT,* 498 (RWE to H. G. O. Blake, November 16, 1857). See Bradley P. Dean, "Natural History, Romanticism, and Thoreau," in *American Wilderness: A New History,* ed. Michael Lewis (Oxford: Oxford University Press, 2007): 78–79.

11. *CC,* 23, 32, 50.

12. Ibid., 79, 139. On October 23, soon after Thoreau and Channing returned to Boston, two men broke in and robbed the Union Wharf Company in Provincetown of $15,000. In the investigation that followed, police tracked Thoreau and Channing, questioning everyone with whom they came into contact, including Newcomb. When Thoreau returned in June 1850, the case was still not cleared, and it's remotely possible that he was even then under suspicion. See James H. Ellis, "The Provincetown Burglary," *TSB* 162 (Winter 1983): 3.

13. *CC,* 98, 137.

14. As of the time of writing, Thoreau's twelve Indian Books—the "Canada &c." volume plus eleven more—remain unpublished except in partial form; an incomplete transcript is available through the Morgan Library.

15. William Ellery Channing II, *Thoreau: The Poet-Naturalist* (Boston: Roberts Brothers, 1873), 55; *Corr.,* 2:35–36 (HDT to Jared Sparks, September 17, 1849; emphasis in the original). Emerson had claimed, and been awarded, the same privilege in 1846 (*LRWE,* 3:335–36).

16. Maria Thoreau to Prudence Ward, December 17, 1849, Thoreau-Sewall Papers, 1790–1917, HM 64937, Huntington Library, San Marino, California; Corr 2:50 (RWE to HDT, February 6, 1850).

17. ABAJ, 227; PEJ, 3:161 (Thoreau's Newburyport host, who gave him the microscope view, was Dr. Henry Coit Perkins), 170–72 (Thoreau's host in Clinton, who gave him the tour of the gingham mills, was Franklin Forbes, the mill's agent). Thoreau's lecture was delivered on January 1, 1851, in a series that included Emerson, Greeley, and Henry Ward Beecher; see TL I, 191–93.

18. Quoted in TL I, 193 (Clinton, Mass.), 194–96 (Portland, Maine).

19. PEJ, 3:43.

20. Ibid., 3:133, 4:32, 3:84.

21. *Days of HT,* 261–63; Henry Petroski, "H. D. Thoreau, Engineer," *Invention and Technology* 5.2 (Fall 1989), 8–16, pp. 14–15; Petroski, *The Pencil: A History of Design and Circumstance* (New York: Knopf, 1990), 148–51; Randall Conrad, "The Machine in the Garden: Re-imagining Thoreau's Plumbago Grinder," *TSB* 243 (Fall 2005): 5–8. The Thoreaus used Eben Wood's mill in Acton, and after 1853, according to Conrad, they used Warren Miles's mills; there may have been others.

22. Maria Thoreau to Prudence Ward, November 15, 1849, Thoreau-Sewall Papers, 1790–1917, HM 64936, Huntington Library, San Marino, California.

23. PEJ, 3:326; *J,* 9:83. Thoreau's herbarium alone eventually included more than nine

hundred specimens; see Ray Angelo, "Thoreau as Botanist: An Appreciation and a Critique," *Arnoldia* 45.3 (Summer 1985): 20.

24. PEJ, 7:168–69. Thoreau gave up the scheme when he found cranberries selling in New York for less than he could buy them in Boston.

25. Thoreau's handbill is reproduced in Milton Meltzer and Walter Harding, *A Thoreau Profile* (New York: Thomas Y. Crowell, 1962), 169, and Patrick Chura, *Thoreau the Land Surveyor* (Gainesville, FL: University Press of Florida, 2010), 85.

26. Chura, *Thoreau the Land Surveyor*, 73–80. A surveyor's chain is one hundred iron links, for a total of four rods, or 66 feet. Thoreau's compass, made by C. G. King Company of Broad Street, Boston, is in the collection of the CFPL; some of his surveying tools are on display at the Concord Museum. The complicated procedure for finding true north and the spiritual use Thoreau made of the results are ably described by Patrick Chura, *Thoreau the Land Surveyor*, 114–21. The Massachusetts Register for 1852 lists Thoreau as a "civil engineer"; see *Thoreau Log*, 240.

27. *Thoreau Log*, 173–74. Thoreau himself was less impressed: "The last two bearings are useless being taken after dark," he underscored. Marcia E. Moss, *A Catalog of Thoreau's Surveys in the Concord Free Public Library*, Thoreau Society Booklet 28 (Geneseo, NY: Thoreau Society, 1976), 12.

28. ABAJ 239 (January 22, 1851).

29. PEJ, 3:134–35, 139, 315.

30. Ibid., 4:77ff; 85. Thoreau had looked forward to this job, but it soured when he found himself adjudicating a nasty boundary dispute. See Chura, *Thoreau the Land Surveyor*, 98–100.

31. PEJ, 4:203–4.

32. *Corr.*, 1:310 (HDT to Sophia Thoreau, October 24, 1847), 315–16 (HDT to RWE, November 14, 1847).

33. PEJ, 3:296–99 (Harvard observatory, July 9, 1851); *Corr.*, 2:23–26 (HDT to Louis Agassiz, June 30, 1849, and Agassiz's reply, July 5, 1849).

34. Ibid., 2–3 (HDT to George Thatcher, February 9, 1849); PEJ, 3:170–77.

35. PEJ, 3:49–53; for an extended reading of the toy waterwheel passage, see Laura Dassow Walls, "Romancing the Real: Thoreau's Technology of Inscription," in *Historical Guide to Henry David Thoreau*, ed. William E. Cain (Oxford: Oxford University Press, 2000), 123–51. The figure of the Aeolian harp invoked here was crucial to Thoreau, who was repeatedly moved to ecstasy by the sound of wind through the telegraph wires strung, in 1852, along the railroad tracks through the Deep Cut. Thoreau built an Aeolian harp small enough to set in a window frame, to bring the wind's song into his family's home; this harp is in the collections of the Concord Museum.

36. *Walden*, 320; PEJ, 4:28. For Thoreau and early Darwin, see Robert D. Richardson Jr., *Henry David Thoreau: A Life of the Mind* (Berkeley: University of California Press, 1986), 240–45. John Aldrich Christie documented 172 separate travel accounts read by Thoreau, 146 of them cover-to-cover, plus collections and periodicals; see *Thoreau as World Traveler* (New York: Columbia University Press, 1965). I have discussed at length Thoreau's reading in the natural sciences in *Seeing New Worlds: Henry David Thoreau and Nineteenth-Century Natural Science* (1995), where I develop my found-

ing analysis of Thoreau's indebtedness to Alexander von Humboldt and the Humboldtian scientific tradition—a tradition I detail in *Passage to Cosmos: Alexander von Humboldt and the Shaping of America* (Chicago: University of Chicago Press, 2009).

37. *Corr.*, 1:94 (Margaret Fuller to HDT, October 18, 1841), 203 (HDT to RWE and LJE, July 8, 1843).

38. When Emerson first learned of her secret family, in October 1849, he assumed they must all come home to America, but by April 1850, with the political situation stabilizing, he begged her to stay: life in Italy would give "new rays of reputation & wonder to you as a star." *LRWE*, 4:168, 199.

39. Charles Capper, *Margaret Fuller: An American Romantic Life, the Public Years* (Oxford: Oxford University Press, 2007), 495–503.

40. "Thoreau's First Draft of His Account of the Wreck of the *Elizabeth* and the Aftermath," in *Corr.*, 2:66–75, in a footnote to Thoreau's July 24, 1850, letter to Emerson. Thoreau wrote up a report based on these notes, which he read to Waldo and Lidian Emerson and Elizabeth Hoar upon his return; this manuscript was scattered, and most of it has yet to be recovered. Part of one leaf is transcribed in Steve Grice, "A Leaf from Thoreau's Fire Island Manuscript," *TSB* 258 (Spring 2007): 1–4.

41. *Corr.*, 2:63–64 (HDT to RWE, July 25, 1850).

42. *LRWE*, 8:254, 4:219.

43. Bayard Taylor, "The Wreck on Fire Island," *New-York Daily Tribune* July 24, 1850, 1; "Thoreau's Account of the Wreck."

44. *PEJ*, 3:99–100; Grice, "Thoreau's Fire Island Manuscript."

45. Smith Oakes and six other men were later charged by the US Marshal's office for being in possession of goods stolen from the *Elizabeth*. See Grice, "Thoreau's Fire Island Manuscript," 2n6; "From Fire Island—Proceedings against the Plunderers of the Elizabeth," *New-York Daily Tribune*, July 31, 1850, 4.

46. *Corr.*, 2:76 (HDT to Charles Sumner, July 29, 1850), 76–77 (Sumner to HDT, July 31, 1850).

47. *PEJ*, 3:95; *Corr.*, 2:78 (HDT to H. G. O. Blake, August 9, 1850).

48. *PEJ*, 3:95; *CC*, 84–85 (cf. *PEJ*, 3:127–28).

49. Ellery Channing quoted in Robert N. Hudspeth, "Dear Friend: Letter Writing in Concord," *Concord Saunterer*, n.s., 11 (2003): 84; *Corr.*, 2:78; *PEJ*, 3:96–97.

50. *Exc.*, 471. Panoramas were then all the rage; Thoreau also went, about this time, to see a panorama of the Rhine and another of the Mississippi. See *PEJ*, 3:181; Joseph J. Moldenhauer, "Thoreau, Hawthorne, and the 'Seven-Mile Panorama,'" *ESQ: A Journal of the American Renaissance* 44.4 (1998): 227–73; and Richard J. Schneider, "Thoreau's Panorama of the Mississippi: Its Identity and Significance," *TSB* 245 (Fall 2003): 5–6.

51. *PEJ*, 3:110.

52. *Exc.*, 101–5.

53. Ibid., 88–89.

54. Ibid., 93–94.

55. Ibid., 103.

56. Ibid., 122–25, 131–32.

57. Ibid., 117 (Thoreau spells them "*snells*"); "Headnote," in *Exc.*, 471–96, p. 474.

58. Ibid., 161.

59. Ibid., 126, 163. See also PEJ, 3:328: "Where there were books only—to find realities."

60. Studies of this florescence in Thoreau's thought and work should begin with Robert Sattelmeyer, *Thoreau's Reading: A Study in Intellectual History with Bibliographical Catalogue* (Princeton, NJ: Princeton University Press, 1988), 92–110, and continue with Richardson, *HDT: Life of the Mind*, esp. 219–23, 279–87.

61. PEJ, 4:7–8 (August 22, 1851); TL I, 202.

62. *Corr.*, 2:102 (Greeley to HDT, March 18, 1852); *Exc.*, 88–89; *Corr.*, 2:139 (Greeley to HDT, January 2, 1853), 145 (HDT to H. G. O. Blake, February 27, 1853).

63. PEJ, 3:131–34 (November 8, 1850), 134–36 (November 9, 1950).

64. Ibid., 141–42.

65. The groundbreaking insight that Thoreau's Journal is, in itself, a complete work of art was first advanced by Sharon Cameron in her influential *Writing Nature: Henry Thoreau's Journal* (Chicago: University of Chicago Press, 1985).

66. Franklin Benjamin Sanborn, *Henry D. Thoreau* (Boston: Houghton Mifflin, 1882), quoted in *THOT*, 132.

67. PEJ, 4:133, 329; W. E. Channing II, *Poet-Naturalist* (1873), 47; Emerson, "Thoreau," 419. See also Channing's detailed, eloquent pages describing Thoreau's exact method of taking field notes and expanding them (*Poet-Naturalist* [1902], 65–66).

68. PEJ, 4:170 ("with these I deal"), 3:150 ("out of my senses"), 151 ("a different sort of man").

69. Ibid., 3:152–54 (November 26, 1850).

70. Ibid., 3:41–42; *Corr.*, 2:48 (Samuel Cabot to HDT, before December 10, 1849); *JMN*, 11:277–78.

71. PEJ, 3:44; *Corr.*, 2:89 (Samuel Cabot to HDT, December 27, 1850). The BSNH's present-day avatar is the Museum of Science, Boston.

72. PEJ, 5:469–70 (March 5, 1853); *Corr.*, 2:151–53 (HDT to Spencer Fullerton Baird, before March 5, 1853), 181–82 (HDT to Spencer Fullerton Baird, December 19, 1853). It has been assumed that Thoreau declined the AAAS membership with disdain and returned the questionnaire only after ignoring it for nearly a year. However, records of the AAAS list him as a member for 1853, and Thoreau himself stated that he returned the questionnaire, which lists his scientific interests, soon after he received it. Despite his private fulminations, Thoreau was interested in the AAAS and was honored by the invitation, which was probably issued by Spencer Fullerton Baird.

73. ABAJ, 238; Thoreau was visiting Alcott on his way to Medford to deliver the lecture "Economy," January 22, 1851.

74. See *JMN*, 11:404 (July 1851) ("pounding beans"), 400 (draft of "captain of a huckleberry party"); Emerson, "Thoreau," 429.

75. *JMN*, 15:352–53.

76. PEJ, 3:148; cf. 192–93, where he rewrites this passage, marking it as a significant moment.

77. Ibid., 198.

78. Ibid., 245 (June 7, 1851).

79. Ibid., 302–3, 329–30. An example of how Thoreau used the sense of touch: in feeling

mullein leaves on a hot day, he noticed that the live ones feel cool, but the dead ones feel warm (ibid., 280).

80. Ibid., 313 ("step to the music"), 306 ("With all your science"), 331 ("But this habit"). Even the experience of having a dentist pull his teeth (which he did on May 12, 1851) became an occasion to explore a new experience—namely, of going under ether, which for Thoreau became an experiment in mind/body relationality: one becomes "a sane mind without organs—groping for organs," and existing "in your roots—like a tree in the winter." He added a puckish warning: "If I have got false teeth, I trust that I have not got a false conscience." (ibid., 218).

81. Ibid., 337.

82. Ibid., 3:338–40. Thomas Blanding details various versions of this story in "Mary Russell Watson's Reminiscences of Thoreau," *Concord Saunterer* 9.2 (June 1974): 1–6.

83. PEJ, 3:341. Thoreau says 1690, but Lawrence D. Geller says 1700. See his *Between Concord and Plymouth: The Transcendentalists and the Watsons* (Concord, MA: Thoreau Foundation; Plymouth, MA: Pilgrim Society, 1973), the source for much of the following information.

84. PEJ, 3:348–49.

85. Ibid., 352; *Days of HT*, 293; W. E. Channing II, *Poet-Naturalist* (1873), 35.

86. PEJ, 3:357; *Walden*, 4. As Thoreau also wrote, a traveler may see "what the oldest inhabitant has not observed" (PEJ, 3:384).

87. Ibid., 4:154–55.

88. Ibid., 200–201.

CHAPTER EIGHT

1. *RP*, 108; PEJ, 8:200.

2. PEJ, 2:123; *RP*, 61.

3. PEJ, 5:120.

4. Ralph Waldo Emerson, *Emerson's Antislavery Writings*, ed. Len Gougeon (New Haven, CT: Yale University Press, 1995), 79.

5. *To Set This World*, 77–78.

6. PEJ, 3:194; *To Set This World*, 80–83.

7. Elizabeth Hoar to Frances Jane Hallett Prichard, April 1851, Prichard, Hoar, and Related Family Papers, vault A45, Prichard unit 2, box 5, folder 11, CFPL; PEJ, 3:204–05, 4:288.

8. PEJ, 3:202–07; Emerson, "Address to the Citizens of Concord" (May 3, 1851), in *Emerson's Antislavery Writings*, 57..

9. Seward gave his speech on March 11, 1850. Albert J. von Frank, *The Trials of Anthony Burns: Freedom and Slavery in Emerson's Boston* (Cambridge, MA: Harvard University Press, 1998), 281–82; see also Wesley T. Mott, ed., *Encyclopedia of Transcendentalism*, s.v. "Higher Law," by Linck C. Johnson, 82–84; and Sandra Harbert Petrulionis, "The 'Higher Law': Then and Now," *TSB* 262 (Spring 2008): 5–7.

10. Quoted in TL I, 199; *Exc.*, 185. See Daniel S. Malachuk, *Two Cities: The Political Thought of American Transcendentalism* (Lawrence: University Press of Kansas, 2016), especially ch. 5, "'So we saunter to the Holy Land': Thoreau and the City of God."

11. PEJ, 4:114–15. Henry Williams's fate is unknown.

12. Ibid., 7:134–35.

13. Moncure Daniel Conway, *Autobiography, Memories and Experiences*, 2 vols. (Boston: Houghton Mifflin, 1904), 1:141; see also Annie Russell Marble, *Thoreau: His Home, Friends, and Books* (New York: Thomas Y. Crowell, 1902), 198–99, although Marble conflates the two incidents.

14. David Wood, *An Observant Eye: The Thoreau Collection at the Concord Museum* (Concord, MA: Concord Museum, 2006), 46–47; the statue is on display at the Concord Museum.

15. PEJ, 7:102–3; *To Set This World*, 94–95.

16. PEJ, 6:212–13. The three men were the Reverend Andrew T. Foss, the Reverend H. C. Wright, and Loring Moody.

17. Margaret Fuller, "The Great Lawsuit," *Dial* 4.1 (July 1843): 10, 14.

18. *Corr.*, 1:199 (HDT to Cynthia Thoreau, July 7, 1843), 211 (HDT to Helen Thoreau, July 21, 1843).

19. *Thoreau Log*, 206; PEJ, 4:233. Smith lectured at the Concord Lyceum on December 31, 1851.

20. PEJ, 4:183–84, 266.

21. "Love," in *EEM*, 270.

22. PEJ, 4:309–10, 426.

23. *JMN*, 13:26–27, 183.

24. *LRWE*, 4:413, 426; *Walden*, 270.

25. *JMN*, 13:20; PEJ, 3:302; see also *Walden*, 267–68.

26. *JMN*, 13:61.

27. PEJ, 5:293; for Thoreau on Channing's dog, see 4:286, 4:20, 6:10, 4:418.

28. Ibid., 4:170 ("moodiest person"), 6:150–51 ("shut them out"), 7:247 (Channing punches cat).

29. George Hendrick, ed., *Remembrances of Concord and the Thoreaus: Letters of Horace Hosmer to Dr. S. A. Jones* (Urbana: University of Illinois Press, 1977), 26; *Walden*, 268. For more on the difficult Ellery Channing, see Frederick T. McGill Jr., *Channing of Concord: A Life of William Ellery Channing II* (New Brunswick, NJ: Rutgers University Press, 1967); and Robert N. Hudspeth, *Ellery Channing* (New York: Twayne, 1973).

30. *Walden*, 268–69, PEJ, 6:101–02.

31. *Thoreau as Seen*, 166, 165.

32. *Walden*, 268–69, see also PEJ, 6:294.

33. *Corr.*, 2:13–14 (Bronson Alcott to "Dear Sir," February 20, 1849).

34. PEJ, 4:451; TL I, 206.

35. PEJ, 4:487; TL I, 206–08; *RP*, 168.

36. TL I, 209–11.

37. PEJ, 3:92; William Ellery Channing II, *Thoreau: The Poet-Naturalist*, ed. F. B. Sanborn (Boston: Charles E. Goodspeed, 1902), 10–11; J. Lyndon Shanley, *The Making*

of "Walden," with the Text of the First Version (Chicago: University of Chicago Press, 1957), 60n7.

38. PEJ, 4:491–92, 582n.

39. Ibid., 4:216. My thanks to Robert Gross for clarifying that school attendance was still, at this time, voluntary in Concord, which means that Johnny's brave choice to go to school was his own (personal communication).

40. PEJ, 4:336–37. For an extended consideration, see my essay "'As You Are Brothers of Mine': Thoreau and the Irish," *New England Quarterly* 88.1 (March 2015): 5–36. Late in November 1850, Thoreau drafted "The Little Irish Boy," a poem modeled on William Blake's "The Little Black Boy" (PEJ, 3:155–56); he also wrote an uncollected essay on Johnny Riordan (J, 3:242–44, January 28, 1852). Both literary works deserve far more attention.

41. *Corr.*, 2:176 (HDT to various recipients, October 12, 1853), 175 (HDT to various recipients, October 12, 1853); PEJ, 7:102–3, 134–35; Flannery quoted in 8:33–34. See also Bradley P. Dean, "Thoreau and Michael Flannery," *The Concord Saunterer* 17.3 (December 1984): 27–33. The man who cheated Flannery, Abiel Wheeler, was the Concord farmer who still bore Henry a grudge for burning his woodlot in 1844.

42. PEJ, 4:194 ("strains of the piano"), Henry S. Salt, *The Life of Henry David Thoreau* (London: Richard Bentley, 1890; revised version of 1908, edited by George Hendrick, Willene Hendrick, and Fritz Oehlschlaeger. Urbana: University of Illinois Press, 1993, 2000), 69; PEJ, 3:325 ("singing from various houses"), 4:134 (mild October evening); J, 8:70 (snow); PEJ, 6:241 (calls Sophia). See also the fine discussion in Michael Sims, *The Adventures of Henry Thoreau: A Young Man's Unlikely Path to Walden Pond* (New York: Bloomsbury, 2014), and especially in Alan D. Hodder, *Thoreau's Ecstatic Witness* (New Haven, CT: Yale University Press, 2001), 184–85; as Hodder observes, Thoreau's "acoustic rapture" served as a leitmotif in his Journal and often led to some of his most searching reflections. Virtually any sound—the locomotive's whistle, the hum of telegraph wires, the song of a robin or a wood thrush, even a dog barking in the distance—could send Thoreau into profound ecstasy.

43. PEJ, 5:188; see also 117, 121–22; 188. Thoreau describes his "botany-box," a straw hat with a scaffolding lining in which he carried his plant specimens, in ibid., 126, and J, 9:157.

44. PEJ, 6:244, 7:30–33.

45. Quoted in Sarah Gertrude Pomeroy, "Sophia Thoreau," in *Little-Known Sisters of Well-Known Men* (Boston: Dana Estes, 1912), 259–61.

46. PEJ, 6:41 (Aunt Maria), 5:417 (Uncle Charles).

47. Ibid., 5:403.

48. Ibid., 4:41, 178.

49. Ibid., 4:269, 392; cf. "Walking," in *Exc.*, 209.

50. Ibid., 7:15, 4:252.

51. Ibid., 4:291; 6:172.

52. Ibid., 4:270–73, 277. The standard source on the composition of *Walden* is Shanley, *Making of "Walden"*; for a useful, concise treatment, see Robert Sattelmeyer, "The Remaking of *Walden*," in *Writing the American Classics*, ed. James Barbour and Tom Quirk

(Chapel Hill: University of North Carolina Press, 1990): 53–78; repr. in Henry David Thoreau, *"Walden," "Civil Disobedience," and Other Writings*, ed. William Rossi (New York: Norton, 3rd edition, 2008), 489–507.

53. For this exchange of letters between Greeley and Thoreau, see *Corr.*, 2:100–104, 111–12 (February 24–July 8, 1852).

54. *Corr.*, 2:137–38 (HDT to Benjamin Marston Watson, December 31, 1852).

55. Ibid., 140 (HDT to H. G. O. Blake, February 27, 1853), PEJ 7:201; PEJ, 6:234 (June), 303 (August), 7:3, 310.

56. PEJ, 8:6; *Corr.*, 2:197–98 (HDT to George Thatcher, February 25, 1854).

57. *Corr.*, 2:140–41 (HDT to H. G. O. Blake, February 27, 1853); PEJ, 7:156.

58. PEJ, 6:236, 245.

59. *MW*, 95.

60. *MW*, 97, 99; PEJ, 7:51–58.

61. PEJ, 7:61–63.

62. Ibid., 66, 69–70.

63. Ibid., 80–82. The identification as Sebattis Dana is according to Fanny Hardy Eckstorm, who identifies his companion as "Swasin (Joachim) Tahmunt." "Notes on Thoreau's 'Maine Woods,'" *TSB* 51 (Spring 1955): 1. Sebattis Dana is not the same person as "Sabattis Solomon," who according to Thoreau had come with Joe Aitteon from Oldtown to the Thatchers, stayed the night with Aitteon in the Thatcher's barn, then gone on his way to stay a few days in Bangor before traveling to Chesuncook to meet up with Joe and John Aitteon to continue moosehunting (ibid., 41).

64. Ibid., 83–86.

65. Ibid., 83–84, 117. On the crucial role of the Penobscot in redirecting Thoreau's thinking, see Phillip Round, "Gentleman Amateur or 'Fellow-Creature'? Thoreau's Maine Woods Flight from Contemporary Natural History," in *Thoreau's World and Ours: A Natural Legacy*, ed. Edmund A. Schofield and Robert C. Baron (Golden, CO: North American Press, 1993), 316–29.

66. PEJ, 7:90, 93; *MW*, 149.

67. PEJ, 7:119; *MW*, 150. This ground-level observation reversed Thoreau's casual condemnation of Indian Island made in 1846, while passing by on a ferry.

68. PEJ 7:95; D. Wood, *Observant Eye*, 54–55. Wood notes that Thoreau's snowshoes, made of ash and maple frames strung with deer rawhide webbing, were a distinctively Indian technology, and though snowshoes were by then being made in Oldtown, this particular pair was probably of Penobscot manufacture.

69. *MW*, 155–56.

70. PEJ, 7:160.

71. TL I, 212–13. The invitation was by Francis Underwood.

72. PEJ, 7:99, 103–7.

73. Ibid., 7:201, 203; Leslie Perrin Wilson, *In History's Embrace: Past and Present in Concord, Massachusetts* (Concord, MA: Concord Free Public Library, 2007), 43–45; Jane Hallett Prichard to Moses B. Prichard, December 15, 1853, Prichard, Hoar, and Related Family Papers, vault A45, Prichard unit 2, box 6, folder 6, CFPL.

74. PEJ, 7:209–10 (tries on snowshoes), 211 (measuring snow), 224, 259 (thaw).

75. Ibid., 224, 233.

76. *Corr.*, 2:192–93 (HDT to H. G. O. Blake, January 21, 1854); PEJ, 7:241 (new coat), 245 (Harris). The court case is detailed in PEJ, 7:349–51; Thoreau had to return on January 26.

77. PEJ, 7:123. For details see Steven Fink, *Prophet in the Marketplace: Thoreau's Development as a Professional Writer* (Princeton, NJ: Princeton University Press, 1992), 211–13.

78. PEJ, 7:176, 216.

79. Ibid., 276 (sand-foliage), 268 (living earth).

80. Ibid., 285–86.

81. Thoreau scholars like to point out that in April 1854, when the Fitchburg Railroad raised its fares from $1.30 to $1.55, the punctilious Thoreau made the change in the proof sheets. See Shanley, *Making of "Walden,"* 32; PEJ, 8:49, 51.

82. PEJ, 8:57, 61, 125.

83. Ibid., 148–54.

84. *To Set This World*, 98–100. See also von Frank, *Trials of Anthony Burns*. Burns was soon purchased by Boston activist Rev. Leonard Grimes. Restored to freedom in Boston, Burns emigrated to Canada. He died from tuberculosis in 1862, some thirteen weeks before Thoreau himself.

85. PEJ, 8:161–62 (cf. 278, on killing a box turtle [*Cistudo*] for science), 164.

86. See Sandra Harbert Petrulionis, "Editorial Savoir Faire: Thoreau Transforms His Journal into 'Slavery in Massachusetts,'" *Resources for American Literary Study* 25.2 (1999): 206–31.

87. *To Set This World*, 103; Bradley P. Dean, "More Context for Thoreau's 'Slavery in Massachusetts,'" *Thoreau Research Newsletter* 1.3 (July 1990): 12.

88. *RP*, 92, 96; Conway, *Autobiography, Memories and Experiences*, 1:184–85; *RP*, 104, 106; von Frank, *Trials of Anthony Burns*, 284. Thoreau did not have time to deliver his entire speech; no record clarifies exactly how much of it, or which part of it, he read aloud.

89. *RP*, 108–9.

90. Thoreau called the familiar white pond lily "our lotus," and linked it explicitly with the sacred Buddhist lotus—and also with Christian symbolism, as on Sabbath mornings in spring when young men would walk to church bearing pond lily blossoms. See, for example, PEJ, 5:149–50, 172.

91. PEJ, 8:161–62; *RP*, 109.

92. *New-York Daily Tribune*, August 2, 1854; Greeley's prefatory paragraph is printed in *Thoreau Log*, 298. For Thoreau's shift from the quietism of "Reform and Reformers" to the "shriller tones of the radical activist," see Linck C. Johnson, "Reforming the Reformers: Emerson, Thoreau, and the Sunday Lectures at Amory Hall, Boston," *ESQ* [*Emerson Society Quarterly*] 37.4 (1991): 280–81.

93. "Historical Introduction," in *RP*, 331–32; PEJ, 8:221.

94. PEJ, 8:247; *Corr.*, 2:213–14 (Charles Scribner, circular letter, May 1854). Scribner's *Cyclopaedia* was published in 1855, and the notice of Thoreau appears in 2:653–56.

95. Fields and Emerson both had already written Richard Bentley, the London publisher, about publishing *Walden* in England, and Fields also sent a copy of *Walden* to Bentley's agent, asking him to find a London publisher. On July 2, Fields sent sample proof sheets to Bentley asking, again, if he would publish it. Bentley was not interested.

Walden was not published in England until 1884; the first new English edition was published in 1886 ("Historical Introduction," in *Walden*, 370).

96. *Corr.*, 2:221 (HDT to H. G. O. Blake, August 8, 1854); PEJ, 8:259. Thoreau used X's to indicate the intensity of such cyclical phenomena as the periodical blooming of plants and onset of fall colors.

97. *Walden*, 4, 8, 16.

98. Quoted by Martin Bickman, *"Walden": Volatile Truths* (New York: Twayne, 1992), 18.

99. The landmark treatment of this dimension of Thoreau's writing is Lawrence Buell, *The Environmental Imagination: Thoreau, Nature Writing, and the Formation of American Culture* (Cambridge, MA: Harvard University Press, 1995).

100. I make the following argument at length in "As You Are Brothers of Mine."

101. *Walden*, 221–22. On the problem of "double consciousness," see Joel Porte, *Consciousness and Culture: Emerson and Thoreau Reviewed* (New Haven, CT: Yale University Press, 2004), 3–10. For the significance of the flute—bequeathed from John to Henry—see "Thoreau's Flute," Louisa May Alcott's elegy for her friend, in *THOT*, 53–54. On Thoreau's subtle process of conversion, signified here by the flute, see Lawrence Buell, "Thoreau and the Natural Environment," in *The Cambridge Companion to Henry David Thoreau*, ed. Joel Myerson (Cambridge: Cambridge University Press, 1995), 186.

102. *Walden*, 223–25; PEJ, 4:291, January 26, 1852 (emphasis in the original).

CHAPTER NINE

1. *LRWE*, 4:460; ABAJ, 273–74.

2. *Corr.*, 2:235–36 (T. H. Higginson to HDT, August 13, 1854). Higginson bought one for himself, the other for Harriet Prescott Spofford, a promising young writer he knew would like it.

3. *Corr.*, 2:238–39 (Richard Fuller to HDT, August 31, 1854), 267 (Charles Sumner to HDT, October 31, 1854); *LRWE*, 4:460.

4. *Thoreau Log*, 327, 330. Hawthorne send two copies of *Walden* to friends in England, one of whom, Monckton Milnes, stayed up until 2:00 a.m. to finish it. See Edward C. Peple Jr., "Hawthorne on Thoreau: 1853–1857," *TSB* 119 (Spring 1972): 2.

5. *Walden* reviews are quoted from Joel Myerson, ed., *Emerson and Thoreau: The Contemporary Reviews* (Cambridge: Cambridge University Press, 1992), 371–406; see also Bradley P. Dean and Gary Scharnhorst, "The Contemporary Reception of *Walden*," *Studies in the American Renaissance* (1990): 293–328.

6. *New-York Daily Tribune*, September 20, 1854; Corr 2:245–46 (HDT to H. G. O. Blake, September 21, 1854; emphasis in the original); J, 7:46, 48. Thoreau had prepared himself for lecturing by studying the lecture styles of others, defining his own goals of truthful sincerity through critiques of his friends; see, for example, PEJ, 4:249–50 ("Noggs," Channing's name for Thoreau, hence a self-critique), 274 (Higginson), 284–85 (Foster), 303–4 (Channing).

7. Apparently a fourth portrait, an ambrotype, was taken on January 17, 1857, but according to Ellen Emerson it was "such a shocking, spectral" picture that she had to return

it. Thoreau was supposed to have had it retaken, but no such image has surfaced. *The Letters of Ellen Tucker Emerson*, ed. Edith E. W. Gregg, 2 vols. (Kent, OH: Kent State University Press, 1982), 1:125.

8. The friend was Eben Loomis. See Thomas Blanding and Walter Harding, *A Thoreau Iconography* (Geneseo, NY: Thoreau Society Booklet 30, 1980), 1–4; and Mark W. Sullivan, *Picturing Thoreau: Henry David Thoreau in American Visual Culture* (Lanham, Maryland: Lexington Books, 2015), 2–8.

9. John Lewis Russell, "Visit to a Locality of the Climbing Fern," *Magazine of Horticulture*, March 1855, 132.

10. PEJ, 8:273–76; *J*, 8:421–25, 11:170–80. See also Ray Angelo, "Thoreau's Climbing Fern Rediscovered," *Arnoldia* 45.3 (Summer 1985): 24–26.

11. *Corr.*, 2:268–69 (Adrien Rouquette to HDT, November 1, 1854), 274 (HDT to Adrien Rouquette, November 13, 1854).

12. *Corr.*, 2:227–31 (Daniel Ricketson to HDT, August 12, 1854), 248–49 (HDT to Daniel Ricketson, October 1, 1854), 256–58 (Daniel Ricketson to HDT, October 12, 1854); Anna Ricketson and Walton Ricketson, *Daniel Ricketson and His Friends* (Boston: Houghton Mifflin, 1902), 280.

13. *Corr.*, 2:275–76 (HDT to Bronson Alcott, November 15, 1854).

14. LRWE, 4:479.

15. On September 29, Spooner came to Concord in person to confirm the arrangement; see Francis B. Dedmond, "James Walter Spooner: Thoreau's Second (though Unacknowledged) Disciple," *Concord Saunterer* 18.2 (December 1985): 35–44; and Annie Root McGrath, "As Long as It Is in Concord," *Concord Saunterer* 12.2 (Summer 1977): 9–11.

16. For a superb discussion of "Moonlight" and of Thoreau's moonlight walks, see David N. Robinson, *Natural Life: Thoreau's Worldly Transcendentalism* (Ithaca, NY: Cornell University Press, 2004), 140–47.

17. TL II, 249–55.

18. *Corr.*, 2:258–59 (HDT to H. G. O. Blake, October 14, 1954); *J*, 7:64–65.

19. *J*, 7:64–65; *Corr.*, 2:272 (Daniel Foster to HDT, November 6, 1854).

20. The surviving correspondence appears in *Corr.*, 2:259–60 (Asa Fairbanks to HDT, October 14, 1854), 264 (Charles B. Bernard to HDT, October 26, 1854), 270 (Asa Fairbanks to HDT, November 6, 1854), 278 (HDT to William E. Sheldon, November 17, 1854), 278 (HDT to Charles B. Bernard, November 20, 1854), 279 (HDT to John D. Milne, November 20, 1854), 280 (Andrew Whitney to HDT, November 27, 1854).

21. *J*, 7:72–73.

22. TL II, 259; *J* 7:74–75; Blanding and Harding, *Thoreau Iconography*, 4–6.

23. *J*, 7:75–76. Fans of Werner Herzog's film *Fitzcarraldo* will recall it was the cast of *I Puritani* that the mad Irish dreamer was bringing to the heart of the Amazon.

24. PEJ, 3:194, *RP*, 174; the Bible quotation is Mark 8:36. See also TL II, 243.

25. *J*, 7:79, 46.

26. *Corr.*, 2:259–60 (Asa Fairbanks to HDT, October 14, 1854); *J*, 7:79; *Corr.*, 2:283 (HDT to H. G. O. Blake, December 19, 1854).

27. *J*, 7:79.

28. *Corr.*, 2:256–58 (D. Ricketson to HDT, October 12, 1854); Ricketson and Ricketson, *Ricketson and Friends*, 280; *Corr.*, 2:289 (HDT to D. Ricketson, December 19, 1854), 290–91 (D. Ricketson to HDT, December 20, 1854).

29. Thomas Blanding, "Daniel Ricketson's Reminiscences of Thoreau," *Concord Saunterer* 8.1 (March 1973): 8–9; for a later version of this story see Ricketson and Ricketson, *Ricketson and His Friends*, 11–12, repr. in *Corr.*, 2:291.

30. *J*, 7:90.

31. TL II, 266; *Corr.*, 2:300–01 (D. Ricketson to HDT, January 9, 1855).

32. *Corr.*, 2:298–99 (HDT to D. Ricketson, January 6, 1855); *J*, 7:92–93. For additional sources for Thoreau's thinking on reforestation, see Robert D. Richardson Jr., *Henry David Thoreau: A Life of the Mind* (Berkeley: University of California Press, 1986), 303–5.

33. TL II, 267–68; *J*, 7:96.

34. *J*, 7:166, 172.

35. Ibid., 171–73, 202, 215.

36. *Corr.*, 2:310 (Franklin Sanborn to HDT, January 30, 1855). The anonymous student was Edwin Morton.

37. Sanborn quoted in *Days of HT*, 353.

38. Leslie Perrin Wilson, *In History's Embrace: Past and Present in Concord, Massachusetts* (Concord, MA: Concord Free Public Library, 2007), 66.

39. *J*, 7:263–67.

40. Ibid., 364–65; *Thoreau as Seen*, 79–80.

41. LRWE, 4:512; *Corr.*, 2:332 (HDT to H.G.O. Blake, June 27, 1855); *J*, 7:417.

42. *J*, 7:417; *Corr.*, 2:333–34 (HDT to H.G.O. Blake, June 27, 1855).

43. *J*, 7:431–43; *Corr.*, 2:337 (HDT to H.G.O. Blake, July 14, 1855).

44. "Historical Introduction," in CC, 262–77; *J*, 7:455.

45. *Corr.*, 2:353 (William D. Ticknor and Company to HDT, September 29, 1855).

46. CHDT, 465–66 (Ticknor and Fields to HDT, n.d.), 532–33 (Ticknor and Fields to HDT, December 15, 1858).

47. Sleepy Hollow was designed in 1855 by pioneer landscape architects Robert Copeland and Horace Cleveland, hired by Emerson and others on the cemetery board to carry out their plans for an open-space public park that would communicate the deep relationship of human mortality to the eternal processes of nature. Both Sleepy Hollow and Emerson's writings were a strong influence on Frederick Law Olmsted; see Wesley T. Mott, ed., *Encyclopedia of Transcendentalism*, s.v. "Landscape Architecture," by Daniel Joseph Nadenicek, 99–100, and "Sleepy Hollow Cemetery," by Nadenicek, 199–200.

48. *J*, 14:109, 7:417. This note, dated September 16, appears in the Journal entry for June 11, showing that Thoreau was by then writing out entries from notes that he had not been strong enough to expand into the Journal. It is possible that during the worst of his illness, Channing was bringing him plants and observations, allowing Thoreau to keep up his Journal record.

49. *Corr.*, 2:345–46 (D. Ricketson to HDT, September 23, 1855), 354 (HDT to D. Ricketson, September 27, 1855), 349 (HDT to H. G. O. Blake, September 26, 1855).

50. Ricketson and Ricketson, *Ricketson and His Friends*, 281–83; *J*, 7:463–82.

51. *Corr.*, 2:354–55 (William Allen to HDT, October 3, 1855); *J*, 7:505 (October 21, 1855).
52. *Corr.*, 2:355–56 (Thomas Cholmondeley to HDT, October 3, 1855).
53. Ibid., 367 (HDT to D. Ricketson, October 16, 1855).
54. ABAJ, 281–82.
55. *J*, 7:485, 495 (oak leaf), 513–14 (old trees).
56. Ibid., 7:502 (wood on the fire); *J*, 8:18, 25 (bookshelves); 7:521 ("eaten in the wind").
57. Ibid., 7:527 (emphasis in the original).
58. Ibid., 8:7–8, 36–37.
59. *Corr.*, 2:378–79 (HDT to Thomas Cholmondeley, November 8 and December 1, 1855); for the packing list, see 371–75 (John Chapman to HDT, October 26, 1855).
60. Ibid., 378–79; 394 (HDT to D. Ricketson, December 25, 1855).
61. *CHDT*, 485 (HDT to Calvin Greene, July 8, 1857).
62. *J*, 8:146, 104–14.
63. Ibid., 8:158, 192–93, 9:178–79.
64. Ibid., 8:217 (March 21, 1856).
65. Ibid., 229–30.
66. *J*, 12:38 (ladder); *J*, 8:269 (spring sap).
67. Ibid., 8:269.
68. Ibid., 315, 335.
69. The CFPL holds the extensive records of the Concord Farmers' Club, including transcripts of their lectures and several volumes of detailed meeting minutes; they offer a rich and underutilized trove of information.
70. Emerson, "Thoreau," 424–25.
71. See *Corr.*, 2:469 (Sarah Alden Bradford Ripley to HDT, September? 1856?): this letter suggests Thoreau and Ripley were discussing the problem of spontaneous generation as early as the fall of 1856.
72. *LRWE*, 5:42.
73. The word *ecology* was not coined until 1866, by Ernst Haeckel. Starting points for information on Thoreau as a pioneer of ecological science include my own *Seeing New Worlds* (1995); Michael Benjamin Berger, *Thoreau's Late Career and "The Dispersion of Seeds": The Saunterer's Synoptic Vision* (Rochester, NY: Camden House, 2000); and Frank Egerton, "History of Ecological Sciences, Part 39: Henry David Thoreau, Ecologist," *Bulletin of the Ecological Society of America* 92.3 (2011): 251–75.
74. *J* 9:115–17 (his 1906 editors deleted Thoreau's too-realistic drawing of the phallic mushroom); *Corr.*, 2:449 (HDT to Calvin Greene, May 31, 1856); 454 (Greene to HDT, June 29, 1856).
75. *Corr.*, 2:440–41 (Horace Greeley to HDT, May 7, 1856), 447 (HDT to H. G. O. Blake, May 21, 1856).
76. *JMN*, 14:76, c. March 1856; *J*, 8:199 (March 4, 1856).
77. *JMN*, 14:91–92; Emerson repeated some of these observations in "Thoreau," 423.
78. Blanding and Harding, *Thoreau Iconography*, 11–19; M. W. Sullivan, *Picturing Thoreau*, 17–21; *Corr.*, 2:452 (HDT to C. Greene, June 21, 1856).
79. George Hendrick, ed., *Remembrances of Concord and the Thoreaus: Letters of Horace Hosmer to Dr. S. A. Jones* (Urbana: University of Illinois Press, 1977), 5–6.

80. Ricketson and Ricketson, *Ricketson and His Friends*, 286–87.

81. *J*, 8:392–94, Ricketson and Ricketson, *Ricketson and His Friends*, 290–94.

82. *J*, 8:390–92.

83. *Corr.*, 2:406–7 (D. Ricketson to HDT, February 26, 1856), 414–15 (D. Ricketson to HDT, March 3, 1856), 420 (HDT to D. Ricketson, March 5, 1856), 424 (D. Ricketson to HDT, March 7, 1856).

84. Ibid., 442 (D. Ricketson to HDT, May 10, 1856; Ricketson did not mail this letter until August 1857); Ricketson and Ricketson, *Ricketson and His Friends*, 285.

85. *J*, 8:199 (March 4, 1856); the second "friend" Thoreau speaks of in this Journal entry is, I am convinced, Ellery Channing.

86. Ricketson and Ricketson, *Ricketson and His Friends*, 297, 209–10. Ricketson's voluminous journal, which he kept from youth until just before his death in 1898, was largely destroyed by his children, Anna and Walton Ricketson. See Don Mortland, "Thoreau's Friend Ricketson: What Manner of Man?" *Concord Saunterer* 18.2 (December 1985): 1–19; and Mortland, "Ellery Channing and Daniel Ricketson: Thoreau's Friends in Conflict," *Concord Saunterer* 19.1 (July 1987): 22–43.

87. *J*, 8:438–39, 444–45.

88. Anonymous, *THOT*, 168; *J*, 8:451–56, with a sequel in 9:26–28.

89. *J*, 9:65; *Corr.*, 2:303–4 (Ann Wetherbee Brown to HDT, January 25, 1855).

90. *CHDT*, 472 (unpublished letter); *Corr.*, 3: [in press, previously unpublished] (HDT to Mary Brown, March 8, 1857).

91. *ABAJ*, 283–85.

92. Carl J. Guarneri, *The Utopian Alternative: Fourierism in Nineteenth-Century America* (Ithaca, NY: Cornell University Press, 1991), 322–26.

93. *Corr.*, 2:477–80 (HDT to Sophia Thoreau, November 1, 1856). For the text of what the spirit moved Thoreau to say, see TL II, 355.

94. *Corr.*, 2:483 (HDT to H. G. O. Blake, November 19, 1856); *ABAL*, 209, *ABAJ*, 287.

95. *ABAJ*, 287–89.

96. Ibid., 290–91, *ABAL*, 210–11; *Corr.*, 2:484 (HDT to H.G.O. Blake, November 19, 1856), 489 (HDT to H.G.O. Blake, December 7, 1856).

97. *Corr.*, 2:483–84 (HDT to H. G. O. Blake, November 19, 1856).

98. *J*, 9:149; *Corr.*, 2:488–89 (HDT to H. G. O. Blake, December 7, 1856).

99. Walter Harding, "Thoreau's Sexuality," *Journal of Homosexuality* 21.3 (1991): 37; Franklin Benjamin Sanborn, "Emerson and His Friends in Concord," *New England Magazine* III (1890), repr. in *Concord Saunterer* 16.1 (Spring 1981): 21–22; *THOT*, 112. Sanborn also claimed that Emerson, Alcott, and Thoreau wanted to invite Whitman to Concord in 1860, but Lidian, Abigail, and Sophia all refused to countenance the invitation (Sanborn, *Life of Thoreau*, 310).

100. *Corr.*, 2:486–87 (HDT to H. G. O. Blake, December 6, 1856).

101. *J*, 9:139, 141.

102. Ibid., 150.

103. Ibid., 151, 160 ("countrymen"), 207 ("exist for joy"), 167 ("grand old poem"), 160 ("nick of time").

104. Ibid., 214 (January 11, 1857).

105. Ibid., 187–90 (December 18, 1856).

106. Ibid., 236–38; TL II, 285.

107. *J*, 9:195, 198.

108. Ibid., 258.

109. Ibid., 210–11 (January 7, 1857).

110. Ibid., 246–47.

111. Ibid., 249–50, 276; *LRWE*, 5:63.

112. See also Harmon Smith, *My Friend, My Friend: The Story of Thoreau's Relationship with Emerson* (Amherst: University of Massachusetts Press, 1999), 165–66.

113. *Corr.*, 2:501–503 (Thomas Cholmondeley to HDT, December 16, 1856).

114. ABAL 1857; Franklin Benjamin Sanborn, *Recollections of Seventy Years*, 2 vols. (Boston: Gorham Press, 1909), 2:397. "Anonymous" remembers another time when the sound of the piano drew Henry downstairs to sing with zest, and soon he began to dance, "all by himself, spinning airily round, displaying most remarkable litheness and agility," until "he finally sprang over the center-table, alighting like a feather on the other side," not the least out of breath, continuing his waltz until his enthusiasm finally abated (*THOT*, 170).

115. Walton Ricketson quoted in Edward Waldo Emerson, *Henry Thoreau as Remembered by a Young Friend* (1917; Concord, MA: Thoreau Foundation, 1968), 145; *CHDT*, 480 (HDT to D. Ricketson, May 13, 1857). Edward Emerson always thought "Tom Bowling" (or "Bowline"), a lament for a sailor lost at sea, "stood in his [Thoreau's] mind for his lost brother, for there was sympathy & admiration and a tear in his voice" whenever he sang it (Harding, *Thoreau as Remembered*, 220).

116. *J*, 7:467–68, 9:335–37; Walter Harding, "Thoreau and Kate Brady," *American Literature* 36.3 (November 1964): 347–49.

117. *CHDT*, 476 (HDT to H. G. O. Blake, April 17, 1857).

118. *J*, 9:377–78, *JMN*, 14:143.

119. *CHDT*, 480 (HDT to D. Ricketson, May 13, 1857); *J*, 9:379.

120. *J*, 9:373–74, *JMN*, 14:144; *J*, 9:391–93.

121. *J*, 9:397–98.

CHAPTER TEN

1. *J*, 9:403; *CHDT*, 484 (HDT to H. G. O. Blake, June 6, 1857); *J*, 9:414–20. See also Ellen Watson in *THOT*, 178–79; she is clearly combining Thoreau's first trip to Clark's Island, in July 1851, with either his Plymouth lecture in 1854 (at which he may have traveled to Clark's Island) or this trip.

2. *J*, 9:420; Francis B. Dedmond, "James Walter Spooner: Thoreau's Second (though Unacknowledged) Disciple," *Concord Saunterer* 18.2 (December 1985): 40.

3. *J*, 9:435–36.

4. Ibid., 439–55.

5. [Isaac Hecker], review of *Cape Cod*, *Catholic World* 2.8 (November 1865): 281.

6. *CC*, 137.

7. Ibid., 59, 147.

8. Ibid., 128, 215.

9. *CHDT*, 485–86 (HDT to George Thatcher, July 11, 1857); *J*, 9:481.

10. Edward S. Burgess Papers, vault A45, Burgess unit 1 [interviews with Edward S. Hoar], folder 4b, CFPL; *J*, 9:402. For a profile of Ed Hoar, see Ray Angelo, "Edward S. Hoar Revealed," *Concord Saunterer* 17.1 (March 1984): 9–16.

11. PEJ transcript (the Princeton edition transcript of Thoreau's Journal) manuscript 23:221 (hereafter cited as PEJ transcript). The 1906 edition of Thoreau's Journal does not print any material that in the editors' judgment was duplicated in *The Maine Woods*; to see Thoreau's original reactions, one must look at the original Journal, which at the date of writing is unpublished but available online at "The Writings of Henry D. Thoreau," http://thoreau.library.ucsb.edu/new_main.html (accessed September 10, 2016).

12. PEJ transcript, 23:221–22; cf. *MW*, 158.

13. PEJ transcript, 23:222.

14. Edward S. Burgess Papers, vault A45, Burgess unit 1, folder 4b, CFPL. Edward Hoar's father's refusal to buy an "Indian" basket gave Thoreau his image in *Walden* for an alternative economic system. For Burgess's interviews with Hoar, see Marcia E. Moss, "Edward S. Hoar's Conversations on Concord with Edward S. Burgess," *Concord Saunterer* 17.1 (March 1984): 17–33.

15. PEJ transcript, 23:361.

16. Ibid., 230 (emphasis in the original); cf *MW*, 162–63. Thoreau remarked that Polis never addressed his clients by name, "while we called him Polis" (PEJ transcript, 23:235).

17. PEJ transcript, 23:237; *MW*, 169.

18. *MW*, 172. In his Journal, Thoreau left a space to insert the name of the "mighty Indian hunter" but finally scrawled in pencil, "I forget" (PEJ transcript, 23:239). See John J. Kucich's important "Lost in the Maine Woods: Henry Thoreau, Joseph Nicolar, and the Penobscot World," *Concord Saunterer*, n.s., 19/20 (2011–12): 22–52; and Phillip Round, "Gentleman Amateur or 'Fellow-Creature'? Thoreau's Maine Woods Flight from Contemporary Natural History," in *Thoreau's World and Ours: A Natural Legacy*, edited by Edmund A. Schofield and Robert C. Baron (Golden, CO: North American Press, 1993), 325–27.

19. PEJ transcript, 23:242, 244–45.

20. Edward S. Burgess Papers, vault A45, Burgess unit 1 [interviews with Edward S. Hoar], folder 4b, CFPL; PEJ transcript, 23:247 and *MW*, 180–81.

21. *MW*, 181.

22. PEJ transcript, 23:251; *MW*, 185.

23. See PEJ transcript, 23:263; cf. *MW*, 193–94. Polis was, observed Thoreau, "very religious," kneeling morning and evening to say his prayers "in a loud voice in Indian" (PEJ transcript, 23:263).

24. PEJ transcript 23:267 and *MW*, 199–200; PEJ transcript, 23:273; *MW*, 168. Polis's sign would today be called an "arborglyph."

25. PEJ transcript, 23:283 and *MW*, 217.

26. PEJ transcript 23:286.

27. Ibid., 304.
28. Ibid., 316; *MW*, 253; Kucich, "Lost in the Maine Woods," 45.
29. PEJ transcript, 23:322; cf. *MW*, 258. Thoreau's published account downplayed both his concerns about Hoar's ability to continue and his own emotional turmoil.
30. PEJ transcript 23:325–26.
31. Ibid., 328–29.
32. Ibid., 331–32.
33. PEJ transcript, 24:356; cf. *MW*, 284.
34. PEJ transcript, 24:358; cf *MW*, 285–86.
35. *MW*, 295–96; PEJ transcript, 24:366.
36. PEJ transcript, 24:354–55; *MW*, 297. Polis offered to sell his canoe to Thoreau, who declined.
37. *MW*, 235–36.
38. See Courtney Traub, "'First-Rate Fellows': Excavating Thoreau's Radical Egalitarian Reflections in a Late Draft of 'Allegash,'" *Concord Saunterer* 23 (2015): 74–96.
39. *CHDT*, 491 (HDT to H. G. O. Blake, August 18, 1857).
40. "Private Journal of John Langdon Sibley of Harvard University Library," 1846–82, 2 vols., 1:443–45, Harvard University Archives, repr. in Keith Walter Cameron, *Transcendentalists and Minerva*, 3 vols. (Hartford, CT: Transcendental Books, 1958), 2:485–86.
41. *THOT*, 79–80; ABAJ, 325, *JMN*, 14:166.
42. See Robert F. Sayre, *Thoreau and the American Indians* (Princeton, NJ: Princeton University Press, 1977), 119.
43. TL II, 291; *CHDT*, 503–4. The person who invited Thoreau for an encore was Rev. Charles C. Shackford.
44. *CHDT*, 504 (HDT to James Russell Lowell, January 23, 1858), 509 (HDT to Lowell, February 22, 1858, and March 5, 1858).
45. Bradley P. Dean and Gary Scharnhorst, "The Contemporary Reception of *Walden*," *Studies in the American Renaissance* (1990): 328; *MW*, 156.
46. *MW*, 121–22; *CHDT*, 515–16 (HDT to Lowell, June 22, 1858), 520–21 (HDT to Lowell, September 1, 1858, and October 4, 1858).
47. *J*, 10:4; *CHDT*, 491 (HDT to H. G. O. Blake, August 18, 1858).
48. *J*, 10:10–13, 14 (the Natick naturalist was Austin Bacon).
49. ABAL, 248. The house cost $600 and the land $345; Alcott's purchase was aided by the annuity Emerson established, to which Thoreau added the less than princely sum of $1. *LRWE*, 5:159–60; *Days of HT*, 380.
50. ABAJ, 307, 326. Anna Alcott and John Pratt were married on May 23, 1860.
51. *To Set This World*, 126–29; *J*, 10:266 (January 28, 1858).
52. *J*, 10:49, 12:343; also *Exc.*, 182. Thoreau may not have remembered the label correctly; *poitrine* means "breast" or "chest." "Squash" would be *gourde* or *courge*.
53. Frances Jane Hallett Prichard (Fanny) to Jane Hallett Prichard, October 22, 1857, Prichard, Hoar, and Related Family Papers, vault A45, Prichard unit 2, box 2, folder 7, CFPL.
54. *J*, 10:92–93; *CHDT*, 496 (HDT to H. G. O. Blake, November 16, 1858).
55. *CHDT*, 500 (D. Ricketson to HDT, December 11, 1858).

56. *J*, 10:233–34, 219.

57. Ibid., 69, 80 (Ruskin); 75–76, 118 (Red Walden). For more on Thoreau and Ruskin, see Robert D. Richardson Jr., *Henry David Thoreau: A Life of the Mind* (Berkeley: University of California Press, 1986), 358–60.

58. *J*, 10:165–65, cf. PEJ transcript, 24:610–11 (November 5, 1857). The 1906 editors, by extracting Thoreau's comments on the "the man of science" from their larger context in the *Maine Woods* material, eliminated the social context of Thoreau's most innovative critique of scientific objectivity.

59. *J*, 10:202, 253–54.

60. PEJ transcript, 25:55 (January 23, 1858).

61. *CHDT*, 495 (HDT to George Thatcher, November 12, 1857), 502 (HDT to Thatcher, January 1, 1858); *Days of HT*, 397.

62. *J*, 10:291–93. The name of Joe Polis's brother is from Fanny Hardy Eckstorm, "Notes on Thoreau's *Maine Woods*," *TSB* 51 (Spring 1955): 1. On Maungwudaus (George Henry), see Donald B. Smith, *Mississauga Portraits: Ojibwe Voices from Nineteenth-Century Canada* (Toronto: University of Toronto Press, 2013), 126–63.

63. *J*, 10:291–95, 313–14.

64. Ibid., 369, 388, 404.

65. *JMN*, 14:203–04; *The Letters of Ellen Tucker Emerson*, ed. Edith E. W. Gregg, 2 vols. (Kent, OH: Kent State University Press, 1982), 1:142.

66. *Corr.*, 3: [in press, previously unpublished letter] (Mary Brown to HDT, April 23, 1858); *CHDT*, 511 (HDT to Marston Watson, April 25, 1858).

67. *J*, 10:142–44; *CHDT*, 491 (HDT to H. G. O. Blake, August 18, 1858), 497–98 (HDT to H. G. O. Blake, November 16, 1858).

68. *J*, 10:452–80. Monadnock is now the generic name for a barren, rocky peak rising from level ground.

69. *J*, 10:467–68, 477–80.

70. Ibid., 11:3–8.

71. Ibid., 16–29.

72. Ibid., 29–49.

73. *CHDT*, 521 (HDT to Ricketson, October 31, 1858), 538 (HDT to Blake, January 1, 1859). Blake seems to have agreed, though Brown admitted he had, rather to his embarrassment, enjoyed it (ibid., 562, Theo Brown to HDT, October 19, 1859).

74. *J*, 11:120.

75. "The wild fruits of the earth disappear before civilization, or are only to be found in large markets." Ibid., 78–79.

76. *Letters of Ellen Tucker Emerson*, 146; Jane Hallett Prichard to Moses B. Prichard, August 17, 1858, Prichard, Hoar, and Related Family Papers, vault A45, Prichard unit 2, box 6, folder 7, CFPL. The connection proved weak and failed in less than a month; not until 1866 did an improved cable allow reliable transatlantic telegraphy.

77. *J*, 11:86–87, 107.

78. Ibid., 170–80; *CHDT*, 521 (HDT to D. Ricketson, October 31, 1858), 527 (D. Ricketson to HDT, November 10, 1858).

79. *CHDT*, 528–29 (T. Cholmondeley to HDT, November 26, 1858); Anna Ricketson and

Walton Ricketson, *Daniel Ricketson and His Friends* (Boston: Houghton Mifflin, 1902), 309–10.

80. *CHDT*, 540 (HDT to H. G. O. Blake, January 19, 1858), 547 (HDT to D. Ricketson, February 12, 1859). Their correspondence continued until Thoreau's death; Cholmondeley, who died in April 1863, did not outlive his American friend by long.

81. *J*, 11:218–21.

82. Ibid., 12:97.

83. *JMN*, 14:158.

84. PEJ, 1:330 (September 4, 1841).

85. *J*, 11:358–59.

86. Ibid., 324–25.

87. Ibid., 396, 435.

88. *CHDT*, 543 (D. Ricketson to HDT, February 9, 1859).

89. *J*, 11:436–37; *CHDT*, 546 (HDT to D. Ricketson, February 12, 1859). See also *Days of HT*, 408, for Thoreau's thanks to Rev. Grindall Reynolds, who conducted the funeral.

90. *J*, 11:437–39, 12:88–93.

91. Ibid., 12:120–23, 175.

92. Ibid., 316 (September 5, 1858); *Days of HT*, 409.

93. *LRWE*, 5:149–50; *CHDT*, 555–56 (HDT to G. Thatcher, August 25, 1859); *J*, 13:272. The selectman's report for 1859 details the town's fears of vandalism; Thoreau's joke would have been widely appreciated.

94. For details, see *CHDT*, 559–60.

95. *J*, 12:344.

96. See also *CHDT*, 541, 545, for Thoreau's donation of five dollars to the Harvard Library, which sum, he told them, exceeded his income "from all sources together for the last four months." Thoreau conducted two annual examinations, on July 13, 1859, and July 13, 1860; the examination was on Asa Gray's *Botanical Text-Book*. For the letters of appointment to the Harvard Committee for Examination in Natural History, see *Corr.*, 3: [in press] for March 28, 1859, June 7, 1859, and June 7, 1860. See also Robert D. Richardson Jr., "Thoreau and Science," in *American Literature and Science*, ed. Robert J. Scholnick (Lexington: University Press of Kentucky, 1992), 123. Other members included his friends John Russell, Marston Watson, Samuel and James Elliot Cabot, Augustus Gould, and future Justice of the Supreme Court Horace Gray Jr.

97. *J*, 12:152–55, 166.

98. *THOT*, 47–48. Dall's lecture was December 14, 1859. See "Caroline Dall in Concord," *TSB* 62 (Winter 1958): 1.

99. TL II, 297; *Letters of Ellen Tucker Emerson*, 1:174; *J*, 12:9.

100. TL II, 299–303.

101. *CHDT*, 555 (HDT to G. Thatcher, August 25, 1859), 558 (HDT to H. G. O. Blake, September 26, 1859).

102. *J*, 11:287; "Report of the Joint Special Committee upon the subject of the Flowage of Meadows on Concord and Sudbury Rivers," January 28, 1860 (Boston: William White, Printer to the State, 1860), 15, 18.

103. *LRWE*, 8:622.

104. Thoreau's "Plan of Concord River from East Sudbury & Billerica Mills, 22.15 Miles" is held by the CFPL (along with associated records), and may be viewed online: http://www.concordlibrary.org/scollect/Thoreau_surveys/107a.htm (accessed September 4, 2016).

105. *J*, 13:149 (Minot Pratt is reporting David Heard's testimony).

106. See Brian Donahue, *The Great Meadow: Farmers and the Land in Colonial Concord* (New Haven, CT: Yale University Press, 2004), 230–34. Donahue documents, in detail, the unintended destruction of the ecological/social order witnessed by Thoreau.

107. *J*, 12:387; Henry David Thoreau, *Wild Fruits: Thoreau's Rediscovered Last Manuscript*, ed. Bradley P. Dean (New York: Norton, 2000), 236–28.

108. Records of the Concord Farmers' Club, 1852–1883, vault A10, unit 3, series 1, vol. 6, 170–72, CFPL.

109. Ralph Waldo Emerson, *Emerson's Antislavery Writings*, ed. Len Gougeon (New Haven, CT: Yale University Press, 1995), 107.

110. *To Set This World*, 114; the petition is reproduced in *Concord Saunterer* 15.4 (Winter 1980): 1–6.

111. Ellen Tucker Emerson, *Life of Lidian Jackson Emerson*, 131.

112. Franklin Benjamin Sanborn, *Recollections of Seventy Years*, 2 vols. (Boston: Gorham Press, 1909), 1:102–8; *To Set This World*, 120–23.

113. *JMN*, 14:125–26; *J*, 12:437. Edward J. Renehan Jr., *The Secret Six: The True Tale of the Men Who Conspired with John Brown* (Columbia: University of South Carolina Press, 1997), 118.

114. *To Set This World*, 127–29. The question is often raised whether Thoreau, or anyone in his circle, knew of Brown's role in the Pottawatomie Massacre, either during Brown's 1857 visit or by the fall of 1859, when in the wake of Harpers Ferry the Pottawatomie Massacre was widely reported in Northeastern newspapers. Thoreau and his allies might have discounted such reports as proslavery propaganda. But Fuller points out that Thoreau's friend T. W. Higginson, one of the Secret Six, certainly knew, for in September 1856, while in Kansas as an agent of the National Kansas Committee, Higginson discussed the murders with the free-state governor of Kansas, Charles Robinson. Like the free-state Kansans he represented, Robinson regarded the murders as beneficial to their cause, for they checked the armed aggression of the proslavery Missouri forces. Higginson later acknowledged his personal discomfort with the massacre; Sanborn claimed not to have known of it. Whether, or how much, Thoreau himself knew of the Pottawatomie Massacre remains an unresolved question. See David G. Fuller, "Thoreau and John Brown's Pottawatomie," *TSB* 210 (Winter 1995): 2–3.

115. *CHDT*, 435–36; *To Set This World*, 125.

116. Brown quoted in *To Set This World*, 127–28; *Days of HT*, 416.

117. *CHDT*, 550 (D. Ricketson to HDT, March 6, 1859); *ABAJ*, 315–16.

118. The phrase is Ricketson's, from *CHDT*, 560 (D. Ricketson to HDT, October 14, 1859).

119. *TL II*, 304–8; *LRWE*, 8:639.

120. *J*, 12:400–402. My interpretation is indebted to Ted A. Smith's penetrating discussion in *Weird John Brown: Divine Violence and the Limits of Ethics* (Stanford, CA: Stanford University Press, 2015). See also Jack Turner, "Thoreau and John Brown," in *A Politi-*

cal Companion to John Brown, ed. Turner (Lexington: University Press of Kentucky, 2009), 151–77.

121. *J,* 12:401–02, October 19, 1859.

122. *J,* 12:404, 406, 420.

123. On the newspaper accounts Thoreau read, see David G. Fuller, "Correcting the Newspapers: Thoreau and 'A Plea for Captain John Brown,'" *Concord Saunterer,* n.s., 5 (Fall 1997): 165–75.

124. *J,* 12:420, 437.

125. Thoreau's words, according to Ralph Waldo Emerson, quoted in TL II, 311–12 (which collects several versions of this same story, including an alternate version told by Edward Emerson).

126. Edward Emerson and Minott Pratt quoted in TL II, 312–13; see also Edward Waldo Emerson, *Henry Thoreau as Remembered by a Young Friend* (1917; Concord, MA: Thoreau Foundation, 1968), 71.

127. *CHDT,* 564 (Charles W. Slack to HDT, October 31, 1859); see also Milton Meltzer and Walter Harding, *A Thoreau Profile* (New York: Thomas Y. Crowell, 1962), which reprints a photograph of the telegram; Emerson quoted in *To Set This World,* 137.

128. Thoreau and Dall quoted in TL II, 316 (emphasis in the original); Howells quoted in ibid., 319 (emphasis added). This source usefully compiles a wide range of responses from newspapers and various unpublished manuscripts.

129. *JMN,* 14:333, n.d. This memorable phrase was not Emerson's; he was quoting Mattie Griffith, abolitionist and woman's rights advocate. For other abolitionists' initial responses to John Brown's insurrection, see *To Set This World,* 135–36.

130. *Corr.,* 3: [in press, previously unpublished letter] (Mary Jane Tappan to HDT, November 7, 1859).

131. ABAJ, 321–22; *CHDT,* 566 (HDT to C. Greene, November 24, 1859). On November 29, 1859, Emerson recorded that Thoreau donated ten dollars to the relief fund for John Brown's family.

132. *J,* 12:447–48, 443.

133. The *Liberator* had published a resolution passed by the American Anti-Slavery Society calling for the friends of freedom to observe Brown's execution with appropriate memorials, and William Lloyd Garrison further recommended church bells be tolled for one hour; see Michael Meyer, "Discord in Concord on the Day of John Brown's Hanging," *TSB* 146 (Winter 1979): 1.

134. *J,* 12:457–58; ABAJ, 322; *J,* 12:443.

135. "John Shepard Keyes's Unpublished Account," *TSB* 143 (Spring 1978): 4; ABAJ, 322; *Days of HT,* 420.

136. For the entire document, see *To Set This World,* 140; and Meyer, "Discord in Concord," 3. Thoreau noted in his Journal that none of those who hung the effigy were long resident in Concord (*J,* 13:15).

137. "Keyes's Unpublished Account."

138. *RP,* 141; ABAJ, 323; the memorial program is reproduced in *RP,* facing page 233. Emerson reimbursed Thoreau the three-dollar printing costs.

139. *To Set This World,* 142. Petrulionis tells the story of Thoreau and Merriam in *To Set*

This World, 1–2; Thoreau tells it in *J*, 13:3–4. For Sanborn's version, see *Thoreau as Seen*, 53–55.

140. *Corr.*, 3: [in press, previously unpublished letter] (James Redpath to HDT, January 5, 1860).

CHAPTER ELEVEN

1. *J*, 13:4–14.

2. Ibid., 30 (Walden pines), 41 (fish in Sleepy Hollow pond), 50 (take care of seeds), 76 (crows and apples), 115 (crow touches the sky).

3. On this "Darwin dinner" and its fateful consequences for the four principals involved, see Randall Fuller, *The Book That Changed America: How Darwin's Theory of Evolution Ignited a Nation* (New York: Viking, 2017).

4. Franklin Benjamin Sanborn to Theodore Parker, January 2, 1860 (Franklin Benjamin Sanborn Papers, vault A35, Sanborn, unit 1, series 3, folder 23, CFPL).

5. Charles Loring Brace, *Races of the Old World: A Manual of Ethnology* (London: Charles Murray, 1863).

6. Thoreau had completed his transcriptions from *Origin of Species* (the British first edition) by February 6, 1860: Henry David Thoreau, "Extracts Mostly upon Natural History," 1856–1861, Berg Collection, New York Public Library. My thanks to Randall Fuller for providing a transcription. See also Fuller, *Book that Changed America*, 126–36.

7. *Walden*, 225; *J*, 13:77; Robert D. Richardson Jr., *Henry David Thoreau: A Life of the Mind* (Berkeley: University of California Press, 1986), 384. Richardson points out that in contrast to *Walden*, Thoreau opened "The Dispersion of Seeds" by citing Pliny on the *unhappiness* of trees such as the cypress that bear no fruit; see "Thoreau and Science," in *American Literature and Science*, ed. Robert J. Scholnick (Lexington: University Press of Kentucky, 1992), 125.

8. ABAJ, 326; Sanborn quoted in TL II, 332–33.

9. *Exc.*, 281, 280, 270–74; Bronson Alcott quoted in TL II, 333.

10. *J*, 13:141, 145.

11. Ibid., 186–87, 192.

12. Amos Bronson Alcott, "Superintendent's Report for the Concord Schools . . . for the Year 1859–60," 11; "Superintendent's Report for the Concord Schools . . . for the year 1860–61," 26, in *Essays on Education by Amos Bronson Alcott*, ed. Walter Harding (Gainesville, FL: Scholars Facsimiles and Reprints, 1960).

13. ABAJ, 326–27; Louisa May Alcott, "Thoreau's Flute," in *THOT*, 55–56.

14. ABAJ, 328; *CHDT*, 582; Sanborn quoted in Philip McFarland, *Hawthorne in Concord* (New York: Grove, 2004), 229.

15. ABAJ, 334–36, 339; Rose Hawthorne quoted in *THOT*, 145–46.

16. Nathaniel Hawthorne, "Septimius Felton," in *The Elixir of Life Manuscripts*, Centenary Edition of the Works of Nathaniel Hawthorne, vol. 13 (Columbus: Ohio State University Press, 1977), 6; see Larry J. Reynolds, *Righteous Violence: Revolution, Slavery, and*

the *American Renaissance* (Athens: University of Georgia Press, 2011), 130.

17. *To Set This World*, 146-48; Annie Brown quoted on 147.
18. Sanborn, *Recollections*, 1:208–10; *To Set This World*, 148–51.
19. *To Set This World*, 151–52; Sanborn, *Recollections*, 1:210–12; *Liberator*, April 13, 1860.
20. Quoted in TL II, 359.
21. J. R. Hinton, who picked up Thoreau's address from him in person when he stopped by the Thoreaus' on his way to North Elba, saw that it was given a place of honor on the program. *RP*, 363–64; TL II, 334–36.
22. *RP*, 147, 152–53.
23. *CHDT*, 585 (HDT to Charles Sumner, July 16, 1860); *Liberator*, July 31, 1860.
24. *J*, 10:74; William Dean Howells, *Literary Friends and Acquaintances* (New York: Harper, 1911), 59–60.
25. *J*, 13:218, 231.
26. For an analysis of these charts and their larger poetics, see the groundbreaking work of Kristen Case, starting with her recent essay "Knowing as Neighboring: Approaching Thoreau's Kalendar," *J19: The Journal of Nineteenth-Century Americanists* 2.1 (Spring 2014): 107–29.
27. *J*, 13:328, 364–67 (emphasis in the original), 14:3.
28. Charles Darwin, *On the Origin of Species by Means of Natural Selection* (London: John Murray, 1859), 73; Thoreau copied a passage from the same page beginning a few lines down from this quotation.
29. *J*, 14:36. Channing, who complained bitterly of the fatigue and filth of camping, nevertheless recounted their Monadnock explorations and debates as the epic climax of his long poem "The Wanderer."
30. *J*, 14:52; *The Letters of Ellen Tucker Emerson*, ed. Edith E. W. Gregg, 2 vols. (Kent, OH: Kent State University Press, 1982), 1:216–17.
31. Jacob Farmer, Concord Farmers' Club Records, Vault A10, Unit 3, series 1, vol 4, p. 130, CFPL (minutes for meeting of April 12, 1860, on "Forest Trees"); Darwin, *Origin*, 74. Thoreau copied into his notes a passage from *Origin* appearing on the same page as Darwin's comment about American forests.
32. *Exc.*, 181–82.
33. TL II, 339–41; *Days of HT*, 33.
34. *CHDT*, 530 (HDT to Horace Greeley, September 29, 1860). Thoreau's unfinished manuscript "Dispersion of Seeds" was eventually published in *Faith in a Seed: "The Dispersion of Seeds" and Other Late Natural History Writings*, ed. Bradley P. Dean (Washington, DC: Island Press, 1993), 23–173.
35. *Corr.*, 3: [in press], Horace Greeley to HDT, December 13, 1860; HDT to Horace Greeley, December 30, 1960; "Are Plants Ever Spontaneously Generated," *New-York Weekly Tribune*, February 2, 1861.
36. *J*, 14:93–94.
37. Ibid., 97 (frost kills everything); 112, 132, 139 (tracking the significance of the seed).
38. Ibid., 146–47 (emphasis in the original); see also Thoreau, *Faith in a Seed*, 101–2, where Thoreau specifically links this phrase, "the development theory," to Darwin. Scholars who have studied Thoreau and evolutionary theory do not doubt that Thoreau's late

work builds on Darwin, and not, say, Robert Chambers's *Vestiges of the Natural History of Creation* (American edition, 1845), which proposed a theory Emerson succinctly called "arrested and progressive development." While Thoreau's notes on Darwin are extensive, his only mention of Chambers (in a Journal entry for September 28, 1851 [PEJ, 4:107]) criticizes the Scottish journalist's "latent infidelity" for "describing that as an exception which is in fact the rule"—or, in Sattelmeyer's words, an exception rather than "a continual state of becoming, where nature is dynamic and evolving." See Robert Sattelmeyer, *Thoreau's Reading: A Study in Intellectual History with Bibliographical Catalogue* (Princeton, NJ: Princeton University Press, 1988), 86–90; Michael Benjamin Berger, *Thoreau's Late Career and "The Dispersion of Seeds": The Saunterer's Synoptic Vision* (Rochester, NY: Camden House, 2000), 48–53; William Rossi, "Evolutionary Theory," in *The Oxford Handbook of Transcendentalism*, ed. Joel Myerson, Sandra Harbert Petrulionis, and Laura Dassow Walls (Oxford: Oxford University Press, 2010), 583–96; and William Howarth, *The Book of Concord: Thoreau's Life as a Writer* (New York: Viking, 1982), 181–97.

39. *J*, 14:148–49.
40. Ibid., 11:299, 14:152.
41. *CHDT*, 579 (HDT to H. G. O. Blake, May 20, 1860).
42. *J*, 14:279–84.
43. Edmund A. Schofield, "The Origin of Thoreau's Fatal Illness," *TSB* 171 (Spring 1985): 2.
44. Quoted in TL II, 349.
45. Quoted in ibid., 352.
46. ABAJ, 330–31; *J*, 14:295, 310 (even as the seed of the giant California redwood is a little thing, "so are all seeds or origins of things"; emphasis added).
47. *J*, 14:310–12.
48. ABAJ, 333–34.
49. *JMN*, 15:112 (February 1861).
50. Francis B. Dedmond, "The Selected Letters of William Ellery Channing the Younger (Part Three)," in *Studies in the American Renaissance* (1991): 289–90.
51. *J*, 14:320; *CHDT*, 609 (HDT to D. Ricketson, March 22, 1861), ABAJ, 337.
52. *CHDT*, 609 (HDT to D. Ricketson, March 22, 1861); *Corr.*, 3: [in press] (HDT to G. Thatcher, March 31, 1861).
53. *Corr.*, 3: [in press] (HDT to G. Thatcher, March 31, 1861).
54. Quoted in *To Set This World*, 154.
55. *Corr.*, 3: [unpublished letter in press] (Parker Pillsbury to HDT, April 9, 1861); *CHDT*, 611 (HDT to Parker Pillsbury, April 10, 1861)
56. *CHDT*, 425 (HDT to C. Greene, May 31, 1856).
57. *CHDT*, 615 (HDT to H. G. O. Blake, May 3, 1861).
58. *Letters of Ellen Tucker Emerson*, 1:250; *CHDT*, 616 (RWE to HDT, May 11, 1861); the list, sadly, is lost.
59. Corinne Hosfeld Smith, *Westward I Go Free: Tracing Thoreau's Last Journey* (Winnipeg: Green Frigate Books, 2012), 62. The following account is deeply indebted to Smith's lively and painstaking reconstruction of Thoreau's trip to Minnesota.
60. *J*, 14:340; Walter Harding, ed., *Thoreau's Minnesota Journey: Two Documents* (Geneseo, NY: Thoreau Society Booklet No. 16, 1962), 47. This booklet prints Harding's tran-

script of Thoreau's "Notes on the Journey West" (held at the Huntington Library, San Marino, California), as well as the letters Horace Mann Jr. wrote home during their excursion to Minnesota; the following account draws from this source as well.

61. *Corr.*, 3: [in press, previously unpublished letter] (HDT to Cynthia and Sophia Thoreau, May 15, 1861); Harding, *Thoreau's Minnesota Journey*, 1.

62. *Thoreau as Seen*, 130–31.

63. Harding, *Thoreau's Minnesota Journey*, 3, 48.

64. Ibid., 4–5.

65. Ibid., 17–18; *Exc.*, 271–72; cf. C. H. Smith, *Westward I Go Free*, 229–31.

66. *CHDT*, 622 (HDT to F. B. Sanborn, June 25, 1861).

67. Harding, *Thoreau's Minnesota Journey*, 12; C. H. Smith, *Westward I Go Free*, 251; for a detailed account of Thoreau's journey aboard the *Frank Steele*, see C. H. Smith, 251-84.

68. *CHDT*, 621 (HDT to F. B. Sanborn, June 25, 1861).

69. Harding, *Thoreau's Minnesota Journey*, 22; C. H. Smith, *Westward I Go Free*, 264.

70. *CHDT*, 621 (HDT to F. B. Sanborn, June 25, 1861). The saddle and the fragile items of Dakota clothing are held by the Concord Museum.

71. Quoted in C. H. Smith, *Westward I Go Free*, 270.

72. Ibid., 285–347; Harding, *Thoreau's Minnesota Journey*, 25–27.

73. *ABAJ*, 340; Daniel Moncure Conway, *Autobiography, Memories and Experiences*, 2 vols. (Boston: Houghton Mifflin, 1904), 1:335; *New-York Tribune*, July 30, 1861.

74. *CHDT*, 593 (D. Ricketson to HDT, October 14, 1860), 599–600 (HDT to D. Ricketson, November 4, 1860), 609 (HDT to D. Ricketson, March 22, 1861); *Corr.*, 3: [in press] (D. Ricketson to HDT, June 30, 1861), *CHDT*, 625 (HDT to D. Ricketson, August 15, 1861); *Corr.*, 3: [in press] (D. Ricketson to HDT, August 16, 1861).

75. Thomas Blanding and Walter Harding, *A Thoreau Iconography* (Geneseo, NY: Thoreau Society Booklet 30, 1980), 20–23; Anna Ricketson and Walton Ricketson, *Daniel Ricketson and His Friends* (Boston: Houghton Mifflin, 1902), 317–19, 147. Ricketson's copy is now held by the Concord Museum; Sophia Thoreau's darker, "stronger" image was stolen in 1910 and has yet to resurface.

76. Ricketson and Ricketson, *Ricketson and His Friends*, 320–22; Dedmond, "Letters of Channing," 302 (October 2, 1861); Annie Russell Marble, *Thoreau: His Home, Friends, and Books* (New York: Thomas Y. Crowell, 1902), 175.

77. Ricketson and Ricketson, *Ricketson and His Friends*, 135; *Thoreau Log*, 599.

78. *CHDT*, 629 (HDT to D. Ricketson, October 14, 1861).

79. *J*, 14:346.

80. Anonymous quoted in *THOT*, 170; *ABAJ*, 343; William Ellery Channing II, *Thoreau: The Poet-Naturalist* (Boston: Roberts Brothers, 1873), 323.

81. Sophia Thoreau to Daniel Ricketson, in Ricketson and Ricketson, *Ricketson and His Friends*, 141–43; *Days of HT*, 462 (musicbox); Alcott brought the apples and cider (*Thoreau Log*, 604).

82. Anonymous quoted in *THOT*, 154–55; Edith Emerson quoted in *Days of HT*, 463 ("I love them as if they were my own").

83. *JMN*, 15:441; Edward S. Burgess Papers, vault A45, Burgess unit 1 [interviews with Edward S. Hoar], folder 4b, CFPL.

84. Sarah Alden Bradford Ripley in *THOT*, 49 ("in a handsome suit of black," letter to So-

phia Thayer, 1862); Ricketson and Ricketson, *Ricketson and His Friends*, 214 ("skating on this river"); Anonymous in *THOT*, 155 ("gray as a rat").

85. Edward Waldo Emerson, *Henry Thoreau as Remembered by a Young Friend* (1917; Concord, MA: Thoreau Foundation, 1968), 117-18 ("I did not know we had ever quarreled"); Parker Pillsbury quoted in *Thoreau as Seen*, 101.

86. E. W. Emerson, *Henry Thoreau as Remembered*, 117 ("it's respectable to leave an estate"); *Corr.*, 3: [in press, previously unpublished letter] (Mary Stearns to HDT, February 23, 1862). Mary Stearns was the wife of George Luther Stearns, one of Brown's "Secret Six," and the niece of Lydia Maria Child.

87. E. Harlow Russell would break these bundles apart and distribute the pages—now worth money as holograph manuscript of the great author—to the winds; Brad Dean would spend much of his own too-short life reassembling the bulk of Thoreau's pages, which he published as *Wild Fruits* (New York: 2000) and *Faith in a Seed* (Washington, DC: Island Press, 1993). For an excellent starting point on *Wild Fruits*, see Lance Newman's illuminating discussion in *Our Common Dwelling: Henry Thoreau, Transcendentalism, and the Class Politics of Nature* (New York: Palgrave Macmillan, 2005), 171-83.

88. On Sophia Thoreau's crucial and largely unrecognized role in editing Thoreau's posthumous publications and in protecting her brother's writings intact for future generations, see Kathy Fedorko, "'Henry's Brilliant Sister': The Pivotal Role of Sophia Thoreau in Her Brother's Posthumous Publications," *ESQ: A Journal of the American Renaissance* 84.2 (2016): 222-56.

89. *CHDT*, 635-36 (HDT to the editors of *Atlantic Monthly*, February 11, 1862), and 640 (HDT to Ticknor and Fields, March 11, 1862); *Exc.*, 241-42. Thoreau had wanted a white oak leaf engraved as well, to appear on the facing page so readers could compare them, but engraving cost so much that he had to make do with one.

90. *Exc.*, 202; both Pillsbury and Channing noted Thoreau was in these weeks censoring out his more cheerful passages. See Pillsbury in *Thoreau as Seen*, 101; Channing quoted in Franklin Benjamin Sanborn, *The Life of Henry David Thoreau* (Boston: Houghton Mifflin, 1917), 171. Blanding established that the handwriting on Thoreau's last two published essays, "Wild Apples" and "The Allegash and East Branch," was Elizabeth Hoar's: see Thomas Blanding, "Beans, Baked and Half-Baked," *Concord Saunterer* 11.3 (Fall 1976) 11-14, 13.

91. Mary P. Sherwood, "Thoreau's Penobscot Indians," *Thoreau Journal Quarterly* 1.1 (January 1969), 6.

92. Ricketson and Ricketson, *Ricketson and His Friends*, 214; *CHDT*, 641 (HDT to Myron Benson, March 21, 1862).

93. *JMN*, 15:246; Ricketson and Ricketson, *Ricketson and His Friends*, 137.

94. W. E. Channing II, *Poet-Naturalist* (1902), 337; W. E. Channing II, *Poet-Naturalist* (1873), 320, 322.

95. *ABAJ*, 346; W. E. Channing II, *Poet-Naturalist* (1902), 343; *CHDT*, 650-51 (D. Ricketson to HDT, May 4, 1862). Walter Harding's quotation from Channing ("'Moose' and 'Indian'") is incorrect (*Days of HT*, 466); Channing wrote "Indians," plural, in both the 1873 and the 1902 editions.

96. *Walden*, 267 ("long-headed farmer"); Mary Hosmer Brown, *Memories of Concord* (Boston: Four Seas, 1926), 105–6.

97. For a full accounting of the controversy over Thoreau's last words, see Kathy Fedorko, "Revisiting Henry's Last Words," *TSB* 295 (Fall 2016): 1–4.

98. *THOT*, 50 (Sarah Ripley's quote), 49 (Sophia Hawthorne's quote).

99. Ricketson and Ricketson, *Ricketson and His Friends*, 138; ABAJ, 348. Alcott's "Readings" were quite a mash-up.

100. Ralph Waldo Emerson, "Thoreau," 431; Sophia Hawthorne quoted in *THOT*, 49. Significantly, at Thoreau's death, the town clerk listed his occupation as "natural historian."

101. *J*, 14:109–10 (October 10, 1860).

102. *LRWE*, 5:278–79; Emerson, "Thoreau," 425. Edward left on his own journey west on May 12, 1862, three days after Thoreau's funeral.

Selected Bibliography

Abelove, Henry. "From Thoreau to Queer Politics," *Yale Journal of Criticism* 6.3 (1993): 17–27.

Adams, Raymond. "Emerson's House at Walden." *Thoreau Society Bulletin* 24 (July 1948): 3–7.

Alcott, Amos Bronson. *Essays on Education by Amos Bronson Alcott.* Edited by Walter Harding. Gainesville, FL: Scholars Facsimiles and Reprints, 1960.

———. *The Journals of Amos Bronson Alcott.* Edited by Odell Shepard. Boston: Little, Brown, 1938. [ABAJ]

———. *The Letters of Amos Bronson Alcott.* Edited by Richard L. Herrnstadt. Ames, Iowa: Iowa State University Press, 1969. [ABAL]

Allen, Gay Wilson. *Waldo Emerson: A Biography.* New York: Viking, 1981.

Angelo, Ray. "Edward S. Hoar Revealed." *Concord Saunterer* 17.1 (March 1984): 9–16.

———. "Thoreau as Botanist: An Appreciation and a Critique." *Arnoldia* 45.3 (Summer 1985): 13–23.

———. "Thoreau's Climbing Fern Rediscovered." *Arnoldia* 45.3 (Summer 1985): 24–26.

Arsić, Branka. *Bird Relics: Grief and Vitalism in Thoreau.* Cambridge, MA: Harvard University Press, 2016.

Bassett, T. D. Seymour. "The Cold Summer of 1816 in Vermont." *New England Galaxy* 15.1 (Summer 1973): 15–19.

Belasco, Susan. "The Dial." In *The Oxford Handbook of Transcendentalism*, edited by Joel Myerson, Sandra Harbert Petrulionis, and Laura Dassow Walls, 373–79. Oxford: Oxford University Press, 2010.

Bennett, Jane. *Thoreau's Nature: Ethics, Politics, and the Wild.* Walnut Creek, CA: Alta Mira Press, 2000.

Bentinck-Smith, William. *The Harvard Book: Selections from Three Centuries.* Cambridge, MA: Harvard University Press, 1960.

Berger, Michael Benjamin. *Thoreau's Late Career and "The Dispersion of Seeds": The Saunterer's Synoptic Vision.* Rochester, NY: Camden House, 2000.

Berkowitz, Morton. "Thoreau, Rice and Vose on the Commercial Spirit." *Thoreau Society Bulletin* 141 (Fall 1977): 1–5.

Bickman, Martin. *Minding American Education: Reclaiming the Tradition of Active Learning.* New York: Teacher's College Press, 2003.

———, ed. *Uncommon Learning: Henry David Thoreau on Education.* Boston: Houghton Mifflin, 1999.

————. *"Walden": Volatile Truths.* New York: Twayne, 1992.

Blancke, Shirley, and Barbara Robinson. *From Musketaquid to Concord: The Native and European Experience.* Concord, MA: Concord Antiquarian Museum, 1985.

Blanding, Thomas. "Beans, Baked and Half-Baked." *Concord Saunterer* 11.3 (Fall 1976): 11–14.

————. "Beans, Baked and Half-Baked (6)." *Concord Saunterer* 12.4 (Winter 1977): 14–15.

————, ed. "Daniel Ricketson's Reminiscences of Thoreau." *Concord Saunterer* 8.1 (March 1973): 6–11.

————. "Mary Russell Watson's Reminiscences of Thoreau." *Concord Saunterer* 9.2 (June 1974): 1–6.

————. "Passages from John Thoreau, Jr.'s Journal." *Thoreau Society Bulletin* 136 (Summer 1976): 4–6.

Blanding, Thomas, and Walter Harding. *A Thoreau Iconography.* Geneseo, NY: Thoreau Society Booklet 30, 1980.

Bode, Carl. *The American Lyceum.* New York: Oxford University Press, 1956.

Borst, Raymond R. *The Thoreau Log: A Documentary Life of Henry David Thoreau, 1817–1862.* New York: G. K. Hall, 1992. [*Thoreau Log*]

Bosco, Ronald A., and Joel Myerson. *The Emerson Brothers: A Fraternal Biography in Letters.* Oxford: Oxford University Press, 2006.

Brain, J. Walter. "Thoreau's Poetic Vision and the Concord Landscape." In *Thoreau's World and Ours: A Natural Legacy,* edited by Edmund A. Schofield and Robert C. Baron, 281–97. Golden, CO: North American Press, 1993.

Broderick, John C. "Thoreau, Alcott, and the Poll Tax." *Studies in Philology* 53.4 (October 1956): 612–26.

Brownson, Orestes. "Independence Day Address at Dedham, Massachusetts." In *Works in Political Philosophy, Vol. 2: 1828–1841,* edited by Gregory S. Butler, 111–24. Wilmington, DE: ISI Books, 2007.

Buell, Lawrence. *The Environmental Imagination: Thoreau, Nature Writing, and the Formation of American Culture.* Cambridge, MA: Harvard University Press, 1995.

————. "Thoreau and the Natural Environment." In *The Cambridge Companion to Henry David Thoreau,* edited by Joel Myerson, 171–93. Cambridge: Cambridge University Press, 1995.

Cafaro, Philip. *Thoreau's Living Ethics: Walden and the Pursuit of Virtue.* Athens: University of Georgia Press, 2005.

Cain, William E., ed. *A Historical Guide to Henry David Thoreau.* Oxford: Oxford University Press, 2000.

Cameron, Kenneth Walter. *Thoreau and His Harvard Classmates.* Hartford, CT: Transcendental Books, 1965.

————. "Thoreau's Early Compositions in the Ancient Languages." *Emerson Society Quarterly* 8.3 (1957): 20–29.

————. *Thoreau's Harvard Years.* Hartford, CT: Transcendental Books, 1966.

————. *Transcendental Apprenticeship: Notes on Young Henry Thoreau's Reading.* Hartford, CT: Transcendental Books, 1976.

————. *Transcendentalists and Minerva.* 3 vols. Hartford, CT: Transcendental Books, 1958.

———. "Young Henry Thoreau in the Annals of the Concord Academy (1829–1833)." *Emerson Society Quarterly* 9.4 (1957): 1–21.

Cameron, Sharon. *Writing Nature: Henry Thoreau's Journal.* Chicago: University of Chicago Press, 1985.

Canby, Henry Seidel. *Thoreau.* Boston: Houghton Mifflin, 1939.

Capper, Charles. *Margaret Fuller: An American Romantic Life, the Private Years.* Oxford: Oxford University Press, 1992.

———. *Margaret Fuller: An American Romantic Life, the Public Years.* Oxford: Oxford University Press, 2007.

Carey, Patrick W. *Orestes Brownson: American Religious Weathervane.* Grand Rapids, MI: William B. Eerdmans, 2004.

Case, Kristen. "Knowing as Neighboring: Approaching Thoreau's Kalendar." *J19: The Journal of Nineteenth-Century Americanists* 2.1 (Spring 2014): 107–29.

———. "Thoreau's Radical Empiricism: The Kalendar, Pragmatism, and Science." In *Thoreauvian Modernities: Transatlantic Conversations on an American Icon,* edited by François Specq, Laura Dassow Walls, and Michel Granger, 187–99. Athens: University of Georgia Press, 2013.

Cavell, Stanley. *The Senses of Walden: An Expanded Edition.* Chicago: University of Chicago Press, 1991.

Channing, William Ellery. *The Works of William E. Channing, D.D.* 6 vols. 8th edition. Boston: James Munroe, 1848.

Channing, William Ellery II. *Poems of Sixty-Five Years.* 1901. New York: Arno Press, 1971.

———. *Thoreau: The Poet-Naturalist.* Boston: Roberts Brothers, 1873.

———. *Thoreau: The Poet-Naturalist.* New edition. Edited by F. B. Sanborn. Boston: Charles E. Goodspeed, 1902.

Christie, John Aldrich. *Thoreau as World Traveler.* New York: Columbia University Press, 1965.

Christy, Arthur. *The Orient in American Transcendentalism: A Study of Emerson, Thoreau, and Alcott.* New York: Columbia University Press, 1932.

Chura, Patrick. *Thoreau the Land Surveyor.* Gainesville: University Press of Florida, 2010.

Conrad, Randall. "The Machine in the Garden: Re-imagining Thoreau's Plumbago Grinder." *Thoreau Society Bulletin* 243 (Fall 2005): 5–8.

———. "Realizing Resistance: Thoreau and the First of August, 1846, at Walden." *Concord Saunterer* 12/13 (2004–5): 165–93.

———. "A Thoreau Christmas." *Thoreau Society Bulletin* 272 (Fall 2010): 3.

Conway, Moncure Daniel. *Autobiography, Memories and Experiences.* 2 vols. Boston: Houghton Mifflin, 1904.

Cooke, George Willis. *An Historical and Biographical Introduction to Accompany the "Dial," in Two Volumes.* New York: Russell and Russell, 1961.

Cosman, Max. "Apropos of John Thoreau." *American Literature* 12.2 (May 1940): 241–43.

Cronon, William. *Changes in the Land: Indians, Colonists, and the Ecology of New England.* New York: Hill and Wang, 1983.

Dean, Bradley P. "More Context for Thoreau's 'Slavery in Massachusetts.'" *Thoreau Research Newsletter* 1.3 (July 1990): 12.

———. "Natural History, Romanticism, and Thoreau." In *American Wilderness: A New History*, edited by Michael Lewis, 73–89. Oxford: Oxford University Press, 2007.

———. "Rediscovery at Walden: The History of Thoreau's Bean-Field." *Concord Saunterer*, n.s., 12/13 (2004–5): 86–137.

———. "Thoreau and Michael Flannery." *Concord Saunterer* 17.3 (Dec. 1984): 27–33.

Dean, Bradley P., and Gary Scharnhorst. "The Contemporary Reception of *Walden*." *Studies in the American Renaissance* (1990): 293–328.

Dean, Bradley P., and Ronald Wesley Hoag. "Thoreau's Lectures after *Walden*: An Annotated Calendar." *Studies in the American Renaissance* (1996): 241–362. [TL I]

———. "Thoreau's Lectures before *Walden*: An Annotated Calendar." *Studies in the American Renaissance* (1995): 127–228. [TL II]

Dedmond, Francis B. "George William Curtis to Christopher Pearse Cranch: Three Unpublished Letters from Concord." *Concord Saunterer* 12.4 (Winter 1977): 1–7.

———. "James Walter Spooner: Thoreau's Second (though Unacknowledged) Disciple." *Concord Saunterer* 18.2 (December 1985): 35–44.

———. "The Selected Letters of William Ellery Channing the Younger (Part Three)." *Studies in the American Renaissance* (1991): 257–343.

———. "'Pretty Free Omissions': Emerson Edits a Thoreau Manuscript for the *Dial*." *Thoreau Society Bulletin* 227 (Spring 1999): 8–9.

Delano, Sterling F. *Brook Farm: The Dark Side of Utopia*. Harvard University Press, 2004.

———. "Thoreau's Visit to Brook Farm." *Thoreau Society Bulletin* 221/222 (Fall 1997/Spring 1998): 1–2.

Delano, Sterling F., and Joel Myerson. "'The General Scapegoat': Thoreau and Concord in 1844." *Thoreau Society Bulletin* 264 (Fall 2008): 1–2.

Dimock, Wai Chee. *Through Other Continents: American Literature across Deep Time*. Princeton, NJ: Princeton University Press, 2006.

Donahue, Brian. *The Great Meadow: Farmers and the Land in Colonial Concord*. New Haven, CT: Yale University Press, 2004.

———. "Henry David Thoreau and the Environment of Concord." In *Thoreau's World and Ours: A Natural Legacy*, edited by Edmund A. Schofield and Robert C. Baron, 181–89. Golden, CO: North American Press, 1993.

Douglass, Frederick. *Narrative of the Life of Frederick Douglass, an American Slave*. In *Autobiographies*, 1–102. New York: Library of America, 1994.

Dowling, David. *Emerson's Protégés: Mentoring and Marketing Transcendentalism's Future*. New Haven, CT: Yale University Press, 2014.

———. *Literary Partnerships and the Marketplace: Writers and Mentors in Nineteenth-Century America*. Baton Rouge: Louisiana State University Press, 2012.

Drew, Bernard A., "Thoreau's Tarn Identified: Guilder Pond." *Concord Saunterer*, n.s., 9 (2001): 126–39.

Egerton, Frank. "History of Ecological Sciences, Part 39: Henry David Thoreau, Ecologist." *Bulletin of the Ecological Society of America* 92.3 (2011): 251–75.

Elliott, Clark A. *Thaddeus William Harris (1795–1856): Nature, Science, and Society in the Life of an American Naturalist*. Bethlehem, PA: Lehigh University Press, 2008.

Ellis, James H. "The Provincetown Burglary." *Thoreau Society Bulletin* 162 (Winter 1983): 3.

Emerson, Edward Waldo. *Henry Thoreau as Remembered by a Young Friend.* 1917. Concord, MA: Thoreau Foundation, 1968.

Emerson, Ellen Tucker. *The Letters of Ellen Tucker Emerson.* Edited by Edith E. W. Gregg. 2 vols. Kent, OH: Kent State University Press, 1982.

———. *The Life of Lidian Jackson Emerson.* East Lansing: Michigan State University Press, 1992.

Emerson, Ralph Waldo. *The Collected Works of Ralph Waldo Emerson.* Edited by Ronald A. Bosco and Joel Myerson. 10 vols. Cambridge, MA: Harvard University Press, 2013.

———. *The Early Lectures of Ralph Waldo Emerson, 1833–1842.* Edited by Stephen E. Whicher, Robert E. Spiller, and Wallace E. Williams. 3 vols. Cambridge, MA: Harvard University Press, 1959–1972.

———. *Emerson's Antislavery Writings.* Edited by Len Gougeon and Joel Myerson. New Haven, CT: Yale University Press, 1995.

———. *Essays and Lectures.* Edited by Joel Porte. New York: Library of America, 1983. [*E&L*]

———. "Henry D. Thoreau." In *Uncollected Prose Writings,* edited by Ronald A. Bosco and Joel Myerson, *The Collected Works of Ralph Waldo Emerson,* 10:411–31.

———. *The Journals and Miscellaneous Notebooks of Ralph Waldo Emerson.* Edited by William Gilman et al. 16 vols. Cambridge, MA: Harvard University Press, 1960–82. [*JMN*]

———. *The Letters of Ralph Waldo Emerson.* Edited by Ralph L. Rusk and Eleanor M. Tilton. 10 vols. New York: Columbia University Press, 1939–91. [*LRWE*]

———. "New Poetry." *Dial* 1.2 (October 1840):220–32.

Emerson, Ralph Waldo, and Thomas Carlyle. *The Correspondence of Emerson and Carlyle.* Edited by Joseph Slater. 2 vols. New York: Columbia University Press, 1964.

Fedorko, Kathy. "'Henry's Brilliant Sister': The Pivotal Role of Sophia Thoreau in Her Brother's Posthumous Publications." *ESQ: A Journal of the American Renaissance* 64.2 (2016): 222–56.

———. "Revisiting Henry's Last Words." *Thoreau Society Bulletin* 295 (Fall 2016): 1–4.

Fink, Steven. *Prophet in the Marketplace: Thoreau's Development as a Professional Writer.* Princeton, NJ: Princeton University Press, 1992.

Fischer, David Hackett, ed. *Concord: The Social History of a New England Town, 1750–1850.* Waltham, MA: Brandeis University, 1983.

Frost, Geneva. "An Early Thoreau's Bangor." *Concord Saunterer* 19.1 (July 1987): 44–53.

Fuller, David G. "Correcting the Newspapers: Thoreau and 'A Plea for Captain John Brown.'" *Concord Saunterer,* n.s., 5 (Fall 1997): 165–75.

———. "Thoreau and John Brown's Pottawatomie." *Thoreau Society Bulletin* 210 (Winter 1995): 2–3.

Fuller, Margaret. "The Great Lawsuit," *Dial* 4.1 (July 1843): 1–47.

Fuller, Randall. *The Book That Changed America: How Darwin's Theory of Evolution Ignited a Nation.* New York: Viking, 2017.

Fuller, Richard. "Visit to the Wachusett, July 1842." *Thoreau Society Bulletin* 129 (Fall 1972): 1–4.

Furtak, Rick Anthony, Jonathan Ellsworth, and James D. Reid, eds. *Thoreau's Importance for Philosophy.* New York: Fordham University Press, 2012.

Geller, Lawrence D. *Between Concord and Plymouth: The Transcendentalists and the Watsons*. Concord, MA: Thoreau Foundation; Plymouth, MA: Pilgrim Society, 1973.

Glick, Wendell. "The Jersey Thoreaus." *Thoreau Society Bulletin* 148 (Summer 1979): 1–5.

Greeley, Dana McLean. "The Grandparents of Henry David Thoreau." *Concord Saunterer* 14.4 (Winter 1979): 2–5.

Grice, Steve. "A Leaf from Thoreau's Fire Island Manuscript." *Thoreau Society Bulletin* 258 (Spring 2007): 1–4.

Griffin, S. G. *A History of the Town of Keene*. Keene, NH: Sentinel Printing, 1904. Accessed September 4, 2015. https://archive.org/details/historyoftownofkoogrif.

Gross, Robert A. "Cosmopolitanism in Concord: The Transcendentalists and Their Neighbors." *Thoreau Society Bulletin* 261 (Winter 2008): 1–4.

———. "Faith in the Boardinghouse: New Views of Thoreau Family Religion." *Thoreau Society Bulletin* 250 (Winter 2005): 1–5.

———. "Helen Thoreau's Anti-Slavery Scrapbook." *Yale Review* 100.1 (January 2012): 103–20.

———. "Men and Women of Fairest Promise: Transcendentalism in Concord." *Concord Saunterer*, n.s., 2.1 (Fall 1994): 5–18.

———. *The Minutemen and Their World*. 1976. 25th Anniversary Edition, New York: Hill and Wang, 2001.

———. "Talk of the Town." *American Scholar* 84.3 (Summer 2015): 31–43.

———. "'That Terrible Thoreau': Concord and Its Hermit." In *A Historical Guide to Henry David Thoreau*, edited by William E. Cain, 181–241. Oxford: Oxford University Press, 2000.

———. "Thoreau and the Laborers of Concord." *Raritan* 33.1 (June 2013): 50–66.

———. *The Transcendentalists and Their World*. New York: Farrar, Straus and Giroux, forthcoming.

Guarneri, Carl J. *The Utopian Alternative: Fourierism in Nineteenth-Century America*. Ithaca, NY: Cornell University Press, 1991.

Gura, Philip. *American Transcendentalism: A History*. New York: Hill and Wang, 2007.

Gustafson, Sandra M. *Imagining Deliberative Democracy in the Early American Republic*. Chicago: University of Chicago Press, 2011.

Hale, Horatio. *Remarks on the Language of the St. John's, or Wlastukweek Indians with a Penobscot Vocabulary*. Boston: 1834. 8 pp.

Harding, Walter, ed. "Amanda Mather's Recollections of Thoreau." *Thoreau Society Bulletin* 188 (Summer 1989): 1–2.

———. *The Days of Henry Thoreau: A Biography*. 1965. New York: Dover, 1982. [*Days of HT*]

———, ed. *Thoreau as Seen by His Contemporaries*. New York: Holt, Rinehart and Winston, 1960; New York: Dover, 1989. [*Thoreau as Seen*]

———. "Thoreau and the Concord Lyceum." *Thoreau Society Bulletin* 30 (January 1950): 2–3.

———. "Thoreau and Kate Brady." *American Literature* 36.3 (November 1964): 347–49.

———. "Thoreau in Emerson's Account Books." *Thoreau Society Bulletin* 159 (Spring 1982): 1–3.

———. "Thoreau Scholarship Today." *Thoreau Society Bulletin* 139 (Spring 1977): 1–2.

———, ed. *Thoreau's Minnesota Journey: Two Documents.* Geneseo, NY: Thoreau Society Booklet No. 16, 1962.

———. "Thoreau's Sexuality." *Journal of Homosexuality* 21.3 (1991): 23–45.

Hartigan, John, Jr. *Aesop's Anthropology: A Multispecies Approach.* Minneapolis: University of Minnesota Press, 2014.

Harrington, C. R., ed. *The Year without a Summer? World Climate in 1816.* Ottawa: Canadian Museum of Nature, 1992.

Hawthorne, Nathaniel. *The American Notebooks.* Columbus: Ohio State University Press, 1932, 1960, 1972.

———. "Septimius Felton." In *The Elixir of Life Manuscripts,* Centenary Edition of the Works of Nathaniel Hawthorne, vol. 13, 3–194. Columbus: Ohio State University Press, 1977.

———. *Tales and Sketches.* New York: Library of America, 1982.

Hendrick, George, ed. *Remembrances of Concord and the Thoreaus: Letters of Horace Hosmer to Dr. S. A. Jones.* Urbana: University of Illinois Press, 1977.

Herrick, Gerri L. "Sophia Thoreau—'Cara Sophia.'" *Concord Saunterer* 13.3 (Fall 1978): 5–12.

Hoagland, Clayton. "The Diary of Thoreau's 'Gentle Boy.'" *New England Quarterly* 28.4 (December 1955): 473–89.

Hoar, George Frisbie. *Autobiography of Seventy Years.* 2 vols. New York: Charles Scribner's Sons, 1903.

Hodder, Alan D. *Thoreau's Ecstatic Witness.* New Haven, CT: Yale University Press, 2001.

Hoeltje, Hubert H. "Thoreau and the Concord Academy," *New England Quarterly* 21.1 (March 1948): 103–9.

[Hosmer, Joseph?] "J. H." "A Rare Reminiscence of Thoreau as a Child." *Thoreau Society Bulletin* 245 (Fall 2003): 1–2.

Howarth, William. *The Book of Concord: Thoreau's Life as a Writer.* New York: Viking, 1982.

Howe, Daniel Walker. *What Hath God Wrought: The Transformation of America, 1815–1848.* Oxford: Oxford University Press, 2007.

Hudson, Edmund. "The Wide Spreading Jones Family." 1917. Reprinted in *Thoreau Society Bulletin* 221 (Fall 1997): 4–12; 222 (Spring 1998): 5.

Hudspeth, Robert N. "Dear Friend: Letter Writing in Concord." *Concord Saunterer,* n.s., 11 (2003): 77–91.

———. *Ellery Channing.* New York: Twayne, 1973.

Irmscher, Christoph. *Louis Agassiz: Creator of American Science.* Boston: Houghton Mifflin, 2013.

Jarvis, Edward. *Traditions and Reminiscences of Concord, Massachusetts, 1779–1878.* Edited by Sarah Chapin. Amherst: University of Massachusetts Press, 1993.

Johnson, Linck C. "The Life and Legacy of Civil Disobedience." In *The Oxford Handbook of Transcendentalism,* edited by Joel Myerson, Sandra Harbert Petrulionis, and Laura Dassow Walls, 629–41. Oxford: Oxford University Press, 2010.

———. "Higher Law." In *Encyclopedia of Transcendentalism*, edited by Wesley T. Mott, 82–84. Westport, CT: Greenwood, 1996.

———. "Reforming the Reformers: Emerson, Thoreau, and the Sunday Lectures at Amory Hall, Boston." *ESQ* [*Emerson Society Quarterly*] 37.4 (1991): 235–89.

———. *Thoreau's Complex Weave: The Writing of "A Week on the Concord and Merrimack Rivers," with the Text of the First Draft.* Charlottesville: University Press of Virginia, 1986.

Judd, Richard W. *Second Nature: An Environmental History of New England.* Amherst: University of Massachusetts Press, 2014.

Keyes, John Shepard. *Autobiography of Hon. John S. Keyes.* Concord, Massachusetts: Concord Free Public Library, 2010. Accessed September 4, 2015, http://www.concordlibrary.org/scollect/Keyes/index.html.

Kohlstedt, Sally Gregory. "Creating a Forum for Science: AAAS in the Nineteenth Century." In *The Establishment of Science in America: 150 Years of the American Association for the Advancement of Science*, edited by Sally Gregory Kohlstedt, Michael M. Sokal, and Bruce V. Lewenstein, 7–49. New Brunswick, NJ: Rutgers University Press, 1999.

Koopman, Louise Osgood. "The Thoreau Romance." *Massachusetts Quarterly* 4.1 (Autumn 1962): 61–67.

Kucich, John J. "Lost in the Maine Woods: Henry Thoreau, Joseph Nicolar, and the Penobscot World." *Concord Saunterer*, n.s., 19/20 (2011–12): 22–52.

Lane, Charles. "Life in the Woods." *Dial* 4.4 (April 1844): 415–25.

———. "State Slavery—Imprisonment of A. Bronson Alcott—Dawn of Liberty." *Liberator*, January 27, 1843. 16.

Lebeaux, Richard M. "From Canby to Richardson: The Last Half-Century of Thoreau Biography." In *Thoreau's World and Ours: A Natural Legacy*, edited by Edmund A. Schofield and Robert C. Baron, 126–35. Golden, CO: North American Press, 1993.

———. *Young Man Thoreau.* 1975. New York: Harper, 1978.

———. *Thoreau's Seasons.* Amherst: University of Massachusetts Press, 1984.

Lemire, Elise. *Black Walden: Slavery and Its Aftermath in Concord, Massachusetts.* Philadelphia: University of Pennsylvania Press, 2009.

Levin, JoAnn Early. "Schools and Schooling in Concord: A Cultural History." In *Concord: The Social History of a New England Town, 1750–1850*, edited by David Hackett Fischer, 343–400. Waltham, MA: Brandeis University, 1983.

Malachuk, Daniel S. *Two Cities: The Political Thought of American Transcendentalism.* Lawrence: University Press of Kansas, 2016.

Marble, Annie Russell. *Thoreau: His Home, Friends and Books.* New York: Thomas Y. Crowell, 1902.

Marx, Leo. *The Machine in the Garden: Technology and the Pastoral Ideal in America.* Oxford: Oxford University Press, 1964.

———. "The Two Thoreaus." In *The Pilot and the Passenger: Essays on Literature, Technology, and Culture in the United States*, edited by Leo Marx, 83–100. Oxford: Oxford University Press, 1988.

Maynard, W. Barksdale. "Emerson's 'Wyman Lot': Forgotten Context for Thoreau's House at Walden." *Concord Saunterer* 12/13 (2004–2005): 60–84.

———. "Thoreau's House at Walden." *Art Bulletin* 81.2 (1999): 303–25.

———. *Walden Pond: A History*. Oxford: Oxford University Press, 2004.

McFarland, Philip. *Hawthorne in Concord*. New York: Grove, 2004

McGill, Frederick T., Jr. *Channing of Concord: A Life of William Ellery Channing II*. New Brunswick, NJ: Rutgers University Press, 1967.

———. "Thoreau and College Discipline." *New England Quarterly* 15.2 (June 1942): 349–53.

McGrath, Anne. "As Long as It Is in Concord." *Concord Saunterer* 12.2 (Summer 1977): 9–11.

———. "Cynthia Dunbar Thoreau." *Concord Saunterer* 14.4 (Winter 1979): 8–14.

Meltzer, Milton, and Walter Harding, *A Thoreau Profile*. New York: Thomas Y. Crowell, 1962.

Mesa-Pelly, Judith Broome. "Thoreau's 'Basket of a Delicate Texture': Weaving History in *A Week*." *Concord Saunterer*, n.s., 4 (Fall 1996): 174–85.

Meyer, Michael. "Discord in Concord on the Day of John Brown's Hanging." *Thoreau Society Bulletin* 146 (Winter 1979): 1–3.

Moldenhauer, Joseph J. "Thoreau, Hawthorne, and the 'Seven-Mile Panorama.'" *ESQ: A Journal of the American Renaissance* 44.4 (1998): 227–73.

Mortland, Don. "Ellery Channing and Daniel Ricketson: Thoreau's Friends in Conflict," *Concord Saunterer* 19.1 (July 1987): 22–43.

———. "Thoreau's Friend Ricketson: What Manner of Man?" *Concord Saunterer* 18.2 (December 1985): 1–19.

Moss, Marcia E. *A Catalog of Thoreau's Surveys in the Concord Free Public Library*, Thoreau Society Booklet 28. Geneseo, NY: Thoreau Society, 1976.

———. "Edward S. Hoar's Conversations on Concord with Edward S. Burgess." *Concord Saunterer* 17.1 (March 1984): 17–33.

Mott, Wesley T., ed. *Biographical Dictionary of Transcendentalism*. Westport, CT: Greenwood, 1996.

———, ed. *The Bonds of Affection: Thoreau on Dogs and Cats*. Amherst: University of Massachusetts Press, 2005.

———. "Education." In *The Oxford Handbook of Transcendentalism*, edited by Joel Myerson, Sandra Harbert Petrulionis, and Laura Dassow Walls, 153–71. Oxford: Oxford University Press, 2010.

———, ed. *Encyclopedia of Transcendentalism*. Westport, CT: Greenwood, 1996.

Munroe, William, Jr. "Memoir of William Munroe." Memoirs of the Concord Social Club. 2nd Series. Cambridge, MA: N.p., 1888.

Myerson, Joel. "A Calendar of Transcendental Club Meetings." *American Literature* 44.2 (May 1972): 197–207.

———, ed. *The Cambridge Companion to Henry David Thoreau*. Cambridge: Cambridge University Press, 1995.

———, ed. *Emerson and Thoreau: The Contemporary Reviews*. Cambridge: Cambridge University Press, 1992.

———. *The New England Transcendentalists and the "Dial": A History of the Magazine and Its Contributors*. Cranbury, NJ: Associated University Presses, 1980.

Myerson, Joel, Sandra Harbert Petrulionis, and Laura Dassow Walls, eds. *The Oxford Handbook of Transcendentalism*. Oxford: Oxford University Press, 2010.

Neufeldt, Leonard N. *The Economist: Henry Thoreau and Enterprise*. New York: Oxford University Press, 1989.

Newman, Lance. *Our Common Dwelling: Henry Thoreau, Transcendentalism, and the Class Politics of Nature*. New York: Palgrave Macmillan, 2005.

Nyren, Dorothy. "The Concord Academic Debating Society." *Massachusetts Review* 4.1 (Autumn 1962): 81–84.

O'Brien, Jean M. *Dispossession by Degrees: Indian Land and Identity in Natick, Massachusetts, 1650–1790* (Cambridge: Cambridge University Press, 1997.

———. *Firsting and Lasting: Writing Indians out of Existence in New England*. Minneapolis: University of Minnesota Press, 2010.

O'Connor, Dick. "Thoreau in the Town School, 1837." *Concord Saunterer*, n.s., 4 (Fall 1996): 150–72.

Oehlschlaeger, Fritz, and George Hendrick, eds. *Toward the Making of Thoreau's Modern Reputation: Selected Correspondence of S. A. Jones, A. W. Hosmer, H. S. Salt, H.G.O. Blake, and D. Ricketson*. Urbana: University of Illinois Press, 1979.

Parel, Anthony J. "Thoreau, Gandhi, and Comparative Political Thought." In *A Political Companion to Henry David Thoreau*, edited by Jack Turner, 372–92. Lexington: University Press of Kentucky, 2009.

Peabody, Andrew Preston. *Harvard Reminiscences*. Boston: Ticknor, 1888.

Peck, H. Daniel. *Thoreau's Morning Work: Memory and Perception in "A Week on the Concord and Merrimack Rivers," the "Journal," and "Walden."* New Haven, CT: Yale University Press, 1990.

Peple, Edward C., Jr., "Hawthorne on Thoreau: 1853–1857." *Thoreau Society Bulletin* 119 (Spring 1972): 1–4.

Petroski, Henry. "H. D. Thoreau, Engineer." *Invention and Technology* 5.2 (Fall 1989): 8–16.

———. *The Pencil: A History of Design and Circumstance*. New York: Knopf, 1990.

Petrulionis, Sandra Harbert. "Editorial Savoir Faire: Thoreau Transforms His Journal into 'Slavery in Massachusetts.'" *Resources for American Literary Study* 25.2 (1999): 206–31.

———. "The 'Higher Law': Then and Now." *Thoreau Society Bulletin* 262 (Spring 2008): 5–7.

———, ed. *Thoreau in His Own Time: A Biographical Chronicle of His Life, Drawn from Recollections, Interviews, and Memoirs by Family, Friends, and Associates*. Iowa City: University of Iowa Press, 2012. [*THOT*]

———. *To Set This World Right: The Antislavery Movement in Thoreau's Concord*. Ithaca, NY: Cornell University Press, 2006. [*To Set This World*]

Petrulionis, Sandra Harbert, and Laura Dassow Walls, eds. *More Day to Dawn: Thoreau's Walden for the Twenty-First Century*. Amherst: University of Massachusetts Press, 2007.

Pomeroy, Sarah Gertrude. "Sophia Thoreau." In *Little-Known Sisters of Well-Known Men*, 253–74. Boston: Dana Estes, 1912.

Porte, Joel. *Consciousness and Culture: Emerson and Thoreau Reviewed*. New Haven, CT: Yale University Press, 2004.

Primack, Richard B. *Walden Warming: Climate Change Comes to Thoreau's Woods*. Chicago: University of Chicago Press, 2014.

Renehan, Edward J., Jr. *The Secret Six: The True Tale of the Men Who Conspired with John Brown*. Columbia: University of South Carolina Press, 1997.

Reynolds, David S. *John Brown, Abolitionist: The Man Who Killed Slavery, Sparked the Civil War, and Seeded Civil Rights*. New York: Knopf, 2005.

———. *Walt Whitman's America: A Cultural Biography*. New York: Knopf, 1995.

Reynolds, Larry J. *Righteous Violence: Revolution, Slavery, and the American Renaissance*. Athens: University of Georgia Press, 2011.

Richardson, Robert D., Jr. *Henry David Thoreau: A Life of the Mind*. Berkeley: University of California Press, 1986.

———. "A Perfect Piece of Stoicism." *Thoreau Society Bulletin* 153 (Fall 1980): 1–5.

———. "Thoreau and Science." In *American Literature and Science*, edited by Robert J. Scholnick, 110–27. Lexington: University Press of Kentucky, 1992.

Ricketson, Anna, and Walton Ricketson. *Daniel Ricketson and His Friends*. Boston: Houghton Mifflin, 1902.

Robbins, Roland Wells. *Discovery at Walden*. 1972. Lincoln, MA: Thoreau Society, 1999.

Robinson, David N. *Natural Life: Thoreau's Worldly Transcendentalism*. Ithaca, NY: Cornell University Press, 2004.

Rosenwald, Lawrence A. "The Theory, Practice, and Influence of Thoreau's Civil Disobedience." In *A Historical Guide to Henry David Thoreau*, edited by William E. Cain, 153–79. Oxford: Oxford University Press, 2000.

Rossi, William. "Evolutionary Theory." In *The Oxford Handbook of Transcendentalism*, edited by Joel Myerson, Sandra Harbert Petrulionis, and Laura Dassow Walls, 582–96. Oxford: Oxford University Press, 2010.

———. "Performing Loss, Elegy, and Transcendental Friendship," *New England Quarterly* 81.2 (June 2008): 252–77.

———. "Poetry and Progress: Thoreau, Lyell, and the Geological Principles of *A Week*." *American Literature* 66.2 (June 1994): 275–300.

———. "Roots, Leaves, and Method: Henry Thoreau and Nineteenth-Century Natural Science." *Journal of the American Studies Association of Texas* 19 (Oct. 1988): 1–22.

Rossi, William, and John T. Lysaker, eds. *Emerson and Thoreau: Figures of Friendship*. Bloomington: Indiana University Press, 2010.

Round, Phillip. "Gentleman Amateur or 'Fellow-Creature'? Thoreau's Maine Woods Flight from Contemporary Natural History." In *Thoreau's World and Ours: A Natural Legacy*, edited by Edmund A. Schofield and Robert C. Baron, 316–29. Golden, CO: North American Press, 1993.

Rusk, Ralph L. *The Life of Ralph Waldo Emerson*. New York: Charles Scribner's Sons, 1949.

Russell, E. Harlow. "Thoreau's Maternal Grandfather Asa Dunbar: Fragments from His Diary and Commonplace Book." *Proceedings of the American Antiquarian Society*, April 19, 1908, 66–76.

Russell, John Lewis. "Visit to a Locality of the Climbing Fern." *Magazine of Horticulture* March 1855, 126–34.

Salt, Henry S. *The Life of Henry David Thoreau*. London: Richard Bentley, 1890; revised version of 1908, edited by George Hendrick, Willene Hendrick, and Fritz Oehlschlaeger. Urbana: University of Illinois Press, 1993, 2000.

Sanborn, Franklin Benjamin. "Emerson and His Friends in Concord," *New England Magazine* III (1890), reprinted in *Concord Saunterer* 16.1 (Spring 1981): 3–22.

———. *Henry D. Thoreau*. Boston: Houghton Mifflin, 1882.

———. *The Life of Henry David Thoreau*. Boston: Houghton Mifflin, 1917.

———. *The Personality of Thoreau*. Boston: Charles E. Goodspeed, 1901.

———. *Recollections of Seventy Years*. 2 vols. Boston: Gorham Press, 1909.

Sattelmeyer, Robert. "Journals." In *The Oxford Handbook of Transcendentalism*, edited by Joel Myerson, Sandra Harbert Petrulionis, and Laura Dassow Walls, 291–308. Oxford: Oxford University Press, 2010.

———. "The Remaking of *Walden*." In *Writing the American Classics*, edited by James Barbour and Tom Quirk, 53–78. Chapel Hill: University of North Carolina Press, 1990, reprinted in *"Walden," "Civil Disobedience," and Other Writings*, by Henry David Thoreau, edited by William Rossi, 489–507. New York: Norton Critical Edition, 3rd edition, 2008.

———. *Thoreau's Reading: A Study in Intellectual History with Bibliographical Catalogue*. Princeton, NJ: Princeton University Press, 1988.

———. "Thoreau and Melville's *Typee*." *American Literature* 52.3 (November 1980): 462–68.

———. "Thoreau's Projected Work on the English Poets." *Studies in the American Renaissance* (1980): 239–57.

———. "'When He Became My Enemy': Emerson and Thoreau, 1848–1849." *New England Quarterly* 62.2 (June 1989): 187–204.

Sayre, Robert F. *Thoreau and the American Indians*. Princeton, NJ: Princeton University Press, 1977.

Schneider, Richard J., ed. *Approaches to Teaching Thoreau's "Walden" and Other Works*. New York: Modern Language Association of America, 1996.

———. *Henry David Thoreau: A Documentary Volume*. Dictionary of Literary Biography 298. Farmington Hills, MI: Gale, 2004.

———. "Thoreau's Panorama of the Mississippi: Its Identity and Significance," *Thoreau Society Bulletin* 245 (Fall 2003): 5–6.

———, ed. *Thoreau's Sense of Place: Essays in American Environmental Writing*. Iowa City: University of Iowa Press, 2000.

Schofield, Edmund A. "'Burnt Woods': Ecological Insights into Thoreau's Unhappy Encounter with Forest Fire." *Thoreau Research Newsletter* 2.3 (July 1991): 1–9.

———. "The Date(s) and Context of Thoreau's Visit to Brook Farm." *Thoreau Society Bulletin* 258 (Spring 2007): 8–10.

———. "Further Particulars on Thoreau's Harvard Scholarship Awards." *Thoreau Society Bulletin* 264 (Fall 2008): 4–6.

———. "The Origin of Thoreau's Fatal Illness." *Thoreau Society Bulletin* 171 (Spring 1985): 1–3.

Schofield, Edmund A., and Robert C. Baron, eds. *Thoreau's World and Ours: A Natural Legacy*. Golden, CO: North American Press, 1993.

Seybold, Ethel. *Thoreau: The Quest and the Classics*. New Haven, CT: Yale University Press, 1951.

———. "The Source of Thoreau's 'Cato-Decius Dialogue.'" *Studies in the American Renaissance* (1994): 245–50.

Shanley, J. Lyndon. *The Making of "Walden," with the Text of the First Version*. Chicago: University of Chicago Press, 1957.

Shattuck, Lemuel. *A History of the Town of Concord*. Boston: Russell, Odiorne; Concord, MA: John Stacy, 1835.

Sherwood, Mary P. "Thoreau's Penobscot Indians." *Thoreau Journal Quarterly* 1.1 (January 1969): 1–13.

Sims, Michael. *The Adventures of Henry Thoreau: A Young Man's Unlikely Path to Walden Pond*. New York: Bloomsbury, 2014.

Smith, Corinne Hosfeld. *Westward I Go Free: Tracing Thoreau's Last Journey*. Winnipeg: Green Frigate Books, 2012.

Smith, Donald B. *Mississauga Portraits: Ojibwe Voices from Nineteenth-Century Canada*. Toronto: University of Toronto Press, 2013.

Smith, Harmon. "Henry Thoreau and Emerson's 'Noble Youths.'" *Concord Saunterer* 17.3 (December 1984): 4–12.

———. *My Friend, My Friend: The Story of Thoreau's Relationship with Emerson*. Amherst: University of Massachusetts Press, 1999.

Smith, Ted A. *Weird John Brown: Divine Violence and the Limits of Ethics*. Stanford, CA: Stanford University Press, 2015.

Solnit, Rebecca. "Mysteries of Thoreau, Unsolved: On the Dirtiness of Laundry and the Strength of Sisters." *Orion*, May–June 2013, 18–23.

Specq, François, Laura Dassow Walls, and Michel Granger, eds. *Thoreauvian Modernities: Transatlantic Conversations on an American Icon*. Athens: University of Georgia Press, 2013.

Stewart, Shawn. "Transcendental Romance Meets the Ministry of Pain: The Thoreau Brothers, Ellen Sewall, and Her Father." *Concord Saunterer*, n.s., 14 (2006): 4–21.

Stowell, Robert E. *A Thoreau Gazetteer*. Princeton, NJ: Princeton University Press, 1970.

Sullivan, Mark W. *Picturing Thoreau: Henry David Thoreau in American Visual Culture*. Lanham, MD: Lexington Books, 2015.

Sullivan, Robert. *The Thoreau You Don't Know: What the Prophet of Environmentalism Really Meant*. New York: HarperCollins, 2009.

Thoreau, Henry David. *Cape Cod*. Edited by Joseph J. Moldenhauer. Princeton, NJ: Princeton University Press, 1988. [CC]

———. *Collected Essays and Poems*. Edited by Elizabeth Hall Witherell. New York: Library of America, 2001. [CEP]

———. *The Collected Poems of Henry Thoreau*. Edited by Carl Bode. Baltimore: Johns Hopkins University Press, 1965.

———. *The Correspondence, Volume 1: 1834–1848*. Edited by Robert N. Hudspeth. Princeton, NJ: Princeton University Press, 2013. [Corr., 1]

———. *The Correspondence, Volume 2: 1849–1856*. Edited by Robert N. Hudspeth. Princeton, NJ: Princeton University Press, forthcoming. [Corr., 2]

———. *The Correspondence, Volume 3: 1857–1862*. Edited by Robert N. Hudspeth. Princeton, NJ: Princeton University Press, forthcoming. [*Corr., 3*]

———. *The Correspondence of Henry David Thoreau*. Edited by Walter Harding and Carl Bode. New York: New York University Press, 1968. [*CHDT*]

———. *Early Essays and Miscellanies*. Edited by Joseph J. Moldenhauer et al. Princeton, NJ: Princeton University Press, 1975. [*EEM*]

———. *Excursions*. Edited by Joseph J. Moldenhauer. Princeton, NJ: Princeton University Press, 2007. [*Exc.*]

———. *Faith in a Seed: "The Dispersion of Seeds" and Other Late Natural History Writings*. Edited by Bradley P. Dean. Washington, DC: Island Press, 1993.

———. *The Journal of Henry D. Thoreau*. 8 vols. to date. Princeton, NJ: Princeton University Press, 1981–. [*PEJ*]

———. *The Journal of Henry David Thoreau*. Edited by Bradford Torrey and Francis Allen. 14 vols. Boston: Houghton Mifflin, 1906; New York: Dover, 1962. [*J*]

———. *Letters to a Spiritual Seeker*. Edited by Bradley P. Dean. New York: Norton, 2004.

———. *The Maine Woods*. Edited by Joseph J. Moldenhauer. Princeton, NJ: Princeton University Press, 1972. [*MW*]

———. *Reform Papers*. Edited by Wendell Glick. Princeton, NJ: Princeton University Press, 1973. [*RP*]

———. *Translations*. Edited by Kevin P. Van Anglen. Princeton, NJ: Princeton University Press, 1986. [*Translations*]

———. *Walden*. Edited by J. Lyndon Shanley. Princeton, NJ: Princeton University Press, 1971. [*Walden*]

———. *Walden: A Fully Annotated Edition*. Edited by Jeffrey S. Cramer. New Haven, CT: Yale University Press, 2004.

———. *"Walden," "Civil Disobedience," and Other Writings*. Edited by William Rossi. New York: Norton Critical Edition, 3rd edition, 2008.

———. *A Week on the Concord and Merrimack Rivers*. Edited by Carl F. Hovde et al. Princeton, NJ: Princeton University Press, 1980. [*Week*]

———. *Wild Fruits: Thoreau's Rediscovered Last Manuscript*. Edited by Bradley P. Dean. New York: Norton, 2000.

Thorson, Robert M. *Walden's Shore: Henry David Thoreau and Nineteenth-Century Science*. Cambridge, MA: Harvard University Press, 2014.

Traub, Courtney. "'First-Rate Fellows': Excavating Thoreau's Radical Egalitarian Reflections in a Late Draft of 'Allegash.'" *Concord Saunterer* 23 (2015): 74–96.

Tufts, Marshall. *A Tour through College*. Boston: Marsh, Capen, and Lyon, 1832.

Turner, Jack, ed. *A Political Companion to Henry David Thoreau*. Lexington: University Press of Kentucky, 2009.

———. "Thoreau and John Brown." In *A Political Companion to Henry David Thoreau*, 151–77. Lexington: University Press of Kentucky, 2009.

Urbanksi, Marie. "Henry David Thoreau and Margaret Fuller." *Thoreau Journal Quarterly* 8.4 (1976): 24–30.

Van Anglen, Kevin P. Introduction to *Translations*, by Henry David Thoreau, 159–233. Edited by Kevin P. Van Anglen. Princeton, NJ: Princeton University Press, 1986.

———. "Thoreau's Epic Ambition: 'A Walk to Wachusett' and the Persistence of the Classics in an Age of Science." In *The Call of Classical Literature in the Romantic Age*. Edited by Kevin P. Van Anglen and James Engell. Edinburgh: Edinburgh University Press, forthcoming.

———. "True Pulpit Power: 'Natural History of Massachusetts' and the Problem of Cultural Authority." *Studies in the American Renaissance* (1990): 119–47.

Van Anglen, Kevin P., and Kristen Case, eds. *Thoreau at 200: Essays and Reassessments*. Cambridge: Cambridge University Press, 2016.

Versluis, Arthur. *American Transcendentalism and Asian Religions*. New York: Oxford University Press, 1993.

Von Frank, Albert J. *The Trials of Anthony Burns: Freedom and Slavery in Emerson's Boston*. Cambridge, MA: Harvard University Press, 1998.

Walls, Laura Dassow. "Articulating a Huckleberry Cosmos: Thoreau's Moral Ecology of Knowledge." In *Thoreau's Importance for Philosophy*, edited by Rich Anthony Furtak and Jonathan Ellsworth, 91–111. Fordham University Press, New York: Fordham University Press, 2012.

———. "'As You Are Brothers of Mine': Thoreau and the Irish." *New England Quarterly* 88.1 (March 2015): 5–36.

———. *Emerson's Life in Science: The Culture of Truth*. Ithaca, NY: Cornell University Press, 2003.

———. Foreword to Corinne Hosfeld Smith, *Westward I Go Free: Tracing Thoreau's Last Journey*. Winnipeg: Green Frigate Books, 2012.

———. "From the Modern to the Ecological: Latour on Walden Pond." In *Ecocritical Theory: New European Approaches*, edited by Axel Goodbody and Kate Rigby, 98–110. Charlottesville: University of Virginia Press, 2011.

———. "Greening Darwin's Century: Humboldt, Thoreau, and the Politics of Hope." *Victorian Review* 36.2 (Fall 2010): 92–103.

———. "The Man Most Alive." Introduction to *Material Faith: Thoreau on Science*, ix–xviii. NY: Houghton Mifflin, 1999.

———. "Of Compass, Chain and Sounding Line: Taking Thoreau's Measure." In *Reasoning in Measurement*, edited by Alfred Nordmann and Nicola Mößner. London: Routledge, 2017.

———. *The Passage to Cosmos: Alexander von Humboldt and the Shaping of America*. Chicago: University of Chicago Press, 2009.

———. "Rethinking Thoreau and the History of American Ecology." With Frank Egerton. *Concord Saunterer*, n.s., 5 (Fall 1997): 4–20.

———. "Romancing the Real: Thoreau's Technology of Inscription." In *Historical Guide to Henry David Thoreau*, edited by William E. Cain, 123–51. Oxford: Oxford University Press, 2000.

———. *Seeing New Worlds: Henry David Thoreau and Nineteenth-Century Natural Science*. Madison: University of Wisconsin Press, 1995.

———. "Textbooks and Texts from the Brooks: Inventing Scientific Authority in America." *American Quarterly* 49.1 (March 1997): 1–25.

———. "*Walden* as Feminist Manifesto." *ISLE: Interdisciplinary Studies in Literature and*

Environment 1.1 (1993):137–44. Reprinted in Henry David Thoreau, *"Walden," "Civil Disobedience," and Other Writings*, third edition, edited by William Rossi, 521–27. New York: Norton, 2008.

Warner, Michael. "Thoreau's Bottom." *Raritan* 11.3 (Winter 1992): 53–79.

———. "Walden's Erotic Economy." In *Comparative American Identities: Race, Sex, and Nationality in the American Text*, edited by Hortense Spillers, 157–74. New York: Routledge, 1991.

Weiss, John. "Thoreau." *Christian Examiner*, July 1865, 96–117.

Wheeler, Joseph C. "Where Thoreau Was Born." *Concord Saunterer*, n.s., 7 (1999): 4–31.

Wheeler, Ruth R. *Concord: Climate for Freedom*. Concord, MA: Concord Antiquarian Society, 1967.

———. "Thoreau Farm." *Thoreau Society Bulletin* 42 (Winter 1953): 2–3.

Whitmore, George. "Friendship in New England: Henry Thoreau. I." *Gai Saber* 1.2 (Summer 1977): 104–11.

———. "Friendship in New England: Henry Thoreau. II." *Gai Saber* 1.3–4 (Summer 1978): 188–202.

Wilson, Leslie Perrin. *In History's Embrace: Past and Present in Concord, Massachusetts*. Concord, MA: Concord Free Public Library, 2007.

———. "'Treasure in My Own Mind': The Diary of Martha Lawrence Prescott, 1834–1836." *Concord Saunterer*, n.s., 11 (2003): 92–152.

Winterer, Caroline. *The Culture of Classicism: Ancient Greece and Rome in American Intellectual Life, 1780–1910*. Baltimore: Johns Hopkins University Press, 2002.

Witherell, Elizabeth Hall. "Thoreau as Poet." In *The Cambridge Companion to Henry David Thoreau*, edited by Joel Myerson, 57–70. Cambridge: Cambridge University Press, 1995.

Wolverton, Nan. "'A Precarious Living': Basket Making and Related Crafts among New England Indians." In *Reinterpreting New England Indians and the Colonial Experience*, edited by Colin G. Calloway and Neal Salisbury, 341–68. Boston: Colonial Society of Massachusetts and the University of Virginia Press, 2003.

Wood, David. *An Observant Eye: The Thoreau Collection at the Concord Museum*. Concord, MA: Concord Museum, 2006.

Wood, Gillen D'Arcy. *Tambora: The Eruption That Changed the World*. Princeton, NJ: Princeton University Press, 2014.

Woodson, Thomas. "Thoreau's Excursion to the Berkshires and Catskills." *ESQ* [*Emerson Society Quarterly*] 21.1 (1975): 82–92.

Index